THE CHECKLIST OF
SPECIES, HYBRIDS
AND CULTIVARS OF
THE GENUS
FUCHSIA

THE CHECKLIST OF SPECIES, HYBRIDS AND CULTIVARS OF THE GENUS FUCHSIA

Incorporating

1976 Addendum 1   1978 Addendum 2

1980 Addendum 3   1982 Addendum 4

Compiled by
Leo B. Boullemier

BLANDFORD PRESS
POOLE · DORSET

First published in the U.K. 1985 by Blandford Press,
Link House, West Street, Poole, Dorset, BH15 1LL.

British Library Cataloguing in Publication Data

Boullemier, Leo B.
   The check list of species, hybrids and cultivars
   of genus fuchsia incorporating 1976 addendum 1,
   1978 addendum 2, 1980 addendum 3, 1984 addendum 4.
   —Rev. ed.   1. Fuchsia—Varieties
   I. Title
   635.9'3344   SB413.F8

Distributed in the United States by
Sterling Publishing Co., Inc.,
2 Park Avenue, New York, N.Y. 10016.

ISBN 0 7137 1594 4

Printed and bound in Great Britain by
Biddles Ltd, Guildford and King's Lynn

CONTENTS

ILLUSTRATIONS

7

PREFACE

The compilation of the first Check List was undertaken with a certain amount of trepidation, realising the colossal task of collating accurate and adequate details of the vast numbers of species, hybrids and cultivars dispersed over many parts of the globe. Indeed, it took about ten years of almost continuous research before it was published in 1975.

However, with the continuous flow of new fuchsia introductions from all parts of the world, the list became out of date almost as soon as the printer's ink had dried and, to keep the list as up to date as possible, addenda were produced in 1976, 1978, 1980 and 1982.

This latest revised edition of the check list is an amalgamation of all the previous material with the descriptions of species, hybrids and cultivars arranged into one alphabetical sequence. Amendments have been made where necessary, new information has been incorporated and descriptions of over 300 new introductions have been added. (New material is indicated by an asterisk throughout.)

It is my sincere hope that this Check List may prove of help and assistance to all those interested in fuchsias, enabling them to check the authenticity of the spelling, origin and the raiser of the numerous cultivars and varieties. The emphasis is upon those fuchsias introduced during this century; little attention has been given to the majority of the old cultivars (many of which are considered to be no longer available or even in cultivation), apart from the recording of the name together with the briefest description and the raiser's name.

My sincere thanks and acknowledgements are accorded to the American Fuchsia Society for their kind permission to use material from their Fuchsia Introduction Booklets and Supplements, to members of the British Fuchsia Society for advice and information, to specialist nurserymen for providing old and current catalogues, to the Dutch Fuchsia Society, to Mr John Wright of Reading University, Mr Mark M. Du Merton O.B.E., B.A. (Cantab.), Mr Robin H. Hillman of Bloxham, Banbury, and to friends and colleagues all over the world.

Leo B. Boullemier
Northampton, 1984

9

INTRODUCTION

CLASSIFICATION

As an introduction to this Check List, a brief mention will be made of the classification of the genus *Fuchsia*, which can be divided into the following categories:

Species

Species are a basic unit of classification, similar individuals of a small natural group of plants separated from other groups by definable characters, and possessing characteristics which indicate a common descent.

Fuchsia is one of 21 genera of the order of Onagraceae and the most important genus from the ornamental viewpoint.

Botanically, *Fuchsia* is divided into several sections, but such considerations are outside the scope of this Check List and, for detailed information, reference should be made to specialized publications such as the *Revision of the Genus Fuchsia* by Dr. P.A. Munz. *Fuchsia* species number approximately one hundred but very few are in cultivation at the present day, as illustrated by the number to be found grown at Botanical Gardens, such as Kew or Edinburgh, totalling no more than fifteen to twenty. Therefore, a very considerable number of the species listed are of botanical interest only.

They are all native to Central and South America, with the exception of a few found in New Zealand and the occasional species from Tahiti.

The plants are of a woody nature, ranging in their natural habitat, from trees such as *F. excorticata*, 30 ft or more high, to prostrate creeping plants such as *F. procumbens* with small petal-less tubular flowers.

The majority are vigorous shrubs, found on high rain-drenched, moisture laden mountain slopes, or in dense evergreen forests or jungles; a few species, such as *F. tunariensis*, as epiphytic with tuberous roots.

The New Zealand species and *F. magellanica* from the mountains of Magellan in Chile are among the hardiest; whilst the leaves and bark of the latter have medicinal uses, the blue pollen of *F. excorticata* is still used by the New Zealand Maori women for face adornment.

Some species have naturalized themselves and, in these islands, *F. magellanica* in particular with its hybrid *riccartonii* can be found growing profusely as hedgerows in Devon and Cornwall and on the West coast of Scotland and Eire, forming a mass of brilliant rich, red and purple flowers.

Hybrids

Plants resulting from a cross between parents genetically unalike, the off-spring from crossing two different species or their variants.

The first known hybrids were raised during the 1820s from crosses with *F. coccinea*, *F. magellanica* and *F. arborescens* and, from that time onward, many British nurserymen became particularly interested, followed by several continental breeders. In the present century, especially after World War 1, the Americans, particularly in California, produced new cultivars and, together with the British hybridists and others, are mainly responsible for the many thousands in existence at the present time.

Triphylla Hybrids and Triphylla Types

The word triphylla means three-leaved, 'tri' meaning three and 'phyllon' meaning leaf from the Greek, differing from the usual fuchsia as the leaves are in sets of three at each set of nodes, instead of the usual two. These hybrids of the first known species *F. triphylla* are among the most beautiful of fuchsias, the majority are the result of crosses between the species *F. triphylla*, *F. fulgens*, *F. corymbiflora* or *F. splendens*. As all the parents are sub-tropical in native habitat, they do need a little more attention, as they are all definitely frost-shy and need the protection of glass for overwintering; needing a minimum of 40°F during the winter months. The foliage is attractive, usually dark green with coloured veins. The flower also differs with its characteristic long tube, its small corolla and petals, resembling a symmetrical star with four points, occasionally found with six points. All are very heavy bloomers, borne in terminal clusters and if sufficient heat and light is provided, can be described as winter flowering. Growth is usually upright and bushy, making excellent subjects for bedding out as half hardies; Thalia and Gartenmeister Bonstedt perhaps being outstanding, most of them will stand more sun than other fuchsias, making good bush plants of considerable size.

Billie Green, Koralle and Gartenmeister Bonstedt can be trained as half or quarter standards, being the most vigorous growers; whereas Mantilla and Trumpeter are excellent subjects for basket work. Unfortunately all are not generally obtainable, even from fuchsia specialist nurserymen, the majority are either in botanical gardens, such as Kew or in private collections.

Cultivars

An assemblage of clearly distinguished cultivated plants, which when reproduced sexually or asexually retain its distinguishing characters, the offspring from crossing species with hybrids, or hybrids with hybrids. The horticultural equivalent of the botanical variety.

Until recent times all new introductions were referred to as varieties, but under the new terminology and to conform with the International usage of terms, the term cultivar is often used to denote a plant variant raised as a seedling or produced by means of a sport or mutation, and constitute the vast majority of fuchsias available from hybridists and nurserymen.

Varieties

Botanically, a group of individuals distinguishable within a species, but insufficiently so to be considered a distinct species, horticulturally any variation of botanical or horticultural origin within a species; applied also to selected forms and hybrids. In the strict sense, the term variety should be specifically applied to variation of the species in wild forms, such as *F. magellanica alba* or *F. m. riccartonii* and should be correctly named as *Fuchsia magellanica* variety *alba* and *Fuchsia magellanica* variety *riccartonii*. It is interesting, however, to observe that the International Code of Nomenclature for Cultivated Plants (1961) uses both the term cultivar and variety as exact equivalents.

FLOWERS

The fuchsia flower is classified into three categories: flowers with four petals only are considered as being SINGLE; flowers with many layers of petals, or those having more than the characteristic number of petals, are classified as DOUBLE; the intermediate category is that of SEMI-DOUBLE and includes flowers with more than four petals, usually five to eight, which cannot be classified as a full double. It is quite common for plants to throw PETALOIDS; whereas the petal is a division of the corolla, a petaloid is a petal-like structure formed when sepals, stamens, or even other organs, assume the part of the petals.

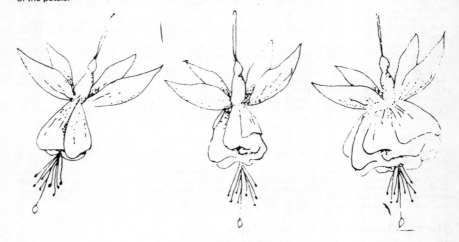

PARENTAGE

The parent stock is quoted throughout the Check List where known, the name of the female (seed bearer) being given first, followed by a multiplication sign followed by the name of the male (pollen bearer). Border Queen for example is a cross between Leonora × Lena Dalton.

Where only one parent is known, or the hybrid or cultivar is a known seedling, the parent is quoted followed by the multiplication sign; Forward Look being a seedling from Margaret Roe and indicated as Margaret Roe × .

HARDINESS

Throughout the Check List reference is made to the hardiness of plants by quoting the letter H. This is only a recommendation according to the locality in which they are grown: some may be perfectly hardy in the South of England but would not stand the winters in the North.

H1 indicates that to grow to perfection, plants need the warmth of greenhouse or glass protection with a minimum temperature of approximately 50°F.
H2 plants require a cool greenhouse or protection, or alternatively, are classified as half-hardy and can be bedded out.
H3 denotes that the plants are hardy and will withstand the winter without lifting.

The duplication of named cultivars will be observed throughout this Check List and confusion in this respect has existed since the earliest days of hybridization. Strenuous efforts were undertaken by the British Fuchsia Society, in an endeavour to unravel the tremendous difficulties in 1965, by the setting up of a Sub Committee to identify and classify existing cultivars.

INTERNATIONAL REGISTRATION OF FUCHSIAS

Certain progress was accomplished, but whilst this Sub Committee was sitting, the American Fuchsia Society was recognised as the International Authority and their work automatically ceased. The American Fuchsia Society is now the International Authority for Fuchsia Registration and Nomenclature by the appointment in 1967 of the International Society for Horticultural Science. This Society solicits the co-operation of all hybridizers throughout the world in common registration of all new fuchsia introductions, in order to eliminate confusion and duplication of cultivar names. The purpose of such registration is to promote uniformity, accuracy and fixity in their naming and is also important for nomenclatural stability. Every cultivar registered with the American Fuchsia Society is allocated an official registered number, which has been quoted throughout the Check List. Any further information on this subject can be obtained from:

American Fuchsia Society,
Hall of Flowers,
Garden Centre of San Francisco,
9th Avenue and Lincoln Way,
San Francisco, California 94122.

HYBRIDISTS, RAISERS AND INTRODUCERS

*PÈRE CHARLES PLUMIER (1646–1704)

The person fuchsia lovers give full praise to is the botanist Father Carol Plumier, who first gave word to the then civilised world, that the fuchsia existed. Several histories of the fuchsia have been written mentioning the fact that Plumier was the first person to describe and draw a fuchsia, *F. triphylla* and he alone honoured Leonhart Fuchs by naming his discovery after him.

Many writers have believed that Plumier was a Brother of the Order of Jesuits, when he was in fact a monk of the Order of Minims, a Strict Order that itself has passed into history.

Charles Plumier, or as he styled himself in Latin, Carolus Plumierus, was born in Marseilles on the 20th April 1646, the son of a turner and engraver. He acquired the technical skills that were to stand him in good stead when, at the age of 16 years, he decided that his vocation was service with the Holy Roman Church.

Plumier, a devout Catholic, did not decide to join the Brotherhood of the most popular Orders of his day, the Jesuits and the Oratorians, but opted for the most strict Order known as the 'Minims'.

This was the Order in which Plumier chose to work, and he became a great botanist of his time.

It was in Rome that Plumier first showed an interest in botany, for it was every Trinity Sunday (the patronal feast of the house of S. Trinita) that the gardens were opened to the public of Rome and a large flower show was staged. The head of the house, besides making just a spectacle of the event, arranged a special display of medicinal herbs to advertise the 'couvent's' pharmacy. Because of the interest displayed by Plumier in this special section, he was allowed to work for a time with the distinguished Italian botanist, Paolo Boccone, and, on his return to France, he continued to study under Pierre-Joseph Garidel, Professor of Botany at the University of Aix-en-Provence.

Plumier was able to exploit his now excellent knowledge of botany when Michel Begon, the Ex-Governor of Saint-Dominico, and at this time the Intendent de la Marine at Marseilles, decided, with Royal consent, that a full botanical survey of the Antilles should be made in order to find new drugs and herbs to combat disease, and to open up the Colonies. The expedition was to be led by a medico-chemist named Surian, who in turn decided to take Plumier along, not only for his knowledge of botany, but also because of his great skill as an engraver. It appears, however, that it was Plumier himself who eventually took charge, for on his return to France he was given a pension, and the title of 'Botaniste du Roy'.

He made further journeys in 1693 and 1695, to both the West Indies and the French possessions in America, to carry out more detailed studies of the flora. It was on his return from the second of these expeditions that Plumier was shipwrecked, and all the specimens that he had collected were lost. These losses included flowers, seeds, dissected portions of animals, including alligator, snakes and a host of other strange things. It may well have been that the first fuchsia could have been introduced to the Old World many years before it actually was, if it had not been for this catastrophe. It was indeed fortunate that Plumier had sent his papers and drawings to France on another ship, and that these arrived safely at their destination.

Not only is he noted in the history of botany as a skilled plant hunter, prolific writer and master engraver, but his skill as turner is also perpetuated by his work on the subject being translated into Russian under the personal supervision of Peter the Great, who introduced much of the French style of architecture into the re-construction of St. Petersburg.

Plumier described the first known fuchsia which he named *Fuchsia triphylla coccinea*, in his study *Nova Plantarum Americanarum Genera*. It was inaccurate in both description and drawing, but it was still this description on which Linnaeus based the genus *Fuchsia* in 1737. Actually it was another Minim, Feullée, himself a pupil of Plumier, who first gave the botanic world the accurate description of *F. triphylla*. Historians put the errors made on this occasion by Plumier down to the fact that the specimens were lost in the wreck and he only had the notes that he made under poor conditions, from which to work.

To Plumier must be attributed the charming custom of naming plants after people. Besides naming *Fuchsia* after Leonhart Fuchs, he named the *Begonia* after Michel Begon, the *Magnolia* after Magnol, and *Lobelia* after Lobel, the Curator of the Botanic Gardens at Oxford.

During his last years, Plumier suffered much ill-health. In 1704, the French King's Physician, Fagon, with the Royal consent, persuaded Plumier to undertake a new expedition with the special task of investigating the culture and properties of the drug, quinine. Waiting to embark, and still weak from his previous illness, he was struck down with pleurisy, and died in a 'cell' at the 'couvent' of Santa-Maria, near Cadiz.

So died a great botanist, and the man who introduced the fuchsia to the then civilised world. Many other plants apart from the fuchsia, that Plumier found and named bear witness to his greatness, and Linnaeus found fit to perpetuate his name by naming that beautiful genus, *Plumierus*, after him.

LIST OF HYBRIDISTS, RAISERS AND INTRODUCERS (1830 TO 1978)

Date quoted is the year of the raiser's first introduction, the other figure
indicates the total number of the raiser's introductions to date.

Name	No.	Nationality	Year
Abermule Nurseries	3	British	1972
Adams, Mrs. V., see Barton's Nursery		American	
Allen, B.W., Birmingham	2	British	1974
Amer, D., Middlesex	1	British	1966
Ann's Garden, see Mrs. A. Gagnon		American	
Antonelli (Bros.), E.B., Santa Cruz, California	12	American	1963
Aranjo, Tony, California	1	American	1975
Atkinson, F.		British	1844
Austin (Medstead Nurseries)	2	British	1963
Baake, H.C., Los Angeles	1	American	1940
Bacher, J.A., Oregon	1	American	1947
Baker, Bernard, Halstead, Essex	19	British	1970
Banheur	1		1873
Banks, Edward, Deal	111	British	1844
Barker	1	British	1841
Barker, D., Wirral, Cheshire	1	British	1973
Barkway	6	British	1846
Barton, Trevor, Auckland, New Zealand	4	N.Z.	1970
Bass	1	British	1847
Baudinat, Meaux	1	French	1850
Baudry, Avranches	2	French	1856
Bausie	1	French	1869
Bees Nurseries (Walker)	1	British	1967
Bell, Y.	2	British	1842
Bellamy	1	British	1978
Bennett, Albert, Ramsgate	1	British	1975
Berkeley Hort, Nursery	5	American	1935
Bernier, Norman, San Bruno, California	2	American	1958
Blackwell, John, Swindon	32	British	1957
Bland, Edward	60	British	1867
Boggis, T.M., and C.A., Norwich	1	British	1975
Bonnet	1	French	1888
Bonstedt, G.	11	German	1904
Brand, Vernon, E., San Leandro, California	14	American	1949
Brazier, J.H., Crosby, Liverpool	1	British	1975
Breary, Bryan, Manchester	1	British	1976
Breitner, Fred, Seattle, Washington	1	American	1970
Brembach	1		1911
Bremer	1	Dutch	1973
Brewster, A.	1	British	1843
Bridger, A.	4	British	1958
Bright, George, Reading	4	British	1910
Brittle	1	British	1857
Broadhurst, N.L., Birmingham	1	British	1974
Brough	1	British	1977
Brown	3	British	1845
Brown, Del, Washington	1	American	1964
Brown, H.A., Chingford, Essex	1	British	1938
Brown, Lowell, H., San Leandro, California	5	American	1936
Brown – Soules	16	American	1951
Bubb, B., Birmingham	1	British	1973
Bugden, George, see Berkeley Hort. Nurseries		American	
Bull, W., Chelsea	54	British	1846
Bundy	1	British	1870
Bunney	2	British	1832
Bürgi – Ott.	2	Swiss	1972
Cannell, H., Swanley	3	British	1900
Carlson, Berger, Poulsbo, Washington	2	American	1971
Carters – Carter & Co., Raynes Park, London	12	British	1869
Castle Nurseries	2	British	1927
Castro, Robert, Oakland, California (see Fuchsia Forest)	53	American	1969
Catt	7	American	1951
Chandler, W.	1	British	1839
Chaté, Paris	1	French	1873
Chatfield	1	British	1973
Cheetham, Hyde, Cheshire	1	British	1977

Cheseldine, J.C., Washington, Tyne & Wear, England	1	British	1975
Chiles	5	American	1953
Churchman	1	British	1887
Clark	2	British	1948
Clark, W.	4	British	1977
Clyne, Mrs. Ivy, E., Uxbridge, Middlesex	18	British	1972
Coals, H.	2	British	1962
Coëne, Ghent	12	Belgian	1853
Colley, T., Leeming Bar, Yorkshire		British	1839
Colville, Dr. Oliver	32	British	1963
Conley	1	American	1953
Copley, Robert & J., Salem, Oregon	12	American	1964
Cormack	1	British	1846
Cornelissen	27	Belgian	1860
Courcelles	1	French	
Cox, New Zealand	1	N.Z.	1940
Creer, Cyril, Middlesex	1	British	1969
Cripps, S., Tunbridge Wells	1	British	1847
Crockett, Mrs. V.L., Bedfordshire, now Ramsgate	11	British	1965
Crousse	14	French	1853
Crumley, Alice, W., San Pablo, California	1	American	1948
Curio	2	Continental	1884
Curtis	2	British	1847
Curtis, T.J., Coventry	10	British	1967
Daglish	1	British	1964
Dale	3	American	1950
Davis, Donald, H., California	2	American	1970
Dawson	3	British	1956
De Graaff	1	Dutch	1976
De Groot	22	Dutch	1967
Decola, A. Marguerite, San Jose, California	1	American	1975
Deegin	1		1868
Demay, Arras	15	French	1865
Dennonveaux	1	French	1857
Dickson, M.	2	British	1846
Diener, R., San Francisco	1	American	1939
Dixon, G.	13	British	1869
Dobbie Forbes	3	British	1888
Doël	2	German	1873
Dominy, F., Exeter	1	British	1852
Doyle	1	British	1899
Doyles, Robert, V., Redcar, Cleveland	1	British	1977
Duschene	1		1912
Dye, Norman, K., Ilford, Essex	1	British	1974
Dyos, Alan, Middlesex	2	British	1978
Eames, Maurice, Edenbridge, Kent	1	British	1976
Eastwood, Washington	1	American	1971
Eden	1	British	1969
Edwards	1	British	1839
Edwards, Ralph, San Francisco	3	American	1948
Eggbrecht	4	German	1868
Elliott	1	British	1899
Elsner	2	German	1878
Endicott	5	British	1965
Epps, C., Maidstone	22	British	1840
Erickson, Robert, San Jose, California	21	American	1957
Ernst	2		1841
Erwin	2	American	1952
Evans and Reeves, Los Angeles, California	63	American	1933
Every	1	British	1849
Fairclo, James (Home Fuchsia Gardens), California	15	American	1944
Farrington, J.W.	1	American	1961
Felton	7	British	1847
Fesco	1	Spanish	1938
Field, Mrs. C.S. (see Soo Yun Field)		American	
Forbes, D., Hawick, Scotland	2	British	1890
Foster, Jack, California	18	American	1972
Fowler	1	British	1846
Foxton	1	British	1845
Francesa, Mrs. Stasko, Fort Bragg, California	9	American	1973
Francis	1	British	1970
Freeman	1	British	1918

Fritz, Arthur, San Francisco	1	American	1968
Frost, Mrs. Madge, Rhodesia	1	Rhodesian	1976
Fry	8	British	1864
Fuchsia Forest – See Castro, Robert		American	
Fuchsia–La Nurseries – see Walker, Roy		American	
Gadsby, Cliff, Breadsall, Derby	87	British	1965–1978
Gagnon, Mrs. Ann, Coos Bay, Oregon	40	American	1962
Gaine, R.	3	British	1845
Garrat	1	British	1844
Garson, Gordon, California	13	American	1938
Gebrider – Teupel	2	German	1904
Gentry, L. and M., California	1	American	1972
Gilbert, W., Birmingham	1	British	1977
Girling, P.	2	British	1846
Golics, J.	1	British	1976
Gordon	1	British	1953
Gorman, Mrs. Mabel, California	22	American	1970
Goyaerts, Mrs.	1	Dutch	Circa 1970
Gray	1	British	1973
Greenacres Fuchsia Gardens (see Luscomb, C.)		American	
Greene	5	British	1862
Greene, Horace, Leicester	3	British	1974
Green, H.A., Monterey, California	8	American	1929
Griffiths	1	British	1974
Grosse, George	2		1864
Gubler, R.D., Surbiton, Surrey	3	British	1974
Guesco, Peter	1	American	1970
Gulliver, Hurstmonceaux	1	British	1840
Gunter	1	British	1970
Haag, W., and R., Arcadia, California	33	American	1945
Hall, Mrs., Margaret, Ponteland	2	British	1973
Halley, N.	5	British	1843
Hammett, C.W., Worcester Park, Surrey	2	British	1967
Handley, Mrs. Enid, F., Derby	42	British	1971
Hanson, Mrs. C., Eureka, California	10	American	1950
Hardcastle, H.B.	1	British	1975
Harland	1	British	1958
Harris, Aubrey	1	British	1977
Harris, Frank, J.T., Winchcombe, Cheltenham	3	British	1974
Harrison, F., Dereham, Norfolk	33	British	1840
Hastings, Mrs. Betty J., Soland Beach, California	2	American	1975
Hatchard	1	British	1974
Hatt	1		1963
Hazard and Hazard, Monterey, California	70	American	1930
Hedlund	1	American	1951
Henderson, D., St. John's Wood, London	43	British	1853
Herron	1	American	1954
Hilton, George, Cattedown, Plymouth	9	British	1976
Hobbs, Leslie, Worthing, Sussex	1	British	1977
Hobbs, Norman, D., Gateley, Cheshire	2	British	1976
Hobson	4	British	1976
Hodges, Raymond, Pacific Grove, California	51	American	1947
Hoeck	2	German	1884
Holmden	1		1953
Holmes, Mrs. E., Midford, Bath	16	British	1966
Holmes, Ron, Edenbridge, Kent	26	British	1970
Homan	2	British	1967
Home Fuchsia Gardens (see Fairclo, James)		American	
Hopgood, G.	1	British	1968
Hopfe	3		1868
Hoppe	2		1868
Howarth, G.	1	British	1976
Howlett, Charles, J., Reading	5	British	1911
Hubbard's Fuchsia Garden	3	American	1967
Ireland	1	American	1954
Ivery	2	British	1846
Jackson	1	British	1846
Jackson, Noel, Tamworth, Staffs.	1	British	1977
Jackson, Robert, D., Altrincham, Cheshire	1	British	1972
Jardine	3	British	1902
Jennings	5	British	1846

Jennings, Ken, Southall, Middlesex ..	..	2	British	1968
Jimenez, Juan, Los Angeles, California	..	1	American	1974
Jones	..	1	British	1862
Jones, I.G.M., Newark, Notts.	..	2	British	1973
Jones, W., Tettenham, Wolverhampton	..	27	British	1958
Keaster, Paul, Huntingham Beach, California	..	1	American	1973
Keiffer, Ray, D., Kirkland, Washington	..	1	American	1962
Kennett, Charles, Walnut Creek, California	..	84	American	1955
Klein	..	1	German	1878
Klese	..	1	German	1911
Knight, G.	..	11	British	1842
Kohene ..	..	2		1874
Köhler	..	7		1927
Kooijman	..	1	Dutch	1972
Krogh, Chad., San Diego, California	..	1	American	1975
Kucchler, Harold, San Landro, California ..	..	9	American	1961
Lagen, Dr. J.B.	..	4	American	1937
Laing, P.	..	2	British	1873
Lampard	..	2	British	1970
Lane, F., Berkhampstead ..	..	1	British	1871
Ledher	..	1	Continental	1891
Lee, B.	..	1	British	1857
Lee, Leo, A., Costa Mesa, California	..	6	American	1945
Leitner, Paul, San Francisco	..	1	American	1946
Lemoine, Nancy, France ..	approx. 445	French	1848
Letheren	..	2	French	1894
Letts	..	4	British	1910
L'Huillier	..	6	French	1864
Lockerbie, Ron, Merimbula, N.S.W. ..	..	4	Australian	1971
Lockyer	..	1	British	1974
Long, A.W.T., Pevensey, Sussex	..	1	British	1972
Longleat Gardens	..	2	British	1966
Lowe, H.	..	15	British	1838
Luscomb, Calvin, Coos Bay, California	..	1	American	1970
Lye, James, Market Lavington	..	68	British	1867
McCormick's Fuchsialand Nursery (see Gorman, Mrs. M.)	..		American	
McParlin, Dr. R., Newcastle-upon-Tyne	..	2	British	1976
Machado, Joseph, Oakland, California	..	13	American	1959
Mahnke	..	2		1912
Manchester University, Manchester ..	..	1	British	1958
Marshall	..	1	British	1975
Martin, George, Oakland, California	..	57	American	1953
May	..	10	British	1841
Mayne ..	..	2	British	1839
Mayle, Henry, Birmingham	..	3	British	1840
Meelley	..	1		1848
Meikle ..	..	1		1916
Melville, T.	..	3	British	1886
Menze ..	..	1		1949
Merrist Wood, Surrey	..	1	British	1968
Mescke, Carl, F., San Jose, California	..	1	American	1977
Middlebrook, W.J.	..	1	British	1975
Miellez ..	..	23	French	1845
Milani, Mrs. Ettori, California	..	1	American	1968
Miller, Ramsgate	..	5	British	1844
Miller	..	1	British	1953
Miller, V.V., Fulham, London	..	7	British	1962
Milne, G.	..	1	British	
Milner	..	1	British	1872
Moir, James, Auckland, New Zealand	..	1	N.Z.	1976
Money, High Wycombe ..	..	1	British	1963
Monk ..	..	3	British	1939
Mouncer, Harold, Satsop, Washington	..	1	American	1961
Mueller, Karl, San Francisco	..	1	American	1975
Munkner, William, San Francisco	..	22	American	1952
Nagel	..	4	German	1847
Napthen, C.W., Cambridge	..	1	British	1978
National Trust, Sharpitor, England	..	1	British	1975
Need	..	7	British	1964
Nelson ..	..	22	American	1940
Nessier, Walter, Colma, California	..	10	American	1948

18

Name	Count	Nationality	Year
Neubronner	1	German	1896
Newberry	2	British	1847
Newton, Robert, L., Corvallis, California	1	German	1973
Nichols	3	British	1846
Niederholzer, Gus, San Francisco	137	American	1938
Nix Nursery (see Ostopkevich, Nick)		American	
Normald, A., Ripon, Yorkshire	2	British	1840
Nuttall, V.T., Brodsworth, Near Doncaster, Yorkshire	1	British	1977
Nutzinger, Karl	24	Austrian	1946
Ocean Bluff Fuchsia Gardens (see Stasko, Mrs. F.)		American	
Olson, Dr. Arther, P., Patterson, California	5	American	1956
Osgood	1		1941
Ostopkevich, Nick, Soquel, California	1	American	1971
Pacey, Robert, Stathern, Melton Mowbray	3	British	1964
Palko, S., Richmond, California	8	American	1976
Palmer	1	British	1891
Pancharian, Joseph, Cupertino, California	7	American	1974
Pape, Nellie, Eureka, California	1	American	1948
Paskesen, Ted, San Francisco	21	American	1965
Passingham	2	British	1846
Pawley	1	British	1846
Pennisi, Michael, San Jose, California	55	American	1967
Pepper, L.	1	American	1952
Peterson – Fuchsia Farms	10	American	1957
Phipps	1	British	1911
Pidwell	1	American	1938
Pince	5	British	1842
Plummer	8	American	1951
Porter, J.V.	1	British	1976
Potney	2	British	1842
Powell, R.E.	1	British	1975
Prentice, Mrs. J.A., Coos Bay, Oregon	27	American	1966
Price	1	British	1883
Pridmore	1	British	1971
Pugh, James, H., Mouldsworth, Chester	16	British	1969
Putley, J., Rayleigh, Essex	2	British	1964
Pybon	3	American	1958
Pyemont	1	British	1974
Rademacher	1	German	1901
Raffill, C.P., Kew, London	4	British	1938
Rapley	3	British	
Rasmussen	1	American	1954
Rawlins, Bernard, W., Hounslow, Middlesex	8	British	1951
Reedstrom, Phil. F., Novato, California	30	American	1943
Rehnelt	3	German	1902
Reichart	1		1866
Reid, Miss Yvonne, M., Lakemba, Sydney	2	Australian	1975
Reimers	5	American	1953
Reiter, Victor, Senior and Junior, San Francisco	90	American	1939
Rendatler	2		1869
Rettengen	2	German	
Reynolds, Edmund, Leyland, Lancashire	1	British	1976
Roberts, M., St. Austell, Cornwall	1	British	1833
Rochfords	1	British	1904
Rodenberg	1	American	
Roe, George, Nottingham	14	British	1966
Rogers	8	British	1845
Rogers	3	British	1899
Rollinson	2	British	1862
Rosecroft Gardens	1	British	1944
Roth	5	American	1956
Rowson	1	British	1887
Rozain – Boucharlet, Lyons, France	70	French	1860
Rudd, T.	1	British	
Rundle, W.	4	British	1833
Rush	3	British	1896
Russell, John	1	British	1960
Ryle, Dr. Matthew	49	British	1970
Salter, John	26	Brit./Fren.	1836
Sankley	5	British	1887
Sauer	3	German	1911

Saunders, Eileen, Godalming, Surrey (see Wagtails)		British	
Sayers, Charles, L., San Jose, California	2	American	1974
Schadendorff	2		1912
Schmidt, William, Palo Alto, California	8	American	1941
Schnabel, Clement, F., San Francisco	59	American	1947
Schneider, Barbara, L., Oxnard, California	1	American	1978
Schofield	1	British	1841
Schulte	1	American	1957
Scott	1	American	1952
Senior, Albert, Birmingham	5	British	1970
Shaw, Mrs. Nora, F., Cupertino, California	3	American	1972
Sheriff	1	British	1847
Shutt, Mrs. Junior	2	American	1968
Simmonds	2	British	1878
Slococks	1	British	1952
Smallwood, Mrs. Jane, A.H., Hythe, Kent	2	British	1973
Smith	51	British	1841
Smith – Aranjo	1	American	1956
Smith, F. and A., Holloway, London	5	British	1866
Smith, G., Dalston	4	British	1844
Smith, J., Trowbridge	1	British	1879
Smith, H., Kegworth, Derby	1	British	1974
Smith, L.A., Christchurch, New Zealand	1	N.Z.	1940
Smith, Mrs. Eileen, Sandwich, Kent	1	British	1969
Smith, Nora, Cupertino, California	2	American	1976
Soo Yun Field, Mrs., Sebastopol, California	71	American	1965
Soules	1	American	1959
Spackman	8	American	1920
Stafford, T.	2	British	1847
Standish, W., Bagshot	9	British	1841
Steevens	12	Dutch	1968
Stewart Walter, Cumnock, Ayrshire	1	British	1971
Stilwell, Don, Hounslow, Middlesex	1	British	1974
Stokes, F., Ipswich	3	British	1848
Storvick, Glen. O., Pacifica, California	1	American	1978
Story, W.H., Newton Abbot, Devon	29	British	1842
Stride	10	British	1873
Strutt	10	British	1867
Stubbs, Mrs. Annabelle, Fort Bragg, California	26	American	1970
Suckley	1	British	1966
Sunderland, Glen, A., Seattle, Washington	3	American	1967
Suzanne Gardens (see Erickson, R.)		American	
Swaffield	1	British	1874
Swales, Fred, Goole, Yorkshire	1	British	1974
Sweet, Mrs. Edward, Constantia, New York	1	American	1961
Tabraham, A.P., St. Mary's, Isles of Scilly	45	British	1974
Tacolneston Nurseries, Norwich	1	British	1973
Tanfield, C.E., South Woodford, London	1	British	1975
Taylor, Arthur, W., Enfield, Middlesex	2	British	1973
Taylor, Mrs. Bertha, O., Richmond, California	1	American	1969
Thame	1	British	1954
Thompson, Buckinghamshire	2	British	1840
Thorne, Thomas	25	British	1953
Thornley, Alf, Preston, Lancashire	27	British	1961
Tiley	3	British	1847
Tiret, H.M., and D., San Francisco	124	American	1947
Tite, L.G., Ilford, Essex	1	British	1975
Todd, H.	3	British	1842
Todman	4	British	
Tolley, Wilf, L., West Heath, Birmingham	16	British	1971–1978
Topperwein, H.	1	German	1977
Travis, James, Bamber Bridge, Preston	40	British	1951
Travis, Susan, Bamber Bridge, Preston	3	British	1959
Tresco Abbey Gardens, Scilly Isles	1	British	
Turner, C.	5	British	1848
Turner, E.T.	4	British	1954
Turville, S.	13	British	1843
Twrdy	40	German	1866
Van der Post	2	Dutch	1968
Van der Grijp	1	Dutch	1968
Van Suchtelen	2	Dutch	1968
Van Wieringen	8	Dutch	1970
Vee Jay Greenhouse, Coos Bay, Oregon	1	American	1978
Veitch, J., Chelsea, London	6	British	1892

Wagtails (see Saunders, E.)	2	British	1969
Walker and Jones, California	27	American	1948
Walker, Roy, A., Long Beach, California	16	American	1953
Walker, Roy, A. (under Fuchsia–La Nursery)	33	American	1952
Waltz, Miss Muriel, Ross, California	65	American	1943
Warren, Cyril, Berkeley, California	2	American	1947
Warscrewiez	6	Belgian	
Watchorn, V. and W., Oceanside, California	1	American	1974
Watson	1	British	1907
Watson	2	British	1967
Wayne	1	British	
Wearle	2	American	1940
Weaver, Ray, Huntingdon Park, California	1	American	1977
Webb	1	British	1949
Weber	1	American	1955
Weinrich	7	German	1863
Weir, Mrs. Penelope, Brighton, Sussex	1	British	1973
Weisel	1	American	1950
Welham	1	British	1842
Wells	1	British	
Westover	1	American	1976
Westover Greenhouses (see Breitner, F.)		American	
Wheeler, S.	7	British	1847
White	1	British	1841
White, R.J., Countesthorpe, Leicester	1	British	1975
Whiteman, H.H., Gloucester	7	British	1941
Williams, B.S., Holloway, London	18	British	1870
Wills, E.J., West Wittering, Sussex	3	British	1966
Wilmore	2	British	1849
Wilson	3	American	1957
Wilson, J.W., Earley, Reading	10	British	1967
Wilson, Stanley, J.	1	British	1965
Wingrove, Edward, Reading	2	British	1966
Woaker, Dorothy, Birmingham	2	British	1975
Wolf	1	German	1911
Wood, W.P., Berrington, Herts.	24	British	1935
Woodley	1	British	1910
Woolley, C.F., Cardiff, Wales	1	British	1978
Wright	1	British	1846
Wright, John A., Atherstone, Warwickshire	4	British	1975
Wright, John O., Reading	3	British	1976
Wyness	4	German	1865
York	9	American	1934
Yorke	1	British	1943
Youell, R., Great Yarmouth	13	British	1840
Young, Charles, A., Kearsley, Bolton	2	British	1975
Young, James, Edinburgh	2	British	1833
Zerland, Fred, Eureka, California	1	American	1977

*EDWARD R.R.G. BANKS, HYBRIDIST (1820–1910)

Edward Banks was a prolific hybridist of fuchsias living at Sholden Hall on the outskirts of Deal in Kent. He did not enjoy good health and took up floriculture as a profession and soon started propagating fuchsias in the large greenhouses, many of which remain to this day. He employed ten gardeners and supplied such famous firms as Henry Cannell Nurseries of Swanley in Kent (of Swanley Gem fame). He also supplied E.G. Henderson of St. John's Wood in London who imported living plants of *F. triphylla* from New York in the late 1870s, presenting one to Kew.

Fuchsias at the time were very expensive; in Cannell's catalogue new varieties were priced at 3 shillings and 6 pence (17½ p) for a rooted cutting, quite a sum of money in those days compared with a labourer's earnings of less than 10 shillings (50p) per week. Banks became one of the largest growers of fuchsias in the world, producing many new cultivars each year. His Forget-Me-Not is the emblem of the British Fuchsia Society and his Mauve Beauty of 1869, both still grown today, won an R.H.S. award of merit.

Edward Banks died at the age of 90 on 11th January 1910 and his death coincided with a wane in popularity of the fuchsia. In the 1930s, the fuchsia enjoyed a revival and it is even more popular today than it was in Banks' time.

Full List of Cultivars Raised and Introduced by Edward Banks

	Date		Date
ALBERT VICTOR		LA PROPHET	1860
ALDERMAN MECHI	1872	LA TRAVIATA	1865
AMERICAN BANNER	1872	LIZZIE HEXHAM	1866
ANTIGONE	1887	LORD DERBY	1868
ARABELLA	1886	LORD ELCHO	1862
AUTOCRACT		LORD FALMOUTH	1866
BACCHUS	1863	LORD MACAULEY	
BANKS FAVOURITE	1855	LUCREAZIA BORGIA	1864
BARONESS BURDETT COULTS	1872	LUCY MILLS	1865
BEAUTY BLOOM	1866	MADAM TREBELLI	1868
BEAUTY (NO. 1)	1866	MAID OF KENT	1855
BEAUTY OF KENT	1867	MARGURETA	1862
BEAUTY OF SHOLDEN	1868	MARS	1863
BEAUTY OF THE BOWER		MARVELLOUS	1866
BLACK PRINCE	1861	MAUVE BEAUTY	1869
BLANCO MARGENATA	1862	MAUVE QUEEN	1872
CATHERINE PARR		MEDORA	1863
CHAMPION	1868	MERRY MAID	1854
CHARLEMAGNE	1885	MINNIE BANKS	
CLIMAX	1855	MISS E. MEARA	
COLONEL HARCOURT		MODEL (NO. 2)	1868
COMET	1862	MONSIEUR RICHARD PAXTON	1872
CONQUEROR	1853	MR. D.T. FISH	1872
CONQUEST	1866	NORTHERN LIGHT (NO. 1)	1864
CONSOLATION	1865	OBERON (NO. 1)	1864
CONSTELLATION	1864	OUR FUTURE QUEEN	1872
COUNT OF CAVOUT	1861	PERFECTION	1848
CYGNE D'ARGENT	1859	PRIDE OF WOOLWICH	
DAY DREAM	1867	PRINCE ALBERT	1855
DON GIOVANNI	1864	PRINCE ALFRED	1853
DONNA JOAQUINA	1852	PRINCE OF ORANGE	
DR. KILLO GIDDINGS		PRINCESS BEATRICE	
DUKE OF EDINBURGH	1872	PRINCESS MARY	
EDITH	1862	PURITANI	1864
ELEGANT ISSING NO. 2	1862	QUEEN OF HANOVER (NO. 2)	
EMBLE MATIC	1863	REVEREND T. WILTSHIRE	
EMPEROR NAPOLEON III	1855	RODERICK DHU	1865
ENOCH ARDEN	1865	ROSE OF CASTILLE	1869
FAIR ORIANA	1857	ROSE OF DENMARK	1864
FAIRY QUEEN	1855	ROSE PHENOMENAL	
FAIREST OF THE FAIR		SCHILLER	
FATHER IGNATIUS	1865	SIGNORA	1862
FAVOURITE		SIR W.G. ARMSTRONG	
FINSBURY VOLUNTEER	1862	SOUVENIR DE CHISWICK	1855
FIRST OF THE DAY	1872	SPLENDOUR	1870
FORGET-ME-NOT	1866	STRIATA PERFECTA	1869
GLORY	1870	STRIATA SPLENDOUR	1872
GLOWWORM		SUNSHINE	1864
GOLDEN CHAINS	1865	THE LORD WARDEN	1862
GRAND SULTAN	1855	THE VILLAGE PETTY	1865
GUIDING STAR	1856	TRUTH	
HERCULES	1872	TRY ME O	1868
J.F. MCELROY		T.T. LAWDEN	
JOHN BRIGHT	1879	VESTA (NO. 1)	
KILLIECRANKIE	1867	VICTOR EMMANUAL	1862
KING OF FUCHSIAS	1863	VOLCANO DI AQUA	1855
KING OF STRIPES	1868	WAR EAGLE	1865
LADY DUMBELLO		WILL SELL	
LA FAVOURITE	1864		

CLIFFORD GADSBY, HYBRIDIST (1920–1978)

With the death of Clifford Gadsby, whilst only 58 years old, on 13th February 1978, the whole fuchsia world will miss an outstanding hybridist, a kind and generous character with a personality who will be difficult to replace. In his own eyes, his greatest achievement was being elected to the British Fuchsia Society Committee in 1971 after 24 years membership, where he served with zeal and contribution and respected by all his co-members. Cliff was a co-opted member of the British Fuchsia Society Floral Committee from 1972 and a full member of that committee since 1977. His knowledge and experience were shared on the British Fuchsia Society Judging Panel Committee since 1973 and his yeoman work on the British Fuchsia Society Committee for Hardy Cultivars took him regularly to R.H.S., Wisley. He was Editor for the British Fuchsia Society from

June 1977, an office he was to hold for 8 months only, but enough time to produce one bulletin and the 1978 Annual – no mean achievement.

Born at Brailsford, a West Derbyshire village, he started gardening at a very early age, being encouraged by his father, whose speciality was the viola.

Even before he was 10 years old he was rooting cuttings from Brilliant and Brutus, finding that road sweepings formed a good rooting medium and studying the root system, always coming top in gardening lessons at school.

Cliff never enjoyed good health and, even at the age of 10, developed tuberculosis and after treatment at Walton Sanatorium, Chesterfield, the specialist, as would be expected, suggested a suitable outside life; this he pursued for many years.

After leaving school, his first job was in the gardens of Brailsford Hall, where his elder brother and father had worked for a long time before; his wage was the staggering figure of 12 shillings, paid only when work was finished at noon on Saturdays. It was now that Cliff really took an interest in fuchsias, growing many of Lemoine's cultivars such as Caledonia, Doctor Foster, Doctor Topinard and Voltaire, together with a very exclusive cultivar, Queen Victoria by Story.

After the outbreak of World War 2, food had to be grown at the expense of flowers, and it was during this period he lost many of his old cultivars and his interest in fuchsias waned.

After World War 2, his interest was renewed and, in 1948, he joined the British Fuchsia Society, just 10 years after its formation. The 1950s saw Cliff really interested in his fuchsias and it was then that he started hybridizing and growing from seed. With no greenhouse, all his early work was performed with plants grown outside and he freely admitted that these early resultant seedlings were anything but beautiful, though some of these hardy seedlings, right up to his death, proved useful as pollen bearers in his later introductions. During this early period of his hybridizing, his name was often quoted and linked with the late W.P. Wood, who had previously carried out such sterling work with hardy cultivars and hardy cultivation. It was in 1963, when he obtained his first greenhouse, that Cliff really concentrated on his hybridizing, becoming particularly interested in producing new cultivars with erect carrying flowers.

He was successful and originally produced two plants with erect flowers and three with plants carrying their flowers horizontally during the latter 1960s and early 1970s. Cliff made his first real breakthrough with Upward Look, raised in 1964 but not released until after extensive trials, being catalogued by both Pacey and Wills in 1968; this cultivar was a cross from Athela × Bon Accorde, the first plant with erect flowers since Bon

Accorde by the Frenchman Crousse in 1861. What is particularly interesting, especially to the pure hybridist, is that the erectness of the flowers in each case came from the pollen parent, not in the first generation, but in the second and third generation.

Two notable introductions released in 1968 were Icecap, the first real improvement upon Snowcap, and that exceptional cultivar, Lady Isobel Barnett, one of the freest flowering cultivars known. There was only one introduction in 1969, that of the hardy Trudy, but 1970 produced 16 introductions and could be quoted as the year of the 'Belles' – Bishop's Belle – Derby Belle – Frosty Bell – Truebell, but these were overshadowed by that lovely pastel blue and pink cultivar Shady Blue; another cultivar to become famous was Margaret Roe, always to be seen since on the showbenches. 1972 saw the first of the Cloverdales, whilst 1973 produced the other famous erect-carrying cultivar, Forward Look. Cloverdale Jewel and Cloverdale Pearl came the next year but the two outstanding cultivars were Plenty, so aptly named, and a breakthrough in the hardies, a large, double red and white, Prosperity. The next few years did not produce many outstanding introductions; maybe we are still waiting for them to prove themselves, which brings us up to the present and past year with five introductions in 1977 and another five in 1978, one of which was named after the city he served so well as a City Councillor – City of Derby. Altogether Cliff raised and introduced 87 cultivars all of which except for five or six have been registered by the A.F.S. This of course does not account for the hundreds upon hundreds of seedlings which never reached his standard of acceptance and were discarded. It is not generally known that Cliff did produce that elusive yellow, a pale primrose double in 1971 and a pale mimosa single in 1972 but he considered they looked nothing but a beautiful fuchsia for colour and, although the single was somewhat attractive with a refined shaped bloom, he did not proceed with them as another fault was the weak habit of growth; he eventually discarded them. Cliff came to the conclusion, which he confirmed to me personally, that breeding a yellow fuchsia, apart from being a novelty, would allow little else and that to breed the desired yellow could prove as dreary at the final stages as the blue rose.

It is true to say that Cliff was one of the greatest and most productive hybridizers of this country and although it could be said that some of his pastel blue and pink raisings were rather similar to another, nevertheless they were all extremely beautiful. It is glad to know that all Cliff's hybridizings notes and records have been handed down to Bob Pacey who intends to start where Cliff left off.

List of Cliff Gadsby Introductions Showing Parentage

	A.F.S. No.	Date	Female (seed bearer) × Male (pollen bearer)
ALBION	1049	1972	Rosedale × Lady Isobel Barnett
ANGELA RIPPON	1423	1977	Christine Clements × Forward Look
ANN PACEY	1479	1978	John Pacey ×
ANTHEA BOND	1311	1975	Cliff's Hardy seedling × Upward Look
ARTHUR COPE	982	1968	Pepi ×
BELVOIR BEAUTY	1279	1975	Cloverdale Jewel ×
BERNARD RAWDIN	973	1970	Upward Look seedling × Caroline
BISHOP'S BELLS	869	1970	Sleigh Bells × Mission Bells

	A.F.S. No.	Date	Female (*seed bearer*) × Male (*pollen bearer*)
BLUE BUSH	1120	1973	Leonora × W. P. Wood × Magellanica Alba
BLUE RANGER	1312	1975	Magenta Flush × Derby Belle
CARL DRUDE		1975	Strawberry Delight × Ice Cap
CHARTWELL	1424	1977	Christine Clements × Cloverdale Pearl
CHATSWORTH	1280	1975	Magenta Flush × Derby Belle
CHRISTINE CLEMENTS		1974	Upward Look × Margaret Roe
CITY OF DERBY	1480	1978	Cliff's Hardy seedling × Bishop's Bells
CLIFFORD GADSBY		1980	
CLIFF'S HARDY	983	1971	Athela × Bon Accorde
CLIFF'S OWN	1425	1977	Christine Clements × Cloverdale Pearl
CLIFF'S UNIQUE	1392	1976	Magenta Flush × Unnamed seedling
CLOVERDALE	1050	1972	
CLOVERDALE DELIGHT	1426	1975	Rosedale × Forward Look
CLOVERDALE JEWEL	1218	1974	Cloverdale × Lady Isobel Barnett
CLOVERDALE JOY	1518	1979	Cloverdale Pearl × Christine Clements
CLOVERDALE PEARL	1219	1974	Unnamed seedling × Grace Darling
CLOVERDALE PRIDE	1519	1979	Seedling × Grace Darling
CLOVERDALE STAR	1393	1976	Unnamed seedling × Cloverdale Pearl
CROWN DERBY	962	1971	Bishop's Bells × Strawberry Delight
DERBY BELLE	876	1970	Upward Look × Caroline
DERBY COUNTESS	1121	1973	Pepi × Sleigh Bells
DERBY IMP	1220	1974	
DERBY STAR		1975	Cliff's Hardy × Shy Look
DIANA WILLS	976	1971	Pepi ×
DR. BRENDAN FREEMAN	1427	1977	Cloverdale Pearl × Grace Darling
EDALE	1281	1975	Joan Pacey × Miss Great Britain
ELIZABETH BROUGHTON		1975	
FLASHLIGHT	977	1971	Flash × Magellanica Alba
FORWARD LOOK	1122	1973	Rosedale × Margaret Roe
FREESTYLE	1313	1975	Lady Isobel Barnett × Bishop's Bells
FROSTY BELL	877	1970	Upward Look × Ting-a-Ling
GARDEN BEAUTY	1481	1978	Chance seedling found growing under Lena
GAY ANNE	1221	1974	Leonora × John Pacey
GAY FUTURE	1314	1975	Cloverdale Pearl × Unnamed seedling
GEORGE ROE	1065	1972	Swingtime × Tom Pacey
GOLD LEAF	1222	1974	Unnamed seedling × Miss Great Britain
GRACE DARLING	1066	1972	Rosedale × Sleigh Bells
HATHERSAGE	1282	1975	Joan Pacey × Prosperity
ICE CAP	971	1968	Snowcap × Bon Accorde
IVAN GADSBY	875	1970	Pepi × Bridesmaid
JEAN BURTON	979	1968	Sleigh Bells × Citation
JOAN PACEY	1067	1972	Rosabel × Sleigh Bells
JOAN'S DELIGHT	1428	1977	Wee Lass × Cloverdale
KARAN	966	1968	Upward Look seedling ×
LADY BOWER	964	1970	Swingtime × Tom Pacey
LADY ISOBEL BARNETT	978	1968	Caroline × Derby Belle (sister seedling)
MAGENTA FLUSH	878	1970	Pepi × Melody
MARGARET ROE	975	1970	Caroline × Derby Belle (sister seedling)
MARGARET THATCHER	1482	1978	Christine Clements × Forward Look
MARTYN SMEDLEY	974	1970	Upward Look × Bon Accorde
MERRY ENGLAND	980	1968	Sleigh Bells × Pepi
MISS GREAT BRITAIN	981	1968	Sleigh Bells × Morning Light
MORNING GLOW	1302	1975	Rosedale × Albion
NICOLINA	1123	1973	Bishop's Bells × White Bride
PAMELA HUTCHINSON	1483	1978	
PLENTY	1223	1974	Cloverdale × Lady Isobel Barnett
PROSPERITY	1224	1974	Bishop's Bells × Strawberry Delight
QUEEN OF DERBY		1975	Rose Bower × Magenta Flush
RACHEL CATHERINE		1979	
RADCLIFFE BEAUTY		1974	Cloverdale × Rosedale
ROBERT HALL	871	1970	Pink Galore × Athela
ROSABELL	970	1968	Upward Look ×
ROSE BOWER	1124	1973	La Fiesta ×
ROSEDALE	1068	1972	Upward Look ×
ROYAL RUBY	972	1971	Pepi × Royal Purple
ROYAL SOVEREIGN	963	1971	Ice Cap ×
SAXONDALE	1125	1973	Trase × Lady Thumb (sister seedling)
SHADY BLUE	880	1970	Upward Look × Caroline
SHERWOOD	1126	1973	Trase × Lady Thumb (sister seedling)
SHY LOOK	1069	1972	Upward Look ×
SKYWAY	965	1971	Jean Burton × Rosabell
SLENDER LADY	879	1970	Pepi × Sleigh Bells
STRAWBERRY DELIGHT	873	1970	Trase × Golden Marinka (sister seedling)

	A.F.S. No.	Date	Female (seed bearer) × Male (pollen bearer)
STRAWBERRY SUPREME	874	1970	Trase × Golden Marinka (sister seedling)
SUNNY SMILES	967	1971	Pink Galore × Athela
SWEET REVENGE	1315	1975	Rose Bower × Magenta Flush
TRUBELL	968	1970	Bishop's Bells
TRUDY	969	1969	Hardy seedling × Chillerton Beauty
UPWARD LOOK	870	1978	Bon Accorde × Athela
VALE OF BELVOIR	1127	1973	Rosedale × Lady Isobel Barnett
WEE LASS	1283	1975	Gambit × Upward Look
WHITE BRIDGE	868	1970	Bridesmaid × Sleigh Bells
WILF TOLLEY	1225	1974	Joan Pacey × Albion

CRISTELL HANSON, GROWER AND HYBRIDIST (1898–1980)

Cristell Hanson, hybridizer and nursery owner of Eureka, California, and for 26 years a member of the American Fuchsia Society, died 30th October 1980 at the age of 82.

Mrs. Hanson originated 49 named cultivars during more than 40 years in the fuchsia nursery business. She registered ten of these with the A.F.S. of which Aunt Juliana and Purple Parasol were the most famous. Cristell imported many of the English cultivars which are now being grown in America. Towards the end of her life it is quoted she once remarked 'I hope that heaven is full of fuchsias'.

Incomplete List of Cristell Hanson Raisings and Introductions

	A.F.S. No.	Date		A.F.S. No.	Date
AMETHYST		Circa 1970	IDA MAE	1324	1976
			LUCILLE	1325	1976
AUNT JULIANA	1320	1950	MAZIE		Circa 1970
AUNT RUTH	1321	1960			
BECKEY		Circa 1970	MISS OKLAHOME	1326	1976
			PRINCESS GRACE	1327	1976
BEN FRANK	1322	1969	PURPLE PARASOL	1328	1976
BLUE FAIRY	1323	1976	REDWOOD BOWL	1329	1976

HAZARD AND HAZARD, HYBRIDISTS

Hugh Hazard and his wife Bessie operated the nursery of Hazard and Hazard in the Pacific Grove, California, for many years in the mid 1900s and were both extremely active as hybridists.

They began raising fuchsias as early as 1923, real pioneers in the American fuchsia field, and had one of the finest collections of fuchsias known at that time. In 1930, they listed 76 cultivars and issued the largest and most complete catalogue. Their first introduction was Hap Hazard in 1930 and they introduced no less than 70 cultivars and were in some way responsible for the revival of the fuchsia in California. Although many of these early introductions may be forgotten, such cultivars as Chang, Flash and Other Fellow, will testify to the skill of the Hazards. Hugh Hazard died in February, 1966, with work unfinished.

Full List of Hazard's Raising and Introductions

	Date		Date		Date
AIRY FAIRY		HARLEQUIN		NOLA	
ALICE (No. 3)		HAUTE MONDE	1930	NORMA (No. 2)	
ALICE EASTWOOD		HERMIONE	1950	OH BOY	
ANNIE LAURIE	1933	INA CLAIRE		OLD DEL MONTE	
BABY BLUE		JOHN McLAREN		OTHER FELLOW	1946
BETTY	1946	JUNO (No. 1)		PAINTED LADY	
CARMEN QUEEN		KITTY O'DAY		PAVLOVA	
CHANG	1946	LAVENDER AND OLD LACE		PAX	
CINDERELLA (No. 1)	1954	LAVENDER BASKET		PERKY	1930
CURLY LOCKS	1950	LEEANNA BELL		POCAHONTAS	
DIANE		MADAME CHANG		QUEENIE	
DR. DAVIS		MADAME VAN DER		RAMBLER (No. 1)	
EVANGELINE		STRASSE	1930	RED RIDING HOOD	
FIRE MARSHALL		MARJORY		RED ROVER	
PARKER	1950	MARY LOU		RHOMBIFOLIA (No. 3)	
FLASH	1930	MRS. DESMOND		ROSE RED	
FRA. ELBERTUS	1941	MRS. H.W. WARE		SANTA CLAUS	
GEORGE BARR	1930	MU LAN		SCINTILLATION	
GLOIRE DE MARCELINE		MUMTAZ		STANFORD	
HAP HAZARD	1930	NANCY LEE		SUZETTE	

	Date					Date
SYDNEY MITCHELL	1948	TOMICO			VINEGAR JOE	
TENOR		TOPSY			WINSOME	1948
TEXAS		TROPHEE			XENIA	
THE BRIDE	1942	UNIQUE (No. 2)		1930	ZENOBIA	

(The number in brackets indicates there are other cultivars of the same name.)

RAYMOND HODGES, HYBRIDIST (1891–1980)

The well known American hybridizer Raymond Hodges died after nearly 4 years of illness on 21st July 1980 at the age of 89. With his wife Merle, Raymond had 68 cultivars most of which were registered with the American Fuchsia Society. Fuchsias were their hobby flower for many years and they were instrumental in making it the official flower of Pacific Grove in California. With so many new beautiful fuchsias now introduced Raymond and his wife were proud to be the forerunners of the open faced fuchsias and the pastels. The most famous introduction was Citation, together with Carmel Blue, both of which were used extensively in England for hybridizing. Other well known introductions include Lilibet, Tinker Bell, Army Nurse and Merle Hodges. A native of Beaver, Utah, Raymond was for many years associated with the Metropolitan Life Insurance Co. in Pacific Grove, California.

Incomplete List of Hodges Raisings and Introductions

	A.F.S. No.	Date		A.F.S. No.	Date
AMERICAN BEAUTY	345	1958	OLD-FASHIONED	342	1958
ARMY NURSE		1947	OREGON TRAIL		1949
BELLE OF SALEM	304	1957	PERIWINKLE	86	1951
BLACK MAGIC	198	1954	PINK POPCORN	243	1955
BLUE BONNET (No. 1)	69	1950	POWDER PUFF	159	1953
BONNY BLUE	341	1958	PUGET SOUND		1949
CARMEL BLUE	247	1956	PURPLE SAGE	87	1951
CHEFFITA	337	1958	RED BUTTONS	481	1961
CHERIE (No. 1)	124	1952	RED CAP	200	1954
CHEROKEE	242	1955	RED SAILS		1947
CITATION	153	1953	ROSIE O'GRADY	453	1960
COLONIAL DAME	245	1956	ROYAL FLUSH	125	1952
COUNTRY COUSIN	125	1952	ROYAL ORCHID	543	1962
DARK SECRET	300	1957	SEPTEMBER MORN	158	1953
HARVEST MOON	338	1958	SHOW OFF	299	1957
HEART THROB	567	1963	SILVER BLUE	298	1957
INDIAN SUMMER	303	1957	SILVER SLIPPER	301	1957
JUNIOR MISS		1950	SMILES	343	1958
LIBERTY BELL	197	1954	SNOW BUNNY	302	1958
LILLIBET	199	1954	SOUTH PACIFIC	85	1951
LILLIAN GRACE PACA	1358	1976	TINKER BELL	244	1955
MADAME QUEEN		1958	TIPTOP	246	1956
MASTER STROKE	297	1957	TWILIGHT	399	1958
MAYFLOWER (No. 2)		1956	WHITE CAPS	340	1958
MERLE HODGES	70	1950	YANKEE-DOODLE	152	1953
MISS CALIFORNIA	71	1950			

(The number in brackets indicates there are other cultivars of the same name.)

HOLMES

British hybridist. When the Check List was compiled all raisings under the name Holmes were attributed to one raiser. It is now confirmed that there are two hybridists of the same name, Mrs. E. Holmes of Combe Hay, Midford, Bath, and Ron Holmes of Edenbridge, Kent. To clarify the position the list of raisings by both hybridists are given below:

List of Mrs. E. Holmes Introductions

	Date		Date
ANN LEE	1970	HELEN CLARE	1973
BEAU NASH	1976	HELLO DOLLY	1969
BEAUTY OF PRUSSIA	1966	IGLOO MAID	1972
COUNTESS OF MARITZA	1977	JESTER	1968
DAVID LOCKYER	1968	JOHN LOCKYER	1969
FLORAL CITY	1974	KATERINA	1968

	Date		Date
LAVENDER KATE	1970	TANYA	1975
SINCERITY	1968	VIOLET BASSETT-BURR	1972

Most of these raisings were introduced by Lockyer of Bristol.

List of Ron Holmes Introductions Showing Parentage

	A.F.S. No.	Date	Female (seed bearer) × Male (pollen bearer)
BEVERLEY	1378	1976	Percy Holmes × • ,
BLUE MINK	1335	1976	Gruss aus dem Bodethal × Dutch Mill
CICELY ANN		1975	
CYRIL HOLMES	1336	1976	Percy Holmes × Hidcote Beauty
DAVID PERRY	1337	1976	
EDEN BEAUTY	1201	1974	Percy Holmes × Achievement
EILEEN SAUNDERS	1202	1974	Percy Holmes × Prodigy
ELLEN MORGAN	1338	1976	Phyllis ×
GRACE	1203	1974	Percy Holmes × Jack Acland
HEATHER HOLMES	1460	1977	Hugh Morgan ×
HUGH MORGAN	1204	1974	Fascination × Pink Flamingo
JACK KING	1461	1977	Sport of General Monk
JOHN FRASER		1977	Percy Holmes ×
JUPITER SEVENTY	1209	1970	Percy Holmes × San Francisco
KENTISH MAID	1339	1976	Percy Holmes ×
KIM	1340	1976	Percy Holmes ×
LIZ	1379	1970	Synonymous with YVONNE
MARGARET SUSAN	1205	1973	Hugh Morgan × Melody
PEPER HAROW	1206	1974	Percy Holmes × Lakeside
PERCY HOLMES	1207	1974	Coachman × Sunset
QUEEN MABS	1341	1976	Percy Holmes ×
RON HOLMES	1462	1977	Percy Holmes ×
RON'S PET	1208	1974	Percy Holmes × Melody
TED'S	1342	1976	Percy Holmes × Hapsburgh
YVONNE			Synonymous with LIZ
YVONNE HOLMES	1210	1974	Percy Holmes × Mr. A. Huggett

JAMES LYE, GROWER, EXHIBITOR, HYBRIDIST

Wherever fuchsias are discussed, the name of James Lye is bound to enter at some stage, for his cultivars, with the beautiful solid, rich, creamy white tube and sepals of a dense, waxlike texture are known as Lye's 'hallmark'. Born in 1830 at Market Lavington (hence the cultivar, Beauty of Lavington) he started work at the age of 12 in the gardens of Clyffe Hall (hence another cultivar, Beauty of Clyffe Hall).

Clyffe Hall was a small estate belonging to the Hon. Mrs. Hay, sister of the Earl of Radnor, and James commenced his apprenticeship under the head gardener, at that time Richard Smith, who was said to be extremely good with trees and vegetables.

James Lye's first duties, it is told, were sweeping and tidying for which he was paid the princely sum of 4 shillings (20p) a week, he did, however, show great promise and whilst learning his trade by the age of 23, was appointed head gardener. At about this time the Trowbridge Horticultural Society was renowned for its annual exhibitions and shows and under the exalted rank of head gardener of an estate, James would naturally attend these events and it is recorded that he was so impressed with the fuchsias on display that around the year 1853, he decided that the fuchsia was the plant to grow and concentrate upon. So much so, that he started exhibiting them himself in 1857 and is reported to have said 'I appear to see a way to improve upon the plant year after

year'. For many years afterwards he became so well known for his pyramid and pillar fuchsias that he was described in 1886 as the Champion Fuchsia Grower in the West of England.

These were wonderful plants which a contemporary account describes as 'plants truly magnificent, eight to ten feet high and four to five feet through the base, the branches feathering down and covering the pots, the foliage robust and healthy in the extreme, and overlaying all a raiment of admirable blossoms'. In W.P. Wood's book, *A Fuchsia Survey*, a photograph shows the grey-bearded James Lye in billy-cock hat with several of these giant pyramids towering over him. It was all the more remarkable when we consider that at Clyffe Hall there was very little glass; he had the use of only one greenhouse for overwintering and starting the specimen plants into growth, but the training and the bringing into bloom with all the finishing touches were done in the open air; this method of cultivation must give modern growers some food for thought. He started hybridizing in the 1860s and his first recorded cultivars were Loveliness (1869), Scarcity (1869) and the fuchsia he named after himself (1869 or 1883), it would seem likely that 1869 is correct and that possibly his first raising was the one he named after himself. Between that year and 1889 no less than 82 different cultivars have been recorded of his raisings. Unfortunately he did not keep many records of his crossings, which

27

seems to be a fault not only with the hybridists of yester year, but with some of the modern hybridists.

Many of his introductions still hold their own among the vast number of cultivars of the present day, such as Amy Lye, Beauty of Trowbridge, Charming, Clipper, Lye's Unique to name but a few. In fact, both Charming and Clipper were given an Award of Merit by the R.H.S. as late as 1929.

Practically all Lye's introductions are of robust, upright growth and all make extremely good plants trained as standards except two cultivars, Jane Lye and Amy Lye; Jane Lye is very lax and almost a trailer, whilst Amy Lye is best described as a spreading lax bush.

The death of James Lye did not mean the end of the interest in fuchsias for his family. His daughter married George Bright of Reading who was a raiser and exhibitor in his own right; his raisings were Coachman (1910), Gordon Potton (1913), Pink Pearl (1919) and White Knight's Gem (1910). George was a worthy follower of James and during the early 1900s was exhibiting pyramids and pillars even better than the master, as photographs with his exhibition plants, particularly of Pink Pearl, prove. Finally it is interesting to record that Lye's granddaughter learned a lot of horticulture from him and eventually married a nurseryman and her own grandchild was none other than that fuchsia personality, the late Tom Thorne.

List of James Lye's Raisings and Introductions

	Date		Date
ALICE PEARSON	1887	LETTY LYE	1877
AMY LYE	1885	LOUISA BALFOUR.	
ANNIE EARL	1887	LOVELINESS	1869
ARABELLE IMPROVED	1871	LOVELY	1887
AURORA		LYE'S ELEGANCE	1884
BEAUTY OF CLYFFE HALL		LYE'S EXCELSIOR	1886
BEAUTY OF LAVINGTON	1886	LYE'S FAVOURITE	1886
BEAUTY OF SWANLEY	1875	LYE'S OWN	1871
BEAUTY OF THE WEST		LYE'S PERFECTION	1886
BEAUTY OF TROWBRIDGE	1881	LYE'S RIVAL	1891
(Introduced by H. Cannell		LYE'S UNIQUE	1886
who refutes the Lye raising		MISS LYE	1877
and quotes J. Smith of		MISS WELCH	
Trowbridge)		MR. BRIGHT	
BEAUTY OF WILTS	1877	MR. F. BRIGHT	1886
BENJAMIN PEARSON	1877	MR. F. GLASS	1886
BLUSHING BRIDE (No. 1)	1877	MRS. F. GLASS	1886
BOUNTIFUL (No. 1)		MRS. GRANT	
CECIL GLASS	1887	MR. HOOPER TAYLOR	
CHARMING	1877	MR. J. HUNTLEY	1874
CLIPPER (No. 2)	1898	MR. J. LYE	1869
CRIMSON GLOBE		MRS. HOBHOUSE	1897
DELICATA (No. 4)	1877	MRS. HOOPER TAYLOR	
DIADEM	1886	MRS. HUNTLEY	1877
DUCHESS OF ALBANY		MRS. J. BRIGHT	1882
ECLIPSE (No. 2)	1897	MRS. J. LYE	1880
ELEGANCE (No. 3)	1877	MRS. KING	
ELLEN LYE		MRS. WILLS	
EMILY BRIGHT	1886	NELLIE	1886
EMILY DOELS		PINK PERFECTION (No. 1)	1879
EMILY LYE		PRIDE OF THE WEST	1871
EMPEROR	1886	ROYAL STANDARD	
EUREKA	1887	SCARCITY	1869
FINAL		SNOWDROP (No. 3)	1897
GEM OF THE WEST		SPITFIRE	
GLORY OF THE DAY		STAR OF WILTS	
HARRIET LYE	1887	SURPRISE (No. 2)	1887
HENRY BROOKS		SWANLEY BEAUTY	1875
HON. MRS. HAY		(see BEAUTY OF	
JAMES HUNTLEY	1877	SWANLEY)	
JAMES LYE	1869	THOMAS KING	1884
JAMES WELCH	1886	WHITE SOUVENIR de	
JANE LYE	1870	CHISWICK	
JOHN BRIGHT	1886	WINIFRED GLASS	1887
JUBILEE (No. 1)	1897	W. R. MOULD	1897

(The number in brackets indicates there are other cultivars of the same name.)

GREGOR MENDEL (1822-1884)

Most fuchsia hybridists will eventually become acquainted in some degree with the laws of biological inheritance or 'mendelism' and may care to read an abridged account of Mendel's life, from which they will be surprised to learn that his favourite flower was indeed the fuchsia.

The modern science of genetics was born in 1900 when research workers investigating heredity discovered that their problems had all been solved 35 years before by an Augustinian Monk experimenting with green peas in his tiny monastery garden somewhere in Moravia.

Father Gregor Mendel was that monk and the statistical laws of biological inheritance he formulated – often known as mendelism – are used now by plant breeders everywhere so that their crosses are not the hit-and-miss business they once were. Johann Mendel came from a long line of gardeners. His father, a smallholder, had improved a little family farm by planting many fruit trees and keeping bees and in these two activities Johann found lifelong hobbies.

Not notably religious, he entered the monastery at Brno Brünn, in what is now Czechoslovakia, because he could not otherwise afford to continue his studies. He assumed the name of Gregor and at 25 became a priest. He tried to qualify as a teacher but failed the examination – surprisingly in natural history.

Nevertheless he was sent to study at Vienna University and then joined the staff at Brno Modern School. In 1856 he failed the teacher's examination again, on this occasion having an argument with the examiner in botany.

Mendel began his famous pea experiments in 1856 in a little strip of the monastery grounds – 120 ft long and just over 20 ft wide – overlooked by the library window and clocktower. Father Gregor's garden still exists, but today it is dominated by a statue of Mendel himself.

Mendel was not very robust in youth and something of a hypochondriac. He hung an Aeolian harp in his garden and if the wind struck a single note he went to fetch his hat.

Boys from his school often visited him in the monastery garden where he explained his experiments to them. In sex matters he called a spade a spade and when they sniggered he reproved them, saying 'These are natural things'. An enlightened attitude indeed for a mid-19th century priest.

He completed his pea experiments in 1863 and in 1865 gave his conclusions at meetings of the local botanical society.

His arguments were beyond the grasp of this audience: there were no questions and no discussion. When the society sent 120 copies of his paper to learned institutions throughout the world, the response was no better.

In 1868, Mendel was elected Abbot. He included his favourite flower, the fuchsia, in his arms as Abbot but thereafter had little time for experiments.

In 1884, he died, a revered prelate, an unrecognised scientist.

EDWARD PASKESEN, HYBRIDIST (-1979)

With the death of Ted Paskesen of San Francisco, California, the fuchsia world has lost another outstanding hybridist.

He was close to achieving a lifetime goal with a double orange fuchsia cultivar and came very near with his Bicentennial in 1976. He was a member of the American Fuchsia Society for 40 years, serving a period as Editor and as Corresponding Secretary; he was also a past president of the San Francisco Branch. In the hybridizing field, he produced 21 introductions with a further four in conjunction with Clem. Schanabel, introducing and developing many beautiful cultivars. He died from a heart attack on 31st January, 1979.

Full List of Paskesen Raisings and Introductions

	A.F.S. No.	Date		A.F.S. No.	Date
BICENTENNIAL	1344	1976	LA PETITE	662	1966
BLUE BOY (No. 2)	958	1971	LOVELY LADY	700	1967
BUTTERCUP	1345	1976	MEDALLION	761	1968
CABLE CAR	762	1968	MILKY WAY	702	1967
CAPRICORN	872	1970	PAINTED DESERT	664	1966
ETERNAL FLAME	959	1971	PREVIEW	827	1969
FAN TAN	1110	1973	ROMANCE	701	1967
HULA GIRL	1023	1972	VICTORIAN	957	1971
ICICLE	760	1968	WIGWAM	663	1966
IGLOO	633	1965	WINDMILL	727	1967
IMPERIAL	826	1969			

Cultivars raised in conjunction with Clem. Schnabel

	A.F.S. No.	Date		A.F.S. No.	Date
ALLEGRA	416	1960	COCKATOO	328	1958
CAPRI	418	1960	EMBARCADERO	532	1962

* GEORGE ROE

List of George Roe Introductions Showing Parentage

	Date	Female (seed bearer) × male (pollen bearer)
ALISON EWART	1977	Eleanor Leytham × Pink Darling
ALISON SWEETMAN	1984	
AMANDA JONES	1981	Bobby Shaftoe × Santa Barbara
BILLIE ROE	1979	Joy Patmore × Brutus
CAROL PEAT	1977	Eleanor Leytham × Pink Darling
CAROL ROE	1977	Eleanor Leytham × Pink Darling
CATHERINE BARTLETT	1983	Carol Peat × Alison Ewart
CELIA SMEDLEY	1970	Joy Patmore × Glitters
CROPWELL BUTLER	1981	Heidi Ann × Cloverdale Jewel
DR. MANSON	1983	Cloverdale Jewel × Glyn Jones
ELEANOR LEYTHAM	1974	Countess of Aberdeen × Pink Darling
ELIZABETH BROWN	1980	Glyn Jones × Neil Clyne
EVANSON'S CHOICE	1980	Snowcap × Cloverdale Pearl
FIRENZ		
FOREST 78	1980	Cloverdale Pearl × Ice Cap
GLYN JONES	1976	Chance Seedling
GRANPA BLEUSS	1970	Sport of Papa Bleuss
HARLEQUIN	1979	Joy Patmore × Ice Cap
HEIDI PURPURN	1976	Heidi Ann × Dollar Princess
JEAN EWART	1981	Mipan × Carol Roe
JUNE BAGLEY	1977	Eleanor Leytham × Pink Darling
KEN JENNINGS	1982	Bobby Shaftoe × Santa Barbara
KHADA	1973	Snowcap × Margaret Roe
LADY THUMB	1966	Sport of Tom Thumb
MAUREEN MUNRO	1980	Alison Ewart × Carol Peat
MICKY GOULT	1981	Bobby Shaftoe × Santa Barbara
NELLIE NUTTALL	1977	Khada × Icecap
PATRICA EWART	1980	Mipam × Meike Meursing
PAUL ROE	1981	Glyn Jones × Brutus
PIRBRIGHT	1982	Glyn Jones × Santa Barbara
PURPLE ANN	1977	Heidi Ann Seedling
RED ACE	1983	
RON EWART	1981	Bobby Shaftoe × Santa Barbara
SHEILA MONTALBETTI	1980	Snowcap × Cloverdale Pearl
SHEILA ORR	1980	Susan Ford × Neil Clyne
SOUTHWELL MINISTER	1980	Glyn Jones × Neil Clyne
RADCLIFFE BEDDER	1980	Neil Clyne × Mipam
VIVIAN MILLER	1980	Cloverdale Jewel × Cloverdale Pearl

Although SANTA BARBARA is quoted as the pollen bearer it is synonymous with LUSTRE.

DR. MATTHEW RYLE, HYBRIDIST (–1981)

The death of Doctor Matthew Ryle of Warkworth, Northumberland, left yet another huge gap amongst the British hybridists. After suffering several strokes, Dr. Ryle finished hybridising in 1979 although a few introductions, notably the beautiful Dusky Beauty, Brenda, Border Reiver and Elise Mitchell appeared later. Dr. Ryle made his name with 53 introductions in the 1970s and had the distinction of being awarded more British Fuchsia Society Awards for new seedlings than any other hybridiser: one Gold, six Silver and two Bronze Certificates of Merit. His Lady Kathleen

Spence in 1975 received the only Gold Certificate ever awarded. His most successful introduction must be Annabel the beautiful creamy-white double, another Silver Certificate award. A great character and a fine gentleman, he will be sadly missed, especially at the Northern Shows and gatherings, that was if you could break the circle of friends usually holding his conversation. Dr. Ryle did very little for his last few years, did not enjoy good health and died as the result of a massive stroke on 31st December 1981. He will be remembered as a great hybridist.

List of Dr. Matthew Ryle Introductions Showing Parentage

	A.F.S. No.	Date	Female (seed bearer) × Male (pollen bearer)
ALISON RYLE	1112	1973	Lena Dalton × Tennessee Waltz
ANDREW RYLE	1239	1975	Pinky × Pink Cloud seedling × Strawberry Delight
ANNABELL (Silver 1977)	1476	1977	Seedling of Coquet Dale, pollen parent unknown
BEAUTY OF BAMBURGH		1970	
BELSAY BEAUTY			
(Silver 1975)	1240	1975	Mrs. L. Lyon × pollen parent unknown
BOBBY SHAFTOE	1113	1973	Parents unknown

	A.F.S. No.	Date	Female (*seed bearer*) × Male (*pollen bearer*)
BORDER BARON		1975	Earl of Beaconsfield × Alison Ryle
BORDER QUEEN	1167	1974	Lenora × Lena Dalton
BORDER REIVER	1574	1980	
BRENDA	1575	1980	
CALLALY PINK	1334	1976	Mrs. L. Lyon × pollen parent unknown
CAMERON RYLE	1024	1972	Lena Dalton × Citation
CHEVIOT PRINCESS (Silver 1977)	1433	1977	Pink Cloud × Lena Dalton seedling × Athela
CHILLINGHAM COUNTESS	1241	1975	Lye's Unique × Citation seedling × Whirlaway seedling × Royal Velvet
COQUET BELL	1114	1973	Lena Dalton × Citation
COQUET DALE	1397	1976	Joe Kusber × Northumbrian Belle
COQUET GOLD	1398	1976	Sport from Belsay Beauty
CUSHIE BUTTERFIELD	1399	1976	Pink Profusion × Northumbrian Belle
DELAVAL LADY	1242	1975	Very complicated parentage involving Earl of Beaconsfield, Lena Dalton, Lye's Unique and Leonora
DIPTON DAINTY	1243	1975	Lye's Unique × Earl of Beaconsfield seedling × Whirlaway seedling × Royal Velvet
DUSKY BEAUTY	1652	1981	
EDEN LADY (Bronze 1975)	1478	1975	Leonora × Lena Dalton
ELISE MITCHELL	1576	1980	
ESCHOTT ELF	1400	1976	Pink Cloud × Lena Dalton seedling × Sonata × Lakeside
GAY DAMOSEL	1434	1977	Viva Ireland × Joe Kusber
GLORORUM	1244	1975	Pink Profusion × Lena Dalton
GREENRIGG BELL	1435	1977	Lena Dalton × Tennessee Waltz seedling × Border Queen
HARRY HOTSPUR	1245	1975	Lena Dalton × Tennessee Waltz seedling × Earl of Beaconsfield seedling × Strawberry Delight
INGRAM MAID	1401	1976	Pink Cloud × Lena Dalton seedling × Sonata
IRENE RYLE	1246	1975	Bobby Shaftoe × Goldcrest
JESSIE RYLE	1247	1975	Complicated parentage involving Howletts Hardy, Ting-a-Ling, Lena Dalton, Pink Cloud, Golden Dawn and Sonata
JOANNE BAKKER (Silver 1977)	1475	1977	Leonora × Ting-a-Ling
LADY KATHLEEN SPENCE (Gold 1976)	1248	1975	Bobby Shaftoe × Schneewitchen
LANGLEY FORD		1975	Coxeen × Mrs. L. Lyon
LINDISFARNE	1168	1974	Parents unknown
LINHOPE SPRITE	1249	1975	Coxeen × Mrs. L. Lyon
MAGGIE LITTLE	1250	1975	Ruthie × Schneewitchen
MINDRUM GOLD	1251	1975	Pink Cloud × Lena Dalton seedling × Sonata seedling × Goldcrest
MITFORD QUEEN (Bronze 1976)	1436	1977	Pink Cloud × Lena Dalton seedling × Sonata × Nancy Lou
NORMAN MITCHINSON (Silver 1976)	1477	1976	Originally known as 5UKB seedling. Parentage unknown
NORTHERN PRIDE	1528	1979	
NORTHUMBRIAN BELLE	1115	1973	Lena Dalton × Citation
PINK LADY (Silver 1976)	1169	1974	Lena Dalton × Citation × unknown pollen parent
PINK SLIPPERS	1252	1975	Complicated parentage involving Earl of Beaconsfield, Lena Dalton, Lye's Unique
PIROUETTE	1402	1976	
PRESIDENT WILF SHARP		1979	Dorothy Woakes ×
RENE	1253	1975	Bon Accorde × Strawberry Delight
ROTHBURY BEAUTY	1474	1977	Seedling from Pink Cloud × Lena Dalton × Lady Kathleen Spence
SIMONSIDE	1437	1977	Pink Lady × Coxeen
SIOBHAM	1403	1976	Joe Kusber × Northumbrian Belle
THORNTON SURPRISE		1975	
TILLMOUTH LASS	1254	1975	Lena Dalton × Tennessee Waltz seedling × Earl of Beaconsfield seedling × Strawberry Delight
TOSSON BELL	1255	1975	Pink Cloud × Lena Dalton seedling × Sonata seedling × Marin Glow
VINDOLANDA	1256	1975	Lena Dalton × Tennessee Waltz × Earl of Beaconsfield seedling × Strawberry Delight

* ANNABELLE STUBBS, HYBRIDIST

Many are familiar with Annabelle's 50 exquisite introductions, including such cultivars as Pink Marshmallow, Applause, Blue Halo and Nancy Lou, but are unfamiliar with the story of Annabelle's life with fuchsias and her three successful nurseries. Born at Troy, Ohio, Annabelle was introduced to fuchsias some 40 years ago by her mother-in-law, who taught her how to take cuttings.

It was not until 20 years later that Annabelle became an avid fuchsia selector/collector and originally purchased plants from Mission Hill's Nursery at three for a dollar in 2 inch pots. Annabelle and her husband first started business in Leucadia with two lath houses and soon Stubb's Fuchsia Nursery moved to a larger nursery in another location in Leucadia. About this time, she met the well known hybridist Roy Walker, who guided her in making her first introduction, Blue Pinwheel, in 1970. Seeking the perfect fuchsia-growing climate, they then moved to the Fort Bragg area of Mendocino County. After 4 years, they sold Annabelle's Fuchsias and returned to the Oceanside–Leucadia area and began their third nursery, Fire Mountain Fuchsias. One of her favourites is Seventh Heaven and the lovely red double, Ada Perry. Her current goal is the development of a big fluffy bloom with orange sepals and a pure blue or purple corolla. Walking down a row of breathtaking hanging baskets, Annabelle points out a huge pink double currently, called Thanksgiving Turkey on account of its late blooming, which could turn out to be a Princess Elaine or perhaps a Queen Guinevere. Annabelle stresses that fuchsias are not shade-loving plants, loving all the light possible without burning. We can expect many more lovely blooms from this remarkable lovely lady.

List of Mrs. Annabelle Stubbs Introductions Showing Parentage

	A.F.S. No.	Date	Female (seed bearer) × Male (pollen bearer)
ADA PERRY	1733	1983	Seventh Heaven × Hula Girl
ANGELS DREAM	1079	1973	Pink Galore × White King
APPLAUSE	1440	1978	(Trade Winds × Dee Dee) × Fan Tan
ARCHIE OWEN	1410	1977	Pink Galore × White King
BLUE HALO	1615	1981	(Trade Winds × Dee Dee) × Capri
BLUE PINWHEEL	902	1970	Esperanza × Self
CHEERS	1499	1979	Applause × (Independence × Bicentennial)
CHERRY JUBILEE	908	1970	Angela Gallegos × Self
CHRISTMAS HOLLY	1411	1977	Mrs. W.P. Wood × Dollar Princess
CONFECTION	1661	1982	Santa Clara × Novella
COPYCAT	1619	1981	
CORSAGE	1500	1979	(Independence × Fluffy Frills) × Fan Tan
CYNDY ROBYN	1662	1982	Applause × Snowfire
DANCING FLAME	1621	1981	Novella × Applause
DAWN THUNDER	1257	1975	Icicle × White King
ERNESTINE	1616	1981	(Trade Winds × Dee Dee) Fan Tan
EUSEBIA	1663	1982	Pepi × (Applause × Bicentennial)
FIRE MOUNTAIN	1536	1980	Novella × (Applause × Bicentennial)
FIRST LADY	1080	1973	Pink Galore × White King
FLUFFY FRILLS	1382	1976	Pink Marshmallow × Frances Keizar
FROSTED AMETHYST	1258	1975	Pink Marshmallow × White King
FUCHSIARAMA	1278	1975	Pink Marshmallow × Jubie Lynn
GAY PARASOL	1501	1979	Applause × Pepi
GOLDEN ANNIVERSARY	1532	1980	Santa Clara × Novella
IMPERIAL FANTASY	1617	1981	Gay Parasol × Pink Marshmallow
INDEPENDENCE	1383	1976	Santa Clara × Self
KATHY'S SPARKLER	1734	1983	Hula Girl × Applause
KNOCKOUT	1622	1981	Bicentennial × Capri
LOVE IN BLOOM	1412	1977	Fan Tan × Shady Lady
MEDALIST	1753	1984	Cyndy Robyn × Trade Winds
MENDOCINO ROSE	1384	1976	Pink Marshmallow × Al. Stettler
MINI SKIRT	1618	1981	Pepi × Applause
MISS LEUCADIA	999	1971	Pink Galore × White King
MISTY PINK	1735	1983	(Bicentennial × Capri) × Blush o'Dawn
NANCY LOU	998	1971	Pink Galore × White King
OVATION	1614	1981	Pepi × Applause
PALE FLAME	1411	1978	(Trade Winds × Dee Dee) × Fan Tan
PINK MARSHMALLOW	996	1971	Pink Galore × Bianca
RED FORMAL	1365	1976	Alice Hoffman × Tolling Bell
ROXANNA BELLE	1760	1984	Cyndy Robyn × Trade Winds
SEVENTH HEAVEN	1620	1981	Pepi × Applause
SHADY LADY	901	1970	Trade Winds × La Niege
SNOWFIRE	1442	1978	Pink Marshmallow × Fan Tan
SNOWY SUMMIT	1259	1975	Pink Marshmallow × White King
SPARKS	1549	1980	Buttercup × Corsage

THOMAS THORNE, AUTHOR AND HYBRIDIST (1906–1969)

Tom Thorne was, in his day, one of the best known authority on fuchsias; his grandfather, known as 'Old George', was a member of the firm Dixon and Sons, nurserymen who ran a nursery with a shop in Moorgate Street, London, as far back as 1830, whilst his grandmother, 'Gran', was a Lye and worked in her early years with England's greatest breeder of fuchsias at the time, the late James Lye. With such a background, there is little wonder he was always interested in fuchsias. The South African War, together with an accident, left Tom an orphan at an early age and he was brought up by his grandparents.

Even from his early boyhood days, he had memories of meeting most of the British and Continental fuchsia hybridists and ever since those boyhood days, kept up to date with every modern advance in the fuchsia. Eleven times he crossed the Atlantic to the United States of America and the Southern Countries, and whenever business allowed, he was among the breeders and collectors of both continents. He resided in Paddington, London, after a sojourn in Chile, and recalled, on one of his expeditions to South America, being trapped under an overturned lorry for a lengthy period of time in the Piscahuanuma Pass in the Peruvian Andes.

Even during the two World Wars he managed to visit various French, Belgian and other continental nurseries. He claims that the largest specimen fuchsia he ever saw was on Garnish Island just off the coast of Cork, Eire, that of a bush of Lena, 8 to 9 ft high with a diameter of 22½ ft and that the smallest single fuchsia outside the species was Venus Victrix, whilst the smallest double was Isis, sometimes called Sylvia, a tiny fully double red and white.

Towards his latter years Tom worked extensively with the species and between 1953 and 1969 raised 26 cultivars of which President Stanley Wilson, Joan Smith (probably the fastest growing cultivar) and Peace were outstanding. He claimed that his outstanding fuchsia was the first white tubed hybrid of *F. triphylla*, which took him over 20 years to produce and was named Bernard Rawlins (1959) but I have never found anyone who has ever seen this supposedly outstanding breakthrough; his description was tube and sepals ebbing white, flushed pink, with bright orange corolla. His book *Fuchsias for all Purposes* was published in the spring of 1959, revised in 1964, but unfortunately is now out of print, but still eagerly sought by fuchsia enthusiasts all over the world. This book contained the only comprehensive Check List since Dr. Essig's list of 1936 and quickly established itself as the Fuchsia Bible; although one supplementary list was published, it soon fell out of date. Tom, in his later years, held a most unusual occupation, that of Queen's Messenger and at all times he had to be within 1 hour's journey of the British Foreign Office. Up to the time of his death, Tom was a successful fuchsia specialist nurseryman at Little Hallingbury in Hertfordshire. He joined the British Fuchsia Society in 1953 and was a regular committee member for many years up to the time of his death, he was a frequent contributor to the Annual, and his articles are still being read today. His illness was fairly protracted and necessitated the amputation of one, if not two, of his legs. He died on 20th December, 1969, in his early sixties – a character difficult to replace in the fuchsia world.

List of Tom Thorne Introductions Showing Parentage

(The number in brackets indicates there are other cultivars of the same name.)

ALFRED THORNLEY

List of Alfred Thornley Introductions Showing Parentage

	A.F.S. No.	Date	Female (seed bearer) × Male (pollen bearer)
BARON BARON	1465	1969	Chang × Liver Bird
BEN HILL		1966	Parentage not known
CYMRU		1966	Parentage not known
DALTON	1008	1971	Hawkshead × Other Fellow
DEEPDALE	1099	1961	White Spider × Blue Gown
DOROTHEA FLOWER	1009	1969	Hawkshead × Venus Victrix
GRAYRIGG	1468	1971	Silverdale × Silverdale
GREAT GABLE		1963	Guinevere × Madame Lantelme
HAVERTHWAITHE	1061	1966	King's Ransom × Hawkshead
HELVELLYN		1962	Parentage not known
KATIE		1962	White Spider × Chillerton Beauty
KENTS BANK	1467	1963	Hawkshead × Falling Stars
LAKESIDE		1967	Parentage not known (could have LYNETTE blood)
LIVER BIRD	1469	1966	Chang × (Self)
LYNETTE		1961	Guinevere × White Spider
MOSEDALE HALL	1216	1974	Silverdale × Silverdale
PENRITH BEACON	1217	1974	Chang × (Self)
PRESTON GUILD	1010	1971	Dorothea Flower × Hawkshead
RAVENSBARROW	1063	1972	Hawkshead × Gruss aus dem Bodethal
SHOT SILK		1964	Pink Galore × Deepdale
SOUTH LAKELAND	1466	1963	Hawkshead × Falling Stars
STRIDING EDGE		1965	Don Peralta × Nightingdale
THORNLEY'S HARDY		1977	Parentage not known
TROUTBECK	1064	1972	Dorothea Flower × Hawkshead
ULVERSTON	1470	1965	Berkeley × (Self)
WARTON CRAG	1100	1973	Jamboree × (Self)
WENNINGTON BECK	1101	1973	Dorothea Flower × (Self)

N.B. As the cultivar HAWKSHEAD (Travis 1962) figures prominently in this list, the parentage of this cultivar is *F. magellanica* var. *molinae* × Venus Victrix, the first white cultivar to be raised by a British hybridist.

WILFRED L. TOLLEY, HYBRIDIST (1918–1978)

The fuchsia world, with the passing of Wilfred Tolley of West Heath, Birmingham on 9th March 1978, lost a hybridist of distinction. Although a gardener all his life, it was not until his later years that he commenced hybridizing with notable success and he will perhaps be remembered most for his introduction, in 1973, of the well-known cultivar, Barbara, named after his wife.

Full List of Wilfred L. Tolley Raisings and Introductions

	A.F.S. No.	Date		A.F.S. No.	Date
AUNTIE MAGGIE	1228	1974	NELLIE'S LANTERN	1157	1973
BABYFACE	1154	1973	RUNNER	1472	1978
BARBARA	1155	1973	SABINA	1158	1971
FLORA (No. 2)	1156	1973	SEVERN QUEEN	1456	1978
FOREST KING	1471	1978	STRIKER	1231	1974
FOXTROT	1229	1974	TEEPEE	1232	1974
GREENFINGER	1230	1974	TUMBLER	1233	1974
ISLE OF MULL	1455	1978	WHITE FALLS	1234	1974

JAMES TRAVIS WMH, HYBRIDIST, NATURALIST AND AUTHOR
(1904–1980)

James Travis, always referred to simply as 'Jimmie', was one of the most knowledgeable growers in the fuchsia world, having spent over 60 years of his life as grower, hybridist, naturalist, lecturer and author. His greatest honour was in 1968 when he became the first person to be honoured by the British Fuchsia Society with the award of the Whiteman Medal of Honour for his services to the fuchsia world in general. His typical Lancastrian humour and accent made him welcome to any fuchsia gathering and his first real interest in fuchsias started in 1921. He bought a collection of six rooted cuttings from Dobbies of Edinburgh for 3 shillings and 6 pence (17½p) which consisted of Mrs. W. Rundle, Dollar Princess, Pink Pearl, Camelia and Golden Treasure; the other one died, but he always maintained that he had never seen a fuchsia to compare with Mrs. W. Rundle.

Jimmie's entry into the nursery business came by accident when he lost the fingers of his left hand at industrial work. He never regretted the plunge and always quoted 'fancy doing something you like and being paid for it'.

At that time the only specialists were Browns of Chingford (still going strong), Hurrans of Gloucester and Haworths of Ipswich and although the British Fuchsia Society formed in 1938 it was not until 1944 that Jimmie made contact and his real opening to the fuchsia world. Here he met such great personalities as W.P. Wood, Anthony Webb and C.J. Howlett, at the age of 92 at one London Show wearing red carpet slippers all the way from Reading 'they are comfortable and why should I at my age conform to society?' Others included C.P. Raffill, W.

Whiteman, all very helpful, but he probably learnt most from Mr. Webb and W.P. Wood.

Naturally his first interest was in cultivars but after seeing the fuchsia species, especially the Encliandras with their fine form and elegance, his aim was to collect these beautiful forms and they became a large part of his life. He would often say 'species and wild plants are perfectly balanced, they must be as they are the results of time infinite'. It was the 'species field' that Jimmie concentrated upon when not commercially occupied on hybridising. Jimmie and his wife organised the British Fuchsia Society stand at Southport for over 30 years and became the mecca for fuchsia people all over the country, eager to hear his words of wisdom.

In his latter years, Jimmie served the British Fuchsia Society well; he was elected to the General Committee in 1968, served on both the Floral Committee and Judging Panel, giving his benefit of years of experience. Although Jimmie raised many fine introductions, it was in his latter years that he really enjoyed the selfing of species, a time expanding matter with many disappointments but grand to prove having produced a correct specimen fuchsia.

His booklet *Fuchsia Culture* ran into over 20 impressions and was responsible for putting countless people on the way to successful fuchsia cultivation. His other great love was that of cricket and woe behold anyone who called or interrupted his concentration when test matches were being played. His death was sudden, from a heart attack at the age of 76 on 5th October 1980. Here was a man whose name was synonymous with fuchsias.

Full List of Travis Raisings and Introductions Showing Parentage

	A.F.S. No.	Date	Parentage
ALICE TRAVIS		1956	F. encliandra × F. hemleyana
ANTHONY WEBB		1956	
ARIEL	1136	1973	
ARTEMIS	1317	1975	
AVOCET	1137	1958	Jules Daloges × Elizabeth Travis
BLUE LAGOON (No. 1)		1958	
BUTTERMERE	1138	1967	Opalescent × Citation
CONISTON WATER	1139	1959	
DERWENTWATER		1961	
ELIZABETH TRAVIS		1956	
EOS	1318	1975	
ERIS	1581	1980	F. encliandra ×
EVENING SKY	1140	1957	
FINGAL'S CAVE		1958	
GEORGE TRAVIS		1956	
GRASMERE		1964	F. cordifolia × F. lycoides
HANORA		1957	
HANORA'S SISTER	1141	1959	Mrs. W. Rundle × Evening Light
HAWKSHEAD	1142	1962	F. magellanica var. molinae × Venus Victrix
IONA	1143	1958	Opalescent × Formosissima
LILIAN ALDERSON	1319	1975	
LITTLE CATBELLS	1582	1980	F. encliandra ×
LITTLE LANGDALE		1967	F. magellanica var. molinae ×
OBERON (No. 2)	1144	1958	
PALLAS ATHENE	1583	1980	F. encliandra ×
PHOEBE TRAVIS		1956	
POSEIDON	1584	1980	F. fulgens var. rubra grandiflora ×
ROBERT DORAN		1956	
RYDAL WATER	1145	1960	Opalescent × Formosissima

	A.F.S. No.	Date	Parentage
SHUNA	1146	1973	Sport of Countess of Aberdeen
SHUNA LINDSAY	1585	1980	
SILVERDALE	1147	1962	*F. magellanica* var. *molinae* × Venus Victrix
SUSAN TRAVIS		1958	
SWAN LAKE (No. 1)		1957	
TARN HAWS		1960	
TEDDY		1957	
TERRY BAYES		1956	
THE TARNS	1148	1962	Venus Victrix ×
TRAVIS'S HARDY		1956	
ULLSWATER	1149	1958	
WALDFEE	1150	1973	*F. michoacanensis* ×
YELENA SUZANNE	1586	1980	*F. arborescens* ×
YOUTH		1958	

(The number in brackets indicates there are other cultivars of the same name).

AWARD-WINNING FUCHSIAS

*LIST OF HYBRIDS – CULTIVARS WITH AMERICAN FUCHSIA SOCIETY CERTIFICATES OF MERIT (1948 to 1973)
(No awards have been made since 1973)

ALASKA	1967	LAURE	1971
ALFIE	1971	LAURIE	1967
ANGEL'S FLIGHT	1960	LEONORA	1964
ANITA	1948	LILLIBET	1956
ANNA	1948	LISA	1968
BERKELEY	1957	LOLITA	1967
BLOOMER GIRL	1954	MAORI MAID	1969
BLUE PINWHEEL	1973	MARIN GLOW	1956
BLUE SATIN	1972	MASQUERADE	1965
BLUE WAVES	1956	MAZDA	1951
BLUSH O' DAWN	1966	MONTEZUMA	1970
BRIDESMAID	1954	NOVELLA	1971
BUTTONS AND BOWS	1965	ORANGE DROPS	1967
CABLE CAR	1971	PAPA BLEUSS	1958
CANDLELIGHT	1963	PAPOOSE	1963
CAPRI	1964	PARKSIDE	1950
CARMEL BLUE	1958	PINK CLOUD	1958
CAVALIER	1955	PINK DOLL	1973
CIRCUS	1970	PINK FAVOURITE	1963
CITATION	1955	PINK FLAMINGO	1964
CITY OF RICHMOND	1958	PINK GALORE	1961
COED	1966	POTENTATE	1956
CRINOLINE	1952	RAMBLING ROSE	1962
CURLEY Q	1964	RED JACKET	1961
DARK EYES	1961	RED SHADOWS	1966
DIANA	1970	RED SPIDER	1948
DOROTHY LOUISE	1954	ROMANCE	1970
DR. JULES WELCH	1951	RUBEO	1949
DR. OLSON	1962	RUFUS	1955
DU BARRY	1952	SAN DIEGO	1968
DUSKY ROSE	1962	SATELLITE	1968
EASTER BONNET	1957	SHARON	1951
ECSTASY	1950	SKYLARK	1958
ENCHANTED	1952	SLEIGH BELLS	1956
FIREBALL	1960	SOPHISTICATED LADY	1968
FIRST LOVE	1960	STELLA MARINA	1953
FLYING CLOUD	1951	STRAWBERRY SUNDAE	1962
FOREVER YOURS	1958	SWINGTIME	1953
FORT BRAGG	1961	SWISS MISS	1965
FRENCHI	1955	THE PHOENIX	1970
GAZEBO	1972	THUNDERBIRD	1960
GEORGANA	1960	TIFFANY	1964
GLORIOUS	1950	TING-A-LING	1962
GOLDEN MARINKA	1960	TINKER BELL	1957
GOV. 'PAT' BROWN	1966	TRANQUILITY	1973
HIDCOTE BEAUTY (Honorary Award)		TREASURE	1949
HIS EXCELLENCY	1962	TUMBLING WATERS	1956
ICICLE	1954	TUTU	1954
ILLUSION	1971	UNCLE CHARLEY	1951
INDIAN MAID	1969	UNCLE JULES	1951
INTREPID	1965	VIOLET GEM	1951
ITALIANO	1973	VOODOO	1951
JACKPOT	1969	WHIRLAWAY	1964
JACK SHAHAN	1969	WHITEMOST	1948
LACE PETTICOATS	1950	WHITE QUEEN (Pennisi 1970)	1973
LADY ANN	1954	YONDER BLUE	1956
LADY BETH	1955	ZIEFIELD GIRL	1969
	1961		

LIST OF HYBRIDS – CULTIVARS WITH BRITISH FUCHSIA SOCIETY AWARDS (1959 to 1983)

ANNABEL	Dr. M. Ryle	Silver Certificate of Merit	1977
*ANN BEL	Dr. M. Ryle	Award of Merit	1983
AUNTIE JINKS	J. Wilson	Bronze Certificate of Merit	1978
BELSAY BEAUTY	Dr. M. Ryle	Silver Certificate of Merit	1975
*BILLY GREEN	Unknown British	First Class Certificate	1982
BLUE ELF	Mrs. M. Hall	Award of Merit and Jones Cup	1972
BOBBY WINGROVE	E.N. Wingrove	Award of Merit	1966
*BORDER QUEEN	Dr. M. Ryle	Award of Merit	1982
BOW STREET	V.V. Miller	Award of Merit and Jones Cup	1970
CARLOTTA	P. Howarth	Bronze Certificate of Merit	1979
CELADORE	Mrs. M. Hall	Silver Certificate of Merit	1979
*CELIA SMEDLEY	G. Roe	First Class Certificate	1982
*CHEVIOT PRINCESS	Dr. M. Ryle	Silver Certificate of Merit	1977
*CITATION	R. Hodges	Highly commended	1982
*CITATION	R. Hodges	Award of Merit	1983
*CLOVERDALE PEARL	C. Gadsby	Award of Merit	1983
COCOANUT ICE	D. Burns	Bronze Certificate of Merit	1978
CONNIE (Dawson)	S.J. Wilson	Award of Merit and Jones Cup	1964
COQUET DALE	Dr. M. Ryle	Silver Certificate of Merit	1978
CRYSTAL STARS	Mrs. I. Clyne	Silver Certificate of Merit	1976
*DISPLAY	Smith	First Class Certificate	1982
EAST ANGLIAN (Thorne)	V.F. Nurseries	Award of Merit and Jones Cup	1960
EDEN LADY	Dr. M. Ryle	Silver Certificate of Merit	1975
ELEANOR LEYTHAM	G. Roe	Bronze Certificate of Merit	1976
ELFIN GLADE	Dr. O. Colville	Award of Merit	1963
*EVA BOERG	Yorke	Award of Merit	1983
*FLIRTATION WALTZ	Waltz	Highly Commended	1982
FUKSIE FOETSIE	H.J. van der Grijp	Bronze Certificate of Merit	1979
*GENII	V. Reiter	Award of Merit	1982
ICEBERG	N. Mitchinson	Silver Certificate of Merit	1980
ICED CHAMPAGNE	K.G. Jennings	Award of Merit and Jones Cup	1968
IRIS AMER	D. Ames	Award of Merit	1966
ISHBELL	W.D. Clark	Award of Merit and Jones Cup	1963
JOANNE BAKKER	Dr. M. Ryle	Silver Certificate of Merit	1977
JOAN SMITH (Thorne)	V.F. Nurseries	Award of Merit and Jones Cup	1959
*JOY PATMORE	E.T. Turner	Highly Commended	1982
JUPITER 70	R. Holmes	Award of Merit	1970
KATHRYN MAIDMENT	C. Creer	Bronze Certificate of Merit	1980
*LA CAMPANELLA	J. Blackwell	Highly Commended	1982
*LADY ISOBEL BARNETT	C. Gadsby	Highly Commended	1982
LADY KATHLEEN SPENCE	Dr. M. Ryle	Gold Certificate of Merit	1976
LEONORA	H. Tiret	Highly Commended	1982
*MARIN GLOW	P.F. Reedstrom	Highly Commended	1982
*MARINKA	Rozain–Boucharlet	First Class Certificate	1982
MARY REYNOLDS	E. Reynolds	Bronze Certificate of Merit	1976
MIEKE MEURSING	G. Hopgood	Award of Merit	1968
*MIEKE MEURSING	G. Hopgood	Award of Merit	1982
MITFORD QUEEN	Dr. M. Ryle	Bronze Certificate of Merit	1976
*MRS POPPLE	Elliott	Award of Merit	1983
NORMAN MITCHINSON	Dr. M. Ryle	Silver Certificate of Merit	1976
NORTHWAY	J. Goliacs	Silver Certificate of Merit	1978
*PACQUESA	Mrs. I. Clyne	Highly Commended	1982
PAT MEARA	V.V. Miller	Award of Merit and Jones Cup	1962
PENNINE	N. Mitchinson	Bronze Certificate of Merit	1979
PINK LADY	Dr. M. Ryle	Silver Certificate of Merit	1976
QUEEN OF BATH	Dr. O. Colville	Award of Merit and Jones Cup	1966
ROYAL VELVET	Waltz	First Class Certificate	1982
SEEDLING B256/75/1	J. Travis	Silver Certificate of Merit	1978
SEEDLING M2	N. Fellow	Bronze Certificate of Merit	1976
*SNOWCAP	D. Henderson	First Class Certificate	1982
SON OF THUMB	R. Gubler	Silver Certificate of Merit	1978

SPANISH RHAPSODY	Dr. O. Colville	Award of Merit and Jones
		Cup 1965
*SWINGTIME	H. Tiret	Award of Merit 1982
*TENNESSEE WALTZ	Walker and Jones	Highly Commended 1982
*TENNESSEE WALTZ	Walker and Jones	Award of Merit 1983
*THALIA	G. Bonstedt	Award of Merit 1982
THE OBSERVER (Coats)	V.F. Nurseries	Award of Merit 1962
*TOM THUMB	Baudinat	Highly Commended 1982
WHITE JOY	D. Burns	Bronze Certificate of Merit 1980
WHITEKNIGHTS AMETHYST	J.O. Wright	Silver Certificate of Merit 1977
WHITEKNIGHTS CASCADE	J.O. Wright	Silver Certificate of Merit 1977
WHITEKNIGHTS RUBY	J.O. Wright	Silver Certificate of Merit 1977
WHITE PIXIE (Merrist Wood)	V.F. Nurseries	Award of Merit 1968

* New information since 1982.

*LIST OF FUCHSIAS WITH ROYAL HORTICULTURAL SOCIETY HARDINESS AWARDS (1928/31)

	Award	Date		Award	Date
ANDENKEN AN			KORALLE	A.M.	1928/31
HEINRICH HENKEL	A.M.	1928/31	GRACILIS	H.C.	1928/31
BALKON	H.C.	1928/31	magellanica var.		
BALLET GIRL	A.M.	1928/31	gracilis	H.C.	1928/31
BEAUTY	H.C.	1928/31	magellanica var.		
CHARMING	A.M.	1928/31	thompsonii	A.M.	1928/31
CLIPPER	H.C.	1928/31	MARINKA	A.M.	1928/31
DAINTY LADY	A.M.	1928/31	MASTERPIECE	A.M.	1928/31
DISPLAY	H.C.	1928/31	MAUVE BEAUTY	A.M.	1928/31
EMILA ZOLA	A.M.	1928/31	MRS. MARSHALL	A.M.	1928/31
FASCINATION	H.C.	1928/31	ROSE OF CASTILE		
GARTENMEISTER			IMPROVED	H.C.	1928/31
BONSTEDT	H.C.	1928/31	SUNRAY	A.M.	1928/31
GOLDEN TREASURE	H.C.	1928/31	THOMPSONII	A.M.	1928/31

A.M. = Award of Merit; H.C. = Highly Commended.

*LIST OF FUCHSIAS WITH ROYAL HORTICULTURAL SOCIETY HARDINESS AWARDS (1962–1978)

The Royal Horticultural Society in co-operation with the British Fuchsia Society has carried out trials of fuchsias for hardiness at their grounds at Wisley, the trials were in three parts, 1960 to 1962, 1963 to 1965 and 1975 to 1978. In each case three young plants of each stock were planted in open ground and left undisturbed for the winters of 1963/4, 1964/5 and 1975/6/7. The plants in the trials were not protected by any overhead covering.

	Award	Date		Award	Date
ABBÉ FARGES	H.C.	1965	GRACILIS VARIEGATA	H.C.	1962
ABUNDANCE	A.M.	1978	GRAF WITTE	A.M.	1978
ADMIRATION (plants grown			ISABEL RYAN	H.C.	1978
in the 1965 trials were			LADY THUMB	F.C.C.	1978
President)			LENA	A.M.	1978
BASHFUL	A.M.	1978	MADAME CORNELISSEN	H.C.	1962
BEACON	H.C.	1978	MADAME CORNELISSEN	F.C.C.	1978
BLUE BONNET	A.M.	1978	magellanica var.		
BRILLIANT	A.M.	1962	gracilis variegata	H.C.	1962
BRUTUS	H.C.	1965	magellanica var. riccartonii	F.C.C.	1978
C.J. HOWLETT	A.M.	1978	magellanica var. thompsonii	A.M.	1965
CHILLERTON BEAUTY	H.C.	1962	MARGARET	H.C.	1962
CHILLERTON BEAUTY	A.M.	1978	MARGARET	A.M.	1965
CLIFF'S HARDY	A.M.	1978	MARGARET BROWN	H.C.	1965
CORALLINA	H.C.	1962	MONSIEUR THIBAND	A.M.	1965
DOLLAR PRINCESS	H.C.	1965	MRS. POPPLE	A.M.	1962
DOROTHY	H.C.	1965	MRS. POPPLE	F.C.C.	1965
DR. FOSTER	H.C.	1962	PEE WEE ROSE	A.M.	1978
DR. FOSTER	A.M.	1965	PHENOMENAL	H.C.	1965
ENFANT PRODIGY			PHRYNE	H.C.	1965
(Synonymous with			PIXIE	H.C.	1978
PRODIGY)	A.M.	1965	PRELUDE (Blackwell)	A.M.	1962
EVA BOERG	A.M.	1962	PRESIDENT (grown in 1965		
EXONIENSIS	H.C.	1962	trials as ADMIRATION)	H.C.	1965

	Award	Date		Award	Date
PRODIGY (Synonymous with			SHARPITOR	H.C.	1978
ENFANT PRODIGY)	A.M.	1965	SUSAN TRAVIS	H.C.	1978
PURPLE SPLENDOUR	H.C.	1978	TENNESSEE WALTZ	H.C.	1965
RICCARTONII	F.C.C.	1978	THOMPSONII	A.M.	1965
RUFUS	A.M.	1978	TOM THUMB	F.C.C.	1962
RUTH	A.M.	1978	TRASE	A.M.	1978
SEALAND PRINCE	A.M.	1965	TRUDY	H.C.	1978

The list differs considerably from the British Fuchsia Society list of hardies which are accepted as hardy plants in B.F.S. shows.

F.C.C. = First Class Certificate; A.M. = Award of Merit; H.C. = Highly Commended.

AVAILABILITY OF FUCHSIAS

Fuchsias Available in Great Britain from Specialist Nurserymen

Addresses of Nurserymen

1. AKER: C. and J.I. Akers, Fountain Nurseries, Fountains, Near Ripon, North Yorkshire. Tel. Sawley (076586) 623
2. BAKER: B. and H.M. Baker, Bourne Brooke Nurseries, Greenstead Green, Halstead, Essex. Tel. Halstead 472900
3. BURGH: Burgh Nurseries, (Norman J. Goodey) Hall Road, Hasketon, Woodbridge, Suffolk. Tel. Grundisburgh (047335) 329
4. CHING: Chingford Nurseries, 20 Chingford Mount Road, South Chingford, London E4.
5. HIGH: High Trees Nurseries, Buckland, Reigate, Surrey. Tel. Reigate 47217
6. JACK: Jackson's Nurseries, Clifton Campville, Near Tamworth, Staffordshire. Tel. (082 786) 307
7. NUTT: V.T. Nuttall, Markham Grange Nursery, Long Lands Lane, Brodsworth, Doncaster. Tel. Doncaster 722390
8. PACEY: R. and J. Pacey, Stathern, Melton Mowbray, Leicestershire. Tel. Harby 60249
9. PENH: Penhalls (Fuchsias) Deeside Gardens, 37 Grain Road, Shaw, Near Oldham, Lancashire. Tel. Shaw 845418
10. PICK: D.N. Pickard, Meadowcroft Nurseries, St Ives Road, Somersham, Huntingham, Cambs. Tel. Ramsey 840454
11. RAIN: Rainbow's Fuchsias, Rainbow End, Mayes Lane, Sandon, Essex. Tel. Danbury 3574
12. RIDD: Fuchsiavale Nurseries, Stanklyn Lane, Summerfield, Kidderminster, Worcs. Tel. Kidderminster (0562) 69444
13. WOOD: Woodbridge Nursery, Don Stilwell, Hibernia Road, Hounslow, Middlesex. Tel. (01 572) 0660

List of Available Fuchsias from Each Nursery

	AKER	BAKER	BURGH	CHING	HIGH	JACK	NUTT	PACEY	PENH	PICK	RAIN	RIDD	WOOD
	1	2	3	4	5	6	7	8	9	10	11	12	13
ABBE FARGES	x	x	x	x	x	x	x	x	x	x	x	x	x
~~ARINGER FAYRE~~													x
~~ABBE FARGES~~													
~~ABUNDANCE (...)~~				x									
ACHIEVEMENT				x	x	x		x	x	x			x
ADMIRATION											x		
AFTER FIVE								x		ʌ			
AILEEN											x		
AINTREE						x					x	x	
ALASKA		x	x		x			x	x	x	x		
ALBION						x		x	x				
ALDHAM												x	
ALFRED RAMBAUD							x						
ALICE ASHTON		x	x		x					x	x		
ALICE HOFFMAN	x	x	x	x	x	x	x	x	x	x	x	x	x
ALICE TRAVIS	x	x		x	x				x				
ALISON EWART					x		x					x	x
ALISON RYLE		x								x		x	
ALLEGRA			.	x	x						x		
alpestris		x		x				x					
ALSA		x											
AL STETTLER			x							x	x		
ALWIN					x							x	
ALYCE LARSON	x	x					x	x				x	x
AMALTHEA													x
AMANDA JONES	x						x						
AMBASSADOR		x	x						x				
AMELIE AUBIN		x		x					x				
AMERICA		x	x										
AMERICANA ELEGANS (See *magellanica americana elegans*)													
AMERICAN FLAMING GLORY			x							x	x		
AMETHYST FIRE													x
AMIGO	x	x								x			
A.M. LARWICK		x											
AMY LYE (LYE)	x	x	x	x	x		x		x	x	x		
ANDRE LE NOSTRE		x							x				
ANDREW						x			x				
ANDREW RYLE	x								x	x		x	
ANDROMEDA					x								
ANGELA							x						
ANGELA LESLIE	x	x			x		x		x				x
ANGELA RIPPON			x		x	x		x		x			x
ANGELINE			x										x
ANGEL'S DREAM										x		x	x
ANGEL'S FLIGHT	x	x	x		x				x	x	x		
ANNABEL		x	x		x	x	x	x		x	x	x	x
ANN LEE		x											
ANNE										x	x		
ANN H. TRIPP	x						x					x	
ANN PACEY								x					
ANN'S BEAUTY			x							x			

	AKER 1	BAKER 2	BURGH 3	CHING 4	HIGH 5	JACK 6	NUTT 7	PACEY 8	PENH 9	PICK 10	RAIN 11	RIDD 12	WOOD 13
ANN'S DELIGHT			x							x			
ANTONIA										x			
APACHE				x									
APHRODITE		x									x		x
APPLAUSE			x					x		x		x	
AQUARIUS										x			
ARABELLA IMPROVED (LYE)									x				
arborescens	x	x		x	x			x	x			x	x
ARCADIA	x											x	
ARCADY									x				
ARCHIE OWEN										x			
ARIEL	x												
ARK ROYAL													x
ARLENDON						x		x	x		x		
ARMY NURSE			x	x					x				x
ARTHUR COPE				x				x					
ATHELA		x		x	x			x		x			
ATLANTIS	x				x								
ATOMIC GLOW		x			x								
AUDRAY		x											
AUNTIE JINKS	x	x	x		x						x	x	x
AUNTIE MAGGIE			x							x			
AUNT JULIANA		x	x										
AURORA SUPERBA		x		x	x			x			x		
AUSTRALIA FAIR		x											
AUTUMNALE (Synonymous with BURNING BUSH)	x	x	x		x	x	x	x	x	x	x	x	x
AVALANCHE		x	x	x									
AVIATOR			x										
AVOCET		x	x	x					x		x		
A.W. TAYLOR		x											
BABY BLUE EYES													x
BABY CHANG			x								x		x
BABY FACE												x	x
BABY PINK			x							x	x	x	x
bacillaris		x		x									x
BAKERS TRI		x											
BALKONKÖNIGIN (Synonymous with BALKON)		x		x									
BALLET GIRL	x	x	x						x		x		x
BARBARA		x	x	x		x	x	x	x	x	x	x	x
BARON de KETTLER			x					x					
BARRY'S QUEEN		x											
BASHFUL			x										
BASKETFUL										x			
BEACON	x	x	x		x		x	x	x	x			x
BEACON ROSA					x								
BEAUTY OF BATH	x	x			x			x			x		
BEAUTY OF CLIFF HALL		x											
BEAUTY OF EXETER		x		x	x			x					x
BEAUTY OF SWANLEY		x		x				x					
BEAUTY OF TROWBRIDGE (LYE)								x					x
BEAUTY QUEEN										x			
BELLA FORBES		x		x					x		x		x
BELLA MIA				x					x	x			

43

	AKER	BAKER	BURGH	CHING	HIGH	JACK	NUTT	PACEY	PENH	PICK	RAIN	RIDD	WOOD
	1	2	3	4	5	6	7	8	9	10	11	12	13
BELL BOTTOMS					x					x			
BELL BUOY				x									
BELLE de LISSE					x						x		
BELLE OF SALEM										x			
BELSAY BEAUTY				x		x		x	x			x	
BELVOIR BEAUTY						x		x	x			x	
BELVOIR ELF								x					
BELVOIR LAKES								x					
BERANGER				x									
BERKELEY													x
BERLINER KIND		x		x		x			x	x			
BERNADETTE													x
BETH ROBLEY			x					x		x	x		
BETSY ROSS		x											
BETTY							x						
BEVERLEY		x		x	x								
BEWITCHED		x										x	
BIANCA												x	x
BICENTENNIAL	x		x		x		x	x		x	x	x	x
BILLIE ROE							x						
BILLY GREEN	x	x	x	x	x	x	x	x	x		x	x	x
BISHOP'S BELLS						x		x	x				
BLACK PRINCE	x									x			
BLANCHE REGINA						x		x			x		x
BLAND'S NEW STRIPED		x		x								x	
BLAZE						x							
BLUE BEAUTY		x		x									
BLUE BOY (Fry)				x									
BLUE BOY (Paskesen)			x							x			
BLUE BUSH						x	x	x					x
BLUE BUTTERFLY		x											
BLUE ELF			x		x				x	x	x		
BLUE GOWN	x	x	x	x						x		x	
BLUE JACKET													x
BLUE LAGOON	x									x			
BLUE MINK		x			x								
BLUE MIST		x											
BLUE PEARL		x					x		x		x		x
BLUE PENDANT										x			
BLUE PETTICOAT										x			
BLUE PINWHEEL		x		x						x	x		
BLUE SAILS								x					
BLUE SATIN			x							x			
BLUE TIT													x
BLUE VEIL	x				x			x					
BLUE WAVES	x	x	x	x	x	x	x		x	x	x	x	x
BLUSH O' DAWN	x	x	x		x		x		x	x	x	x	x
BOBBY BOY		x											
BOBBY SHAFTOE		x	x		x			x	x		x	x	x
BOBBY WINGROVE		x											x
BOBOLINK		x								x		x	x
BOB'S CHOICE								x					
BOERHAAVE		x											

	AKER	BAKER	BURGH	CHING	HIGH	JACK	NUTT	PACEY	PENH	PICK	RAIN	RIDD	WOOD
	1	2	3	4	5	6	7	8	9	10	11	12	13
boliviania	x	x		x	x			x	x				
BON ACCORDE	x	x	x		x				x	x	x	x	x
BONANZA		x								x	x		
BON BON		x	x	x	x				x	x	x	x	x
BONITA							x		x				
BONNIE LASS		x			x								
BORA BORA	x	x								x			
BORDER QUEEN	x	x	x	x	x	x		x	x	x		x	x
BORDER REIVER												x	
BOSUN'S NORAH											x		
BOUFFANT		x		x	x			x	x	x			
BOUNTIFUL	x				x		x		x		x	x	x
BOUQUET				x	x			x	x				x
BOW BELLS						x		x					
BRANDT'S 500 CLUB		x		x	x				x		x	x	
BREEDER'S DREAM		x										x	
BRENDA		x	x		x			x				x	x
BRENDA PRITCHARD								x					
BRENTWOOD		x											
BRIDAL PINK									x				
BRIDAL VEIL		x										x	
BRIDESMAID		x	x	x	x				x	x		x	x
BRIG O'DOON		x								x			
BRILLIANT		x	x								x		
BRITISH STERLING						x		x					
BRIXHAM ORPHEUS				x									
BRODSWORTH							x						
BRUTUS	x	x	x	x	x			x	x		x	x	x
BUBBLE HANGER		x							x	x			
BUDDHA			x		x					x	x		
BUNNY		x	x		x		x				x		
BURNING BUSH (Synonymous with AUTUMNALE)			x							x			
BUTTERCUP		x		x	x			x		x	x	x	x
BUTTERFLY										x			x
BUTTERMERE													x
BUTTONS & BOWS									x				
CABALLERO		x								x			x
CABLE CAR										x			
CADMUS									x				
CAESAR	x	x	x		x		x		x	x			x
CALEDONIA	x	x		x					x				
CALLALY PINK				x	x		x						
CAMBRIDGE LOUIE		x	x		x		x				x		x
CAMERON RYLE	x							x	x	x			
CANDLELIGHT		x			x				x		x	x	
CANDY STRIPE									x				
CAPITOLA										x			
CAPRI	x	x								x			
CAPRICORN			x							x			
CARA MIA				x							x	x	x
CARDINAL	x			x					x				
CARDINAL FARGES	x		x	x	x		x	x	x			x	x
CARIOCA		x		x					x				

45

	AKER	BAKER	BURGH	CHING	HIGH	JACK	NUTT	PACEY	PENH	PICK	RAIN	RIDD	WOOD
	1	2	3	4	5	6	7	8	9	10	11	12	13
CARL DRUDE					x								
CARMEL BLUE		x	x	x		x			x	x	x		x
CARMEN		x											
CARMEN MARIA				x		x		x		x			
CARNIVAL		x	x		x					x		x	
CAROLE PUGH										x			
CAROLE ROE							x						x
CAROLINE	x	x	x	x	x	x		x	x		x	x	x
CAROL PEAT							x						x
CASCADE		x	x	x	x	x	x	x	x	x	x	x	x
CATALINA				x					x				
CATHE MACDOUGALL		x											x
CATHERINE CLAIRE			x							x		x	x
CECIL GLASS (Lye)		x											
CELADORE								x				x	x
CELIA SMEDLEY	x	x	x	x	x	x	x	x	x	x	x	x	x
CENTRE PIECE		x			x								
CHANDLERII	x								x				
CHANG		x	x	x	x				x		x		x
CHARLIE GARDINER		x											
CHARLIE GIRL		x									x		
CHARLOTTE						x							
CHARMING (Lye)	x	x	x	x		x			x			x	x
CHARTWELL								x					
CHE BELLA													x
CHECKERBOARD	x	x	x	x	x	x		x	x	x	x	x	x
CHECKMATE		x		x								x	
CHEERS		x			x		x		x				
CHESSBOARD		x											
CHEVIOT PRINCESS	x											x	x
CHILLERTON BEAUTY	x		x	x	x	x		x	x	x			
CHINA DOLL		x	x		x				x	x	x		x
CHINA LANTERN	x	x		x			x	x	x	x	x		
CHRISTINE PUGH										x	x		
CHRISTMAS ELF		x		x					x	x	x		x
CHRISTY										x			
CICELY ANN											x		
CINNABARINA									x				x
CIRCE		x					x						
CIRCUS		x						x		x	x		
CITATION	x	x	x	x	x	x	x	x	x	x	x		x
CITY OF DERBY		x		x				x					
C.J. HOWLETT				x									
CLAIRE de LUNE		x	x							x			x
CLAIRE EVANS									x				
CLARET CUP									x				
CLEOPATRA													x
CLIFFORD GADSBY					x			x				x	
CLIFFORD ROYLE									x				
CLIFF'S HARDY					x		x	x	x				
CLIFF'S OWN									x		x		x
CLIFF'S UNIQUE					x			x				x	x
CLIFTON BEAUTY			x			x					x		x

46

	AKER	BAKER	BURGH	CHING	HIGH	JACK	NUTT	PACEY	PENH	PICK	RAIN	RIDD	WOOD
	1	2	3	4	5	6	7	8	9	10	11	12	13
CLIFTON BELLE						x							
CLIFTON CHARM						x							
CLIPPER (Lye)				x					x				
CLOTH OF GOLD	x	x	x	x		x			x	x	x	x	x
CLOVERDALE DELIGHT					x							x	x
CLOVERDALE JEWEL	x	x	x		x	x	x	x	x			x	x
CLOVERDALE JOY			x									x	x
CLOVERDALE PEARL	x	x	x	x	x	x	x	x	x	x	x	x	x
CLOVERDALE PRIDE	x											x	x
CLOVERDALE STAR						x			x				
COACHMAN	x	x		x	x	x			x	x	x	x	x
COCCINEA (*See magellanica* var. *coccinea*)													
colimae											x		
COLLINGWOOD	x	x		x	x				x				
COME DANCING								x	x			x	x
COMET		x	x	x		x			x	x	x		
CONCHILLA		x											
CONISTON WATER		x							x				
CONNIE		x											
CONSPICUA		x		x					x				x
CONSTANCE	x		x	x		x			x	x	x	x	
CONSTELLATION (Sohnabel)	x	x	x		x	x	x	x	x	x	x		
CONTRAMINE				x									
COQUET BELL	x	x			x	x		x	x			x	x
COQUET DALE	x					x	x	x			x	x	x
COQUET GOLD							x						
CORALLE (see KORALLE)													
CORALLINA	x	x	x	x					x	x	x		x
CORAL SEAS		x		x						x			
cordifolia	x	x		x	x			x	x		x		x
CORE 'N GRATIO		x							x	x	x		
CORSAGE			x						x	x	x		
CORSAIR		x					x						x
corymbiflora	x	x		x	x				x		x		x
corymbiflora alba	x	x		x	x			x	x				
COSMOPOLITAN		x											
COSTA BRAVA									x				
COTTON CANDY		x			x			x	x	x		x	x
COUNTESS OF ABERDEEN		x	x	x	x	x			x		x	x	x
COUNTESS OF MARITZA			x										
COUNTRY GIRL								x				x	
COURT JESTER		x			x				x	x			
COXEEN		x	x						x				
CRACKERJACK		x	x					x	x	x	x		x
CRESCENDO				x					x				
CRINOLINE		x			x	x							
CROPWELL BUTLER						x							
CRUSADER	x		x	x	x		x			x		x	x
CRYSTAL BLUE		x								x			
CRYSTAL STARS					x			x					
CUPID		x		x					x				
CURLY Q	x	x							x		x		
CURTAIN CALL	x	x		x					x	x			x

	AKER	BAKER	BURGH	CHING	HIGH	JACK	NUTT	PACEY	PENH	PICK	RAIN	RIDD	WOOD
	1	2	3	4	5	6	7	8	9	10	11	12	13
CYMRU									x		x		
DAINTY				x									
DAINTY LADY		x								x			
DAISY BELL	x	x	x		x	x		x	x	x	x	x	x
DALTON		x	x	x									x
DANISH PASTRY					x				x		x		
DANNY BOY		x			x		x		x	x	x		
DAPHNE ARLENE (Synonymous with SHUNA)											x		
DARK EYES	x	x	x	x	x	x	x	x	x	x	x	x	x
DARK SECRET		x			x				x	x			
DARK SPIDER			x		x								
DAVID ALSTON		x			x				x				
DAVID LOCKYER									x				
DAVID PERRY					x								
DAWN	x	x									x		x
DAWN SKY									x				
DAWN THUNDER										x			
DAY STAR		x											
DEBBY		x											
DEBEN ROSE			x										
decussata		x							x				x
DEE COPLEY		x										x	
DEE DEE									x				
DELILAH						x							
denticulata (Synonymous with F. serratifolia)		x		x			x	x	x		x		
DERBY BELL									x				
DERBY IMP			x		x			x	x	x			
DEUTSCHER KAISER									x				
DEVAVAL LADY			x					x					
DIABLO		x	x							x	x	x	
DIANA		x								x		x	
DIE FLEDERMAUS	x												
DILLY DILLY									x	x			
DIPTON DAINTY		x							x				x
DISCOLOR (See magellanica var. discolor)		x							x				x
DISPLAY	x	x	x	x	x	x		x	x	x	x	x	x
DOC		x											
DOCTOR		x											
DOCTOR JILL										x			
DOLLAR PRINCESS	x	x	x	x	x		x		x	x	x	x	x
DOMINIANA		x			x				x		x		x
DON PERALTA		x											
DOPEY			x										
DORBETT										x			
DORIS FORD					x								
DOROTHEA FLOWER		x		x	x				x	x			x
DOROTHY				x									
DOROTHY LOUISE					x				x				
DRAME		x			x		x		x	x	x		
DR. BRENDEN FREEMAN					x	x		x					
DR. FOSTER		x	x								x	x	
DR. OLSON		x								x			
DR. TOPINARD		x		x									x

	AKER	BAKER	BURGH	CHING	HIGH	JACK	NUTT	PACEY	PENH	PICK	RAIN	RIDD	WOOD
	1	2	3	4	5	6	7	8	9	10	11	12	13
DRUM MAJOR		x											
DUBARRY		x		x									
DUCHESS OF ALBANY	x	x		x	x	x			x	x	x		
DUKE OF WELLINGTON	x	x		x									
DULCIE ELIZABETH		x	x						x			x	x
DUNROBIN BEDDER				x					x				
DUSKY BEAUTY				x								x	
DUSKY ROSE	x	x			x	x		x	x				
DUTCH MILL		x	x	x	x		x		x		x		
DUTCH SHOES											x		
EARL OF BEACONSFIELD				x	x				x	x			x
EAST ANGLIAN		x											
EASTER BONNET	x			x					x	x	x		
EBBTIDE		x											
EDALE						x			x			x	
EDEN DAWN							x						
EDEN LADY			x				x						
EDITH EMERY				x			x						x
ED LAGARDE	x	x			x	x	x				x		x
EILEEN RAFFILL		x		x									
EILEEN SAUNDERS		x											
EL CAMINO		x								x	x		
EL CID		x		x							x		
ELEANOR CLARK				x						x			
ELEANOR LEYTHAM			x		x		x	x			x		x
ELEANOR RAWLINS		x	x	x		x	x	x					
ELFIN GLADE		x						x	x				
ELFREDA							x						
ELIZABETH BROWN						x							
ELIZABETH TRAVIS		x			x								
ELIZABETH (Whiteman)		x		x					x	x			
EL MATADOR									x				
ELSA				x		x		x	x		x		
ELSIE MITCHELL								x					
EMPRESS OF PRUSSIA		x	x	x	x				x		x		x
ENCHANTED		x									x		
ENCHANTRESS									x				
encliandra	x												x
ENCLIANDRA MEXIAE											x		
ENFANTE PRODIGUE (See L'ENFANTE PRODIGUE)													
EPSII				x									
ERICA SHARP				x									
ESCHOTT ELF			x		x						x		
ESTELLE MARIE	x	x	x	x	x	x	x		x			x	x
ESTHER										x			
ESTHER DEVINE							x					x	
ETERNAL FLAME		x	x				x	x		x	x	x	
ETHEL										x			
ETHEL WILSON			x										
EVA BOERG		x			x		x		x		x	x	
EVANSON'S CHOICE	x						x						
EVA PENHALL									x				
EVELYN LITTLE				x									

	AKER	BAKER	BURGH	CHING	HIGH	JACK	NUTT	PACEY	PENH	PICK	RAIN	RIDD	WOOD
	1	2	3	4	5	6	7	8	9	10	11	12	13
EVENING SKY		x											
EVENSONG			x		x		x	x	x			x	x
excorticata				x					x				
FAIR COP										x			
FALLING STARS	x	x		x	x				x	x			
FANCY PANTS					x				x	x			
FAN DANCER		x	x						x	x			
FANDANGO											x		
FANFARE	x	x		x	x				x		x		x
FAN TAN										x			
FASCINATION	x	x	x	x		x	x	x	x	x	x	x	x
FASHION		x		x					x				
FAVOURITE		x		x						x	x		
FENROTHER FAIRY		x										x	
FESTIVAL									x				
FESTOON		x											
FIERY SPIDER		x			x								
FIONA		x	x	x	x	x		x	x	x	x	x	x
FIRE LITE		x											
FIRENZI							x						
FIRE OPAL										x			
FIRST KISS					x					x			
FIRST LADY	x						x			x		x	
FIRST LOVE			x							x	x	x	x
FLAMBOYANT										x			
FLAME		x		x					x				
FLAMING GLORY										x			
FLAMINGO					x								
FLAREPATH					x								
FLASH	x	x	x	x	x	x	x	x	x	x	x		x
FLASHLIGHT									x				
FLAVIA		x								x			
FLIRTATION WALTZ	x	x	x	x	x	x	x	x	x	x	x	x	x
FLOCON de NEIGE		x							x				
FLORA										x		x	
FLORAL CITY		x											
FLORENCE TAYLOR						x		x					
FLORENCE TURNER		x								x	x		x
FLORENTINA	x	x				x	x		x				
FLUFFY FRILLS			x							x		x	x
FLUFFY RUFFLES			x										
FLYAWAY		x											x
FLY-BY-NIGHT		x		x					x		x		
FLYING CLOUD	x	x	x	x	x		x		x	x	x	x	x
FOLIES BERGERE										x			
FOREST KING	x										x	x	
FOREST 78						x							
FORGET ME NOT		x		x	x	x			x	x	x		x
FORMOSISSIMA									x				
FORT BRAGG					x				x				
FORWARD LOOK							x			x			
FOUNTAINS ABBEY	x												
FOXTROT					x			x		x	x	x	x

	AKER	BAKER	BURGH	CHING	HIGH	JACK	NUTT	PACEY	PENH	PICK	RAIN	RIDD	WOOD
	1	2	3	4	5	6	7	8	9	10	11	12	13
FRANCES		x											
FRANCOIS VILLON					x								
FRAU HILDE RADEMACHER		x											
FREEFALL		x											
FRENCHI										x			
FROSTED AMETHYST	x									x			
FROSTED FLAME					x	x						x	x
FRÜHLING		x											x
FUCHSIA FAN			x							x			
FUKSIE FOETSIE													x
fulgens				x	x				x				
fulgens var. *gesneriana*		x		x			x	x		x			
fulgens var. *rubra grandiflora*		x		x			x						x
FULGENS SPECIOSA (See SPECIOSA)													
FUR ELISE		x								x			
FUTURA										x			
GALA		x											
GARDEN NEWS	x		x		x						x	x	x
GARTENMEISTER BONSTEDT	x	x	x	x	x	x		x	x	x			x
GAY ANNE	x					x		x		x			
GAY DOMOZEL	x												x
GAY FANDANGO	x	x	x					x		x	x	x	
GAY FUTURE													x
GAY PARASOL										x			
GAY PAREE		x						x	x				
GAY SENORITA		x						x	x				
GAZEBO										x			
GAZETTE		x											
gehrigeri		x											
GEISHA GIRL			x							x	x		
GENERAL MONK	x	x		x	x				x		x		x
GENERAL WAVELL								x	x				x
GENII	x	x	x	x	x		x	x	x		x	x	x
GEORGANA		x			x				x				x
GEORGE BARR													x
GEORGE JOHNSON									x		x		
GEORGE ROE	x												
GEORGE TRAVIS		x											
GEORGIA PEACH										x			
GIANT PINK ENCHANTED		x			x								
GILDA					x	x					x		
GINA					x								
GLADIATOR		x								x	x		x
GLENBY					x	x				x	x		x
GLENDALE			x					x	x				
GLENN MARY										x			
GLITTERS	x	x			x		x	x	x		x		
GLOBOSA (See *magellanica* var. *globosa*)													
GLOIRE de MARCHE			x										
GLORORUM				x									x
GLOW		x		x									
GLOWING EMBERS	x	x											
GLYN JONES							x						

51

	AKER	BAKER	BURGH	CHING	HIGH	JACK	NUTT	PACEY	PENH	PICK	RAIN	RIDD	WOOD
	1	2	3	4	5	6	7	8	9	10	11	12	13
GOLD BROCADE										x			
GOLD CREST	x	x											
GOLDEN BORDER QUEEN (Synonymous with BARRY'S QUEEN)	x								x				
GOLDEN DAWN (HAAG)		x	x		x	x		x	x	x	x		x
GOLDEN LA CAMPANELLA (Synonymous with PRINCESS PAT)	x												
GOLDEN LENA			x		x			x				x	x
GOLDEN MARINKA	x	x	x		x	x	x		x	x	x	x	x
GOLDEN SWINGTIME			x		x						x		
GOLDEN TREASURE	x			x			x			x		x	x
GOLDEN WEST													x
GOLD LEAF					x			x		x			x
GOLDSWORTH BEAUTY				x									
GOLONDRINA		x									x		
GOODY GOODY	x	x	x	x									
GOV. PAT BROWN		x											
GRACE				x									
GRACE DARLING		x	x					x					x
GRACILIS TRICOLOR (See TRICOLORII)													
GRACILIS VARIEGATA (See *magellanica* var. *gracilis variegata*)													
GRAF WITTE									x				
GRAND PRIX	x							x		x			
GRAND SLAM										x			
GRASMERE					x						x		
GRAY DAWN										x			
GRAYRIGG													x
GREENFINGERS					x					x			
GREEN 'N GOLD		x						x	x		x		
GREENRIGG BELL	x												
GRIFFIN									x				
GROENE KAN'S GLORIE					x								
GROOVY										x			
GRUMPY			x										
GRUSS aus dem BODETHAL		x			x				x		x		x
GUINEVERE	x	x	x							x			
GUSTAVE DORE		x		x									
GUY DAUPHINE	x	x											
GYPSY GIRL	x				x			x	x				
GYPSY PRINCE		x								x			
GYPSY QUEEN										x			
HALLOWEEN									x				
HANNA											x		
HANORA									x				
HAPPY		x									x		
HAPPY FELLOW		x		x	x					x			
HAPSBURGH		x									x		
HARLEQUIN							x						
HARMONY		x											
HARRIET										x			
HARRIET LYE (Lye)				x									
HARRY DUNNETT		x											
HARRY GRAY			x								x	x	
HARRY HOTSPUR								x					
HATHERSAGE						x							x

52

	AKER	BAKER	BURGH	CHING	HIGH	JACK	NUTT	PACEY	PENH	PICK	RAIN	RIDD	WOOD
	1	2	3	4	5	6	7	8	9	10	11	12	13
HAVERTHWAITE									x				
HAWAIIAN NIGHT		x								x	x		
HAWKSHEAD	x								x		x		
HEALDSBURG										x			
HEART THROB		x											
HEATHER HOBBS				x									
HEBE		x								x			
HEIDI ANN	x		x	x	x	x	x	x	x	x	x	x	x
HEIDI WEISS (Synonymous with WHITE ANN)	x		x		x	x							
HEINRICH HEINKEL	x	x	x	x	x		x	x	x		x		x
HEIRLOOM							x			x			x
HELEN CLARE		x							x			x	
hemsleyana	x			x									x
HENRIETTA ERNST									x				
HENRI POINCARE	x			x									
HERALD		x										x	
HERALD ANGELS							x						
HERBÉ de JACQUES											x		
HERITAGE		x		x	x					x			
HERON		x										x	
HESTON BLUE					x		x			x			x
HEYDON													x
H.G. BROWN		x				x			x				
hidalgensis													x
HIDCOTE BEAUTY	x	x		x			x		x		x	x	
HIGH PEAK	x			x		x	x						x
HI-JINKS										x			
HILARY				x									
HINDU BELLE		x			x				x		x		
HIS EXCELLENCY		x											
HOBSON													x
HOBSON'S CHOICE													x
HOLLYWOOD PARK		x		x						x			
HOMBRE										x			
HONEYMOON				x									
HORATIO						x		x			x	x	
HOWLETT'S HARDY	x	x	x	x	x		x		x	x	x	x	
HULA GIRL	x	x			x	x	x	x		x			x
ICEBERG					x	x	x						x
ICECAP								x		x			
ICE CREAM SODA		x		x									
ICED CHAMPAGNE	x	x	x	x	x	x	x		x	x	x		
ICHIBAN					x								x
ICICLE										x			
IDA DIXON (Synonymous with IDA)		x									x		
IGLOO										x			
IGLOO MAID	x	x	x		x	x		x	x	x	x	x	x
ILSE													x
IMPUDENCE		x		x	x			x	x		x		
INA	x												
INDEPENDENCE								x		x			x
INDIAN MAID	x	x	x	x	x	x	x	x	x	x		x	
INDIAN PRINCESS			x										

53

	AKER	BAKER	BURGH	CHING	HIGH	JACK	NUTT	PACEY	PENH	PICK	RAIN	RIDD	WOOD
	1	2	3	4	5	6	7	8	9	10	11	12	13
INGRAM MAID	x				x		x						
INTERLUDE		x											
INTREPID										x			
INVASION										x			
IRIS AMER		x		x	x		x		x	x	x		
ISHBEL					x								
ISIS					x								
ISLE OF MULL	x				x			x				x	x
ITALIANO				x		x		x		x			
JACK ACLAND					x				x				x
JACK POT		x			x				x	x			
JACK SHAHAN		x	x	x	x	x		x	x	x	x		
JAMBOREE	x	x	x		x					x	x		
JAMES LYE (Lye)		x		x					x				
JAMES TRAVIS (Thorne)		x								x	x		
JANDEL										x			
JANE LYE (Lye)		x		x					x				
JEAN													x
JEAN BURTON										x			
JEAN CAMPBELL		x		x									
JEANETTE BROADHURST										x			
JEAN EWART							x						
JENNIE RACHAEL									x				
JENNIFER HAMPSON													x
JESSIMATE	x							x				x	
JET FIRE		x									x		
JOAN COOPER		x	x	x	x				x		x		x
JOAN GILBERT			x									x	x
JOANNE (Pugh)										x			
JOANNE BAKKER								x			x		
JOAN PACEY	x	x		x	x	x	x	x	x	x	x		
JOAN'S DELIGHT						x		x					
JOAN SMITH		x		x		x	x	x					
JOE KUSBER	x	x			x		x			x		x	x
JOHN LOCKYER		x											
JOHN MARSH		x											
JOHNNY									x				
JOHN SUCKLEY		x							x				x
JOKER					x								
JOS'E JOAN								x		x	x		
JOSEPH HOLMES					x								
JOY PATMORE	x	x	x		x	x	x	x	x	x	x	x	x
JUBIE-LIN										x			
JULES DALOGES		x		x									
JULIE HORTON													x
JUNE REVELL						x							
JUNO		x		x						x	x		
JUPITER 70		x		x	x					x	x		
JUSTIN'S PRIDE							x	x					
KALEIDOSCOPE		x								x		x	
KATHLEEN (Pugh)										x	x		
KATHRYN MAIDMENT													x
KATHY LOUISE										x			

	AKER	BAKER	BURGH	CHING	HIGH	JACK	NUTT	PACEY	PENH	PICK	RAIN	RIDD	WOOD
	1	2	3	4	5	6	7	8	9	10	11	12	13
KATRINA		x											
KEEPSAKE		x							x			x	
KEGWORTH				x									
KEGWORTH BEAUTY									x				
KEGWORTH CARNIVAL		x				x		x	x				
KEGWORTH DELIGHT					x	x		x					
KEGWORTH SUPREME						x		x	x				
KEN JENNINGS						x							
KENNY HOLMES					x								
KENTISH MAID											x		
KERNAN ROBSON	x	x						x	x				x
KERRY ANN							x					x	
KEYSTONE	x	x		x	x				x				
KHADA					x				x				
KIMBERLEY		x		x									
KIM HAMPSON													x
KING GEORGE V									x				
KING OF HEARTS		x											
KING OF SIAM				x					x				
KINGS RANSOM		x	x	x	x	x	x	x	x	x		x	
KIWI	x	x	x		x					x	x		
KOLDING PERLE		x			x								
KOMEET					x								
KON-TIKI					x								
KORALLE (Synonymous with CORALLE)	x		x	x	x			x	x	x	x	x	x
KWINTET		x	x		x						x		
LA BERGÈRE					x						x		
LA BIANCA		x			x					x			
LA CAMPANELLA	x	x	x		x	x	x	x	x	x	x	x	x
LACE PETTICOATS		x			x						x		
LADY ANN			x							x		x	
LADY BARTLE FRERE				x									
LADY BETH		x			x				x				
LADY BOOTHBY		x		x					x				x
LADY ISOBEL BARNETT	x	x	x		x	x		x	x	x	x		x
LADY KATHLEEN SPENCE			x		x	x	x	x	x		x		x
LADY RAMSEY		x											
LADY THUMB	x	x	x	x	x	x	x	x	x			x	x
LA FIESTA		x									x	x	x
LA FRANCE	x	x		x						x	x		
LAGA					x								
LAKELAND PRINCESS		x										x	
LAKESIDE	x	x	x						x		x		x
LALEHAM LASS													x
LA NEIGE		x	x		x					x	x		x
L'ARLESIENNE		x			x				x				
LA ROSITA		x			x					x		x	x
LASSIE	x	x				x		x	x				
LAURA	x		x			x	x						x
LAURIE										x	x		
LAVENDER GIRL									x				
LAVENDER KATE		x				x					x	x	
LAVENDER LADY	x									x			

55

	AKER	BAKER	BURGH	CHING	HIGH	JACK	NUTT	PACEY	PENH	PICK	RAIN	RIDD	WOOD
	1	2	3	4	5	6	7	8	9	10	11	12	13
LAZY LADY		x											
LEIBREIZ		x			x				x	x			x
LENA		x	x	x	x	x	x		x	x	x		x
LENA DALTON	x	x	x	x	x		x	x	x	x	x	x	x
L'ENFANTE PRODIGUE				x			x		x		x		
LEONORA	x	x	x	x	x		x	x	x	x	x	x	x
LEONORA ROSE													x
LETTY LYE (Lye)				x									
LEVERHULME	x	x		x		x			x	x	x		x
LIBRA										x			
LIEBESTRAUME (Niederholzer)		x							x				
LILAC		x											
LILAC DAINTY													x
LILACLUSTRE	x	x			x	x	x	x	x	x		x	x
LILAC PRINCESS						x		x				x	
LILAC QUEEN		x											
LILAC SCEPTRE													x
LILIAN LAMPARD													x
LILLIBET		x			x					x	x	x	
LINDA GOULDING		x											
LINDISFARNE		x	x		x	x		x	x	x	x	x	x
LISA			x		x					x			
LITTLE BEAUTY	x								x	x			x
LITTLE BIT										x			
LITTLE FELLOW								x					
LITTLE GENE		x											
LITTLE JEWEL	x											x	x
LITTLE LANGDALE									x				
LITTLE RONNIE			x							x			
LIZ		x			x								
LOEKY			x		x								
LOLITA		x	x		x				x	x		x	
LOLLYPOP										x			
LONELY BALLERINA									x				
LONGIPENDUNCULATA (See *magellanica* var. *longipendunculata*)													
LORD BYRON	x	x		x					x	x	x		
LORD LONSDALE		x	x	x					x	x			
LORD ROBERTS			x						x				
LORNA DOONE										x			
LOTHARIO										x			x
LOTTIE HOBBY								x	x		x	x	x
LOUISE EMERSHAW	x	x					x	x		x	x	x	x
LOUISE FAUCON									x				
LOVABLE		x			x					x		x	x
LOVELINESS (Lye)	x	x		x					x	x	x		
loxensis	x	x			x		x			x			x
LUCINDA												x	
LUCKY STRIKE					x								x
LUCY DYOS													x
LUNAR LIGHT										x			
LUSCIOUS					x						x		
LUSTRE		x		x					x				
LUSTRE IMPROVED				x									

56

	AKER	BAKER	BURGH	CHING	HIGH	JACK	NUTT	PACEY	PENH	PICK	RAIN	RIDD	WOOD
	1	2	3	4	5	6	7	8	9	10	11	12	13
lycoides	x	x	x					x	x				x
LYE'S EXCELSIOR (Lye)		x		x					x		x		x
LYE'S FAVOURITE (Lye)				x									
LYE'S OWN (Lye)					x				x				
LYE'S UNIQUE (Lye)			x	x	x	x	x	x				x	x
LYNDA	x												
LYNN ELLEN		x											
LYRIC										x			
MACHU PICCHU					x								
MACROSTEMMA TRICOLOR								x					
MADAME CORNELLISEN	x	x	x	x	x	x	x		x	x			x
MADAME van der STRASSE					x					x			
MADEMOISELLE										x			
magellanica var. *alba* (synonymous with *molinae*)	x	x	x	x	x		x	x	x	x	x		x
magellanica var. *americana elegans*				x					x				
magellanica var. *conica*	x												
magellanica var. *discolor*				x									
magellanica var. *globosa*		x						x	x				
magellanica var. *gracilis*				x		x							
magellanica var. *gracilis variegata*	x	x	x	x	x				x	x	x	x	
magellanica var. *longipendunculata*				x					x				
magellanica var. *macrostemma*				x									
magellanica var. *prostrata*									x				
magellanica var. *pumila*				x			x	x	x		x		
magellanica var. *riccartonii*	x	x		x			x	x		x			
magellanica var. *thompsonii*				x									x
MAGENTA FLUSH	x				x			x		x			
MAGENTA MAGIC									x				
MAGGIE LITTLE			x						x				
MAGIC FLUTE						x					x	x	x
MAHARAJA		x	x							x	x		
MAJOR HEAPHY		x		x	x			x	x				
MAMA BLEUSS		x	x	x					x				
MANDARIN		x			x			x	x			x	
MANTILLA (A.F.S. No. 1)		x		x	x	x	x	x	x	x			x
MARDI GRAS		x											
MARGARET	x	x	x	x	x		x	x	x	x	x		
MARGARET ROE		x	x	x	x	x	x	x	x	x			x
MARGARET ROSE					x			x	x			x	x
MARGARET THATCHER								x					
MARGERET BROWN		x	x	x	x		x		x				
MARGERY BLAKE		x		x	x								x
MARGHARITA				x									
MARIETTA										x			
MARIN BELLE		x			x								
MARIN GLOW	x	x	x		x	x	x	x	x	x		x	x
MARINKA	x	x	x	x	x	x	x	x	x	x	x	x	x
MARS					x								
MARTINA									x				
MARTINS MIDNIGHT	x						x		x		x		x
MARTY		x											
MARTYN SMEDLEY			x						x	x			
MARY	x	x	x	x	x			x	x		x		x

	AKER	BAKER	BURGH	CHING	HIGH	JACK	NUTT	PACEY	PENH	PICK	RAIN	RIDD	WOOD
	1	2	3	4	5	6	7	8	9	10	11	12	13
MARY ELLEN										x			
MARY JOAN							x						
MARY KIPLING							x						
MARY LOCKYER		x	x			x			x				
MARY POPPINS	x				x						x		
MARY THORNE		x							x		x		x
MAUREEN MUNRO							x						
MAYFAYRE									x				
MAYFIELD								x					
MEADOWLARK	x										x	x	
MEDUSA					x								
MEG								x					
MELODY	x	x		x					x	x			x
MELODY ANN		x								x			
MELTING MOMENTS											x		
MENDOCINO MINI											x		
MENDOCINO ROSE			x							x			
MEPHISTO				x					x				
MERCURIUS					x								
MERRY ENGLAND					x								
MERRY MARY	x	x	x	x	x			x		x			x
MEXICALI ROSE				x									
MIA VAN DER ZEE					x								
michoacanensis				x					x				x
MICKY GOULT					x								
microphylla		x			x				x		x		x
MIDNIGHT SUN		x											
MIEKE MEURSING	x	x	x	x	x	x	x	x	x	x	x	x	x
MING		x		x					x		x		
minimiflora	x			x	x				x		x	x	x
MINNESOTA		x											
MINUET				x									
MIPAM					x								x
MISS CALIFORNIA	x	x	x	x	x			x	x	x	x	x	x
MISS GREAT BRITAIN										x	x		
MISSION BELLS	x	x	x	x	x	x		x	x	x	x	x	x
MISS LEUCADIA										x			
MISS VALLEJO		x	x		x					x			
MISS WASHINGTON			x						x	x	x		
MISTY BLUE													x
MME. DANJOUX				x									
MME. EVA BOYE		x											
MME. van der STRASSE									x				
MOLESWORTH	x	x		x	x	x		x	x	x	x		
MONEY SPINNER		x							x				
MONSIEUR GLADSTONE									x				
MONSIEUR JOULE					x				x				
MONSIEUR THIBAUT			x	x	x				x				
MONTEREY										x			
MONTE ROSA					x							x	
MONTEZUMA					x								
MONUMENT									x				
MOONLIGHT SONATA				x			x			x	x	x	

	AKER	BAKER	BURGH	CHING	HIGH	JACK	NUTT	PACEY	PENH	PICK	RAIN	RIDD	WOOD
	1	2	3	4	5	6	7	8	9	10	11	12	13
MOONRAKER		x			x							x	x
MOORLAND BEAUTY										x			
MORNING GLOW								x					x
MORNING LIGHT		x	x		x		x		x		x		
MORNING MIST				x									
MOSEDALE HALL									x				
MOTH BLUE	x	x	x		x								
MOUNTAIN MIST					x	x			x				
MR. A. HUGGETT				x					x		x		x
MR. BIG										x			
MRS. CHURCHILL										x			
MRS. J.D. FREDERICKS													x
MRS. LAWRENCE LYONS		x		x									
MRS. LOVELL SWISHER	x	x	x	x	x	x		x	x	x	x	x	x
MRS. MARSHALL		x		x			x		x	x	x	x	x
MRS. MINNIE PUGH										x	x		
MRS. PALMER					x								
MRS. POPPLE	x	x	x	x	x	x	x	x	x	x	x	x	x
MRS. SUSAN PUGH										x			
MRS. VICTOR REITER		x								x			
MRS. W.P. WOOD				x				x					
MRS. W. RUNDLE		x		x	x			x		x			x
MR. W. RUNDLE		x		x	x			x					x
MURIEL		x		x	x			x		x	x		
MY BEAUTY												x	x
MY FAIR LADY		x						x		x	x		
MY HONEY		x					x			x		x	
MY LOVE										x			
MY VALENTINE		x								x			
NANCY LOU	x		x	x	x	x	x	x	x	x	x	x	x
NATNE DANCER		x							x	x			
NAUTILUS		x								x			
NAVAJO								x					
NEIL CLYNE		x									x		x
NELL GWYN		x			x					x		x	x
NELLIE NUTTALL	x	x	x		x	x						x	x
NETTALA													x
NEUE WELT		x						x					
NEW FASCINATION		x			x			x					
NEW HOPE										x			
NICOLA		x			x								
NICOLA JANE	x	x	x	x	x		x	x	x		x		x
NICOLETTE					x								
NIEL								x					
NIGHTINGALE		x						x					x
NIKKI					x								
NINA WILLS		x			x			x					
NIOBE		x											
NO NAME		x											
NORMANDY BELL	x	x		x		x		x	x	x			x
NORMAN MITCHINSON							x					x	x
NORTHERN PRIDE			x									x	x
NORTHUMBRIAN BELL	x	x				x		x					x

	AKER	BAKER	BURGH	CHING	HIGH	JACK	NUTT	PACEY	PENH	PICK	RAIN	RIDD	WOOD
	1	2	3	4	5	6	7	8	9	10	11	12	13
NORTHWAY			x		x	x			x			x	x
NORVELL GILLESPIE		x								x		x	
NOVATO			x	x					x				
NOVELLA		x	x							x	x	x	
NOYO STAR								x		x			
NUTSHELL					x								
OCEAN BEACH					x						x		
ODDFELLOW													x
OLD ROSE												x	
OLIVE SMITH								x				x	
OLYMPIC LASS		x											x
OMEOMY								x				x	
OPALESCENT	x								x				
ORANGE CRUSH	x	x	x	x	x			x	x			x	x
ORANGE CRYSTAL						x		x					
ORANGE DROPS			x	x	x				x	x			x
ORANGE FLARE	x			x	x	x			x		x	x	x
ORANGE GLOW				x					x				
ORANGE MIRAGE	x		x	x	x			x	x				x
ORANGY									x				
ORIENTAL LACE													x
ORIENTAL SUNRISE	x		x					x		x	x		
O SOLE MIO										x			
OTHER FELLOW	x	x	x		x		x		x		x		x
PACIFIC GROVE		x											
PACIFIC QUEEN		x							x	x			
PACQUESA	x		x		x		x	x	x		x	x	x
PAMELA HUTCHINSON								x			x		
PAN AMERICA		x											
paniculata		x			x								
PANTALOONS		x											
PAPA BLUESS		x		x	x		x	x	x				x
PAPOOSE	x	x	x	x			x	x	x				x
PARASOL	x							x				x	
PARTY FROCK	x	x	x	x	x			x	x				x
parviflora		x						x					
PASSING CLOUD										x			
PASTEL		x											
PATHETIQUE									x				x
PATHFINDER					x								
PAT MEARA		x							x				
PATRICIA		x		x									
PATRICIA ANN												x	
PATRICIA BARGETT							x						
PATTY EVANS		x		x									
PAULA JANE					x								x
PAUL CAMBON		x		x					x				
PAULINE RAWLINS		x											
PAUL ROE						x							
PEACE		x								x			
PEARL FARMER								x					
PEARLY QUEEN													x
PEBBLE BEACH				x									

	AKER	BAKER	BURGH	CHING	HIGH	JACK	NUTT	PACEY	PENH	PICK	RAIN	RIDD	WOOD
	1	2	3	4	5	6	7	8	9	10	11	12	13
PEE WEE ROSE		x		x					x				
PEGGY ANN										x			
PEGGY KING		x			x				x				
PELORIA	x	x		x					x		x		
PENNINE												x	
PEPER HAROW		x		x									
PEPI		x	x	x	x				x		x		
PEPPERMINT STICK	x	x	x		x	x	x	x	x	x	x	x	x
PERIWINKLE									x				
PERKY PINK		x	x		x			x	x		x	x	x
PERRY PARK	x	x				x		x		x		x	
PERSONALITY		x			x					x			
PETER PAN									x				x
PETITE		x											
PETIT POINT					x								
PHARAOH									x				
PHENOMENAL		x			x				x				x
PHYLLIS	x	x	x	x		x	x		x	x	x	x	x
PHYRNE		x		x									
PICK OF THE POPS									x				
PINCH ME	x	x	x				x	x	x	x	x	x	x
PINK AURORA									x				
PINK BALLET										x			
PINK BALLET GIRL		x		x					x	x			
PINK BON ACCORDE			x	x	x		x		x		x	x	x
PINK CHIFFON										x			
PINK CLOUD		x			x		x		x		x		
PINK DARLING		x	x	x	x	x	x	x	x	x		x	x
PINK DESSERT		x						x					
PINK DOLL										x			
PINK FAIRY			x		x		x		x	x	x	x	
PINK FLAMINGO		x	x		x		x		x	x	x		x
PINK GALORE	x	x	x		x		x	x	x	x	x	x	x
PINK GOON													x
PINK JADE		x		x	x				x	x	x		
PINK LADY	x												
PINK MARSHMALLOW	x				x	x		x	x	x	x	x	x
PINK PEARL		x		x		x			x	x			x
PINK PROFUSION		x											
PINK QUARTET	x	x		x	x		x	x	x	x	x	x	x
PINK RUFFLES					x								
PINK TEMPTATION		x		x	x					x			
PINTO		x											
PINWHEEL		x											
PIRBRIGHT						x							
PIXIE	x	x	x	x	x	x	x	x	x		x		x
PLAYBOY											x		
PLAYFORD		x											
PLENTY		x	x		x			x		x	x	x	x
PORT ARTHUR		x			x			x	x				
POSTILJON					x								
POSY													x
POTNEY'S TRICOLOR	x												

61

	AKER	BAKER	BURGH	CHING	HIGH	JACK	NUTT	PACEY	PENH	PICK	RAIN	RIDD	WOOD
	1	2	3	4	5	6	7	8	9	10	11	12	13
POWDER PUFF			x		x						x		x
PRELUDE	x	x							x				
PRESIDENT		x		x					x				
PRESIDENT B.W. RAWLINS		x			x								
PRESIDENT ELLIOT		x		x							x		
PRESIDENT LEO BOULLEMIER					x								
PRESIDENT MARGARET SLATER		x	x	x	x						x	x	x
PRESIDENT ROOSEVELT						x		x	x				x
PRESIDENT STANLEY WILSON	x	x			x				x				x
PRESIDENT WILF SHARP	x		x						x			x	
PRESTON GUILD	x	x	x	x	x		x		x		x		x
PRETTY BELINDA													x
PRETTY GRANDPA										x			
PRIDE OF THE WEST (Lye)		x									x		
PRINCE OF ORANGE	x	x	x						x	x	x		x
PRINCE OF PEACE								x					
PRINCESSITA		x										x	x
PRINCESS PAT (Synonymous with GOLDEN LA CAMPANELLA)								x					
PRINCE SYRAY					x								x
procumbens	x	x		x	x				x		x		x
PRODIGY (Synonymous with L'ENFANTE PRODIGUE)													
PROFUSION											x		
PROSPERITY	x	x			x	x	x	x	x			x	x
PROSTRATA (See *magellanica* var. *prostrata*)													
PUMILIA (See *magellanica* var. *pumila*)													
PURPLE ANN							x						
PURPLE HEART		x					x		x	x			
PURPLE PROFUSION	x												
PUT'S FOLLY		x		x	x			x	x		x	x	
QUASAR										x			
QUEEN MABS		x											
QUEEN MARY		x	x						x		x		
QUEEN OF BATH									x				
QUEEN OF DERBY			x		x			x					
QUEEN OF HEARTS	x									x			
QUEENS PARK		x											
QUEEN VICTORIA		x											
QUERY		x											
RACHEL CATHERINE		x									x	x	
RADCLIFFE BEAUTY		x					x						
R.A.F.		x	x	x	x	x			x	x	x	x	x
RAHNEE							x						
RAINTREE LEGEND	x												
RAMBLING ROSE	x	x	x	x	x	x			x	x		x	x
RASPBERRY	x	x	x	x	x	x			x	x	x	x	x
RASPBERRY SURPRISE					x								
RATAE BEAUTY								x					
RAVENS BARROW			x						x				
RAZZLE DAZZLE	x	x	x										x
READING SHOW			x										
RED JACKET	x	x	x						x	x	x		
RED PETTICOAT										x			
RED RIBBONS		x			x				x				

	AKER	BAKER	BURGH	CHING	HIGH	JACK	NUTT	PACEY	PENH	PICK	RAIN	RIDD	WOOD
	1	2	3	4	5	6	7	8	9	10	11	12	13
RED RUM			x		x								x
RED SHADOWS		x			x	x		x	x	x	x		
RED SPIDER	x	x	x		x		x	x	x	x	x	x	
RED STAR									x				
RED WING									x				
REGAL ROSE				x							x		
RENE									x				
REV. DOCTOR BROWN		x		x	x								
REV. ELLIOTT (Synonymous with PRESIDENT ELLIOTT)													
RICCARTONII (See *magellanica* var. *riccartonii*)													
RIDESTAR	x	x	x	x	x	x	x		x	x	x	x	x
RIGOLETTO						x							
RINGWOOD MARKET			x		x						x		
ROBERT DORAN									x				
ROBERT HALL										x			
ROBIN (Kennett)										x			
ROBIN PACEY								x					
ROLLA		x		x	x								
ROMANCE		x				x	x			x			
ROMNEY GIRL													x
RON EWART							x						
RON HOLMES					x								
RON'S PET					x								
ROSABELL									x				
ROSALIND	x												
ROSE AYLETT		x		x					x				
ROSE BOWER				x				x	x				
ROSE BRADWARDINE		x		x									
ROSE BUD		x			x					x	x		
ROSE CHURCHILL					x			x					
ROSECROFT BEAUTY	x	x	x		x	x			x				
ROSE OF CASTILE	x	x	x	x		x		x				x	x
ROSE OF CASTILE IMPROVED	x	x		x	x	x		x	x	x	x		
ROSE OF DENMARK		x		x	x						x	x	
ROSE OF PHENOMENAL					x				x				
ROSE REVERIE		x	x										
ROSY FRILLS		x				x		x				x	x
ROSY MORN		x											
ROTHBURY BEAUTY	x											x	
ROUGH SILK		x			x						x		x
ROYAL CROWN		x											
ROYAL PINK										x			
ROYAL PURPLE		x		x	x				x				
ROYAL SERENADE											x		
ROYAL SOVEREIGN	x				x								
ROYAL TOUCH			x		x				x	x		x	x
ROYAL VELVET	x	x	x	x	x	x	x	x	x	x	x	x	
ROYAL WEDDING		x											
ROY WALKER		x			x			x	x			x	x
RUBEO													x
RUFFLED PETTICOATS													x
RUFFLES		x	x		x					x	x		x
RUFUS	x	x	x	x	x	x		x	x	x	x	x	x

	AKER	BAKER	BURGH	CHING	HIGH	JACK	NUTT	PACEY	PENH	PICK	RAIN	RIDD	WOOD
	1	2	3	4	5	6	7	8	9	10	11	12	13
RUNNER												x	
RUTHIE		x	x							x			
RUTH KING		x		x						x		x	x
RUTLAND WATER									x			x	
SALLY										x			
SALLY ANN		x											x
SALMON GLOW						x							
SAMPAN										x			
SAMSON		x		x					x		x		
sanctae-rosae				x					x				x
SANDBOY			x				x		x			x	
SAN DIEGO	x												
SANDY												x	
SAN FRANCISCO		x											
SAN LEANDRO		x	x						x	x			
SAN MATEO		x								x			
SAN PABLO			x							x	x		
SANTA BARBARA													
SANTA CRUZ	x	x	x	x					x		x‍		x
SANTA LUCIA	x	x		x						x			
SANTA MARIA									x				
SANTA MONICA		x											
SAPPHIRE		x									x		
SARAH (Curtis)			x										
SARA HELEN		x									x		
SARAH JANE		x	x	x								x	x
SARONG		x							x	x	x		
SATELLITE	x	x			x	x	x		x	x	x		x
SATURNUS		x	x		x								x
SCARCITY (Lye)	x	x		x	x								
SCHNEEBALL		x			x						x		
SCHNEEWITTCHEN		x	x						x				
SCHNEEWITTCHER		x											
SCOTCH HEATHER											x		
SEAFORTH		x		x					x				
SEALAND PRINCE	x		x										
SEA SHELLS	x	x			x				x				x
SEBASTOPOL	x		x				x	x					
SENSATION									x				
SERENDIPITY										x			
serratifolia (Synonymous with *F. denticulata*)		x		x			x	x	x		x		
SEVENTEEN									x				
SEVERN QUEEN								x				x	
SHADES OF SPACE										x			
SHADY BLUE					x			x	x				
SHADY LADY										x			
SHANGRI-LA		x							x				
SHANLEY								x	x				x
SHARPITOR											x		
SHAWNEE										x			
SHEILA ORR							x						
SHELL PINK													
SHELLY LYNN			x							x	x		x

64

	AKER	BAKER	BURGH	CHING	HIGH	JACK	NUTT	PACEY	PENH	PICK	RAIN	RIDD	WOOD
	1	2	3	4	5	6	7	8	9	10	11	12	13
SHERL ANN									x				
SHIRLEY THOMPSON					x								
SHOOTING STAR		x									x		
SHUNA (Synonymous with DAPHNE ARLENE)												x	
SHY LADY			x		x					x		x	
SHY LOOK								x	x				
SIERRA BLUE	x	x			x					x	x		
SILVERDALE	x			x					x				
SILVER JUBILEE	x								x			x	x
simplicicaulis	x	x		x					x				
SIOBHAN						x		x					
SIREN		x											
SISTER GINNY			x							x	x		
SLEEPY			x								x		
SLEIGH BELLS	x	x	x		x		x	x	x		x		x
SLENDER LADY								x	x				
SNEEZY		x									x		
SNOWCAP	x	x	x	x	x	x	x	x	x	x	x	x	x
SNOWDRIFT	x	x	x		x		x	x	x	x			
SNOWFIRE										x		x	x
SNOWSTORM	x		x			x	x						
SNOW WHITE		x											
SNOWY SUMMITT										x	x		
SO BIG					x			x					
SOLDIER OF FORTUNE					x								
SOLITAIRE												x	x
SOMBRERO										x			
SONATA	x	x			x			x		x	x		
SON OF THUMB	x				x						x	x	x
SOPHISTICATED LADY	x	x	x		x	x	x	x		x		x	x
SOUTHGATE	x	x	x	x	x				x		x	x	x
SOUTHLANDERS													x
SOUTH SEAS		x		x						x			
SOUTHWELL MINSTER							x						
SPANISH RHAPSODY									x				
SPECIOSA	x							x	x				
SPION KOP		x			x		x	x	x			x	x
splendens	x	x	x					x					x
SPRING BELLS					x								
SQUARE PEG													x
STANLEY CASH		x				x		x		x	x	x	x
STARDUST		x	x		x	x							x
STARGAZER		x											
STARLET										x			
STARLIGHT									x				
STAR OF PINK	x		x							x		x	x
STELLA ANN	x	x	x		x		x	x			x		x
STELLA MARINA		x		x									
STEVE WRIGHT													x
STORMY SUNSET													x
STRAWBERRY DELIGHT	x	x	x		x	x	x	x	x		x	x	x
STRAWBERRY FIZZ					x								
STRAWBERRY SUNDAE		x	x		x					x			

	AKER	BAKER	BURGH	CHING	HIGH	JACK	NUTT	PACEY	PENH	PICK	RAIN	RIDD	WOOD
	1	2	3	4	5	6	7	8	9	10	11	12	13
STREAMLINER										x			
STRIKER										x			
STRING OF PEARLS	x		x		x	x	x	x		x	x		
STUDENT PRINCE								x					
SUGAR ALMOND					x								
SUGAR BLUES		x											
SUGAR PLUM								x					
SUMMER SNOW			x		x			x					x
SUNDANCE						x	x				x		
SUNKISSED	x	x		x	x						x		
SUNNY SMILES					x			x					
SUNRAY	x	x	x	x	x			x	x	x	x		x
SUNRISE									x				
SUNSET	x	x		x	x			x	x				
SUSAN FORD			x				x	x			x		
SUSAN GREEN							x						
SUSAN TANDY			x										
SUSAN TRAVIS	x	x		x	x		x			x	x		x
SUSAN YOUNG							x						
SUSIE OLCESE		x		x	x						x		
SWANLEY BEAUTY													x
SWANLEY GEM	x	x	x	x	x		x	x		x	x		x
SWANLEY YELLOW		x		x	x			x					x
SWEETHEART (van Wieringen)		x			x	x		x				x	x
SWEET LEILANI	x	x		x				x		x	x		x
SWEET SERENADE								x					
SWEET SIXTEEN								x					
SWINGTIME	x	x	x	x	x	x	x	x	x	x	x	x	x
S' WONDERFUL	x	x		x						x			
SYLVIA (VEITCH)				x									
SYLVY													x
SYMPHONY		x	x		x			x	x				
TABU										x			
TADDLE	x		x		x								
TAFFETA BOW								x		x	x		x
TAFFY											x		
TAHITI									x				
TAMWORTH	x	x	x			x	x			x		x	x
TANGERINE	x	x		x		x		x	x		x		
TANHOUSE									x				
TANYA BRIDGER		x			x				x				
TAUSENDSCHÖN											x		
TED HEATH			x								x		x
TELEVISION	x				x						x		
TEMPTATION		x		x	x	x		x	x	x		x	x
TENNESSEE WALTZ	x	x	x	x	x	x	x	x	x	x	x	x	x
TEXAS LONGHORN		x	x		x		x		x	x	x		x
THALIA	x	x	x	x	x	x	x	x	x	x	x	x	x
THAMES VALLEY			x										x
THAT'S IT		x											
THE ARISTOCRAT		x			x					x	x	x	x
THE DOCTOR				x	x	x				x	x	x	
THE JESTER		x											

66

	AKER	BAKER	BURGH	CHING	HIGH	JACK	NUTT	PACEY	PENH	PICK	RAIN	RIDD	WOOD
	1	2	3	4	5	6	7	8	9	10	11	12	13
THE MADAME		x											
THE MARVEL		x											
THE PHOENIX					x						x		x
THE RIVAL	x									x	x		
THÉROIGNE de MERICOURT		x		x									
THE SPOILER			x										
THE TARNS	x	x			x						x		
THE 13th STAR										x			
THIS ENGLAND		x											
THOMPSONII (See *magellanica* var. *thompsonii*)													
THORNLEY'S HARDY	x				x		x	x	x	x			x
THREE CHEERS	x	x									x		
THUNDERBIRD		x	x							x			
thymifolia				x					x				
TIARA		x											
TIFFANY		x											
TIMLIN BRENED	x	x						x	x				
TIMOTHY HAMMETT				x									
TINA HEAD					x								
TINA MARIE					x								
TING-A-LING	x	x	x	x	x	x	x	x	x	x	x	x	x
TINKER BELL		x	x	x	x					x			
TOBY BRIDGER	x	x							x				
TOLLING BELL	x	x		x	x	x		x	x	x	x	x	x
TOM H. OLIVER		x							x				
TOM THORNE		x											
TOM THUMB	x	x	x		x	x	x	x	x	x		x	x
TOM WEST	x	x	x										x
TOM WOODS	x									x			
TOPAZ		x											
TOPPER		x					x			x	x		
TOP SCORE					x								
TORCH	x	x		x	x	x	x	x	x	x	x	x	x
TOSCA		x									x		
TOSSON BELL									x				
TOUR EIFFEL					x								x
TRADEWINDS		x								x			
TRAIL BLAZER	x	x	x	x	x	x	x		x		x	x	x
TRAILING QUEEN		x	x	x		x	x		x		x		
TRANQUILITY													
TRASE	x	x	x		x		x	x		x	x		x
TRAUDCHON BONSTEDT	x	x		x	x			x	x	x	x		x
TREASURE		x		x					x				
TRESCO									x				
TREWINCE TWILIGHT		x			x			x	x			x	
TRICOLORII		x			x			x	x				x
triphylla					x				x				
TRISHA									x				
TRISTESSE		x	x		x		x	x		x	x	x	x
TROIKA					x								
TROPICANA	x	x	x						x	x	x		
TROPIC SUNSET					x				x	x			
TROUBADOR			x						x	x			

	AKER	BAKER	BURGH	CHING	HIGH	JACK	NUTT	PACEY	PENH	PICK	RAIN	RIDD	WOOD
	1	2	3	4	5	6	7	8	9	10	11	12	13
TROUTBECK				x					x		x		
TRUDY	x	x		x	x		x						
TRUMPETER	x	x	x	x	x	x	x	x	x	x	x		x
TUMBLER										x		x	
TUMBLING WATERS										x			
TUONELLA	x	x	x	x	x	x		x	x	x	x		
TURANDOT	x									x			
TUTONE	x					x			x				
TWINKLING STARS		x		x	x							x	x
U.F.O.		x		x					x		x		x
ULLSWATER		x		x					x		x		x
ULTRAMAR		x											
UNCLE CHARLIE		x		x	x				x				
UNCLE JULES										x			
UNCLE NICKI									x				
UNCLE STEVE		x								x	x		
UNIQUE							x		x				
UPWARD LOOK	x	x	x		x	x			x		x		
VAILENT		x		x									
VALENTINE		x											
VALE OF BELVOIR				x				x					
VALERIE												x	
VALERIE ANN	x	x								x			
VANESSA JACKSON			x			x		x					
VANITY FAIR		x			x								
VICTORIAN										x			
VICTORY		x											
VIENNA WALTZ										x			
VINCENT d' INDY				x									
VIOLACEA										x			
VIOLET BASSETT BURR		x			x						x		
VIOLET GEM	x		x	x	x					x	x		
VIOLET ROSETTE		x		x					x	x			
VIOLET SZARBO					x								
VIVA IRELAND		x	x	x		x	x		x		x		
VIVIAN MILLER						x							
VIVIEN COLVILLE											x		
VIVIEN HARRIS	x					x		x					
VIVIEN LEE				x									x
VOGUE		x		x							x		
VOLTAIRE		x		x									
VOODOO	x	x	x		x		x		x		x	x	x
VULCAN (Pugh)										x			
WALDFEE	x		x		x								x
WALSINGHAM	x	x					x					x	x
WAR DANCE			x							x	x		
WAR PAINT		x							x				
WARTON GRAIG	x											x	
WAVENEY WALTZ					x								
WAVE OF LIFE	x			x					x		x		x
WAXEN BEAUTY					x				x			x	x
WEE ONE			x										
WEE LASS							x	x					

68

	AKER	BAKER	BURGH	CHING	HIGH	JACK	NUTT	PACEY	PENH	PICK	RAIN	RIDD	WOOD
	1	2	3	4	5	6	7	8	9	10	11	12	13
WELSH DRAGON		x								x			
WENDY HARRIS						x		x		x		x	
WENNINGTON BECK	x												
WESTERGEEST			x		x								
WESTMINSTER CHIMES					x	x						x	x
WEST WONG								x					
WHIRLAWAY		x	x		x		x		x				x
WHIRLIGIG										x			
WHITE ANN (Synonymous with HEIDI WEISS)				x					x		x	x	x
WHITE BOUQUET												x	
WHITE BRIDE			x										
WHITE CLOVE													x
WHITE FALLS								x		x		x	
WHITE GALORE	x						x		x	x		x	
WHITE GOLD		x											
WHITE JOY					x								x
WHITE KING		x	x		x		x			x	x		x
WHITE PHENOMENAL								x					
WHITE PIXIE	x	x	x		x	x			x	x	x		x
WHITE QUEEN		x				x		x	x				x
WHITE SPIDER	x	x	x	x	x		x		x	x			x
WHITE STAR					x								
WILD and BEAUTIFUL			x							x	x	x	
WILDFIRE		x	x	x	x						x	x	x
WILF TOLLEY							x						
WILSONS PEARLS			x										
WILTON WINKIE					x								
WINE & ROSES		x								x			
WINGROVE'S MAMMOTH								x					
WINGS OF SONG	x	x			x	x			x	x			x
WINIFRED					x								
WINSTON CHURCHILL	x	x	x		x	x	x	x	x	x	x	x	x
WITCHINGHAM													x
WOOD VIOLET	x		x							x			
YANKEE CLIPPER										x			
YONDER BLUE			x							x			
YOSINET									x				
YULETIDE					x								
YVONNE HOLMES					x								
ZIEGFIELD GIRL		x	x		x					x	x		
ZODY'S DANTE				x									

*FUCHSIA SPECIES AVAILABLE IN GREAT BRITAIN AND THE UNITED STATES OF AMERICA

According to Philip A. Munz, in his *A Revision of the Genus Fuchsia*, the genus contains some 100 species, but only a proportion are in present day cultivation. The following list details those available in Great Britain and in the United States of America, although others may still be found in private collections.

Species Available in Great Britain and the U.S.A.

F. alpestris (see F. regia)
F. arborescens
F. bacillaris
F. boliviana
F. colimae
F. cordifolia
F. corymbiflora
F. corymbiflora ssp. alba
F. decussata
F. denticulata
F. encliandra
F. excorticata
F. fulgens
    var. gesneriana
    var. rubra grandiflora
F. gehrigeri
F. hemslyana
F. hidalgensis

F. loxensis
F. lycoides
F. magellanica
    var. alba
    var. americana elegans
    var. conica
    var. discolor
    var. globosa
    var. gracilis
    var. gracilis variegata
    var. longipedunculata
    var. macrostemma
    var. pumila
    var. riccartonii
    var. thompsonii
    var. tricolor
F. michoacanensis
F. microphylla
F. minimiflora

F. paniculata
F. parviflora
F. procumbens
F. regia var. alpestris
F. sanctae-rosae
F. simplicicaulis
F. skutchiana
F. splendens
F. thymifolia
F. triphylla

Additional Species Available in the U.S.A.

F. asplundii
F. ayavacensis

F. canescens

F. dependens

F. aff. fischerii

F. hartwegii
F. hitchcockii
F. jiminezii

F. macrophylla
F. magellanica
F. membranacea
F. microphylla ssp. chiapensis

F. nigricans

F. scabriuscula
F. sessilifolia
F. smithii

F. tillertiana
F. tincta
F. vulcanica
F. venusta
F. wurdockii

*ORIGINAL FUCHSIA CULTIVARS IMPORTED INTO THE UNITED STATES OF AMERICA

The cultivars listed below were imported in December 1930, from H.A. Brown of Chingford, Essex, by George Budgen's Nursery of Berkeley, California. From the 51 plants sent over, Budgen successfully grew on 48.

AURORA SUPERBA
BALKON
BRUTUS
CALEDONIA
CARNEA
COCCINEA FLOREAN
CUPID
COUNTESS OF ABERDEEN
COVENT GARDEN
DANIEL LAMBERT
DUCHESS OF ALBANY
FLOCON DE NEIGE
GARTENMEISTER BONSTEDT
HERON
ISTAR
JULES DALOGES
KORALLE
LADY HEYTESBURY
LONGIPENDUNCULATA
LUSTRE IMPROVED
MARINKA
MARVEL
MARY
MASTERPIECE

MAUVE BEAUTY
MISS B. HESSE
MISS JOAN HADDOCK
MME. CORNELISSEN
MOLESWORTH
MRS. MARSHALL
MRS. (W.) RUNDLE
PASTEUR
PINK BALLET GIRL
PINK PEARL
PRINCE OF MAY
PUMILA
ROLLA
ROSE OF DENMARK
ROYAL PURPLE
STARLIGHT
SUNRAY
THALIA
THE DOCTOR
TRAILING QUEEN
TRAUDCHEN BONSTEDT
VALIANT
VENUS VICTRIX
WAVE OF LIFE

FUCHSIAS FOR SPECIFIC PURPOSES

FUCHSIAS FOR TRAINING AS BONSAI OR MINIATURE TYPES OF GROWTH

Suitable Cultivars and Species

ABBÉ FARGES
APRIL
ALICE HOFFMAN
BABY BALLERINA
BABY CHANG
BEACON
BLUETTE
BON ACCORDE
BOUQUET
CALEDONIA
CARNEA
CHANCE ENCOUNTER
CHRISTMAS ELF
CLOVERDALE JEWEL
COUNTESS OF ABERDEEN
COXEEN
DAVID
DERBY IMP
DUNROBIN BEDDER
ELEANOR LEYTHAM
ELF
ELLEN DIANE
ERIS
ESTELLE MARIE
FIFI
FLASHLIGHT
GOLDEN GATE
GOLDEN MARINKA
GRUSS AUS DEM BODETHAL
GUSTAVE DORE
HAVERTHWAITE
ISIS
JAMES TRAVIS (Travis)
JESTER
JEWEL
JINGLE BELLS
JOAN'S DELIGHT
KHADA
LADY THUMB

LAVENDER LACE
LITTLE CATBELLS
LUSTRE
LUZELLA
lycoides
magellanica var.
    gracilis variegata
MARGERY BLAKE
MAUREEN MUNRO
MAUVE WISP
MENDOCINO MINI
minutiflora
NEUE WELT
OBERON
OCEAN MIST
OTHER FELLOW
PALLAS ATHENE
PAPOOSE
PEE WEE ROSE
POWDER PUFF (Tabraham)
PRETTY BABY
procumbens
PUMILA
RAVENSBARROW
SAXONDALE
SHEILA MONTALBETTI
SHEILA ORR
SHERWOOD
SON OF THUMB
TINKER BELL
TINY TIM (Walker)
TITANIA (Travis)
TOM THUMB
TOM WEST
TRICOLORII
WALDFEE
WEE LASS
WINDMILL

FUCHSIAS FOR TRAINING AS CLIMBERS

In Britain, fuchsias may be grown with advantage as greenhouse climbers by training up a main stem along the rafters of the greenhouse. The flowers hanging down are thus seen to advantage. They should be treated like grape vines, pruning back to the main stem every year and cleaning the bark of the stem during the winter. In America, particularly California, under ideal growing conditions, many ordinary cultivars are grown as climbers against trelliswork to 6 or 8 ft. Strong vigorous varieties should be selected from the following.

List of Suitable Cultivars and Species

*ABINGER FAYRE
boliviana
corymbiflora
ELIZABETH (Whiteman)
GIANT CASCADE
JOAN SMITH
LADY BOOTHBY
MURIEL
PRIDE OF SHEFFIELD
PRIDE OF THE WEST
RAMBLER

RED FORMAL
REGAL
regia
regia var. *alpestris*
ROSE OF CASTILE
ROSE OF CASTILE IMPROVED
ROSE PILLAR
ROYAL PURPLE
SWISS MISS
WESTWOOD
WISTERIA

FUCHSIAS AS HEDGES

It is doubtful whether the fuchsia as a hardy plant, and especially when grown as a hedge, has ever been utilised to its full potential and provided it is not planted in a frost pocket, it should survive in almost every part of the British Isles, although the southern districts have proved to be more acceptable. Many fuchsia enthusiasts may have been influenced by witnessing the hedgerows of Devon and Cornwall, the west coast of Scotland, in County Kerry on the west coast of Ireland which include the species *F. magellanica* with its variants *Alba* (molinae), *Globosa*, *Gracilis*, *Riccartonii* and *Thompsonii* all of which have naturalised themselves in those parts of the world and flower from July to the end of September.

The fuchsia can be used as a low hedge, or for edging or dividing purposes and, if suitable cultivars are selected, a sizeable screen or hedge can be grown to several feet. Climatic conditions naturally have a bearing upon the ideal place where a hedge can be grown; this could be described as cool, moist but humid, and where a certain amount of shade is experienced for some time of the day. Hot dry winds should be avoided as these will cause scorching and the drying out of the leaves. Hardies for hedges will grow in most soils but preparation of the site is necessary before actual planting. Fuchsias, although shallow rooters at the top, need a deep cool root run and deep digging to break up the subsoil found at two spits deep; should this subsoil be loose, the addition of material such as peat or humus of some description is necessary. If, on the other hand, the subsoil is of a clayey and heavy nature, gravel or sand will be necessary to prevent waterlogging. Naturally if farmyard manure is obtainable, this should be worked into the bottom spit. Late autumn or early winter is the ideal time to make this initial preparation so that the soil can weather before planting. When returning the first spit, any moisture-retaining material, such as peat, spent hops, humus or manure, can be used to advantage.

The actual planting should take place as soon as the danger of frosts has disappeared in the South and Midlands by the end of May, but in the North of England, growers should wait another fortnight or so. It is advisable to order your plants from the nurseryman well in advance and to take delivery in pots no smaller than 3½ in, remembering that nowadays we can obtain hardy plants in other colours than red and purple. Should the grower have the necessary facilities to grow the plants on to 4¼ in or 5 in pots, then the chances of success will be greatly increased, but attention must be paid to ensure that, whenever the plants are planted out, they have been successfully hardened off; otherwise a great check will be experienced, with foliage turning bronzy and leaves falling off. Hardening off can easily be established by transferring the plants, in their pots to a suitable garden frame, 2 or 3 weeks prior to planting, gradually increasing the exposure from a completely closed frame to a stage of ventilation when the top light can be removed entirely, except for the nights when frosts can be expected.

Planting distances will vary according to the vigour of the cultivars, but generally 18 in is a good spacing distance. The depth of planting is important and plants should be planted at least 2 inches below the soil level to protect those vital roots from subsequent frost damage; planting should be firm with no air pockets; the heel of the boot trod lightly around the plants is quite sufficient.

No fertilizer or feeding is necessary at this time although a little bonemeal dug in around the roots will be beneficial.

The object of planting in May or June is to let the plants become well established during the summer so as to prepare them for the forthcoming winter conditions. On no account should any hardy fuchsias be planted in August or the autumn months of September and October as they will not have sufficient time to become established and are certain to be lost during the winter.

A nice warm humid atmosphere at the time of planting is ideal and plants should be well watered in. Should dry, or even drought, conditions prevail after planting, the newly planted fuchsias will have to be watered regularly to prevent the soil drying out and, if possible, plants should be sprayed overhead on evenings after 5 pm.

Although fuchsias are gross feeders, only moderate feeding should be carried out during the first summer, commencing with a weak feed with the concentration upon nitrogen some 3 or 4 weeks after planting; fortnightly feeds with same concentration can then be carried out during the growing season.

During the first winter, it is advantageous to cover the base of the plants with some protective material, such as peat, sand, leaves or weathered ashes, to protect the roots from any likely frosts. This should then be removed in the spring.

No pruning should be undertaken in the autumn or during the first winter, leaving all the growth made during the summer intact; this will give a certain amount of protection against any unkindly weather and, in any case, most of the growth will be lost.

Pruning should take place when the new growth appears at the base of the plants in the early or late spring; then prune right down to ground level or to those shoots or eyes that appear a little way up the stems or laterals according to the grower's choice. It will be the second summer before the hedge will realize the growth and colour expected. Feeding can be stepped up considerably during this second year, firstly with feed concentrating on nitrogen and then switching over to a feed with the emphasis on the potash content, as buds and flowers appear. Finally, it should be emphasised that, when once established, hardies do resent being moved or having their roots disturbed and, as they are shallow rooters, any weeding should be done by hand at the expense of the conventional hoe.

List of Suitable Varieties and Cultivars

BRILLIANT (2½)
Very vigorous, scarlet and violet-magenta flowers.

CALEDONIA (2)
Rather dwarf habit, cerise and crimson flowers, almost a self, ideal for the low hedge, upright and graceful cultivar.

CHILLERTON BEAUTY (2 to 3)	Pale rose-pink and mauvish-violet flowers, small flowers very profuse, extremely vigorous, excellent for medium-sized hedge.
CLIFF'S HARDY (2½)	Light crimson and violet flowers, one of the more recent cultivars for training as a hedge, very acceptable.
CORALLINA (3)	Scarlet and purple, extremely vigorous, foliage has bronzy tint, very old cultivar with large flowers.
DOROTHY (3 to 4)	Very vigorous with medium-sized flowers, bright crimson and violet flowers.
DRAME (2)	Semi-double with rather a spreading habit, foliage is attractive yellow-green.
DR. FOSTER (3½)	Scarlet and violet flowers, probably the largest flower in the whole range of hardies, extremely fine cultivar.
E.A. BABBS (1½)	Suitable for low hedge or edging with small flowers, crimson and deep rose colouring very prolific.
ENFANTE PRODIGUE (3)	Often quoted as L'Enfante Prodigue or just Prodigue. Semi-double crimson and purple flowers very similar to Margaret, extremely hardy and most suitable for medium hedge.
FLASH (2½)	Almost a self in colour magenta-red, flowers small but very profuse, foliage is light green, very vigorous growth.
FLORENCE TURNER (3)	Pale pink and white with pink-purple corolla, medium-sized flowers, a welcome introduction to the hardies.
GRAF WITTE (3)	Carmine purple and rosy-mauve with yellowish-green foliage, beautifully formed flowers of substance and size.
JEWEL (1½)	Ideal for the low hedge or edging, carmine and purple, long flowers borne on long pedicels.
JOAN COOPER (3)	Pale rose-opal and cherry red flowers, unusual colouring for hardy lightish green foliage, smallish flowers.
LADY THUMB (1)	Semi-double, carmine and white, ideal for edging, very small flowers identical to Tom Thumb except for colouring.
MADAME CORNELISSEN (3)	Welcome colour change from the red and purple, semi-double flowers will even grow to higher than 3 ft under ideal conditions.
magellanica var. alba (6 to 10)	Correct name is molinae, small flowers with white tube and very pale lilac sepals and corolla, reaches great height and proportions with age, needs restricted root run for profusion of bloom.
magellanica var. globosa (5 to 6)	Scarlet and purple flowers, small but profuse.
magellanica var. gracilis (4 to 5)	Most attractive with its rampant and arching type of growth, small red and purple flowers with a deeper purple, has more of a spreading habit.
magellanica var. riccartonii (4 to 6)	Probably the best known of the hardies, scarlet and dark purple flowers, small but in profusion, bronze to reddish cast on foliage.
magellanica var. thompsonii (4 to 5)	Small flowers but in profusion, brightly coloured scarlet and palish purple.
MARGARET (3 to 4)	Semi-double carmine-scarlet and violet flowers, large for a hardy cultivar, very vigorous.
MARGARET BROWN (2 to 3)	Rose-pink and light rose colouring, flowers are small but very profuse, very suitable for a low hedge.
MRS. POPPLE (2 to 3)	Scarlet and violet-purple, flowers are larger than the average hardy and one of the very best hardy cultivars, very erect.
MRS. W.P. WOOD (4 to 5)	Pale pink with white corolla, very small flowers but very profuse, lightish green foliage, extremely vigorous, considered to be an improvement upon alba.
PHYLLIS (3)	Semi-double, waxy-rose and rosy-cerise flowers, very stiff and upright, ideal for medium hedge.
PIXIE (2 to 3)	Pale cerise and rosy-mauve medium-sized flowers, yellowish-green foliage, very vigorous, makes good small hedge.
PROSPERITY (3)	Possibly the only double flowered cultivar suitable for hedges. Crimson and rose with white overtones, most welcome introduction to the hardies.
TOM THUMB (1)	Carmine and mauve, very small flowers but very profuse, ideal for edging, produced a sport Lady Thumb.
TRASE (1½)	Carmine-cerise and white, medium-sized blooms, very delightful cultivar and suitable only for low hedge.
WHITE PIXIE (3)	Reddish-carmine and white, small flowers but very free foliage, yellow-green with crimson veins, very attractive for medium hedge.

(The figures quoted in brackets are the height in feet which they are likely to attain.)

ORNAMENTAL AND VARIEGATED FUCHSIAS

Some confusion may occur if it is not understood what constitutes ornamental or variegated foliage in classes calling for this type of cultivar. Although the British Fuchsia Society does not lay down any definition, it is generally accepted that variegated foliage is defined as having two or more distinct colours, typical examples are Autumnale with its golden and coppery-red leaves changing to dark red and salmon, mahogany and russet and Golden Marinka with the attractive cream edges and patches on a medium yellow or green leaf.

Ornamental is not so easily defined, being cultivars with foliage grown for their beauty which includes those cultivars with foliage distinctly yellow, usually described as golden and sometimes accompanied with red veining. Examples of ornamental are those cultivars with lime-green or yellow-green leaves, or foliage with a blush or overlay of a second colour such as Golden Treasure and Cloth of Gold.

The cultivar President falls into a group with blush overlay, having a reddened or bronzed addition to a basic green leaf and is a typical cultivar that can lose its ornamental value with maturity or incorrect conditions.

Red-veined foliage is not recognised as ornamental or variegated unless some additional characteristics are present. Most ornamental and variegated cultivars are not free-flowering, but as foliage is the essential consideration, flowers are not necessary, but if present are appraised as an asset.

The following cultural information may be of assistance for cultivating ornamental foliage fuchsias. The whole range of ornamental fuchsias are very sensitive to light and correct cultivation, their colour will vary considerably, dependant upon the degree of sunlight or shade they receive, they will tolerate full sunlight and warmer conditions, but if heavily shaded, the colour of the foliage is greatly reduced. Feeding or the lack of feeding can also produce different results and to obtain the best effect, it is suggested that a fertiliser with a high nitrogen content be used, rather than one with high potash. Care must be taken with spraying and watering, on account of easy marking of the foliage if overhead spraying is practised and on the whole, they prefer to have their compost on the dry side, almost to the drying out stage before the next watering, leaf drop can be troublesome if the plants are overwatered especially in the early stages of growth, particularly with peat based composts, as the plants are prone to damp off at the base.

The most important aspect, however, is the light factor.

Finally, judges can only assess what they actually see on the showbench, and it is of little consequence whether catalogue, book or check list, describes the cultivar, if the ornamental or variegated characteristics are not present, the reason for some members' exhibits being N.A.S. or ignored, without understanding just why.

List of Suitable Cultivars

ACUBEAFOLIA
AUTUMNALE
*BARRY'S QUEEN
(synonymous with
GOLDEN BORDER
QUEEN)
BLUE AND GOLD
BURNING BUSH
CANARY BIRD
CANDY ROSE
CARL DRUDE
*CAROL ANN
CLOTH OF GOLD
*COL
COQUET GOLD
*CORALLINA VARIEGATA
CRIMSON BEDDER
DAISY BELL
DAYBREAK
DAY BY DAY
DOMINYANA
DUNROBIN CASTLE
*EDEN PRINCESS
FIREFALL
GENII
GILDA
GILT EDGE
*GOLD BROCADE
GOLDCREST
*GOLD DUST
*GOLDEN BORDER QUEEN
(synonymous with
BARRY'S QUEEN)
GOLDEN CHAINS
*GOLDEN CLOVERDALE
PEARL
*GOLDEN DRAME
*GOLDEN EDEN LADY
GOLDEN FLEECE
GOLDEN GATE
GOLDEN GLORY
*GOLDEN JESSIMAE

*GOLDEN JEWEL
*GOLDEN LA CAMPANELLA
(synonymous with
PRINCESS PAT)
GOLDEN LENA
GOLDEN MANTLE
GOLDEN MARINKA
*GOLDEN MELODY
*GOLDEN PENNYASKEW
*GOLDEN QUEEN
*GOLDEN RUNNER
*GOLDEN SNOWCAP
*GOLDEN SWINGTIME
*GOLDEN TOLLING BELL
GOLDEN TREASURE
GOLDEN VIOLET
*GOLDEN WEDDING
*GOLDERS GREEN
GOLDILOCKS
GOLD LEAF
GOV: PAT BROWN
GRACILIS VARIEGATED
GRAF WITTE
GREEN 'N GOLD
*GRIFFIN
*HARVEST GLOW
*HERALD ANGELS
HERBÉ DE JACQUES
*JANET WILLIAMS
JUDY
*LEMACTO
LITTLE RASCAL
METEOR
MEXICALI ROSE
MR. WEST
MUNTAZ
*MY DELIGHT
*NANANICE
*ORNAMENTAL PEARL
PINK LEMONADE
*POP WHITLOCK
POTNEY'S TRICOLOUR

PRESIDENT
*PRINCESS PAT (synonymous
  with GOLDEN LA
  CAMPANELLA)
ROSECROFT BEAUTY
SAMSON
SANTA CLARA
*SCARLET RIBBONS
SHARPITOR
*SHIRLEY
STRAWBERRY DELIGHT
SUNRAY

THE SMALL WOMAN
*TOLEMAC
TOM WEST
TRICOLORII
TROPIC SUNSET
*VARIEGATED SNOWCAP
*VARIEGATED TOLLING BELL
*VARIEGATED WHITE JOY
WAVE OF LIFE
WHITE GOLD
WHITEKNIGHTS GLISTER
WHITE PIXIE

The most attractive and easily obtainable include Autumnale (Burning Bush), Cloth of Gold, Golden Marinka, Golden Treasure and Sunray.

SPORTS AND MUTATIONS

Nature has been responsible for seeding, cross-seeding and reproducing its many species and one important aspect of natural plant change is the result of mutating or sporting. When this change or alteration occurs it is a sudden variation, producing offspring differing from its parents due to changes within the chromosomes or genes, a natural break from the recognized character.

Sports and mutations are a form of a plant which arise spontaneously from an existing root or shoot stock, but which are unlike the original.

Some fuchsias have changed their leaf colouring through mutation, whilst the flowers remain the same as the original plant, typical examples being *F. magellanica* var. *gracilis variegata* with its silvery variegated foliage and Golden Marinka with foliage of a bright hue, slashed creamy-gold and banded, quite distinct from their parents.

Most sports are, however, best exemplified by corolla colour changes and such mutations are generally from a dark colour to a lighter colour, such as Lady Thumb from Tom Thumb and Cardinal Farges from Abbé Farges, but very occasionally the procedure can be reversed.

Both sports and mutations are interesting phenomena resulting in many worthwhile new additions to the vast list of cultivars; the first doubles, the first white corollas and the first marbling effects, together with the first white-tubed (Venus Victrix) were all the result of natural mutations.

Lists of Sports and Mutations

Sport	From	Sport	From
*ALAN'S GOLD	Swingtime	GOLDEN LENA	Lena
*AMY MARIE	Blue Eyes	GOLDEN MARINKA	Marinka
*ARCADIA GOLD	Swingtime	*GOLDEN PENNY ASKEW	Brilliant
ARTHUR YOUNG	King's Ransom	GOLDEN SNOWCAP	Snowcap
AUNT JULIANA	Uncle Jules	GOLDEN SWINGTIME	Swingtime
BACHELOR GIRL	Bewitched	*GOLDEN WEDDING	Pirbright
BARRY'S QUEEN	Border Queen	GONDOLIER	Fluorescent
BELLE-LAVON	Clara Beth.	GRANPA BLEUSS	Papa Bleuss
BERYL'S CHOICE	Georgana	GREEN 'N' GOLD	Glendale
*BOB PAISLEY	Spion Kop	GREY WALKER	Beryl's Choice
BOLERO BLANCO	Bolero	*HAMPSHIRE BLUE	Carmel Blue
CARDINAL FARGES	Abbé Farges	*HAMPSHIRE PRINCE	Prince of Peace
CARMEN MARIA	Leonora	HAZEL MARSH	His Excellency
*CAROL ANN	White Ann	HEIDI WEISS	Heidi Ann
CATALINA	Gypsy Queen	HERBE DE JACQUES	Corallina
CENTURY 21	Amapola	HOLLYDALE	Winston
CHECKERS	Checkerboard		Churchill
CHECKMATE	Checkerboard	HOLLYDALE SPORT	Hollydale
CLOTH OF GOLD	Souvenir de	JACK KING	General Monk
	Chiswick	JAYNE LOUISE MILLS	Dutch Mill
COLUMBIA	America	JEANETTE BROADHURST	Cascade
CONSTANCE	Pink Pearl	JOHN MARSH	Shalimar
COOS BAY PIRATE	Nonpareil	JUBILEE	Phenomenal
COQUET GOLD	Belsay Beauty	JUDY	Amapola
COUNTESS OF HOPE-		JULIA DITRICH	City of Pacifica
TOWN	Phenomenal	*JUNE'S JOY	Seaforth
DAPHNE ARLENE	Countess of	KING OF HEARTS	Queen of Hearts
	Aberdeen	*LADY DOROTHY	Beacon
DAY BY DAY	Emile Zola	LADY THUMB	Tom Thumb
DEBRA HAMPSON	Dark Eyes	*LEMACTO	Camelot
*EGMOUNT TRAIL	Oregon Trail	LEONORA ROSE	Leonora
ELEANOR CLARK	Symphony	*LIEMER'S LANTAERN	Dusky Rose
ELIZABETH BREARY	Symphony	LILIAN LAMPARD	Marin Glow
ETHEL SANGSTER	Tower of	LITTLE RONNIE	Lorna Doone
	London	LORNA DOONE	General Monk
FLIRTATION	Lucky Strike	MARGARET SWALES	La Fiesta
FROST'S MIDAS TOUCH	Display	MARION YOUNG	La France
GAN	Army Nurse	MARY CLARE	Blue Moon
GAY MELAINE	Constance	MAUVE POINCARE	Henry Poincare
*GITA NUNES	Vienna Waltz	MISS NEW YORK	Swingtime
GOLDEN BORDER QUEEN	Border Queen	MISS WASHINGTON	Fort Bragg
*GOLDEN CLOVERDALE		MME. CAROLYN	Purple
PEARL	Cloverdale Pearl		Phenomenal
GOLDEN DRAME	Drame	MRS. GEORGE MARTIN	Prince of Orange
*GOLDEN EDEN LADY	Eden Lady	MRS. LAWRENCE LYONS	Nonpareil
*GOLDEN JEWEL	Cloverdale	MT. HOOD	Gypsy Queen
	Jewel	NETTALA	Chang
*GOLDEN JESSIMAE	Jessimae	NEVILLE YOUNG	His Excellency
GOLDEN LA		NIKKI	Elizabeth
CAMPANELLA	La Campanella		(Whiteman)

77

Sport	From	Sport	From
NINA WILLS	Forget-Me-Not	SPORT OF BORA BORA	Bora Bora
NOVAR	Flirtation	SPRING BELLS	Snowcap
OREGON	America	SUSAN YOUNG	Blue Pearl
*ORNAMENTAL PEARL	Cloverdale Pearl	SUZY	Bonanza
PINCH ME NOT	Pinch Me	TED'S RAINBOW	Unknown
PINK DELIGHT	Guinevere	THE SMALL WOMAN	Lovable
PINK PHOENIX	The Phoenix	THIS ENGLAND	La France
PINK SPORT OF		TIFFANY (Pyemont)	Leonora
BONANZA (SUZY)	Bonanza	*TOLEMAC	Camelot
PINK TEMPTATION	Temptation	TOM WOODS	La Campanella
PIXIE	Graf Witte	TREWINCE TWILIGHT	Marin Glow
*POP WHITLOCK	Border Queen	*VARIEGATED TOLLING	
PRINCESS PAT	La Campanella	BELL	Tolling Bell
ROSE CHURCHILL	Winston	*VARIEGATED WHITE JOY	White Joy
	Churchill	VARTY'S PRIDE	Swingtime
ROSECROFT BEAUTY	Snowcap	VIENNA WALTZ	Dusky Rose
SAN JOSE	San Pablo	WHITE ANN	Heidi Ann
SAN PABLO	San Mateo	WHITEKNIGHTS GLISTER	*F. magellanica*
SEQUOIA	Honeymoon		var. *molinae* ×
SHUNA	Countess of		*F. fulgens*
	Aberdeen	WHITE PIXIE	Pixie
SON OF THUMB	Tom Thumb	WHITE WONDER	Gypsy Queen
SPECIAL SAMPAN	Sampan	WILLIAMETTE	San Pablo

Alphabetical List of Species, Hybrids and Cultivars

ALPHABETICAL LIST OF SPECIES, HYBRIDS AND CULTIVARS

In this list hybrid and cultivar names appear in **bold** and specific names in ***bold italic***. Introductions made since the publication of Addendum 4 to the original Checklist are marked with an asterisk.

A1. Double. Tube and sepals, pale pink; corolla pale blue centre with pink and blue petaloids, fading to lavender with age, very full. Large flowers, free, growth trailer. Castro – American – 1969 – A.F.S. No. 837.

Abbé David. Lemoine – French – 1909.

Abbé Farges. Semi-double. Tube and reflexed sepals, light cerise; corolla rosy-lilac, flowers small but profuse, small, medium green foliage, stems rather brittle and easily broken. Awarded H.C. by R.H.S. 1965 in hardy trials. Growth upright and bushy. Accepted by B.F.S. as showbench hardy. Lemoine – French – 1901.

Abbé Farges

Abbess. Semi-double to double. White tube, white sepals touched pink near tips, rather broad reflexed and curls at tips. Corolla pale purple ageing to light purple with maturity. Medium sized blooms with pink stamens and short pink pistil. Dark green foliage with crimson mid-rib. Growth upright, stiff tall and strong. British introduction not widely known and exclusive to Southern Counties. Homan – British – 1967.

Abd-El-Kader. Lemoine – French 1880.

Abel Cárriere. Single. Lemoine – French – 1868.

Aberdeen Gold. Synonymous with Golden Treasure.

Abinger Fayre. Semi-double. Tube and sepals pink; corolla dark magenta, pink at base, style and filaments pink. Seedling from Gay Fandango. Strong habit of growth as of its parent but more self-branching, almost too vigorous for pot work and could be considered suitable as a climber. Not in commercial production and originated from the Guildford Fuchsia Society. Growth lax upright or trailer. Gay Fandango ×. Pridmore – British – 1971.

A Bit of Red. Double. Short tube and sepals, bright red; corolla white, blushed with red and with darker red veriegations at base, with dark red veins. Flowers large and full. Growth trailer. Soo Yun – American – 1969 – A.F.S. No. 850.

abrupta. Tube scarlet, sepals scarlet; corolla mauvish-scarlet. Longish flowers, borne in terminal, pendant clusters. Low flat shrub. Johnston – 1925 – Peru.

*Abt. Koloman Holzinger. Double. Tube and sepals pink; corolla white. Medium sized blooms

very early and very free flowering. Short growth. Probably named after the Abbot of the monastery where Nutzinger was head gardener at Admont, Austria. El Camino × Bernadette. Nutzinger – Austrian – 1965.

Abundance. Single. Tube and sepals, rich cerise; corolla purple with small cerise petaloids. Medium sized flowers freely produced, growth is vigorous and bushy, with spreading habit, hardy in Southern England. Todd – British – 1870.

Abundance. Single to semi-double. Tube and sepals, rose-pink; corolla pale bishop-blue almost white at base of petals. Flowers medium size, compact and free. Growth trailer, suitable for baskets. Received R.H.S. Award of Merit at Wisley Hardy Trials 1975–78. Niederholzer – American – 1944.

Acantha. Semi-double. Tube and sepals, light rose; corolla ivory-white flushed pale pink at edge of petals. Flowers medium size and free. Growth upright bush. Dickson – British – 1846.

Accent. Single to semi-double. Tube pink, sepals have tinges of pink which accent a purple centre. Corolla deep purple, fading to deep magenta forming a pattern. Flowers are small, growth lax bush or trailer. Kennet – American – 1969 – A.F.S. No. 862.

Achievement. Single. Tube and recurved sepals, reddish-cerise; corolla reddish-purple, scarlet at base, bright and effective, beautiful shape. Flowers medium to large and very free. Foliage yellowish-green, growth upright, bushy and self branching. A cultivar for the beginner. Accepted by B.F.S. as showbench hardy. (Synonymous with Goliath Twrdy 1866?). Melville – British – 1886.

Achievement

Achievement – Charming. To distinguish between these two similar cultivars the following characteristics may be useful. Achievement foliage has red vein in the leaf whilst the sepals are somewhat narrower and longer than Charming. Charming sepals are well reflexed and the foliage has a definite light green colour at the tips of the leaves.

Acidalie. Single. Red and white. Demay – French – 1865.

Acteon. Double. Demay – French – 1872.

Adagio. Double. Tube and sepals, rosy-red; corolla claret-red. Trailing or semi-trailing habit. Tiret – American – 1961 – A.F.S. No. 485.

Adam Koch. Double. Red and violet-red striped. Weinrich – German – 1863.

*Ada Perry. Double. Scarlet tube (R.H.S. 53B) ¾ in long by ¼ in wide, sepals scarlet (R.H.S. 43C) on top, deeper scarlet (R.H.S. 43B) underneath, horizontal with recurved tips 1¾ in long by ⅞ in wide. Corolla blue-purple (R.H.S. 78A) streaked cardinal-red, maturing to rose (R.H.S. 58B) 1½ in long by 2¾ in wide. Large blooms, almost fully flared with serrated edges; petaloids bluish-rose, streaked scarlet, some attached to sepals. Stamens are red, extend 1 in below corolla, pistil extends 1¼ in below corolla with pink style and flesh stigma. Dark green foliage (R.H.S. 146A) 3½ in long by 2 in wide, ovated with serrulate edges. Growth lax upright on stiff trailer. Raised and tested for 3 years in Oceanside, California before release. Trademarked in California. Named after a well known American horticultural journalist. Seventh Heaven × Hula Girl. Stubbs – American – 1983 – A.F.S. No. 1733.

Addison. Bland – British – 1881.

Adelaide. Knight – British – 1858.

*Adelaide Tutt. Double. Carmine tube, sepals carmine, paler towards tips, rose-pink underneath. Corolla white, veined carmine. Largish blooms with long narrow sepals which twist and curl, carmine stamens and rose-pink style. Medium green foliage with crimson mid-rib. Growth lax upright; very suitable for patio container work. Raised in the vicinity of Guildford, Surrey. Weeks – British – 1980.

A. Delean. Rozain-Boucharlat – French 1860.

A. de Neuville. Lemoine – French – 1888.

Adine. Bland – British – 1878.

Admirable. Single. Cherry-red and red, almost a self. Harrison – British – 1840.

Admirable. Semi-double. Rose-pink and dark rose. Knight – British – 1842.

Admirable Obry. Lemoine – French – 1891.

Admiral Aube. Lemoine – French – 1891.

Admiration. Single. Tube and sepals, bright red, tipped with yellowish-green; corolla Indian lake; flowers long and of medium size. Growth lax bush habit, hardy in most districts. One of W. P. Wood's early introductions and little favoured today. Seedling × Mrs. Marshall (letter from W. P. Wood 1952). Wood – British – 1940.

Admiration – President. These two similar cultivars are often confused with one another and at one time Admiration was grown under hardy trials as President. The telling difference is that Admiration is much less robust than President and the key is the yellow tips to the sepals of Admiration. Admiration received an award of merit from the R.H.S. at their 1965 Wisley Trials although the actual plant grown was President.

Adolphe Weich. Double. Red and violet-rose. Lemoine – French – 1867.

Adolphina. Semi-double. Scarlet and purple. Stafford – British – 1847.

*Adonis. Semi-double. Short pink tube, white sepals on upper surface, pale pink stripe underneath, 1¾ in long by ½ in wide. Corolla deep lavender 1½ in wide by 1¾ in long. Largish blooms with bright pink stamens. Medium green foliage, large with spear-shaped and slightly serrated leaves. Growth medium upright, will produce a good bush. Raised and tested for 4 years in the vicinity of Timperley, Cheshire before release. Howarth – British – 1983 – A.F.S. No. 1712.

Adria. Single. Rosy-red, long tubed. *F.fulgens* × Conspicua. Lowe – British – 1875.

Adrien Marie. Lemoine – French – 1894.

Aerostat. Lemoine – French – 1889 or 1894.

A.F. Shulte. Double. Tube and sepals, bright-red; corolla bright red outer petals, whilst the inner petals are deep blue. Growth upright bush. Named after a past President of the American Fuchsia Society. Martin – American – 1959 – A.F.S. No. 367.

After Five. Single to semi-double. Tube white, short and thin, sepals white and straight when mature. Corolla is short, open deep red-burgundy, fades to lighter shade of red, varies in shape. Foliage small and dark green. Growth upright and self-branching. Castro – American – 1972 – A.F.S. No. 1028.

Afterglow. Single. Tube and sepals crimson; corolla of same colour, crimson self. Medium size blooms and quite free. Growth is lax bush. Wood – British – 1951.

Afterglow. Double. Tube creamy, recurved sepals creamy, colouring to pale rose with age; corolla light flame. Flowers of medium size opening from cream coloured buds into frilly, unfading pale flame. Growth is bushy and medium vigour. Reiter – American – 1954 – A.F.S. No. 211.

Agamemnon. Double. Red and purple. Wyness – German – 1865.

Agnes. Semi-double. Red and purple. Youell – British – 1845.

Agnes. Single. White and red. Story – British – 1851.

Agnes Reeves. Single. Tube and sepals, pale red, long corolla white, veined rose at base. Medium sized blooms and very free. Growth upright and bushy. Evans and Reeves – American – 1939.

Agnes Sorel. Lemoine – French – 1882.

Aida Lorraine. Double. Short crimson tube, recurled, medium sized crimson sepals; white corolla, veined and splotched crimson. Medium sized blooms, full skirted with crimson striped petaloids, crimson stamens and pistil, best colour develops in sun, needs frequent stopping, heavy blooms make it trail. Growth natural trailer, good for basket or lax bush. Smith, N.F. – American – 1976 – A.F.S. No. 1359.

Aileen. Double. Short tube, uniform light green; sepals pale green, darker at the tips, corolla of medium size, cerise, lighter at base. Dark green foliage of medium size. Growth medium upright or trailer. Soo Yun – American – 1972 – A.F.S. No. 1040.

Aimé Millet. Lemoine – French – 1891.

Aintree. Single. Tube ivory and slender; sepals slightly suffused rose. Corolla vivid rose-madder. Growth upright but habit is also horizontal.

Named after the famous British Racecourse. Need
– British – 1964.

*Airball. Single. White tube (R.H.S. 157C) $\frac{1}{2}$ in
long, half up sepals 2 in by $\frac{1}{2}$ in wide magenta
(R.H.S. 66D) on top, slightly darker (R.H.S. 66C)
underneath, tipped green and recurved. Half
flared squared corolla $\frac{3}{4}$ in long by $\frac{3}{4}$ in wide,
opening magenta (R.H.S. 66B) maturing to
fuchsia-purple (R.H.S. 67C). Medium sized flowers with fuchsia-purple filaments and anthers,
white style and stigma. Light green foliage
(R.H.S. 138A) slightly lighter (R.H.S. 138B) underneath. Cordate shaped leaves $1\frac{1}{2}$ in long by 1
in wide, veins, stems and branches green. Growth
medium upright, will make good standard or
upright, prefers full sun and cold hardy to 30°F.
Very similar to Edith Emery except a true single
and much easier to grow. Tested and grown in
the vicinity of Worthing before registration. Seedling × Edith Emery. Hobbs, L. – British – 1984 –
A.F.S. No. 1772.

Airy Fairy. Single. Long slender tube and sepals
red; corolla dark blue-violet. Growth tall, upright
bush. Hazard and Hazard – American – date unknown.

Aladdin. Semi-double. Tube and sepals, bright
red; corolla white. Medium sized flowers and free,
growth upright. Price – American – 1956.

Alameda. Double. Tube and sepals, dark red;
corolla white, slightly veined crimson at base.
Dark green foliage, growth upright bush. Niederholzer-Waltz – American – 1950 – A.F.S. No. 55.

*Alan Ayckbourn. Single. New seedling raised
by Dave Clark of Merseyside to commemorate the
centenary of the Scarborough Horticultural
Society. Baby pink tube, sepals baby pink are reflexed to cover the short tube. Corolla is startling
white, medium sized flowers bell shaped and prolific in flowering. Growth lax upright, short-
jointed and self-branching with two flowers in
every leaf axil. Ideal cultivar for $3\frac{1}{2}$ in or 5 in pots
and well in the exhibition category. Named after
the internationally renowned playwright, raised in
the vicinity of Merseyside, North England, and
introduced by Studley Royal Nurseries, Ripon,
Yorkshire. Clark, D. – British – 1985.

*Alan Dyos. Single. Rich pink tube, sepals are
broad and upswept, rich pink. Corolla rich pink
with short and flared petals, almost a pink self.
Small flowers held well out and very floriferous.
Growth small upright, vigorous and bushy, good
for bush, shrub or standard. Raised in the vicinity
of Middlesex and introduced by Woodbridge
Nurseries of Hounslow, Middlesex, in 1984. Dyos
– British – 1984.

*Alan's Gold. Double. Little known cultivar
from the South of England, which appears to be
another sport from Swingtime and synonymous
with Golden Swingtime. Finder unknown –
British – ca 1984.

Alaska. Double. Short white tube, sepals white
tinged with pale blue at tips; corolla white, edged
pale blue. Medium sized blooms and very free,
growth trailer. Roth – American – 1956.

Alaska. Double. Tube pure white, sepals white,
slightly tipped green. Corolla white, large and
fluffy. Very free flowering for a white double. Darkish green foliage; growth upright bush, slow
grower. Probably one of the purest of the whites.
Extremely popular, probably because the cultivar
is usually the first large double listed in nursery-

men's catalogue. A.F.S. Cert. of Merit 1967.
Schnabel – American – 1963 – A.F.S. No. 585.

Alata. Single. Red and purple. Smith – British –
1846.

Alba. See *magellanica*.

Alba coccinea. Single. White and red. Henaer-
son – British – 1867.

Alberta. Double. Red and purple. Bull – British
– Date unknown.

Albert Delpit. Lemoine – French – 1893.

Albert Memorial. Double. Red and purple.
Bland – British – 1871.

Albert Victor. Single. Red and purple, almost
black. Banks – British – Date unknown.

Albino. Single. Pink and vermilion. Slater –
British and French – 1838.

Albinose. Single. Rose pink and vermilion. Salter – British and French – 1838.

Albion. Single. Long tube neyron-rose; sepals
pointed and held right back to tube, neyron-rose.
Corolla hyacinth-blue passing to spectrum-violet;
fading to mallow-purple; medium size, open
saucer shape. Perfectly shaped flowers and extremely free. Growth medium, upright bush. Pollen parent Lady Isobel-Barnett. Gadsby – British
– 1972 – A.F.S. No. 1049.

Alcan Skies. Double. Tube and sepals pink;
corolla grey-blue, marbled with coral; flowers are
exceptionally large and free. Heat resistant,
growth trailer. Peterson-Fuchsia Farms – American – 1959 – A.F.S. No. 373.

Al Castro. Semi-double. Tube and sepals white;
corolla peachy-pink with white marbling on outer
petals, flaring out with age. Growth trailing. Castro – American – 1971 – A.F.S. No. 948.

Alderman. Single. Pinkish-red and dark purple.
Rudd – British – Date unknown.

Alderman Mechi. Single. Red and purple.
Banks – British – 1872.

Aldham. Double. Tube and sepals white, tinged
pink underneath with maturity, sepals are reflexed. Corolla is virgin-white, almost a self.
Medium sized blooms, very profuse flowering,
very full double making a welcome addition to
the 'whites'. Red stamens and pistil, red veined
leaves with serrated edges. Growth lax upright
and very suitable for either basketwork or weeping standards, makes dense basket. Named after
and introduced by Aldham Garden House Nurseries of Colchester in 1979. Shelley Lyn × self.
Dunnett – British – 1978 – A.F.S. No. 1514.

*Alerta Logue. Double. Short thick white tube;
sepals are white blush pink on top, pink-orange
underneath held half up 2 in long by $\frac{1}{2}$ in wide.
Three-quarters flared corolla opens pale red-
orange (R.H.S. 39B) maturing to dark red-orange
(R.H.S. 45D) 1 in long by 1 in wide with petal
margins turning up. Medium sized blooms with
pink filaments and white anthers, pistil has light
pink style and white stigma. Ovate shaped foliage,
serrated with acute tip leaves 2 in long by 1 in
wide, light green (R.H.S. 138A). Growth lax
upright or stiff trailer, very heat tolerant and pest
resistant; will make good basket with weights.
Raised in the vicinity of Downey and Oxnard,
California and trademarked in California. Parentage unknown. Anonymous raiser but registered

by Betty Cole of Downey. Raiser unknown – American – 1984 – A.F.S. No. 1758.

Alexandra Dumas. Lemoine – French – 1895.

Alexandrina. Double. Red and white. Veitch – British – Date unknown.

Alfie. Double. Tube and sepals red; corolla deep purple. Growth trailer. A.F.S. Cert. of Merit 1971. Tiret – American – 1968 – A.F.S. No. 792.

Alfred Dumesnil. Double. Red and violet. Lemoine – French – 1882.

Alfred Fouillee. Lemoine – French – 1898.

Alfred Neymarck. Lemoine – French – 1907.

Alfred Picard. Lemoine – French – 1906.

Alfred Rambaud. Double. Tube and sepals, rich scarlet; corolla violet-purple fades with age. Flowers are large and free, an old cultivar still seen on the showbench. Growth upright and bushy. Lemoine – French – 1896.

Alf's Pet. Single. Long thin white tube, sepals blush-white with green tips on top and azalea-pink (R.H.S. 41C) with green tips underneath, held at 45° angle below horizontal and recurve up. Corolla scarlet (R.H.S. 43B) and mandarin red (R.H.S. 40B) at the base. Small square flowers, pleated, with very long pistil, pink with yellow stigma, short anthers are blush-white. Mid green (R.H.S. 137B) foliage, cordate leaves with little serration. Growth small self-branching upright, will make good bush, standard or decorative. Holmes, R. – British – 1980 – A.F.S. No. 1555.

Alf Thornley. Double. Short pink tube, neyron-rose (R.H.S. 55) sepals held half up with recurved green tips. Corolla near perfect in form, creamy-white (R.H.S. 155D) maturing to dull-white. Medium sized blooms very full and reminiscent of a carnation, almost perfect form, two flowers in each leaf axil. Foliage mid-green (R.H.S. 138A). Growth upright and bushy, self-branching, will produce an excellent show plant. A fuchsia of almost perfect form, shape and habit. Named after well known hybridist and B.F.S. judge. Raised and tested in the vicinity of Merseyside for 3 years before release and introduced by Porter of Southport. Seedling from Lilac Lustre × . Clark, D. – British – 1981 – A.F.S. No. 1742.

Ali Baba. Double. Tube and sepals crimson; corolla rose-magenta. Medium sized blooms and very free, growth upright and bushy. Price – American – 1957.

Alice. Single. Red and white-blushed rose. Bull – British – 1873.

Alice. Double. Rose and white. Rozain-Boucharlat – French – 1913.

Alice. Semi-double. Tube and sepals, rich pink; corolla purple. Growth trailer. Hazard and Hazard – American – Date unknown.

Alice Ashton. Double. Tube and sepals pink; corolla porcelain-blue. Growth trailer. Tiret – American – 1971 – A.F.S. No. 991.

Alice Eastwood. Semi-double. Tube crepy-white, sepals crepy-white washed rose-red. Corolla white, veined rose-red at base. Flowers fairly large and free, growth upright bush. Named after one of the founders of the American Fuchsia Society in 1929. Hazard and Hazard – American – Date unknown.

Alice Hallmark. Single. Tube and reflexed sepals pink; corolla flat and open, small four petals, apple blossom pink. Tiny foliage, growth upright and bushy, when bedded out resembles a miniature rose. Hardy. York – American – 1954.

Alice Hoffman. Semi-double. Tube and sepals rose; corolla white, veined rose, flowers are small but very profuse, small foliage of bronzy-green colour, growth upright, compact and bushy, height 1½ to 2 ft. Accepted by B.F.S. as showbench hardy. Klese – German – 1911.

Alice Hoffman

Alice Kling. Single. Deep red self of medium size. Vigorous grower, main stem has many small side laterals which are covered with blooms all season. A true climber which will reach 20 ft in California. Heat tolerant. Wilson – American – 1959 – A.F.S. No. 413.

Alice Pearson. Single. Tube and sepals, waxy-white; corolla crimson, lovely colour contrast, medium size blooms, very free, early flowering. Growth upright bush, old cultivar worth seeking. Lye – British – 1887.

Alice Travis. Semi-double to double. Tube and sepals, carmine-cerise; horizontal when opened, broad sepals of full substance. Corolla deep violet-blue, very rich colour, large blooms and very free. Good pyramid habit. Travis, J. – British – 1956.

Alison. Single. Tube and sepals rose-pink; corolla bright purple on opening, maturing later to clover, pink at base. Large flowers, very free and bell shaped. Curtis – British – 1972.

Alison Ewart. Single. Tube neyron-rose, sepals neyron-rose tipped green; corolla mauve, flushed pink. Small flowers but very free. Foliage dark-green with bronze sheen and red veining. Growth upright and bushy inherited from Eleanor Leytham. Eleanor Leytham × Pink Darling. Roe – British – 1977.

Alison Reynolds. Double. Tube rose-Bengal, sepals clear rose-Bengal (R.H.S. 144D) on lower surface, shading to pink and cream with green tips on upper surface, sepals held 45° above horizontal. Violet (R.H.S. 74B). Medium sized blooms with pink stamens and white pistil. Mid-green (R.H.S. 137B). Small to medium foliage. Growth is medium upright, will train as bush or other tall types of training, best colour develops in shade. Tested for 3 years in the vicinity of Leyland, Lancashire, before release. Reynolds – British – 1982 – A.F.S. No. 1679.

Alison Ryle. Semi-double. Short tube, fuchsia pink, sepals brilliant fuchsia pink, pale at tips. Corolla deep lavender-blue, flushed very pale mauve with rose veins, fades with age, deeper colour around corolla edges. Medium size blooms and free flowering. Foliage dark green, oval with serrated edges. Good bedder, will take full sun. Growth medium, upright bush. Raised by Dr. M. Ryle and introduced by R. Atkinson of Consett. Lena Dalton × Tennessee Waltz. Ryle–Atkinson – British – 1968 – A.F.S. No. 1112.

*Alison Sweetman. Single. Longish tube and sepals, bright crimson held horizontally. Corolla beetroot-purple. Medium sized flowers freely produced. Growth upright, vigorous and very tall; similar growth to Angela Rippon only taller. Very disappointing cultivar with its long jointed laterals needing early support. Just another red and purple with no outstanding feature. Raised and tested before release in the vicinity of Nottingham. Named after the wife of the best known fuchsia personality in New Zealand. Introduced by Jackson's Nurseries of Tamworth in 1984. Roe – British – 1984.

Alitan. Double. Tube and sepals coral-red, corolla violet. Growth upright. Freeman – British – 1918.

Allegra. Double. Tube and reflexed sepals, medium rose. Corolla loose and flaring is a lively rose-bengal. Grower describes as a new development in flower form, 'the shattered form with large blooms which retain perfection of form, the colour shadings (tone on tone) are subtle, yet vibrant'. Growth, arching type trailer, heat tolerant. Submitted by Mrs. M. Slater for R.H.S. Hardy Trials 1975–78 but received no award. Schnabel-Paskesen – American – 1960 – A.F.S. No. 416.

Allurement. Double. Tube and sepals red; corolla blue, splashed pink. Large blooms, fairly free for size, growth upright bush. Tiret – American – 1968.

Aloha. Single. Tube and sepals white, tipped green; corolla light purple. Medium size flowers. Growth upright and bushy. Niederholzer – American – 1947.

Alpestris. Single. Tube and sepals deep red; corolla dusky-purple. Very small flowers tend to drop prematurely under wrong conditions. Foliage has reddish tinge. Growth very rampant and almost too vigorous for pot work. Refer to regia.

Alpestris Reevesi. Single. Habit is similar to F.magellanica gracilis, with larger and thicker foliage, evergreen, flowers similar and larger. F.alpestris × seedling of F.m. virgata. Evans and Reeves – American – 1937.

Alpha. Double. Red and violet-blue. G. Smith – British – 1872.

Alphand. Double. Red and purple. Lemoine – French – 1899.

Alphonse Daudet. Double. Red and violet. Lemoine – French – 1880.

Alphonse Karr. Lemoine – French – 1891.

Alsace. Double. Red and rosy-white. Rozain – Boucharlat – French – 1913.

Alsace-Lorraine. Double. Red and violet. Lemoine – French – 1874.

Alsa Garnet. Double. Tube white, sepals.white, tipped green and slightly flushed pink; corolla rich, garnet-red and fairly large. Growth is cascade, vigorous and fast. Thorne – British – 1965.

Alsternixe. Single. Tube and sepals deep red; corolla blue. Very sturdy grower suitable for garden and balcony. Gesäuseperle × F. gracilis. Nutzinger – Austrian – 1971.

Al Stettler. Double. Short tube and sepals, pink and white; corolla deep rose and salmon, large blooms and very showy. Growth upright. Pennisi – American – 1968 – A.F.S. No. 746.

Altair. Double. Red and violet. Freeman – British – 1918.

alternans. (Sessé and Mocino 1828). Synonymous with F. thymifolia.

Alwin. Semi-double. Tube and sepals neyron-rose. Short, thick tube and reflexing sepals. Corolla is white, red veined and tightly fluted. Medium-sized flowers, very floriferous and carried outward. Growth upright and bushy, short jointed, makes extremely good bush or shrub and ideal for the showbench. Introduced by Wills Fuchsias Ltd in 1977. La Campanella × Leibreiz. Clyne – British – 1976.

Alyce Larson. Double. Tube and sepals white, tipped pink; corolla white. Natural trailer, makes good basket. Tiret – American – 1972 – A.F.S. No. 1070.

*Amalia Kirchmayr. Semi-double. Tube and sepals red; corolla white with red veining. Growth short upright. Nutzinger – Austrian – 1973.

Amalie Twrdy. Double, Red and purple. Twrdy – German – 1870.

Amalthea. Semi-double. Short tube rose-madder wide boat-shaped sepals rose-madder (R.H.S. 55A) are held high, opal pink and tipped green. Corolla lilac-mauve (R.H.S. 85B) flushed rose at base with red veins. Medium sized blooms, very colourful at all stages showing characteristics of both parents, very free flowering. Foliage medium green with pointed leaves. Growth upright, free branching, short jointed 1⅜in between joints, red wood. Introduced by Woodbridge Nurseries, D. Stilwell in 1979. Coquet Bell × Blush O' Dawn. Clitheroe – British – 1979.

Amanda. Single. Red and purple. Harrison – British – 1853.

*Amanda Bridgland. Double. Short thick greenish tube ½ in by ¼ in is fluted, streaked rosy-red. Horizontally held sepals 1⅜ in by ⁷⁄₁₆ in are greenish-white on top, slightly rosy-red underneath, tipped green and slightly recurved. Corolla opens deep blue, streaked pink at base, maturing to mauve-blue with pink 1⁷⁄₁₀ in by 1½ in. Medium sized blooms very tight with fluted petals, quarter flared; petals are smooth, turned under and fluted, pink filaments and crimson anthers, white style and stigma. Foliage lightish green with ovate shaped leaves 2 in–2½ in by 1½ in. Growth small upright, self-branching very suitable for bush or decorative, needs little stopping, very attractive cultivar. Raised in the vicinity of Fareham, Hampshire, tested for 3 years before release and introduced by Kerrielyn Fuchsias of Cambridge in 1985. Speedbird × Preston Guild. Bridgland – British – 1985 – A.F.S. No. 1822.

Amanda Jones. Single. Short white bulbous tube with touch of soft pink, sepals white and soft pink on top, old rose colour underneath, held at angle of 45°. Corolla soft mauve-pink with very little veining. Small flowers 1½ in long by 1¼ in wide, long pedicel but flowers are not held erect like its sister seedling, Micky Goult, and although free flowering is not so prolific. Much darker in colours than Micky Goult and a lovely cultivar.

Light green foliage with ovate-cordate leaves 2 in long by 1¼ in wide. Growth upright and bushy, fairly short jointed, responds well to frequent pinching. Another of the raiser's introductions destined for the showbench. No trace of Bobby Shaftoe, one of its parents, but has the nodding characteristic of Santa Barbara (syn. Lustre) even holding its pistil on one side. Raised in the vicinity of Nottingham before release to Markham Grange Nurseries of Doncaster who introduced in 1981. Bobby Shaftoe × Santa Barbara (syn. Lustre). Roe – British – 1981.

Amandine Hans. Lemoine – French – 1862.

Amapola. Semi-double. Tube and sepals, dark pink; corolla rose-purple. Large blooms, growth trailer. Dale – American – 1950.

Amato. Semi-double. Red and crimson. Knight – British – 1842.

Amazing Grace. Double, Candy pink tube, up-turned sepals candy pink, tipped green. Corolla Wedgewood-blue, flushed candy-pink at base, turning lilac with maturity. Medium sized blooms, free and fully flared. Large foliage, dark green, growth upright and bushy. Cheseldine – British – 1975 – A.F.S. No. 1288.

Amazing Mary. Semi-double. Long light red tube, light red sepals which arch back. Corolla very dark red, large blooms very much like its parent. Dark green foliage. Growth tall, upright and vigorous, very suitable for standard. Raised and introduced by Hill Top Fuchsia Nurseries of Atherstone in 1980. Marinka × . Wright, J.A. – British – 1980 – A.F.S. No. 1596.

Amazone. Double. Red and white. Twrdy – German – 1874.

Ambassador. Single. Tube and sepals, rose-madder with white flush; corolla violet-purple fading to peony-purple. Blooms are large and very free, growth upright and bushy. Imported from England by Walker-Jones. W, Jones (British) – Machado (American) – 1962 – A.F.S. No. 502.

Ambroise Verschaffelt. Double. Red and purple. Cornelissen – Belgian – 1866.

Amelia Aoban. Single. White and cerise. This cultivar could be Amelie Aubin. Reedstrom – American – 1943.

Ameliaux. Single. Tube and sepals rose; corolla pale pink, growth upright bush. Raiser unknown – British – Date unknown.

Amelie Aubin. Single. Tube very long and thick, waxy-white; sepals waxy-white, tipped green. Corolla rosy-cerise, white at base. Foliage lightish green, a cultivar remarkable for size and quality of its flower, needs frequent stopping and staking for bush training. Growth is lax bush or trailer. One of the superb old cultivars, which should be in every collection. Synonymous with Gesause-perle (Nutzinger 1946) according to Dutch Fuchsia Technical Commission. Eggbrecht – German – 1884.

America. Single. Tube very thin and long, white at base; gradually changing to rose-madder on outside of sepals, crimson on inside with greenish-white tips. Corolla deep crimson. Flowers large and very free. Growth trailer, very lax. Golondrina × Rundle. Niederholzer – American – 1941.

americana elegans. Single. Tube and sepals cerise; corolla purple. Flowers small but very free.

Growth upright and bushy, but tends to straggle. Hardy, suitable for hedges 3 to 4 ft high. Accepted by B.F.S. as showbench hardy. Raiser unknown – Date unknown. (See also *magellanica*.)

American Beauty. Double. Long offset tube, light pink, curled sepals bengal-rose; corolla pendant shaped, glowing rose, spreads as flower matures, petals diluted to near white at base. Foliage dark green. Growth strong growing cascade. Hodges – American – 1958 – A.F.S. No. 345.

American Festival. Semi-double. Tube and sepals, pale pink; corolla claret and rose, large blooms. Growth upright and vigorous. Schnabel – American – 1948.

American Flaming Glory. Double. Tube and sepals pink, corolla purple toning to flaming red, edged with pink and orange. Largish blooms but very free for size, growth lax upright, will trail for basketwork with weights. Introduced by Meadowcroft Nurseries of Huntingdon. Martin – American – 1962.

Amethyst. Semi-double. Red and purple. Brown – British – 1845.

Amethyst. Double. Tube and sepals, pale red; corolla purple, flowers large and free. Growth upright bushy and vigorous. Identical in every way with Brown's Amethyst. Tiret – American – 1941.

Amethyst Fire. Double. Tube and sepals red; corolla amethyst-blue, heavily splashed pink. Large blooms, flowering continuously, dark green foliage. Growth upright and bushy, very strong and vigorous, medium height 1½ to 2 ft, hardy in Southern England and Scilly Isles. Tabraham – British – 1975.

Amigo. Single to semi-double. Tube and sepals salmon; corolla dark purple with deep salmon and light patches of coral. Flowers of medium size and very showy. Growth upright. Kennett – American – 1969 – A.F.S. No. 863.

Ami Hoste. Double. Red and two shades of violet. Lemoine – French – 1863.

Amiral Coubert. Lemoine – French – 1884.

Amiral Evans. Lemoine – French – 1908.

Amiral Moit. Lemoine – French – 1886.

A.M. Larwick. Tube and sepals, rich carmine; corolla purplish-mauve. Flowers free and of medium size; foliage medium green with crimson mid-rib. Growth upright and bushy. Suitable for all types of training. Accepted by B.F.S. as showbench hardy. L.A. Smith – New Zealand – 1940.

Amoena. Double. Red and purple. Twrdy – German – 1866.

Amori Mia. Double. Short tube red; sepals medium red inside, rose outside. Corolla dark fuchsia, marbled in rose. Large blooms, heat resistant. Growth trailer. Pennisi – American – 1970 – A.F.S. No. 891.

Amphion. Double. Red and purple. Bull – British – 1872.

ampliata (Bentham 1845). Synonymous with *F. ayavacensis.*

Amy Lye. Single. Tube creamy-wax, sepals white, tipped green; corolla coral-orange, medium size blooms very free and early. Foliage dark green with crimson mid-rib. Growth very vigorous, best described as spreading, lax bush, needs early stopping. Good for standard and all tall training. This cultivar is almost identical with White Queen. Lye – British – 1885.

Amy Marie. Double. Thick short light red tube, sepals $1\frac{1}{2}$ in by $\frac{3}{4}$ in wide light red, shiny on upperside, crepe textured on lowerside and held above the horizontal. Blush-pink corolla 1 in long by 2 in wide has long and short petals that fold and curl to form full corolla. Dark pink veins extend almost to bottom of petals. Medium sized blooms, best colour develops in shade. Dark green foliage 2 in long by $1\frac{1}{2}$ in wide, red veined. Growth trailer, but needs weights for basketwork. Tested 3 years in the vicinity of Portland, Oregon, U.S.A. before release. Very similar, especially in shape, to Swingtime and Yuletide; also to Dark Eyes except for colour. Sport from the unregistered Blue Eyes, not to be confused with Blue Eyes (Reedstrom 1954). The unregistered Blue Eyes is probably a sport of Dark Eyes and could be synonymous with Debra Hampson (Hilton 1976). Curtis – American – A.F.S. No. 1683 – 1982.

Amythyst. Double. Tube and sepals amethyst; corolla same colouring. Growth lax upright, will trail for basketwork. Correct spelling could be Amethyst which would add to the confusion of other cultivars by the same name. Originates from California. Hanson – American – *ca* 1970.

Andenken an Heinrich Henkel. Triphylla single. One of the most beautiful of the Triphylla hybrids and synonymous with Heinrich Henkel. Very long tube lovely rosy-crimson, flushed with faint cinnabar; short petals bright crimson. Dark reddish-green foliage, flushed purplish-red with roundish-ovate leaves. Like most triphylla hybrids is continuous in flowering in long terminal racemes, growth is upright but a trifle lax, distinctly unusual for a Triphylla. Various dates have been quoted for either the raising or the introduction, but history reads that in 1895 *F. triphylla* was introduced into German botanical gardens and *Moellers Deutsch Gaertner Zeitung* drew the attention of plant breeders to this species. *Fuchsia triphylla* is the type genus and the first fuchsia known to science. It was on this species that Father Carol Plumier (1646–1704) founded the genus *Fuchsia* in 1703 and named the plant he found in the West Indies '*Fuchsia triphylla flore coccinea*' and published a somewhat crude drawing of it. Linnaeus, who only knew the plant from Plumier's publication, reduced the name to *Fuchsia triphylla*, but later on as the bulk of the species were found in South America, Plumier's plant was forgotten until around 1873 when Thomas Hogg of New York introduced seeds from St. Domingo, where Plumier had originally found Triphylla. Thus 170 years after the plant had been described and figured, it was introduced into cultivation.

In 1882 the plant was introduced into England by the firm of G.G. Henderson and Sons from America and was recommended by Moeller in Erfurt as a promising object to the plant breeders.

This suggestion was promptly taken up, but the crosses were chiefly made with *F. triphylla* and *F. corymbiflora.*

A hybridizer by the name of Alwin Berger at the Botanic Garden at Greifswald in 1896 had several small specimens of *F. triphylla* and crossed the flowers of one with the pollen of a white flowered and long tubular hybrid variety, thought to be

Andenken an Heinrich Henkel

Edelstein, referred to as a 'White Rademacher'. Four fruits ripened during the following winter and in the spring of 1897 Berger handed them over to Mr. F. Rehnelt of the Botanic Gardens in Giesen in order that he might grow them on.

The seeds germinated quickly and in June, before Berger left for Italy, a number of promising seedlings were obtained which were all very similar. The following year, 1898, the young seedlings were planted out in the Botanic Garden at Giessen and there attracted the attention of Mr. Henkel from Darmstadt, who immediately acquired the whole set for a small sum and put the variety into trade under the long name of Andenken an Heinrich Henkel.

A. a. H. Henkel is perfectly intermediate between its parents; it shows the roundish-ovate leaves of the pollen plant and the rich, dark colour of the flower is changed from the hard cinnabar of the mother parent through the white of the pollen parent to a fine brilliant, rosy-crimson with a slight cinnabar hue.

Like all the hybrid descendants of *F. triphylla*, A. a. H. Henkel has inherited from the species, the habit of abundant and continuous flowering in long terminal racemes. It succeeds equally well in the cool greenhouse, as in the open, where it revels in the sun and is generally at its best towards the autumn, is very frost shy and must be protected during the winter with a minimum temperature of 40°F. Reliable German sources quote parentage as *F. corymbiflora* × Magnifica. Would therefore become a Triphylla type.

André Gill. Lemoine – French – 1882.

andreii. Tube green, sepals green and red; corolla red. Small flowers, low shrub. Johnston – 1935 – Ecuador.

André le Nostre. Double. Tube and sepals cerise; tube is extra long for this type of bloom. Corolla violet-purple, large blooms and free. Growth upright and bushy. Old cultivar still grown today and outstanding. Lemoine – French – 1909.

Andrew. Single. Tube cream, sepals pale madder; corolla very pale Tyrian-purple. Medium size blooms, growth upright and bushy. Watson – British – 1967.

*Andrew Carnegie. Double. Tube and sepals crimson, sepals held over corolla with upturned tips. Corolla white, veined cerise, very full and frilly. Largish blooms which fade quickly and drop prematurely, cerise stamens. Medium green foliage and serrated leaves. Growth lax bush, a cultivar which sends branches out sideways in spite of frequent pinching, vigorous and self-branching; best results in cool conditions. Named after the founder of the Public Library system. Very old cultivar, date not certain, could be circa 1865. Demay – French – *ca* 1865.

Andrew Ryle. Single. Short crimson tube, crimson sepals, shiny on upperside, held horizontally and well curved. White corolla with central crimson vein from base to half way down petals. Small dainty flowers, very free, best colour in sun. Small foliage, growth small, upright bush, self-branching. Pinky × Pink Cloud seedling × Strawberry Delight. Ryle – British – 1975 – A.F.S. No. 1239.

*Andrina. Double. White tube $\frac{3}{4}$in long, sepals white and fully turned up, 1 in long by $\frac{1}{2}$ in wide. Corolla silver-lavender, 1 in long. Medium sized blooms, very similar in shape to White Spider with pink stamens $1\frac{1}{2}$ in long, white pistil $2\frac{1}{4}$ in long and bright yellow stigma. Dark green foliage, small $1\frac{1}{2}$ in long by $\frac{5}{8}$ in wide. Growth small compact and upright and short-jointed, extremely good as a bedder. Raised and tested for 4 years in the vicinity of Timperley, Cheshire before release. Lena Dalton × White Spider. Howarth – British – 1983 – A.F.S. No. 1717.

Andromeda. Salter – British & French – 1841.

Andromeda. Single. Light red tube, sepals light-red stand out horizontal. Corolla lilac with red veining, small to average flowers. Growth upright and bushy. *F. regia* var. *typica* × Upward Look. De Groot – Dutch – Date unknown.

*Andy Cracolice. Double. White tube, sepals white tipped green, crepey white underneath $2\frac{1}{2}$ in long by 1 in wide, fully reflexed with recurved tips. Corolla purple-blue maturing to wine colours 1 in to $1\frac{1}{2}$ in long by $\frac{3}{4}$ in to 1 in wide. Largish blooms with pink marbling near base of sepals, dark pink stamens extend almost 2 in below corolla, pale pink style and white stigma extending almost 2 in below corolla. Medium green foliage wtih yellow cast maturing to dark green 3 in to 4 in long, ovate. Growth stiff trailer, will make good basket with weights; will need support for bush plant. Prefers warmth and heat tolerant if shaded. Raised and tested for 3 years in vicinity of Cuperino, California before release. Ambassador × White King. Smith, N.F. – American – 1983 – A.F.S. No. 1736.

Andy Pandy. Single. Thin short tube is flesh-pink; narrow pale pink sepals, deeper pink on lowerside, each sepal approximately $\frac{3}{4}$ in long and held horizontally. Corolla reddish-orange, flushed pink at the base. Smallish flowers with red stamens and white pistil. Light green foliage with small rounded serrated leaves. Growth natural trailer, will make excellent basket and takes full sun. Tested for 3 years in the vicinity of Cardiff, South Wales before release. Adams – British – 1982 – A.F.S. No. 1686.

Angel. Semi-double. Tube and sepals white, with pink cast when mature; corolla white. Foliage medium, light green on reddish branches, when in new growth. Growth lax bush, will trail. Hybridized in 1963. Gorman – American – 1970 – A.F.S. No. 928.

Angela. Double. Tube and sepals deep pink, corolla pale pink. Large blooms with lovely colour combination. Growth lax. Introduced by Mark-

ham Grange Nursery of Doncaster. Raiser and date unknown – *ca* 1970's.

Angela Gallegos. Double. White tube and sepals; corolla plum-royal blue. Growth lax upright, can be trained as basket, originates from California. Araujo – American – *ca* 1970.

Angela Leslie. Double. Tube pink, sepals recurving, pink, tipped pea green; deeper pink underneath. Corolla deep pink, further enhanced by small spots and veins of rose colouring. Growth upright and bushy, needs staking to support the heavy blooms. Showclass cultivar. Tiret – American – 1959 – A.F.S. No. 382.

Angela Rippon. Single. China rose tube, sepals waxy china-rose (R.H.S. 58D) with green tips. Corolla wisteria blue passing to Imperial purple (R.H.S. 92A). Medium-sized flowers freely produced, carried out horizontal from close-jointed bush. Growth upright and bushy. Self-branching, will produce good bush and all tall types of training. Tested for 4 years before release and named after the well known British television news reader. Christine Clements × Forward Look. Gadsby – British – 1977 – A.F.S. No. 1423.

Angelina Braemt. Double. Red and white. Cornelissen – Belgian – 1868.

Angeline. Double. Very long thin white tube, white sepals flushed pink with green tips, long and thin fully recurving. Corolla campanula-violet (R.H.S. 82C) flecked with pink (R.H.S. 65D). Medium sized blooms, very full double and very free, the outstanding characteristic is the unusual coloured corolla on a very long thin tube. Growth trailer, vigorous and short jointed. Self-branching and suitable for basketwork. Introduced by Aldham Garden House Nurseries of Colchester, 1979. Shelley Lyn × self. Dunnett – British – 1979 – A.F.S. No. 1515.

Angel Island. Double. Long white tube gives way to dainty, upturned white sepals; corolla white. Dark green foliage, makes excellent background for the frosty-white blooms, medium to large sized flowers. Growth trailer. Needs heat. Reedstrom – American – 1957 – A.F.S. No. 305.

Angel's Dream. Double. Tube and sepals, clear soft pink; corolla white, pink markings towards centre, petals serrated, mature bloom is flaring, lacy and frilly. Foliage dark green, veined red with red stems. Heavy bloomer, long trailer with blooms all the way down the branches. Trailer. Similar to Angels Flight but not related. Stubbs – American – 1973 – A.F.S. No. 1079.

Angel's Flight. Double. Long white tube, sepals deep pink, wide, which turn back the full length of tube. Corolla white, centre petals and shorter side skirt petals. Extra long, deep pink stamens. Growth low bush or trailer. Martin – American – 1957 A.F.S. No. 320.

Angel's Flight – Beauty of Bath. These two lovely pink and white cultivars are frequently confused with each other and unless individual blooms are placed side by side it is understandable to see why. Angel's Flight (Martin – American – 1957) and Beauty of Bath (Colville – British – 1965) are both doubles with almost the same shape corolla. A.F.'s tube is thinner and shorter, but the main difference is in the sepals, both are pink, deeper at the base and edge but B. of B. are tipped green and do not twist and curl which is a characteristic of A.F. and unusual. Both corollas are white but A.F.'s is veined pale pink whereas the other is pure white and the whole corolla does not taper like the other. Another difference is the long pistil of Angel's Flight which is white and the long tapering bud, growth is a lax upright which will trail whereas Beauty of Bath is upright and bushy responding to frequent pinching, both cultivars are well worth growing.

Anita. Double. Tube and sepals red; corolla violet splashed red, large blooms. Growth very vigorous, upright to 8 ft in height in California. A.F.S. Cert. of Merit. 1948. Niederholzer – American – 1946.

Anna. Double. Tube and sepals carmine; corolla magenta, carmine at base, almost a self. Blooms are very large and long. Foliage dark green and large. Growth trailer. A.F.S. Cert. of Merit. 1948. Reiter – American – 1945.

Annabel. Double. Annabel by Dr. M. Ryle formerly known as seedling 49D is a most welcome good double to the range of near whites. The white tube is rather long and striped pink, the long broadish sepals are white, slightly flushed pink which curl at the tips and are recurved held well out from the tube, pink at base. The white double corolla is veined pink, long and very full, very free flowering for a double cultivar, pink stamens and light pink style with lightish green foliage. The growth is upright but although inclined to be lax is strong enough to carry the heavy blooms which hang in clusters. This cultivar was submitted to the B.F.S. Floral Committee at Manchester 1977 who were most impressed with the shape and quality of the blooms together with the good natural growth and awarded the plant a Silver Certificate of Merit. Annabel certainly shows the excellent qualities of parent Nancy Luo without the pink sepals. This should be a welcome addition to the exhibitors who are looking for a good show class white double. Ingram Maid × Nancy Luo. Ryle – British – 1977 – A.F.S. No. 1476.

Anna Hohl. Single. Tube and sepals light red; corolla soft pink. Average size flowers with pink stamens and style. Growth upright and bushy. Grown and cultivated in the Netherlands. Raiser unknown – Date unknown.

Anna Magnani. Single. Light red tube, sepals light red gradually becoming white at tips, tipped green, pink underneath. Corolla deep pink-red, the sepals are short in comparison with the rest of flower, pink stamens and light pink style. Growth lax bush. Steevens – Dutch – Date unknown.

Anna Marie. Double. Tube and sepals scarlet; corolla violet, outer petals splotched with pink. Large blooms and free. Growth upright, tall and vigorous. Munkner – American – 1952.

Anna Pavlova. Double. Very long red tube, sepals red; corolla white and pale pink, very compact and ruffled. The outstanding feature of this cultivar is its long tube with the short, solid compact corolla. Growth upright and lax. Best grown as H1. Colville – British – 1966.

Anna Roth. Double. Tube and sepals red; corolla dark red, large blooms and free. Growth upright bush. Niederholzer – American – 1945.

Anne. Single. Long thin tube, very pale cerise; sepals long and spreading, pale cerise. Corolla mauve-cerise long and tight. Foliage medium green, finely serrated. Growth upright bush, makes good standard. Harris – British – 1974 – A.F.S. No. 1211.

Annette Barbier. Semi-double. Tube and sepals, light pink, very small tube; corolla white. Growth upright bush. Pennisi – American – 1968 – A.F.S. No. 747.

Ann Howard Tripp. Single to semi-double. Short thick white tube with faint stripe, white sepals held at the horizontal, edged and tinged with palest pink, tipped green. Corolla white, very lightly veined pink held well clear of foliage. Medium sized flowers almost a white self, very similar to Ting-a-Ling, very strong pedicel. Produces two flowers in each leaf axil, exceptionally free flowering, could be described as a pure white Lady Isobel Barnett with adequate shading. Pale green foliage, leaves of new growth yellow changing with maturity. Growth upright, very vigorous and self-branching, requires 11 weeks stopping period. Raised and tested in the vicinity of Merseyside for 3 years before release. Introduced by John Ridding of Kidderminster in 1982. Lady Isobel Barnett × Joy Patmore. Clark, D. (Merseyside) – British – 1982 – A.F.S. No. 1701.

Annie. Single. White and carmine. Green – British – 1862.

Annie Earle. Single. Tube waxy-cream; sepals waxy-cream with green tip, corolla carmine-scarlet, medium size blooms very free, and early. Growth upright vigorous bush, good for standard. Another good Lye cultivar, seldom seen these days. Lye – British – 1887.

Annie Laurie. Double. Tube and sepals red; corolla deep violet, large flowers with petaloid anthers, fairly free. Grow lax bush, will trail. Hazard and Hazard – American – 1933.

Anniversary. Double. Short tube and sepals, deep coral; corolla variegations of red, purple and orange. Large blooms and fairly free, dark green foliage. Growth bush or trailer, needs support for bush cultivation. Walker – American – 1969 – A.F.S. No. 836.

Ann Lee. Double. Tube and sepals red, long sepals; corolla rich violet-blue, very rich colouring. Growth upright and bushy. Holmes, E. – British – 1970.

Ann Pacey. Double. Short, thick, white tube, broad sepals pink, tipped green with neyron-rose underside. Corolla phlox-pink at base shading to pale neyron-rose. Medium to large blooms free flowering for a double. Growth upright, self branching, medium height, vigorous, will make good bush, standard or decorative. Best colour in shade, tested for 6 years in Midlands before release. Joan Pacey × . Gadsby – British – 1978 – A.F.S. No. 1479.

Ann Porter. Single. White tube, sepals white veined red, corolla aster-violet. Medium sized flowers, growth upright and bushy. Introduced by the raiser in the vicinity of Southport, England. Porter – British – 1978.

Ann's Beauty. Double. Thin, white tube, 1 in long, $\frac{5}{8}$ in diameter, triphylla form, sepals neyron-rose $2\frac{1}{2}$ in long and 1 in wide, edges curve inward slightly, very light green tips, upper side lighter colour than underside. Violet-purple corolla with neyron-rose variegation, with slight flare. Large blooms, prefers heat, best colour in sun, dark blue stamens and pistil, beige stigma. Large, dark green foliage with red stems and branches. Growth trailer, makes good basket. Soo Yun – American – 1976 – A.F.S. No. 1352.

Ann's Delight. Double. Tube and long sepals, bright pink of heavy crepe texture; corolla large but loose, orchid-pink. Petals are spoon type and out-lying at base of corolla. Beautiful and different cultivar. Leathery green foliage. Growth upright and strong. Needs heat. Gagnon – American – 1962 – A.F.S. No. 507.

Ann Sothern. Double. White tube, white sepals with tinge of pink; corolla white. Small petite blooms, growth trailer, suitable for baskets. Araujo – American – 1975.

Antagoniste. Single. White and vermilion Brittle – British – 1857.

Anthea Bond. Single. Short tube spiraea-red, long slender sepals measuring 4 in across, spiraea-red, recurving at tips. Corolla wisteria-blue, lighter at base. Long tapering flowers with rolled petals, very free flowering. Dainty spear-shaped, dark green foliage, growth medium upright bush, self-branching and exceptionally well branched and short jointed. Raised by Cliff Gadsby and introduced by Fuchsialand Nurseries, Birmingham, 1975. Cliff's Hardy seedling × Upward Look. Gadsby – British – 1975 – A.F.S. No. 1311.

Anthea Day. Double. Tube and sepals rich waxy red, corolla blush pink. Medium sized blooms, very early and free flowering all through the season. Growth upright and bushy, best grown as H2. Introduced by C.S. Lockyer of Bristol in 1981. Pink Cloud × Pink Quartet. Day – British – 1981.

Anthony Webb. Double. Short ivory tube, sepals ivory, tipped green, flushed rose underneath and reflexed. Corolla campanula-blue and pale lavender. Medium to large blooms. Growth vigorous and of scandent habit. Travis, J. – British – 1956.

Antigone. Single. Tube and sepals white, with touches of pink; corolla pinkish-orange. Early bloomer, medium size and very free. Dark green foliage, growth upright and bushy. Still listed by some specialist growers. Banks – British – 1887.

*Antonella Merrills. Single. Long thin tube salmon-pink, petal margins are wavy; sepals pale pink on top, light salmon-pink underneath, $\frac{2}{3}$ in long by $\frac{1}{4}$ in wide, horizontally held with green tips and reflexed. Quarter flared corolla opens deep salmon-pink maturing slightly paler; slightly pyramidal shaped corolla $\frac{1}{2}$ in long by $\frac{1}{2}$ in wide. Smallish flowers with salmon-pink filaments and white anthers, mid-green foliage with ovate leaves 2 in long by $1\frac{1}{4}$ in wide. Growth is lax upright or stiff trailer; needs frequent pinching to obtain bushy plant; does not tolerate overhead watering. Raised in the vicinity of Worksop, Nottinghamshire. Coachman × Lye's Unique. Caunt – British – 1984 – A.F.S. No. 1763.

Antonia. Single. Tube pale pink, sepals pale pink flushed with cerise, deeper on the inside, spreading. Corolla cerise and bell shaped. Long pistil and short stamens. Growth upright and bushy. Good bedder. Harris – British – 1974 – A.F.S. No. 1213.

Apache. Double. Tube and sepals rosy-red. Corolla lilac, over splashed with pink. Medium sized blooms and free flowering for double. Growth upright and bushy. Introduced by High Trees Nurseries of Reigate, Surrey, in 1980. Blue Lagoon × Phyllis. Hobson – British – 1973.

apetala. Orange-scarlet tube, reddish-orange sepals; no corolla. Very few flowers, approximately 2 in long, borne near the apex of the branchlets. Vine-like shrub, up to 3 ft in native habitat. Synonymous with *F. insignis.* Ruiz and Pavón – 1802 – Ecuador and Peru.

Aphrid. Double. Tube has alternative stripes of pink and white; sepals deep pink, short and spreading. Corolla white with pink veins, tight and compact. Growth upright and bushy. Harris – British – 1974 – A.F.S. No. 1212.

Aphrodite. Double. Tube and sepals pink; corolla pure white, long and full. Large blooms very prolific, similar to Angel's Flight only larger. Growth upright and vigorous, will make a good standard, best grown as H1. Colville – British – 1964.

apiculata (Johnston 1925). Synonymous with *F. loxensis.*

Applause. Double. Short, thick pale carmine tube, very broad carmine sepals up to an inch across have pale streak down middle and curve slightly at maturity. Deep orange-red corolla, wide spreading with many petals. Huge blooms very beautiful, bright colour which need staking as a bush, best colour in shade. As a basket must be trained very early due to heavy vigorous growth. Dark green foliage, will trail with weights. Tested for 3 years at Fort Bragg, California before release. Stubbs – American – 1978 – A.F.S. No. 1440.

Apple Blossom. Single. Tube and sepals, shell-pink; corolla pink, almost a self. Petite, single flaring blooms, dark green foliage. Growth low spreading and vigorous. Heat tolerant. Schnabel–Paskesen – American – Originally introduced 1953 – Reintroduced 1960 – A.F.S. No. 417.

Appollo. Single. Tube and sepals, pale pink; corolla pale blue, medium size blooms and long. Growth trailer. Haag – American – 1950.

Apricose. Single. Tube and sepals, shrimp-pink; corolla rose, lighter at base, medium sized flowers and free. Growth upright and bushy, makes a large plant. Niederholzer – American – 1944.

Apricot. Single. Tube and sepals, pink and orange; corolla apricot, unusual colouring. Medium sized blooms and free. Growth trailer. Reedstrom – American – 1943.

April. Single. Tube and sepals bright red, corolla violet, flowers very small but very free. Growth dwarf, bushy and compact, very similar to Carnea, very suitable for rockery or border. Good bedder, hardy. Raised by W.P. Wood and introduced by H.A. Brown in 1935. Pumila × Mrs. King. Wood – British – 1935.

April Showers. Semi-double. Tube and sepals, rose-madder; corolla light magenta-purple. Medium sized flowers and free. Growth lax bush, will trail with weights. Fuchsia-La – American – Date unknown.

Aquarilla. Single. Tube ivory, sepals cream; corolla orchid-blue and rosy-lilac. Growth upright and bushy. Raiser unknown – British – Date unknown.

Aquarius. Single. Tube and sepals, light pink, tipped green, darker pink on underside; corolla pink, bell shaped. Foliage medium size with serrated edges. Growth upright and bushy. Soo Yun – American – 1971 – A.F.S. No. 946.

Arabella. Single. White and dark rose. Banks – British – 1866.

Arabella Improved. Single. Tube and reflexed sepals, waxy-cream; corolla rosy-cerise. Medium size blooms and free. Growth upright bush, vigorous. Although Lye used Arabella as a parent has no resemblance, still grown and very good. James Lye × Arabella. Lye – British – 1871.

Arago. Semi-double. Carmine and red. Harrison – British – 1842.

Arantgarde. Rozain-Boucharlat – French – 1913.

Arborea. Single. Rose and red. Smith – British – 1841.

arborea (Sessé and Mocino 1887). Synonymous with *F. arborescens.*

arborescens. Rose to magenta tube, sepals reddish to wine purple; corolla lavender on lilac as long as sepals. Flowers are borne in corymbose panicles. Large foliage with laurel-like leaves, paler underneath, leaves are opposite sometimes in threes. Sometimes referred to as the lilac fuchsia on account of the mass effect of the flowers having the appearance of a lilac spray, hence the synonymous name of *F. syringaeflora.* Grand subject for planting out in cool conservatory. Small or large tree attaining a height of 25 to 30 ft on the lofty mountains of South Mexico. Synonymous with *F. arborea, F. hamellioides* and *F. syringaeflora.* Sims – 1865 – Central America particularly in South Mexico and Guatemala.

var. **megalantha**.

arborescens – paniculata. To distinguish between these similar species see *paniculata.*

Arcadia. Single. Red cerise tube, thick of medium length, red-cerise sepals, long broadish and slightly upturned. Corolla of true magenta colour with long compact petals which do not flare. Largish flowers attractive and good, magenta stamens and pistil, heat tolerant. Pale green foliage, serrated and oval shape. Growth upright, stems are long and thin and with weights would basket. Introduced by J. Ridding in 1979 after the raiser's death. Tolley – British – 1979 – A.F.S. No. 1520.

*****Arcadia Gold.** Double. Short tube and sepals rich, shiny red of crepe texture, inside of petals rosy-red. Very full corolla is milky-white, but sparkling colours, faintly veined pink. Medium to large blooms of exceptional quality and very showy. Foliage is variegated and differs from all other sports from the same cultivar Swingtime which have golden foliage. Growth is lax, will produce fine full or half basket; rather on the stiff side, responds well to pinching and well within the showbench category. Found in the vicinity of Middlesborough, Co. Cleveland, and introduced exclusively by Arcadia Nurseries of Nunthorpe, Middlesbrough in 1985. Sport of Swingtime. Birch (locator) – British – 1985.

Arcady. Single. Tube and sepals, pink suffused salmon, tipped green. Corolla deep rose, edged salmon. Growth upright and free branching habit. Colville – British – 1968.

Archiduchesse Marie Thérèse. Double. Red and purple. Twrdy – German – 1866.

Archie Owen. Double. Tube soft pink, sepals are of the same colour medium long with average taper, reflex on maturity. Corolla of many petals soft pink. Medium to small leaves are dark green with reddish tinges and red veins. Growth natural trailer will make good basket, tested for 6 years in California before release. Stubbs – American – 1977 – A.F.S. No. 1410.

*****Architect Ludwig Mercher.** Semi-double. Tube and sepals red; corolla white with pink veining. Growth medium upright. Nutzinger – Austrian – 1977.

Arctic Night. Double. Tube and sepals deep red; corolla petunia-purple. Medium sized blooms and free. Growth upright and bushy. Fuchsia-La – American – 1964.

Ariel. Single. Tube magenta, sepals magenta with green tips, very pointed, spreading not reflexed. Corolla deep magenta-pink, Breviflorae type, petals reflexed. Foliage deep green, deeply cut serrated margin, glossy. Flowers tiny, very floriferous. Growth upright, makes good self-branching medium standard, bush, decorative, miniature or bonsai. Breviflorae hybrid *F.encliandra × F.hemsleyana.* Travis, J. – British – 1970 – A.F.S. No. 1136.

Ark Royal. Double. Tube bright red, sepals bright red, tipped white. Corolla white splashed red at the base with occasional red splash on petals. Large blooms and very free for size of bloom, growth upright and bushy. Introduced by Woodbridge Nurseries of Hounslow in 1980. Swingtime × Joy Patmore. Dyos – British – 1980.

Arlendon. Semi-double. Tube and sepals bright red, corolla white slightly veined cerise, flowers larger than Snowcap. Named by the raiser after his three sons, Arthur, Leonard and Donald. This cultivar was previously known as Snowcap Improved. Introduced by R. Pacey in 1979. Green-Horce – British – 1974 or 1975.

Arlequin. Single. White and rosy-carmine. Lemoine – French – 1884.

Arlequin. Rozain-Boucharlat – French – 1913.

Armand Carrel. Lemoine – French – 1882.

Armand Gautier. Lemoine – French 1904.

Army Nurse. Semi-double. Tube and sepals, deep carmine; corolla bluish-violet, flushed pink at base, veined pink. Flowers small but profuse, growth upright, bushy and vigorous. Accepted by B.F.S. as showbench hardy. Hodges – American – 1947.

Artemis. Single. Long thin white tube, sepals white with very pale green tips, spreading but not reflexed. White corolla, Encliandra type, flared but not reflexed. Very small flowers, very floriferous with good display of large purple to black berries. Small foliage, dense and serrated, typical Encliandra type foliage. Growth natural trailer, self branching will also produce medium upright bush. Travis, J. – British – 1975 – A.F.S. No. 1317.

*****Arthur Bland.** Semi-double. Short rose-purple tube, half up pale rose-purple sepals $1\frac{1}{2}$ in long by $\frac{1}{3}$ in wide with recurved tips. Corolla opens spectrum-violet maturing to imperial-purple $\frac{3}{4}$ in long by 1 in wide. Medium sized blooms are non-flaring and bell shaped with violet petaloids, splashed mauve, magenta filaments, anthers and pistil. Pale lime green foliage with cordate leaves $1\frac{1}{2}$ in long by 1 in wide; veins and stems are red with deep red branches. Growth self-branching lax upright or stiff trailer with excellent contrast between foliage and blooms. Raised and tested for 8 years in vicinity of Rotherham, Northern England before being introduced by Castledyke Fuchsias of Wildmore, New York, Lincolnshire in 1984. Border Queen × Army Nurse. Lamb – British – 1984 – A.F.S. No. 1770.

Arthur Cope. Semi-double. Tube long and white; sepals waxy-white. Corolla spiraea-red, flushed rose-red and splashed white. Large blooms and free, growth vigorous and spreading makes a good bedder, prefers shade. Gadsby – British – 1968 – A.F.S. No. 982.

Arthur Fritz. Double. Tube and sepals, Chinese-red; corolla deep burgundy, variegated with orange and pink. Flowers large and free. Growth upright. Pennisi – American – 1967 – A.F.S. No. 712.

Arthur Young. Double. Thin, white tube of medium size, long, broad, recurving sepals, white, with extreme tip green. Corolla has four inner petals of Imperial-purple with outer petals, white, flushed rose and purple. Medium sized blooms, small outer petaloids white, flushed rose with some almost purple, sepals recurve to hide tube, pale rose stamens with white pistil. Best colour in shade, growth semi-trailer but will make good bush, standard or decorative. Sport of King's Ransom. Young – British – 1976 – A.F.S. No. 1396.

Artistic. Fry – British – 1864.

Artus. Double. Tube and sepals, rosy-scarlet; corolla pure white, has very square appearance which makes it unusual and unique. Flowers large and free. Growth upright, vigorous and bushy. Crousse – French – Date unknown.

asperifolia. Dark red tube, red sepals; scarlet corolla. Smallish flowers approximately one inch long, free, borne in terminal racemes. Low shrub and spreading. Kause – 1905 – Peru and Brazil.

aspiazui. Blood-red tube, red sepals; corolla reddish-scarlet. Small flowers borne in pendant clusters. Upright shrub up to 6 or 7 ft. Macbride – 1941 – Peru.

asplundii. Tube orange-red, sepals red; corolla brick-red. Long flowers produced solitary in the leaf axils with small foliage. Small upright shrub. Macbride – 1941 – Peru.

Astoria. Single. Tube and sepals bright red; corolla light lilac streaked with carmine. Small flowers, growth upright and bushy. Cultivar which seems to be exclusive to California. Raiser unknown – American – *ca* 1960.

Astronaut. Single. Very striking cultivar of unusual colouring introduced by Ron Winkley of Birmingham about 1972. Raiser unknown – British – 1972.

Athela. Single. Tube creamy-pink, sepals pink; corolla salmon-pink deepening in colour at base, edged pale pink. Flowers medium and free, early bloomer. Growth upright bush. Gadsby crossed this cultivar with Bon Accorde to obtain a new break-through with Upward Look in 1968. Rolla × Mrs. Rundle. Whiteman – British – 1942.

Athene. Single. Tube and sepals white, shaded Tyrian-rose; corolla rose, flowers medium and long. Growth trailer, heat resistant. Warren – American – 1947.

Athenes. Lemoine – French – 1911.

Atkinsoniana. Single. Tube and sepals, bright scarlet; corolla rich purple, long, medium sized flowers and very free. Growth upright and hardy. One of the first hybrids, claimed to be an improved *globosa.* Lowe – British – 1838. (See also *magellanica* var. *globosa.*)

Atlantis. Semi-double. Short tube white and thick; sepals white, flushed pale pink inside. Corolla lilac, with deeper shade at edge of petals. Foliage dark green, well serrated. Growth lax bush, self branching, makes good standard, will trail with weights. Handley – British – 1974 – A.F.S. No. 1190.

Atomic Glow. Double. Tube pale pink; sepals pale orange, tipped green, deeper colour underneath. Corolla glowing pink with orange tint. Early bloomer, medium in size, blooms in flushes. Growth lax bush or trailer. Machado – American – 1963 – A.F.S. No. 561.

Atropurpurea plena. Lemoine – French – 1858.

atrorubra (Johnston 1925). Synonymous with *F. sylvatica.*

Attraction. Single. Red and purple. Bland – British – 1881.

Attractor. Standish – British – 1841.

Aucubefolia. Single. Long red tube and sepals, sepals are held at the horizontal; corolla red. Flowers are a red self and freely produced for a variegated foliage cultivar. Foliage is very ornamental having greater merit than its flowers, the leaves have a creamy-white and conspicuous central blotch. R.H.S. First Class Certificate at R.H.S. Chiswick Trials 1875. Henderson – British – *ca* 1870.

Audoti. Single. Red and purple. Salter – British and French – 1841.

Audray. Single. Very short green tube, long thin sepals spinel red (R.H.S. 54B) shading to neyron-rose (R.H.S. 55C) with white markings and tipped green, the unusual characteristic of the sepals is the shapening like an outline of a pagoda and curling. Corolla spectrum-violet (R.H.S. 82B) edged with imperial-purple. Medium sized tubular shaped flowers, very free flowering which take full sun. Medium foliage with lanceolate leaves, serrated edges and pale veins, light green (R.H.S. 143B). Growth is self-branching natural trailer, making good basket or standard. Tested for three years in the vicinity of Woodbridge, East Coast of England before release. Introduced by Burgh Nurseries of Woodbridge, Suffolk in 1982. Deben Rose cross. Dunnett – British – 1982 – A.F.S. No. 1705.

Audrey Chez. Double. Long thin flesh-coloured tube, sepals pink inside and pale pink outside, thick textured, narrow pointed. Corolla very short only ½ inch long, deep pink and varied orange, orange base with pink tips. Small blooms with pink stamens and pale pink pistil, cupped shaped. Light green foliage, pointed and narrow leaves. Growth trailer, self-branching suitable as basket or weeping standard. Cheseldine – British – 1979 – A.F.S. No. 1505.

Audrey Thill. Double. Small deep pink tube, pink sepals with lighter tips turning to rose, long, curl over tube. Corolla light blue, changing to rose-orchid with maturity. Small blooms, very free, ten blooms to a cluster, flare out and rather loose, long stamens and pistil. Small dark green foliage with wiry branches. Growth natural trailer, beautiful basket cultivar. Flash × .Prentice – America – 1975 – A.F.S. No. 1299.

Auguste Flemeng. Double. Red and purple. Lemoine – French – 1884.

Auguste Hardy. Double. Red and purple. Lemoine – French – 1892.

Auguste Holmes. Lemoine – French – 1903.

Auguste Lemarchand. Crousse – French – 1864.

Auguste Renold. Single, Red and purple. Still in cultivation per Arthur W. Taylor in England. Lemoine – French – 1886.

Auguste Zaubitz. Double. Red and white. L'Huillier – French – 1864.

Augustin Thierry. Lemoine – French – 1888.

Auld Reekie. Double. Tube and sepals rose opal; corolla aconite-violet. Large blooms, very full double. Growth upright and spreading. Introduced by R. Pacey. Named by late Tom Thorne. Jones – British – 1960s.

Aunt Chloe. Double. Tube and curved sepals, deep phlox-pink; corolla purple-blue, deep phlox-pink at base. Bright green foliage with serrated edges. Growth lax bush, vigorous, can be made to trail. Ewing – American – 1953 – A.F.S. No. 150.

Auntie Elsie. Single. Long violet tube, smokey-violet sepals which arch back. Corolla cherry-red, large flowers. Light green foliage, growth tall, upright and vigorous, very suitable as bush. Raised and introduced by Hill Top Fuchsia Nurseries of Atherstone in 1980. Barbara × . Wright, J.A. – British – 1980 – A.F.S. No. 1597.

Auntie Jinks. Single. Tube pink-red, sepals white, edged cerise; corolla purple, but best described as cerise-purple with white shading. Smallish blooms but extremely floriferous and attractive, pink style, pale pink filaments. Small mid-green foliage with pointed leaves. Growth pendulous, excellent cultivar for basketwork despite its parent, similar in many ways to La Campanella with more compact growth. Checkerboard self seedling, grown and tested at Reading. Wilson, J.W. – British – 1970.

Auntie Maggie. Single. Tube flesh pink; sepals topside pink, underside pale geranium-pink with paler tips, coiled right back. Corolla Indian-red, close barrel shaped. Medium size blooms and profuse, foliage pale green; oval, pointed and serrated. Growth upright, makes good bush, standard or decorative. Seedling of Mrs. Marshall. Tolley – British – 1974 – A.F.S. No. 1228.

Aunt Juliana. Double. Tube short red, upturned red sepals; corolla pale lavender-blue, all red stamens and pistil. Beautiful colouring, blooms large and free. Growth lax bush or trailer, needs support as bush, would make a good basket. Probably the best pastel blue. Sport of Uncle Jules. Hanson – American – 1950 – A.F.S. No. 1320.

Aunt Priscilla. Double. Thick white tube, sepals white to faint pink on upper surface, crepey-white on lower surface. Corolla dusky-rose with petals of smoky-lavender edges, white veins at the base with white steak down the centre. Large blooms and fairly free for size with fat white buds, best colour in shade, stamens and pistil are long and white with faint tinge of pink. Large foliage medium green and makes lax branches. Growth

medium upright, but can be made a lax bush, needing weights if used for basketwork. Tested for 2 years in the vicinity of Cupestino, California, U.S.A. before release. Pepi × unnamed white double. Smith, Nora – American – 1982 – A.F.S. No. 1703.

Aunt Ruth. Double. Short, medium thick red tube, long and curved red sepals; short corolla is violet with streaks of red and white. Medium sized blooms and fairly free for double, dark green foliage. Growth upright and bushy, self-branching medium size, will make good bush. Introduced in 1960 but not registered until 1976. Hanson – American – 1960 – A.F.S. No. 1321.

Aurantia. Single. Bronze-vermilion self. Hybrid of *F.fulgens.* Tiley – British – 1847.

Aurea. See *magellanica.*

Aurea Superba. See Aurora Superba.

Aurora Borealis. Single. Tube and sepals soft pink, sepals are narrow and tipped green; corolla orange-red. Growth upright. Seems to be exclusive to California where it is thought to be identical to Speciosa which is now confirmed to be a hybrid from *F. splendens × F. fulgens.*

Aurora Superba. Single. Tube and sepals, light apricot colour, sepals droop at first, but become horizontal with maturity. Corolla deep orange-peach, almost self coloured. Exquisite flowers medium in size, length from seed pod to end of stigma approximately 5 in and fairly profuse. Soft light green foliage, broad at base, tapering to a point, characteristic is the saw toothed edge, curling foliage and very bad leaf curl. Growth is rather lax but bushy, needs heat for perfection, best grown as H1. Will produce a good standard or pyramid, can be a disappointing cultivar for the beginner. This cultivar is often confused with Lord Lonsdale which has longer flowers, more robust foliage, slightly lighter coloured corolla with larger petals, less green at the sepal tips, better grower and more free in flowering. Although this cultivar has always been considered to be a British raising, from information given in the *Journal of Horticulture* 1879 p 117, it could be otherwise: 'Aurea Superba' raised in America and distributed by Cannell, the nearest approach to yellow'. From this information would appear to be American and Aurea Superba could be the correct spelling.

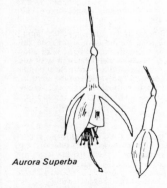

Aurora Superba

Austerlitz. Double. Red and violet. Demay – French – 1869.

Australia Fair. Double. Tube and sepals, bright red; corolla white, flushed and veined red. Large blooms and free. Growth upright and bushy, needs support for the heavy blooms. Rawlins – British – 1954.

austromontana. Reddish-orange self, long tubular flowers approximately 1 to 1½ in long. Dark green foliage, tall upright shrub reaching several feet in height. Synonymous with *F. serratifolia* (Hook 1845). Johnston – 1939 – Peru.

Autumnale. Single. Tube and sepals, scarlet-rose; corolla purple, medium sized flowers, quite free, late in flowering. Smallish but shiny foliage, golden and coppery-red, leaves start as green and yellow, but change to dark red and salmon with splashes of yellow. Growth is stiff, habit lax, more horizontal than vertical. Considerable confusion with this cultivar, Burning Bush and Rubens. Would appear that Rubens is the correct name for all three. Meteor – European – Date unknown – 1880?

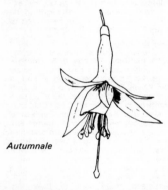

Autumnale

Autumn Red. Single. Rose-Bengal tube, sepals rose-Bengal (R.H.S. 25); corolla beetroot-purple (R.H.S. 830/2) fading to Tyrian-purple (R.H.S. 727/2) and beetroot-purple petaloids. Medium sized flowers, heat tolerant, best colour in shade, light green foliage 3¼ in × 1¾ in wide. with red stems. Growth natural trailer good for basket or weeping standard. Raised in vicinity of Sebastopol, California. Introduced and registered by Mrs. Soo Yun Field. De Francisco – American – 1979 – A.F.S. No. 1496.

Ava Ellen. Single. Rose tube medium length and thickness, rose sepals with light rose tips. Corolla is fluorescent fuchsia colour with slight orange at base. Medium sized flowers with rose stamens and pistil hanging an inch below corolla, best colour in sun. Growth tall upright, very fast growing will make large bush in first year, requires lots of room and very little pinching. Tested for 2 years in vicinity of Coos Bay, Oregan. Vee Jay Greenhouse – American – 1978 – A.F.S. No. 1464.

Avalanche. Double. Tube and sepals scarlet; corolla purplish-violet shaded and splashed carmine. Needs staking as a bush for the large, full blooms. Growth is lax bush or trailer. Accepted by the B.F.S. as a show-bench hardy. Henderson – British – 1869.

Avalanche. Double. Carmine and white. G. Smith – British – 1870.

Avalanche. Double. Tube white, sepals white, edged in rose, gradually spreads to entire sepal as flowers matures. Corolla white and star shaped. Blooms produced in clusters at tip of branches. Better as a second year plant. Growth lax bush and willowy, will trail with weights. Schnabel – American – 1954 – A.F.S. No. 194.

Avalon. Single. Tube and sepals white; sepals horizontal, corolla rose-lilac and of medium size. Growth upright, vigorous and bushy, heat resistant. Evans and Reeves – American – 1946.

Ave Maria. Double. White tube, sepals white with greenish tinge at tips; corolla white with markings of pink at base. Medium sized blooms and fairly free, growth, upright bush. Reiter – American – 1945.

Aviator. Single. Tube and sepals red, twisted sepals; corolla long, ivory white. Large flowers freely produced. Growth strong, upright bush. Diener – American – 1939.

Avocet. Single. Short tube crimson; sepals crimson, crepe-like, long, pointed and reflexed. Corolla white with red veining at petal base, tight barrel shape. Pistil much exerted, pedicel extremely long. Foliage dark green with red veins. Growth upright and bushy, self-branching suitable for standard, pyramid or decorative. Jules Daloges × Elizabeth Travis. Travis, J. – British – 1958 – A.F.S. No. 1137.

Avon Gem. Single. Tube and sepals red; corolla purple to magenta. Medium sized flowers, very free flowering with narrow corolla. Growth tall, upright and vigorous, very suitable as a standard. Best grown as H2. Raised by John Lockyer and introduced by his father C.S. Lockyer in 1978. Lockyer – British – 1978.

A. W. Taylor. Single or semi-double. Tube white, sepals white, pink at base, tipped green. Corolla pale lilac-blue, ageing to rosy-lavender; foliage bluish-green. Growth upright and bushy. Named after a President of the Metropolitan Essex Fuchsia Society. Brentwood × Party Frock. Thorne – British – 1969.

ayavancensis. Deep red tube, bulbous at base, red sepals; scarlet corolla. Upright shrub. Synonymous with *F. ampliata*. Kris – 1823 – Peru and Ecuador.

Azalea. Renamed Electra.

Aztec. Double. Tube and sepals, rich red; corolla vivid violet. Flowers large and free, foliage deep green with touch of red. Growth tall and vigorous, up to 6 ft in California. Graphic × unknown seedling. Evans and Reeves – American – 1937.

Baby. Single. Tube and sepals scarlet; corolla phlox-purple. Grown upright and bushy. Could be an American introduction. Raiser and date unknown.

Baby Ann. Single. Tube and sepals rose; corolla pale pink. Small flowers and very free, growth upright and bushy, rather dwarf habit. Introduced by California Nursery – American – Date unknown.

Baby Ann. Single. Light pink tube, light pink sepals, very narrow ¾ in long, very pointed with extreme tip pale green, sepals spread out stiffly emphasizing the brightness of the corolla. Bright rose corolla of fluorescent colouring. Small flowers, very free, petals flare out on maturity but colour remains clear, rose stamens and extra long pistil. Dark green foliage, shiny with red stems and sawtoothed leaves. Growth small upright bush, suitable as a small standard. Hybridizer unknown, introduced by Westover Greenhouse of Seattle. Raiser unknown/Westover – American – 1976 – A.F.S. No. 1330.

Baby Ballerina. Single. Short thin tube, pale green to pale pink, long green tipped sepals turn straight up, coloured pale ivory-green, flushed pink on outside, glowing bright pink on inside. Short dark purple corolla fading to rosy-magenta. Smallish flowers, petals are concave giving full effect. Small dark green foliage with short internodes. Self-branching bush, will trail with weights and suitable for bush, basket or even bonsai. Tested for 10 years before release in vicinity of Sebastopol. Soo Yun Field – American – 1980 – A.F.S. No. 1545.

Baby Belle. Single. Light Bengal-red tube $\frac{1}{4}$ × $\frac{3}{8}$ in long, $\frac{1}{2}$ in × $2\frac{3}{8}$ in long sepals light Bengal-red on lower surface, slightly lighter on upper surface. White corolla with pink veins 1 in wide × $1\frac{1}{8}$ in long. Medium sized flowers with pink stamens and light pink pistil $2\frac{3}{8}$ in long. Light green foliage 1 in wide × $2\frac{1}{8}$ in long leaves. Growth small upright, heat tolerant if shaded. Introduced by Soo Yun Fuchsia Gardens in 1980. De Francisco – American – 1980 – A.F.S. No. 1565.

Baby Blue. Single. Tube and sepals scarlet; corolla clear blue; similar to *F. m.* var. *gracilis*. Growth upright and stiff. Hardy. Hazard and Hazard – American – Date unknown.

Baby Blue Eyes. Single. Tube and sepals red, corolla dark lavender; small flowers but profuse. Growth upright, compact bush. Erecta × Wood Violet. Plummer – America – 1952.

Baby Bunting. Single. Tube and sepals, pale rose, corolla pale lavender-blue; flowers small and profuse. Foliage yellowish-green. Growth lax bush. Rolla × Venus Victrix. Lagen – American – 1938.

Baby Chang. Single. Orange-red tube, sepals orange-red, tipped green; corolla brilliant orange. Very small almost miniature flowers, extremely profuse, identical to Chang but with natural trailing habit, needs frequent stopping. Hazard and Hazard – American – 1950. (See also p. 313.)

Baby Dark Eyes. Single. Short red tube, red sepals curve inward, giving square effect; corolla purple with pink centre. Small flowers, very profuse, buds and blooms are like little dark eyes with four distinct cups. Dark green foliage, growth lax bush, self-branching will also produce medium bush. Francesca – American – 1975 – A.F.S. No. 1289.

Baby Doll. Double. Tube and sepals white; corolla amethyst-violet. Growth restrained and bushy. Reiter – American – 1949 – A.F.S. No. 31.

Baby Face. Double. Tube and sepals pink; corolla white. Blooms are large for a double and fairly free. Growth upright and fairly bushy. Introduced by R. Winkley in 1972. Senior – British – 1971.

Babyface. Double. Short, thin tube baby pink; sepals baby pink, green tipped and reflexed. Corolla creamy-white, fluffy and full, eight petaloids. Foliage pale green, slightly crimped. Medium size blooms, late to bloom. Growth upright and bushy,

self-branching not a tall grower. Tolley – British – 1973 – A.F.S. No. 1154.

Baby Lilac. Double. Short white tube; sepals white with green tips. Corolla light pinkish-lilac which flares out. Blooms are large and box type. Growth trailer. Pennisi – American – 1970 – A.F.S. No. 889.

Babylon. Single. Tube pale pink, sepals long and reflexed to stem, pale pink; corolla long bell-shaped, magenta-rose, large blooms. Small, bright green foliage. Growth good natural trailer. Handley – British – 1973 – A.F.S. No. 1131.

Baby Pink. Double. Long, thin, triphylla type tube, white with slight tinge of green; sepals very light pink with light green tips, cup shape $\frac{1}{2}$ in wide × $1\frac{1}{8}$ in long, curving up and then down. Corolla very light pink with dark pink vein to the base and darker pink at base. Medium sized blooms, very compact, petals flare out slightly, four petals form four swirls in centre, bright pink stamens, white pistil. Dark green foliage with light green veins and red stems, edges of leaves smooth until maturity when serrated. Growth semi-trailer, self branching, very heavy bloomer, good for basket. Soo Yun – American – 1976 – A.F.S. No. 1355.

Baby Storm King. Synonymous with Conspicua.

Bacchus. Single. Red and purple. Banks – British – 1863.

Baccus. Rozain-Boucharlat – French – 1913.

Bachelor Girl. Semi-double. Tube and sepals white, tipped with green, flushed palest pink inside. Corolla pale mallow. Flowers large, long and free. Growth trailer. Sport of Bewitched. Schmidt-Tiret – American – 1952 – A.F.S. No. 141.

bacillaris. Red tube, rose sepals and corolla. Tiny flowers no larger than $\frac{1}{4}$ in borne solitary in the leaf axils, sepals reflex back to tube. Very small foliage which can be hairy on upper surface. Belongs to the Breviflorae section (Encliandra). Upright shrub reaching 4 to 6 ft in Mexico. Considered to be hardy in most districts. Lindley – 1832 – Mexico.

Bagworthy Water. Single. Long tube and curling sepals, salmon-orange. Corolla claret-rose, fading to neyron-rose with age. Medium sized blooms and free. Growth lax bush or trailer. Endicott – British – 1972.

Baker's Boy. Synonymous with Rough Silk.

Baker's Tri. Triphylla type single. Long tube, geranium lake, sepals venetian pink tipped green, pointed. Corolla spinel-red, blossoms like little almonds, partly hidden. Growth trailer, very unusual habit and appearance for triphylla type. Baker – Dunnett – British – 1974 – A.F.S. No. 1197.

Balalaika. Double. Tube deep bright red, lighter near ovary, long and thin. Sepals deep bright red, pale green tips, long slender, reflexed to tube. Corolla deep purple with irregular red streaks, turns deep lavender with maturity. Medium sized blooms and very profuse. Light green foliage, slightly serrated. Growth natural trailer, makes good basket. Foster – American – 1973 – A.F.S. No. 1083.

Bali Hi. Double. Broad tube and upturned sepals, white. Corolla starts violet-blue, opens to mauve-blue. Medium sized blooms and profuse.

Growth trailer. Tiret – American – 1955 – A.F.S. 234.

Balkönkoningen. Single. Tube pale pink, sepals pale pink, tipped green, deeper pink underneath; corolla deep shade of pink. Smallish blooms but free, smallish foliage with crimson mid-rib and veins. Growth cascade, long, thin trailing stems, can be disappointing, does not like excessive watering. R.H.S. H.C. Cert. 1929. Usually abbreviated to Balkon which is incorrect. Cultivar grown in the Netherlands under this name is a single red and purple and is probably Achievement. Neubronner – German – 1896.

Balkonönigen. Considerable confusion exists with this German cultivar and the correct spelling could be: Balkonkönigin translated into English as Balcony Queen; OR Balkonkönig translated into English as Balcony King.

Ballarat. Synonymous with Coxeen in Australia.

Ballerina. Single. Tube and sepals, ivory-pink; corolla clear pink with rose edges. Medium sized blooms and fairly profuse. Growth is vigorous but brittle, up to 6 ft in California; very rarely seen or grown in this country. This is not the Ballerina the uninitiated conjure in their minds at the mention of the word fuchsia. Rolla × Display. Niederholzer – American – 1939.

Ballet Girl. Double. Tube and sepals, bright cerise; corolla white, veined cerise at base of sepals. Reflexed sepals with a very full corolla, large and free. Growth upright, vigorous and bushy, usually grown as bush, but will produce a good half or full standard. R.H.S. Award of Merit 1929. Another cultivar the uninitiated describe as their early introduction to fuchsias; consequently plants supplied under this name are not always correct. Even the true Ballet Girl can be disappointing and has been replaced with such cultivars as Swingtime etc. Veitch – British – 1894.

Ballet Girl

Ball of Fire. Double. Tube and sepals, bright red; corolla bright red with fiery orange-red overtones, compact and excellent form. Dark green foliage with slight red veining. Growth trailer, will produce good basket or weeping standard. Reedstrom – American – 1957 – A.F.S. No. 306.

Bambi. Double. Short, rose bengal tube, short, rose sepals ¾ in × ½ in wide with slight cup shape. Corolla dark mallow purple with rose bengal veining 1½ in × ¾ in wide. Medium-sized blooms loosely petalled with rose bengal stamens and pistil. Light green foliage, heat tolerant if shaded. Small upright, bushy, growth, tested for 5 years in vicin-

ity of Sebastopol, California. Soo Yun Field – American – 1978 – A.F.S. No. 1449.

Banks Favourite. Banks – British – 1855.

Barbara. Single. One of the most recent introductions, creating an early impact, especially when trained as a standard. Raised in 1971 by one of the Midlands' outstanding fuchsia characters, with features which could be easily mistaken for Harry Wheatcroft, Wilfred L. Tolley of Birmingham, and introduced upon the market by R. Winkley, who possesses a good eye for outstanding material. Barbara is a seedling from that outstanding, but old cultivar Display, tested in the vicinity of Birmingham for 6 years before release. Tolley raised two other cultivars around the same time as Barbara, Flora and Sabina, but neither reached the same limelight. Colouring is most attractive, commanding a second look even from the most discerning; a single cultivar, the tube is pale pink and short, sepals pale pink and slightly upturned whilst the corolla, which is semi-flared and shortish, a delightful colouring of cherry and tangerine-pink, with stamens and pistil of the same shade. Does tend to drop its flowers rather quickly, but is self cleaning, dropping its seed pods at the same time. Growth is very upright and extremely vigorous, has a spreading habit and doubtful whether a good bush specimen would be achieved, excels when trained as a medium standard and consider it would produce an excellent pyramid or pillar. Foliage is pale, dull green of medium size, but its outstanding feature is the abundance of bloom, produced at every joint. Barbara is one of the cultivars which will tolerate full sun, made a terrific impact when exhibited by W. Gilbert at 1972 B.F.S. Midland Show with an outstanding specimen, trained as a half standard. Classified as a very good exhibitor's cultivar, will perform with distinction in the open garden, border or as a bedder. Best grown as H2. Display × unknown. Tolley – British – 1971 – A.F.S. No. 1155.

Barbara Pennisi. Double. Tube, variegated pink and white, sepals and corolla purple, variegated with salmon and pink. Large flowers and free. Light yellowish-green foliage. Growth trailer. Pennisi – American – 1968 – A.F.S. No. 748.

Barbe-bleue. Lemoine – French – 1864.

Barcelona. Double. Red and violet. Henderson – British – 1873.

*Barnet Fair. Double. Short bright red tube, bright-red sepals. Corolla palest pink with distinct red veining. Medium sized blooms and very full; free flowering for a double. Growth lax with arching type of growth. Raised in the vicinity of Middlesex and introduced by Woodbridge Nurseries of Hounslow, Middlesex in 1984. Chosen by and named after the Barnet Fuchsia Society. Dyos – British – 1984.

Baron Baron. Single. Tube claret-rose (R.H.S. 50B), sepals claret-rose (R.H.S. 50B) tipped green; corolla claret-rose. Smallish flowers, same size as Chang, stamens are soft pink. This cultivar was named after the Manchester Radio Gardener's Questionmaster by request. Although raised in 1969 was not released or introduced until 1978. Chang × Liver Bird, Thornley – British – 1969 – A.F.S. No. 1465.

Baron de Ketteler. Double. Tube and sepals, rich crimson; corolla intense purple, light pink centre, very large blooms and fairly free. Growth upright, bushy and sturdy. Still listed by specialist nuserymen. Lemoine – French – 1901.

Baroness Burdett Coults. Single. White and vermilion. Banks – British – 1872.

Baron Gros. Lemoine – French – 1861.

˚Baroque Pearl. Double. Tube greenish-white fading to rose, sepals ivory-white with pink blush, pink underneath, tipped green. Corolla lavender-lilac with pink base to full rosy-lilac. Medium sized blooms and quite free flowering. Growth upright and bushy. Raised in Holland in the vicinity of Lisse. Parentage unknown. de Graaff – Dutch – 1979.

Barrington. Double. Tube and sepals, rosy-red; corolla pink. Medium sized blooms and profuse. Growth small bush, heat resistant. Reiter – American – 1947.

Barrington. Double. Tube and sepals, rosy-red; corolla silvery-pink. Medium sized blooms and fairly free for double, growth trailer. Menze – unknown – 1949.

Barry's Queen. Single. Short thin tube, sepals rhodamine-pink, tipped green, neyron-rose underneath flaring and upturned. Corolla amethyst-violet, flushed pale pink with dark pink veining. Colour slightly lighter than its sister seedling, Eden Lady. Identical to Border Queen except for its brilliant yellow foliage without any variegation. Border Queen like other sports, produced identical sports in different places, almost at the same time. Found by Barry Sheppard of Ipswich in 1980 and introduced by Baker's of Halstead in 1982. Identical to Golden Border Queen found in 1979 by Penhalls Nurseries of Shaw Oldham, and introduced by them in 1981. Sheppard – British – 1980.

Bartholdi. Lemoine– French – 1887.

Bashful. Double. Tube and sepals deep pink; corolla white, veined pink. Small blooms, very free, deep green foliage. Growth upright and bushy, strong and stiff, dwarf, only 9 to 15 in high, hardy in Southern England, raised in the Scilly Isles. Received R.H.S. Award of Merit at Wisley Hardy Trials 1975–78. Tabraham – British – 1974

Basketfull. Double. Tube and sepals pink, corolla white and pink. Medium sized blooms, growth trailer, very suitable for basketwork. Introduced by Rainbow's Fuchsias of Sandon, Essex in 1981. Raiser and date unknown – ca 1970s.

Basket Strawberry Festival. Double. Tube and sepals red; corolla light rose-pink. Flowers similar to New Fascination, but growth is lax bush, described in America as beautiful semi-trailer. Extra hardy in America. Haag – American – 1956.

Baudouin. Single. Cerise and red. Salter – British and French – 1848.

Bay Fair. Double. Tube pink, sepals deep pink, darker pink at base, blending out to pale pink and tipped green. Corolla white, flushed pink at base of petals. Flowers large and free. Growth trailer. Kuechler – American – 1961 – A.F.S. No. 488.

Bayou Blue. Double. Tube light pink, sepals very long and curling, light pink; corolla lavender-blue to pale lavender, stays fairly tight. Large blooms, beautiful pastel shades. Growth trailer. Kennett – American – 1967 – A.F.S. No. 738.

Beacon. Single. Tube and sepals, deep pink; corolla bright mauvish-pink. Medium sized flowers, very free. Darkish green foliage with waved edges. Growth upright, bushy and compact. Always in bloom, as a bush plant, still seen on the showbench, could be confused with Display. Very good old cultivar. Submitted by G. Roe of Nottingham for R.H.S. Hardy Trials at Wisley 1975–78 and received Highly Commended Certificate. Bull – British – 1871.

Beacon Rosa. Single. Tube rather long, pink-red, sepals pink-red; corolla pink lightly veined red. Medium-sized flowers with pink stamens and style, short style. Foliage is similar to Beacon, growth upright and bushy, branches out well. Bürgi-Ott. – Swiss – 1972.

Beacon Superior. Single. Tube and sepals red; corolla purple. Large flowers with upright growth. Bürgi-Ott. – Swiss – Date unknown.

˚Bealings. Double. Waxy-white tube, sepals waxy-white turning faintly pink with maturity and running backwards. Corolla is intense violet. Fully double medium sized blooms; huge numbers for a double. Growth tall upright with large number of side shoots, suitable for most types of upright cultivation. Foliage mid-green with smaller than average leaves. Raised in the vicinity of Ipswich, Suffolk and introduced by B. and H.M. Baker of Halstead, Essex in 1983. Goulding – British – 1983 – A.F.S. No. 1723.

Beatrice. Knight – British – 1858.

Beatrice. Bland – British – 1877.

Beau Marchais. Single. Red and purple. Named after the famous French playwright. Lemoine – French – 1897.

Beau Nash. Single. Medium-length tube, very pale pink, sepals are long and of much deeper pink; corolla fuchsia-purple. Smallish flowers, very free flowering and early, growth upright and bushy, small, neat and compact. Holmes, E. – British – 1976.

Beaute Parfait. Single. White and pink. Harrison – British – 1844.

Beauty. Double. Red and purple. Banks – British – 1866.

Beauty. Single. Rose and purple. Sankey – British – 1877.

Beauty Bloom. Single. Red and blue. Banks – British – 1866.

Beauty 'n' Blue. Double. Short thick tube rose-red, sepals 1 7/8 in long and 1/2 in wide curving up tight, rose-red with creped rose-Bengal bottom side. Corolla amethyst-violet fading to roseine-purple at base. Largish blooms wavy and open 3/4 in long × 1 3/4 in wide with petaloids attached to sepals, dark pink stamens and white-pink pistil. Growth trailer, self-branching, very early and heavy. Prolonged bloomer. Soo Yun Field – American – 1979 – A.F.S. No. 1491.

Beauty 'n' Red. Double. Pinkish-white tube 1/4 in × 1/2 in long, reflexed sepals cardinal red (H.C.C. 822) on upper surface, carmine-rose. Corolla beetroot-purple (H.C.C. 830/2) 2 in wide × 1 1/2 in long. Largish blooms with eight or more petaloids and pink pistil 2 3/4 in long. Dark green foliage with red stems, leaves 2 7/8 in wide × 4 3/4 in long. Growth lax upright, will make good basket, bush or standard. Introduced by Soo Yun

Fuchsia Gardens in 1980. De Francisco – American – 1980 – A.F.S. No. 1560.

Beauty of Bamburgh. Single. Bright vermilion-magenta self. Growth upright and bushy. Ryle – British – 1970.

Beauty of Banks. Single. Tube and sepals scarlet, corolla white. Growth upright and bushy, hardy in Northern England, Wells – British – Date unknown.

Beauty of Bath. Double. Tube pale pink, sepals pale pink, deeper at base, edged bright pink with green tips. Corolla pure white, flowers large and well formed, very free for large double. Growth upright and bushy. Very similar to Angel's Flight, best grown as H1. Colville – British – 1965.

Beauty of Bath – Angel's Flight. To distinguish between these two similar cultivars, see Angel's Flight – Beauty of Bath.

Beauty of Clapham. Single. White and red. Henderson – British – 1867.

Beauty of Cleveland. Double. Purple and white. Date of introduction not known but listed by H.A. Brown in 1938. Wayne – British – Date unknown.

Beauty of Clyffe Hall. Single. White and pink. Lye – British – Date unknown. Confusion exists with this cultivar and another called Beauty of Cliff Hall attributed to Monk in 1944 with colour descriptions exactly the same. It was thought the original Beauty of Clyffe Hall attributed to Lye was out of cultivation but is listed by an American nurseryman with the following description, 'dwarf bush or basket cultivar, pink corolla, sepals very light pink underneath, outside and tube waxy-white' a typical Lye description. Beauty of Cliff Hall by Monk is listed and distributed by an English nurseryman, but it is extremely likely that the two cultivars are the same, which is confirmed with the first reference to Beauty of Clyffe Hall being quoted in Nicholson's List of recommended varieties in the 1885 *Encyclopedia of Gardening* and the entry in Dr. Essig's List 'blush-white and carmine pink' and quoting Cannell's List 1881 and 1888 as reference.

Beauty of Exeter. Semi-double. Tube and sepals, light rosy-salmon; corolla deeper shade of rosy salmon, almost a self. Flowers are large and free, lovely blooms and very early. Growth lax bush, old cultivar still in cultivation. Used extensively for hybridising and one of the few introductions by the raiser. Letheren – French – 1890.

Beauty of Exmouth. Double. Tube and sepals reddish-cerise; corolla white veined cerise. Growth upright bush. Veitch – British – 1892.

Beauty of Kent. Single. Tube and sepals red; corolla rich purple, ageing to rose. Growth upright bush. Banks – British – 1867.

Beauty of Lavington. Single. White and carmine. Lye – British – Date unknown.

Beauty of Leeds. Double. Pink and red. Nichols – British – Date unknown.

Beauty of Prussia. Double. Tube and sepals scarlet; corolla scarlet lake, veined scarlet. Medium sized blooms and free, dark shiny foliage. Growth upright bush. Holmes, E. – British – 1966.

Beauty of Sholden. Single. Red and purple. Banks – British – 1868.

Beauty of St. Leonards. Single. White and purple. Knight – British – 1847.

Beauty of Swanley. Single. Long waxy-white tube and sepals, slightly tinted blush; corolla soft rose-pink. Medium sized blooms and free. Growth, spreading bush, inclines to straggle. When first introduced was known as Hebe and known in America as Villa Hebe. Lye – British – 1875.

Beauty of the West. Single. Light coloured blooms. Lye – British – 1878.

Beauty of Trowbridge. Single. Creamy-white tube, thick and waxy, recurved sepals, waxy creamy-white, corolla rosy-cerise. Medium sized flowers, early and very free, beautiful clear cut colours. Growth upright, bushy and vigorous, produces fine standard, should be grown more, responds to frequent stopping. This cultivar was considered to be one of James Lye's raisings but the *Gardener's Chronicle* of 1879 quotes it as one of two new cultivars introduced by H. Cannell and, whilst attributed to James Lye, was subsequently refuted and stated to be raised by Mr. J. Smith of Trowbridge.

Beauty of Trowbridge – Mrs. Marshall. To distinguish between these two similar cultivars the following information may be useful. Whilst Mrs. Marshall is best described as a rosy-cerise corolla, Beauty of Trowbridge is more pinkish-orange, whilst the petals are shorter. The main difference is in the foliage, the leaves of B. of T. are longer, more deeply serrated but with fewer teeth. The growth of the two cultivars is somewhat different, whereas B. of T. is vigorous and upright suitable for the training of all tall shapes, especially as a standard, the growth of Mrs. Marshall again vigorous and sturdy, can be trained to most shapes, even as a basket which in itself describes the growth as being somewhat lax.

Beauty of Wilts. Single. Tube and sepals white; corolla scarlet, petals with darker edge. Arabella Improved × James Lye. Lye – British – Date unknown.

Beauty Queen. Double. Tube red, with lighter red veins, sepals light red, dark red veins, light green tips, fold back around tube. Corolla violet-purple, red at base fading to mallow-purple. Medium sized blooms, no petaloids and free. Dark green foliage with red stems and branches. Growth trailer, suitable for basket with weights. Soo Yun – America – 1974 – A.F.S. No. 1181.

Beckey. Double. Tube and sepals dark rose; corolla light violet with touch of red. Medium sized blooms and very free. Growth trailer, cultivar appears to be exclusive to California and is unregistered. Hanson – American – ca 1970.

Bee Keesey. Double. Tube white, thick and short; sepals white with green tips, long, standing straight out. Corolla wisteria-blue with white variegations, large, full, box type. Growth, trailer with weights, easily trained as a weeping standard. Pennisi – American – 1972 – A.F.S. No. 1045.

Be Happy. Single. Tube and sepals white; corolla pinkish-lilac. Rather small flowers, small wide spreading bush. van Wieringen – Dutch – 1970.

Bella. Single. White and crimson. Youell – British – 1861.

Bella Blu. Double. Short tube, white and pink; sepals white, variegated with pink. Corolla blue, variegated with white. Very large blooms, growth upright and bushy. Pennisi – American – 1968 – A.F.S. No. 749.

Bella Forbes. Double. Tube and sepals cerise; corolla creamy-white, lightly veined cerise. Very full double, largish blooms, flowers in flushes. Old cultivar but first class, one of the few cultivars from Scotland. Growth upright and vigorous, easily grown as bush or standard. Forbes – British – 1890.

Bella Forbes

Bella Mia. Single. Short tube flesh coloured; sepals flesh coloured, tipped white. Corolla ochre-red and very firm, very much like Cara Mia. Foliage large, spear-shaped. Growth tall upright. Machado – American – 1963 – A.F.S. No. 562.

Bellbottoms. Single. Tube light salmon; sepals pale orange to salmon, long, thin and curl back. Corolla first opens to purple with coral base, fading to smoky-orange with age, bell shape. Medium sized blooms and free, foliage very light green, turning very dark in later stages. Growth upright and bushy. Castro – American – 1972 – A.F.S. No. 1029.

Bell Buoy. Single. Tube and sepals, bright red; corolla dark bluish-purple, flared. Medium sized blooms and very free, holds its colour in sun. Growth good self-branching bush, easily trained as standard, pyramid, pillar or cordon. Has taken 15° of frost in Southern England. Smallwood – British – 1973 – A.F.S. No. 1075.

Belle de Lisse. Double. Tube and sepals cream; corolla pink. Medium sized blooms, best grown as H1 will not take sun. Growth lax, needs frequent pinching and not considered suitable as a standard, definitely frost shy. Introduced by Wills Fuchsia Nurseries in 1979. de Graaff – Dutch – 1976.

Belle de Spa. Single. Orange-pink long tube, orange-pink sepals, lighter colour towards the tips, tipped green. Corolla orange-red with rather short stamens and style, pink. Foliage mid-green with bronzy leaves. Medium-sized flower, with beautiful rich colouring. Growth natural trailer. This cultivar is grown and cultivated in the Netherlands. Raiser and date unknown.

Belle-La Von. Double. Tube white, sepals white crepe, with green tips; corolla medium dark blue, holds its colour. Dark foliage. Growth trailer. Sport of Clara Beth. Gagnon – American – 1968 – A.F.S. No. 781.

Belle of New York. Semi-double. Cerise and purple. Felton – British – 1847.

Belle of Salem. Single. Medium tube and long sepals, bright rosy-red; corolla beautiful new shade of pink, heavily veined bright rosy-red bell shaped, profuse bloomer throughout the summer. Foliage small and dark green. Growth trailer and vigorous. Hodges – American – 1957 – A.F.S. No. 304.

Bellissima. Single. Tube and sepals, bright red; corolla deep purple. Large flowers, growth tall, upright and bushy. Niederholzer – American – 1957.

Bellona. Single. Dark crimson. *F.fulgens* × Venus Victrix. Lowe – British – 1875.

Bells of Rozelle. Single. Tube and sepals, rosy-pink; corolla large bell-shaped, light pink, streaked with rose. Small foliage, growth trailer. Prentice – American – 1969 – A.F.S. No. 854.

Bells of St. Mary. Double. Tube and sepals, bright red; corolla mauvish-white. Growth upright bush. York – American – 1943.

Belmont. Single. Tube and sepals, turkey-red; corolla purple. Growth upright. Niederholzer – American – 1946.

Belsay Beauty. Semi-double. Short tube rhodamine-pink, sepals rhodamine-pink underneath, topside whitish with rhodamine-pink shading, short and fat. Corolla violet, fading to cyclamen-purple. Medium sized flowers with short plum buds, few small petaloids violet, streaked with rhodamine-pink, contrast of new and old flowers create pleasing aspect. Mid to light green, smooth foliage, growth natural trailer but will produce good bush. Awarded the B.F.S. Silver Cert. of Merit at Manchester 1975. Introduced by Jackson's Nurseries of Tamworth in 1979. Ryle – British – 1975 – A.F.S. No. 1240.

Belvedere. Double. Tube dark pink, sepals dark pink to red, turn back over thick tube; corolla pale blue, mottled with dark pink, mass of short, pink petaloids. Fades from blue to palest purple with age. Blooms very large and fairly free. Growth upright and bushy. Reedstrom – American – 1960 – A.F.S. No. 421.

Belvoir Beauty. Semi-double. Short white tube, flushed green, sepals white with green tips, broad, waxy with crepe effect and held well up. Corolla white at base shading through pale wisteria with distinct blue-bird blue edge to each petal. Medium sized flowers, free, very neat, most attractive pastel shades with added beauty of picotee edge. Light green foliage, growth medium upright bush. Gadsby – British – 1975 – A.F.S. No. 1279.

Belvoir Belle. Single. Tube and sepals rich-red, corolla lilac-blue, veined red. Medium-sized flowers, raiser describes the sepals as coming away in pairs and not the usual four square, growth upright and bushy. Pacey – British – 1966.

Belvoir Elf. Single. Tube Tyrian-purple, sepals Tyrian-purple heavily tipped green, curve upwards. Corolla violet-purple. Medium sized flowers, very neat and free flowering. Growth upright and bushy, compact and short-jointed very suitable as pot plant or summer bedder. Raised in the vicinity of Melton Mowbray, Leicestershire. Raised and introduced by R. and J. Pacey of Stathern, Melton Mowbray in 1982. Pacey – British – 1982.

Belvoir Lakes. Single. Tube and sepals spinel-red, sepals are tipped green. Corolla imperial-purple, rose-purple at base of petals with red veining. Medium sized flowers and very free flowering. Growth is bushy and compact. Introduced by the raiser in 1980. Pacey – British – 1980.

*Ben. Double. Crimson tube $\frac{3}{4}$ in long, horizontally held crimson sepals $2\frac{1}{2}$ in long by 1 in wide with recurved tips. Corolla lilac-purple (R.H.S. 70B) splashed with crimson (R.H.S. 52A), $1\frac{1}{2}$ in across. Largish blooms are fully flared and square size, crimson filaments and blue (R.H.S. 92D) anthers; pistil extends $1\frac{1}{2}$ in below corolla with crimson style and stigma. Elliptic shaped foliage with dark green leaves, 4 in long by 2 in wide. Growth medium upright, heat tolerant and prefers warm conditions although it is considered extremely hardy in New Zealand. Raised in the vicinity of New Plymouth, New Zealand. Tiki × unknown seedling. Brightwell – New Zealand – 1984 – A.F.S. No. 1748.

Ben Frank. Double. Thick red tube, long red sepals; violet corolla. Medium-sized blooms, most unusual as petals roll back and look like rolled ribbons, red stamens and pistil. Large dark green foliage with reddish cast. Growth upright, will make good bush plant, best colour in shade. Introduced in 1969 but not registered until 1976. Hanson – American – 1969 – A.F.S. No. 1322.

Bengali. Double. Red and purple. Rozain-Boucharlat – French – 1911.

Ben Hill. Double. Short tube and sepal base, rose madder, sepals white, tipped green, with underside shell pink. Corolla very pale, shell pink with rose flushed at base. Large blooms, growth upright bush. Named after a founder of the British Columbia Fuchsia Society. Thornley – British – 1966.

Ben Hur. Double. Tube and sepals pink; corolla purple, marbled with contrasting shades of pink and white. Very large flowers. Growth trailer or lax bush. Martin – American – 1963 – A.F.S. No. 571.

Benita. Triphylla type single. Long thin tube, bright scarlet self. Foliage, deep bronze-green. Growth lax and dwarfish. Gartenmeister Bonstedt × *F. splendens*. Rogers – British – 1912.

Benjamin Pearson. Single. Red and purple. Lye – British – 1887.

Beranger. Double. Red and purple. Hardy cultivar. Lemoine – French – 1862 or 1899.

*Berbanella. Double. Little known Dutch cultivar except for parentage. La Campanella seedling. *ca* 1980.

*Berba's Trio. Double. Very unusual cultivar classified as a novelty, basket cultivar with medium-sized blooms and instability in the chromosomes controlling flower colour. Calyx is always red but in some flowers the corolla is white, in others a rich blue-purple, whilst others are half white and half purple-blue. Raised in the vicinity of Lochem, Netherlands. La Campanella × Bridesmaid. Bats – Wesseling – Dutch – 1983.

*Berg Nemf. Single. Little known Dutch species hybrid, the name meaning 'wood-nymph'. Introduced by Lechlade Fuchsia Nursery of Lechlade in 1984. *F. sessilifolia* × *F. fulgens*. Raiser unknown – Dutch – *ca* 1980.

Berkeley. Double. Tube and sepals, pale rose; sepals are large and recurved, corolla brilliant Tyrian-rose. Large blooms, globular in shape and very profuse. Growth upright or lax bush. Named after City of Berkeley, California, whose official flower is the fuchsia. A.F.S. Cert. of Merit. Reiter – American – 1955 – A.F.S. No. 233.

Berliner Kind. Double. Tube and sepals, cerise-scarlet; corolla white, veined with pink at base. Small flowers but very free, growth low bush and small. Schneewittchen × Goliath. Eggbrecht – German – 1882.

Bernadette. Double. Tube and sepals, pale rose; corolla veronica-blue, medium sized blooms and free. Small dark green foliage, growth upright bush, with stiff lateral branches. Schnabel – American – 1950 – A.F.S. No. 52.

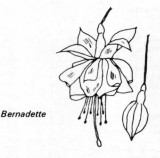

Bernadette

Bernard Allen. Allen – British – 1976.

Bernard Rawdin. Single. Tube and sepals, rose-red; corolla cyclamen-purple, wide bell shaped blooms, very free. Growth upright, medium bush, prefers partial shade. Not to be confused with Bernard Rawlins which is *F. triphylla* hybrid. Upward Look × Caroline. Gadsby – British – 1968 – A.F.S. No. 973.

Bernard Rawlins. Triphylla single. Long tube, white flushed pink; petals bright orange, very free. Growth upright. Not to be confused with Bernard Rawdin by Gadsby 1970. *F. triphylla* × . Thorne – British – 1959. (See also p. 313.)

Bertha Lee. Single. Tube and sepals, dark pink; corolla irregular, pink streaked red. Long blooms and very free, foliage small holly shaped, dark green. Growth trailer. Lee – American – 1945.

Bertnay. Double. Tube and sepals, dull cerise; corolla dark reddish-purple, large flowers and free. Growth upright and vigorous. Old cultivar still grown, but not listed by many nurserymen. Salter – British and French – 1837?

Bertrade. Double. Red and white. Lemoine – French – 1906.

*Beryle Bamford. Double. Long white tube streaked phlox-pink, white flushed phlox-pink sepals held half down, green tipped and recurved $1\frac{1}{2}$ in long by $\frac{3}{4}$ in wide. Corolla white flushed phlox-pink (R.H.S. 62B) 1 in long by 2 in wide. Large blooms fully flared with phlox-pink filaments and blue (R.H.S. 92D) anthers, white style and stigma. Elliptic shaped foliage with emerald-green leaves (R.H.S. 134A) and light green veins and stems $3\frac{1}{2}$ in long by $1\frac{1}{2}$ in wide. Growth upright, and bushy; raiser claims cultivar is extremely easy to grow. Raised in the vicinity of New Plymouth, New Zealand. Parentage un-

Beryl's Choice. Double. Short $\frac{1}{2}$ in long pink tube, broad 1 in long reflexed sepals are pink, tipped light green on top, dark crepe pink tipped light green underneath. Corolla light mauve-pink $1\frac{1}{2}$ in wide deeper pink with maturity, deep rose blotching at base $1\frac{1}{4}$ in long petals, outer petals streaked rose-pink. Large blooms with long rose-red stamens, mauve-pink pistil. Foliage is lighter green than Georgana but very much larger. Growth medium bushy upright, the deep orchid colour of its parent is completely missing. Tested in vicinity of Montrose, Victoria, Australia. Sport of Georgana. Richardson, N.B. and L.M. – Australian – 1980 – A.F.S. No. 1531.

Bessie Emmerson. Single. Just another undistinguished red and purple cultivar. McParlin – British – 1976.

Bessie Royle. Single. Long light red tube, pink sepals, strong with upward curl. Corolla blue shading to pink near sepals. Medium sized flowers with wavy petals, pink stamens and pistil and red stigma. Dark green foliage, oval leaves, growth upright will make good bush, requires early pinching. Raised in vicinity of Manchester. Royle – British – 1979 – A.F.S. No. 1523.

Best Wishes. Single. Deep Bengal-red tube $\frac{1}{4}$ in long, deep Bengal-red sepals turn completely over tube $\frac{1}{4}$ in $\times$ $1\frac{3}{8}$ in long. White corolla with deep Bengal-red veining $1\frac{1}{2}$ in wide $\times 1\frac{1}{4}$ in long. Medium sized flowers which can produce double blooms with petaloids, stamens and pistil Bengal-red, pistil $2\frac{1}{4}$ in long. Light green foliage, leaves 1 in wide $\times$ 2 in long. Growth medium upright, suitable for bush, standard or pyramid. Introduced by Soo Yun Fuchsia Gardens in 1980. De Francisco – American – 1980 – A.F.S. No. 1560.

Beth Robley. Double. Tube and sepals salmon; corolla salmon-orange. Growth trailer. Tiret – American – 1971 – A.F.S. No. 992.

Betsy. Double. Tube and sepals deep pink: corolla dark burgundy. Medium sized blooms and fairly free, growth upright and bushy. Curtis – British – *ca* 1972.

Betsy Ross. Double. Tube red, white sepals, long and upturned; corolla blue spectrum-violet. Medium sized blooms and free. Growth lax bush, will trail for basket and produce an excellent espalier. Walker and Jones – American – 1954.

Bettanne. Single. Cultivar very similar to Phyllis. Phyllis seedling. Hardcastle – British – 1975.

Bette Ann Peterson. Double. Proportionately short rose tube of medium thickness, slightly recurved sepals, rose with lavender tint and tipped green. Corolla slightly fluorescent rose-purple with rose at base. Small to medium sized blooms, blue-green foliage, growth natural trailer, will make good basket without weights. Raised in the vicinity of Coos Bay, Oregon, U.S.A. Vee Jay Greenhouse – American – 1981 – A.F.S. No. 1624.

Betty. Semi-double. Tube and sepals, rose-red; corolla rich creamy-white, veined rose-red. Small blooms, but very free. Growth trailing habit, suitable for baskets. Hazard and Hazard – American – 1946.

Betty Ann. Single. Tube and sepals waxy-white with pinkish cast; corolla coral-salmon. Medium

sized flowers, growth trailer suitable for basket. Appears to be exclusive to California. Raiser and date unknown – *ca* 1960.

Betty Keizer. Single. Long tube creamy-white, sepals orange-red; corolla orange-red. Blooms are heavy and large. Growth trailer. Gagnon – American – 1968 – A.F.S. No. 783.

Betty's Choice. Single. Tube and sepals pink; corolla mauve. Very similar to Cloverdale only a little larger, colouring is almost identical. Sepals are more reflexed and a little lighter in colour, showing more of the corolla, attractive but no real breakthrough, habit is upright and bushy. Parentage: Cloverdale × General Monk. Sayers, E. – British – 1979.

Beulah Fay. Double. Tube and sepals, red with underside rose, corolla deep violet-blue, petals turn upward like the sepals. Large blooms with unusually long stamens, 4 in long. Growth trailer. Peterson-Fuchsia Farms – American – 1959 – A.F.S. No. 372.

Beverley. Single. Short, medium thick tube, empire-rose (R.H.S. 48D), striped empire-rose (R.H.S. 48C); neyron-rose (R.H.S. 55A) sepals with green tip, creped inside, medium sized, narrow and flicking upwards in graceful curve. Fuchsia-purple (R.H.S. 67A) corolla with neyron-rose (R.H.S. 55A) at base. Medium sized flowers, bell shaped, very short stamens and very long pistil. Heavily serrated, cordate foliage, midgreen on top, lighter underneath, growth upright and bushy, vigorous, fast growing cultivar, good for all upright forms of training. Percy Holmes ×. Holmes, R. – British – 1976 – A.F.S. No. 1378.

Beverley Hills. Single. Tube and long sepals, shell-pink with white stripe, tipped white, deep rose on underside. Corolla vivid burgundy-red, large flowers and free. Growth upright, vigorous and bushy. Santa Monica × Grenadine. Evans and Reeves – American – 1936.

Beverley Wilson. Double. Light pink tube, sepals light rose at base, shading to white at tip. Corolla light blue with outer petals, marbled with light rose, pleated with a square shape. Small foliage. Growth trailer. Prentice – American – 1967 – A.F.S. No. 720.

Bewitched. Semi-double. Tube and long sepals, white outside, flushed pale pink inside; corolla dubonnet-purple, flushed white at base. Large blooms and free, heat tolerant. Growth lax bush and vigorous, can be made to trail. Tiret – American – 1951 – A.F.S. No. 94.

Bianca. Double. Short tube and sepals white; corolla white, large blooms. Growth trailer. Pennisi – American – 1967 – A.F.S. No. 715.

Bianca Marginata. Single. White and rose. Banks – British – 1862.

Bicentennial. Double. Thin, white tube approximately 1 in long, sepals Indian-orange (R.H.S. 32A) inside, salmon-orange outside. Corolla centre is (R.H.S. 51A) magenta, surrounded by Indian-orange (R.H.S. 32A) petals and petaloids. Medium sized blooms, fairly free, pale magenta stamens, orange colour shows brightest if given some sun. Growth semi-trailer, self branching, good for either basketwork or standard. Named after the American Bicentennial Year. Paskesen – American – 1976 – A.F.S. No. 1344.

*Biddy Lester. Single. Short thin tube $\frac{3}{8}$ in long by $\frac{7}{16}$ in wide is neyron-rose (R.H.S. 58C), fully

---

known. Brightwell – New Zealand – 1984 – A.F.S. No. 1749.

up sepals 1 in long by ¾ in wide neyron-rose (R.H.S. 58C) striped rose-red (R.H.S. 58B) on top, crepey rose-red underneath, reflexed and tipped green. Corolla opens deep mallow-purple (R.H.S. 72A), pale pink at base with central vein rose-red, maturing slightly paler. Smallish flowers are quarter flared with practically colour fast and long blooming flowers. Mid-green foliage 1½ in long by ¾ in wide cordate shaped leaves, veins are light green and stems green flushed pink. Growth self-branching small upright bush, short jointed, will make good upright, standard, pillar or even bonsai, very profuse flowering. Raised in the vicinity of Edenbridge, Kent. String of Pearls by seedling. Holmes, R. – British – 1984 – A.F.S. No. 1783.

biflora (Sessé and Mocino 1894). Synonymous with *F. michoacanensis*.

Big Blue Boy. Double. White tube, sepals white on top, pale pink on underside with green tips, standing out straight until mature, then turn upward. Corolla deep purple, fading to dark burgundy-purple. Large blooms and free, large foliage. Growth upright bush. Gorman – American – 1970 – A.F.S. No. 935.

Big King. Double. Tube and sepals, dark red; corolla very dark purple. Very large blooms, growth upright and extremely vigorous, up to 6 to 7 ft in California. Gorman – American – 1970 – A.F.S. No. 936.

Billie Roe. Single. Tube and sepals cardinal-red (H.C.C. 821/1); sepals same colouring held well back. Corolla pansy colour (H.C.C. 180) heavily veined cardinal-red. Medium sized flowers with red style and yellow stigma hard, robust flowers. Growth upright, strong and bushy. Introduction by V.T. Nuttall of Doncaster in 1979. Joy Patmore × Brutus. Roe – British – 1979.

Bill's Lucky Thirteen. Single. Proportionately short red tube of medium thickness, red sepals 1½ in long curve up slightly. Purple corolla stays rolled approximately ½ in wide, each petal red at base with light lavender edges. Medium sized flowers, dark green foliage 1½ in to 2 in oblong leaves slightly serrated. Growth tall upright, will make good bush or shrub. Raised in the vicinity of Coos Bay, Oregon, U.S.A. Vee Jay Greenhouse – American – 1981 – A.F.S. No. 1623.

Billy Green. Triphylla type single. Long tube, pinkish-salmon self, extremely profuse. Foliage olive green, growth upright, vigorous and bushy. Has been dominating the showbenches in recent years. Raised in Surrey by unknown raiser and introduced by Bernard Rawlins. F3 hybrid with *F. triphylla* Andenken an Heinrich Henkel and Leverkusen blood. Raiser unknown – British – 1966.

Billy King. No further details except that the cultivar which originates from South Africa is grown and cultivated in the Netherlands. Raiser and date unknown.

Bingo. Semi-double to double. Tube and sepals white; corolla reddish-pink, with white marbling and long petals. Growth trailer or lax bush. Castro – American – 1971 – A.F.S. No. 949.

Bird of Paradise. Bland – British – 1870.

*Birthday Girl. Double. Little known unregistered cultivar with pale pink tube with darker streak, pale pink sepals and pink corolla. Very frilly flowers almost serrated edges to petals. Raised and introduced by Stansborough Nurseries of El-

burton, Plymouth, Devon. Stansborough Nurseries – British – *ca* 1980.

Bishop's Bells. Semi-double. Tube rose-red, sepals are very long and a feature of the flower, rose-red, lighter colour at tip and tipped green. Corolla bishop's-violet ageing to reddish-purple, veined rose. Delightful cultivar, large blooms, sepals often measuring 2½ in and a flower over 5 in across. Growth upright bush, strong. Caroline ×. Gadsby – British – 1970 – A.F.S. No. 869.

Bishop's Robe. Double. Tube light pink, sepals light pink, with white stripe running through each sepal. Corolla campanula-violet with a row of petaloids, bishop's-violet in colour. Large flowers and free. Growth upright and strong. Machado – American – 1960 – A.F.S. No. 448.

Bittersweet. Double. Tube pale pink, sepals pale pink and white, upperside white. Corolla outer petals rose, with salmon to orange marbling, purple centre fades to rose. Large blooms. Growth trailer or lax bush. Kennett – American – 1971 – A.F.S. No. 953.

Black Beauty. Double. Tube and sepals, dark red; corolla very deep purple. Large blooms. Growth upright and vigorous. Fairclo – American – 1952.

Black Eyes. Double. Short tube and sepals, deep rose; corolla white. Flowers large and free, unusual feature is the production of black pollen when mature, hence the name. Growth upright and bushy. Brown-Soules – American – 1953.

Black Magic. Double. Tube deep red, sepals are broad and recurved, deepest red. Corolla very deep purple almost black, wide-spreading, curled and twisted petals. Largish blooms and very free, very similar to Purple Sage. Growth upright and bushy. Hodges – American – 1954 – A.F.S. No. 198.

Black Pearl. Single. Tube and sepals, turkey red; corolla deep purple. Medium size blooms, very long. Growth trailer. Niederholzer – American – 1946.

Black Prince. Single. Red and purple. Synonymous with Gruss au dem Bodethal. Banks – British – 1861.

Black Princess. Semi-double. Tube and sepals red; corolla deep purple, streaked red and very open. Large flowers and early bloomer. Growth upright bush. Niederholzer – American – 1940.

Blanche. Single. Pink and carmine. Harrison – British – 1842.

Blanche de Castille. Lemoine – French – 1899.

Blanche Regina. Double. Tube and sepals white, sepals are reflexed, crepe on inside. Corolla amethyst-violet, changing to rhodamine-purple with age. Medium sized blooms, very free and continuous. Flower feature is the long stamens and pistil, producing a tassel-like appearance. Growth self-branching, natural trailer. La Campanella × Flirtation Waltz. Clyne – British – 1974 – A.F.S. No. 1175.

Bland's New Striped. Single. Tube and recurved sepals cerise; corolla rich purple with rugged streaks of pink down centre of each petal. Flowers medium to large and free. Growth upright and bushy. Another old cultivar still grown at the present time. Bland – British – 1872.

Blaze. Single. Light coral tube, sepals light coral (R.H.S. 43D) outside with deeper coral (R.H.S. 43C) inside are of medium length and width. Corolla is coral (R.H.S. 44C) at base, blending to flame (R.H.S. 46D). Flowers are long with overlapping petals and with long sepals held well out from tube. Medium coral stamens and pistil. Foliage mid-green with flushed bronze leaves. Early flowering, freely produced of medium to large flowers. Growth trailer, self-branching, tested for 7 years before release. Handley – British – 1977 – A.F.S. No. 1413.

Blaze. Single. Tube and sepals rich red; corolla rich plum-purple. Large flowers, heavy and profuse bloomer with expanded corolla. Growth upright and bushy. Raiser and date unknown. Australian cultivar. Although growth is rather upright and bushy, this cultivar is synonymous with Marinka in Australia.

*Blessed Event. Semi-double. Tube and sepals pink, corolla mauve with pink petaloids. Largish flowers freely produced; growth upright and bushy. Raised in the vicinity of Merimbula, New South Wales, Australia. Lockesbie – Australia *ca* 1975.

Blonda. Single to semi-double. Rose and carmine. Smith – British – 1841.

Blondine. Single. White tube and upturned sepals, light pink; corolla pale lilac. Growth upright and bushy. Brown-Soules – American – 1953.

Bloomer Girl. Double. Short tube and long sepals, bright carmine; corolla palest pink, carmine at base, overlaid with extra pleated petals of same colour, veined carmine. Bell shaped blooms, large and free. Growth trailer. Waltz – American – 1951 – A.F.S. No. 105.

Blossom Time. Single. Waxy-white tube and long curved, upturned sepals. Corolla soft pink, large blooms and free flowering, heat tolerant. Growth lax bush, strong grower, will trail. Tiret – American – 1952 – A.F.S. No. 142.

*Blowick. Single. Tube and sepals pinky-white. Corolla mallow-purple. Medium sized flowers and very easy to grow. Growth upright and bushy, can be trained to almost any shape. Raised in the vicinity of Southport and tested for 5 years before release. Introduced by J.V. Porter of Southport in 1984. Porter – British – 1984.

Blue Adonis. Double. Tube and heavy sepals, shell-pink; corolla light orchid-blue. Large blooms and free. Growth upright. Haag – American – 1949.

Blue and Gold. Double. Tube and sepals, palest pink; corolla mauve-blue. Flowers are large, full and free. Foliage is lemon-yellow of medium size. Growth upright. This cultivar is a welcome addition to the variegated foliage section, with flowers other than red and purple. Best grown as H1. Reedstrom – American – 1956 – A.F.S. No. 254.

Blue Beauty. Double. Short tube, sepals held moderately erect, red. Corolla bluish-violet, flowers very full and free. Growth upright and vigorous, good bush plant and easily trained as standard. Aptly named and still holds its own with the newer cultivars. Bull – British – 1854.

Blue Bells. Semi-double. Short tube and upturned sepals rose; corolla light blue, red at base and red veins. Flowers of medium size are bell shaped, very free and early. Growth medium upright bush. Brown and Soules – American – 1952 – A.F.S. No. 135.

Blue Bird. Semi-double. Short tube and long pointed, slender sepals, snowy-white. Corolla of deepest violet-blue, scalloped edges which overlap, attached to base of sepals, extra petals as flower matures, these turn a rosy hue whilst the corolla petals stay folded, large blooms. Growth trailer. Best grown as H1. Waltz – American – 1957 – A.F.S. No. 309.

Blue Bonnet. Single. Tube and broad, upturned sepals, bright red; corolla purple-blue, veined red. Flowers are large and flared, very free. Growth trailer. Hodges – American – 1950 – A.F.S. No. 69.

Blue Bonnet. Double. Tube and sepals red; corolla deep blue. Medium sized blooms in great profusion for hardy cultivar. Deep green foliage. Growth upright and bushy yet dainty, height 1½ to 2 ft, hardy in Southern England, raised in the Scilly Isles. Received the R.H.S. Award of Merit at the Wisley Hardy Trials 1975–78. Should not be confused with Blue Bonnet raised by the American Hodges in 1950. Tabraham – British – 1974.

Blue Boy. Single. Tube and sepals, deep rose-pink; corolla clear violet-blue. Small flowers but very profuse, very early bloomer. Growth upright and bushy, makes an ideal bedder. Correct name could be The Blue Boy after the famous painting. Fry – British – 1889.

Blue Boy. Double. Short tube and short sepals are white, tinted pink. Corolla deep violet-blue with pink shading at base. Large flowers, growth upright bush. Not to be confused with Big Blue Boy by Gorman 1970. Paskesen – American – 1971 – A.F.S. No. 958.

Blue Bush. Single. Tube rosy-red, sepals long and held out from corolla, rosy-red. Corolla blue bird-blue fading to bishop's-violet with rose veins. Flowers medium sized and very free. Growth upright bush, very vigorous and self-branching, will take full sun. Tested by raiser for five years in central England and proved hardy, suitable cultivar for hedges, height 3 to 4 ft. Gadsby – British – 1973 – A.F.S. No. 1120.

Blue Butterfly. Semi-double. Short tube and long sepals white. Corolla deep violet-blue, splashed with white. Blooms are medium to large, as they mature inner petals open wide, turning to lush orchid shade with blue undertones. Foliage dark green, growth trailer, best grown as H1. Waltz – American – 1960 – A.F.S. No. 438.

Blue Dancing Doll. Single. Tube and sepals, bright red; corolla purple to blue. Medium sized flowers and free growth lax bush. Raiser unknown – American – 1930.

Blue Danube. Double. Tube and sepals rosy-pink; corolla blue, marbled blue and red. Large blooms and free. Growth lax bush. Reiter – American– 1938.

Blue Doll. Single. An American introduction of which little is known except for the pink sepals and blue corolla with upright growth. Raiser and date unknown – *ca* 1960.

Blue Elf. Single. Tube and sepals, rose-pink, crepe effect on underside, curl back to tube with twist, short and narrow. Corolla light blue with violet edges, flushed very pale blue at base, rose-pink veins, fades to pale mauve with brilliant heavy edges. Flowers medium bell shaped. Foliage olive green with distinct red veins and serrated edges. Growth upright and bushy. Winner of Jones Cup B.F.S. London 1972 also the B.F.S. Award of Merit. Raised by Mrs. Margaret Hall and introduced by R. Atkinson of Consett. Hall-Atkinson – British – 1968 – A.F.S. No. 1116.

Blue Eyes. Double. Tube and sepals, pale pink; corolla bright blue. Flowers large and free. Growth lax bush, will trail, cultivar that will stand frequent stopping. Reedstrom – American – 1954 – A.F.S. No. 205.

Blue Fairy. Double. White tube, long white sepals curl outwards; corolla light blue. Medium sized blooms, very full and fairly free, best colour in shade, prefers warmth for best results. Growth natural trailer, makes good basket. Hanson – American – 1976 – A.F.S. No. 1323.

Blue Flame. Single. Tube and sepals crimson; corolla campanula-violet, streaked with pale rose-madder. Flowers medium and free. Growth upright and bushy. Niederholzer – American – 1948 – A.F.S. No. 15.

Blue Gem. Single. Tube and sepals cerise, corolla lilac-blue. Very large flowers and free, growth upright and bushy. Raiser unknown – British – *ca* 1970.

Blue Gown. Double. Tube and sepals cerise; corolla bluish-purple, splashed pink and carmine. Large blooms free and beautiful, early flowerer. Growth upright and vigorous, good as bush, will produce excellent standard. Very old cultivar. Accepted by B.F.S. as showbench hardy. Milne – British – Date unknown.

Blue Halo. Double. Proportionately short pinkish-ivory tube, thin. Curving, long broad sepals white with pink markings at base. Corolla white to pale pink with each petal edged in blue shading to purple. Medium sized blooms and free for size, dark green foliage, leaves $2\frac{1}{2}$ in by $1\frac{1}{4}$ in wide with red veining. Lanceolate to ovate with ovate to cordate base, acute to rounded tip and serrated margin. Growth trailer, will make good basket with weights. Trademarked in California, raised in the vicinity of Fort Bragg, Oxnard and Oceanside, California, U.S.A. Stubbs – American – 1981 – A.F.S. No. 1615.

***Blue Ice.** Single. Rose-pink tube $\frac{3}{8}$ in long by $\frac{1}{8}$ in wide, fully up sepals rose-pink (R.H.S. 52C) on top, crepey rose-pink underneath, $1\frac{1}{2}$ in long by $\frac{3}{8}$ in wide with recurved tips, twisting at ends. Pale lavender-blue corolla (R.H.S. 91A) veined rose and maturing to pale lavender (R.H.S. 78B) flushed white at base, $\frac{3}{4}$ in long by $1\frac{3}{4}$ in wide. Medium sized flowers three quarters to full flaring of beautiful delicate colouring, symmetrical and considered to be of different colour combination. Yellow-green foliage (R.H.S. 146C) with elliptic shaped leaves $1\frac{3}{4}$ in long by $\frac{9}{10}$ in wide, acute tipped and obtuse base, veins very pale green with brownish-red stems and dark red branches. Growth small upright, will make good upright, bushy, very compact and short-jointed. Raised in the vicinity of Ponteland, Newcastle-upon-Tyne. Blue Elf × Mayfield. Hall – British – 1984 – A.F.S. No. 1766.

Blue Jacket. Semi-double. Tube and sepals crimson, sepals curl right back to tube. Corolla dark blue ageing to purple with maturity. Medium sized blooms and very free. Growth upright, bushy and self-branching. Introduced by Woodbridge Nurseries of Hounslow in 1980. Joy Patmore × Madame Cornelissen. Dyos – British – 1980.

Blue Lace. Double. Tube and sepals red; corolla blue. Large blooms, continuous flowering, dark green foliage. Growth upright and bushy, strong branching habit, height 2 to $2\frac{1}{2}$ ft, hardy in Southern England, raised in the Scilly Isles. Tabraham – British – 1974.

Blue Lagoon. Double. Short tube and broad, recurving sepals, bright red; corolla rich, deep purple, cast on blue. Full double, spreads out to large size as it opens. Growth upright bush. Travis, J. – British – 1958.

Blue Lagoon. Double. Tube and sepals, rosy-red. corolla medium blue. Very large blooms. Growth upright. Needs H1 for best results. Tiret – American – 1961 – A.F.S. No. 482.

Blue Mink. Single. Short, thick tube crimson (R.H.S. 52A), narrowing at waist, sepals are crimson (R.H.S. 52A), creped inside, broad and medium in length, reflexing and twisting around short tube. Corolla dark violet shading to violet (R.H.S. 86A) towards base, rose-red (R.H.S. 58B) at base, veined crimson (R.H.S. 52A). Medium sized flowers consisting of four petals of classic shape, forming long, slightly flared bell, cardinal-red (R.H.S. 53C) stamens and very long pistil. Growth small upright and bushy, self branching with dwarfish habit. Parentage: Gruss aus dem Bodethal × Dutch Mill. Holmes, R. – British – 1976 – A.F.S. No. 1335.

***Blue Mirage.** Double. Tube and sepals white, sepals are held horizontally, long and broad. Corolla aster-violet; large fully double blooms and quite free flowering. Growth upright and bushy. Raised in the vicinity of Bardney, Lincolnshire and introduced by Pacey's Nurseries of Melton Mowbray, Leicestershire in 1984. Bellamy – British – 1984.

Blue Mist. Double. Tube and sepals, rosy-pink; corolla blue and pink. Growth trailer. Tiret – American – 1964 – A.F.S. No. 595.

Blue Moon. Semi-double. Short tube and sepals, bright red; corolla clear blue. Medium sized flowers and free. Growth upright and vigorous up to 6 ft in California. Created much attention when first introduced, first of the tri-colours. Rolla × Heron. Niederholzer – American – 1938.

Blue Mulan. Single. Tube and sepals, clear pink; corolla orchid-blue. Flowers very free and medium sized. Growth upright and bushy. Nelson – American – 1953.

Blue 'n' White. Double. Short wavy tube and long, broad sepals, white tinted blush, tipped pale green. Corolla lilac-blue, outer, smaller petals overlaid phlox-pink. Flowers are large and spreading, fairly free. Growth trailer. Brand – American – 1960 – A.F.S. No. 420.

Blue Pearl. Double. Tube and heavy, broad arching sepals, pink, tipped green; corolla violet-blue. Blooms are of good substance and free. Growth lax bush, can be made to trail. Almost identical to Pinwheel. Martin – American – 1955 – A.F.S. No. 325.

Blue Pendant. Double. Tube and sepals, pale Tyrian-rose, tipped green; corolla campanula-violet with blue cast. Medium flowers and small foliage. Growth lax bush. Brown – American – 1949.

Blue Peter. Semi-double. Pink and blue. Rogers – British – 1899.

Blue Petticoat. Double. Tube and sepals white, palest blush on inside; corolla beautiful shade of silvery lilac-lavender, turning to orchid-pink with age. Medium sized blooms, growth trailer. Evans and Reeves – American – 1954 – – A.F.S. No. 216.

Blue Phenomenal. Double, Scarlet and blue. Lemoine – French – 1871.

Blue Pinwheel. Single. Short red tube, sepals red and long, curling to form pinwheel. Corolla orchid-blue and long shape. Colour medium size, small dark foliage. Growth trailer. A.F.S. Cert. of Merit 1973. Stubbs – American – 1970 – A.F.S. No.902.

Blue Q. Single. Red and pale blue cultivar with little distinguishing features from unknown parents. Cheetham – British – 1977.

Blue Ranger. Semi-double. Long thick crimson tube, crimson sepals, broad and waxy, slightly curved back. Corolla blue-bird blue shading to hyacinth-blue, fading to violet. Medium to large flowers and free flowering, best colour in shade. Medium sized foliage, spear shaped, growth upright and bushy, self-branching, vigorous and strong. Gadsby – British – 1974 – A.F.S. No.1312.

Blue Rhythm. Semi-double. Tube and recurved sepals, dawn-pink, peach on outer side. Corolla dauphine's-violet, shading to peach-white at base with overlaying petaloids of same colour. Flowers of exquisite colouring, largish and free. Growth upright and bushy. Lee – American – 1953 – A.F.S. No.147.

Blue Ribbon. Double. Tube pale pink, sepals pale pink which cling to corolla. Square corolla, white. Large lush foliage. Growth lax bush or trailer. Fuchsia-La – American – 1967 – A.F.S. No.695.

Blue Sails. Single. Tube neyron-rose, sepals neyron-rose deeper on underside. Corolla dark violet-blue fading to fuchsia-purple, white at base of petals. Growth upright and bushy, short-jointed and vigorous enough to be suitable for training as standards. Medium sized flowers and raised in the vicinity of Melton Mowbray, Leicestershire. Raised and introduced by R. and J. Pacey of Stathern, Melton Mowbray in 1982. Pacey – British – 1982.

Blue Satin. Double. Short tube, long sepals, glistening white; corolla indigo-blue shading to white at base, giving a satiny sheen. Blooms grow larger and more flaring after opening. Dark green foliage. Growth lax bush or trailer. A.F.S. Cert. of Merit 1972. Best grown as H1. Walker – American – 1969 – A.F.S. No. 835.

Blue Skies. Single. Tube and sepal rose; corolla blue-violet. Small flowers and free. Growth upright and bushy-. Nessier – American – 1948.

Blue Sleighbells. Single. Tube and sepals white; corolla lavender-blue and bell shaped. Growth upright and bushy. Barton – New Zealand – 1970 – A.F.S. No. 915.

Blue Sultan. Double. Tube and sepals red, short and broad. Corolla dark violet with peraloids splashed pink, attached to sepals. Large blooms of good substance. Growth trailer. Martin – American – 1956 – A.F.S. No. 281.

Blue Tit. Single. Red tube, reflexed sepals also red. Corolla violet, veined red on pale pink splash at base of petals. Small flowers but very floriferous. Growth upright, vigorous bush and hardy in Southern England. Raised in the vicinity of Banstead, Surrey and introduced by Woodbridge Nurseries of Hounslow, Middlesex, in 1982. Hobson – British – 1982.

Bluette. Double. Tube and sepals red; corolla blue edged with pink. Long and narrow blooms, quite small but very free. Growth upright bush. Schmidt – American – 1949.

Blue Veil. Double. Pure white tube, broad sepals pure white; corolla lobelia-blue. Large blooms with red stamens, very full and well shaped, sepals do not turn pink with maturity, lovely colour combination. Growth strong trailer. Introduced by the raiser in 1980. Pacey – British – 1980.

Blue Waves. Double. Short tube very pale pink, upturned sepals neyron-rose. Corolla deep campanula-violet, decided blue overtone, wavy petals. Blooms fairly large and free, outer petals of corolla splashed neyron-rose, centre remaining deep violet-blue, matures opening into loose waved form, holds colour. Growth upright and bushy, makes good standard. A.F.S. Cert. of Merit 1968. Waltz – American – 1954 – A.F.S. No. 201.

Blue Waves

Blush. Single. Tube pink, short white-backed pink sepals. Corolla very pale pink. Foliage light green. Growth upright bush. Brown and Soules – American – 1953.

Blushing Beauty. Double. Bengal-red tube $\frac{1}{4}$ in wide × $\frac{3}{8}$ in long, sepals Bengal-red $\frac{5}{8}$ in wide × 1$\frac{1}{4}$ in long. Pale pink corolla 1$\frac{1}{2}$ in wide × $\frac{3}{4}$ in long. Medium sized blooms with four pale pink petaloids, pink pistil 2$\frac{1}{8}$ in long and light pink stigma. Light green foliage with leaves $\frac{5}{8}$ in wide × 1 in long. Growth medium upright will make good bush, prefers warmth for best results. Introduced by Soo Yun Fuchsia Gardens in 1980. De Francisco – American – 1980 – A.F.S. No. 1559.

Blushing Bride. Single. Pink and violet. Lye – British – Date unknown.

Blushing Bride. Semi-double. Tube and sepals pale pink; corolla white. Large blooms and free. Growth upright bush. Jones – British – 1960.

Blush o' Dawn. Double. This exceptional cultivar was raised in America by George Martin of California in 1962 and considered by the raiser to be his best introduction to date. Fuchsia enthusiasts are indeed indebted to Martin, who in addition to raising Blush o' Dawn, has given us Orange Drops, Sophisticated Lady and Coral Seas, amongst the 20 odd introductions, all registered by the A.F.S. Blush o' Dawn is a double, with tube and sepals of waxy-white with a green tip, the very full corolla is a most unusual colour combination, a delicate colouring of silver-grey and lavender-blue, quite different from the other blues. Although not an early bloomer, the flowers which are quite free, are long lasting and would excel as a cut bloom exhibit. Foliage is medium green and attractive; growth is bushy and responds well to frequent pinching. This outstanding cultivar is undoubtedly one of the best and most delicate of the pastel shades, but can only be grown to perfection with the protection of the greenhouse and needs a shady position. Grown in the fuchsia border, needs shade and like all the pastels is susceptible to frost. The only fault found with this cultivar is that, unless grown fairly hard, it does lack the vigour of a good bush plant, although it will make a good conical, with careful cultivation. However, consider it fairly universal as, with careful training, it can be used as a stiff trailer and with the weight of the heavy blooms will make an excellent half basket or full basket. Capable of making a beautiful small or medium standard, but would anticipate it lacking the essential qualities for achieving a full standard. A.F.S. Cert. of Merit 1966. Martin – American – 1962 – A.F.S. No. 516.

Blush o' Dawn

Bobby Boy. Double. Tube and sepals reddish-rose; corolla bluish-rose, fades to rose with touches of orange on outer petals. Small blooms but very profuse, have the appearance of a small rose. Growth lax bush. Fuchsia Forest – American – 1965 – A.F.S. No. 625.

Bobby Shaftoe. Semi-double. Tube clear frosty-white, flushed palest pink and short. Sepals clear frosty-white, crepe effect underside, flushed palest pink with lemon tips. Corolla clear frosty-white, flushed palest pink with pink veins, flared and ruffled to form four flutes. Blooms medium in size, profuse, heavy flowerer into late season. Foliage mid to light green, oval and smooth. Growth medium bush, upright and self-branching. Ryle-Atkinson – British – 1973 – A.F.S. No. 1113.

Bobby Wingrove. Single. Tube and sepals red, tipped green; corolla turkey-red. Small flowering cultivar very like a miniature Rufus, but rather more pleasing colour. Extremely prolific, always in bloom, almost impossible to find cutting without flowers. Growth upright and bushy. B.F.S. Award of Merit 1966. Wingrove – British – 1966.

Bob Kennedy. Double. Tube and sepals white, tipped with green; corolla white. Large blooms and small foliage, will stand heat. Growth trailer. Pennisi – American – 1969 – A.F.S. No. 812.

Bo Bo. Double. Short red tube, red sepals. Corolla purple shaded magenta at the base, area from the centre of petal to tip is dark rose. Small to medium sized blooms, dark green foliage, ovate in shape with entire to slightly serrate margins, veins are red through first half of leaf. Growth medium upright will make good bush. Originates from the Coos Bay area of California. Adkins – American – 1980 – A.F.S. No. 1587.

Bobolink. Double. Tube and upturned sepals, flesh-pink; corolla intense blue-violet. Blooms large and free but described as loose double. Growth upright, vigorous and bushy. Evans and Reeves – American – 1953 – A.F.S. No. 182.

*Bob Paisley. Double. Rose-red short tube $\frac{1}{2}$ in to $\frac{3}{4}$ in long by $\frac{3}{8}$ in wide, horizontally held sepals rose-red (R.H.S. 58B) on top, crimson (R.H.S. 52A) underneath with recurved tips $1\frac{7}{16}$ in long by $\frac{3}{4}$ in wide. Corolla opens mallow-purple (R.H.S. 73C) maturing with age to rose-purple (R.H.S. 68B) $1\frac{1}{2}$ in long by $2\frac{1}{4}$ in wide. Fully flared largish blooms, very early flowering and profuse, rose-purple (R.H.S. 57A) filaments and deep rose anthers (R.H.S. 58A). Dark green (R.H.S. 137C) foliage, much lighter green underneath, elliptic leaves $2\frac{1}{4}$ in long by 1 in wide. Growth small upright and bushy, excellent for both upright or standard, responds to frequent pinching, tolerates full sun. Sport of Spion Kop. Found in the vicinity of Ormskirk, Lancashire. Sinton Nurseries – British – 1984 – A.F.S. No. 1798.

Bob's Choice. Single. White tube, sepals white flushed china-rose, tipped green. Corolla white, veined rose-purple at base of petals. Large flowers, very neat and free flowering. Growth upright and bushy, compact and vigorous enough for the training as standard. Raised in the vicinity of Melton Mowbray for 3 years before release. Raised and introduced by R. and J. Pacey of Stathern, Melton Mowbray in 1982. Pacey – British – 1982.

*Bodensee. Semi-double. Tube and sepals red; corolla dark blue. Growth medium upright. Nutzinger – Austrian – 1970.

Boerhaave. Single. Tube and sepals deep red; corolla deep rose to rosy-purple. Blooms large and free. Feature of the flower is the terrifically long tube and seed pod with reflexed sepals held well away from the tube, very long thin tapering buds and long pistil. Growth upright and bushy, one of the few Dutch introductions. van Wieringen – Dutch – 1970.

Bolero. Double. Tube and sepals, bright red; corolla dark plum-purple. Large blooms, growth upright and vigorous. Niederholzer – American – 1942 or prior.

Bolero Blanco. Double. Tube and sepals red; corolla white. Large blooms, growth upright and bushy. Sport of Bolero. Nelson – American – 1954.

boliviana. Belongs to the Eufuchsia section of species, the largest section consisting of approximately 58 species. The *boliviana* attributed to Britton 1890 is synonymous with *F. sanctae-rosae*. Dark red tube with dark red sepals, the corolla is also dark red shading to light red. The flowers are very beautiful, long and narrow and are borne in clusters showing up well against the lightish green foliage. After flowering produces masses of attractive crimson red berries which are quite edible and rich in vitamins.

The lightish green foliage has elliptic to ovate leaves, rounded at base, acuminate at apex and may be opposite, alternate or ternate and are rather paler on the undersides.

The species resembles, could almost be described as belonging to the Corymbiflora group, both in colour of flowers and general appearance but is much more compact and dwarfer in habit than *F. corymbiflora*.

In this country it is best planted out in the border during the early summer in good soil in a moist shady position. The resultant clump can be lifted like a chrysanthemum in the autumn and carefully potted up, it will then continue to flower under glass, but this is one of the species which needs fairly brisk heat and is definitely frost shy during the winter. In its natural habitat will attain 12 ft and over, with an open branching habit and as the name suggest originated from Bolivia in South America, although it is also found in Argentina, Guatemala and Ecuador, often at an elevation of 9000 to 10,000 ft.

This species is well worth cultivating and one of the most beautiful of the species. Bakers, Chingford Nurseries, Pacey and Akers all currently list as being available.

Some authorities quote discovery by Roezl in 1873, others by Carr in 1876.

Boliviana Alba. Single. Pure white flowers, very long and very free, with bright green foliage. Species type bloom and habit. Nelson – American – 1955.

Bon Accorde. Single. One of the most unusual cultivars in cultivation, Bon Accorde is far from ordinary, in as much as its delicate blooms stand out erect, in contrast to any typical fuchsia flower. This charming cultivar was raised by the Frenchman Crousse in 1861. Single flower, the tube and sepals are waxy, ivory-white and the corolla of a delicate pale purple, suffused white, exceptionally free-flowering and small in size. Growth is bushy and very upright, in fact when grown cool, is stiff and strong; best grown as H2. Bon Accorde is not self-branching and when grown under glass, needs frequent pinching, especially in the early stages of growth; if left to its own devices will quickly become leggy. Would consider this cultivar too stiff for the training of a full standard as the laterals do not hang graciously; it will, however, make a delightful quarter or half-standard, especially when used as an outside bedder as a "dot" plant. One of the finest beds of half standards of Bon Accorde is to be seen at Chester Zoo. When grown as a bush plant, needs only a central stake and like most fuchsias responds well to feeding, especially with potash whilst in bud and flower. This cultivar should not be confused with Pink Bon Accorde introduced by Tom Thorne in 1959, considered by many to be a sport of Bon Accorde, but unfortunately does not possess the same upright habit and is nearly a self pink. Cliff Gadsby of Derby has executed much hybridizing with Bon Accorde and the first cross, Bon Accorde × Athela in 1968, produced Upward Look, which although a very nice cultivar, has not

the same delicate colouring; has since raised other cultivars with Bon Accorde parentage. Bon Accorde did find its way over to America many years ago and was sent back to England as a new introduction, under the name of Erecta Novelty. Bon Accorde is a cultivar which should be in every fuchsia collector's selection. Crousse – French – 1861.

Bon Accorde

Bonanza. Double. Tube and sepals, spinel-pink; corolla spectrum-violet, fading to petunia-purple with maturity. Medium sized blooms and fairly free, growth lax bush. Fuchsia-La – American – 1963.

Bon Bon. Double. Long tube greenish-white, sepals pale pink, deeper pink underneath; corolla very pale pink. Medium size blooms, very free and tight, grown under shade can be almost self white. Small glossy foliage. Growth lax bush or trailer, self-branching best grown as H1. Kennett – American – 1963 – A.F.S. No. 592.

Bonita. Double. Tube and sepals. light pink, sepals shading to white on topside, underside China-rose. Corolla orchid-purple. Medium blooms and dark green foliage. Growth trailer, strong grower makes a wonderful basket. Fuchsia-La – American – 1972 – A.F.S. No. 1021.

Bonnie Lass. Double. Tube and reflexed sepals, frosty-white outside and palest pink underside. Corolla clear lilac fading to pleasing shade of rose. medium size blooms and very free, small, dark green foliage. Growth upright bush, beautiful and unusual cultivar. Waltz – American – 1962 – A.F.S. No. 522.

Bonnie Sue. Double. Pink tube, rosy-pink sepals tipped green and held horizontally to tube. Corolla rosy-red with dark rose edge on each petal, lighter at base. Medium sized blooms and quite free with flowering. Dark green small to medium foliage with serrated edges and ovate shape. Growth trailer, this cultivar was originally introduced in California about 1965 in the Coos Bay area with little details. Adkins – American – 1980 – A.F.S. No. 1550.

Bonny. Double. Tube and sepals rosy-red; corolla white. Medium sized blooms, fairly free, ruffled appearance, same petaloids are veined rosy-red. Growth upright bush and very compact, excellent for pot work, best as H2. Introduced by C.S. Lockyer in 1978. Holmes, E.M. – British – 1978.

Bonny Blue. Double. Short waxy tube and broad white sepals, sepals shiny-white outside, pink at base, crepe texture inside with a light carmine flush. Corolla of rolled petals, lovely medium silvery-blue. Large blooms beautifully

proportioned. Growth upright. Hodges –
American – 1958 – A.F.S. No. 341.

Bo Peep. Semi-double. Tube and sepals, white
to faint pink, corolla orchid-blue. Small flowers
and free. Growth small low bush. Schnabel –
American – 1948.

Bora Bora. Double. Tube white faintly pink, sepals white, corolla purplish-blue fading to
pinkish-purple with small green petaloids, lightish
green foliage. Growth trailer. Not an easy cultivar,
needs plenty of ventilation, buds fail to open with
wrong conditions, can produce a basket 5 ft
across. Tiret – American – 1966 A.F.S. No. 688.

Border Baron. Single. Tube and sepals carmine,
purple corolla, light carmine at base, filaments and
style are carmine. Foliage yellowish-green with
crimson mid rib. Flowers are profuse on each side
shoot. Growth upright and very bushy, may be
proved to be hardy. Ryle – British – 1975 – Not
registered.

Border Queen. Single. Short thin tube, sepals
rhodamine-pink tipped pea green, underside
neyron-rose, veins darker rose, flare out with tips
turned up. Corolla amethyst-violet, flushed pale
pink with dark pink veins, fading to white at base,
bell shaped. Foliage medium green, stems reddish, leaves smooth. Growth upright and self-
branching. A sister seedling to Eden Lady, only
difference is that Eden Lady is a little darker. Leonora × Lena Dalton. Ryle-Atkinson – British –
1974 – A.F.S. No. 1167.

Border Reiver. Single. Neyron-rose tube,
semi-reflexed sepals neyron-rose on upper surface, vermilion underneath. Corolla cardinal red,
medium sized flowers with pink filaments, ruby-
red anthers, extremely floriferous and outstanding
colouring. Dark green foliage, ovate with obtuse
leaf tip, lobed leaf base and serrate margins.
Leaves medium to large in size, growth tall,
upright bush, will take full sun in north-east England. Introduced by J.E. Ridding, Fuchsiavale
Nurseries, Kidderminster, in 1980. Ryle – British
– 1980 – A.F.S. No. 1574.

'Bornemanns Beste. Triphylla type single. Little known orange-red triphylla probably raised by
Carl Bonstedt and listed in German literature. A
particularly strong growing plant and interesting
to record that all triphylla hybrids raised by Carl
Bonstedt were introduced on the market by his
friend Georg Bornemann, a nurseryman of Blan-
kenburg in the Harz region of Germany. Introduced into Britain in 1984 by B. and H.M. Bakers
of Halstead, Essex, having acquired from the
President of the Dutch Society, N. Aalhuizen, in
the summer of 1983.

Boson's Norah. Single. Long tube salmon
orange, sepals salmon orange. Corolla salmon.
Medium sized flowers almost a self, feature is the
long tube. Growth upright bush, introduced by
Wills Fuchsias Ltd. of West Wittering in 1980.
Granger – British – 1979.

Boudoir. Double. Tube and sepals cream, tipped
green; corolla pale violet, changing to pink at
base. Dark foliage with crimson mid-rib. Large
blooms fairly free and of neat, puffy shape.
Growth lax bush, not an easy cultivar. Reiter –
American – 1954 – A.F.S. No. 212.

Bouffant. Single. Tube and sepals red; corolla
white, veined rosy-red. Large blooms and very
free. Growth cascade trailer. Tiret – American –
1949 – A.F.S. No. 32.

Boule de Neige. Double. Tube and sepals
white, tinged with pink and tipped green; corolla
white, tinged pink, almost a self. Growth trailer,
suitable for basket. Little known cultivar and
appears to be exclusive to California. Raiser and
date unknown – *ca* 1960.

Bounteous. Single. New white cultivar with little information other than parentage: Orange
Drops × Bobby Shaftoe. Exhibited in the Midlands
1981 by John Kirby of Sutton Coalfield. Bambrick
– British – 1981.

Bountiful. Single. Arabella Improved × James
Lye. Lye – British – Date unknown.

Bountiful. Double. Tube and sepals, palest pink,
tipped green. Corolla milky-white, pink veining at
base of sepals. Full, globular blooms early and
continuous, very free, with the weight of blooms
needs support as bush plant. Growth upright and
bushy. Munkner – American – 1963 – A.F.S. No.
564.

Bouquet. Double. Tube and sepals red; corolla
violet, ageing to reddish-purple. Small flowers but
very profuse, small foliage, requires little stopping,
self-branching. Growth upright, bushy and dwarf.
Hardy cultivar to a height of 1½ ft. Accepted by the
B.F.S. as a showbench hardy. Myrtifolia × . Lemoine – French – 1893.

Bouquet

Bow Bells. Single to semi-double. Short white
tube, long white sepals, tipped green. Corolla magenta, white at base, long over-lapping petals.
Large flowers of good substance, prolific and
early bloomer, needs support as bush plant.
Growth upright, self-branching, spreading bush.
Handley – British – 1972 – A.F.S. No. 1051.

Bow Street. Single. Tube and sepals, cherry-
red; corolla rich glowing red, almost a self.
Medium sized flowers and free, growth upright
and bushy. Winner of the B.F.S. Jones Cup 1970
also the B.F.S. Award of Merit. Named after the
famous Police Station in London. Miller, V.V. –
British – 1970.

bracelinae. Tube and sepals red; corolla purple.
Very small flowers, borne in leaf axils, found in
State of Espiritu Santo. Munz – 1943 – Brazil.

Bradley 'G'. Double. Long tube deep pink, sepals deep rose-pink, long, narrow and pointed.
Corolla light purple, veined rose-pink with outer
petals rose-pink. Foliage long and narrow with
pointed ends and serrated edges. Growth upright
bush. Luscomb – American – 1970 – A.F.S. No.
918.

Brandt's 500 Club. Single. Tube and sepals,
pale cerise; corolla cerise shaded orange, almost
a self colour, very long sepals. Large blooms and
free. Growth upright and bushy. Brand – American – 1955.

Bransby. Rozain-Boucharlet – French – 1913.

Bravado. Double. Tube and sepals red; corolla periwinkle-blue, splashed rosy-red at base, fading to Spanish-red. Large blooms and free. Growth lax bush or trailer. Fuchsia-Forest-Castro – American – 1960 – A.F.S. No. 425.

Brazier. Semi-double. Tube and sepals carmine; corolla deep carmine, almost a self, heat resistant. growth lax bush or stiff trailer. Reiter – American – 1947.

Breeder's Dream. Double. Tube and sepals white. flushed pink, tipped light green. Corolla phlox-purple. Large flowers and fairly free. Growth upright and bushy. Jones – British – 1961.

Brenda. Double. Short, thick tube is palest pink, reflexed sepals white, tinged pink. Corolla is two shades of pink. Medium to large sized blooms with ruby-red stamens, held well clear of petals, very eye-catching flowers. Dark green foliage, ovate to cordate with acute leaf tips, lobed leaf base, mostly entire leaf margins and slightly crinkled, medium to large. Growth tall, upright and bushy, self-branching will make excellent bush. Introduced by J.E. Ridding Fuchsiavale Nurseries, Kidderminster, in 1980. Ryle – British – 1980 – A.F.S. No. 1575.

Brenda Lee Peterson. Double. Short flesh-coloured tube, sepals light rose tipped green on upper surface, light rose underneath, sepals lay across the top of corolla and do not curve up or down. Corolla pastel purple, marbled pastel pink and white. Large blooms, quite free for size. Medium green foliage with red stems, growth natural trailer will make good basket. Originates from the Coos Bay area of California. Vee Jay Greenhouse and Nursery – American – 1980 – A.F.S. No. 1590.

Brenda Megan Hill. Single. Short tube in blush-pink, long, horizontal held sepals blush-pink on upperside, coral-pink on the underside. Deep lavender corolla with pink overtones. Medium sized flowers with rounded petals overlapping with lighter colour at the base of the petals, deepening to the edge, heat tolerant if shaded. Mid-green foliage, flat leaves, ovate and slightly serrated. Growth tall, upright and bushy. Tested for 5 years in the vicinity of Colchester, South East Coast of England before release. Hill – British – 1982 – A.F.S. No. 1671.

Brenda Pritchard. Semi-double. Tube and sepals, neyron-rose; corolla red-purple, flecked carmine-rose. Large flowers and free, growth trailer. Marshall – British – 1975.

Brennus. Single. Red and purple. Salter – British and French – 1841.

Brennus. Lemoine – French – 1867.

Brentwood. Semi-double. Tube and sepals, waxy-white, tipped green. Corolla near white, edged pale green. Medium size blooms very charming, flowers in flushes. Growth low bush, compact but not very vigorous. Used by the late Tom Thorne extensively for hydridizing and probably the first of the near whites. Rolla × Duchess of Albany. Evans and Reeves – American – 1936.

Brewsterii. Single. Scarlet and purple. Brewster – British – 1843.

Brian Young. Semi-double. Short to medium eau-de-nil tube is thin, green tipped sepals re-

curve back and cover both tube and ovary, white (R.H.S. 159D) on top flushed pale pink rose underneath and tipped white. Corolla purple (R.H.S. 93C). Medium sized blooms flared, one pair of purple petaloids attached to each sepal, rose stamens and white pistil. Foliage is narrow and long, medium green (R.H.S. 137A). Growth lax medium upright, will make good basket, bush or standard. Originally from the vicinity of Kearsley, Bolton. Susan Young × Arthur Young. Young – British – 1980 – A.F.S. No. 1566.

Bridal Bouquet. Single. Tube and sepals white, tinged with pink; corolla waxy-white. Medium sized flowers and very free, growth upright and bushy. Raiser unknown – New Zealand – Date unknown.

Bridal Pink. Double. Short tube pink, sepals long, light pink with light green tips which are slightly frosted and tend to curve and recurve lengthwise. Corolla fluffy pink with light pink overlays. Growth trailer. Copley Gardens – American – 1968 – A.F.S. No. 768.

Bridal Veil. Double. Tube and sepals white, tipped green; corolla creamy-white. Small dark green, glossy foliage, large blooms, continuous flowerer and heat resistant. Growth trailer. Best grown as H1. Waltz – American – 1963 – A.F.S. No. 586.

Bridesmaid. Double. Thick tube and broad, recurving sepals white, light carmine-blush; inside sepals phlox-pink. Corolla pale lilac-orchid, deepening toward petal edges. Medium size blooms, very free. Growth medium upright bush. Show-class cultivar always to be seen on the show-bench, but has lost favour with present exhibitors. Tiret – American – 1952 – A.F.S. No. 143.

Bridesmaid

Brigadoon. Double. Tube pink, long, broad recurved sepals pink, inside sepals of crepe texture, light green tips. Corolla violet-blue, overlaid and marbled near base with fuchsia pink. Blooms are large and free. Growth upright bush, willowy grower. Erickson – American – 1957 – A.F.S. No. 322.

Bright Eyes. Double. Short tube light red, sepals light red tipped green, short and broad, reflexed to tube. Corolla blue, with four swirls in centre with outer petals flaring to form skirt. Heavy bloomer from early to late in season. Growth semi-trailer, basket or lax bush. Soo Yun – American – 1973 – A.F.S. No. 1093.

*Brighton Belle. Single. Triphylla type hybrid. Very long tube rosy-red, sepals are short rosy-red but the petals of the corolla are nearer to a salmon-pink. Flowers are typical of terminal flowering parentage which will take full sun. Foliage is mid green, the leaves carrying a slight patina. Growth upright and self-branching. Raised in the vicinity of Ipswich and introduced by the raiser, Gouldings Fuchsias of Ipswich, in 1985. One of a series of new introductions named after famous trains in 1985. Goulding – British – 1985.

Brighton Express. Double. Rose-bengal tube, medium sepals rose-bengal, flare out to 180° of corolla. Corolla white with rose-bengal overcast, veined rose-bengal. Medium sized blooms, fairly free, petals curl slightly and flare, has a double skirted look, rose-bengal stamens and pistil. Growth semi-trailer, good for basket with weights or lax bush. Foster – American – 1976 – A.F.S. No. 1346.

Brilliant. Single. Tube and sepals scarlet, sepals are recurved, corolla violet-magenta, veined red. Medium sized flowers, very free. Growth upright bush, very vigorous, not self-branching, needs frequent pinching. Good bedder and produces excellent standard. Accepted by the B.F.S. as a showbench hardy. Bull – British – 1865.

Brilliant. Single. Red and white. Henderson – British – 1867.

Brilliantissima. Single. Greenish-white tube, reflexed sepals and dark crimson corolla, very fine in colour, but rather small. Received R.H.S. First Class Certificate at Chiswick Trials 1875. Henderson – British – *ca* 1870.

Britannia. Semi-double. Red and purple. Smith – British – 1846.

British Festival. Single. Tube and sepals dark red; corolla reddish-purple. medium sized flowers and very free, growth upright and bushy. Catt – British – 1951.

British Queen. Single. Rose-pink and red. Jennings – British – 1846.

British Sterling. Semi-double. Thick, short tube white, sepals white top-side, rosy-pink underside, tipped green, short, broad and reflexed to tube. Corolla lavender with faint rose cast, delicately veined pink, small with slight flair. Growth upright and bushy. Foster – American – 1973 – A.F.S. No. 1084.

Brixham Orpheus. Single. Proportionately medium length tube Venetian-pink (R.H.S. 49C) of medium thickness. Long sepals held out to just below horizontal, outer surface Venetian-pink (R.H.S. 49C), inner surface azalea-pink (R.H.S. 38A), tipped green turning up slightly. Blood red corolla (R.H.S. 45D) with lighter flecks changing to mandarin-red (R.H.S. 40C) at base. Medium sized flowers with very long pistil and large yellow stigma. Mid-green foliage with cordate leaves, stems pale green. Growth upright and bushy, self branching and tall, will however trail with weights, good as lax bush or standard. Tested for five years before release in vicinity of Edenbridge, Kent, England. Introduced by High Trees Nurseries of Reigate in 1981. Holmes R. – British – 1981 – A.F.S. No. 1643.

Brodsworth. Single. Tube and sepals cherry-red to scarlet; corolla deep purple. Medium-sized flowers and very free, considered to be an improvement upon Mrs. Popple which itself is an outstanding hardy cultivar. Growth upright, bushy, vigorous and hardy. Introduced by V.T. Nuttall of Markham Grange Nursery 1978. Mrs. Popple × Neue Welt. Nuttall – British – 1977.

Bronte Bell. Double. Short tube, variegated pink and white. sepals of the same colour, tipped green; sepals are horizontal with crinkled appearance. Corolla white, small, ruffled, full and flared. Small slender foliage. Growth lax bush, will trail, very heat resistant up to 115°F in California. Foster – American – 1972 – A.F.S. No. 1039.

*Brookwood Joy. Double. White tube ¾ in by ¼ in wide, sepals white tipped green, blush-pink underneath horizontally held with recurved tips, 1½in long by ⅞ in wide. Corolla hyacinth-blue (R.H.S. 90C) marbled phlox-pink (R.H.S. 62B). Medium sized blooms, fully double and half flared with deep pink stamens, pale pink style and creamy-white stigma. Medium sized foliage, lighter green underneath, ovate and serrated 2 in long by 1 in leaves with acute tip. Growth lax upright on stiff trailer; needs frequent stopping and grown very cool to produce good bush plant. Raised and grown in the vicinity of Birmingham before release. Introduced by Fuchsiavale Nurseries of Kidderminister in 1983. Stanley Cash × Joan Gilbert. Gilbert – British – 1983 – A.F.S. No. 1743.

Bruna. Double. Red and white. Twrdy – German – 1872.

*Brunette. Little known Dutch cultivar other than the parentage. Mephisto ×. de Graaff – Dutch – 1982.

Brutus. Single. Short tube and recurving sepals, rich cerise; corolla rich dark purple, ageing to reddish-purple. Medium sized flowers, very profuse and early bloomer. Growth upright, vigorous and bushy. Versatile for all types of training especially pyramid, pillar, espalier and standards. This is a cultivar which can throw semi-double blooms. One of the very good old cultivars, hardy in most parts of southern England. Lemoine – France – 1897.

Brutus

Bubble Hanger. Single. Tube and sepals, pale pink; corolla rose-madder, concave petals. Large flowers and free. Growth trailer, vigorous. Niederholzer – American – 1946.

Buddha. Semi-double. Tube and sepals, rich wine colour; corolla rich wine, self colour. Growth upright. Fuchsia-La – American – 1968 – A.F.S. No. 799.

Buffon. Double. Scarlet and white. Lemoine – French – 1890.

Buisson Blanc. Double. Cerise and white. Rozain-Boucharlat – French – 1913.

Bulgarie. Double. Red and purple. Lemoine – French – 1886.

Bunker Boy. Double. Thick waxy tube and long, broad upturned sepals, white, flushed palest carmine. Corolla long and fluted, white at base, deepening to geranium-lake at petal edges, smaller outer petals marbled fuchsia pink. Large blooms and free. Growth upright and bushy. Best as H1. Tiret – American – 1952 – A.F.S. No. 144.

Bunny. Semi-double. Tube and sepals cerise; corolla lilac-pink, edged with darker shade of violet-rose with a very distinct picotée edging. Growth upright and bushy. Need – British – 1965.

Burbank. Single. Long tube and sepals crimson; corolla dark crimson, streaked pink. Large blooms. Growth upright bush. Niederholzer – American – 1946.

Burgundian. Double. Tube and granular sepals, deep carmine; corolla maroon with dark red shadings. Large blooms rather short and spreading. Most unusual colouring described as dusky-oxblood. Growth lax bush. Gypsy Queen × unnamed seedling. Schnabel – American – 1955 – A.F.S. No. 221.

Burning Bush. Synonymous with Autumnale and Rubens.

Burnouf. Lemoine – French – 1876.

Bussiere. Lemoine – French – 1876.

Buttercup. Single. Short tube pale tinted pink, orange tinted sepals on inside, stand straight out, but curve slightly inward at tips. Corolla consists of four flaring orange (R.H.S. 32C) petals. Medium-sized flowers, heat tolerant if shaded. Growth medium upright, good for bush or standard. Paskesen – American – 1976 – A.F.S. No. 1345.

Butterfly. Single. Crimson and red. Stride – British – 1902.

Butterfly. Tube and recurved sepals, Bengal-rose; corolla Bengal-rose, crimson at base, almost a self. Flowers are large and free. Growth trailer. Reiter – American – 1942.

Buttermere. Single. Short tube, rose with greenish veins stripes, sepals rich rose-pink tipped eau-de-nil, long, narrow, reflexed and spiral in older flower. Corolla lavender-purple with silver sheen at base of petals, deep purple edge on petals, young flowers square in cross section, petals open almost flat. Foliage deep green, red mid-vein and serrated. Growth self-branching bush. Opalescent × Citation. Travis, J. – British – 1967 – A.F.S. No. 1138.

Buttons & Bows. Double. Tube and sepals red; corolla very full, white, opening to cup shape. Foliage small and stiff. Growth upright bush. A.F.S. Cert. of Merit 1965. Machado – American – 1962 – A.F.S. No. 499.

Buxifolia floreplena. Lemoine – French – 1869.

Buzenval. Lemoine – French – 1887.

Byzance. Lemoine – French – 1911.

Caballero. Double. Tube and sepals, salmon pink; corolla bluish-purple to violet with splashes of salmon-pink on outer petals, petaloids vary from white to red. Large double blooms. Growth lax bush or trailer. Kennett – American – 1965 – A.F.S. No. 638.

Cabaret. Double. Tube and sepals white, flushed palest pink inside. Corolla bright magenta,

streaked with pink from base of each petal, has pencilled vermilion edge. Large blooms, early and prolific. Growth trailer, self-branching. Handley – British – 1971 – A.F.S. No. 984.

Cable Car. Double. Short heavy white tube; sepals very faint pink with darker pink tips. Corolla multi-hued, orchid fading to mixed hues of rose. Foliage dark green with red veining. Growth upright and vigorous up to 6 ft in California, can trail. A.F.S. Cert. of Merit 1971. Paskesen – American – 1968 – A.F.S. No. 762.

Cadmus. Single. Tube and reflexed sepals cerise; corolla white. Medium sized blooms free and early. Growth upright bush. Rozain-Boucharlat – French – 1928.

Caesar. Double. Tube and sepals red; corolla purple fading to burgundy, petals curl to a rose shaped bloom. Large flowers and fairly free. Growth lax bush or trailer. Can be disappointing if conditions do not suit. Fuchsia Forest – America – 1967 – A.F.S. No. 722.

Cairey. Double. Tube and sepals white to shell-pink; corolla lavender-blue. Medium sized blooms, growth upright and bushy. Raiser unknown – British – Date unknown.

Calchas. Lemoine – French – 1911.

Caledonia. Single. Very long cerise tube, sepals cerise, do not reflex; corolla crimson, almost a self. Flowers of medium size and very free. Growth upright and very bushy, ideal for low hedge, height 2 ft. Accepted by the B.F.S. as showbench hardy. Lemoine – French – 1899.

Calico. Single. Tube and sepals, Tyrian-rose; corolla wide, flaring, cobalt-violet with heart of white. Medium sized blooms and free. Growth small bush and upright. Nessier – American – 1952 – A.F.S. NO. 116.

California. Single. Tube and sepals, orange-pink; corolla bright orange. Flowers medium and free, light green foliage. Growth upright and vigorous up to 9 ft in California, good for standards. Fireflush × unnamed seedling. Evans and Reeves – American – 1936.

California Beauty. Single. Short tube rhodamine-purple (H.C.C. 29/3) $\frac{1}{4}$ in long × $\frac{1}{8}$ in wide, sepals green tipped with upper surface rhodamine-purple (H.C.C. 29/3) and white underneath $1\frac{1}{8}$ in long × $\frac{1}{4}$ in wide. Corolla fuchsia-purple (H.C.C. 28/1) with pink stamens and white pistil with yellow tip $1\frac{1}{4}$ in long. Light green foliage, leaves 1 in long × $\frac{3}{8}$ in wide. Growth natural trailer, originated from the area of Sebastopol, California. Soo Yun Field – American – 1980 – A.F.S. No. 1546.

California Centennial. Double. Tube and long sepals, rosy-red; corolla violet and dark purple. Very large blooms and fairly free. Growth trailer. Walker and Jones – American – 1949.

California Queen. Double. Tube orange, sepals dark orange on tips, light orange on bottom; corolla madder red. Growth trailer. Pennisi – American – 1971 – A.F.S. No. 1013.

Callaly Pink. Single. White, striped shell-pink tube, sepals white, flushed pink, reflect upwards; corolla shell-pink (R.H.S. 62D). Medium sized flowers very compact and very beautiful, created great attraction when first shown at Manchester 1974. Growth upright and bushy will make good bush or standard. Received B.F.S. Certificate of

Preliminary Acceptance at Manchester 1974. Very similar to Pink Dessert; introduced by Jackson's Nurseries of Tamworth in 1979. Seedling from Mrs. Lawrence Lyons. Ryle – British – 1974 – A.F.S. No. 1334.

Calypso. Double. Tube rosy-cream, sepals are broad and long, recurving completely, displaying an even unfading Tyrian-rose inner surface. Large petals open widely, outer surface the same colour of the sepals, the outer edges of the large petals are marbled with flecks of white and masses of deep cyclamen-purple and amethyst-violet. Large heavy blooms need support unless trained as a basket. Growth trailer. Best grown as H1. Reiter – American – 1956 – A.F.S. No. 275.

Cambridge Louie. Single. Thin tube pinky-orange, sepals pinky-orange, underside of darker shade. Corolla rosy-pink with darker edges, medium-sized flowers, very floriferous. Foliage rather small, light green. Growth upright and bushy, raised by Napthan in 1977 and introduced by D. Stilwell in 1978. Named after a delightful lady Mrs. Louise Napthen of Cambridge who although totally blind extremely active with fuchsias at all levels. Established as an exhibitor's banker. Lady Isobel Barnett × Mr. A. Huggett. Napthen – British – 1977 – A.F.S. No. 1473.

Camelia. Double. Cerise and white, Rozain–Boucharlat – French – 1928.

Camelia Flammarion. Double. Red and violet. Rozain-Boucharlat – French – 1912.

*Camelot. Single. Short, thick white to pink tube, sepals white very pale pink underneath, fully reflexed with recurved tips. Corolla white to very pale pink, with pink veining. Medium sized flowers, bell shaped and very free. Mid-green foliage with larger than average leaves. Growth medium upright, vigorous and self-branching; will produce excellent bush or standard. Best grown in shade protected from bees. Has produced two sports: Lemacto and Tolemac. Raised and tested in the vicinity of Ipswich, East of England for 2 years before release, introduced by B. and H.M. Baker Nurseries of Halstead in 1983. Goulding – British – 1983 – A.F.S. No. 1724.

Cameo. Semi-double. Tube and sepals, pale rose-madder; corolla delicate pink. Small flowers but profuse. Growth low bush and upright. Schnabel – American – 1950 – A.F.S. No. 53.

Cameron. Single. Red and blue. Bull – British – 1872.

Cameron Ryle. Semi-double. Short tube white, sepals frosty-white, pink to red overcast, tipped green, horizontal to full reflex over tube. Corolla very dark bluish-purple, inside palish pink, fading to magenta with age. Medium size blooms and profuse, resembles Citation. Growth lax bush, can be trained as basket, Lena Dalton × Citation, Ryle-Atkinson – British – 1971 – A.F.S. No. 1024.

Camille. Double. Tube crimson, sepals short and cupped, fully reflexed, coloured crimson. Corolla rose-bengal. Huge flowers of classic shape and spreading. Growth upright, sturdy bush. Schnabel – American – 1956 – A.F.S. No. 264.

campos-portoi. Tube and sepals red; purple corolla. Small flowers, not very free. Shrub on mountain heights of 7000 ft or more, State of Rio de Janeiro. Pilger and Schuize - 1935 – Brazil.

Canary Bird. Single. Variegated foliage. Bull – British – 1873.

Can Can. Double. Short thick tube pink, sepals pink, broad and reflexed. Corolla white, veined pink, short, full and fluffy. Medium sized pastel blooms, early and prolific. Dark green foliage with bronze flash in centre of leaves, veined red. Growth upright and bushy. Handley – British – 1973 – A.F.S. No. 1132.

Candelabra. Semi-double. Tube and sepals, greyish-white; sepals are long curling up tightly at base of corolla. Dark blue corolla with streaks of white and reddish-pink. Flowers are long and free, growth trailer and cascading. Fuchsia Forest – Castro – America – 1962 – A.F.S. No. 512.

Candidissima. Single. White and rose-pink. Halley – British – 1843.

Candlelight. Double. Tube and upturned sepals, pure white outside, slightly flushed pink underside. Corolla rose, with overlapping petals of very dark purple-lilac, fading into bright carmine-red. Large blooms and free, growth, medium bush, upright and self-branching. Waltz – American – 1959 – A.F.S. No. 391.

Candy Floss. Double. Tube and sepals pink; corolla pink with deeper pink markings. Large blooms, growth upright and bushy. Barton – American – 1970 – A.F.S. No. 916.

Candy Rose. Double. Short tube and sepals, bright red, heavy crepe; corolla pale pink with deep pink stripes. Medium sized blooms resemble a small rosebud. Bronze-green foliage, growth upright and bushy, Gagnon – American – 1964 – A.F.S. No. 600.

Candy Stripe. Single. Tube and sepals, pale pink, deeper on underside, sepals curl upwards. Corolla pink changing to pale violet with age. Medium sized blooms, feature of the flower is the very large ovary and thick pedicel. Growth upright and bushy. Queen of Hearts × Bridesmaid. Reliable sources quote raiser as Dr. R.M. Harper of Barnstaple and not Endicott. Endicott – British – 1965.

canescens. Deep scarlet tube, purplish at base, sepals deep scarlet; corolla scarlet. Strong upright shrub up to 7 ft in natural habit. Synonymous with *F. vulcanica*. Bentham – 1845 – Colombia and Ecuador.

Cannell's Gem. Single. Red and white, Bland – British – 1873.

Capistrano. Double. Tube and sepals, vivid red; corolla pure white with slight red veining. Large blooms, heavy and floriferous, early. One of the showiest of the red and whites. Growth upright and bushy. Best as H1. Evans – American – 1954.

Capitaine Binger. Lemoine – French – 1894.

Capitaine Boynton. Double. Red and purple. Lemoine – French – 1878.

Capitaine Tilho. Lemoine – French – 1907.

Capitola. Double. Tube and sepals, light pink to white, tipped green. Corolla beautiful shade of orange-rose. Growth trailer. Antonelli – American – 1971 – A.F.S. No. 1003.

Capri. Double. Short thick tube and broad granular sepals, glistening white. Corolla deep blue-violet, heavy petalled. Blooms are huge and of distinctive beauty, but not an easy grower. Growth lax upright or trailer. Best as H1, week growth, A.F.S. Cert. of Merit, 1964. Schnabel-Paskesen – American – 1960 – A.F.S. No. 418.

Caprice. Single. Long tube pale rose-madder, sepals of the same colour; short corolla petunia-purple. Small flowers but free. Growth trailer. Sister seedling to Coquette. Niederholzer – American – 1945.

Capricorn. Double. Short tube very pale pink, sepals white, swinging back in classic form, petals rather long. Corolla rich blue-violet, flushed white at base with long petals. Growth vigorous trailer. Paskesen – American – 1970 – A.F.S. No. 872.

caracanensis (Fielding and Gardner 1844). Synonymous with *F. hirtella.*

Cara Mia. Semi-double. Tube pale pink, sepals long and graceful, palest rose-pink, slim, pointed and reflexed. Corolla deepest crimson and globular shaped. Medium sized blooms, very profuse along entire length of branch. Growth trailer. Schnabel – American – 1957 – A.F.S. No. 288.

Cardinal. Single. Tube and sepals, dark red; corolla, rich dark red, almost a self. Lightish green foliage. Growth extremely vigorous and upright, suitable as climber, will reach 10 to 12 ft in California. Santa Monica × President. Evans and Reeves – American – 1938.

Cardinal Farges. Semi-double. Tube and reflexed sepals, pale cerise; corolla white, lightly veined cerise. Flowers are quite small but profuse. Growth upright, bushy and vigorous, similar in every way to Abbé Farges, has the same small fault, rather brittle growth. Show class cultivar. Accepted by B.F.S. as showbench hardy. Sport of Abbé Farges. Rawlins – British – 1958.

***Carefree.** Double. Tube and sepals white, sepals tipped green and flushed pink, very broad. Corolla very pale pink flushed rose-Bengal at base of petals. Medium sized blooms with very rich coloured corolla, free flowering for a double. Raised in the vicinity of Melton Mowbray, Leicestershire and introduced by the raisers, Pacey's Nurseries, in 1984. Pacey – British – 1984.

Cargundy. Double. Tube and sepals cardinal-red; corolla burgundy. Large blooms and large dark green foliage. Growth upright. Reedstrom – American – 1952 – A.F.S. No. 108

Carillon. Semi-double to double. Tube and sepals, scarlet-cerise; corolla dark plum, striped pink and rose. Large blooms, free and early. Growth upright bush. Old cultivar still in cultivation. Rozain-Boucharlat – French – 1913.

Carillon van Amsterdam. Single. Long, slender tube, red; long, slender sepals red with green tips, stand out at the horizontal. Corolla dark red with pink stamens and style. Medium-sized flowers and foliage. Growth lax bush or trailer. van Wieringen – Dutch – 1970.

Carin Harrer. Double. Tube and sepals deep red; corolla purple-blue. Medium-sized flowers and fairly free. Koralle × Golden Glow. Nutzinger – Austrian – 1973.

Carioca. Single. Tube and sepals, pale rosy-red, tipped green; corolla rosy-red with some purple shadings. Flowers large and spreading, with serrated petals, free and early. Growth lax bush, will trail and heat resistant. Schmidt – American – 1951 – A.F.S. No. 98.

Cark. Semi-double. Short tube flesh pink, sepals neyron-rose (R.H.S. 55) of good shape, tipped green, folding back to tube. Corolla two shades of blue, blue to violet (R.H.S. 85A). Medium sized blooms with petals of different lengths. Growth self-branching medium upright, ideal for good bush. Takes full sun near Preston but best colour develops in shade. Tested for 4 years in the vicinity of Preston before release. Lilac Lustre self. Thornley – British – 1981 – A.F.S. No. 1635.

Carla. Single. Tube and sepals, pale flesh; corolla carmine. Small blooms and free. Growth trailer. Niederholzer – American – 1943.

Carl Drude. Semi-double. Tube and sepals, cardinal-red; corolla white with red veins. Medium sized flowers and very free. Seedling from Strawberry Delight with the same golden-bronze foliage. Growth upright and bushy but with dwarfer habit, very compact. Strawberry Delight × . Gadsby – British – 1975.

***Carlisle Bells.** Single. Tube is palest pink striped carmine, short ¼in long by ¼in wide. Reflexed sepals white flushed pale pink underneath, 2in long × ¾in wide with recurved tips. Corolla bishops-violet shading to pale pink at base of each petal, maturing to spectrum-violet, petals 1in long by 1½in wide. Medium sized flowers, very free flowering and similar shape to Mission Bells and Citation, especially in bud form. Pale pink stamens cherry red anthers and pale pink pistil. Dark green foliage with cordate leaves 2in long by 1½in wide, obtuse tips. Growth medium upright, bushy and self-branching; will produce good bush or standard, prefers being grown cool. Will make 6in pot on current growth from January cutting. Raiser considers this cultivar to be his best introduction. Raised in the vicinity of Carlisle, Cumbria, and introduced by Fuchsiavale Nurseries of Kidderminster in 1983. Mitchinson – British – 1983 – A.F.S. No. 1744.

Carlotta. Single. Pale pink tube ½in long, long, waxy sepals bright red, tipped green 1¼in long. Corolla cerise flushed pink and of good substance. Long bell-shaped flowers 1⅛in long with deep pink stamens and very long pistil 2in. Small mid-green foliage with serrated leaves. Growth medium upright and bushy, originates from the vicinity of Cheshire. Awarded the Bronze Certificate of Merit at B.F.S. Northern Show, 1979. Display × Gay Fandango. Howarth – British – 1980 – A.F.S. No. 1577.

***Carl Wallace.** Double. Tube and sepals rosy-red, corolla violet-purple. Medium sized blooms, very full and rosette shaped, free flowering. Growth upright and vigorous, will make good bush or shrub and standard. Named after a well known London successful exhibitor. Raised and tested in the vicinity of Banstead in Surrey. Introduced by Homestead Nurseries of Uxbridge, Middlesex in 1984. Hobson – British – 1984.

Carmel. Single. Tube and sepals, pale pink; corolla vermilion. Small flowers. Growth trailer. Niederholzer – American – 1948.

Carmel Blue. Single. Long greenish-white narrow tube, outspread white sepals, flushed palest blush on underside, tipped pale green. Corolla beautiful blue and long. Medium sized blooms, very free. Growth upright and bushy. A.F.S. Cert. of Merit 196? Hodges – American – 1956 – A.F.S. No. 247.

Carmen. Semi-double. Tube and sepals cerise; corolla purple. Very small flowers and profuse. Growth upright and dwarf, suitable for rockery.

Accepted by the B.F.S. as showbench hardy. Myrtifolia ×. Lemoine – French – 1893.

Carmen. Single. Tube and recurving sepals, very bright pink, corolla beautiful campanula-blue, flaring, outer petals are mottled pink. Growth lax bush. Blackwell – British – 1966.

Carmencita. Semi-double. Tube and sepals, bright scarlet; corolla pure white, veined red. Medium sized flowers and free, growth upright and bushy. Raiser unknown – American – 1935.

Carmen Maria. Single. Pink tube, sepals long, narow, real pink, standing straight up. Corolla four overlapping petals of baby pink with deeper pink veins. Medium sized blooms, very heavy flowerer of perfect shape. Growth lax bush or trailer. A.F.S. Cert. of Merit 1973. Sport of Leonora. Breitner – American – 1970 – A.F.S. No. 907.

Carmen Queen. Single. Tube and sepals, dark red; corolla reddish-mauve. Growth upright bush. Hazard and Hazard – American – Date unknown.

Carmen Sylva. Lemoine – French – 1899.

Carminata. Bland. – British – 1877.

Carmine Queen. Single. Carmine and mauve. Berkeley Hort. Nursery – American – 1935.

Carnea. Single. Tube and sepals scarlet; corolla purple. Small flowers and small foliage, free bloomer. Growth upright and dwarf. Petite. Accepted by the B.F.S. as showbench hardy. Smith – British – 1861.

Carnival. Double. Long white tube, glistening frosty-white sepals, outer sides tinted delicate pea-green. Corolla brilliant spiraea-red and very long. Large blooms, free and early. Growth lax bush or trailer. Tiret – American – 1956 – A.F.S. No. 250.

*Carol Ann. Single. Very short white tube, white sepals rather broad and held horizontally with slight pink flush. White corolla, medium sized flowers, perfect in shape, bell shaped with the slightest of pink tinge. Foliage is bright golden yellow and differs from Variegated White Joy by Dyos. Growth is upright, bushy and short jointed. Found by Charles Gardiner in the vicinity of Attleborough, Norfolk and tested for 3 years before release. Sport of White Joy. Gardiner – British – 1985.

Carol Elizabeth. Single. Short tube dusky pink, sepals dusky pink, tipped green, horizontal to fully reflexed over tube. Corolla royal purple, fades slightly with age, lavender-mauve tinge at base, bell shaped. Very small flowers, growth tall upright and vigorous, up to 6 to 8 ft in California. Much better as second year plant. Shaw – American – 1972 – A.F.S. No. 1035.

Carole Pugh. Double. Long thin tube, orient-pink, sepals orchid-pink, frosted inside; corolla amethyst-violet, base of petals mallow-purple. Medium sized blooms with twelve petals and four petaloids, very free for double, best colour in shade. Growth self-branching, natural trailer, willowy type of cultivar. Pugh – British – 1975 – A.F.S. No. 1235.

Caroline. Single. Tube and sepals cream, flushed pink; corolla campanula-violet, maturing to pale cyclamen-purple, pale pink at base. Flowers large and free, shows the parentage of Citation. Growth upright. Probably Viv Miller's best

introduction, perfect in every way. Citation ×. Miller, V.V. – British – 1967.

Carol Peat. Single. Tube and sepals neyron-rose, tipped green; corolla pink. Small flowers but very profuse, growth upright and bushy, very strong and vigorous. This cultivar was first introduced as June Bagley in the Birmingham Show Seedling Class 1976. Eleanor Leytham × Pink Darling. Roe – British – 1976.

Carol Roe. Single. Short thick tube creamy-white, sepals light pink topside, pale rose-pink underside, tipped green and held almost horizontal. Corolla rosy-pink, pale pink pistil with creamy-white stigma. medium-sized flower of good substance showing colouring of both parents. Light-green foliage, growth upright and bushy with a constant supply of buds, very attractive. First appeared at Birmingham and Nottingham 1976 Shows. Eleanor Leytham × Pink Darling. Roe – British – 1976.

Carousel. Double. Tube and sepals crimson; corolla white, medium sized flowers and free. Growth upright and bushy. Evans – American – 1954

Carpeaux. Lemoine – French – 1876.

Cartmel. Single. White tube flushed pink, narrow, white, flushed pink, narrow, white, flushed pink sepals which fold back to cover tube. Corolla spectrum-violet (R.H.S. 82B). Smallish to medium sized flowers with pink stamens (R.H.S. 185D). Growth medium upright, will make good bush and any tall type of training, will take full sun near Preston but best colour in shade. Tested for 4 years in vicinity of Preston before release, named after beauty spot in Lake District of Cumbria. Hawkshead × Dorothea Flower. Thornley – British – 1981 – A.F.S. No. 1636.

Cascade. Single. Tube and long slender sepals white, heavily flushed with carmine; corolla deep carmine. Blooms medium in size but extremely floriferous. Growth very pendulous and cascading, excellent for basket work and exhibiting. One fault is the exclusion of blooms on top growth, but profuse on the trails. Sister seedling of Claret Cup and Halloween. Rolla × Amy Lye. Lagen – American – 1937.

Cascade

Cassandra. Single. Tube and sepals, turkey-red; corolla rich purple. Large blooms and free. Growth upright bush. Niederholzer – American – 1946.

Cassandra. Single. Pink tube, sepals pale pink, tipped green, deeper pink underneath. Corolla pale mauvish-pink. Flowers medium sized and free, described as a pink Ting-A-Ling. Hangs on to its seed pods, not an easy cultivar, but pleasing and enchanting. Growth upright. Senior – British – 1970.

Castelar. Lemoine – French – 1880.

Castle Beauty. Double. Red and white, Castle Nurseries – British – 1927.

Catalina. Double. Tube and sepals, rich crimson; corolla snowy-white. Extremely large blooms but not very free, dark green foliage. Growth tall, upright and vigorous. Identical to White Wonder and Mt. Hood. Sport of Gypsy Queen. Evans and Reeves – American – 1937.

Catherine Anne. Double. Pale pink self. Large flowers especially for a double, delightful pink and unusual. Tested for 3 years in the Merseyside area before release. Growth lax upright. The raiser introduced only five cultivars all of them exceptionally fine and outstanding for their pastel colouring. Introduced by R. Winkley in 1972. Senior – British – 1972.

*Catherine Bartlett. Single. Short tube white flushed very pale rose, sepals white flushed very pale rose, held well at the horizontal with recurved tips. Corolla beautiful shade of rose with very little veining but lighter shade at base of petals. Smallish flowers 1⅞ in by 1¾ in wide, corolla ½ in long by ⅝ in wide, very dainty, very similar colouring to Lye's Loveliness, very floriferous. Light green foliage with ovate leaves 1¾ in long by 1⅛ in wide and obtuse tips with serrate edging. Growth upright, bushy and compact, short-jointed, strong grower. Raised in the vicinity of Nottingham and introduced by Jackson's Nurseries of Tamworth in 1983. Named after the daughter of the current editor of the British Fuchsia Society. Carol Peat × Alison Ewart. Roe – British – 1983.

Catherine Claire. Double. Tube and sepals carmine; corolla rose-madder. Large blooms and fairly free for double, growth upright and bushy, excellent cultivar for training as a standard. Clyne – British – 1974.

Catherine Parr. Single. White and rose-scarlet. Banks – British – 1848.

Cathie MacDougall. Double. Tube and upswept sepals cerise; corolla violet-blue, marbled and striped various shades of blue and pink. Medium sized blooms, heavy bloomer. Growth trailer and cascade. Best grown as H1. Named to commemorate the visit of Mrs. Mark MacDougall to the 1959 B.F.S. in London. Thorne – British – 1960 – A.F.S. No. 454.

Cathy Miller. Double. Tube and sepals, bright red; corolla soft purple or orchid. Medium sized blooms and very free for double, growth upright and bushy. Miller – British – 1953.

Cavalier. Single. Tube and long twisted sepals, pale carmine-pink; corolla long bell shaped, petunia-purple, shading to rhodamine at base. Large blooms and free, early flowering. Growth trailer, cascading. Schnabel – American – 1953 – A.F.S. No. 188.

Cecile. Double. Thick light pink tube, deep rose-pink sepals curl back covering tube and ovary, tipped light green. Corolla lavender-blue, pink at base. Medium sized blooms one inch long by two inches wide, tightly ruffled and pleated. Cordate shaped foliage 1 in × 2½ in. Growth

natural trailer, without weights will make good basket, best colour in shade. Tested for 5 years in vicinity of Carlsbad, California before release where it will be trademarked. Whitfield – American – 1981 – A.F.S. No. 1609.

Cecil Glass. Single. Tube and sepals white, flushed pink; corolla magenta-pink. Early flowerer of medium size, free. Growth low bush. Not one of Lye's best introductions, but still in cultivation. Lye – British – 1887.

Celadore. Double. Candy-pink tube (R.H.S. 52C), horizontally held sepals luminous candy-pink (R.H.S. 52C) on upper surface and crepe textured candy-pink on inner surface, tipped eau-de-nil. Corolla luminous candy-pink (R.H.S. 55B). Medium sized blooms 1½ in long by 2½ in across, complete bloom is 4½ in across, stamens and pistil just protrude from corolla. Deep green (R.H.S. 146A) foliage, 2 in × 1½ in wide heart shaped leaves, central vein shaded pink for ¾ of length. Growth natural trailer without weights, vigorous beautiful new basket cultivar will make good weeping standard or pillar. Awarded Silver Certificate of Merit B.F.S. Northern Show 1979. Tested for 9 years in vicinity of Northumberland N.E. England before release. Introduced by R. and J. Pacey of Melton Mowbray in 1981. Pink Galore × Blush O'Dawn. Hall – British – 1981 – A.F.S. No. 1613.

Celebrity. Double. Rose and violet. Jones, W. – British – 1960.

Celebrity. Double. Tube and sepals red; corolla white. Very large flowers but not very free. Growth trailer, strong grower. Fuchsia-La – American – 1967 – A.F.S. No. 696.

Celestial. Double. Red and cream. Jones – British– 1960.

Celia Smedley. Single. George Roe's outstanding introduction to date; cultivar yet to be registered, raised and introduced at Nottingham in 1970, can be described as a breakthrough in colour combination. Celia Smedley is a single cultivar with neyron-rose tube and sepals, while the corolla is a vivid currant-red, flowers are somewhat larger than medium size, but freely produced, largish leaves of medium green. Parentage is Joy Patmore × Glitters; named after George Roe's daughter. As a hybridist, he believes in the motto 'a few but good' borne out with his other introductions Lady Thumb (1967) and Khada (1973). Growth is extremely vigorous and produces an excellent bush, suitable for exhibition; would like to see if this variety will respond to training as standard. Growth is so strong and robust, that it will produce a sizeable bush plant in its first year, can take a 6 in pot with current growth, if moved on quickly during the potting-on stages. Very easy to root, responds to frequent pinching, which is essential and necessary to counteract its only disadvantage, this cultivar does make very heavy wood, even during its first year and will not respond to cultivation, unless it is repotted in the early spring. With the excessive wood it creates, is a cultivar that will benefit being left lying on its side during its period of rest, to induce that desirable growth from the base. Celia Smedley inherits more of her blood from Joy Patmore than its other parent, for that reason is rather frost shy, best grown as H2. Makes a magnificent tub specimen for the patio, a third year plant with good cultivation can obtain a width and height of over 4 ft. Joy Patmore × Glitters. Roe – British – 1970.

Céline Mantaland. Lemoine – French – 1891.

Centinela. Semi-double. Tube and sepals rose; corolla magenta mauve. Small blooms but free. Growth trailer. Baake–American – 1940.

Centrepiece. Semi-double. Tube and sepals red; corolla starts opening with four pink petaloids surrounding lavender-blue petals, then petaloids flare out and centre keeps growing to a long corolla. Large blooms for a semi-double and free. Growth lax bush or trailer. Best as H1. Fuchsia Forest – American – 1964 – A.F.S. No. 604.

Century 21. Semi-double. Tube and sepals, coral-rose. Corolla two tone brilliant orchid. Large blooms. Growth trailer. Sport of Amapola. Keiffer – American – 1962 – A.F.S. No. 496

Cérès. Single. White and rose. Demay – French – 1872.

Ceri. Single. Tube and sepals white, corolla white faintly tinged with pink. Medium sized flowers very freely produced, early blooms, just another near white to add to the long list without being outstanding. Growth upright and bushy. Introduced by C.S. Lockyer at Chelsea Show 1980. Holmes, E. – British – 1980.

Cerrig. Single. Pale pink tube, clear rose-pink sepals held tight from corolla. Deep rose corolla slightly flared. Medium sized flowers with purple stamens and pistil, very pleasing colour contrast. Largish foliage, broad, leathery leaves with red mid-rib. Growth tall upright, will make good bush, standard or pillar. Raised in vicinity of Timperley, Manchester. Howarth – British – 1979 – A.F.S. No. 1529.

Cervantes. Lemoine – French – 1889.

cestroides. Dark red tube, sepals greenish-red; no corolla. Few flowers which are smallish, borne in short lateral racemes. Erect shrub attaining 10 ft and more in natural habitat. Schulze-Menz – 1940 – Peru.

C.F. Newman. Double. Short tube and reflexed sepals bright crimson, corolla bright purple flecked with rose. Large blooms. Growth upright. Probably one of the first Australian introductions raised and introduced by C.F. Newman & Sons of Houghton, South Australia. Newman – Australian – *ca* 1894.

Champion. Single. Cerise and dark cerise. Banks – British – 1868.

Champion of the World. Semi-double. Very old but reliable information states the tube and sepals as coral-red, tipped green with the corolla of pure purple expanding to nearly 2½ in in breadth; Sepals broad and well reflexed. Growth upright and bushy. Seldom seen at present time. At the time of introduction said to have carried the largest flowers of any cultivar. Received First Class Certificate at the R.H.S. Chiswick Trials in 1975. Bland – British – 1863 or 1871.

Chance Encounter. Single. Pink tube maturing to darker pink, ⅜ in to ½ in long. Sepals are white and oval, corolla white. Small flowers the total length of which are slightly longer than the tube and typical of an Encliandra crossing. Fine fernlike foliage, dark green with short internodes. Growth self-branching natural trailer will make good basket, very unusual cultivar. Encliandra cross,

originated from the area of Onard, California. Schneider – American – 1980 – A.F.S. No. 1589.

Chandelier. Single. Long tube and long slender sepals, white with faint pink blush. Corolla lilac-purple. Medium sized flowers, very free. Growth upright. Jones – British/Machado – American – 1961 – A.F.S. No. 501.

Chandlerii. See *magellanica* var. *globosa*.

Chandlerii. Single. Tube and sepals, creamy-white, corolla orange-scarlet. Medium to large flowers and free. Growth upright and bushy. Will make a good standard. One of the oldest of cultivars and still in cultivation. Globosa × . Chandler – British – 1839.

Chang. Single. Tube orange-red, sepals orange-red, tipped green, paler underneath; corolla brilliant orange. Flowers are small but profuse. Growth upright bush and vigorous, must be stopped frequently in early stages, can be a disappointing cultivar, susceptible to botrytis if overwatered. Flowers better out of doors. *F.cordifolia* hybrid. Hazard and Hazard – America – 1946.

Chantilly. Double. Reddish tube and white sepals; corolla white with many short petaloids, touched with pink, giving the blooms an overall lacy appearance. Growth upright, needs early pinching. Kennett – American – 1962 – A.F.S. No. 538.

Charlemagne. Banks – British – 1885.

Charles Abraham. Single. Tube and sepals red; corolla purple. Medium sized blooms and free. Growth upright bush. Niederholzer – American – 1944.

Charles Blanc. Lemoine – French – 1882..

Charles Darwin. Single. Carmine and ochre-yellow. Dominyana × *F.serratifolia*. Lemoine – French – 1878.

Charles Drew. Single or semi-double. Tube and sepals scarlet; corolla purple, veined scarlet. Growth upright and bushy. Hardy in Southern England. Money – British – 1963.

Charles Garnier. Double. Red and purple. Lemoine – French – 1899.

Charles Hooton. Single. Pink and red. Brown – British – 1847.

Charles Klein. Triphylla single. Long tube, slightly funnel shaped, cinnabar-red; petals crimson. Dark green foliage, flushed red. Growth upright. *F. triphylla* × . Klein – German – Date unknown.

Charles Samoureux. Lemoine – French – 1899.

Charles XII. Lemoine – French – 1862.

Charlie Gardiner. Single. Short salmon-pink tube, long and rather thin sepals are salmon-pink which reflex 45° above horizontal. Corolla rose-apricot and large for an orange. Medium to largish flowers, spreading bell shaped and extremely free, stamens are rose-apricot, will take full sun, best colour develops in sun. Medium green foliage with smooth leaves and entire edges. Growth is self-branching upright which can also be lax, makes good bush plant and may require weights for basketwork. Tested for 3 years in the vicinity of Ipswich, Suffolk before release. Named after a well known and prominent showman and exhibitor. Introduced by Baker's Nurseries of Halstead,

Essex, in 1982. Goulding – British – 1982 – A.F.S. No. 1672.

Charlie Girl. Double. Short pink tube, rose-pink sepals open right out covering tube; corolla lilac-blue, paler at base, veined rose. Medium sized blooms, free flowering, opening out well to form perfect shape. Growth upright bush, strong grower. Tanfield – British – 1970 – A.F.S. No. 1277.

Charlie S. Field. Double. Light pink tube ¼ in wide × ½ in long, sepals rose-Bengal (H.C.C. 25/2), tipped green ¾ in wide × 1⅛ in long. White corolla with pink variegations 2 in wide × 1⅛ in long. Largish blooms with eight petaloids rose-Bengal and ⅛ in shorter than petals, pink pistil 2½ in long with white stigma. Dark green foliage 1¾ in wide by ¾ in long leaves. Growth natural trailer, originates from the Sebastopol area of California. Introduced by Soo Yun Fuchsia Gardens in 1980. Palko – American – 1980 – A.F.S. No. 1564.

Charlotte. Single. Rose-pink tube, rose-pink sepals which arch from base of tube, broad with blunted points. Corolla rose-pink curled and ruffled, medium sized flowers and early, buds are square box-shaped, short rose-pink stamens. Foliage light green with well serrated leaves and dark red stems. Growth medium upright, bushy, short jointed, will make good bush or standard. Hanley – British – 1976 – A.F.S. No. 1366.

Charlotte Taylor. Double. Pink tube, broad slightly recurved sepals white with small blotch of crimson at point of separation. Corolla opens wedgewood-blue aging to rose-magenta with lilac on maturity. Medium sized blooms, four centre petals surrounded by many fluted petals which stand away from the centre. Light green foliage, growth medium upright, will make fine bush plant, heat tolerant if shaded. Tested for 5 years in the vicinity of Colchester, Essex before release. Hill – British – 1981 – A.F.S. No. 1628.

Charm. Single. Tube and sepals carmine, corolla rose-purple. Growth upright and bushy, hardy. Appears to be exclusive to the Midlands of England. Listed and introduced by J.A. Wright of Hilltop Nurseries, Atherstone. Raiser unknown – British – ca 1970s.

Charming. Single. Tube carmine, sepals reddish-cerise, well reflexed, corolla rosy-purple, cerise at base. Foliage slightly yellowish, very light at tips of leaf. Medium sized flowers, very free. Growth upright and bushy. One of Lye's best introductions with its classic bloom, easy to cultivate, should be in the beginners 'top ten'. Accepted by the B.F.S. as showbench hardy.

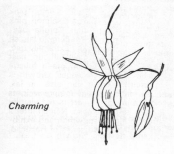

Charming

R.H.S. Award of Merit 1929. Arabella Improved × James Lye. Lye – British – 1895.

Charming – Achievement. To distinguish between these two similar cultivars see Achievement.

Charming – Drame. These two cultivars are often confused with each other, mainly on account of the similar foliage, which in both instances is yellowish-green, although with age the foliage of Drame does turn to green, whereas the foliage of Charming remains almost the same. There should be little cause for confusion with the flower, as Charming raised by James Lye in 1895, is a single and Drame raised by Lemoine in France in 1880 is a semi-double, although it can produce single flowers according to treatment and situation.

Charming's flower is almost a classic bloom, whereas Drame's is fuller and shorter, the tube of Charming is much longer than Drame. The colouring of both cultivars is very similar and could be lumped up very conveniently as red and purple, however, Charming is more carmine and purple ageing to reddish-purple than Drame which is scarlet and reddish-purple with a scarlet base. The sepals of Drame are not reflexed as much as Charming and the pistil of Drame is much longer and darker in colour. Drame's blooms will drop much earlier and easier than Charming, especially if grown under glass. The real marked difference between the cultivars is the habit of growth, for whilst Charming can be described truly as upright and bushy, Drame, although of similar growth, is easily distinguished by the low spreading habit and Drame is much hardier than Charming, which can be understood by the fact that it is a seedling from *F.m.*var. *riccartonii*, whereas Charming's parents are Arabella Improved × James Lye. Both cultivars are accepted by the B.F.S. as hardies on the showbench, Charming was awarded an Award of Merit by the R.H.S. in 1929, and is probably Lye's best introduction.

Chartwell. Single. White tube, long recurved sepals held well out from corolla are rhodamine-pink (R.H.S. 62A) with green tip. Corolla wistaria-blue (R.H.S. 92A) on a lighter base. Medium-sized flowers and very free, will take full sun. Growth upright and bushy of medium size, prefers warmth for best results, very good bedder, could be proved to be hardy, tested for 3 years in the Midlands before release. Christine Clement × Cloverdale Pearl. Gadsby – British – 1977 – A.F.S. No. 1424.

Chastity. Bland – British – 1881.

Chateau Briand. Semi-double. Rose and scarlet. Lemoine – French – 1847..

Chatsworth. Single. Crimson tube, waxy sepals neyron-rose on underside, crimson on top; corolla magenta-rose. Large open bell shaped flowers, free, prefers shade for best colour. Growth upright and bushy, self-branching. Magenta Flush × Derby Belle. Gadsby – British – 1975 – A.F.S. No. 1280.

Che Bella. Single. Tube pink, sepals pink outside currant-red inside which stand out horizontally from the tube. Corolla currant-red, large flowers and very free. Growth upright and extremely vigorous very suitable for tall training. Introduced by Woodbridge Nurseries of Hounslow in 1980. Hobson × Celia Smedley. Dyos – British – 1980.

Checkerboard. Single. Long tube red, sepals slightly recurved, start red and change abruptly to white. Corolla red but deeper than tube, white at base. Flowers are long and of medium size, blooms drop very quickly but hardly noticed with the great profusion; flowers very early and always in bloom. Growth upright and vigorous, easily in the show class category. Makes a good conical, pyramid or stiff standard. Excellent cultivar in every way. Walker and Jones – American – 1948.

Checkers. Single. Tube red, sepals white, creped and reflexed; corolla cupped, magenta around edge of petals, shading to white at base. Small blooms but free. Growth lax bush, will trail. Sport of Checkerboard. Eastwood – American – 1971 – A.F.S. No. 988.

Checkmate. Single. Short pale striped pink tube, short pale magenta-pink sepals slightly upturned. Corolla Indian-magenta. Medium sized flowers, semi-flared with Indian-magenta stamens and pistil, extremely floriferous producing many falling laterals from a single upright stem. Very different from its parent. Medium to dark green foliage, ovate with obtuse leaf tip, lobed leaf base and slightly serrate leaf margins. Growth self-branching lax upright, will make fine weeping standard. Originated from the vicinity of Birmingham and introduced after Tolley's death. Introduced by J.E. Ridding of Fuchsiavale Nurseries, Kidderminster, in 1980. Sport of Checkerboard. Tolley – British – 1980 – A.F.S. No. 1540.

Cheerful. Single. Tube and sepals pink; corolla bright blue. Medium sized blooms and free. Growth upright bush. Niederholzer – American – Date unknown.

Cheerie. Single. Tube and sepals cerise; corolla white. Small flowers and very free, growth upright and bushy, dwarf habit. H.A. Brown – British – 1939.

Cheerio. Double. Tube and sepals white, tipped green; corolla deep pink with touch of lavender. Small flowers. Growth lax bush. Kennett – American – 1967 – A.F.S. No. 739.

Cheers. Double. Light coral-pink tube, sepals broad and sharply pointed, streaked pale pink along centre, coral-pink (R.H.S. 48D) outside, R.H.S. 43D underside. Orange-red (R.H.S. 44B) corolla mixed with R.H.S. 40D. Medium sized blooms with proportionately short corolla but very full with over forty petals. Dark green foliage with rather coarsely serrated leaves. Growth lax upright, will trail with weights, vigorous grower. Trademarked in California, introduced into England by D.N. Pickard of Huntingdon in 1979. Stubbs – American – 1979 – A.F.S. No. 1499.

Cheffita. Double. Tube deep pink, broad outspread sepals deep pink; corolla opens purplish, then turns to rosy hue with smoky overcast towards petal edges. Large blooms and prolific. Similar to a larger Cherokee. Growth lax bush or trailer. Hodges – American – 1959 – A.F.S. No. 337.

Cherie. Double. Tube and sepals cherry-red; corolla white. Medium-sized blooms, growth lax bush. Not to be confused with Cherie raised by Hodges in 1952. Lampard – British – 1970.

Cherie. Single. Tube and long upturned sepals, rosy-red; corolla bluish-purple, near white at base, petals roll in at edges, prominently veined. Free bloomer of medium size. Growth medium

upright. Hodges – American – 1952 – A.F.S. No. 124.

Cherokee. Double. Tube and upturned sepals, deep pink; corolla opens purplish turns to rosy hue with smoky overcast towards petal edges, large centre petals and smaller outer petals, many pleated. Large flowers of unusual shape and very free. Dark green foliage. Growth lax bush or trailer, can be trained as espalier. Hodges – American – 1955 – A.F.S. No. 242.

Cherry. Semi-double. Tube and sepal, deep rose; corolla pale pink. Medium size blooms and free. Growth upright. Reiter – American – 1942.

Cherry Jubilee. Double. Tube and sepals, cherry red; corolla burgundy. Large blooms, dark green foliage. Growth upright. Stubbs – American – 1970 – A.F.S. No. 908.

Cherry Pie. Single. Tube and sepals cherry red, corolla mauve fading to pink. Small flowers borne in great profusion. Dark green foliage, growth upright, makes lovely rounded bush, height is only 6 in to 9 in, miniature and suitable for troughs, rockeries and window boxes. One of a whole series of new hardy miniatures raised in Scilly Isles. Tabraham – British – 1982.

Cherry Ripe. Single. Tube and sepals, cherry red; corolla dark cherry. Medium sized blooms and free. Growth upright and bushy. Travis, J. – British – 1951.

Chessboard. Single. Pink tube, long sepals starting with pink colouring, middle section white, tipped green. Corolla magenta, edged crimson. Medium to large flowers, extremely free and very similar to Checkerboard but larger. This cultivar is much superior to Checkerboard with no loss of vigour in the plant, growth upright, strong and vigorous. Colville – British – 1975.

Cheviot Princess. Single. This cultivar is a recent introduction from the prolific hybridiser Dr. Matthew Ryle, the moment you see this cultivar you are impressed with the beautiful luminous flowers making the whole plant become alive. Short white tube with slight bulge, sepals are long also white in colour, recurved and held well out at the horizontal. Corolla is ruby red (R.H.S. 61A) in the early stage maturing to spiraea-red, flowers are single, very free flowering which hang in trusses with a delightful pretty colour change, rose-pink stamens and white style, bell-shaped corolla. Very good foliage and excellent habit of growth which is self-branching and bushy, tall upright. Tested for 3 years in the North East of England before being entered in the Seedling Class at Manchester 1977 where it received a Silver Certificate of Merit; with its extremely luminous characteristic could have been named better; the Athela parentage is quite pronounced. The parentage is rather complicated firstly with a Pink Cloud × Lena Dalton cross followed by a seedling from the latter cross and then crossed with Athela. Dr. Ryle has now raised some 50 introductions and this cultivar is definitely here to stay for some considerable time. Pink Cloud × Lena Dalton seedling × Athela. Ryle – British – 1977 – A.F.S. No. 1433.

chiapensis. Synonymous with *F. michoacanensis.* Brandg – 1914.

Chic. Single. Tube and sepals, light pink to coral; corolla burgundy-red; long and stays closed for a long time. Large flowers. Growth lax bush or trailer. Fuchsia Forest – American – 1964 – A.F.S. No. 605.

Chicago. Double. Carmine and white. Henderson – British – 1873.

Chi-Chi. Double. Little information known about this American introduction except it is a pink self, raised by Walker and introduced by Tony Araujo, with upright growth. Walker – American – 1973.

Chickadee. Single. Tube and sepals creamy-white, tipped green; corolla lavender-pink. Medium sized flowers and like most pastels needs shade for good colouring. Growth upright, little known about this unregistered American introduction. Raiser and date unknown – American – ca 1960.

Chief. Double. Tube and sepals, dark red; corolla dark purple, streaked red. Large blooms and free. Growth upright bush. Evans and Reeves – American – 1943.

Chief Seattle. Double. Short, thick tube, pink to cream, sepals creamy-white or very pale pink fading to white at tips, crepe-like texture spread out at first and then turn straight up. Corolla carmine-rose edged with touch of violet. Large blooms, fairly free for size, four centre petals drop below the rest of corolla which is made up of double layer of petals in a billowy skirt style, petaloids flare out under the sepals. Foliage smaller than normal with red stems. Growth semi-trailer, self-branching, good for basket or standard. Registered by Westover Greenhouse Nurseries. Sutherland – American – 1976 – A.F.S. No. 1395.

Childwall. Single. Longish tube and broad sepals, creamy-wax, flushed pink. Corolla rose with deeper edging. Large blooms and floriferous. Growth upright. Need – British – 1964.

Chillerton Beauty. Single. Tube and sepals, pale rose-pink, tipped green; corolla mauvish-violet slightly veined pink. Small flowers but very free, growth upright and bushy. Suitable cultivar for a medium sized hedge with a height of 3 ft. Often confused with Query and General Tom Thumb. Named after Chillerton, Isle of Wight. Re-submitted by Jackman's Nurseries Ltd. of Woking for the R.H.S. Wisley Hardy Trials 1975–78 who upgraded their H.C.C. in 1962 to an Award of Merit. Accepted by the B.F.S. as showbench hardy. Bass – British – 1847.

Chillingham Countess. Single. Long thin tube rhodamine-pink, sepals phlox-pink, long and carried just above the horizontal, curved slightly upwards. Corolla violet-blue, shading to pink near base of petals, fading to purple-violet. Long flowers, very compact with anthers carried well clear of corolla, long white stigma, large and free flowering. Growth medium upright bush, good for bush or standard. Lye's Unique × Citation seedling × Whirlaway seedling × Royal Velvet. Ryle – British – 1975 – A.F.S. No. 1241.

Chimes. Single. Red tube, sepals flushed rose; corolla white at base, darkening to dianthus-purple at margins. Largish blooms do not fade with age. Large light green foliage. Growth trailer, can be trained to scandent growth. Kennett and Ross – American – 1955 – A.F.S. No. 241.

China Doll. Double. Tube and sepals, cerise red; corolla white faintly veined red. Growth trailer. Walker and Jones – American – 1950.

China Lantern. Single. Tube deep pink and shiny, sepals white, tipped green. Corolla rosy-pink, white at base. Medium sized flowers and free, dark green foliage. Growth upright but lax. Submitted by Mrs. M. Slater in the R.H.S. Wisley Hardy Trials 1975–78 but received no award. Raiser unknown – American – 1953?

Chinois. Salter – British and French – 1840.

Chiquita. Double. Tube and sepal, rosy-pink; corolla pale rosy-orchid. Medium size blooms and very free. Small crinkly grass-green foliage. Growth trailer and cascading, unusual feature is the non production of berries. Reiter – American – 1955 – A.F.S. No. 232.

chloroloba (Johnston 1939). Synonymous with *F. tuberosa.*

Choir Girl. Double. Tube and sepals red; corolla white, veined red at base. Medium-sized blooms with red stamens and style. Foliage lightish green. Growth upright and bushy. Cultivar grown and cultivated in the Netherlands. Raiser and date unknown.

Christian IX. Lemoine – French – 1863.

Christine Clements. Single. Tube and sepals, China-pink; corolla wisteria-blue maturing to gentian-blue. Medium sized flowers very free and held well out from plant, long tapering buds. Growth medium bush with spreading habit. Gadsby – British – 1974.

Christine Gatske. Double. Tube and sepals, pale pink, corolla deep blue splashed with pale pink, changing to rosy-lavender. Large blooms and very profuse, light green foliage turns darker. Growth trailer. Prentice – American – 1967 – A.F.S. No. 721.

Christine Pugh. Double. Tube phlox-pink; sepals rhodamine-pink, tipped pale green, frosted inside and recurving. Corolla phlox-purple. Largish blooms and free, twelve petals with four petaloids, appear to glow when in full bloom. Growth medium upright bush, good for all tall types of training. Pugh – British – 1975 – A.F.S. No. 1236.

Christmas Cheer. Single. Tube and sepals white; corolla bluish-purple. Growth upright, little known about this unregistered American introduction, appears to be exclusive to California. Raiser and date unknown – American – ca 1960.

Christmas Elf. Single. Tube and sepals, bright red, sepals fully reflexed encircling the ovary. Corolla near white, red veined. Small dark foliage, small flowers, very profuse, sterile and self-cleaning. Growth upright, compact and dwarf, eminently suitable for training as bonsai or miniature decorative Hardy. Jingle Bells ×. Gentry – American – A.F.S. No. 1027.

Christmas Gem. Triphylla single. Very long tube, reddish-vermilion, petals orange-red, very free but late. Reddish-bronze foliage, flushed red underneath, red stems. Growth upright best grown as H1. *F. triphylla × F. serratifolia.* Rottengen – German. Date unknown.

Christmas Holly. Double. Thin red tube, thin bright red sepals open straight but turn up at maturity. Corolla deep purple, streaked crimson. Small blooms have uneven deep purple petaloids. Foliage is holly-like with deeply serrated edges, hence the name. Growth is upright and bushy about 2 ft high. Suitable for bush, shrub or small standard. Tested for 3 years in California before release. Stubbs – American – 1977 – A.F.S. No. 1411.

Christmas Ribbons. Double. Tube rhodonite-red, short sepals rodonite-red which curl to tube. Corolla campanula-violet with rhodonite-red veins. Flowers are small and compact, but free. Growth upright and bushy, heat resistant. Foster – American – 1974 – A.F.S. No. 1170.

Christophe Colomb. Double. Red and carmine. Lemoine – French – 1893.

Christopher Hammett. Double. Scarlet tube, long, reflexed sepals scarlet; corolla scarlet turning to purple. Very free bloomer of medium size. Dark green foliage, disease and pest resistant. Growth upright, suitable for bush or standard. Tennessee Waltz × Heron. Hammett – British – 1966 – A.F.S. No. 1025.

Christy. Double. Tube clear pink, short upturned sepals clear pink. Corolla has a skirt of salmon-pink, mottled with white, four large creamy-white petals protrude from the centre. Foliage dark green on reddish stems. Growth upright bush, self branching. Antonelli – American – 1963 – A.F.S. No. 559.

Chrysanthea. Double. Tube and sepals red; corolla purple. Very large blooms but extremely loose. Growth trailer, basket type. Niederholzer – American – 1945.

*Churchtown. Semi-double. Tube and sepals rhodamine-pink. Corolla roseine-purple edged deep fuchsia-purple. Medium sized blooms, very beautiful and free flowering. Very easy to grow, shapes well with showbench potential. Growth upright and bushy. Raised in the vicinity of Southport and tested for 3 years before release. Introduced by the raiser, J.V. Porter of Southport in 1984. Porter – British – 1984.

Cicely Ann. Single. Long thin crimson tube (R.H.S. 52A) upswept sepals crimson (R.H.S. 52A) on outside with yellow-green tip and crimson inside. Corolla mallow-purple (R.H.S. 42A) crimson at base, veined crimson with extremely fine crimson edging. Medium-sized flowers with neat semi-flared bell shape, crimson stamens, white anthers, long pale crimson pistil and white stigma, will take full sun. Growth natural trailer, self-branching, tested for 6 years in Kent before release. Registered in 1977. Holmes, R. – British – 1975 – A.F.S. No. 1418.

Cigarette. Single. Tube and sepals, rose-pink, corolla pink, long and edged with greyish-blue. Small flowers and very free, growth small low bush. Nelson – American – Date unknown.

Cigarette. The fuchsia grown in South Africa under the name of Cigarette is synonymous with Andenken an Heinrich Henkel and is not the Cigarette by Nelson of America.

Cinderella (Waltz). Synonymous with Silverado.

Cinderella. Single. Tube and sepals red; corolla white. Small flowers and bronzy foliage. Growth upright. Very similar to Alice Hoffman. Hazard and Hazard – American – 1954.

Cindy. Single. Tube and sepals rosy-carmine; corolla rosy-magenta. Medium sized flowers early and free. Growth upright and bushy. Longleat Gardens – British – 1966.

Cinnabarina (Reflexta). Single. Small bushy plant with orange-scarlet flowers, reflexed sepals. The shape of Harebells. Suitable for rockery, also known as Reflexta and Reflextus. Breviflorae hybrid. Raiser unknown – 1829?

*Cinnamon. Double. Orange tube $\frac{7}{16}$ in by $\frac{3}{4}$ in wide. Sepals orange held horizontally with recurved tips 1$\frac{1}{2}$ in long by $\frac{5}{8}$ in wide. Corolla reddish-orange with orange streaks, half flared 1 in long by 2 in wide. Medium-sized blooms with numerous petaloids, reddish-orange stamens held inside corolla. Medium green foliage with cordate leaves and acute tipped, 2$\frac{3}{4}$ in long × 1$\frac{3}{4}$ in wide. Growth natural trailer, will make excellent basket or weeping standard, prefers being grown cool. Raised and tested for 3 years in the vicinity of Pacifica, California. Storvick – American – 1983 – A.F.S. No. 1740.

Circe. Semi-double. Tube and sepals, pale pink; corolla of four, light blue petals that fade to pale lavender, pink petaloids surround the petals which spread open almost flat. Large flowers very profuse. Growth upright. Kennett–American – 1965 – A.F.S. No. 639.

Circus. Single. Tube and sepals, pinkish-coral; corolla has base of coral-pink, shading to bright magenta-orange. Medium and profuse bloomer. Growth upright, tall and fast. Fuchsia Forest – American – 1967 – A.F.S. No. 723.

Cissbury Ring. Single. White tube, sepals white with slight neyron-rose blush (R.H.S. 55C) held at the horizontal, with tips held downward. Sepals have distinctive green tip on upperside but with purple (R.H.S. 71B) tip on the lowerside. Corolla beetroot red-purple (R.H.S. 71B). Small to medium sized flowers almost square shape and very free flowering. Light green medium sized foliage. Growth is natural trailer, making excellent basket. Tested for 3 years in the vicinity of Worthing, South Coast of England before release. Hobbs, L. – British – 1982 – A.F.S. No. 1676.

Citation. Single. Tube light to rose-pink, sepals upturned of same colour; corolla white, veined light pink at base. Large flowers with four petals flaring wide to saucer-shape, wide open and very free, beautiful shaped blooms. Growth upright and bushy. One of the best introductions from America, and created a sensation when first introduced, well in the showcase cultivars, it is one, however, that either grows well or not at all, needs H1 for perfect results. Hodges – American – 1953 – A.F.S. No. 153.

City of Alameda. Double. Tube and reflexed sepals, deep rose; corolla pink, streaked with rose. Small flowers very profuse, small foliage. Growth low bush and compact, heat resistant. Olson – American – 1957 – A.F.S. No. 326.

City of Derby. Single. Crimson tube, waxy crimson sepals with spiky effect, held well up and curved over, long and narrow. Corolla campanula-violet on lighter base. Large open saucer-shaped flowers, very free. Growth upright and bushy. One of the last introductions by a great hybridist and named after his native City having for many years sat upon its Council. Cliff's Hardy seedling × Bishop's Bells. Gadsby – British – 1978 – A.F.S. No. 1480.

*City of Leicester. Single. Tube rose-Bengal, sepals rose-Bengal tipped green. Corolla pale violet-purple, heavily veined imperial-purple. Medium sized flowers and very free flowering.

Growth upright and bushy, well within the exhibition category, short jointed and very suitable for bush or shrub. Very impressive and outstanding cultivar. Raised in the vicinity of Melton Mowbray, Leicestershire and introduced by the raiser, Pacey's Nurseries, in 1984. Pacey – British – 1984.

City of Millbrae. Double. Tube rose, very wide sepals, bright rose with bright green tips. Corolla soft orchid-blue to bright rose at base of folded petals, opens to form a square bloom. Growth trailer. Martin – American – 1958 – A.F.S. No. 365.

City of Pacifica. Double. Tube and sepals white; corolla pale blue. Large blooms not very free. Growth upright. Reedstrom – American – 1962 – A.F.S. No. 546.

City of Portland. Double. Carmine tube, broad granular sepals carmine; corolla petunia-purple with light carmine marbling. Large blooms, free and early. Growth upright. Schnabel – American – 1950 – A.F.S. No. 51.

City of Richmond. Double. Tube and upturned sepals white, delicately flushed. Corolla pale pink. Medium size blooms, spreading corolla and very free, early flowerer. Growth upright bush. A.F.S. Cert. of Merit 196?. Schnabel – American – 1956 – A.F.S. No. 265.

C.J. Howlett. Single. Tube and sepals reddish-pink, tipped green; corolla bluish-carmine, pink at base. Early bloomer, smallish flowers freely produced, can come semi-double. Growth upright and bushy, good bedder. Submitted by Mrs. M. Slater for the R.H.S. Wisley Hardy Trials 1975–78 and received the Award of Merit. Howlett – British – 1911.

Clair de Lune. Single. Salmon and salmon-orange. This delightful cultivar has bronzy foliage and trailing growth, very seldom seen or grown but well worth searching the catalogues. Currently listed by Meadowcroft Nurseries and Don Stilwell. Rozaine-Boucharlat – French – 1880?

Clair de Lune – Coachman. These two cultivars with single flowers excel in the orange colour range, could easily be confused with each other and are also very similar to the American cultivar Shanley. Clair de Lune is French raised by Rozain-Boucharlat *ca* 1880 and considered to be the most beautiful with its long straight tube $1\frac{5}{8}$in long, whereas Coachman's tube is slightly tapered and much shorter $\frac{7}{8}$in long. The colouring of C. de L. is delicate apricot-salmon and salmon-orange, whereas Coachman is pale salmon and rich orange-vermilion. The length of the flowers from seed pod to end of stigma $2\frac{1}{2}$ in and $1\frac{3}{4}$ in respectively; both have long pedicels $1\frac{3}{4}$ in long. C. de L.'s petals are fluted with narrow sepals, Coachman's petals are not fluted with broader sepals held at the horizontal compared with C. de L. sepals although held horizontal are slightly upturned. The attractive cream anthers and stigma with pale pink filaments contrast somewhat with Coachman's pale mauve anthers, cream stigma and darker pinkish-red filaments.

Whilst the foliage of each cultivar is almost identical in size and shape 3 in × $2\frac{1}{4}$ in C. de L. is much darker, slightly bronzed on the underneath with many serrations, Coachman's leaves are lightish green and slightly serrated, with petiole 1 in long against the other cultivar's $1\frac{1}{2}$ in long.

The habit of growth is almost identical, lax bush which makes for suitability for the training as half baskets or baskets, but would need help and supports for training as bush, would imagine both would excel as a half weeping standard.

Claire Evans. Double. White tube, sepals white, tinted shell-pink on underside; corolla opens light blue, fades to rosy-mauve. Large flowers and free, early flowerer. Growth upright and bushy, compact. Evans and Reeves – American – 1951 – A.F.S. No. 102.

Clara. Double. White tube, white sepals tinted shell-pink on underside; corolla light violet-blue fades to rosy-mauve. Medium size blooms and very free. Growth upright. Brown-Soules – American – 1952.

Clara Beth. Double. Short white tube, sepals short and pointed, heavy white crepe with green tips. Corolla medium blue, fades to lavender shade as bloom loosens. Medium sized blooms. Growth trailer. Gagnon – American – 1965 – A.F.S. No. 621.

Clara G. Meservey. Single. Short tube, light green, sepals light pink with light green tips on top, white underneath splashed darker pink $1\frac{1}{2}$ in long and $\frac{5}{8}$in wide, light green at tube. Corolla purple shading to lighter purple at base, medium sized flowers, very compact with long petals $\frac{7}{8}$in long evenly overlapping each other, light purple stamens, light purple pistil with white stigma. Foliage light green with red stems, growth medium upright, self-branching will make good bush or standard. Registered by Soo Yun's Fuchsia Gardens. Palko – American – 1976 – A.F.S. No. 1350.

Clare Evans. Double. Tube and sepals white shading to shell pink. Corolla mauvish blue, medium to large blooms, flowers very early. Growth spreading bush, very easy, will produce good show plant. This cultivar prefers slight heat, better as H1. Evans – British – 1938.

Claret Cup. Single. Carmine and red. Smith, F. – British – 1896.

Claret Cup. Single. Tube and sepals, creamy-pink; corolla deep Tyrian-rose, large flowers and free. Growth cascading trailer. Sister seedling to Cascade and Halloween. Sometimes called Giant Cascade. Rolla × Amy Lye. Lagen – American – 1940.

Clarinda. Bland – British – 1880.

Clarion. Double. Tube and sepals crimson; corolla rose-Bengal. Large blooms, fairly free. Growth upright and vigorous. Reiter – American – 1949 – A.F.S. No. 27.

Clarisse. Single. White and rose. Bull – British – 1870.

Classic Jean. Double. Longish tube white, fluted with very slight tinge of pink, sepals are fairly broad, white with tinge of pink, tipped green, fully upturned held away from tube and corolla. Corolla white with delicate tinge of pink, almost a white self. Medium sized blooms, colour held without fading for a long period, unusual for a white, pink stamens, pistil lighter shade of pink. Light green foliage, growth is inclined to be lax but makes a good bush and should be suitable for basket. An outstanding cultivar and a most welcome addition to the 'whites'. Created great attention at the 1979 Midland Shows. Nancy Lou × Nancy Lou. Bambrick – British – 1977.

Classy. Double. Tube and reflexed sepals white; corolla red when first open, becomes bright red at maturity, white marbling. Dark green foliage with red veining. Very heavy bloomer, growth upright and bushy. Castro American – 1973 – A.F.S. No. 1102.

Claude de Lorraine. Double. Red and mauve. Lemoine – French – 1873.

Cleopatra. Double. Tube and sepals red; corolla blue, fades to lavender, very full. Very large blooms, very free. Growth lax bush or trailer. Martin – American – 1964 – A.F.S. No. 607.

Clevedon. Single. Pink tube, bright pink sepals which arch back gracefully. Corolla lilac with red veining. Large flowers much larger than parent. Large foliage, growth tall upright and bushy. Semi-hardy, originates from the vicinity of Warwickshire. Snowcap ×. Wright, J.A. – British – 1980 – A.F.S. No. 1598.

Clifford Gadsby. Double. Tube and sepals are pale spiraea, green tipped sepals, changing to deeper shade as flower reaches maturity. Corolla rose-Bengal, large blooms and free for size. Growth bushy and compact. This is the last of Gadsby's seedlings to bear his name and is appropriately named after himself. Introduced by R. and J. Pacey Nurseries in 1980. Gadsby – British – 1980.

Clifford Royle. Single. Long red tube, red sepals very substantial and curl back to tube. Corolla white, pink veined and is proportionately long. Medium sized flowers with red stamens and pink pistil, light pink stigma. Dark green foliage with slender leaves. Growth upright bushy and open. Raised in the vicinity of Manchester. Royle – British – 1979 – A.F.S. No. 1524.

Cliff's Hardy. Single. Tube and sepals, light crimson, tipped green; corolla campanula-violet, paler at base, veined scarlet. Medium size flowers, free, blooms held erect. Growth upright and bushy. Accepted by the B.F.S. as showbench hardy. Very hardy, height 2½ to 3 ft. Submitted by Wills Fuchsia Nurseries in the R.H.S. Wisley Hardy Trials 1975–78 and received the Award of Merit. Athela × Bon Accorde. Gadsby – British – 1966 – A.F.S. No. 983.

Cliff's Own. Single. White tube, waxy-white sepals, pale pink underside and tipped green. Corolla hyacinth-blue (R.H.S. 91A) passing to a delicate pale violet. Small to medium-sized pastel shaded flowers, very lovely, the free light blue flowers show off the light green foliage, heat tolerant in shade. Growth upright and bushy, best results in small pots, fine cultivar for 3½ in pot classes. Tested for 4 years before release, must be good for the raiser to consider it his own. Christine Clements × Cloverdale Pearl. Gadsby – British – 1977 – A.F.S. No. 1425.

Cliff's Unique. Double. Short, thick, light pink tube; broad and thick, waxy-white sepals flushed pink with green tip. Gentian-blue (R.H.S. 94D) corolla maturing to light violet-pink (R.H.S. 84B). Medium sized blooms, well formed, resembling camelia flower, early and prolific, best colour in shade. Another break-through for the raiser as this cultivar is understood to be the first known double to carry blooms erect, more pronounced when grown cool or in the open. Growth upright and bushy, tested for 4 years near Derby before release. Gadsby – British – 1976 – A.F.S. No. 1392.

Clifton Beauty. Double. Thick white tube, sepals creamy-pink; corolla rosy-purple with crimson pencilled edges, outer petals heavily streaked with salmon. Large blooms, early and prolific, very full with closely packed petals, retain shape with age, best colour in sun. Growth semi-trailer, suitable for tall pots, tubs and baskets. Handley – British – 1975 – A.F.S. No. 1272.

Clifton Belle. Double. Long and white tube, sepals white, tinged palest pink inside, long and reflexed to stem. Corolla brilliant magenta, petals of even length. Medium sized blooms and free. Growth upright and bushy. Handley – British – 1974 – A.F.S. No. 1191.

Clifton Charm. Single. Short waxy-cerise tube (R.H.S. 52B), bright cerise thick crepey sepals are reflexed to tube ½ in wide × 1½ in long. Corolla deep lilac (R.H.S. 78B) at edge, blending to rose-pink at base of petals. Medium sized flowers with 1 in bell shaped corolla, overlapping petals have deep red picotee edges and veining with long pistil and cerise stamens. Mid to dark green foliage 2½ in long × 1½ in lightly serrated, dark red short-jointed stems. Growth upright, will make good bush, standard or decorative. A new and welcome addition to the hardies, will take full sun where it develops best colours. Tested for 10 years in the vicinity of Derby, Central England, before release. Introduced by Jackson's Nurseries of Tamworth in 1981. Handley – British – 1981 – A.F.S. No. 1626.

Climax. Single. White and crimson. Gaines – British – 1846.

Clio. Semi-double. Red and purple. Harrison – British – 1846.

Clio. Triphylla single. Triphylla hybrid with no further details other than the raisers name and date of introduction, not to be confused with Harrison's cultivar of 1846. Bonstedt – German – 1906.

Clipper. Single. Tube and recurving sepals cerise; corolla rich claret. Early bloomer, medium size and very frree. Growth upright bush, very vigorous makes fine standard. R.H.S. H.C. 1929. Lye – British – 1897.

Cloche Bleu. Rozain-Boucharlat – French – 1934.

Close Call. Double. Tube and sepals red; corolla dark bluish-purple. Growth lax bush or trailer. Gorman – American – 1970 – A.F.S. No. 926.

Cloth of Gold. Single. Tube and sepals red; corolla purple. Small to medium sized flowers, very late, not very free. Cultivated for its delightful foliage, golden ageing to green flushed with bronze, rosy-red on reverse side. Growth bushy. Flowers can come semi-double. Sport of Souvenir de Chiswick. Stafford – British – 1863.

Clouds. Single. Tube and sepals deep pink; corolla lavender-blue. Medium sized flowers in great profusion, pale green foliage, growth upright and bushy, strong spreading habit, height 1½ to 2 ft, hardy in Southern England, raised in the Scilly Isles. Submitted by the raiser for R.H.S. Wisley Hardy Trials 1975–78 but received no award. Tabraham – British – 1974.

Cloverdale. Single. Short thin crimson tube, sepals crimson; corolla cornflower-blue fading to cyclamen-purple. Small flowers and very profuse. Growth upright, dwarf up to 12 in and bushy. Ideal as edging bedder, excellent cultivar for 3½ in pot showbench classes. Shoots freely produced from base of plant. Gadsby – British – 1972 – A.F.S. No. 1050.

Cloverdale Delight. Semi-double. Pink tube, soft pink sepals held well back to tube. Bell shaped corolla wistaria-blue (R.H.S. 92A) fading to violet. Medium-sized blooms, bell shaped, very neat and well displayed, best colour in shade. Growth upright and bushy of medium height easy to train and shape. The less known of the seven 'Cloverdale' introductions, but very beautiful. Tested for 6 years in Central England before release. Rosedale × Forward Look. Gadsby – British – 1975 – A.F.S. No. 1426.

Cloverdale Jewel. Semi-double. Tube and sepals held well back to tube, neyron-rose. Corolla wisteria-blue with rose veining, passing to violet-blue. Medium sized blooms, very floriferous, early flowerer, the few petaloids turning a single to semi-double. Growth upright and bushy. Cloverdale × Lady Isobel Barnett. Gadsby – British – 1974 – A.F.S. No. 1218.

Cloverdale Joy. Single. White tube, white sepals with tinge of pink, held well out. Corolla violet (R.H.S. 84A). Medium sized blooms, lovely colour combination and very attractive. Growth upright, strong compact bush, best colour in shade, introduced by J. Ridding in 1979 after the hybridiser's death. Cloverdale Pearl × Christine Clements. Gadsby – British – 1979 – A.F.S. No. 1518.

Cloverdale Pearl. Single. White tube, sepals rhodamine-pink, shading to white, tipped green, curving back towards tube. Corolla white of medium size and well formed, free bloomer. Growth self-branching bush. Unnamed seedling × Grace Darling. Gadsby – British – 1974 – A.F.S. No. 1219.

Cloverdale Pride. Single. Pale pink tube, sepals rose-Bengal (R.H.S. 61D) are upturned and curve back. Corolla cyclamen (R.H.S. 74B). Medium sized flowers, well formed, best colour in shade. Growth upright will make good bush. Introduced by J. Ridding in 1979 after the hybridizer's death. Seedling × Grace Darling. Gadsby – British – 1979 – A.F.S. No. 1519.

Cloverdale Star. Single. Pale pink tube, white sepals with underside flushed pink, sepals are long and held well up. Corolla wisteria-blue on lighter base. Smallish flowers with uniform shape, very prolific and early, very delightful cultivar in every way. Small foliage with wiry growth, growth small upright, bushy, excellent cultivar for 3½ in pot classes. Gadsby – British – 1976 – A.F.S. No. 1393.

Coachman. Single. Tube and sepals, pale salmon; corolla rich orange-vermilion. Medium sized blooms, very free and early, beautiful clear colouring, blooms in flushes. Growth lax bush and vigorous, excels as a half basket, excellent cultivar in every way. Bright – British – 1910?

Coachman – Clair de Lune. To distinguish between these two cultivars see Clair de Lune – Coachman.

coccinea. Tube and sepals red; violet and purple corolla. Flowers and foliage similar to *F. magellanica*, leaves slightly broader and narrow off to a more pointed apex, flowers are borne axillary and sepals are longer. Upright shrub, very hardy. Synonymous with *F. elegans, F. pendula* and *F.*

pubescens. Kew – 1789 – Brazil. (See also *magellanica* var. *globosa*.)

Cockatoo. Double. Tube and sepals, lovely deep-rosy-red; corolla clear white with bright red veins. Flaring corolla, free blooming with small foliage. Growth upright and bushy, heat resistant. Schnabel-Paskesen – American – 1958 – A.F.S. No. 328.

Cocky. Single. Tube and sepals, dark geranium-lake; corolla petunia-purple. Small blooms, very free. Growth upright and bushy. Niederholzer – American – 1946.

Coco. Double. Tube white, sepals white tinged with red on top, light brick-red underside, tipped light green. Corolla ruby-red with red variegation at base. Growth lax bush or trailer. Soo Yun – American – 1968 – A.F.S. No. 765.

Coconut Ice. Single. Tube and sepals white, sepals are well reflexed rose (R.H.S. 56B) outside and R.H.S. 56D inside. Corolla white with rose-pink veining (R.H.S. 55C). Medium sized flowers and long, an improvement upon Cloverdale Pearl with its very vigorous and upright growth. Possesses the best characteristics of both its parents, could be described as an upright Cloverdale Pearl, three leaves at each node. Received B.F.S. Bronze Certificate of Merit as a seedling B.F.S. Show, London, 1978. Introduced by Wills Nurseries in 1979, raised in the vicinity of Bungay, Suffolk. Ice Champagne × Cloverdale Pearl. Burns – British – 1979 – A.F.S. No. 1513.

Coed. Double. Long white tube, sepals broad and outspreading, purest white. Corolla smoky-rose with orange undertone, some petals are marbled white. Very attractive colour contrast. Growth lax bush or trailer best as H1, very weak. Cert. Of Merit 1966. Erickson – American – 1962 – A.F.S. No. 539.

*Col.** Semi-double. Sport from Snowcap with exactly the same red and white characteristics as its parent except for the variegated yellow foliage. Introduced by Laburnum Nurseries, Leicester, in 1983.

colensoi (Section IV Skinnera). Another New Zealand species, not so well known as *F. excorticata* or *F. procumbens*. A small branching and erect shrub, found from the Waikato area of New Zealand as far South as Stewart Island and is found growing up to an altitude of 1500 ft.

The tube has the usual New Zealand species peculiar restriction near the base, is green in colour, sepals greenish to reddish; the corolla is purple and in New Zealand flowers between October and February. The smallish flowers have the same unusual appearance of the other New Zealand species, the foliage is somewhat similar to *F. excorticata* with green on the upper sides, white beneath and smooth on both sides. This species is reasonably hardy in this country, but very rarely offered even by the fuchsia specialist nurserymen and to be found very occasionally in this country in Botanical Gardens. Hooker – 1867 – North Island New Zealand.

Coleridge. Lemoine – French – 1877.

Colibri. Single. Red and purple. *F.coccinea* × . Lemoine – French – 1898.

colimae. Tube greenish-white, white sepals; mauvish-white corolla. Tiny flowers borne solitary in the leaf axils. Very similar to *F. minimiflora* except for the colouring of the flowers. Member of the Breviflorae section (Encliandra). Upright shrub. Munz – 1943 – Mexico.

Colin Sir Campbell. Wheeler – British – 1858.

Colleen. Double. Tube and sepals, very light green, darker at tips. Corolla and orchid, growth medium bush. Soo Yun – American – 1970 – A.F.S. No. 911.

Collen Bawn. Single. Red and blue. Rollinson – British – 1862.

Collingwood. Double. Tube and sepals, pure white; corolla pale pink. Large blooms, growth upright bush. Niederholzer – American – 1945.

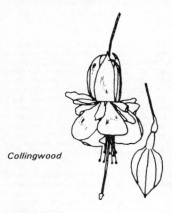

Collingwood

Colombine. Double. Tube and sepals, waxy-white; corolla flaring of rhodamine-purple. Medium size blooms early and free. Growth upright and bushy. One of the first batch of introductions to be registered with the A.F.S. under the No. 29. Raised by Victor Reiter Jr. Reiter – American – 1949.

Colonel Branlieres. Lemoine – French – 1908.

Colonel de Trentinian. Lemoine – French – 1899.

Colonel Dominé. Double. Rose and white. Lemoine – French – 1886.

Colonial Dame. Double. Tube pink, short outspread sepals, rose-pink, tipped green. Corolla light to medium pink. Large flowers, growth lax bush or trailer, willowy. Hodges – American – 1956 – A.F.S. No. 245.

Colossal. Double. Tube and sepals pink; corolla rich blue with streaks of pink extending downward from sepals. As name implies, blooms are extra large, but not very free. Growth trailer. Fuchsia La – American – 1968 – A.F.S. No. 800.

Colossus. Single. Red and purple. Standish – British – 1841.

Colossus. Double. Red and purple. Formosa Elegans × F. corymbiflora. Smith – British – 1862.

Colossus. Bland – British – 1880.

Columbia. Single. Tube and sepals, white flushed pink; corolla deep rich crimson. Identical to America except tube and outside sepals are white. Growth trailer. Sport of America. Raiser unknown – American – Date unknown.

Coma. Bull – British – 1873.

Come Dancing. Double. Short tube deep pink, sepals long and broad, deep pink, tipped yellow-green. Corolla magenta-rose, salmon rose at base, large flowers, well shaped buds. Bright green foliage, rounded and crinkled. Growth semi-trailer, makes good basket or standard. Handley – British – 1972 – A.F.S. No. 1052.

Comet. Single. Red and violet-blue. Banks – British – 1862.

Comet. Double. Tube and sepals red; corolla purplish-blue. Growth upright, unusual colouring. Tiret – American – 1963 – A.F.S. No. 575.

Commandant Marchand. Lemoine – French – 1899.

Commandant Taillant. Double. Red and white. Lemoine – French – 1874.

Commander Burnham. Single. Short crimson tube, sepals pointed and flaring, crimson. Corolla magenta, shading to lighter shade of magenta toward the base of petals, each petal has distinctive narrow border of darker magenta. Medium sized blooms,very free. Growth lax bush or trailer, heat resistant. Olson – American – 1956 – A.F.S. No. 249.

Commander-in-Chief. Double. Tube and sepals carmine; corolla purple. Huge blooms not very free, similar to Reiter's Giant but larger and more evenly pale coloured. Growth arching and scandent. Sister seedling of Reiters Giant. Reiter – American – 1942.

Compacta. Single. Pink and purple. Barkway – British – 1847.

Compacta. Double. Red self. Smith – British – 1866.

Companion. Double. Long, thin rose-Bengal tube, sepals rose-Bengal have slight downward curve $\frac{3}{4}$in × $\frac{3}{8}$in wide. Corolla marshmallow-white with spiraea-red stripe, smallish flowers for a double $\frac{3}{4}$in × $\frac{3}{4}$in wide with rose-Bengal stamens and pistil, pistil curves upward, very heavy bloomer. Olive green foliage, growth tall and upright, will make good basket or standard, tested for 3 years in vicinity of Richmond, California. Registered in 1978 by Soo Yun Field. Palko – American – 1978 – A.F.S. No. 1443.

Comte de Flandre. Double. Red and purple. Cornelissen – Belgian – 1868.

Comte de Lopinau. Double. Red and purple. Crousse – French – 1869.

Comte de Medici Spada. Double. Red and blue. Lemoine – French – 1859.

Comte Leon Tolstoi. Double. Red and purple. Lemoine – French – 1893.

Comtesse de Flandre. Red and white. Cornelissen – Belgian – 1868.

Comte Witte. Lemoine – French – 1906.

concertifolia. Dark red tube, red sepals flushed green; corolla red. Small flowers, very sparse, very small foliage. Upright bushy shrub. Synonymous with F. dolicantha. Fielding and Gardner – 1844 – Peru and Brazil.

Conchilla. Single to semi-double. Short tube and sepals pale pink; corolla amethyst-violet, changing to rhodamine-purple. Medium flowers and free. Growth upright and bushy, sturdy. Margarita × Rolla. Niederholzer – American – 1941.

Concile. Single. White and pink. Lemoine – French – 1870.

*Concorde. Double. Tube and sepals rose, corolla blue. Large blooms, growth upright and bushy. Raised in the vicinity of Merimbula, New South Wales, Australia. Lockerbie – Australian – *ca* 1975.

Concordia. Single. Red and purple. Wave of Life × *F.fulgens*. Lowe – British – 1875.

Confection. Double. Thin greenish-white tube, broad sepals are white to blush-pink, tipped green which stand out and turn back to tube. Corolla white with faint pink at base of petals. Large fluffy blooms and fairly free for size, pink stamens, best colour in filtered light. Dark green foliage with large 3 in long × 2 in wide leaves, faintly serrated with pronounced pointed tip. Growth lax bush, will make good basket with weights and support needed for bush training to carry the large blooms. Tested for 4 years in the vicinity of Fort Bragg and Oceanside, California, U.S.A., before release. Trademarked in California. Stubbs – American – 1982 – A.F.S. No. 1661.

Confetti. Double. Short tube and sepals pink; corolla bright violet-blue with shorter outer petals of red, pink and white, many petaloids resembling fat confetti balls. Medium sized blooms and very profuse. Growth bush. Martin – American – 1965 – A.F.S. No. 629.

Conica. See *magellanica*.

Coniston Water. Single. Tube soft rosy-pink, very long recurving sepals, soft rose. Corolla deep lavender-blue. Large pagoda shaped blooms, dark green, ovate foliage. Growth upright and bushy. Travis – British – 1959 – A.F.S. No. 1139.

Connie. Double. Tube and sepals cerise-red, corolla white flushed pale purple. Medium-sized flowers, petals fold into four parts. Growth upright, vigorous and tall. Winner of Jones Cup 1964 and also B.F.S. Award of Merit. Submitted by Mrs. M. Slater for R.H.S. Wisley Hardy Trials 1975–78 but received no award. One of Stanley Wilson's few cultivars for the showbench and introduced by him. Dawson – British – 1961.

Conqueror. Semi-double. Vermilion and purple. Salter – British and French – 1846.

Conqueror. Single. Red and purple. Youell – British – 1848.

Conqueror. Semi-double. Red and purple. Banks – British – 1853.

Conquest. Single. Red self. Banks – British – 1866.

Consolation. Single. Carmine and blue. Banks – British – 1865.

Conspicua. Single. Tube and sepals, bright scarlet; corolla milky-white, slightly veined scarlet. Flowers are small but very profuse and can come semi-double. Growth upright and bushy, excels as an outside bedder. Accepted by B.F.S. as showbench hardy. Smith, G. – British – 1863.

Conspicua Arborea. Single. Pink and red. Smith, F. – British – 1867.

Conspicuous. Double. Tube pale rose, sepals pale rose, recurved changing abruptly to a lighter shade of China-rose on the tube. Corolla clear China-rose and very compact. Very lush compact foliage. Growth trailer. Tiret – American – 1956 – A.F.S. No. 251.

*Constable Country. Semi-double. Short thick tube orient-pink (R.H.S. 36D) ½in long by ½in wide, horizontally held sepals neyron-rose (R.H.S. 55B) ¾in long by ½in wide with reflexed tips. Corolla opens violet (R.H.S. 84A) maturing to cyclamen-purple (R.H.S. 74B) ¾in long, some mottling at maturity. Quarter flared and thick bell shaped, medium-sized blooms, two or three blooms carried in each leaf axil near periment. Dark green foliage (R.H.S. 137A) carrying hint of blue in the green leaves 2¼in long by 1 in wide. Growth lax upright or stiff basket, short-jointed with side shoots in abundance, ideal for hanging pots or baskets, may need weights. Heavy feeder and much better as second year plant, very easy rooter. Raised in the vicinity of Ipswich and introduced by the raisers, Gouldings Fuchsias of Ipswich, in 1984. Goulding – British – 1984 – A.F.S. No. 1777.

Constance. Double. Tube and sepals, soft pink; corolla bluish-mauve, tinted pink. Medium sized blooms, very free, very similar to Pink Pearl from which it is a seedling, except the corolla of different colouring. Often sports back to Pink Pearl, sometimes confused with James Lye. Growth upright, and bushy very easy and in the showclass category, better as second year plant. Found by George Budgen of Berkeley Horticultural Nursery in 1935 and named after his daughter. A double pink and blue, shaded pink, a sport of Pink Pearl differing only in colour. Accepted by the B.F.S. as showbench hardy. Berkeley Hort. Nursery – America – 1935.

Constance – James Lye. The following information is intended to be of assistance in distinguishing between these two very similar cultivars. James Lye has slightly larger blooms with slightly longer tube, Constance colouring is deeper especially the corolla in a young bloom; James Lye is a little darker colouring on top side of sepals. Constance sepals tips show slight tinge of green, whereas James Lye has a pronounced darker light cerise colouring at tips. James Lye stalk is longer, much earlier in flowering and freer in bloom, but tends to drop blooms early, but with the profusion of flower is always in bloom until the autumn. James Lye is self cleaning as it drops both flower pod and stalk.

Constellation. Single. *F. corymbiflora* × *F. fulgens*. Miller – British – 1844.

Constellation. Single. Red and purple. Banks – British – 1864.

Constellation. Double. White tube, sepals white, tipped green. Corolla creamy-white, backed by clear white pointed sepals. Large blooms and more perfectly formed than Flying Cloud, very free for a white double, but susceptible to botrytis, a failing with most whites. Early bloomer and free, growth medium bush, best grown as H1. Schnabel – American – 1957 – A.F.S. No. 289.

*Consuella. Double. Tube and sepals salmon, corolla carmine overlaid with salmon-orange. Largish blooms and quite free flowering. Growth trailer, suitable for basketwork. Raised in the vicinity of Merimbula, New South Wales, Australia. Lockerbie – Australian – *ca* 1975.

Contessa. Double. Short pale green tube, sepals thick and reflexed to stem, white. Corolla orchid-rose, flecked white and pink, very full. Large blooms and free, growth medium bush and upright. Handley – British – 1972 – A.F.S. No. 1053.

*Continental. Semi-double or double. Short white tube, sepals are longer, white on upper surface but flushed pink underneath, recurving. Corolla pink with rose coloured margins. Medium sized blooms with picotée edged petals, multi-flowering is common, held prominently near the branch ends. Growth is upright and stiff, very suitable for bush or standard training. Raised in the vicinity of Ipswich, Suffolk and introduced by the raiser. Gouldings Fuchsias of Ipswich in 1985. One of a series of ten new introductions named after famous trains in 1985 and a cultivar for those looking for the unusual. Goulding – British – 1985.

Contramine. Single. Tube light rose, sepals white, flushed rose tipped green. Corolla light purple-base with rose at base. Medium sized flowers and very free, foliage red veins and stems. Growth lax bush. Introduced by Wills Fuchsias Ltd. of West Wittering in 1980. La Campanella ×. de Graaff – Dutch – 1978.

Convent Garden White. Single. Tube and sepals creamy-white; corolla rosy-cerise. Medium-sized flowers, free and early. Growth is spreading habit. Doël – German – Date unknown.

Coos Bay. Double. Short tube and sepals, dark red; corolla deep blue, very full with petals having folded look, fades to rosy-purple. Very large blooms, lax bush or trailer. Prentice – American – 1971 – A.F.S. No. 989.

Coos Bay Pirate. Single. Short tube rose in colour, dark rose sepals, tipped green, wide flaring up toward stem at maturity. Medium sized flowers, corolla purple fading to red-violet, some petals twisted occasionally. Growth natural trailer without weights. Raised in vicinity of Oregon, California. Sport of Nonpariel. Vee Jay Greenhouse – American – 1979 – A.F.S. No. 1510.

Coos Cutie. Double. Tube and sepals pink, tipped green; corolla, large centre petals white, surrounding petals pink and white. Large blooms and almost continuous, growth trailer. Gagnon – American – 1963 – A.F.S. No. 556.

Coppelia. Semi-double. Tube and sepals, carmine-pink; corolla bright purple, changing to plum-purple with age. Light coloured foliage. Growth lax bush or trailer. Blackwell – British – 1964.

Copycat. Single. Rose to red tube, horizontally held pointed sepals of the same colour. Blue corolla, almost miniature flowers under 1 in. Dark to medium green foliage with lanceolate leaves 1¾ in long by ⅞ in acute tip, ovate base and slightly serrated margin. Growth tall upright, will make good bush on standard, best colour develops in filtered sun. Tested for 4 years in the vicinity of Fort Bragg, Oxnard and Oceanside, California before release. Stubbs – American – 1981 – A.F.S. No. 1619.

Coquet Bell. Single to semi-double. Short tube and sepals, rose-madder, slightly tipped green. Corolla pale mauve flushed rose-mauve at base, with distinctive red veins, bell shaped with slightly wavy edge. Medium sized blooms, very free and of intense colouring. Growth upright, bushy and self-branching. Lena Dalton × Citation. Ryle-Atkinson – British – 1973 – A.F.S. No. 1114.

Coquet Dale. Double. Short tube, whitish-rose; short, wide neyron-rose (R.H.S. 55B) sepals, held well up above horizontal. Corolla is lilac (R.H.S. 76A), medium sized blooms slightly flared with one or two lilac petaloids and red anthers. Growth medium upright, sturdy and vigorous, good for bush or standard, raised in Northumberland. Joe Kusber × Northumbrian Belle. Ryle – British – 1976 – A.F.S. No. 1397.

Coquet Gold. Single. Pinkish-white tube, sepals white and pink on topside and pink underneath, thick and held horizontally. Violet-purple (R.H.S. 77B) corolla, medium sized flowers with square looking corolla initially, at maturity corolla is bell-shaped with edges flaring out, white anthers. Lettuce-green (R.H.S. 144A) foliage, some leaves yellow-citron green (R.H.S. 151A), most leaves tipped with yellow along edges but sometimes yellow for ¾ of surface. Growth medium upright, self-branching and bushy, will make good bush or standard and with careful training, good basket, as with most variegated foliage cultivars, best colour develops in sun. Sport from Belsay Beauty by the same raiser. Ryle – British – 1976 – A.F.S. No. 1398.

Coquette. Double. Carmine and red. Williams – British – 1873.

Coquette. Single. Tube and sepals red; corolla purple, small flowers and free. Sister seedling to Caprice. Growth lax bush or trailer. Niederholzer – American – 1943.

Cora Belle. Double. Long white tube, sepals white, long and tipped light green. Corolla blue turns to orchid with white base. Petals are long and wide, veined light colour. Light coloured foliage and large, very free bloomer. Growth trailer. Gagnon – American – 1965 – A.F.S. No. 623.

Cora Brant. Single. Short thick tube and wide-spreading sepals, solid crimson; corolla rose-madder, tinged geranium-lake and flaring. Large flowers and free. Growth upright and bushy. Aviator × Sunset × Libuse. Niederholzer – American – 1941.

Cora Elsey. Semi-double. Short tube and up-turned sepals, pink. Corolla blush pink, with darker pink veins, bell shaped. Grow lax bush or trailer. Copley Gardens – American – 1967 – A.F.S. No. 743.

Cora Engleman. Single. White and red. Stride – British – 1902.

Coral. Single. Tube and sepals rosy-red; corolla rosy-red. Medium-sized flowers and very free. Growth upright and bushy. Fuchsia-La (Walker) – American – 1957.

Coralle. Synonymous with Koralle.

Corallina. Single. Tube scarlet, non reflexing sepals scarlet; corolla rich purple, pink at base. Medium sized blooms and free, darkish green foliage with bronzy tint. Growth lax spreading bush, very vigorous, suitable for hedges height up to 3 feet. Accepted by the B.F.S. as showbench hardy. Exoniensis × *F. montana*. According to Munz *F. montana* is synonymous with *F. var. globosa var. coccinea*. Exoniensis is *F. cordifolia* × *F. globosa* and both the hybrids are almost identical. Pince – British – 1844.

*Corallina Variegata. Single. Scarlet tube with non reflexing scarlet sepals; rich purple corolla, pink at base. Identical to Corallina except for the variegated foliage, leaves are green with distinct centre edge, extremely attractive. One of the few

Belgian fuchsias, raised at the Institut Horticole at Liège, Belgium, introduced into Britain by Leo Boullemier in 1983. Verdeur – Belgian – 1979.

Coral Rose. Double. Tube and sepals coral-pink, corolla rose-pink. Small double blooms, extremely free flowering for a double. Olive green foliage, growth prostrate and compact, very suitable for rockeries and window boxes, height 6 to 9 in. One of a series of hardy miniatures raised in the Scilly Isles. Tabraham – British – 1982.

Coral Seas. Single. Tube and sepals, salmon-pink to orange; corolla burnt orange, splashed salmon. Medium size blooms and free, colouring can be most disappointing, dirty burnt orange. Growth cascade trailer, best as H1. Martin – American – 1966 – A.F.S. No. 672.

cordifolia. Tube dark scarlet, sepals scarlet with extended green tips; corolla combination of green, yellow and white. Very close to *F. splendens*, distinguishing character is the stamens which barely protrude beyond the tube and are borne axillary. Leaves are almost as broad as long. Medium sized shrub, found at elevation of 10,000 ft. Bontham – 1841 – Guatemala.

Core'ngrato. Double. Long tube pale coral, sepals pale coral outside, frosty salmon-pink inside. Corolla opens light burgundy-purple, changes almost to salmon-burgundy with salmon-pink splashes at base of petals. Petals are veined and edged. Medium sized blooms and free, growth upright and vigorous. Blackwell – British – 1964.

Corentine. Salter – British and French – 1841.

Corinthe. Lemoine – French – 1911

Cormackii. Semi-double. Carmine self. Cormack – British – 1846.

Corne d'Abondance. *F.venusta × F.boliviana.* Lemoine – French – 1894.

Cornéilla. Double. Red and purple. Lemoine – French – 1897.

Cornelis Steevens. Single to semi-double. Long white tube flushed soft pink, sepals white flushed soft pink, tipped green. Corolla deep pink-red, lighter colour at base. Medium to large flowers with pink stamens and style. Dark green foliage, growth natural trailer. Steevens – Dutch – 1968.

Coronation. Double. Short tube and long, narrow sepals waxy-white, flushed soft pink on underside. Corolla a rosy-raspberry, wide and spreading. Large flowers, free and early. Growth upright. Tiret – American – 1953 – A.F.S. No. 154.

Coronet. Semi-double. White tube, sepals white on top, pink on underside. Corolla a blue fading to lavender with pink marbling. Symmetrical shaped blooms, large for semi-double. Growth upright. Kennett – American – 1968 – A.F.S. No. 778.

Corpus Christie. Double. Tube and upturned sepals, rosy-red; corolla soft lilac-lavender, overlaid with flesh-pink petals at base. Growth upright. Walker and Jones – American – 1953.

Corsage. Double. Ivory-pink tube, ivory-pink to pale salmon sepals, salmon inside, short and standing straight out until fully mature, then straight against tube. Orange-coral corolla, rather short but very full, rosette type with up to thirty or more petals. Flowers are very suitable for corsages as sepals are proportionately short and do not recurve. Foliage with red stems on new growth. Growth semi-trailer, prefers warmth for best colour. Raised in California in vicinity of Fort Bragg and Oxnard, trademarked in California. Introduced into England by D.N. Pickard of Huntingdon in 1979. Stubbs – American – 1979 – A.F.S. No. 1500.

Corsair. Double. Tube and sepals white; corolla sky-blue fading to light purple, centre is white, the white running up centre of each petal, outer petals white with purple marbling. Extra large blooms, striking contrast of colours. Growth lax bush or trailer. Kennett – American – 1965 – A.F.S. No. 640.

corymbiflora. Long scarlet tube, sepals scarlet; corolla coral-red. Long flowers borne in large terminal racemes, very showy. Growth is not free branching, foliage much larger than most species, leaves are opposite, softly pubescent with long stalks. Grows to advantage when planted out and trained up a pillar in a cool conservatory. In its natural habitat will reach 15 ft or more. Synonymous with *F. dependens*, *F. macropetala* and *F. volutina*. Ruiz and Pavón – 1802 – Peru.

alba. Identical to *F. corymbiflora* but with white tube and sepals and with a deep red corolla. Confusion existed with this species as it was considered to be raised by Mr. Salter of Hammersmith and Versailles and then considered to be a variant discovered and introduced by the French grower Courcelles in 1850, but has since been recorded that it is a natural variant discovered by Bentham in 1845 in South Africa. Bentham – 1845 – Ecuador.

Cosmopolitan. Double. Tube pink, sepals deep rose-pink; corolla white, flushed pale pink, splashed and veined rose-pink, coral-pink twisted petaloids. Large blooms and free. Growth lax bush or trailer. Fuchsia Forest, Castro – American – 1960 – A.F.S. No. 426.

Costa Brava. Single. Tube and sepals red; corolla burgundy-red. Large blooms for a single, excellent shape. Foliage very light green and extremely large. Growth upright vigorous and fast. Best grown as H1. Colville – British – 1973.

Costa Mesa. Single to semi-double. Tube and long recurring sepals, bright pink; corolla rose-bengal. Medium to large flowers, fairly free. Growth upright and bushy. Fuchsia-La – American – 1952.

Cote d'Azur. Rozain-Boucharlat – French – 1912.

Cottinghamii. Single. Tube and sepals coral-red; corolla glowing crimson, flowers succeeded by glossy purple-brown bead-like fruits. Very small flowers, belongs to the Breviflorae section of cultivars. Little information available. Raiser unknown – Date unknown.

Cotton Candy. Double. Tube white with tinge of pink, sepals white, tipped green, touch of pink underneath. Corolla pale pink, veined light cerise pink. Largish blooms full and fluffy, sepals recurve and curl to tube, easy cultivar to shape. Foliage dark to medium green, growth upright can become lax with wrong conditions. Tiret – American – 1962 – A.F.S. No. 529.

Countess. Knight – British – 1858.

Countess of Aberdeen. Single. Tube and sepals, very pale pink; corolla creamy-white flushed pale pink, very pale pink in shade almost white, but rich pink in full sun. Small blooms but very profuse. Growth upright and bushy but rather stiff, needs early pinching to produce blooms for summer shows, can be disappointing if not given the right conditions. Show class category, capable of magnificent specimens. Best grown as H1. Dobbie Forbes – British – 1888.

Countess of Burlington. Double. Red and white. Story – British – 1856.

Countess of Cornwallis. Single. White and rose. Epps – British – 1846.

Countess of Hopetoun. Double. Tube and sepals red, corolla white with red veining. Growth lax will make good basket. Sport of Phenomenal and located at the Melbourne Botanic Gardens in Australia in 1888. Named after the wife of Lord Hopetoun, an English peer who held high office at one time in Australia. Still listed and grown in Australia. Introducer unknown – Australian – 1888.

Countess of Maritza. Double. Short tube pale pink, sepals are broad and long, pale pink. Corolla lilac. Growth upright and bushy, best grown as H2. This cultivar was grown at Lockyer's Nurseries, Bristol for sometime prior to release. Holmes, E. – British – 1977.

Count of Cavour. Single. Red and purple. Banks – British – 1861.

Country Cousin. Semi-double. Short tube and upturned sepals, deep red, corolla violet-purple, near white at centre, heavily veined flesh colour. Saucer shaped blooms, five to six petals, spreading. Growth medium upright bush. Hodges – American – 1952 – A.F.S. No. 125.

Country Fair. Single. Tube and sepals red; corolla white. Miniature blooms, very free with a full corolla. Light green foliage, growth trailer, self-branching, needs no pinching. Hubbard – American – 1967 – A.F.S. No. 703.

Country Girl. Single. Flesh-pink tube, flesh-pink sepals are longish and thin sometimes twist. Corolla pink-Bengal, medium sized blooms, almost a pink self with its pink-Bengal stamens and pistil. Light green foliage, ovate and longish leaves. Growth upright and bushy, tall, suitable as bush or standard, short-jointed and strong grower. Raised in the vicinity of Birmingham. Introduced by J. Ridding in 1979 after the raiser's death. Auntie Maggie × seedling. Tolley – British – 1979 – A.F.S. No. 1521.

Court Jester. Double. Short tube rosy-red, sepals creped rosy-red. Corolla royal purple, pink-coral petaloids overlay the satin sheen centre, giving an effect of a jester's costume. Large blooms almost continuous, free. Growth upright and bushy, very easy. Seedling from Lady Beth (Martin 1958). Fuchsia Forest, Castro – American – 1960 – A.F.S. No. 427.

***Cove Bay.** Single. Short greenish-pink tube ⅜in by ½in, half up white sepals overlaid green on top, white with pink base underneath, 1 in long by ¼in wide, recurved and tipped green. Corolla opens Violet (R.H.S. 84A) with white base, maturing to imperial-purple (R.H.S. 78A) ¾in long by 1 in wide. Quarter flared medium sized flowers with violet petaloids with white base ⅜in long by ⅛in wide with distinct colouring for a hardy, pink filaments and white anthers, with long banana shaped buds. Foliage is green (R.H.S. 137B) on top, slightly lighter (R.H.S. 138B) underneath, leaves 1¾in long by ¾in wide with serrulate margins. Growth small upright, will make good upright or standard and cold weather hardy to 26°F. Raised in the vicinity of Woodbridge, Suffolk. Norman Mitchinson ×. Dunnett – British – 1984 – A.F.S. No. 1761.

Covent Garden. Single. Long, rich waxy white tube, sepals waxy white, glossy rich, long and rather slender, held almost at the horizontal. Corolla rich rose, fairly large flowers which could be mistaken for one of Lye's introductions with the same waxy tube and sepals, very similar to Loveliness. Growth lax bush will produce good basket, this cultivar is still very popular in California. Spackman – American – 1936.

Cover Girl. Semi-double. Tube and sepals, bright red; corolla rich blue, blending of white at base of petals. Growth upright. Haag and Son – American – 1953.

Coxeen. Single. Tube dull red, sepals white; corolla rosy-pink. Small blooms, very free. Growth, trailer, very thin. Old basket cultivar. Raiser and date unknown (Could be Howlett – British – 1936).

Coza. Double. White tube tinged pink, sepals white, tinged pink underneath, crepe-like texture, wide tapered, turning upward. Corolla rosy-violet. Light green, long oval foliage. Growth trailer. Carlson – American – 1971 – A.F.S. No. 941.

Crackerjack. Single or semi-double. Tube and sepals white, faintly flushed pink. Corolla pale blue, ageing to pale mauve with white centre, veined pink. Large blooms very long petals, free flowering. Light green foliage. Growth cascade and very lax, makes excellent basket, will produce a good weeping standard. Fuchsia-La – American – 1961.

Craigana. Semi-double. Red and purple. Youell – British – 1840.

Crane. Single. Tube and sepals white; corolla reddish-purple. Very showy blooms and floriferous. Growth upright, bushy and vigorous and self-branching. Evans – American – 1954.

Crater Lake Blue. Single. Short tube and sepals white, shaded pink with green tips. Corolla blue. Medium sized blooms, star shaped, very free. Growth lax bush or trailer. Prentice – American – 1970 – A.F.S. No. 883.

Crazy Quilt. Single. Pink tube, upturned sepals palest green on outside, shell-pink underside. Corolla pale pink with purple blotches, spreading habit. Dark green foliage. Growth upright and bushy. Reedstrom – American – 1957 – A.F.S. No. 307.

Creampuff. Doubles. Long slender tube pale pink, slightly curved, sepals pale pink becoming white at tips. Corolla creamy-white with delicate pink overlay on outer folded petals. Large frilled blooms, fairly free. Growth trailer, very good grower and similar to So Big. Kennett – American – 1960 – A.F.S. No. 428.

Creole. Semi-double. Tube and sepals, bright red; corolla blood-red and maroon. Large blooms, growth trailer. Schnabel – American – 1949 – A.F.S. No. 23.

Crepe Suzette. Semi-double. Short tube, outer sepals white, inner sepals white flushed pink. Corolla violet-blue, nicely scalloped, opening semi-flat and surrounded by smaller petals.

Medium sized flowers and small foliage. Growth upright, compact bush. Kennett and Ross – American – 1956 – A.F.S. No. 260.

Crescendo. Double. Tube and sepals, turkey-red; corolla outer third, peony-purple, margin and two-thirds turkey-red. Medium sized blooms early and free. Growth upright and shrubby. Mme. d'Anjon × Mrs Victor Reiter. Reiter (Senior) – American – 1942.

Creusa. Single. Red and purple. Bland – British – 1880.

Crimson Globe. Single. Red and purple. Lye – British – Date unknown.

Crinoline. Double. Tube and sepals, rosy-white, tipped with green, corolla clear pale rose. Growth upright, makes a lot of heavy wood, lovely but temperamental. A.F.S. Cert. of Merit 195?. Reiter – American – 1950 – A.F.S. No. 58.

Cristal. Double. Cerise and white. Rozain-Boucharlat – French – 1925.

Criterion. Single. Red and purple. Smith – British – 1849.

Criterion. Semi-double. Red and purple Williams – British – 1881.

Croce-Spinelli. Lemoine – French – 1876.

Cropwell Butler. Single. Tube and sepals rosy-red, tube is short and thick, sepals held horizontal. Corolla campanula-violet. No unusual colour combination and very similar to existing cultivars. Medium sized flower but very floriferous. Growth upright and bushy, raised in the vicinity of Nottingham. Introduced by Jackson's Nurseries of Tamworth in 1981. Heidi Ann × Cloverdale Jewel. Roe – British – 1981.

*Cross Check. Little known Dutch cultivar other than the parentage: Checkerboard × Achievement. Brouwer – Dutch – 1982.

Crown Derby. Double. Tube and sepals, waxy-crimson; corolla centre petals white with outer petaloids crimson, showing distinct colour combination. Medium sized blooms and very profuse. Growth upright bush. Gadsby – British – 1970 – A.F.S. No. 962.

Crown Jewel. Double. Flesh coloured tube, long broad sepals faintly blushed, Corolla glowing rose, spreading and ruffled. Growth upright and willowy. Schmidt – American – 1953 – A.F.S. No. 151.

Crown of Fuchsia. Variegated foliage. Carter – British – 1870.

Crown Prince of Prussia. Double. Red and purple. Henderson – British – 1871.

Crusader. Double. Tube and sepals, frosty-white; corolla deep purple. Growth trailer. Tiret – American – 1967 – A.F.S. No. 733.

Crystal. Double. Red and white. Strutt – British – 1913.

Crystal Blue. Single to semi-double. Tube white to pale pink, sepals crisp-white, tipped green. Corolla clear violet-blue, occasional petaloids white or pink. Medium sized blooms, fairly free, foliage medium green with faint greyish cast. Growth lax bush or trailer. Kennett – American – 1962 – A.F.S. No. 537.

Crystal Rose. Double. Tube and sepals, bright rose; corolla pink-lilac orchid, form with centre petals downward. Growth trailer. Martin – American – 1959 – A.F.S. No. 368.

Crystal Stars. Semi-double. Short, thick greenish-white heavily flushed red tube, white reflexed sepals; white corolla. Smallish flowers, very free, neat and slightly flared, best colour in shade. Medium to small oval-shaped spinach-green foliage. Growth medium upright, bushy and self-branching. Awarded the B.F.S. Silver Certificate of Merit at London 1975. Ting-a-Ling × (La Campanella × Flirtation Waltz). Clyne – British – 1974 – A.F.S. No. 1362.

C.T. LeHew. Semi-double. Tube and sepals white to pale pink, corolla violet-blue. Growth lax bush or trailer. Named after a well known personality in the A.F.S. The notes of the raiser read 'one cross was made in 1951, the seed parent was Blue Pendant crossed with Prima Donna; from this cross thirty-eight seedlings were grown, all of which flowered in 1952. One seedling (52–10) a single to semi-double cultivar with pink sepals and flaring lilac-blue corolla. Kennett – American – 1953 – A.F.S. No. 653.

cuatrecasasii. Tube bright red, sepals scarlet; corolla scarlet. Small flowers, very sparse, borne in terminal racemes. Small upright shrub. Munz – 1943 – Colombia.

C.U.L. Newman. Single. Tube and sepals rich, glossy crimson, corolla bluish purple. Large flowers and at the time of introduction considered to be one of the best. Probably one of the first Australian introductions raised and introduced by C.F. Newman & Sons of Houghton, South Australia. Newman – Australian – ca 1894.

Cunning. Double. Tube and narrow sepals rose; corolla pale orchid with petals scalloped and edged with deeper orchid. Medium sized blooms and very profuse. Originally named Cutie. Brand – American – 1956 – A.F.S. No. 278.

Cupertino. Single. Long thin tube, white with pale tinge of pink, white sepals with pale green tips, downward to horizontal, not reflexed. Corolla reddish with mauve overtones, tight bell shaped. Similar to Checkerboard, medium sized blooms. Growth trailer. Checkerboard ×. Shaw – American – 1972 – A.F.S. No. 1033.

Cupid. Single. Tube and sepals, light scarlet-cerise; corolla pale bluish-magenta. Small to medium flowers, very free. Growth medium bush, upright and vigorous. Almost hardy in most districts. Wood – British – 1946.

Curiosity. Double. Red and purple. Henderson – British – 1872.

Curlew. Double. Tube and sepals, long and flesh tinted, corolla white. Growth semi-trailer. Evans and Reeves – American – 1951 – A.F.S. No. 104.

Curley Top. Single. Tube and sepals pale cerise, sepals are fully reflexed which curl over. Corolla violet-blue, medium-sized flowers and very free, can come semi-double. Growth upright and bushy, best grown as H2. The ore and only cultivar by this raiser. Thame – British – 1954.

Curly Goldtop. Single. Tube and sepals, palish-rose; corolla sky-blue. Large blooms and free. Golden foliage changing to deep green with age. Most attractive cultivar. Growth lax bush or trailer. Party Frock × Brentwood. Thorne – British – 1968.

Curly Locks. Single. Tube and sepals, deep pink; corolla purple. Small flowers, very free. Growth dwarf upright. Hazard and Hazard – American – 1950.

Curly Q. Single. Tube whitish-carmine; sepals pale carmine, reflexed perfectly into circles which lie against the tube. Corolla of four rolled petals, violet-purple. Unusually small foliage, grey-green with dark purple stems. Feature of the blooms is the completely folding back of the sepals, hence the name. Growth lax bush or trailer, can be trained for bush basket, espalier or small standards. Charming cultivar, heavy bloomer, quaint and pert. A.F.S. Cert. of Merit 1964. Kennett – American – 1961 – A.F.S. No. 474.

Curly Wurly. Single. Tube and sepals, turkey red; sepals are oddly curled, corolla bell shaped, very dark violet-purple, lighter at base with red streaks. Large flowers. Growth upright bush. 1915 × Aviator. Niederholzer – American – 1941.

Curtain Call. Double. Tube and sepals, pinkish-carmine; corolla ranging from deep rose-bengal to crimson, with serrated edging. Large blooms and very free, four blossoms produced in leaf axils instead of the usual two. Growth lax bush or trailer. Munkner – American – 1961 – A.F.S. No. 479.

Curtisii. Semi-double. Red and purple. Curtis – British – 1847.

curviflora (Bentham 1845). Synonymous with *F. petiolaris.*

Cushie Butterfield. Double. Carmine-rose tube, carmine-rose (R.H.S. 52C) sepals, held horizontally with slight upward curve. French-rose (R.H.S. 49D) corolla. Medium sized blooms with markedly frilled edge and several small French-rose petaloids, bright red stamens and pistil stand well clear of corolla. Best colour in sun makes a dainty, elegant bush. Growth medium upright, bushy and self-branching. Almost identical to Siobham but with very full corolla. Pink Profusion × Northumbrian Belle. Ryle – British – 1976 – A.F.S. No. 1399.

Customa. Semi-double. Tube and sepals rich rose-pink; corolla white with deep pink edge. Medium sized flowers and very free. Growth cascade, needs heat for best results. Roth – American – 1956.

Custozza. Double. Red and white. Twrdy – German – 1867.

Cutie. See Cunning.

Cygne d'Argent. Single. Chalice white. Banks – British – 1857.

cylindracea. Deep red tube, deep red sepals; lighter red corolla. Tiny flowers. Borne solitary in the leaf axials. Foliage is partly shiny on top side leaves, hairy underneath. Belongs to the Breviflorae section (Encliandra). Strong upright shrub, reaching a height of 15 ft in its native Mexico. Lindley – 1838 – Mexico.

Cymru. Double. Short tube wild silk, sepals ivory, reflexed and broad; corolla very compact and full with narrow cylindrical petals, shell pink. This rather large white double was raised from the same group as Ben Hill. The raiser gave the seedling to James Travis who retained it with permission and named it. Parentage unknown although we do know that Thornley used the cultivar Nightingale for breeding purposes and, as

the flower is of the Nightingale type, it could have that blood. Thornley – British – 1966.

Cyndy Robyn. Double. Short flesh coloured tube, long, broad sepals flesh to pink colour (R.H.S. 48C) which curve up with maturity. Corolla rose to red (R.H.S. 51A) turning to coral-red with warm climates. Large flaring blooms which are fairly free, with few petaloids same colour as corolla, long pointed buds are flesh to pink. Dark green foliage is large with 3 in long × 1¾ in leaves, red central vein, serrated edges and sharply pointed top. Growth natural trailer, very suitable for basketwork without the need of weights. Tested for 2 years in the vicinity of Oceanside, California, U.S.A., before release. Trademarked in California. Stubbs – American – 1982 – A.F.S. No. 1662.

Cyril Holmes. Additional information released by raiser. Single. Thick, waxy-white tube, sepals blush-white with green tip, scarlet (R.H.S. 43D) inside, held out from tube slightly below horizontal. Corolla rowanberry (R.H.S. 42A) with capsicum-red (R.H.S. 33A) at base. Medium sized flowers of four distinct petals, crinkled and forming squarish corolla. Soft green (R.H.S. 138B) foliage, growth medium upright, bushy and self-branching. Percy Holmes × Hidcote Beauty. Holmes, R. – British – 1973 – A.F.S. No. 1336.

cyrtandroides. Tube rosy-red, sepals rosy red; corolla bright magenta. Tiny flowers no more than half an inch long. Growth reaches treelike proportions of 16 ft and more in Mexico. Synonymous with *F. volutina.* Moore – 1940 – Mexico.

Daddy Gene. Double. Tube and sepals pale white; corolla purple fading to rose. Growth trailer. Gallegos – American – 1975.

*Daddy Longley. Single. Very long thin tube cream, cream sepals held at angle of 45° below horizontal with tips recurved. Reddish-orange corolla. Short stamens and long pistil. Flowers are similar to Elizabeth (Whiteman). Little known cultivar which could be of Belgian origin. Raiser unknown – *ca* 1983.

Dainty. Single. Tube and sepals cerise; corolla bluish-mauve. Flowers are medium sized open and flared. Growth upright and bushy. Raiser unknown – British – Date unknown.

Dainty Damosel. Semi-double. Short waxy-pink tube, short, sturdy, clear white sepals, Corolla deepest cobalt-violet fades to mallow-purple. Largish flowers and free, heat tolerant. Growth upright bush. Schnabel – American – 1953 – A.F.S. No. 187.

Dainty Dinah. Single. Tube creamy-pink, sepals white flushed pink, upturned. Corolla creamy-pink, shading to cyclamen-pink towards edge, veined deep orange, conical, open form with well rounded petals. Foliage long pointed leaves of crinkled form with serrated edges. Medium size blooms and free. Growth upright and self-branching. Dye – British – 1974 – A.F.S. No. 1165.

Dainty Lady. Semi-double. Tube and sepals cerise; corolla white, veined cerise at base. Medium sized blooms and free. Growth upright bushy and neat, good bedder. R.H.S. Award of Merit. Lowe – British 1838? This cultivar was confused with La France which is surprising as the colouring is different.

Dainty Maid. Double. Tube and sepals carmine; corolla white, veined pink at base. Small blooms but very free for double, compact corolla and compressed. Growth low bush. Raiser unknown – American – Date unknown.

Daisy Bell. Single. Long white tube with orange cast, sepals pale orange, shading to apple green at tip, lanceolate in form measuring only ⅝ in to ⅞ in, sepals at maturity are straight and held at the horizontal. Corolla is vermillion shading to pale orange at base ⅝ in in diameter. Small flowers, the four petals arranged in close whorl forming a narrow cone ⅝ in in diameter and depth, pink stamens and pistil, cream anthers and stigma. Small foliage 1⅜ × 3 in medium green, lighter green on lower surface. Growth natural trailer, self-branching and vigorous, heavy blooming cultivar making compact plant with minimum of pinching, makes exceptionally good basket. Although grown in San José, California for over 15 years before being registered, did not appear in this country until the London and Birmingham Shows of 1976. Raiser unknown but introduced and registered by Miescke – American – 1977 – A.F.S. No. 1420.

Dalliance. Single. Waxy rose tube, sepals waxy rose flushed cerise underneath; corolla rosy-cerise. Medium sized flowers and free growth medium to low bush. Ledher – Continental – 1891?

Dalstonia. Single. Cream and carmine. Smith – British – 1841.

Dalton. Single. Tube and sepals, flesh-pink corolla venetian-pink, tipped green. Medium sized blooms of extra good substance, very free. Growth upright and bushy, should make a good standard. Hawkshead × Other Fellow. Thornley – British – 1971 – A.F.S. No. 1008.

Daly City. Double. Tube and wide, thick sepals red. Corolla has outer rim of petals deep blue, with colour graduating to rose-pink in centre, causing blooms to appear fluorescent. Large blooms and free. Growth upright bush. Martin – American – 1957 – A.F.S. No. 317.

Damson. Single. Tube and sepals red; corolla extremely dark colour hence the name, blackish-purple. Very long flowers with long corolla, free flowering. Growth upright and bushy. Raiser unknown – American – Date unknown.

Dancing Flame. Double. Short thick tube, pale orange to flesh colour with darker stripes. Slightly recurving and rather narrow sepals, orange inside and slightly paler on top side, sepals are the same length as corolla. Orange-carmine corolla with deep orange-carmine centre, outer petals infused lighter orange. Medium sized blooms with flaring corolla pink to orange stamens with grey-mauve anthers. Large foliage 3¼ in long × 2 in wide leaves, ovate, with acute tip and serrated margin. Growth trailer, but weights required, will make either good upright bush or basket. First blooms seem to come mostly semi-double changing to double. Tested for 4 years in vicinity of Fort Bragg, Oxnard and Oceanside, California, before release where it will be trademarked. Stubbs – American – 1981 – A.F.S. No. 1621.

Dancing Girl. This cultivar is known by the name of Dancing Girl for Emile de Wildeman (Lemoine).

Dandy Lady. Double. Short tube and sepals pink; corolla white with petaloids around base.

Large blooms, growth trailer. Pennisi – American – 1969 – A.F.S. No. 861.

Daniel Lambert. Single. Red and blue. Lee – British – 1857.

Danish Pastry. Single. Tube and sepals, coral with green tips, corolla lavender to salmon red. Large blooms, growth lax bush or trailer. Fuchsia Forest – American – 1968 – A.F.S. No. 771.

Danny Boy. Double. Tube and sepals, pale red; corolla red. Huge blooms not very free, nice colour change. Growth upright. Tiret – American – 1961 – A.F.S. No. 483.

Dante. Double. Red and purple. Demay – French – 1871.

Dante. Single. Tube and sepals red; corolla rich purple. Largish flowers and very free, growth upright and bushy. Not to be confused with Dante by Demay. Travis, J. – British – Date unknown (about 1970).

Danube Blue. Double. Red and blue. Rozain-Boucharlat – French – 1912.

Daphne Arlene. Single. Tube and sepals waxy-white with tinge of pink, sepals are broad and short; corolla coral pink. Small flowers, very profuse, identical to Shuna by Travis 1973. Growth and foliage is identical to Countess of Aberdeen, both Daphne Arlene and Shuna are sports from Countess of Aberdeen. Makes good show plant. Introduced by Wills Fuchsia Nurseries in 1979. Putley – British – 1948.

Darcie Morton. Semi-double. Light red tube, large red sepals turn completely back to stem; corolla red, veined white. Medium sized flowers, compact and pixie-like, early and heavy bloomer, best colour in shade. Medium- to small foliage, growth trailer, natural and self-branching. Copley, R. and J. – American – 1976 – A.F.S. No. 1389.

Darin Maddy. Double. Pink tube, broad sepals shell-pink with white tip, underside of darker shade than upperside. Corolla shell-pink. Large to medium sized blooms, very compact, needs frequent pinching. Large foliage, growth semi-trailer. Copley, R. and J. – American – 1976 – A.F.S. No. 1391.

Dariway. Single. Short pale pink tube, pale pink sepals reflexed at 45° below horizontal. Corolla mauve, pink at base. Small flowers and very free blooming. Dark green foliage, ovate with serrulate margins, new stems are reddish. Growth medium upright. Originated from the Coos Bay area of California, introduced about 1965 with little detail. Adkins – American – 1980 – A.F.S. No. 1551.

Dark Eyes. Double. Short tube and short broad upturned sepals, deep red. Corolla violet-blue, petals curled and rolled. Medium sized blooms and free. Growth upright bush. A.F.S. Cert. of Merit 1961. Erickson – American – 1958 – A.F.S. No. 351.

Dark Night. Double. Tube and sepals, currant-red; corolla spectrum-violet, heavily flushed with cherry. Blooms are full and very free, small foliage. Growth medium bush. Hardy in Huntingdonshire. Crockett – British – 1967 – A.F.S. No. 823.

Dark Secret. Double. Short greenish tube, heavy broad upturned sepals, waxy-white outside, pale pink and crepe texture inside. Corolla deep violet, few outer petals marked with phlox-pink. Medium size blooms, very dark foliage, growth medium bush and upright. Hodges – American – 1957 – A.F.S. No. 300.

Dark Secret

Dark Spider. Single. Long tube rich rosy-red, sepal red. Corolla rose ageing to red with maturity. Growth natural trailer, will make good basket. Raised in the Netherlands and introduced by High Trees Nurseries of Reigate in 1981. Brutus×. de Graaff – Dutch – 1980.

Darlene. Semi-double. Long white tube, sepals white, tinted rose. Corolla purple with white centre, fading to orchid-purple. Large blooms and very free, growth upright and sturdy. Scott – American – 1952.

Darling. Single. Tube and sepals rose-pink; corolla rosy-purple. Smallish flowers and very free. Growth upright and bushy medium-size. Raiser unknown – British – 1899.

Dartmoor Pixie. Single. Tube and sepals rhodonite-red; corolla plum-purple, pink at base with red veining. Medium-sized flowers, self cleaning and prolific flowerer. Growth trailer, very suitable for basketwork. Hilton – British – 1978.

David. Single. Tube and sepals cerise; corolla rich purple. Small flowers but free, same colouring as Pumila. Growth upright short and bushy. Ideal as bedder and edging, hardy. Pumila × Venus Victrix. Wood – British – 1937.

David Alston. Double. Tube and sepals crimson; corolla white, veined and flushed carmine. Large blooms very full and free, need support. Growth upright and bushy. The raiser and date of introduction are more likely to be Forbes – British – 1906 than Lemoine – French – 1910.

David Blaine. Double. Short tube and sepals, deep pink, corolla deep lilac. Growth trailer. Fritz – American – 1968 – A.F.S. No. 797.

David Chez. Double. Short red tube, long pointed sepals red. Corolla purple, flushed pink at base. Medium sized blooms with short stamens and long gold tipped pistil, light green ovary. Dark green foliage, long narrow leaves 2 in long, veins stand out. Growth lax upright, will make good basket with weights or small to medium standard. Tested for 5 years in the vicinity of Washington, N.E. England, Tyne and Wear before release. Cheseldine – British – 1981 – A.F.S. No. 1612.

David Lockyer. Double. Tube and sepals white; corolla bright red stripped with white. Feature of the flower is the secondary skirt from centre of corolla extending below normal corolla length, making very large blooms. Growth upright. Holmes, E. – British – 1968.

David Perry. Single. Short, thin tube, cardinal-red (R.H.S. 53C), elongated spear-shaped sepals, cardinal-red (R.H.S. 53C). Corolla fuchsia-purple (R.H.S. 67B), becomes neyron-rose (R.H.S. 55A) at base, veined cardinal-red fading to fuchsia-purple. Medium sized flowers, very free, consists of four well-shaped petals forming a neat slightly-flared bell with pistil showing just below corolla, longer stamens, very little fading. Growth medium upright, bushy and self-branching, needs little training, excellent cultivar for pot work. Holmes, R. – British – 1976 – A.F.S. No. 1337.

David Strutt. Semi-double. Rose-pink and violet. Strutt – British – 1867.

Dawn. Single. Tube and sepals white, tipped green; corolla pale violet, pale at base. Medium sized blooms and free. Growth upright and bushy. Baker – British – 1970.

Dawn Sky. Double. Tube and sepals, neyron-rose; corolla heliotrope with neyron-rose at base, all fading to petunia-purple. Large flowers and free. Growth spreading bush and vigorous. Crocket – British – 1967 – A.F.S. No. 824.

Dawn Thunder. Double. Thin flesh coloured tube, sepals pink, very broad and long; corolla dusky-pink and purple, fading to rose and coral. Huge blooms, fairly free for size, most petals serrated, when matured have smoky effect. Dark green foliage, growth lax bush, will trail with weights. Stubbs – American – 1975 – A.F.S. No. 1257.

Daybreak. Single. Tube and sepals red; corolla purple. Small flowers, fairly free, golden-green foliage, growth medium bush. Raiser unknown – British – Date unknown.

Day by Day. Single. Tube and sepals scarlet, lighter at tips; corolla rosy-purple. Foliage variegated green, cream and cerise. Growth upright and bushy. Sport of Emile Zola. Wagtails – British – 1971.

Day Dream. Double. Red and purple. Banks – British – 1867.

Day Dream. Semi-double. Thin rose tube, sepals rose; corolla light blue mottled white with long pink and white petals among the blue. Large flowers and free. Growth upright and bushy. Brown-Soules – American – 1952 – A.F.S. No. 133.

Day Star. Single. Tube and sepals, pale rose-opal; corolla magenta-rose. Large flowers growth upright and bushy. Baker – British – 1970.

*D-Day 44. Double. Cream (R.H.S. 158A) tube; white sepals with pink outer edge, fairly large 1½ in long by ¾ in wide and waxy. Corolla white, veined pink (R.H.S. 65D) on edges. Medium sized blooms, fully flared bright rose stamens and shell pink pistil, like all whites will mark. Foliage mid-green with serrated finely toothed leaves 2¾ in long by 1¼ in wide. Growth medium upright will make good bush, standard or decorative, also good summer bedder and a lovely contrast to other cultivars. The outstanding characteristic is the delicate pink edging to the crisp sepals. Tested for 3 years and raised in the vicinity of

Chaddesden, Derbyshire. Introduced by Jackson's Nurseries of Tamworth in 1985. Bobby Shaftoe × Stanley Cash. Redfern – British – 1985.

Dealbata. See also *magellanica* var. *globosa*.

Deane Le Baron. Double. Tube and sepals, rosy-pink; corolla violet-purple. Growth trailer. Tiret – American – 1969 – A.F.S. No. 828.

De Athay. Single. Pink and purple. Lemoine – French – 1890.

Debbie 'C'. Semi-double to double. Tube and sepals, bright rose; corolla bell shaped, pink heavily veined red. Medium size blooms, early and very free, small foliage. Growth trailer. Copley – American – 1966 – A.F.S. No. 693.

Debby. Double. Tube rose-bengal, wide recurving sepals rose-bengal; corolla heliotrope-blue, fading to cobalt-violet. Flowers free and largish. Growth upright and bushy. Nessier – American – 1952 – A.F.S. No. 117.

*Deben Petite. Single. Encliandra type of introduction with tiny red flowers. A species hybrid which could attain treelike proportions, raised in the vicinity of Woodbridge, Suffolk, and introduced by Lechlade Fuchsia Nursery of Lechlade in 1984. Waldfee × *F. arborescens*? Dunnett – British – *ca* 1975.

Deben Rose. Single. Tube delicate shade of azalea-pink (R.H.S. 38B). Long, slender, slightly recurved sepals spinel-red (R.H.S. 54C), tipped green, Corolla mallow (R.H.S. 72C) edge, spinel-red (R.H.S. 54A). Medium sized flowers with red stamens and pistil, very prolific and early. Growth natural trailer without weights, vigorous grower, will make a standard in 10 months and due to the rapid growth can be trained to most shapes. Raised in the vicinity of south-east England. Introduced by Aldham Garden House Nurseries of Colchester in 1979. La Campanella × Shady Lady. Dunnett – British – 1979 – A.F.S. No. 1516.

Debonair. Double. Tube and sepals, pale pink; corolla various shades of lilac and rose. Large flowers, growth lax bush or trailer. Kennett – American – 1964 – A.F.S. No. 611.

De Bono's Pride. Double. Short thin tube ivory-white overlaid and veined pink, sepals shade from white at tips to pink near tube on top, green (R.H.S. 150A) at tips to pink near tube on underneath. Sepals flare back to 45° from tube at maturity. Corolla red-purple (R.H.S. 72A) at outer edge fading to R.H.S. 61D at base. Small neat blooms with four petaloids same colour as petals but smaller, short crimson stamens and very long pink pistil. Small dark green foliage, ovate to cordate with serrated edges. Growth medium upright bush, carries auxiliary buds and very prolific bloomer. Originates from the vicinity of Southampton. De Bono – British – 1980 – A.F.S. No. 1535.

Deborah. Double. Tube and sepals, rosy-white; corolla orangy-red. Growth trailer. Tiret – American – 1970 – A.F.S. No. 897.

*Debra. Double. Short white tube, sepals white, flushed pink underneath, tipped green. Corolla pale violet-purple. Medium sized blooms and quite free flowering. Growth medium upright. Raised in the vicinity of Plymouth, Devon. Mrs. Hilton × Merry Mary. Hilton – British – 1984.

Debra Hampson. Double. Short, thick, deep red tube, short, broad, upturned deep red sepals; mauve corolla. Medium sized blooms with curled and rolled petals, will stand both sun and shade, heat tolerant if shaded. Dark green foliage with red centre vein. Growth upright, bushy and self-branching. Sport from Dark Eyes. Hilton – British – 1976 – A.F.S. No. 1374.

Debutante. Double. Tube and sepals pink; corolla pink, pink self. Medium sized blooms and free, growth low bush. Schnabel – American – 1949 – A.F.S. No. 26.

De Candolle. Dominyana × *F.serratifolia*. Lemoine – French – 1878.

De Cherville. Double. Red and purple. Lemoine – French – 1896.

decidua. Tube and sepal reddish-vermilion; corolla vermilion. Flowers are borne in short racemose, lateral panicles. Low spreading shrub, deciduous at time of flowering. Standley – 1929 – Mexico.

decussata. Red tube, sepals red with green tips; corolla reddish-purple. Smallish normal flowers, produced with the greatest of ease. Upright shrub growing to a height of 10 to 12 ft in its natural habitat. Synonymous with *F. fontinalis, F. fusea* and *F. scandens*. Ruiz and Pavón - 1802 – Chile and Peru.

*Dedham Vale. Single. Orient-pink (R.H.S. 36D) tube $\frac{1}{4}$in long by $\frac{1}{2}$in wide, half up sepals 1$\frac{1}{4}$in long by $\frac{1}{2}$in wide, pale neyron-rose (R.H.S. 56B) on top, paler (R.H.S. 55B) underneath with recurved tips. Corolla violet (R.H.S. 84A) maturing to methyl-violet (R.H.S. 85C). Quarter flared medium sized flowers with pleated square corolla carrying three or more in each leaf axil, neyron-rose filaments and magenta-rose (R.H.S. 64B) anthers, long thin buds are pointed. Small foliage matt green (R.H.S. 138A) with ovate leaves 1$\frac{1}{2}$in long by $\frac{1}{2}$in wide. Growth self-branching small upright, versatile for upright, standard, pyramid, pillar, miniature or bonsai, with plenty of side shoots. Raised in the vicinity of Ipswich and introduced by the raiser, Gouldings Fuchsias of Ipswich, in 1984. Goulding – British – 1984 – A.F.S. No. 1778.

Dee Copley. Double. Tube and broad sepals, bright red; corolla deep purple mottled red at base. Unusual colouring, large blooms extremely profuse, dark green foliage. Growth upright and sturdy. Copley Gardens – American – 1964 – A.F.S. No. 617.

Dee Dee. Double. Tube and sepals white, sepals long, curved and tipped green; corolla rosy-purple. Medium sized blooms with light green foliage, free flowering. Growth natural trailer, makes good basket. Walker – American – 1974 – A.F.S. No. 1179.

De Ell. Semi-double. Short thin tube dawn pink, green tipped sepals 1$\frac{1}{2}$in long × $\frac{3}{4}$in wide are carmine-rose (R.H.S. 52C) on top, dawn pink (R.H.S. 49A) underneath. Corolla bishop's violet (R.H.S. 81A) fading to cyclamen purple (R.H.S. 74A) with maturity. Medium sized blooms which flare open to 1$\frac{1}{4}$in long × 1$\frac{1}{2}$in wide, petaloids attached to front and back of petals same colour as corolla. Dark green foliage (R.H.S. 136A) with red stems, leaves 2$\frac{1}{2}$in long × 1$\frac{1}{2}$in wide. Growth natural trailer, originates from the Puget Sound area of Washington. Introduced by Linda Tancey

133

of Kent, Washington, in 1980. Eastwood – American – 1980 – A.F.S. No. 1568.

Deepdale. Double. Tube rose-bengal, ivory sepals flushed pink, green tips, opening almost horizontal. Corolla spectrum-violet, changing when grown in shade to campanula-violet. Medium sized blooms and free, very good pastel shade colouring. Growth upright and bushy, heat resistant. White Spider × Blue Gown. Thornley – British – 1961 – A.F.S. No. 1099.

***Deep Pink Lady.** Wrongly named cultivar in the South of England. Synonymous with Phyllis.

Defiance. Single. Pale crimson self. Smith – British – 1842.

De Goncourt. Single. White and coral-red. Lemoine – French – 1896.

Delaval Lady. Single. Carmine tube striped with darker shade, long thin sepals, neyron rose underneath, with darker colour shading on white, shiny upperside, dropping to angle of 45° with slight twist. Corolla rhodamine-pink. Long graceful flowers, free, hold colour and remain compact with age, best colour in shade. Growth upright and bushy. Complicated parentage involving Earl of Beaconsfield, Lena Dalton, Lye's Unique and Leonora. Ryle – British – 1975 – A.F.S. No. 1242.

Delicata. Single. Pink and purple. Barkway – British – 1846.

Delicata. Single. White and purple. Newberry – British – 1847.

Delicata. Single. Pink and red. Standish – British – 1848.

Delicata. Single. White and mauve. Lye – British – Date unknown.

***Delicia.** Single. Short white tube ½in long, half up sepals crimson (R.H.S. 43D) on top, carmine (R.H.S. 52B) underneath, 1¼in long by ⅜in wide with recurved tips. Corolla opens imperial-purple (R.H.S. 78A) maturing slightly paler (R.H.S. 78B), 1⅛in long by ¾in wide. Medium sized flowers non flaring and square shape, fuchsia-purple filaments and anthers, rose style and stigma, colour held longer than both parents. Forest-green (R.H.S. 136A) foliage with ovate leaves 2½in long by 1½in wide, obtuse tips and rounded bases, white veins, magenta stems. Growth small upright, will make good bush, upright, standard or decorative, sister seedling of Doreen Redfern. Raised in the vicinity of Chaddesden, Derbyshire and tested for 4 years before release. Cloverdale Pearl × Marin Glow. Redfern – British – 1984 – A.F.S. No. 1794.

Delight. Single. Tube and sepals clear crimson, sepals are reflexed; corolla pure white with rosy streaks near the base. Very large flowers and free blooming. Growth upright and bushy. Awarded First Class Certificate by the R.H.S. at Chiswick Trials 1873. Smith – British – *ca* 1870.

Delight. SIngle. Red and purple. Sankey – British – 1887.

Delightful. Single. Tube and sepals pink; corolla white and violet. Medium sized blooms and free. Growth upright and bushy. Niederholzer – American – 1946.

Delilah. Double. Tube and sepals, rose-pink, sepals reflexed to stem; corolla violet, flecked pink and white, matures to rosy-magenta, full and short; Growth medium upright bush, short jointed. Handley – British – 1974 – A.F.S. No. 1192.

Délos. Lemoine – French – 1911.

Dels Spring King. Double. Tube and sepals, shiny red; corolla milky-white. Variegated foliage. Growth trailer. Del Brown – American – 1964 – A.F.S. No. 618.

Delta. Double. Tube and sepals red; corolla blue. Largish blooms and free, cupped shape. Growth trailer, needs heat. Raiser unknown – American – Date unknown.

Delta Rae. Single. Short rose-pink tube, rose sepals tipped light green and held out 45° below horizontal. Corolla rosy-red with dark red borders on each petal. Medium sized flowers, medium to large foliage, new growth shows bronze tinges, red stems and veins. Growth natural trailer. Originates from the Coos Bay area of Oregon, introduced in 1965 with little details. Adkins – American – 1980 – A.F.S. No. 1552.

***Deltaschön.** Little known Dutch cultivar other than the parentage: sport from Jäusendschön. Felix – Dutch – 1982.

Democrat. Double. Tube and sepals white and rose; corolla purple. Growth upright and bushy. Jones, W. – British – 1960.

De Montaliviet. Double. Red and purple. Lemoine – French – 1879.

Démosthène. Double. Red and purple. Lemoine – French – 1874.

denticulata. Long reddish-pink tube, sepals of the same colour, tipped green; corolla red. Very large foliage and together with *F. fulgens* the largest foliage within the species. Requires heat, flowers late in the season. Strong upright bush. Synonymous with *F. grandiflora, F. serratifolia* (Ruiz and Pavón 1802) and *F. tasconiiflora.* Ruiz and Pavón – 1802 – Peru and Bolivia.

Whiteknights Goblin. Single. Long tube crimson lake gradually enlarging from a slightly swollen base. Diameter at mouth of tube 1¼in ×¼in . Emerald-green sepals are lanceolate 1 in ×¼in. Corolla scarlet obovate petals typically 1 in ×¼in. Foliage very dark green with dark red undersides and veining. Twigs deep mahogany red, leaves lanceolate typically 6 in × 1⅜in. Growth medium self-branching upright, will make good bush. A national variant of *F. denticulata* grown from South American seed and differs from the norm in its very dark green leaves and mahogany veins and twigs. Tested under glass in the University of Reading, South England before release. Wright, J.O. – British – 1981 – A.F.S. No. 1631.

dependens (Hook 1837). Synonymous with *F. corymbiflora.*

De Pleiden. (The Pleiades). Single. Tube and sepals pinkish-white; corolla pinkish-white. Small flowers and stand somewhat erect. Growth small, upright bush. Saturnus × Bon Accorde. De Groot – Dutch – 1974?.

Député Berlet. Double. Red and purple. Lemoine – French – 1881.

Député Teutsch. Vermilion and red. Lemoine – French – 1874.

Député Voix. Lemoine – French – 1884.

De Quatrefages. Lemoine – French – 1892.

Derby Belle. Single. Tube and sepals white, flushed rose; corolla cyclamen-purple, flushed magenta. Medium sized bell-shaped blooms, very free, pale green foliage. Growth medium bush. Upward Look × Caroline. Gadsby – British – 1970 – A.F.S. No. 876.

Derby Countess. Single. Long white tube, sepals waxy-white, large, held well out; corolla violet-purple. Exceptionally large blooms, five inches from sepal tips across whole flower, good novelty for collectors of large cultivars, late flowering. Growth upright bush, heat tolerant. Sleigh Bells ×. Gadsby – British – 1973 – A.F.S. No. 1121.

Derby Imp. Single. Thin crimson tube of medium length, sepals crimson (R.H.S. 52A) with underside rose-red (R.H.S. 58B). Corolla violet-blue (R.H.S. 93A) Maturing with age to violet-purple (R.H.S. 97A). Flowers small but dainty, extremely free and exceptionally early and will take full sun. Foliage small and wiry of mid-green colour. Growth best described as semi-trailing, needs frequent and regular pinching as will make long trails if left to its own devices; would make a good basket if weights are provided and adaptable to most forms of training. Falls into the category of small flowered cultivars with corresponding growth and can be used for miniature or even bonsai work. Good for 3½ in pot work and one of many cultivars favoured very successfully by Ron Venables of Birmingham for exhibition work in recent years. Although not one of Cliff Gadsby's best introductions, is nevertheless worth a place in the exhibitor's selection of cultivars and although Cliff Gadsby raised some 82 new introductions from 1968 to 1977 Derby Imp and Cloverdale are the only two he cannot quote the parentage. It was tested for 3 years at Derby before being registered and its way into the commercial field was to say the least, unusual. Derby Imp was just another of the hundreds of cultivars growing about in Cliff's own garden and fancied by Jim Wills on one of his visits as a likely cultivar for market work about 1973, otherwise it would never have found itself in the world wide selection of present day fuchsias. Gadsby – British – 1974 – A.F.S. No. 1220.

Derby Star. Single. Tube and sepals white with flush of pink; corolla wistaria blue on white base passing to violet-blue. Medium-sized flowers, held out horizontal on long stems, showing spiking effect. Growth spreading bush with very branching habit. Taken up by Wills Fuchsia Nursery but not introduced until 1977. Cliff's Hardy × Shy Look. Gadsby – British – 1975.

Derwentwater. Double. Tube and sepals, pale pink, paling to white with green shading at tips. Corolla soft lilac with delicate pink at base, very full. Growth upright bush. Travis, J. – British – 1961.

Desdomena. Double. Pink-peach self. Harrison – British – 1853.

Desert Rose. Double. Tube and sepals carmine; corolla globular shaped, rosy-purple splashed with carmine. Growth upright and bushy. Tiret – American – 1946.

Desert Sunset. Double. Short white tube, flushed pink, sepals rosy shade, rather broad and curl upward. Corolla smoky-rose with splashes of coral and coppery tones, turn a brilliant crimson as flower matures, which looks as if two different plants. Medium to large blooms and very free.

Growth semi-trailer. Waltz – American – 1956 – A.F.S. No. 268.

Desideratum. Double. Red and purple. Henderson – British – 1874.

Deutsche Kaiserin. Semi-double. Red-carmine self. Weinrich – German – 1870.

Deutsche Perle. Single. Tube and sepals are white with crimson corolla and medium-sized flowers. Growth is medium upright bush. This cultivar is synonymous with Water Nymph on the continent, especially in the Netherlands. A magnificent coloured photograph of a huge plant can be found in Gerda Manthey's book on p. 70. Twrdy – German – 1874.

Devonshire Dumpling. Single. Short thick tube white, sepals neyron-rose, tipped green. Corolla white, outer petals flushed pink. Large flowers and very prolific. Growth trailer, will make exceptional basket. Raised in the vicinity of Plymouth, England. Hilton – British – 1981.

Diablo. Double. Tube and sepals white, corolla burgundy-red. Growth trailer. Tiret – American – 1961 – A.F.S. No. 484.

Diabolo. Double. Tube and sepals waxy-white with green tip; corolla lilac and purple, shading to carmine-red. Very large blooms and fairly free for size. Growth strong and vigorous. This cultivar has been listed and supplied for a few years by Bakers of Halstead, England, and is different to Tiret's Diablo. Raiser unknown – Date unknown.

Diadem. Double. Red and purple. Smith – British – 1865.

Diadem. Semi-double. Tube and sepals white; corolla peony-purple. Medium sized flowers with large foliage. Growth upright and still. Reiter – American – 1946.

Diadème. Double. Carmine and white. Demay – French – 1873.

Diamant. Double. Scarlet and white. Story – British – 1862.

Diament. Double. Tube and sepals scarlet; corolla white, streaked with carmine. Growth upright and bushy. This cultivar appears to be exclusive to California and could be Diamant (Story 1862) with a slightly different spelling. Raiser and date unknown.

*Diamond Fire. Double. Tube and sepals bright red; corolla brilliant white. Large fully double blooms 2½ in long, prolific flowering for a double. Growth upright, vigorous and strong yet compact and short jointed. Dark green foliage; described as a beautiful plant. Hardy in Southern England, raised and introduced in the Isles of Scilly by Tabraham's Nurseries. Ultimate height 2 to 2½ ft. Tabraham – British – 1984.

Diana. Double. Tube greenish-white, sepals white with touch of very pale pink, tipped green. Corolla light marbled lavender which fades to bright old rose. Large flowers and free, light green foliage. Growth trailer A.F.S. Cert. of Merit 1970. Kennett – American – 1967 – A.F.S. No. 740.

Diana Wills. Double. Tube and sepals, waxy-white, heavily tipped green; corolla spiraea-red, flushed white and China-rose, fading to ruby-red. Growth medium bush, prefers semi-shade. Gadsby – British – 1968 – A.F.S. No. 976.

*Diana Wright. Single. Long, thin cylindrical tube, flesh-pink (R.H.S. 36A) ⅞ in by 1/16 in, sepals reflexed and held slightly below the horizontal are pink (R.H.S. 55C) tipped green $\frac{1}{10}$ in by $\frac{1}{8}$ in . Corolla phlox-pink (R.H.S. 62B) $\frac{3}{8}$ in by $\frac{7}{16}$ in with no flaring. Filaments palest pink, cream anthers, palest pink pistil and cream stigma. Dark green (R.H.S. 139A) foliage paler underneath (R.H.S. 139C) acute-obtuse leaves $2\frac{1}{8}$ in by 1 in, heavily serrated. Growth small upright, self-branching, good for bush or standard, hardy to 15°F. in Southern England. Best colour in bright light, tested for 5 years unprotected in the vicinity of Reading. Deeper pink than Whiteknights Blush and more floriferous and colourful than *F. magellanica alba*. *F. magellanica alba* × *F. fulgens* (F3). Wright, J.O. – British – 1984 – A.F.S. No. 1787.

Diane. Single. Tube and sepals, waxy-white; corolla cameo-pink. Medium sized blooms, free, growth upright bush. Hazard and Hazard – American – Date unknown.

Dianthus. Double. Tube and sepals carmine; corolla deep purple with mottled carmine. Growth lax bush, will trial for basketwork. Unregistered American cultivar exclusive to California. Raiser and date unknown.

Diawillis. Single. Tube and sepals, pale rose; corolla pale Tyrian-rose. Medium sized flowers and free. Growth upright bush. Niederholzer – American – 1947.

Dickie Doo. Semi-double. Long pink tube, sepals pink and flared; corolla bishops-violet, marbled white towards top and sweeping down middle of petals. Long flared flowers very profuse. Growth natural trailer, strong grower. Araujo-Bishop – American – 1975 – A.F.S. No. 1304.

Dictator. Bull – British – 1871.

Dido. Double. Tube and sepals rose-pink, sepals are broad and upturned but held away from tube, long fluted tube. Corolla lavender, pale pink at base, veined rose. Small blooms but quite free flowering not an outstanding cultivar but neat and attractive. Small foliage medium green. Growth upright and bushy. Francis – British – 1974.

Die Fledermaus. Double. Tube and sepals scarlet; corolla, violet-blue. Growth trailer Blackwell – British – 1967.

Dilly-Dilly. Double. Tube and sepals pink; corolla lilac. Flowers largish and free, growth semitrailer. Tiret – American – 1963 – A.F.S. No. 577.

Dimples. Double. Short red tube is thick, sepals red, slightly reflexed but do not curl $\frac{1}{2}$ in to $\frac{3}{4}$ in long. Corolla white with light red veining on each petal. Small blooms approximately 1 in diameter. Medium green foliage with red main stems. Growth self-branching trailer, will make basket with weights, good for upright or standard training. Best colour develops in shade, tested for 3 years in vicinity of the coastal area of Pacifica, California, before release. Storvick – American – 1981 – A.F.S. No. 1629.

Dipton Dainty. Semi-double. Short tube rhodamine-pink, sepals rhodamine-pink, curve slightly upward. Corolla wisteria-blue, shading to lighter colour. Medium sized flowers, free flowering, delicate colouring, petaloids flecked and striped with phlox-pink, best colour in shade. Growth upright and bushy. Raised by Dr. M. Ryle but not released until introduced by C.S. Lockyer (Fuchsias) of Bristol in 1979. Lye's Unique × Earl of Beaconsfield seedling × Whirlaway seedling ×

Royal Velvet. Ryle – British – 1975 – A.F.S. No. 1243.

Dirk van Delen. Single. Pink tube, pink sepals with green tips; corolla light purple-pink. Medium-sized flower and free, dark green foliage. Growth upright bush or standard. Steevens – Dutch – 1971?

Discolor. See *magellanica*.

Display. Single. This cultivar is a particularly, lovely fuchsia which should be in every collection; a cultivar any beginner can cultivate with success. Raised in England by Smith in 1881, still holds its own with modern cultivars with distinction. Almost a self pink, single, tube and sepals are rose-pink whilst the corolla is of a deeper pink. One of the best all round fuchsias in cultivation, capable of being trained to any shape, except a basket; excels as a bush plant, but makes an excellent standard, conical, pillar or pyramid. One of the few that can be grown in the house, provided it receives full light and atmosphere not too dry; holds its blooms for long periods and was one of the prominent cultivars, together with Ballet Girl, Achievement, Mrs. Marshall and Emile de Wildeman (Fascination) during the hey day of the fuchsia, the late Victorian and early Edwardian days. The blooms are unusual in shape and description as 'coolie's hats', because of the saucer shaped corolla, borne in great profusion. One of the first to flower and continues to bloom, without flushes, throughout the entire season. With its vigorous root system is one of the best types for bedding out and, although not classified as a hardy, will stand all but the worst of winters, provided precautions are taken to cover the base of the plant with suitable material during the coldest months. Foliage is of medium size and attracts very few pests. Display is self-branching; two pinches are sufficient to make a bush plant which can be quite sizeable, even in its first year, however, to grow to showbench standards, where it excels as a bush plant, regular pinching back is needed and, if well cultivated, will need very little or no staking. Old cultivar, grown everywhere and likely to be cultivated for many more years in the future, deserves more than the old Certificate of Highly Commended by the R.H.S. many years ago. Accepted by the B.F.S. as showbench hardy. Grown and cultivated in the Netherlands as Frau Ida Noach. Smith – British – 1881.

Dixie. Double. Tube and sepals, bright red opening rectangularly; corolla deep blue, opens with an outer skirt of rose coloured petals. Growth trailer, self-branching. Martin – American – 1957 – A.F.S. No. 319.

Dobbie's Bedder. This cultivar is synonymous with Dunrobin Bedder.

Doc. Single. Tube and sepals red; corolla pale purple. Small flowers but extremely free and continuous, deep green foliage. Growth upright and bushy, strong and branching, dwarf, only 9 to 15 in high. Hardy in Southern England, raised in the Scilly Isles. Tabraham – British – 1974.

Doctor. See **The Doctor.**

Doctor Brenden Freeman. Single. Pale pink tube, sepals rhodamine-pink (R.H.S. 62A) shading to phlox-pink; corolla white. Medium-sized flowers, free bloomer and improvement upon its parents, requires usual protection, best colours develop in shade. Growth medium upright, bushy, will make good bush, shrub or decorative. Tested

136

for 4 years before release. Cloverdale Pearl × Grace Darling. Gadsby – British – 1977 – A.F.S. No. 1427.

Doctor Hessel. Single. Red and purple. Williams – British – 1873.

Doctor Jill. Double. Short tube red-purple (R.H.S. 65B), sepals red-purple (R.H.S. 62B) reflex completely on to tube $1\frac{1}{2}$ in × $1\frac{2}{3}$ in wide. Corolla red-purple (R.H.S. 65C) veined (R.H.S. 66A) $1\frac{1}{2}$ in in length and width. Medium-sized blooms with red-purple (R.H.S. 68A) stamens and pistil, best colour in shade. Growth medium upright and bushy, will make good standard or bush. Named for one of raiser's granddaughters and tested 2 years in vicinity of Chester before release. Seedling from Chang. Pugh – British – 1978 – A.F.S. No. 1457.

Doctor O'Connor. Double. Tube and sepals, bright red; corolla deep purple. Large blooms, flat and compact. Growth upright. Soo Yun Field – American – 1965 – A.F.S. No. 644.

Doctor S. A. Appel. Single. Tube and sepals red; sepals are tipped green; corolla dark violet-purple. Medium-sized flowers, good flowerer. Named after a well known personality in the Dutch Fuchsia world and in Dutch Horticulture. Steevens – Dutch – 1968.

Dodie. Double. Bright red tube, sepals also bright red, narrow and completely reflexed. Corolla deep purple splashed cerise spreads with maturity. Small compact blooms, dark green foliage, narrow slightly serrated leaves. Growth trailer and self-branching. Originates from the Pacifica area of California. Stosvick – American – 1980 – A.F.S. No. 1543.

dolicantha (Krause 1905). Synonymous with *F. concertifolia*.

Dollar Princess. Double. Tube and sepals cerise; corolla rich purple. Flowers rather small for a double, but very profuse and of perfect shape, very early bloomer. Growth upright and vigorous, excels as bush plant but can be trained to almost all shapes, particularly good for pyramid or standard. One of the real old cultivars which any grower can cultivate with ease, very often named backwards, as Princess Dollar. Lemoine – French – 1912.

Dollar Princess

Dollarprinzessin. Synonymous in the Netherlands with Dollar Princess.

Dollie Pausch. Double. Tube and broad upturned sepals, deep rosy-red; corolla creamy-white with red veining near base of petals. Large blooms and dark green foliage, vigorous grower.

Growth lax bush or trailer. Cannot hold its own against Lassie or Swingtime. Olson – American – 1962 – A.F.S. No. 495.

Dolly Varden. Semi-double. Short white tube flushed pink, white sepals. Corolla lilac-blue, maturing to pinkish-lavender. Large flowers and very free. Growth lax bush or trailer. Martin-Soules – American – 1953 – A.F.S. No. 174.

Dolores. Single. Self coloured carmine-rose, medium sized flowers, very free. Growth trailer. Niederholzer – American – 1944.

Domingo. Double. Red and purple. Bull – British – 1872.

Dominyana. Single. Long tube, small sepals, small corolla, rich scarlet self. Long trumpet shaped flowers, very free, borne in terminal clusters. Dark bronzy-purple foliage, one of the very early hybrids from *F.serratifolia*. Growth upright and bushy, needs H1 cultivation. *F.spectabilis* × *F.serratifolia*. Dominy – British – 1852.

*** Donaunixe.** Single. Tube and sepals red; corolla blue. Medium-sized flowers will take full sun. Koralle × *F. boliviana*. Nutzinger – Austrian – 1971.

*** Donauweibchen.** Double. Tube and sepals cherry-red; corolla white. Small blooms but very free flowering. Growth short upright. Koralle × *F. boliviana*. Nutzinger – Austrian – 1971.

Don Giovanni. Single. Red and purple. Banks – British – 1864.

Donna Marie. Single. Tube and sepals pale pink; corolla salmon. Medium sized flowers and very free. Growth natural trailer. Tiret – American – 1969 – A.F.S. No. 829.

Donna Olivia. Single. Tube and sepals white, tipped eau-de-nil; corolla white. Medium sized flowers and free. Growth upright makes thinnish bush. Manchester University – British – 1958.

Don Pedro. Single. Crimson self. Twrdy – German – 1872.

Don Peralta. Single to semi-double. Tube, sepals and corolla coloured red; colouring much the same as Anna. Flowers are large and long. Growth upright, vigorous, makes heavy wood. Tiret – American – 1950 – A.F.S. No. 62.

Dopy. Double. Tube and sepals red; corolla purple, tinged with pink. Small blooms but very free, dark green foliage. Growth upright and bushy yet dainty, dwarf, only 9 to 15 in in height. Hardy in Southern England, raised in the Scilly Isles. Tabraham – British – 1974.

Dorbett. Red tube, red sepals. Corolla white, veined red, medium sized flowers, true single two flowers produced in each leaf axil. Medium green foliage, growth upright and bushy, very self-branching. Raised in the vicinity of Merseyside for 3 years before release. Introduced by Meadowcroft Nurseries of Huntingdon in 1980. Meike Meursing × Citation. Clark, D. (Merseyside) – British – 1979.

*** Doreen Redfern.** Single. Short white tube $\frac{1}{2}$ in long by $\frac{1}{4}$ in wide. White sepals on upper surface, pale lilac (R.H.S. 73D) underneath, tipped green, held well above the horizontal with reflexed tips. Non flaring rounded corolla opens methyl-violet (R.H.S. 85B) maturing to violet-purple (R.H.S. 77B) $1\frac{3}{4}$ in long by $\frac{3}{4}$ in wide. Pale lilac filaments and anthers, white style and stigma, medium sized flowers with long pointed buds. Dark green

(R.H.S. 137B) foliage with cordate leaves 1⅜ in long by 1 in wide, veins and stems white with pale green branches. Growth small upright, will make good bush or standard; sister seedling to Delicia. Raised in the vicinity of Chaddesden, Derbyshire, and introduced by R. and J. Pacey of Melton Mowbray in 1983. Cloverdale Pearl × Marin Glow. Redfern – British – 1984 – A.F.S. No. 1795.

Doris Ford. Single. Greenish-white tube, sepals greenish-white flushed pink. Corolla lavender-blue flushed pink at base. Medium sized flowers delightful colour combination and very free. Named after a very successful South of England exhibitor of the 1970s. Growth upright, bushy and self-branching. Introduced by High Trees Nurseries of Reigate, Surrey, in 1981. Clyne – British – 1981.

Doris Francis. Semi-double or double. Tube and sepals, deep rose-pink, paler underneath. Corolla pale orchid-pink, veined rose-pink. Growth lax bush, needs support when grown as bush. Francis – British – 1970.

Dorothea Flower. Single. White thin tube, sepals white with faint flesh-pink, deeper at underside. Corolla violet-blue with pink flush at base. Long flowers, fairly small but profuse, needs cool cultivation. Growth upright and bushy. Named after Miss D. Flower founder of the Dorking Fuchsia Society. Sister seedling to Oxenholme released in 1980. Hawkshead × Venus Victrix. Thornley – British – 1969 – A.F.S. No. 1009.

Dorothea Foubert. Semi-double. Red and purple. Lemoine – French – 1902.

Dorothy. Single. Tube and sepals, bright crimson, sepals violet veined red. Medium sized flowers and free, growth upright and bushy, hardy in southern districts, suitable for low hedges, height 3 ft. Accepted by the B.F.S. as showbench hardy. Wood – British – 1946.

Dorothy Louise. Double. Pale pink self. Medium sized blooms and very free, growth upright or arching trailer. Schnabel – American – 1952 – A.F.S. No. 113.

Dorothy Plater. Double. Red and purple. Strutt – British – 1886.

Dorothy Woakes. Double. Short tube, rosy-carmine, sepals rosy-carmine. Corolla pale rose-pink with deeper rose-pink veining. Large flowers, very prolific, growth upright and bushy. Bubb-Gay – British – 1973 – A.F.S. No. 1153.

Dotti. Double. Short, red tube, rosy-red sepals, completely reflexed; corolla deep purple, flocked pink at base, fading to rose at maturity. Smallish blooms for a double with flaring corolla and smaller than its parent Dollar Princess, rosy-red, flaring stamens with pink pistil. Dark green foliage, medium-sized leaves. Blooms are only half the size of Dollar Princess but more profuse and continuous flowering. Growth lax upright, responds to any type of training, will trail with weights, used for corsage work in America. Tested for 3 years in California coastal area. Dollar Princess × Jingle Bells. Storvick – American – 1978 – A.F.S. No. 1485.

Dovecot. Double. Short thick tube and sepals rose-pink, corolla rose-violet. Medium sized blooms neat and very compact. Growth low bush. Need – British – 1964.

Dragonfly. Double. Tube cherry, sepals cherry with reverse side rose-madder. Corolla dauphin's violet, veined and flushed rosy-madder. Large flowers and free, light green foliage. Growth upright. Crockett – British – 1965 – A.F.S. No. 819.

Drake 400. Double. Medium sized tube pale carmine, sepals carmine which twist around tube. Corolla imperial-purple, heavily flushed carmine. Medium sized blooms and very free for a double. Growth upright, raised in the vicinity of Plymouth, England. Hilton – British – 1981.

*Drake's Drum. Double. Medium sized carmine-rose tube, sepals carmine-rose. Corolla violet-purple with claret-rose flushed petaloids. Medium sized blooms and extremely free flowering for double. Growth natural trailer, raised in the vicinity of Plymouth, Devon. Whirly Bird × Bicentennial. Hilton – British – 1984.

*Drama Girl. Double. Tube and sepals, pale pink, corolla blue with pink marbling. medium sized blooms, growth trailer very suitable for basketwork. Raised in the vicinity of merimbula, New South Wales, Australia. Lockerbie – Australian – ca 1975.

Dr. A.M. De Cola. Double. Tube and sepals, pink inside and white outside, tipped green. Corolla long and coloured three shades of rose with orange variegations. Large flowers but very small foliage. Growth lax bush or trailer. Pennisi – American – 1969 – A.F.S. No. 814.

Drame. Semi-double. Tube and sepals scarlet; corolla violet-purple. Medium sized blooms and very free, with yellowish-green foliage. Growth upright bushy and spreading. Hardy in most districts. Suitable for low hedge up to 2 ft. Accepted by the B.F.S. as showbench hardy. Riccartonii ×. Lemoine – French – 1880.

Drame

Drame – Charming. To distinguish between these two similar cultivars see Charming.

Dr. Behring. Double. Red and purple. Lemoine – French – 1902.

Dr. Bornet. Lemoine – French – 1912.

Dr. Bowman. Single. Tube deep pink, sepals pale pink, tinged blue, edged deeper blue. Corolla orchid-pink. Flowers very small, star shaped, similar to species. Foliage is similar to *F.cordifolia*. Growth upright and vigorous. Named after Paul Bowman, M.D., hybridiser in America of rhododendrons and other plants. Francesca – American – 1973 – A.F.S. No. 1098.

Dr. Crevaux. Lemoine – French – 1880.

Dr. Davis. Double. Tube and sepals pink; corolla light cream. Medium sized blooms and free. Growth medium upright Hazard and Hazard – American – Date unknown.

Dreadnought. Smith – British – 1864.

Dreadnought. Double. Red and purple. Felton – British – 1870.

Dream. Single. Tube and sepals, deep pink, tipped green; corolla old rose. Medium sized flowers and free. Growth upright and rampant up to 8 ft in California, makes it suitable as a climber. Munker – American – 1952.

Dream Girl. Double. Tube and sepals, bright red; corolla orchid-rose. Large blooms, early and free. Growth lax bush or trailer. Haag – American – 1955.

Dr. Ennis. Double. Tube and sepals carmine, crepy texture; corolla violet-blue with a touch of carmine, turning a bright hue as it matures. Large blooms resembling a big rose, heavy bloomer and of very heavy texture. Dark green foliage. Growth trailer. Gagnon – American – 1964 – A.F.S. No. 601.

Dresden. Semi-double. Tube and sepals, neyron-rose; corolla mauve, outside petals neyron-rose. Medium sized flowers and free. Growth upright and bushy. Niederholzer – American – 1946.

Dr. Foster. Single. Tube and sepals scarlet; corolla violet. Large flowers and free. Growth upright and bushy, hardy in Southern districts. Feature of this cultivar is that it is probably the largest flower for a hardy, suitable for a low hedge of up to 3 ft. Accepted by the B.F.S. as showbench hardy. Lemoine – French – 1899.

Dr. Fournier. Lemoine – French – 1905.

Dr. Godron. Single. Dominyana × *F.serratifolia*. Lemoine – French – 1878.

Dr. Jephson. White and dark purple. Newberry – British – Date unknown.

Dr. Johannsen. Lemoine – French – 1904.

Dr. John Gallivey. Double. Long tube and sepals, rose-madder; corolla white. Large flowers and free. Growth upright and erect, firm grower. Mrs. Gladstone × Amy Lye. Reiter – American – 1940.

Dr. Jules Welch. Double. White tube, sepals and outer petals watermelon-pink, corolla blue-violet. Large blooms and free. Growth upright and vigorous. Evans and Reeves – American – 1946 – A.F.S. No. 45.

Dr. Kelly. Double. Tube and sepals, light pink; corolla orchid with serrated edges. Foliage light green and large. Growth lax bush or trailer. Soo Yun Field – American – 1966 – A.F.S. No. 682.

*Dr. Manson. Single. Tapering tube carmine-rose, sepals completely upswept with tips recurved carmine-rose, tipped green, but neither tube or ovary hidden. Very open corolla violet shading to pale pink at base with veining. Medium sized flowers of typical Cloverdale Pearl shape, true single with pink filaments and pistil. cream anthers and stigma. 2 in long by 1¼ in wide, fairly free flowering. Medium green foliage with ovate leaves 2¼ in by 1¼ in wide. Growth very upright, tall and bushy, makes good shape with minimum of pinching, fairly short jointed. Raised in the vicinity of Nottingham before release to Jackson's Nurseries of Tamworth, who introduced it in 1983. Cloverdale Pearl × Glyn Jones. Roe – British – 1983.

Dr. Olson. Double. Tube and upturned sepals, bright red; corolla palest orchid-pink with large centre petals surrounded by shorter, spreading petals, heavily overlaid mallow-purple with salmon flush. Large blooms, free blooming. Growth trailer. A.F.S. Cert. of Merit 1962. Olson-Mrs. D. Lyon – American – 1959 – A.F.S. No. 412.

Dr. Prillieux. Lemoine – French – 1890.

Dr. Rahn. Double. Tube and upturned wide sepals, waxy carmine-rose. Corolla purple, veined at base with rose, often has extra short rose petals. Large blooms and very profuse. Growth upright and tall. Brand – American – 1956 – A.F.S. No. 279.

Dr. Ruben. Double. White tube, sepals white with pink blush underneath, white with green tips on topside. Corolla and petaloids purple with streakings of pink, white at base. Growth upright and bushy. Unregistered American introduction which appears to be grown only in California. Raiser and date unknown.

Dr. Topinard. Single. Tube and sepals rose, corolla white, veined rose. Medium sized flowers, very free, corolla is flared and open, similar to Display. Growth upright and bushy. Very fine old cultivar, chosen by Northampton Fuchsia Society as their emblem for lapel badge. Lemoine – French – 1890.

Drum Major. Semi-double. Tube and sepals, white with green tip. Corolla magnolia-purple with crimson flecks. Flowers large and free. Growth upright and bushy. Baker – British – 1970.

Dr. Vance. Double. Tube red, sepals vivid red and recurved; corolla dark violet and cerise. Large flowers, free and loose, dark green foliage. Growth upright bushy and vigorous. Evans and Reeves – American – 1935.

Dr. Wm. R. Vizzard. Double. Deep red tube, large sepals, broad and upturned, deep red. Corolla snowy-white with deep red veining. Large flowers and free, dark green foliage. Growth trailer. Chiles – American – 1953 – A.F.S. No. 163.

Du Barry. Double. Tube and reflexed sepals, softest pink, corolla purple to fuchsia with smaller outside petals marbled flesh-pink. Large blooms and fairly free. Growth upright and vigorous. A.F.S. Cert. of Merit. Tiret – American – 1950 – A.F.S. No. 63.

Duc D'Aumale. Lemoine – French – 1896.

Duc de Crillon. Cornelissen – Belgian – 1866.

Duchess. Single. White and purple. Carter – British – 1870.

Duchesse de Geroldstein. Single. Tube and sepals palish-carmine; corolla bluish-pink. Medium-sized flowers and very free. Growth upright and bushy. Eggbrecht – German – 1868.

Duchess of Albany. Single. Tube waxy-cream, sepals whitish-pink and recurving; corolla pinkish-cerise. Medium sized flowers and free, with bright green foliage. Growth upright bush and vigorous, makes an excellent standard. Elegant and attractive. Rundle – British – 1891.

Duchess of Chatelaine. Double. Tube and thick sepals pink; corolla rich creamy-white, could be described as a pink and white Swingtime. Extra large blooms and free. Growth lax bush or trailer, makes fine basket. Haag – American – 1955.

Duchess of Edinburgh. Double. Tube and sepals cerise; corolla white, veined cerise. Flowers very full, medium sized and free. Growth upright bush. Seems to have passed out of cultivation. Rundle – British – 1892.

Duchess of Fife. Single or semi-double. Tube and sepals pale scarlet; corolla rosy-lilac. Smallish flowers and very free. Growth upright and busy. Synonymous with Monsieur Joule (Lemoine 1890). Clark – British – 1948.

Duchess of Gloucester. Semi-double. Red and purple. Standish – British – 1848.

Duchess of Lancaster. Single. White and pink. Henderson – British – 1853.

Duchess of Sutherland. Single. No other details available other than the colouring – pale lilac. Gaines – British – 1845.

Duet. Double. Long red tube, bright pink (R.H.S. 56A) sepals 1¾in long × ⅝in wide which recurve to cover the tube. Pale raspberry-pink (R.H.S. 56A) corolla, flushed bright pink and lightly veined. Large blooms 1¼in long × 1½in wide some of the petals form a bell shape with remainder irregularly arranged, petaloids 1 in long same colour as corolla, stamens and pistil red (R.H.S. 55A). Foliage spring green (R.H.S. 146A) with large leaves 2½in long × 2 in wide, serrated and prominent veins with pink central vein. Growth is natural trailer, will make basket without weights. Tested for 10 years in the vicinity of Northumberland, N.E. England, before release. Hall – British – 1982 – A.F.S. No. 1664.

Duke of Cornwall. Single. Almost pink self. Passingham – British – 1847.

Duke of Edinburgh. Single. Red and purple. Banks . British – 1872.

Duke of Norfolk. Semi-double. White and purple. Barkway – British – 1846.

Duke of Wellington. Semi-double. Red and purple. Epps – British – 1845.

Duke of Wellington. Double. Tube and sepals carmine; corolla violet-purple, pink at base, veined cerise. Huge blooms very much like Enchanted. Growth upright and vigorous. Haag – American – 1956.

Duke of York. Single. Pink and purple. Still in cultivation and very similar to Mrs. Popple but corolla tends to saucer shape and is lighter blue. Miller – British – 1845.

Dulcie Elizabeth. Double. Tube and reflexed sepals, neyron-rose; corolla powder-blue, flecked deep rose and shell-pink, flares out. Parsley green foliage. Growth upright and bushy self-branching. Tennessee Waltz × Winston Churchill. Clyne-Aimes – British – 1974 – A.F.S. No. 1227.

Dulcinea. Double. Tube and extra long sepals red; corolla white. Large blooms, fairly free. Growth medium upright. Edwards – American – 1948.

*Dulwich. Double. Advance information before release under another name. Medium tube pink and fluted, sepals light pink on top, slightly darker pink underneath, broad for size, fully recurved but held well away from both tube and ovary, long pedicel. Corolla white slightly veined pink, full double and tight typical shape of Heidi Ann. First cultivar of the Heidi Ann class but with totally different colouring, dark pink stamens, brown anthers and stigma. Darkish green foliage with ovate leaves 1¼in long by ⅞in wide and acute tip. Growth upright, bushy and short jointed, similar growth to Heidi Ann. Raised in the vicinity of Merseyside and at present undergoing tests and trials on the showbench before being renamed. Clark, D. – British – to be released.

Dunois. Single. Tube and sepals crimson, corolla purple. Medium sized flowers and free. Growth upright bush. Niederholzer – American – 1943.

Dunrobin Bedder. Single. Tube and sepals scarlet, corolla dark purple. Very small flowers but very free. Growth dwarf and spreading, suitable for rockery or edging border, hardy. Accepted by the B.F.S. as showbench hardy. Variant of *F.globosa*. Synonymous with Dobbie's Bedder. Melville – British – 1890. (See also *magellanica* var. *globosa*.)

Dunrobin Castle. Variant of *globosa* with pale green and bright coral-red foliage. Neville – British – Date unknown. (See also *magellanica* var. *globosa*.)

Duplex. Double. Red and purple. This cultivar together with Multiplex are considered to be the first double flowered hybrids and mutations. Story – British – 1850.

Durango. Double. Rich, vivid-red self. Largish to medium blooms and free for double. Foliage is red veined with red stems, growth cascade, this cultivar could also be described as a 'double Marinka'. York – American – 1934.

Dusk. Double. Tube and sepals, palest blush-pink, underside of sepals slightly darker pink. Corolla pale blue, shades to pink at base of petals. Growth trailer, natural and fast. Reedstrom – American – 1958 – A.F.S. No. 357.

Dusk. No other details available other than it is a miniature cultivar and should not be confused with Dusk by Reedstrom 1958. Pugh – British – 1977.

Dusky Beauty. Single. Tube neyron-rose, horizontally held sepals neyron-rose. Corolla pale purple with pink cast and deeper pink edges. Small flowers very prolific, best colour in shade. Medium to dark green foliage, ovate with obtuse leaf tip. Growth small upright, will make good bush and fine exhibition cultivar. Exhibited with great success by Norman Mitchinson at B.F.S. Northern Show, Manchester 1980 before release. Raised in Northumberland and vicinity but tested for 4 years in the vicinity of Kidderminster before being introduced by Fuchsiavale Nurseries of Kidderminster in 1981. Ryle – British – 1981 – A.F.S. No. 1652.

Dusky Boy. Single. Tube and sepals rich-red; corolla Trojan-red. Flowers long and free with long tube. Growth upright bushy. Jones, W. – British – 1960.

Dusky Falls. Double. Tube and sepals red; corolla dusky-red. Growth upright and bushy. Jones, W. – British – 1960.

Dusky Rose. Double. Tube deep pink, long sepals which curl at tips, clear deep coral-pink. Corolla lovely shade of rose with coral-pink splashes. Large blooms changing to raspberry-rose and opens into a fluffy, ruffled bloom with age. Dark green foliage, heat resistant. Growth trailer, makes a good wall basket or full basket. A.F.S. Cert. of Merit 1962. Waltz – American – 1960 – A.F.S. No. 439.

Dutch Bonnet. Double. Tube and pointed sepals, waxy-white, curve up as a dutch bonnet. Corolla deep violet-blue. Growth lax bush or trailer. Martin – American – 1958 – A.F.S. No. 361.

Dutch Mill. Single. Tube and sepals, bright rose-Bengal, sepals are long and curled. Corolla bell shaped, veronica-blue. Medium sized blooms and free. Growth upright bush. Peterson – American – 1962.

Dutch Shoes Double. Short tube and sepals, rose with pink tips. Corolla rose. Growth trailer. Pennisi – American – 1970 – A.F.S. No. 895.

Dynamic. Double. Red self, medium-sized blooms very similar to San Leandro. Not to be confused with Dynamic by Kuechler 1962. Walker – American – 1959.

Dynamic. Double. Tube rose, sepals wide, rose on inside and near white, tipped with green on outside. Corolla blue, marbled pink, very profuse bloomer. Bright green foliage. Growth upright bush. Kuechler – American – 1962 – A.F.S. No. 506.

E.A. Babbs. Single. Tube and sepals crimson; corolla deep rose. Small flowers but very free. Growth upright and bushy, suitable for low hedge, hardy. Wood – British – 1949.

Earl of Beaconsfield. Single. Features very long tube, thick and very substantial, slightly bulbous in the middle, salmon-pink with a touch of carmine with a waxy-like texture. Sepals salmon-pink delicately tipped green, recurved with a little tight curl. Fluted corolla is salmon-orange and short in comparison to the tube, stamens are short and pink in colour whilst the style is salmon-pink. The flowers are single and very free for the size which is between 4 and 4½ in long. Another fine old cultivar worth searching for, raised by P. Laing in 1878 and as far as the flower is concerned in a class of its own. Together with Mrs. Marshall, Display, Scarcity and Ballet Girl was used extensively by the Home Counties nurserymen in the glorious days of the fuchsia (1880 to 1914) and sent to Covent Garden market in great quantities. Both Mr. Rundle (1896) and Mrs. Rundle (1883) are reputed to be seedlings from the Earl of Beaconsfield and when all three flowers are side by side, would be easy to substantiate the claim. The raiser only introduced one other cultivar named Laing's Hybrid in 1873 which was a red self and a seedling from *F. fulgens*. Always in bloom and very early, flowers can be obtained by the end of June and under normal conditions last longer than most. Foliage is a little large and lightish green, growth a little disappointing and needs careful cultivation for training as a bush, needs tight pinching in the early stages of growth, but would imagine a fine standard could be obtained. A cultivar well worth adding to any grower's selection, you may have to search diligently as not many nurserymen list it, although it is still currently obtainable both from Chingford Nurseries and Woodbridge Nurseries. From information gathered from *The Garden* 1876, Vol. IX,

p. 607 and 1877, Vol. XI, p. 98, it would appear that Earl of Beaconsfield and Laing's Hybrid are synonymous. The cross is *F. fulgens* × Perfection (Banks). Laing – British – 1878.

East Anglian. Single to semi-double. Tube flesh-pink, sepals pink streaked carmine; corolla rose, flushed orange, white at base. Largish blooms, very free, the whole bloom is waxy and of great substance. Growth lax upright. Winner of the B.F.S. Jones Cup 1960 and B.F.S. Award of Merit. Thorne – British – 1960.

Easter Bonnet. Double. Short tube flushed rose, broad frosty upturned sepals, shading from deep pink at base of petals to pale pink, tipped green. Corolla a dusky rose-pink, deeper shade at base of petals. Beautiful buds, opening into wide-spreading ruffled cup shaped blooms, ageing to deeper shade of rose. Dark green foliage. A.F.S. Cert. of Merit. Waltz – American – 1955 – A.F.S. No. 225.

***Easterling.** Single. Tube and sepals ivory-white, sepals are recurving with maturity. Corolla rosy-red. medium sized flowers and very floriferous. Medium green foliage with leaf margins serrated. Growth upright and bushy, early stopping produces well shaped plant with plenty of side shoots, large show plants made with little trouble, the bi-coloured flowers making splendid impact. Raised in the vicinity of Ipswich, Suffolk, and introduced by the raiser, Gouldings Fuchsias of Ipswich, in 1985. One of a series of ten new introductions named after famous trains in 1985. Goulding – British – 1985.

Ebbtide. Double. Tube and recurved sepals, light pink inside, white outside. Corolla light blue and phlox-pink, changing to pastel lavender and phlox-pink with age. Large spreading blooms, very early. Growth trailer, very vigorous. Erickson-Lewis – American – 1959 – A.F.S. No. 405.

Eclipse. Double. Red and purple. Smith – British – 1881.

Eclipse. Single. Tube and sepals, waxy-white; corolla rose-carmine. Medium sized blooms, very free and early. Growth upright and bushy, produces excellent standard. Lye – British – 1897 – A.F.S. No. 9.

Ecstasy. Double. Tube and sepals, neyron-rose, tipped green; corolla hyacinth-blue, splashed phlox-pink. Large flowers and free, growth semi-trailer. One of the first to be registered with the A.F.S. 1948, the first year of registrations. Tiret – American – 1948.

Edale. Single. Light pink, thick tube, sepals rhodamine-pink; corolla spectrum-violet, shading to Imperial-purple. Large flowers and free, best colour in shade. Growth medium upright and bushy. Joan Pacey × Miss Great Britain. Gadsby – British – 1975 – A.F.S. No. 1281.

Edelstein. Double. Red and white. Grosse – British – 1864.

Edelweiss. Double. Red and white. Henderson – British – 1882.

Eden. Double. Short tube and sepals, light pink; corolla a light blue, variegated with blue, pink and white with touches of purple. Large blooms, not very free. Growth trailer. Pennisi – American – 1968 – A.F.S. No. 757.

Eden Beauty. Single. Tube carmine, sepals carmine outside, crimson inside, tipped green, curve up gracefully. Corolla fuchsia-purple, veined red, fades to magenta-rose. Large bell shaped blooms and very profuse. Growth natural self-branching trailer, will make good basket or weeping standard. Named for the Edenbridge Fuchsia Society. Percy Holmes × Achievement. Holmes, R. – British – 1974 – A.F.S. No. 1201.

*Eden Dawn. Single. Pale pink tube (R.H.S. 36D). Sepals are a paler pink (R.H.S. 36D) slightly reflexed. Corolla pale pink (R.H.S. 36B). Medium sized flowers almost a pure pink self, bell shaped. Foliage is almond-green (R.H.S. 138B), medium sized with slightly serrated leaves. Growth medium upright, will produce excellent bush or standard. Raised and tested for 4 years in the vicinity of Carlisle, Cumbria, before release. Introduced by Markham Grange Nurseries of Doncaster in 1982. Mitchinson – British – 1983 – A.F.S. No. 1720.

Eden Lady. Single. Short, thin pale rose tube. Amaranth rose (R.H.S. 65A) sepals, deeper colour underneath with the whole shading to white at tips, upturned from the horizontal and held well clear of the tube and corolla. Hyacinth-blue (R.H.S. 91A) corolla with slight rose colouring at base of petals. Medium-sized flowers, best colour in shade, ruby-red (R.H.S. 61A) stamens with pale rose pistil, exceptionally free flowering. Growth upright, self-branching and bushy, short jointed and easy cultivar to grow. Awarded the B.F.S. Bronze Certificate of Merit at Manchester 1975. This cultivar is a sister seedling to Border Queen and the only difference is that Eden Lady is a little darker in colour. Leonora × Lena Dalton. Ryle – British – 1975 – A.F.S. No. 1478.

*Eden Princess. Single. Tube and sepals are reddish-pink, corolla rich mallow-purple. Medium to largish flowers freely produced. Foliage is golden-honey coloured with red veining on fresh growth. Growth is upright and bushy; will produce excellent standard. Raised in the vicinity of Cumbria in the North of England and introduced by Fuchsiavale Nurseries of Kidderminster in 1983. Mitchinson – British – 1984.

Edith. Single. Red and purple. Banks – British – 1862.

Edith Emery. Semi-double. Short and thick waxy-white tube, white sepals are reflexed with crepe reverse. Corolla amethyst-violet, fading to rhodamine-purple. Short neat flowers, profuse flowering and of medium size. Smallish foliage with broad spinach-green leaves. Growth upright, bushy, self-branching and short jointed. La Campanella × Flirtation Waltz. Clyne – British – 1975 – A.F.S. No. 1284.

Edith Jack. Double. Tube and sepals deep pink, corolla lilac-blue. Very large blooms for a double which flowers in profusion. Dark green foliage, growth dainty, compact upright, ultimate height 1½ ft to 2 ft. Hardy in Southern England. Raised in the Scilly Isles. Tabraham, A.P. and E.V. – British – 1980.

Edith Pohley. Semi-double. Short tube and sepals, light 'salmon-pink, upturned sepals. Corolla pinkish-blue, medium sized blooms. Growth upright and bushy. Brown and Soules – American – 1951 – A.F.S. No. 75.

Edith Russell. Double. Tube and sepals, salmon-pink; corolla salmon-pink, violet at base.

Very small flowers, with petals folding over like a rosebud, very free. Very small foliage. Growth trailer. York – American – 1952 – A.F.S. No. 137.

Edith Summerville. Single. Long narrow tube, pale crimson, sepals the same colour. Corolla pale petunia. Bell shaped blooms, medium sized and free. Growth upright bush. Miller – British – 1970.

Ed Largarde. Double. Short tube and sepals white; corolla deep blue. Large flowers. Growth trailer. Pennisi – American – 1967 – A.F.S. No. 713.

Edmond About. Lemoine – French – 1888.

Edmond Perrier. Lemoine – French – 1904.

Edna May. Single. Pink and white striped tube, white sepals with blush of pink on underside. Corolla cream with scarlet anthers. Medium sized flowers, very free flowering, edge of sepals scarlet when given full light, can best be described as a white Border Queen. Dark green foliage, growth lax bush, habit is similar to Border Queen. Named after the raiser's wife, raised in the vicinity of Merseyside for four years before release. Seedling of Border Queen ×. Clark, D. – British – 1982.

Edouard Andre. Dominyana × *F.serratifolia*. Lemoine – French – 1878.

Edwardsii. Salter – British and French – 1841.

*Egmont Blue. Single. Pale pink tube with darker pink veining, half up sepals ivory tinged on top, white edged light violet underneath with recurved tips 1¾ in long by ½ in wide. Corolla opens campanula-violet (R.H.S. 82C) splashed pink and white at base, maturing to cyclamen-purple (R.H.S. 74A) with a lighter base. Three quartered flared medium sized flowers with pink filaments and garnet-lake anthers (R.H.S. 67C) white style and stigma, buds are long and slightly curved. Parsley green (R.H.S. 150D) foliage lighter green (R.H.S. 196A) underneath ovate leaves 2 in long by 1 in wide. Growth medium upright and bushy, will make good bush, upright or standard. Raised in the vicinity of Mount Egmont, New Plymouth, New Zealand and introduced by Gro-Wel Fuchsias. Proffit – New Zealand – 1984 – A.F.S. No. 1751.

*Egmont Trail. Single. Thin crimson tube, fully up sepals crimson 1½ in long by ¾ in wide and recurved tips. Corolla white heavily veined crimson (R.H.S. 52A). Medium sized flowers fully flared same shape as its parent, crimson filament, anthers, style and stigma, pistil extends 3 in below corolla. Lanceolate shaped foliage with 3 in long by 1¾ in wide leaves with serrulate margins, acute tips and rounded base, dark green (R.H.S. 152A) lighter green (R.H.S. 152D) underneath. Growth medium upright, bushy, good for bush or standard. Found in the vicinity of Mount Egmont, New Plymouth, New Zealand and introduced by Gro-Wel Fuchsias. Sport of Oregon Trail (Hodges 1949). Proffit – New Zealand – 1984 – A.F.S. No. 1752.

Eileen Pearson. Double. Pink and blue. Rozain-Boucharlat – French – 1910.

Eileen Raffill. Single. Tube rosy-cerise, sepals white with pale pink, tipped green. Corolla pale purple, rosy-pink at base. Medium sized blooms and free. Growth lax upright. Rafill – British – 1944.

Eileen Saunders. Single. Tube carmine, lined crimson, long sepals crimson, tipped green, reflexed to cover long slightly curved tube. Corolla fuchsia-purple, base carmine, veined crimson. Bell shaped blooms with four neatly shaped petals, feature of the flower is the distinct curving of the tube with reflexed sepals, giving the bloom a quaint clean cut look. Growth upright and bushy. Named after the author of the Wagtails series of fuchsia publications. Percy Holmes × Prodigy. Holmes, R. – British – 1974 – A.F.S. No. 1202.

E. Joubert. Double. Carmine and white. Lemoine – French – 1908.

Elaine. Single. Tube and sepals, rose-pink; corolla lavender. Medium sized blooms and free. Growth upright bush. Little Beauty × .Berkeley Hort. Nurseries – American – 1935.

Elaine Allen. Semi-double. Tube and sepals, neyron-rose, sepals held well out from corolla. Corolla magenta-rose, lighter at base. Large open saucer shaped blooms, pale green foliage. Growth upright and bushy. Albion × Rosedale. Allen – British – 1974 – A.F.S. No. 1214.

Elalie. Salter – British and French – 1841.

El Camino. Double. Tube rosy-red, short broad upturned sepals rosy-red; corolla white, heavily flushed and veined rose. Large blooms with large centre petals and smaller spreading outer petals. Deep green foliage. Growth upright and bushy. Lee – American – 1955.

El Cid. Single. Tube and sepals, deep red; corolla burgundy-red. Compact well shaped blooms, very profuse and of medium size. Growth upright and bushy, hardy. Accepted by the B.F.S. as showbench hardy. Empress of Prussia × .Colville – British – 1966.

Eleanor Carmino. Double. Tube and sepals, rosy-red; corolla white, flushed and veined rose. Medum sized blooms and free. Growth upright bush. Lee – American – 1955.

Eleanor Clark. Single. Tube phlox-pink with deeper pink stripes, sepals also phlox-pink and fully reflexed with maturity. Corolla shell-pink, medium sized flowers freely produced and gracefully shaped. Light to medium green foliage, ovate with obtuse leaf tip, lobed leaf base and serrate leaf margins. Growth medium upright, makes excellent bush, best colour in shade. Originates from the vicinity of Liverpool. Introduced by J.E. Ridding of Fuchsiavale Nurseries, Kidderminster, in 1980. Sport of Symphony. Clark, D. – British – 1980 – A.F.S. No. 1539.

Eleanor Crowther. Double. Tube and sepals dark rose; corolla pink, veined rose at base. Medium-sized blooms, very free for a double. Growth upright and arching bush. Duschene – Nationality unknown – 1912.

Eleanor Leytham. Single. Tube and sepals white, flushed pink; corolla pink, edged deeper pink. Small flowers but very profuse. Growth upright, bushy and compact, rather stiff, can be described as a pink Countess of Aberdeen. Named after a great lady of the British Fuchsia world B.F.S. Certificate of Preliminary Acceptance, Birmingham 1974, B.F.S. Bronze Certificate of Merit 1976, B.F.S. Show Birmingham. Countess of Aberdeen × Pink Darling. Roe – British – 1973.

Eleanor Rawlins. Single. Tube and sepals carmine; corolla magenta changing to carmine at base. Blooms very free and of medium size, light-

ish green foliage. Growth upright, bushy and hardy, excellent bedder. Accepted by the B.F.S. as showbench hardy. Wood – British – 1954.

Electra. Double. Tube and sepals red; corolla palest pink almost white, veined rose. Large flowers with wide open centre, free. Growth upright bush. This cultivar was originally named Azalea. Niederholzer – American – 1944.

Elegance. Single. Cream and pink. Turville – British – 1849.

Elegance. *F. fulgens* × Sultan. Lowe – British – 1875.

Elegance. Single. Red and blue. Arabella Improved × James Lye. Lye – British – Date unknown.

Elegans (Salisbury 1791). Synonymous with *F. magellanica* var. *globosa* var. *coccinea*.

Elegant. Myrtifolia × . Lemoine – French – 1893.

Elegantissima. Single. White and scarlet. Banks – British – 1862.

Elegantissima. Single. Red and purple. Smith – British – 1880.

Elf. Single. Tube and sepals red; corolla cherry red. Small flowers borne in profusion, foliage dark green. Growth upright, bushy and very compact, height 6 to 9 in, real miniature, suitable for rockeries, window boxes and troughs. One of a series of new hardy miniatures raised in the Scilly Isles. Tabraham – British – 1976.

Elfin. Single. Tube and sepals, faint pink; corolla pure white with faint carmine lines. Very small flowers, very profuse. Growth upright bush. Rolla × . Niederholzer – American – 1941.

Elfin Glade. Single. Tube and sepals, pink with rosy tint, corolla pinkish-mauve, paling at base, veined pink. Medium sized blooms and free, similar but larger and rather deeper colour than Margaret Brown. Growth upright and bushy. Accepted by the B.F.S. as showbench hardy. B.F.S. Award of Merit 1963. Colville – British – 1963.

Elfrida. Double. Red and purple. Miellez – French – 1871.

Elfriede Ott. Semi-double. Flowers salmon-pink; most unusual, and best described as like a double triphylla. Foliage dark green inherited from its parent Koralle. Very free flowering. One of the last raisings by the Austrian hybridist who died in 1976. Introduced in 1980 by Wills Fuchsia Ltd. of West Wittering. Koralle × *F. splendens*. Nutzinger – Austrian – 1976.

Eliane. Lemoine – French – 1913.

Elina. Double. Tube and sepals, white with green tips; corolla dark lilac. Small foliage, medium sized blooms. Growth trailer. Pennisi – American – 1969 – A.F.S. No. 815.

Elisabeth. Double. Tube and sepals light red; corolla light blue. Flowers are like tiny roses but not very free. El Camino × Winston Churchill. Nutzinger – Austrian – 1966.

Elise Chez. Double. Short thick tube pale green, sepals cream, flushed magenta at base, 1½ in to 2 in long upturned long and with pointed green tips. Corolla flushed cream turning to grey-blue with maturity. Largish blooms with rounded petals and very small petaloids same colour as corolla, cream stamens, long pistil with cream stigma. Olive green foliage with slight variegation at edges, large leaves 3 in long × 1½ in wide. Growth self-branching medium upright, will make basket with weights, or bush and standard. Tested for 3 years in the vicinity of Washington, Tyne and Wear, England before release. Registered by D. Thorp. Jo Chez cross. Cheseldine – British – 1982 – A.F.S. No. 1664.

Elite. Double. Tube and sepals light crimson-rose; corolla Imperial purple. Medium-sized blooms not very free, top petals variegated with light rose. Growth natural trailer. Walker – American – 1953.

Elizabeth. Single. Very long tube, rose-opal, sepals rose-opal, tipped green; corolla deep rich rose with salmon-pink shading. Long slender flowers and free, very similar to Mrs. W. Rundle, but Elizabeth growth is more vigorous. Growth upright and very vigorous, will make a greenhouse climber. Whiteman – British – 1941?

Elizabeth. Double. Tube and sepals, rosy-pink; corolla pastel pink. Large flowers, growth trailer. Tiret – American – 1970 – A.F.S. No. 898.

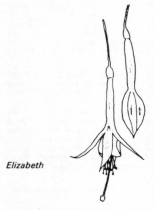

Elizabeth

Elizabeth Breary. Semi-double. Tube and incurved sepals pale pink; corolla deeper shade of pink, very slightly flushed rose. Medium-sized flowers and very free. Growth upright and bushy. Sport from Constance and almost identical in every way to Pink Pearl. Breary – British – 1976.

Elizabeth Broughton. Single. Tube and sepals, neyron-rose; corolla violet-purple with deep pure white markings in centre. Small flowers, very free, growth upright and bushy. Gadsby – British – 1975.

Elizabeth Brown. Semi-double. Short tube and medium sepals neyron-rose (H.C.C. 623) tipped green, sepals fold back slightly. Corolla spectrum-violet (H.C.C. 735/1). Medium sized blooms, growth strong, vigorous and bushy 12 in to 15 in in height. Glyn Jones × Neil Clyne. Roe – British – 1980.

Elizabeth Campbell. Double. Thick crimson tube, short, broad crimson sepals held horizontally with lower surface crepe textured. Corolla deep luminous purple, splashed crimson. Medium sized blooms showing definite characteristics of Royal Velvet, tightly ruffled 1¼ in long with short

crimson stamens. Medium green foliage leaves 2 in long oval shaped with red stems. Growth self-branching medium upright, will make good bush or standard. Tested for 2 years in the vicinity of Midlothian, Scotland before release. Royal Velvet × Fascination. McGuigan – British – 1982 – A.F.S. No. 1681.

Elizabeth Marshall. Double. Red and white. Simmonds – British – 1904.

Elizabeth Travis. Double. Tube and long sepals, pale pink, edged deep rose, recurving at tips. White corolla, petals are longer than the usual ones of its type. Large flowers and free. Growth upright, vigorous. Travis, J. – British – 1956.

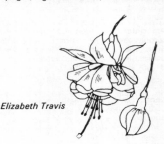

Elizabeth Travis

Elk Horn. Double. Tube and sepals carmine; corolla deep pink with serrated edges. Large flowers. Growth upright. Brand – American – 1949 – A.F.S. No. 49.

Ellen. Single. White and vermilion. Cripps – British – 1847.

Ellen Cant. Semi-double. Rose-pink and pink. Dixon – British – 1897.

Ellen Diane. Single. Pale red tube, long, thin and tiny sepals, fuchsia red. Corolla rosy-purple. Flowers are miniature in size, bell shaped, stamens and pistil do not extend below corolla, many blooms have five petals and five sepals, resembling a tiny red star. Foliage medium size, rather wrinkled. Growth upright and bushy, excellent cultivar for miniature or bonsai cultivation. Shaw – American – 1973 – A.F.S. No. 1034.

Ellen Morgan. Double. Short, thin tube, blush-white with green lining; sepals blush-white outside, tipped green with green line down centre, flushed neyron-rose (R.H.S. 55C), neyron-rose inside, blush-white at base. Mallow-purple (R.H.S. 72C) corolla, neyron-rose (R.H.S. 55C) at base, veined rose-Bengal (R.H.S. 67B) fading to ruby-red (R.H.S. 61B). Medium sized blooms with occasional petaloids, neatly flaring skirt of 16 or more petals, very fine stamens are longer than pistil. Growth medium upright, bushy and self-branching, excellent for all types of training also as outside bedder. Phyllis ×. Holmes, R. – British – 1976 – A.F.S. No. 1338.

Ellen Tidmarsh. Single. Pink and rose. Stride – British – 1904.

Elliott's Variety. Single. Tube and sepals and corolla very pale pink making it a true self. Medium sized flower with very tall growth and upright. Hardy cultivar, appears to be exclusive to the Home Counties of England. Raiser unknown – British – date unknown.

144

Elma Oliver. Double. Tube bright rose, long twisted sepals bright rose on inside, lighter shade outside. Corolla dusky-rose. Bright green foliage, growth trailer, heat tolerant. Kuechler – American – 1962 – A.F.S. No. 503.

El Matador. Semi-double to double. Tube and sepals, pink to salmon shade; corolla dark shades of purple and burgundy with streaks of salmon. Flowers are large, petals flare out wide, extra long pistil, very long buds. Growth trailer, makes beautiful basket. Kennett – American – 1965 – A.F.S. No. 641.

Elm City. Double. Tube and sepals red; corolla very dark purple, striped red at base. Small flowers and free. Growth upright, dwarf habit. Berkeley Hort. Nurseries – American – 1935.

Elsa. Semi-double. Tube and sepals, flesh colour, corolla rosy-magenta, ageing to light purple. Flowers are largish and free, very early. Growth upright and bushy. This cultivar is always confused with Eva Boerg, Hapsburgh, Lena and Madame Eva Boye. Raiser unknown – British – Date unknown.

Elsa – Lena. To distinguish between these two almost identical cultivars: one fundamental difference is the relative length of the pistil and the stamens. In the case of Elsa, the pistil is longer than the stamens, whereas Lena stamens are longer than the pistil. Another small difference is in the sepals, in the case of Elsa they lay around or 'hood over' the corolla.

Elsie. This is the name given to the cultivar Beauty of Swanley in California.

Elsie Blackmore. Semi-double. White and purple. Carters – British – 1908.

Elsie Mitchell. Double. Pink tube, sepals pink at base, shaded to white and tipped green, semi-reflexed. Corolla sea-lavender with pleasing effect of a pink haze. Medium sized blooms with anthers and stamens that protrude well from the petals. Medium green foliage, ovate with obtuse leaf tip, ovate leaf base and senate leaf margins. Growth medium upright, will make good bush, self-branching similar habit to Border Queen, best colour develops in shade. Originates from Northumberland. Introduced by J.E. Ridding of Fuchsiavale Nurseries, Kidderminster, in 1980. Ryle – British – 1980 – A.F.S. No. 1576.

Elsie Vert. Double. Red and purple. Lemoine – French – 1898.

Elysée. Single. Red and purple. Riccartonii×. Lemoine – French – 1886.

Elysia. Single. Tube and sepals dark red; corolla rich claret. Large flowers very free and early, best colours in shade, dislikes hot conditions. Growth upright, strong vigorous and bushy. Raiser unknown – American – Date unknown.

Embarcadero. Double. Tube and sepals, light pink, tipped with rose; corolla muted purple, fading to dusky flaring rose. Extra long blooms with medium sized foliage. Growth trailer. Schnabel-Paskeson – American – 1962 – A.F.S. No. 532.

Emberglow. Double. Carmine tube, recurving sepals, carmine-rose, tipped pea green. Corolla lilac-purple, changing to smoky hue of China-rose and spiraea-red. Medium size blooms and lush deep green foliage. Growth trailer. Tiret – American – 1957 – A.F.S. No. 295.

Emblematic. Single. Red and purple. Banks – British – 1863.

Emelita. Semi-double. Long scarlet tube, extremely long sepals of the same colour; corolla light blue to violet, whether the raiser is prone to exaggeration or not, but claims the blooms to be the size of a tea cup, with the appearance of an orchid. Dark green foliage, growth upright. Munkner – American – 1954.

Emile Bayard. Lemoine – French – 1892.

Emile de Wildeman. (Synonymous with Fascination). Double. Probably the best cultivar raised by the great hybridist Lemoine of Nancy in 1905. Although generally referred to as Fascination, was introduced as Emile de Wildeman and catalogued as such, was for some time erroneously known in England as Rose Ballet Girl and in America as Irwin's Great Pink. The tube and sepals are rich waxy-red, with a very full double corolla of blush-pink, heavily flushed rose-pink and veined cerise, the flowers which are freely produced are large and hold their colour. The filaments and style are cerise and the foliage of medium green. Growth is upright and vigorous, excels as a bush plant, will make a fine pyramid and can produce a good standard, although in this shape, the rather stiff growth of the laterals can be under strain to support the weight of the flowers. The saying 'you cannot beat an old good un' is very true of this cultivar, which is a leader in its own class, very easy to grow and responds to correct timing for show purposes. A cultivar which can easily be flowered early in the season, prefers a warm start and will continue to bloom until autumn. Belongs to the Edwardian era of Ballet Girl, Achievement, Scarcity and Mrs. Marshall, all of which hold their own amongst the newcomers of today, very suitable for growing indoors and will hold its bloom and bud in the dry atmosphere, if necessary. Although it prefers life underglass and best grown as H2, it is equally at home being bedded out in the border. Once the beginner has been successful with the singles, this cultivar should be on his list as an easy double and, although not seen very often these days on the showbench, a well grown plant will take a lot of beating. Has received a Highly Commended Certificate from the R.H.S. and will still continue to stand the test of time. This cultivar should not be confused with New Fascination, raised by Niederholzer in 1940 with similar colouring but a little darker and not so full a corolla, or so compact, but with much more upturned sepals. Lemoine – French – 1905.

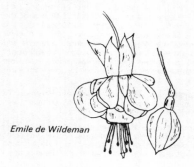

Emile de Wildeman

145

Emile Eskmann. Lemoine – French – 1903.

Emile Laurent. Double. Rose and white. Lemoine – French – 1904.

Emile Lemoine. Double. Pink and blue. Lemoine – French – 1907.

Emile Richebourg. Lemoine – French – 1894.

Emile Zola. Single. Tube scarlet cerise, reflexed sepals scarlet-cerise; corolla bright rosy-magenta. Flowers are medium sized, bell shaped open corolla and fairly free. Growth is upright and bushy, vigorous and almost hardy. Awarded R.H.S. Award of Merit in 1929, resubmitted by Chingford Nurseries for R.H.S. Wisley Hardy Trials 1975–78 but received no further award. Lemoine – French – 1910.

Emilie. Semi-double. Tube and sepals, coral-pink; corolla fuchsia-rose and peach. Medium sized flowers and free. Growth semi-trailer. Nessier – American – 1948

Emily Bright. Single. White and carmine. Lye – British – 1892.

Emma. Semi-double. Red coloured. Rufus × R.A.F. Griffiths – British – 1974.

Emma Calve. Double. Cerise and white. Lemoine – French – 1912.

Emma O'Neill. Semi-double. Tube and sepals ivory, flushed neyron-rose; corolla flushed plox-pink, white at base, petals faintly darker edged. Medium sized blooms. Growth upright and bushy. Schnabel – American – 1952 – A.F.S. No. 110.

Empereur des Fuchsias. Double. Red and white. Cornelissen – Belgian – 1863.

Empereur Napoleon III. Single. Red and purple. Banks – British – 1855.

Emperor. Single. Red and purple. Bull – British – 1867.

Emperor of Brazil. Double. Red and purple. Williams – British – 1872.

Empress. Single. White and purple. Halley – British – 1846.

Empress Eugénie. Single. Crimson and white. Story – British – 1850.

Empress of Germany. Single. Red and purple. Williams – British – 1871.

Empress of Prussia. Single. Tube and sepals, glowing scarlet; corolla reddish-magenta, paler at base. Largish flowers for a hardy and very free; outstanding feature being that every joint carries 6 to 8 blooms instead of the customary two. Growth upright and bushy up to 3 ft, one of the outstanding hardy cultivars, accepted by the B.F.S. as showbench hardy. Was found in 1958 growing in a West Country garden where it had been growing for 60 years. Raiser's name thought to be lost in the realms of antiquity at the time Bernard Rawlins reintroduced. Hoppe – British – 1868.

Empress of Prussia–General Voyron. To distinguish between these two cultivars see General Voyron–Empress of Prussia.

Empress of Prussia – Monsieur Thibaut. These two similar cultivars can easily be confused with one another, the distinguishing features are the corolla. E. of P. corolla is straight whereas the corolla of M.T. is rather the shape of Display.

Enchanted. Double. Short tube and sepals, rosy-red; corolla campanula-blue, outer petals overlaid with fuchsia-pink. Fairly large blooms and free. Growth lax bush or trailer. A.F.S. Cert. of Merit. Sister seedling of Swingtime. Titanic × Yuletide. Tiret – American – 1951 – A.F.S. No. 95.

Enchantress. Double. Scarlet and white. Bland – British – 1869.

Enchantress. Double. Tube and sepals carmine; corolla lavender-pink. Large blooms, fairly free. Growth upright. Raiser unknown – American – Date unknown.

encliandra. Red tube, reddish sepals; purplish-red corolla. Tiny flowers with fern-like foliage. Upright shrub, rampant grower, can attain a height of many feet in Mexico. Synonymous with *F. parviflora* (Hemsley 1880) Steudel – 1840 – Mexico.

Encore. Double. Tube and sepals, pure white; corolla amethyst, mottled with pink, fading to clear white at base, blending into the sepals. Large blooms, fairly free and compact. Growth natural trailer, makes a lovely basket, needs shade. Reedstrom – American – 1960 – A.F.S. No. 422.

Enfante Prodigue (also known as Prodigue). Semi-double. Tube and sepals crimson; corolla bluish-purple, ageing to magenta, pink at base. Medium sized flowers and free, very similar to Margaret. Growth upright and bushy, hardy. Accepted by the B.F.S. as showbench hardy. Submitted under the name of Prodigy for the R.H.S. Wisley Hardy Trials 1975–78 and, although it received the Award of Merit in 1965, received no further award. Riccartonii ×. Lemoine – French – 1887.

*Engelmann's Giant. Double. Tube and sepals rose, corolla white with heavy rose veining. Largish blooms and very free flowering. Growth upright and bushy. Raised in the vicinity of Merimbula, New South Wales, Australia. Lockerbie – Australian – *ca* 1975.

Enid. Double. Tube and sepals crimson; corolla plum-purple. Largish blooms and fairly free, slow grower. Growth medium upright, bushy and self-branching. Whiteman – British – 1941.

Enoch Arden. Double. Red and purple. Banks – British – 1865.

Ensign. No details available for this cultivar except that it could be another name for Display in Kenya. Information contained in a letter from L.R. Gillespie 22/1/51 in Nairobi.

Eos. Single. Long thin white tube, sepals phlox-pink, deltoid and much reflexed; corolla Tyrian-purple, Breviflora type, much recurved. Tiny flowers, very free flowering with very long pistil, produces display of black-purple berries with maturity. Foliage typical Encliandra with ovate, slightly serrated leaves. Growth semi-trailer, self-branching and bushy, good for all types of training. Travis, J. – British – 1975 – A.F.S. No. 1318.

Eppsii. Single. Tube waxy-pink, long and non-recurving sepals, rosy-cerise, tipped green; rosy-magenta corolla. Medium sized flowers, very free, light green foliage. Growth upright and bushy, suitable for pyramid or standard. Epps – British – 1844.

Erecta. Single. Tube and sepals red; corolla pale blue changing to pink along the edges. Small erect flowers and fairly free. Growth upright and bushy, hardy in some districts. *F.fulgens* × *F.fulgens* var.*rubra grandiflora*. Maye – German – 1841.

Erecta Novelty. Synonymous with Bon Accorde.

Erica Sharp. Double. Tube and sepals, palish-crimson; corolla rose-madder, fading to deep crimson with age. Medium sized blooms, very free with twisted sepals. Growth upright and bushy. Named after a past assistant Secretary/Treasurer of the B.F.S. Thorne – British – 1967.

***Erich Mehlis.** Single. Tube and sepals dark red; corolla dark blue. Small flowers very free flowering. Growth small, neat and dwarf, suitable for the rockery. Nutzinger – Austrian – 1976.

Erika. Single. Cerise self, medium sized flowers, very slender. Growth upright and strong. Hatchard – British – 1974.

***Erika Köth.** Triphylla type single. Long tubed orange triphylla type hybrid. Small flowers with strong upright growth; sister seedling to Lilo Vogt. Koralle × *F. boliviana*. Nutzinger – Austrian – 1976.

Eris. Single. Deep rose, thin tube ⅛ in long, deep rose sepals ⅜ in wide with lighter colour on the underside, slightly recurved above the horizontal. Corolla light rose, very small flowers with very small petals pressed against the sepals. Prominent pistil has spreading rose stigma, total length of flower is only ⅞ in. Diamond shaped, deeply toothed foliage, light green and fernlike, large black berries. Growth tall and upright, self-branching, best colour develops in shade. Originates from the area of Preston, Lancashire. Encliandra cross. Travis, J. – British – 1980 – A.F.S. No. 1581.

Ernestine. Double. Flesh coloured tube, curving sepals of medium width, flesh to orangy-pink. Corolla pale orangy-scarlet, (R.H.S. 43C). Medium to large sized blooms with full flaring petals, slightly serrated with lighter colouration on outer petals. Medium green foliage 2½ in long × 1½ in ovate leaves with lobed base, obtuse tip and serrated margin. Growth medium upright, will make good bush, best colour in filtered sun. Tested for 6 years in vicinity of Fort Bragg, Oxnard and Oceanside, California before release where it will be trademarked. Stubbs – American – 1981 – A.F.S. No. 1616.

Ernest Renan. Single. White and rose. Lemoine – French – 1888.

Ernie's Choice. Double. Tube and sepals pink; corolla mauve, although the flowers are larger than General Monk, the colouring is not so intense, both the sepals and the corolla of lighter colour. Corolla is not so tight as General Monk but an attractive bell-shaped. Very nice cultivar but too similar to Cloverdale to be outstanding, growth upright and bushy. Cloverdale × General Monk. Sayers – British – 1979.

Eroica. Single. Short, thick, salmon-pink tube, red sepals, 1½ in long held high from corolla and swept up at tips. Corolla 1½ in long opens claret but quickly turns red. Large flowers, very free flowering, with pink stamens, very long pink pistil

2 in long. Flowers unique in the way in which they change in a self colour. Light green, spear-shaped foliage with serrated leaves. Raised in the vicinity of Manchester. Howarth – British – 1979 – A.F.S. No. 1530.

Eros. Triphylla single. Long tube, creamy salmon-pink; petals salmon-red, very free. Pale green foliage, veined purple. Growth upright and dwarfish, best as HI. *F. triphylla* ×. Bonstedt – German – 1906.

Errol. Double. Tube and sepals scarlet; corolla pink. Large flowers, fairly free, heat resistant. Growth upright. Brand – American – 1949 – A.F.S. No. 46.

Escallopia. Single. Tube and sepals red; corolla rich violet, ageing to purple. Large blooms, early and free, flared and petals scalloped. Growth upright bush. Niederholzer – American – 1939.

Eschott Elf. Single. Thin, white tube, flushed pink, long, thin sepals, white flushed pink, reflexed close up against stem at maturity; white corolla. Small flowers very prolific, long and bell shaped with ruby-red anthers and pistil, stamens are held well clear of corolla. Growth natural trailer. Introduced by Jackson's Nurseries of Tamworth in 1979. Pink Cloud × Lena Dalton seedling × Sonata × Lakeside. Ryle – British – 1976 – A.F.S. No. 1400.

Escondido. Double. Tube pale pink, long flaring sepals light pink, tipped green. Corolla light violet, fading to lilac with age. Large flowers, very free and of crisp appearance, with loose corolla. Growth upright and bushy. Evans and Reeves – American – 1952.

Esme Tabraham. Double. Tube and sepals deep pink, sepals are reflexed. Corolla rose-pink veined red. Large blooms and very free flowering for a double. Dark green foliage, growth upright, strong and bushy considered by the raiser to be outstanding cultivar, with ultimate height of 1½ to 2 ft. Hardy in Southern England. Raised in the Scilly Isles. Tabraham, A.P. and E.V. – British – 1980.

Espana. Single. Short thick tube, white with pink cast, extra long slender and tapered sepals, white with pale rosy cast topside, underside pink and greenish tips. Corolla pink at base, deepening to deeper rosy-pink at tips of petals. Medium sized blooms, open slowly and compact. Bright medium green foliage with deep rose stems. Growth trailer. Foster – American – 1973 – A.F.S. No. 1085.

Espartero. Epps – British – 1840.

Espérance. Double. Red and purple. Riccartonii ×. Lemoine – French – 1889.

Esperanza. Single. Tube and sepals, dark rose-madder; corolla pale fuchsia-purple. Medium sized flowers, free, similar to Abbé Farges. Growth upright and shrubby grower. *F.lycoides* ×. Reiter – American – 1942.

Esteem. Smith – British – 1848.

Estelle. Bull – British – 1872.

Estelle Marie. Single. Tube greenish-white short and thick, stamens pink, pistil pink. Sepals white with very prominent green tips, standing straight up, ¾ in wide and 1 in long. Corolla opens blue-violet, matures to violet with white at base of petals. Four petals form a cup with overlap of about ⅛ in. Foliage dark green, leaves oval and of good substance. Growth upright and sturdy, self-branching with typical Bon Accorde habit of carrying flowers erect, very clean appearance. Cultivar is excellent for 3½ in pot work, creating considerable attention on the 1975 Birmingham showbenches when shown by Ron Venables. This delightful cultivar is very similar to Enid Handley's Martina (1971) but flowers are smaller. The summer of 1976 did however produce many mutations; one example carried as many as twelve sepals, twenty-four stamens and three pistils and more mutations were seen on the 1976 and 1977 showbenches. Although the parentage is not established, it is confidently considered to be of Bon Accorde descendancy and the raiser, being American, quotes Erecta Novelty; tested for 8 years in Corvallis, Oregon, and 2 years in the vicinity of Seattle, Washington, before release. Newton – American – 1973 – A.F.S. No. 1082.

Esther. Double. Short thick tube, white, globular and ribbed, sepals semi-recurved, pure white tipped green, frosted underneath. Corolla purple-violet. Medium sized blooms, very free, best colour in shade. Growth upright and bushy. Pugh – British – 1974 – A.F.S. No. 1188.

Esther Devine. Single. Crimson tube, broad sepals rich crimson, held well back from tube. Corolla wistaria-blue veined fuchsia-purple at base of petals. Very large flower and free flowering, growth upright and bushy, will make good bush, very clean and good shape. Raised in the vicinity of Melton Morbray, Leicestershire, before release and introduced by R. and J. Pacey in 1981. Pacey – British – 1981.

Esther Fearon. Double. Red and pink. Story – British – 1861.

Esther Nelson. Double. Tube and sepals, deep red; corolla orchid-purple to pink. Medium sized flowers and free. Growth willowy trailer. Nelson – American – 1951 – A.F.S. No. 175.

Estrella. Single. Tube and upcurved, sepals rose; corolla violet-purple. Large flowers, free, growth upright bush. 1915 × Aviator. Niederholzer – American – 1941.

Estrellita. Single. Tube and long sepals pink; corolla white with lightest pink veining. Flowers medium sized are long and tight, free. Growth upright and bushy. Tiret – American – 1950 – A.F.S. No. 67.

Eternal Flame. Semi-double. Flowers not too large, with an extra petaloid or two, has a very nice colour combination; smokey-rose corolla, streaked orange and salmon colour at the base. Tube and sepals are dark salmon-pink, tipped green with orange underneath. The foliage is attractive and darkish-green whilst the growth is excellent, being upright and bushy, unusual for an American. This cultivar could be aptly named by the raiser Ted Paskesen of San Francisco, California. With a little extra cultivation and some heat this cultivar will flower during the winter and certainly continues with its bloom well into the autumn. Very heavy bloomer both in the border and under glass, several nurserymen list this outstanding cultivar including Jacksons and Pickard (Meadowcroft Nurseries). Paskesen – American – 1941 – A.F.S. No. 959.

Ethel. Single. White and violet. Bull – British – 1872.

Ethel. Semi-double to double. White tube, sepals white with green tips on top side, pale pink on underside. Corolla lavender centre with pink petaloids on outside. Large blooms, fairly free, growth upright and bushy. Martin – American – 1967 – A.F.S. No. 726.

Ethel Grother. Double. Long red tube, sepals red, tending to curl around corolla. Rosy-pink corolla, striped with red. Small foliage and medium sized blooms, free. Growth trailer. Prentice – American – 1968 – A.F.S. No. 790.

Ethel May. Double. Tube bright crimson, curled sepals bright crimson; corolla rich violet, occasionally marked with cerise. Large flaring blooms and dark green foliage. Growth upright, bushy and vigorous. Aztec × Graphic. Evans and Reeves – American – 1940.

Ethel Sangster. Double. Rose and violet. Sport from Tower of London. Spackman – Unknown – 1920.

*Ethel Weeks. Semi-double. Tube and sepals red, corolla white and pink. Medium sized blooms, originally known as Seedling No. 412. Growth trailer, raised in the vicinity of Guildford, Surrey. Weeks – British – 1982.

Ethel Wilson. Single. Short pale pink tube ¼ in long, sepals pale pink, shading to white tip; corolla pink base darkening to cerise. Medium sized flowers and very free, white style with pink stem, filaments pale cerise. Mid-green foliage growth upright, bushy and hardy, tested in Reading area for several years as H3. Mrs. Marshall self seedling. Wilson, J.W. – British – 1967.

Etienne Larny. Lemoine – French – 1906.

Ettori M. Milani. Double. Tube white, sepals white, with tint of green at tips, short and wide, extending straight out to form box shape. Corolla white with light pink veins and compact. Shiny dark green foliage. Growth trailer. Milani – American – 1968 – A.F.S. No. 798.

Eugéne Bourcier. Lemoine – French – 1862.

Eugéne Delaplanche. Lemoine – French – 1891.

Eugéne Verconsin. Lemoine – French – 1892.

Eureka. Red and purple. Lye – British – 1887.

Europa. Double. Red and white. Twrdy – German – 1872.

*Eurydice. No details except it is a cultivar listed by C.S. Lockyer of Bristol in 1983.

Eusebia. Double. White tube, long sepals white fading to rose and recurve. Corolla red (R.H.S. 54A), full flaring blooms rather short. Dark green foliage with large leaves 3¼ in long × 1¾ in wide with sharp tip. Growth self-branching medium upright, making good bush on standard, best colour in filtered light. Tested for 2 years in the vicinity of Oceanside, California, U.S.A. Trademarked in California. Stubbs – American – 1982 – A.F.S. No. 1663.

Eva Boerg. Single to semi-double. Tube greenish-white, sepals pinkish-white, tipped green, pink underneath; corolla pinkish-purple, paling at base and splashed pink. Medium sized flowers and free, often confused with Lena, Hapsburg, Elsa and Madame Eva Boye. Foliage lightish-green, growth lax, low bush. Received R.H.S. Award of Merit at Wisley Hardy Trials 1960–62; re-submitted by L.R. Russell Ltd for 1975–78 trials but received no further award. Yorke – British – 1943.

Evangeline. Single. Tube and sepals, pure white; corolla pink. Very small flowers but profuse. Growth trailer. Hazard and Hazard – American – Date unknown.

Evanson's Choice. Single. Tube and sepals crimson (H.C.C. 22), sepals held horizontally. Corolla Venetian-pink (H.C.C. 420/2). Medium sized, slender flowers. Growth tall and vigorous, very suitable for standard training. Snowcap × Cloverdale Pearl. Roe – British – 1980.

Eva Penhall. Single. Tube and sepals deep pink, corolla violet shading to pink at base. Medium sized flowers. Little known cultivar appears to be exclusive to the north of England. Chance seedling, raised and introduced by Penhall's Fuchsia Deeside Gardens of Shaw, Oldham, in 1980. Penhall – British – 1976.

Evelyn Kern. Double. Short tube deep rose, sepals deep rose. Corolla violet-blue with pink marbling at base of petals. Large flowers, fairly free, dark green foliage, heat resistant. Growth trailer. Kuechler – American – 1962 – A.F.S. No. 504.

Evelyn Steele Little. Single. Tube and sepals, rosy-red; corolla lavender-pink, flecked magenta. Medium sized flowers and free but has the habit of dropping flowers before maturity. Growth cascade trailer, named after one of the earliest American hybridizers. Greene – American – 1930.

Evening Light. Double. Short tube and sepals white, tinted underneath with pink. Corolla violet. Large flowers with large, white globular buds, free. Growth upright and vigorous. Evans and Reeves – American – 1954 – A.F.S. No. 219.

Evening Shadows. Double. Short white tube, stiff, broad sepals white on top side, lower surface white, flushed purple. Corolla deep purple, outer petals marbled pink. Medium sized blooms with dark green foliage. Growth upright, vigorous and stiff. Kennett and Ross – American – 1957 – A.F.S. No. 284.

Evening Sky. Double. Long thin tube, eau-de-nil, flushed rose-bengal, long linear sepals of the same colour, much reflexed. Corolla violet, flushed ruby at opening, with paler flush of ruby, pink and orange, resembling evening hues in sky. Large full double flowers, compact and free. Dark green, obovate foliage. Growth natural trailer, self-branching. Travis, J. – British – 1957 – A.F.S. No. 1140.

Evening Star. Single. White and violet. Henderson – British – 1868.

Evensong. Single. Self white, with touch of pink at base of sepals, sepals reflect back to cover tube. Medium sized blooms and free, foliage lightish-green. Raiser claims this to be the first self white cultivar to be raised by a British hybridist, but Hawkshead by Travis 1962 has prior claim. Growth upright, compact bush, best grown as H1. Colville – British – 1967.

*Excalibur. Single. Short pale pink tube, sepals pink which open just about horizontal. Corolla baby pink with pink petaloids carried within the petals. Smallish flowers almost a pink self, unusual, give the effect of being double blooms with a ruffled appearance. Mid to dark green foliage, small leaves have irregular margins and can bend backwards. Growth small upright with many side shoots, will produce excellent bush. Raised and tested for 2 years before release in the vicinity of Ipswich, East of England. Introduced by B. and

H.M. Baker of Halstead, Essex in 1983. Goulding – British – 1983 – A.F.S. No. 1725.

Excellent. Double. Red and purple. Smith – British – 1865.

Excelsior. Single. Tube and sepals red; corolla purple with carmine centre. Medium sized flowers, early and free with wide open corolla. Growth upright. Niederholzer – American – 1942.

excorticata (Section IV Skinnera). Appears to have been first raised in this country in a certain Mr. Colvill's nursery from seeds collected in New Zealand by a Mr. Richardson in the early part of the nineteenth century; discovered around 1824. This is a deciduous tree fuchsia which grows on the edge of forests in New Zealand, particularly North Island, up to 3000 ft and forms a tree of some 40 to 50 ft in height, in favourable conditions making a trunk 3 ft or more in diameter.

It is one of the commonest trees of the New Zealand bush with its short gnarled trunk and is easily recognized by the characteristic cinnamon-brown bark that hangs in long strips. Will grow so large that, in New Zealand, it is grown as a cover for massive banks of rhododendrons. Tube and sepals start green turning to purplish-red, the corolla is a very dark purple almost black. The small flowers of unusual appearance and distinct in shape only about 1½ in long, are few in number, pendulus, on a slender stem growing from the axils of the leaves. In New Zealand they bloom in August to December with masses of pollen produced on the blue anthers which are level with the large, globular, yellow stigma. The pollen carried on alternate anthers, is bright blue in colour, used in the olden days by the young Maori maidens as a face powder, this custom may have arisen from seeing the foreheads of the tuis and other mectar-sucking birds, bright with viscid pollen. The bark is paper thin, reddish-brown in colour, the leaves are very distinct and tapered 1½ in to 4 in in length, dark green and glossy topside and silver green or tawny underneath, shiny and sometimes whitish. The fruit is an oval berry with many seeds, dark purplish in colour still eaten by the Maori Children and are called 'Konini'. The tree is known to the Maoris as the 'Kotuhutuhu' and the wood is extremely hard with a wavy grain, sought after by woodworkers for ornamental work. This species is hardy in some parts of the British Isles, mainly in the south-west counties and can produce large specimens, although it is not very widely grown, will also make a good bush plant with training. Currently obtainable from Akers of Ripon and Lechlade Fuchsias of Swindon.

purpurescens. There is also another form with leaves of a distinct purple colouring and silvery undersides, which give it a decorative value.

Exoniensis. Single. Longish tube crimson-carmine, longish sepals which expand freely crimson-carmine; corolla rich crimson-purple. Pendant habit and very hardy very suitable as an outside bedder. Seedling raised in the Exeter Nursery of Lucombe, Pince & Co., the result of a cross between *F. cordifolia* × *F. globosa* and obtained London Horticultural Society Certificate of Merit 1843. Almost identical with Corallina sent out by the same firm in 1844 the result of crossing Exoniensis with *F. montana*. Pince – British – 1842.

Exotic. Double. Tube and broad sepals carmine, tipped with green. Corolla orangy-carmine, large flowers and heat resistant. Growth upright. Fuchsia-La – American – 1959.

Exquisite. Single. Pink and rose. Fowler – British – 1846.

Exquisite. Single. Long white tube, sepals shaded pink, corolla rose-lavender. Flowers borne in great clusters and extremely early. Growth upright and vigorous, up to 8 ft in California. Munkner – American – 1954

Eyecatcher. Double. Tube rose-pink (R.H.S. 55A), short, broad sepals rose-pink (R.H.S. 55A) outside and deep rose (R.H.S. 55B) inside. Corolla is white with deep rose (R.H.S. 58B) at base, veined lighter rose (R.H.S. 58C). Very full blooms, free flowering and early, rose-pink stamens, best colour in shade, four blooms at each leaf joint. Growth upright and bushy, self-branching and close jointed, good exhibition cultivar, tested for 3 years before release. Seedling from Snowcap. Jackson, N. – British – 1977 – A.F.S. No. 1416.

Fabulous. Double. Long, medium thick, Tyrian-purple tube, Tyrian-purple sepals $\frac{1}{2}$ in wide × $\frac{7}{8}$ in long, curving upward with white and yellow tips. Spiraea-red corolla fading to magenta rose at the sepals, 1 in long × 1$\frac{3}{8}$ in wide. Medium-sized blooms, very free for a double, heat tolerant if shaded, best colour develops in shade. Growth natural trailer without weights, self-branching. Tested for 4 years in vicinity of Richmond, California. Registered by Soo Yun Field in 1978. Palko – American – 1978 – A.F.S. No. 1444.

Fair Cop. Semi-double. Short white tube, sepals pure white, becoming overlaid with pink, recurving, slightly frosted underneath. Corolla purple, flowers medium sized, resemble tulips in shape when beginning to open, this is characteristic. Growth upright and bushy. Pugh – British – 1974 – A.F.S. No. 1189.

Fair Maid. Semi-double. White and purple. Rogers – British – 1847.

Fair Oriana. Single. White and red. Banks – British – 1857.

Fairy. Single. Pink and rose. Youell – British – 1840.

*Fairy Bell. Double. Short pink tube, sepals candy-pink with recurving tips 1$\frac{1}{2}$ in long. Corolla white 1$\frac{1}{2}$ in long. Medium sized blooms, slightly bell shaped, stamens and pistil candy-pink. Medium green foliage with slightly serrated leaves 3 in long by 2$\frac{1}{8}$ in wide. Growth medium upright; will make good bush or standard, will take full sun in Cheshire. Igloo Maid × Swingtime. Raised and tested for 5 years in the vicinity of Timperley, Cheshire, before release. Howarth – British – 1983 – A.F.S. No. 1713.

Fairyland. Double. Long white tube, sepals, pink, tipped green and flare upward. Corolla variegated amethyst violet. Medium-sized blooms with magenta-pink stamens and chrome yellow stigma, best colour in shade, very heavy bloomer. Medium green foliage with slightly serrated leaves. Growth tall upright and bushy. Tested for 5 years in Sebastopol, California before release. Soo Yun Field – American – 1977 – A.F.S. No. 1405.

Fairy Lights. No details available other than the cultivar is a miniature, details to be announced later. Pugh – British – 1977.

Fairy Princess. Double. Pink tube, thick wide sepals pink, tipped green; corolla orchid-blue, lightly marbled pink at base of petals. Large flowers and free, opens square shaped. Growth upright bush. Martin – American – 1957 – A.F.S. No. 318.

Fairy Queen. Single. White and rosy-carmine. Henderson – British – 1863.

Fairy Queen. Semi-double. Tube and sepals, light pink; corolla ivory-white. Medium sized blooms, free and with light green foliage. Growth upright bushy and vigorous, up to 6 ft in California. Rolla × Fascination. Evans and Reeves – American – 1937.

Fairytales. Semi-double. Short tube candy-pink, fully reflexed sepals candy-pink. Corolla candy-pink. Medium sized blooms, very free. Growth trailer, very short internodes. Australian introduction. Lockerbie – Australian – 1972 – A.F.S. No. 1047.

*Falklands. Semi-double. Thick white blushed pink tube, half down sepals white shaded roseine (R.H.S. 68C) on top, roseine underneath 1$\frac{1}{2}$ in long by $\frac{1}{4}$ in wide with reflexed tips. Corolla opens fuchsia-purple (R.H.S. 67B) maturing to rose-Bengal (R.H.S. 57B) $\frac{3}{4}$ in long by 1$\frac{1}{4}$ in wide. Half flared medium sized blooms, claimed to be a new colour in hardy fuchsias with pink filaments and white anthers and stigma. Green foliage (R.H.S. 137A) slightly lighter (R.H.S. 138B) underneath, leaves 2 in long by 1 in wide with serrulate margins, acute tips and rounded bases, green veins and pink stems. Growth self-branching small upright, will make good bush or upright. Cold weather hardy to 26°F in South East England. Raised in the vicinity of Woodbridge, Suffolk. Lye's Unique × F. fulgens. Dunnett – British – 1984 – A.F.S. No. 1762.

Falling Stars. Single. Tube and pleated sepals, pale scarlet; corolla turkey-red with slight orange tint. Perfectly shaped flowers, very clean appearance, very free, well in the showclass category. Growth lax upright, needs a lot of early pinching, excels as a half basket, will produce a good standard. Its fault lays in the splitting of the basal stems. Cross between an old cultivar similar to Morning Mist × Cascade. Reiter (Sr) – American – 1941.

Fallowfield. Double. Tube and sepals, pale pink; corolla white, medium sized flowers and free. Growth upright bush. Harland – British – 1958.

Fame. Single. Red and violet. Bull – British – 1846.

Fancy Fair. Double. Tube and sepals, rich pink; corolla pale pink. Large flowers, fairly free, similar to San Jose. Growth trailer. Martin – American – 1959 – A.F.S. No. 369.

Fancy Flute. Single. White tube, sepals white, thick and crisp; corolla magenta, velvety petals, fluted and flared. Flowers medium sized, very free and heat resistant. Growth upright and bushy. Handley – British – 1972 – A.F.S. No. 1054.

Fancy Pants. Double. Tube and sepals, bright red; corolla purple, fading to beautiful reddish hue. Large blooms and free, very easy cultivar to grow, heat resistant. Pale green foliage. Growth lax bush or trailer. Reedstrom – American – 1961 – A.F.S. No. 489.

Fan Dancer. Semi-double. Tube and sepals, reddish-carmine, corolla light orchid-blue with mixture of pink and red. Medium sized blooms and free, sepals form a rectangular shape. Growth lax bush or trailer. Seedling of Crystal Rose (Martin 1959). Fuchsia Forest, Castro – American – 1962 – A.F.S. No. 513.

Fandango. Single. Tube and sepals, very pale geranium-lake, darker inside; corolla Tyrian rose-maroon. Medium sized flowers, free and early. Growth trailer. Princessita × Mrs. Rundle. Niederholzer – American – 1941.

Fanfare. Single. Long tube and short sepals scarlet, short corolla turkey-red. Tubular flowers three inches long, not very free, late bloomer can even be winter blooming. Large deep green foliage. Growth climbing or drooping, most unusual type of growth, perverse in temper, will grow several feet if left unstopped, but even if stopped will never produce a bushy plant, better as second year plant, well worth persevering for the lovely exotic blooms. Best grown as H1 but makes excellent plant in the border a half hardy bedder. *F.denticulata × F.leptopoda.* Reiter (Sr) – American – 1941.

Fanfare

Fantaisie Impromptue. Single. Tube and sepals carmine; corolla violet, veined carmine, largish flowers and free, growth upright. Blackwell – British – 1959.

Fan Tan. Double. Short tube pale pink, sepals white to very pale off-white, pale pink tips, reflexed. Corolla reddish-orange, slight marbled at base of outer petals. Growth upright and vigorous, tall. Paskesen – American – 1973 – A.F.S. No. 1110.

Fantasy. Semi-double. Short white tube, upturned sepals flushed pink outside, fuchsia-pink inside. Corolla has four large petals, palest orchid-pink at centre, shading to deep purple at edges, also overlaid smaller petals of similar colour. Medium sized blooms which opens flat, free. Growth upright and vigorous, tall. Waltz – American – 1951 – A.F.S. No. 106.

Fascination. Synonymous with Emile de Wildeman.

Fashion. Semi-double. White tube with upturned sepals, coloured rose, flushed pink on outside. Corolla deep methyl-violet, marbled mauve with extra thin overlaying petals of rose. Medium flowers and free. Growth upright and bushy. Niederholzer-Waltz – American – 1951 – A.F.S. No. 91.

Father Ignatius. Single. Red and purple. Banks – British – 1865.

Faust. Demay – French – 1868.

Favourite. Single. Tube and sepals, flesh-pink; corolla rosy-red with white at base. Largish blooms and free. Velvety texture green foliage; growth upright and bushy, needs frequent pinching, lovely old cultivar still grown today, but not particularly robust. Bland – British – 1868.

Felicièn David. Lemoine – French – 1894.

Felix Dubois. Lemoine – French – 1894.

Femina. Lemoine – French – 1913.

*Fenman. Single. Thick flesh-pink tube half the length of the sepals, flesh-pink sepals and recurving. Corolla pink, very large flowers, long and thickly textured, sometimes irregular in outline, very floriferous. Growth upright and bushy, particularly suitable for training as standard. An easy cultivar with flowers which do not mark easily and more robust than most of its type. Raised in the vicinity of Ipswich, Suffolk, and introduced by raiser, Gouldings Fuchsias of Ipswich, in 1985. One of a series of ten new introductions named after famous trains in 1985. Goulding – British – 1985.

Fenrother Fairy. Single. Tube and sepals white, flushed pink; corolla shell pink. Medium-sized flowers. This cultivar was formerly known as seedling 46B and considered to be too similar to other cultivars, especially Cally Pink, the flowers are rather untidy. Dwarf habit of growth. Blue Satin × Royal Velvet. Ryle – British – 1977.

Ferdinand Mahnke. Single. Tube and sepals red; corolla white. Fairly small flowers and free. Synonymous with Flocon de Neige (Lemoine 1884). Mahnke – German – 1912.

Fernrother Fairy. Single. Thin tube polished slightly pinky-white; white flushed pink sepals, green tipped held horizontally with upward curve, upper side of sepals are polished looking, with matt finish. Corolla pale pink (R.H.S. 62D). Medium sized flowers with magenta (R.H.S. 66D) stamens and white stigma. Formerly known as seedling 46B, submitted in seedling class B.F.S. Manchester Show, 1977, but considered to be too similar to other cultivars especially the raiser's Cally Pink. Small, dainty, dwarf plant, growth small upright and bushy. Raised in vicinity of Northumberland. Introduced by J. Ridding in 1979. Blue Satin × Royal Velvet. Ryle – British – 1979 – A.F.S. No. 1527.

Festival. Semi-double. Tube and sepals, pale pink; corolla claret-rose. Medium sized flowers and free. Growth upright bush. Schnabel – American – 1948 – A.F.S. No. 4.

Festoon. Single. Pale pink tube, sepals pink with green tip. Corolla China-rose at base, darkening to magenta-rose. Very small flowers but prolific. Growth upright, strong and bushy. Baker – British – 1970.

Fiddlesticks. Single. Long thin white tube, flushed pale pink, sepals very pale rose with very pale pink at tips, long and narrow with slight twist, never curl, stick straight out at maturity. Corolla deep rosy-red, pink at base, petals stay fairly tight. Dark green foliage, coarse looking, easy grower. Growth lax bush or trailer. Castro – American – 1973 – A.F.S. No. 1103.

Fiery Spider. Single. Long thin tube carmine, sepals long and narrow, pale salmon, tipped green. Corolla crimson with pronounced orange flush. Flowers are long and thin, early and very free. Growth cascading trailer, not very free branching, needs early and frequent pinching. Excellent basket cultivar, resents over watering and needs more than the average plants to fill the basket. Eye catching, good, and aptly named. Munker – American – 1960 – A.F.S. No. 452.

Fiesta Flares. Single. Thin crimson tube, crimson (R.H.S. 52A) sepals recurved and tipped green, Corolla ruby-red (R.H.S. 61A) streaked crimson (R.H.S. 52A). Medium sized flowers with flat petals and little flaring, stamens and pistil crimson with petaloids occasionally attached, best colour in shade. Medium to light green foliage (R.H.S. 44A) leaves red veined with shallow serrations. Growth natural trailer, making excellent basket. Tested for 3 years in vicinity of Rancho Palo Verdes, California, U.S.A. before release. Drapkin – American – 1982 – A.F.S. No. 1710.

Fifi. Single. Tube white, sepals curl upward, upper sepals flushed pink. Corolla soft violet-blue with colour fading to white at base of petals. Flowers are small and very free with rolled corolla. Growth upright miniature, bushy, suitable as small standard or bonsai training. Martin – American – 1958 – A.F.S. No. 362.

*Filigrain. Little known Dutch cultivar other than the parentage: Madame Cornelissen × Caledonia. Brouwer – Dutch – 1982.

filipes (Rusby 1927). Synonymous with *F. sanctae-rosae.*

Fille de L'Air. Single Red and white. Lemoine – French – 1862.

Fille des Champs. Lemoine – French – 1887.

Fingal's Cave. Double. Long thinnish tube crimson, sepals very long and pointed, crimson, recurving showing light green tips. Corolla deep amethyst. Flowers are large and free. Growth upright. Travis, J. – British – 1958.

Finsbury Volunteer. Single. Red and purple. Banks – British – 1862.

Fintelmannii. *F.globosa* × *F.fulgens.* Nagel – British – 1847.

Fiona. Single. Tube and long elegant sepals white, tipped green; corolla attractive blue, paling to light reddish-purple with age, white flush at base. Flowers are long and free, growth lax upright, needs early support. Winner of the B.F.S. Jones Cup 1958 and Award of Merit. Clark, W. – British – 1958.

Fireball. Double. Short tube and broad upturned sepals, bright carmine, tipped green. Corolla ruddy-purple with splashes of carmine at base of petals as flower matures, some petals turn dark bluish-purple, which again change into a red of great brilliancy. Flowers are large and unusual for its many colour changes as flower matures. Growth trailer. Waltz – American – 1957 – A.F.S. No. 310.

Fire Bird. Semi-double. Tube and sepals red; corolla deep red, almost a self. Growth natural trailer. Walker – American – 1962.

Firebird. Single. Carmine-red self-coloured cultivar. Medium sized flowers, very free. Growth lax and vigorous suitable either as hanger or climber, will take sun. Not to be confused with Firebird by Roy Walker, 1962. This cultivar was submitted to the B.F.S. London 1978 Seedling Class but was not impressive. Introduced by Wills Fuchsia Nurseries in 1979. Meur. Goyarts' × . de Graaff – Dutch – 1976.

Firefall. Single. Clear carmine self. Large flowers and free with ruddy-bronze foliage. Growth trailer. Autumnale × Mrs. Rundle. Reiter – American – 1939.

Fireflush. Single. Tube and sepals, rosy-red, corolla orangy-apricot. Medium sized flowers and free. Growth upright bush. Waltz – American – 1943.

Firefly. Single. Almost a self with sepals and corolla of vivid red. Medium sized flowers and free. Growth tall, stiff upright, but brittle. Pride of Exeter × Rolla. Niederholzer – American – 1940.

Fireglow. Double. Slender, near white tube and light rose sepals, corolla rosy-red with shorter petals of lighter shade. Largish flowers and free. Growth trailer. Nelson. – American – 1953 – A.F.S. No. 180.

Fire King. Turville – British – 1843.

Firelite. Double. Tube and pointed sepals white, sepals curl on edges. Corolla brilliant glowing carnival red which does not fade. Flowers are fluffy and flaring with a wonderful colour contrast. Light green foliage. Growth lax bush or trailer. Waltz – American – 1965 – A.F.S. No. 654.

Fire Marshall Parker. Double. Tube and sepals red; corolla deep purple, streaked flame-red. Large flowers and fairly free. Growth tall upright. Hazard and Hazard – American – 1950.

Fire Mountain. Double. Flesh-coloured tube, medium pale orange-pink sepals, straight to slightly curved. Corolla orange-carmine, shaded orange on outer petals. Large, compact blooms, compact when first opens, spreading with maturity. Medium green foliage with 2 in × 3 in long serrated leaves, red veins and stems on new growth. Long slender buds, immature plant may have single to semi-double blooms, best colour developed in filtered sun. Originates from the area of Fort Bragg in California. Stubbs – American – 1980 – A.F.S. No. 1536.

*Firenza. Double. Short pink tube, deep rose-pink sepals held at the horizontal 1½ in by ¾ in wide. Corolla deep lavender flushed bright pink, splashed lavender 1½ in by 2 in wide. Medium sized blooms with rose-pink stamens 1 in long and pink pistil 2 in long. Yellowish-green foliage pointed with serrated edges and slight veining. Growth medium upright, self-branching, will produce good bush or standard, takes full sun in Timperley. This cultivar should not be confused with Firenzi by G. Roe. Igloo Maid × Joan Gilbert. Raised and tested for 4 years in the vicinity of Timperley, Cheshire. Howarth – British – 1983 – A.F.S. No. 1714.

Firenzi. Single. Ruby-red and crimson cultivar. Introduced by V.T. Nuttall of Brodsworth, Doncaster in 1981. Roe – British – 1981.

Fire Opal. Single to semi-double. Red tube and sepals; corolla deep blue. Heavy bloomer with long lasting blooms, turning to rosy hue with maturity. Foliage is large, bronzy-green. Growth trailer. Gagnon – American – 1963 – A.F.S. No. 552.

Firmin Gèmier. Lemoine – French – 1914.

First Kiss. Single. Tube rose-pink, sepals white flushed pink. Corolla soft candy-pink. Medium sized flowers which age to a pale pink self with maturity. Growth upright, introduced by Wills Fuchsias Ltd. of West Wittering in 1980. La Campanella × . de Graaff – Dutch – 1978.

First Lady. Double. Pink tube, sepals deep pink to coral, lift above corolla, slightly recurved. Corolla deep clear pink, slightly flaring, some petals serrated. Large blooms, round and full of unusually heavy substance, very free, classic double. Medium foliage, dark green with red stems and red vein down leaf to centre. Growth lax bush or trailer. Named after Mrs. Richard Nixon of America, during her term of office as President's wife. Stubbs – American – 1973 – A.F.S. No. 1080.

First Light. Single. White tube, white sepals slightly flushed pink and reflexed; corolla lovely soft pink. Medium sized flowers and free, growth lax bush, will produce good standard. Baker – British – 1974.

First Love. Double. Tube and sepals white, long sepals, lower surface very crepe and flushed pink. Corolla clear orchid, outer petals spreading with marbling of pink and white. Large blooms of loose form, free. Lightish green foliage. Growth trailer. Kennett and Ross – American – 1957 – A.F.S. No. 283.

First of the Day. Single. Red and purple. Banks – British – 1872.

*First Success. Single. Little known Dutch species hybrid introduced by Lechlade Fuchsia Nursery of Lechlade in 1984. *F. paniculata × F. splendens.* Weeda – Dutch – *ca* 1983.

fischerii. Tube reddish green, sepals reddish-green; corolla purple. Small flowers, little known of this species, one of the last to be discovered. McBride – 1941 – Brazil.

Flair. Double. Tube and sepals white; corolla raspberry-pink. Large blooms and free. Growth trailer. Tiret – American – 1961 – A.F.S. No. 486.

Flambeau. Double. Red and purple. Rozain-Boucharlat – French – 1904.

Flamboyant. Semi-double. Reddish short tube, sepals waxy-white on outside, flushed with pink inside. Corolla cerise to purple, flaring at maturity. Foliage large, glossy deep green. Growth trailer. Kennett – American – 1959 – A.F.S. No. 400.

Flame. Single. Ivory tube and sepals; corolla reddish-orange. Medium size blooms and free. Growth upright bush. Niederholzer – American – 1941.

Flamenco. Single. Rose-pink tube, sepals rose-pink, very long and slender. Corolla darker rose, flowers medium sized, very free and long, feature of the flower is the exceptionally long buds. Growth willowy bush. Niederholzer – American – 1940.

Flame of Bath. Single. Salmon-pink tube and sepals; corolla orangy-cerise. Medium sized blooms and very free. Growth lax upright. Colville – British – 1967.

Flaming Beauty. Double. Long slender tube, light crimson, sepals light crimson; corolla slightly darker, almost a crimson self. Large blooms and free, dark green foliage with serrated edges. Growth upright and bushy. Soo Yun – American – 1972 – A.F.S. No. 1041.

Flaming Glory. Double. Tube greenish-white, sepals pale pink, tipped green, pink underneath. Corolla purple to flaming red centre, outer edges of pink and orange. Large flowers of very unusual colouring, with light green foliage. Growth trailer, best as H1. Martin – American – 1962 – A.F.S. No. 517.

Flamingo. Single. Self-coloured pinkish-orange. Medium sized flowers, very free. Growth upright and bushy. Colouring is identical to the long-necked, heavy-billed bird. Not to be confused with the cultivar of the same name by J.V. Porter (1976). Introduced by Wills Fuchsia Nurseries in 1979. Duke of York × . de Graaff – Dutch – 1976.

Flamingo. Semi-double. Short pink tube narrows to top of sepals, pink line runs down the edge of sepal to tip. Upturned sepals are white, lightly tinged pink. Corolla white with pinky-red stamens, very long pink pistil and white stigma. Small to medium flowers, very free and most unusual with four extra stamens attached to sepals, creating a most unusual flower, giving the appearance of petaloids. It will be interesting to see whether this new characteristic is permanent. Foliage and growth is similar or almost identical to that of its parent. La Campanella seedling. Porter – British – 1976.

Flarepath. Single. Tube and sepals deep pink; corolla rose-madder. Medium sized flowers, growth upright and bushy and is a chance seedling. Introduced by High Trees Nurseries of Reigate, Surrey, in 1980. Hobson – British – 1976.

Flash. Single. Tube and sepals, light magenta, corolla light magenta-red, almost a self. Flowers are small but profuse, foliage light green and small. Growth upright and bushy up to 2½ ft, very vigorous, can be grown to very large specimen plants for the showbench. Accepted by the B.F.S. as showbench hardy. Submitted by Wills Nurseries for the R.H.S. Wisley Hardy Trials 1975–78 but received no award. Hazard and Hazard – American – 1930?

Flashlight. Single. Tube and sepals, pale pink, tipped green; corolla pale rose-purple. Flowers are small, very free, *F.magellanica* var. *alba* cross which seems to have eliminated the pale lilac. Growth dwarf bush, height 12 in, prefers semi-shade, hardy. Submitted by Wills Nurseries and Mrs. E. Saunders for the R.H.S. Wisley Hardy Trials 1975–78 but received no award. Flash × *F.magellanica* var. *alba*. Gadsby – British – 1968 – A.F.S. No. 977.

Flavescens. Single. White and vermilion. Meillez – French – 1849.

Flavia. Double. Tube and sepals pink; corolla deep lilac. Large flowers, fairly free, growth trailer. Tiret – American – 1971 – A.F.S. No. 993.

Flek. Double. Light pink tube, sepals light pink, tipped rose; corolla pink, also tipped, rose. Medium sized blooms and free, sepals are pointed, standing straight out, best colour in shade. Growth upright and bushy. Mueller – American – 1975 – A.F.S. No. 1308.

Fleur Bleue. Lemoine – French – 1901.

Fleur Rouge. Single. Red and purple. Lemoine – French – 1885.

Flim Flam. Single. Tube and sepals creamy-white, corolla red. Medium sized flowers, growth upright and bushy. Cultivar which prefers a cool position. Introduced by Wills Fuchsia Nurseries of Sussex in 1979. de Graaff – Dutch – 1976.

Flirtation. Double. Tube and sepals pale rose-madder, corolla very pale petunia-purple petals picotée edged. Large flowers and fairly free. Growth upright bush. Sport of Lucky Strike. Leitner – American – 1946.

Flirtation Waltz. Double. This is one of the many cultivars from the prolific Waltz 'stable' in California, raised and inroduced in 1962, registered by the A.F.S. under No. 523. This cultivar possesses nearly everything that produces an ideal fuchsia; flowers are double, tube and wide spreading sepals are creamy-white, flushed pink, whilst the corolla is of shell-pink, deepening somewhat with maturity. Extremely free flowering, with medium sized blooms of great substance, easily obtained by mid July. Growth is vigorous and upright, requires little training to produce a well shaped bush plant, does not respond to excessive stopping, but is very free in flowering for a double. Good foliage and a first class cultivar for the showbench, but care has to be exercised with the blooms, which bruise very easily. Will produce a magnificent standard. As a delicate, pastel colouring cultivar, does not flower well as a bedder and if subjected to excessive moisture, corolla will unfortunately turn brown; under glass is a cultivar which must not be sprayed after bud stage. Fairly easy to overwinter and one of the first to break into leaf in the early spring. In America, the flowers being of exceptional substance, are ideal for the making of corsages. This is a cultivar which should endure for ever. Waltz – American – 1962 – A.F.S. No. 523.

Flocon de Neige. Single. Tube and sepals cerise; corolla creamy-white, faintly veined cerise. Medium sized blooms, very free, like Ballet Girl can be disappointing, dislikes too much moisture. Growth upright and bushy, still grown but has lost its early popularity. Synonymous with Ferdinand Mahnke. Lemoine – French – 1884.

Flora. Single. Carmine and purple. Harrison – British – 1856.

Flora. Semi-double. Tube and long, thin, turned back sepals bright cerise; corolla pale violet with pink veins. Large blooms, fairly floriferous, similar colouring to Alison Ryle almost as large as Texas Longhorn and flares like Mission Bells, two petaloids make this a semi-double. Foliage yellowish-green with red veins. Growth upright, suitable for any training except basket. Tennessee Waltz ×. Tolley – British – 1971 – A.F.S. No. 1156.

Floradora. Double. Short tube and broad pagoda type sepals, neyron-rose; corolla deep victorian-violet, flushed rose at base. Medium sized blooms and free, early. Growth upright and bushy. Waltz – American – 1951 – A.F.S. No. 107.

Floral Art. Single. Tube and sepals red, corolla white flushed pink. Medium sized flowers and very free. Growth upright and bushy appears to be exclusive to the Border Counties of England.

Listed and introduced by Caldew Bank Nurseries of Carlisle. Raiser unknown – British – *ca* 1970s.

Floral City. Double. Tube and sepals, very pale pink; corolla pale lilac. Medium sized blooms and free, delightful, delicate pastel colouring, well in the showclass category. Growth upright and bushy. Holmes – British – 1974.

Flora Rugh. Single. Tube and sepals carmine; corolla orchid-blue, flowers medium sized and free. Growth upright and bushy. Gagnon – American – 1963 – A.F.S. No. 554.

Florence. Single. Rose and purple. Epps – British – 1840.

*Florence Mary Abbott. Single. Very short white tube, bulbous and striped pink; long, narrow, pointed, recurving sepals white with the slightest tinge of pink. Sepals held well away from tube and corolla, almost horizontal, fully exposing delightful corolla. Corolla pure white with no veining, a true single with neatly folded petals, smallish flowers 2 in long, flowering in the leaf axil well before those on terminal laterals. Very free flowering with white pistil but disappointing small stamens, brownish in colour, best colour develops in shade although little discolouration occurs in wind or sun. Whitest cultivar for some considerable period, a dainty, elegant, young lady, well within the exhibition class. Not prone to botrytis as most 'whites' and pastel shaded cultivars. Light green foliage with obovate leaves 2 in long by 1 in wide and obtuse tipped, medium sized with reddish mid-rib running half down each leaf. Upright growth, short-jointed and self-branching, produces basal shoots. Whole plant has a very clean appearance and refreshing effect. Parentage not known, raised in the vicinity of Ipswich, Suffolk, and introduced by B. and H.M. Baker of Halstead, Essex, in 1983. Goulding – British – 1983 – A.F.S. No. 1726.

Florence Nightingale. Semi-double. Red and white. Pince – British – 1842.

Florence Taylor. Double. Tube and sepals deep blood-red; corolla fuchsia-purple, mottled rose-red. Large ruffled blooms, fairly free for a double. Growth trailer. Introduced by R. Pacey in 1979. Harris – British – 1978.

Florence Turner. Single. Tube pale pink, sepals white; corolla pale pinkish-purple. Flowers of medium size, early and free. Growth upright and bushy, excellent as a bedder. Accepted by the B.F.S. as showbench hardy. First introduced by E.T. Turner in new seedling class at B.F.S. London Show 1955. Has since proved an outstanding hardy cultivar. Rolla × Forget-Me-Not. Turner – British – 1955.

Florentina. Double. Tube and sepals, frosty-white, corolla smoky burgundy-red. Large blooms fairly free, created great interest when first introduced from America. Growth lax bush or trailer. Tiret – American – 1960 – A.F.S. No. 432.

Florian. Single. Red and purple. Hardy cultivar. *F.coccinea* × Lemoine – French – 1897.

Floribunda. Single. Red and purple. Turville – British – 1847.

Floribunda. Single. Red and white. Bland – British – 1872.

Flossie Fant. Double. Tube white, flushed pink, sepals whitish-pink; corolla white with very faint pink lines. Flowers are large, blooms open up to resemble an orchid and long lasting. Growth trailer. Gagnon – American – 1964 – A.F.S. No. 599.

Flossie Mae. Double. Short, thin, red tube, sepals red, long somewhat slender, reflexed to stem. Corolla white, red veined. Large blooms, fairly free, pendulous and fairly compact. Foliage medium green, deep red stems, delicately serrated. Growth trailer. Foster – American – 1973 – A.F.S. No. 1086.

*Flowerdream. Dutch introduction for 1983. Raised in the vicinity of Amersfoort, Netherlands. Merry Mary × Bora Bora. Rijff – Dutch – 1983.

Fluffy Frills. Double. Short, dark pink tube, broad sepals claret-rose darker on outside, of heavy substance, and when mature lift above corolla. Amaranth-pink (R.H.S. 68A) corolla, large to medium sized blooms, very ruffled and frilly, needs frequent pinching for best results. Dark green foliage with red veined leaves and red stems, growth semi-trailer, needs weights for basket work. Stubbs – American – 1976 – A.F.S. No. 1382.

Fluffy Ruffles. Double. Tube and sepals, rosy-red, corolla white. Large fluffy blooms, fairly free. Growth trailer. Copley – American – 1966 – A.F.S. No. 692.

Fluorescent. Double. Tube and sepals white, tipped green. Corolla orchid, blushed white at base, short outer petals roseine-purple. Flowers are long and large, fairly free, growth lax bush or trailer. Walker and Jones – American – 1952.

Flyaway. Double. Short tube and reflexing sepals, white with reverse, frosty rose-madder. Corolla spectrum-violet, with rose-madder flush at base of petals, fading to orchid-purple. Blooms are large and free. Growth upright and bushy. Crockett – British – 1965 – A.F.S. No. 820.

Fly-by-Night. Double. Tube and sepals cherry; corolla fuchsia purple, flushed and edged deep royal purple, with cherry shading at base of petals. Blooms are large and free, long bloom period. Growth upright and bushy. Crockett – British – 1965 – A.F.S. No. 821.

Flying Cloud. Double. Tube and sepals white, tipped green, faintly pink underneath; corolla white, touched pink at base. Flowers are largish and very free, probably the best white double, the degree of whiteness depends upon the amount of shade afforded. When grown in full sun, the pink-colouring is most pronounced, well in the show-class category. Growth lax upright and spreading, always seems to prefer growing horizontally. Elegant beauty, first of the best near whites, has two faults, produces hard wood cuttings difficult to strike and like most whites, easily falls to botrytis. Reiter – American 1949 – A.F.S. No. 27.

Flying Saucer. Double. Tube and sepals, bright red, sepals held out vertical. Corolla deep purple. Flowers are large with wide-open corolla and free. Growth upright and bushy. Haag – American – 1955.

*Flying Scotsman. Double. Short, thick tubes which redden with age, sepals are pale pink inside and rather darker pink outside, recurve tightly. Large blooms for a double cultivar with red corolla and white streaks with occasional petaloids. Growth is upright, vigorous and strong, multi-flowered and suitable for either bush or standard. Raised in the vicinity of Ipswich, Suffolk, and

introduced by the raiser, Gouldings Fuchsias of Ipswich, in 1985. One of a series of 10 new introductions named after famous trains in 1985. Goulding – British – 1985.

Folies Bergere. Double. Tube and sepals pink; corolla pink and lavender. Large flowers, lovely pastel colour combination, fairly free. Growth trailer. Fuchsia Forest – American – 1968 – A.F.S. No. 769.

Fondant. Double. Pink tube, sepals frosty-candy pink held horizontally. Corolla pure white without any veining. Medium sized blooms very free flowering with very long pink pistil. Dark green foliage, small glossy leaves. Growth small upright, self-branching, will make good bush or standard, can take full sun. Originates from the area of Timperley, Cheshire. Swingtime × Seventeen. Howarth – British – 1980 – A.F.S. No. 1578.

fontinalis (MacBride 1940). Synonymous with *F. decussata.*

Forester. Double. Red and purple. Brown – British – 1938.

Forest King. Single. Magenta tube, sepals magenta are flat, broad and green tipped but not upturned. Corolla magenta-violet, medium to large flowers, barrel-shaped, almost a self, best colour in shade. Dark green foliage, long, ovate leaves with red mid-rib and few serrations. Growth natural semi-trailer, short jointed, will make good basket without weights or standard. Tested for 4 years in Birmingham area before release. This cultivar was originally known as The Forester but the name was not accepted by the A.F.S. and subsequently changed, one of the last introductions by the raiser before he died in 1978. Tolley – British – 1978 – A.F.S. No. 1471.

Forest 78. Single. Tube and sepals rhodanite-red (H.C.C. 0022), sepals fold back almost hiding the tube. Corolla white with slight red veining. Medium sized flowers, extremely floriferous, charming and pleasing. Growth is inclined to be lax making the cultivar ideal for either tub or basket training. Named after the famous football club, Nottingham Forest, after their European Cup victory. Cloverdale Pearl × Ice Cap. Roe – British – 1980.

Forever Yours. Semi-double. Tube pale rose, sepals are long and graceful, recurved pale rose fading to delicate pale green at tips. Corolla campanula-violet, heavily marbled at base with light pink and rose-madder. Large flowers, free, early and continual. Growth lax bush or trailer. A.F.S. Cert. of Merit. Tiret – American – 1956 – A.F.S. No. 252.

Forget-Me-Not. Single. Tube and sepals, pale flesh-pink, corolla palish-blue. Very small flowers,

Forget-Me-Not
(Banks 1866)

155

early and very free. Growth upright and bushy, needs frequent and early pinching. Appears to be considerable confusion with this cultivar and the one by Niederholzer. Generally accepted that Banks introduction is the correct cultivar and somewhat proved by the fact that Banks was grown in England for many years before 1940. Adopted by the British Fuchsia Society as their emblem. Banks – British – 1866.

Forget-Me-Not. Single. Tube and sepals, pale pink, corolla pale blue. Small flowers and free, growth upright and bushy. Considered to be identical with Banks 1866 cultivar. *F. macrostemma* var. *alba* ×. (Synonymous with *F. magellanica* var. *molinae* or *F. magellanica* var. *alba*) Niederholzer – American – 1940.

Forget-Me-Not. A rather small, dainty bloom, tube and sepals pink; corolla forget-me-not blue, paling with age, claimed by G. Niederholzer but it was raised by Banks in 1869. Tom Thorne reference in his book on page 58.

Are there two cultivars named Forget-Me-Not or is there only one? The Check List is cluttered with duplications and multi entries, but the example of Forget-Me-Not almost defies clarification as all the following entries are supposed to be authentic. Arthur Taylor of Enfield states he cannot find a reference to Banks 'FMN' as red and rich-blue as stated by Essig and infers the reference as being incorrect. Cannell's catalogue refers to 'FMN' as pale pink and palish-blue. Essigs reference refers to a list of 1861 whereas Banks did not raise the cultivar until 1866 and it is known that Forget-Me-Not has been grown in this country by Arthur Taylor at Enfield since the 1920s which is long before a Gus. Niederholzer introduction. We can only conclude that Gus. Niederholzer in America, by a lucky chance, made a similar cross to Banks and obtained very similar results. It is known that Niederholzer was a great hybridizer, who went right back to the species and did his hybridizing under correct sterile conditions. Susan Travis writing in the 1973 B.F.S. Annual made reference to a rumour that Forget-Me-Not was stolen from Banks by Niederholzer in 1940 however, this was completely untrue and continues by stating that Banks 'FMN' raised approximately 1866 is red and purple with crimson strips (not now in circulation) and the Niederholzer version has a pale pink tube and sepals with a pale blue corolla. All very confusing, however, one thing is certain and that is the British Fuchsia Society use this cultivar as their emblem on badges etc., but the actual colouring leaves a lot to be desired and is no help to identification.

Forgotten Dreams. Semi-double. Tube and sepals, coral shade with deeper markings, corolla dusky-purple. Growth lax bush or trailer. Blackwell – British – 1962.

Formosa. Bland – British – 1882.

Formosa. Double. Carmine and purple. Harrison – British – Date unknown.

Formosa. Single. Tube and sepals rose; corolla purple. Smallish flowers with rose coloured stamens and pistil. Growth lax bush, will trail with weights. Cultivar grown in California and could be any one of four early British introductions of the same name and description. Raiser and date unknown.

Formosa Elegens. Thompson – British – 1841.

Formosa Elegens. Single. Pink and cerise. Story – British – 1850.

Formose. Lemoine – French – 1885.

Formosissima. Single. White and violet. Girling – British – 1846.

Fort Bragg. Double. Tube and broad upturned sepals rose; corolla pale lavender-rose with bluish tinge, petals slightly veined with rose. Large flowers and fairly free, growth natural trailer. A.F.S. Cert. of Merit 1961. Sport of Enchanted. Waltz – American – 1957 – A.F.S. No. 314.

Fortuna. Double. Red and white. Lowe – British – 1875.

Forward Look. Single. Short, thick tube, light pink, sepals China-rose, tipped green, held well back. Corolla wisteria-blue fading to violet. Medium sized blooms, held out horizontal from plant. Growth upright and bushy, makes good self branching bush or any upright training shape, close jointed. Winner of seedling class B.F.S. Northern Show 1972. Margaret Roe ×. Gadsby – British – 1972 – A.F.S. No. 1122.

Fountains Abbey. Double. White tube, sepals pinkish-white on uppersides, baby-pink underneath, tipped green. Corolla delightful colour of lavender-blue, flushed and veined pink from the base inherited from one of its parents Blush O' Dawn. Medium sized blooms and very free for a double, long, pinkish-white stigma with red stamens. Growth lax, may need a little support when trained as a bush. Delightful cultivar and named after the famous Abbey ruins in North Yorkshire. Raised and introduced by C. and J.I. Akers of Fountains Abbey Nurseries of Ripon, North Yorkshire in 1982. Coquet Bell × Blush O' Dawn. Akers – British – 1981.

Foxtrot. Semi-double. Short tube and sepals pale cerise, tipped green, stand well out. Corolla pale lavender, pink base. Flowers medium sized, very free, open and semi-flared. Foliage flat pale green, rather small. Growth upright and bushy. Tennessee-Waltz ×. Tolley – British – 1974 – A.F.S. No. 1229.

Fra. Elbertus. Double. Tube and sepals red, very pointed at ends; corolla violet with fine lavender edge. Large flowers, fairly free, foliage golden veined. Growth upright. Hazard and Hazard – American – 1941.

Frances. Semi-double. Tube and sepals rose-pink with green tips; corolla blue with pink base changing to clover. Medium-sized flowers, free flowering, growth upright and bushy. Curtis – British – 1967.

Frances Keizer. Double. Tube and sepals red, heavily creped sepals; corolla deep rose. Flowers large and free, have five sepals most of the time. Growth trailer. Gagnon – American – 1967 – A.F.S. No. 709.

Frances Lo Bue. Double. Short tube, short sepals white on top, light pink on reverse side. Corolla fuchsia variegated-pink around base, with pink petaloids at base. Foliage pale green and small. Growth upright. Pennisi – American – 1969 – A.F.S. No. 860.

Francis Magnard. Lemoine – French – 1879.

Francisque Sarcey. Double. Red and purple. Lemoine – French – 1879.

François Boucher. Lemoine – French – 1910.

François Devos. Double. Red and purple. Seedling from Deutschekarserrin. Coene – Belgian – 1869.

Francois Villon. Single. Long creamy-white tube with slight curve, creamy-white sepals held at the horizontal slightly upturned. Corolla cerise-red, medium sized flowers could be mistaken for a Lye's cultivar and similar to Mrs. Marshall. The outstanding feature of the flower is the extremely long pistil and its floriferousness. Introduced by Wills Fuchsias Ltd. of West Wittering in 1980. La Campanella×. de Graaff – Dutch – 1978.

Frank E. Henry. Semi-double. Tube and sepals pale flesh pink; corolla pure white. Large blooms, fairly free. Growth upright and bushy. Raiser unknown – American – Date unknown.

Frankie. Double. Light pink tube, sepals are the same colour and arch well back. Corolla mottled blue and red, small blooms very similar to its parent. Dark green foliage with medium sized leaves. Growth upright and bushy, will make good bush or standard, best colour develops in sun. Originates from the vicinity of Warwickshire. Seedling of Winston Churchill. Wright, J.A. – British – 1980 – A.F.S. No. 1599.

Franklin. Double. Red and purple. Demay – French – 1872.

*****Frank Saunders.** Single. White tube, short and unswept sepals white. Corolla lilac-pink, smallish flowers very attractive pastel shaded cultivar, flowers push up and out. Small dark green foliage. Growth small upright and vigorous, makes an excellent shrub with dense growth, also good for standard. Named after a popular fuchsia personality in South-East England. Raised in the vicinity of Middlesex and introduced by Woodbridge Nurseries of Hounslow, Middlesex, in 1984. Dyos – British – 1984.

Frank Unsworth. Double. Short white tube, white sepals which fly back covering tube, tipped green. Corolla white with slight pink flush at base of petals. Small fully double blooms, two blooms produced in each leaf axil. Small foliage, dark green. Growth lax bush very self-branching lending itself admirably to basket work. Raised and tested for 3 years in the vicinity of Merseyside before release. Seedling of Bobby Shaftoe×. Clark, D. (Merseyside) – British – 1982.

François Devos. Double. Red and purple. Seedling from Deutschekarserrin. Coene – Belgian – 1869.

*****Franz Noszian.** Double. Tube and sepals red; corolla white with touch of pink. Medium-sized blooms, very free flowering. Growth vigorous and strong, medium upright, excels as a standard. Koralle × F. boliviana × F. splendens. Nutzinger – Austrian – 1976.

Frau Emma Tauper. Double. Tube and sepals, coral-red; corolla white veined red, medium sized flowers and free. Growth upright bush, name changed to Storm King when introduced into America. Letheren – French – 1894.

Frau Hilde Rademacher. Double. Tube and sepals, rich red; corolla lilac-blue, splashed cerise. Medium sized flowers, very free, delightful tight double. Growth lax bush and spreading, hardy in most districts. Deserves to become more popular, good old cultivar. From H. Rademacher nursery in Mülheim-Ruhr. Henriette Ernst × Monkemeyer. Rademacher – German – 1925.

Frau Ida Noach. Synonymous in the Netherlands with Display.

Frau Hilde Rademacher

Frauline Bonstedt. Triphylla type single. Long tube, rose-vermilion self. Sage-green foliage, bluish-purple underneath. Growth upright. Bonstedt – German – 1904.

Frau Ria Mehlis. Double. Tube and sepals pure white; corolla pure white. Although this is described as a pure white cultivar would suggest it contains an element of pink colouring. Smallish flowers, early and very free. El Camino × F.corymbiflora alba. Nutzinger – Austrian – 1968.

Frau Wurth. Double. Tube and sepals dark red; corolla white veined red at base. Medium-sized blooms with pink stamens and pistil, very round buds. Growth upright, bushy and branching. Although not confirmed the raiser is thought to be: Nutzinger – Austrian – Date unknown.

Frederick Passy. Lemoine – French – 1902.

Fred's First. Double. Tube carmine-rose, sepals carmine-rose are curled fully covering ovary when fully open. Corolla violet, tinged with pink at base. Medium-sized blooms, well shaped with carmine-rose stamens and long, bright pink pistil. Growth medium upright, self-branching and bushy, makes good bush or pyramid. Will take full sun, but best colour in shade. Tested for 3 years in vicinity of Cardiff before release, fully hardy and very suitable for training as a standard. Woolley – British – 1978 – A.F.S. No. 1488.

Freedom. Double. Tube and sepals, bright red; corolla dark blue, marbled with red and white. Medium sized blooms compact and free. Growth lax bush or trailer. Martin – American – 1961 – A.F.S. No. 462.

Freefall. Single. Tube and sepals pale rose-opal, China-rose corolla. Flowers large and long. Growth cascade. Baker – British – 1970.

Freestyle. Single. Long and thick tube, rose-bengal, sepals rose-bengal, long and held well up and out. Corolla Imperial-purple, lighter colour at base. Large bell-shaped flowers, similar in shape to Lady Isobel Barnet, but much larger, very free, best colour in shade. Medium to large deep green foliage. Growth tall upright and bushy, vigorous. Lady Isobel Barnett × Bishop's Bells. Gadsby – British – 1975 – A.F.S. No. 1313.

Frenchi. Double. Tube flushed white, wide recurved sepals, salmon-pink; corolla silvery-blue and pale mauve with splashes of pink. Large flowers and free, growth upright and bushy. Waltz – American – 1953 – A.F.S. No. 166.

Frère Orban. Lemoine – French – 1896.

Fried Harms. Single. White-chalice. Weinrich – German – 1870..

Frilly Brentwood. Semi-double. Tube and sepals, pale pink; corolla pale blue and pink, marbled white. Medium sized flowers and free, frilly and fluffed. Growth upright bush. Greene – American – 1932.

Friso. Double. Tube and sepals white; corolla marbled white with pale blue. Large blooms, fairly free, growth trailer. Roth – American – 1957.

Fritz Kreisler. Single to semi-double. Tube and sepals crimson; corolla rhodamine-purple. Medium sized flowers and free. Growth upright bush. Niederholzer – American – 1944.

Frolic. Single to semi-double. Tube light pink, long broad sepals flesh outside, light pink underside, tipped green. Corolla soft mallow-pink, large open spreading flowers, very free blooming. Growth trailer, heat resistant. Erickson – American – 1962 – A.F.S. No. 540.

Frosted Amethyst. Double. Bright red tube, long and broad, bright red sepals; corolla amethyst-purple, streaked red, pink, and very pale amethyst. Large blooms, free for size, opens in classic double form, sepal colour extends into outer petals of corolla, serrated petals, centre elongates and outer petals flare. Growth semi-trailer. Stubbs – American – 1975 – A.F.S. No. 1258.

Frosted Flame. Single. White tube, sepals white, lightly flushed palest pink inside, long and narrow, held well out, tips curl upwards. Corolla bright flame with deeper edge, pale pink near tube. Long barrel shaped flowers with overlapping petals, early, large and profuse. Bright green foliage, growth natural trailer. Handley – British – 1975 – A.F.S. No. 1273.

Frostiana. Double. White tube, sepals white on top, flushed pink, which fades to deep pink with undersides white flushed pink, sepals proportionately long and reflex upon opening. Corolla lilac with some petals splashed pink 1½ in to 2 in wide. Large blooms and substantive, occasional petaloids are lilac splashed pink. Dark green foliage with short and rounded leaves furrowed on veins. Growth semi-trailer, raised and tested for 16 years in the vicinity of San Jose, California, before release. Raised by Robert Erickson and introduced by C.L. Sayers of California. Erickson – American – 1979 – A.F.S. No. 1517.

Frost's Midas Touch. Single. Flower is a self, the same colour as Display but smaller with longer tube and sepals that do not recurve. Corolla is small and not the saucer shape as Display. Foliage is beautiful gold and green variegated. Habit of growth is upright and bushy, identical to its parent. Sport of Display. Frost – Rhodesian – 1979 – A.F.S. No. 1599.

Frosty. Single. Tube and sepals, dark crimson; corolla white, veined red. Large blooms heavily creped and free. Growth trailer. Niederholzer – American – 1947.

Frosty Bell. Single. Tube and sepals, bright pink; corolla pure white, veined pink. Bell shaped flowers much like Ting-a-Ling. Foliage is very dark, glossy, and very large. Growth upright and bushy. Upward Look × Ting-a-Ling. Gadsby – British – 1970 – A.F.S. No. 877.

Frühling. Double. Tube and sepals light red; corolla purple-blue with white and light blue. Large blooms, fairly free and early. Elsner – German or Austrian – 1878.

Fuchsia Fan. Double. Short tube red, sepals red on both sides; corolla deep fuchsia, variegated red. Large blooms with small foliage. Growth trailer. Pennisi – American – 1968 – A.F.S. No. 759.

Fuchsia King. Double. Short tube and sepals same colouring as corolla, fuchsia shade turning to deep rose, marbled pink. Large flowers, fairly free with small foliage. Growth trailer. Pennisi – American – 1969 – A.F.S. No. 817.

Fuchsia Mike. Semi-double. Short tube and sepals bright red; corolla purple to carmine. Medium sized blooms, fairly free and pointed. Foliage, heavily dark veined leaves, growth upright, bushy and vigorous. Conley – American – 1953 – A.F.S. No. 149.

Fuchsiarama. Double. Short and thick tube red, sepals red, broad and long, reflex slightly at first, reflex to tube with maturity. Corolla deep blue-purple, streaked red, fading to magenta and pink. Large blooms of classic form, fairly free for size, round and full, petals lift and flare, outstanding feature is the very long pistil. Dark green foliage, veined red with serrated edges. Growth semi-trailer. Jubie-Lin × Pink Marshmallow. Stubbs-Barnes and Ebeling – American – 1975 – A.F.S. No. 1278.

Fuksie Foetsie. Single. Tube and sepals ivory-white shading to flesh-pink. Corolla white ageing to pink with maturity. Received the B.F.S. Bronze Certificate of Merit at the R.H.S. London Show, 1979. *F. microphylla* seedling. van de Grijp – Dutch – 1979.

* Fuksie Vort. Single. Light pink tube maturing to rosy-red, sepals greenish-white ageing to rosy-red. Corolla white maturing to rosy-red. Small miniature flowers but very free, Breviflorae type. Small foliage, light green highly serrated. Growth upright and bushy. Dutch cultivar very rarely seen outside Holland. van der Grijp – Dutch – 1973.

fulgens. Long tube. Light vermilion-red, sepals yellowish to greenish with red base; corolla bright vermilion. Extremely attractive flowers, very long, pendulous and borne at the extreme ends of the branches in long and lasting clusters. Foliage is light sage-green, darker on upper sides, large with hairy leaves; the largest of any known fuchsia measuring some 9 in. One of the species with thickened tuberous roots. Upright shrub up to 4 ft. Described as the aristocrat of the genus. De Candolle – 1828 – Mexico.

var. *carminata rosea.* Tube and sepals rosy-carmine; vermilion corolla, similar in habit.

var. *gesneriana.* Similar flowers but habit of growth is rather lax with shorter flower tube. Native to Guatemala.

var. *multiflora pumila.* Dwarf in growth habit and very free flowering; flowers are not as long.

var. *rubra grandiflora.* Very long tubed flowers with similar habit of growth, but the most beautiful. Native to Guatemala and Salvador.

Fulgens Speciosa. Refer to Speciosa for detailed description and information.

Funk Brentano. Double. Red and purple. Rozain-Boucharlat – French – 1908.

Fur Elise. Double. Pink tube, white sepals pink underneath; corolla pale lavender-blue, ageing to pale purple. Light green foliage. Growth lax upright, needs support as bush. Blackwell – British – 1968.

furfuracea. Tube red, sepals red; corolla purplish-red. Smallish to medium sized flowers, sparse, borne in terminal racemes. Flat, bushy shrub. Johnston – 1925 – Bolivia.

Furst Otto zu Wernigerode. Triphylla single. Long tube, rosy-pink; petals pale vermilion, very free. Foliage pale green, velvety leaves, bluish colour underneath. Growth upright. *F. triphylla* × Surprise. Gireoud – Germany – 1898.

fusea (Krause 1906). Synonymous with *F. decussata.*

Futura. Double. Pink tube, pink sepals very long, twist in futuristic fashion, hence the name. Corolla outer petals are pleated, pink overlaid and splashed blue, stay tight and grow very long before flaring to blue inner petals. Large blooms and fairly free for large double. Growth natural trailer. Kennett – American – 1969 – A.F.S. No. 864.

Gabriel Bonvalot. Lemoine – French – 1899.

Gabriel Rose. Single. Tube and sepals pale pink; corolla clear sky blue. Medium-sized flowers, growth upright and bushy. Hardy in Southern England, raised in the Scilly Isles. Tabraham – British – 1978.

Gaiety. Single. Red and purple. Sankey – British – 1887.

Gaiety. Double. Tube and sepals, bright crimson; corolla rose-bengal. Medium sized flowers and free. Growth low bush. Schnabel – American – 1952 – A.F.S. No. 111.

Gala. Double. Tube and sepals, light pink to salmon, tipped green; corolla blue centre surrounded by petals in shades of pink, lavender and salmon. Large flowers, fairly free but late in blooming. Growth lax bush or trailer. Martin – American – 1966 – A.F.S. No. 673.

*Galadriel. Little known Dutch cultivar other than the parentage: Mephisto × Countess of Aberdeen. de Graaff – Dutch – 1982.

*Galahad. Single. Short white tube, white sepals tipped green, fully reflexed with recurved tips when mature. Corolla rose-pink. Largish flowers are long and slightly flared, the feature of these flowers is the phenomenal flowering capacity and are of the Lye type. Foliage mid-green of medium size with some red in the leaf veins and young growth. Growth upright, strong arching and self-branching, will produce bush or standard and possibly basket with weights. Heat tolerant if shaded. Raised and tested for 2 years in the vicinity of Ipswich, East of England and introduced by B. and H.M. Baker of Halsted, Essex in 1983. Goulding – British – 1983 – A.F.S. No. 1727.

Galatea. Double. Red and purple. Bland – British – 1878.

Galathea. Single. Tube and sepals, pale pink; corolla deep pink. Large flowers and free. Growth upright and bushy. Niederholzer – American – 1946.

Galli Curci. Single. Tube and sepals, waxy shell-pink, stained rose-pink on reverse; corolla pink, suffused with violet-pink. Growth lax bush, spreading and weeping. Evans and Reeves – American – 1942.

Gambette. Lemoine – French – 1876.

Gambit. Single. Short crimson tube, reflexed sepals crimson; corolla white, lightly veined pink with overlapping petals. Flowers are small, very free, four blooms at each pair of leaf axils, sepals begin to separate when buds are small. Small foliage, makes excellent pot plant. Growth upright and bushy. Handley – British – 1971 – A.F.S. No. 985.

Gan. Double. Tube and sepals cerise; corolla blue. Medium sized blooms and free, growth upright and bushy. Considered to be a sport of Army Nurse. Abermule Nurseries – British – 1972.

Gardena. Double. Tube and sepals red; corolla white. Large blooms and free. Growth trailer. Fairclo – American – 1946.

Garden Beauty. Double. Rose-red tube, broad and waxy rose-red sepals; corolla violet-blue, flushed carmine and neyron-rose. Large blooms with fourteen petals, distinct red stamens and quite free for a double. Growth upright, bushy, medium height, branches arch due to weight of blooms and needs some support when grown as bush. Tested for 10 years in the Midlands of England and received no protection and classified as hardy in that area. Parentage not known but was a seedling found growing in open ground under a plant of Lena. Gadsby – British – 1978 – A.F.S. No. 1481.

Garden Grove. Double. Tube pinkish-green turning to green at base, sepals creamish-green on top, light pink underneath, tipped green. Corolla various shades of pink, with centre petals forming cup with many short petals. Flowers are large, fairly free, very long stamens. Growth upright. Gorman – American – 1970 – A.F.S. No. 919.

Garden News. Double. Short, thick, pink (R.H.S. 52D) tube, sepals (R.H.S. 52D) pink on outside and frosty rose-pink (R.H.S. 52C), broad, short and of good substance, well arched from base of corolla. Corolla is shades of magenta-rose (R.H.S. 57B and 61C), base of petals rose-pink (R.H.S. 52C). Large blooms of attractive shape mainly in fours at each pair of leaf axils, continuous flowering. Mid-green foliage, lightly serrated, growth tall, upright bush with large proportion of three-leaved stems, self branching will make good bush or decorative, will take full sun where colour best develops. Tested for 10 years in vicinity of Central England, 8 of which testing as hardy. Named by invitation from the British National Gardening Publication. Handley – British – 1978 – A.F.S. No. 4553.

Garibaldi. Single. Red and purple. Henderson – British – 1868.

garleppiana. Greenish-pink tube, sepals pink; no corolla. Produces only three or four very lovely flowers on leafless stems, borne in the axils of the main branches. Tall, epiphytic shrub up to 3 or 4 ft with thickened tuberous roots. Kuntze and Wittmach – 1893 – Bolivia and Peru.

Garnet. Single. Tube and sepals red; corolla deep red, almost a self. Medium sized flowers and very free, early. Growth strong upright bush. Niederholzer – American – 1946.

Garnier Pagès. Double. Red and purple. Lemoine – French – 1896.

Garrechien. Single/Double. Tube and sepals carmine-pink; corolla indigo-blue. Medium-sized flowers, very suitable cultivar for pot work. De Groot – Dutch – 1967.

Gartendirektor Hample. Triphylla type single. Long tube, brick-red; long petals, pale crimson. Bronze-green foliage. Growth upright. Sauer – German – 1911.

Garteninspektor Monkemeyer. Triphylla type single. Very long tube, dull red; petals cinnamon and short. Very dark green foliage; growth upright. Sauer – German – 1912.

Gartenmeister Bonstedt. Triphylla single. Long tube, orange brick-red self, very free. Flowers are almost identical to Thalia, the distinguishing feature separating the two is the pronounced bulge in the tube of Gartenmeister. Foliage dark bronzy-red. Growth upright and very vigorous, will stand sun and heat and with 50°F plus, will bloom well into the winter. Received H.C. certificate R.H.S. 1929. Has been known to be called Late Perfection. *F. triphylla* × .Bonstedt – German – 1905.

Gartenstadt Bruck/Mur. Double. Tube and sepals red; corolla purple. Landaver Schoenheit × *F.boliviana.* Nutzinger – Austrian – 1968.

*Gartenstadt Landau. Double. Tube and sepals dark red; corolla dark blue. Medium-sized blooms, free flowering. Growth strong vigorous, medium upright. El Camino × Bernadette. Nutzinger – Austrian – 1965.

Gaspar. Bland – British – 1880.

Gaston Cazalio. Rozain-Boucharlat – French – 1911.

Gavarni. Lemoine – French – 1867.

Gay Anne. Semi-double. Tube claret-rose, sepals claret-rose, underside crimson, held well back. Corolla mallow-pink, distinct edging of magenta-rose. Flowers long, well shaped and open, free, may be described as a single, but some blooms have five petals. Growth lax bush or trailer, self-branching. Named in honour of Princess Anne at the time of her wedding. Leonora × Joan Pacey. Gadsby – British – 1973 – A.F.S. No. 1221.

Gay Damosel. Double. Pink tube, long, thin sepals are neyron-rose (R.H.S. 55B). Corolla ruby red (R.H.S. 61A) at lower edges of petals fading to white at base. Medium-sized blooms, best colour in shade, rhodonite-red stamens and pistil. Foliage forest-green (R.H.S. 138A). Growth medium upright, bushy and self-branching, very graceful bush or shrub. Tested for 2 years in North East England before release. Viva Ireland × Joe Kusber. Ryle – British – 1977 – A.F.S. No. 1434.

Gay Darr. Double. Tube and narrow sepals, reddish-white, thin line of red around edges. Corolla orchid-blue. Flowers large and fairly free. Growth trailer. Soo Yun Field – American – 1965 – A.F.S. No. 643.

Gaye Lynne. Semi-double. Tube and long sepals, white on outer side, light pink underneath. Corolla smoky-blue. Flowers medium sized, free and long lasting, fading to various orchid shades. Small light green foliage. Growth natural trailer. Martin – American – 1960 – A.F.S. No. 443.

Gay Fandango. Double. Tube and long, broad spreading sepals carmine; corolla rose. Large flowers and free, petals of the corolla in tiers.

Growth upright and bushy, makes good standard. Nelson – American – 1951 – A.F.S. No. 176.

Gay Future. Single. Short thin white tube, sepals white, lightly flushed neyron-rose, tipped green, recurving and held horizontally. Corolla violet shading to white. Medium sized flowers, bell shaped, similar to Martin Glow but with stronger colour contrast and with a deeper violet than Estelle Marie, very free flowering. Deep green foliage with distinctive serrated leaves. Growth natural trailer but will produce good bush, self-branching. Cloverdale Pearl × .Gadsby – British – 1975 – A.F.S. No. 1314.

Gay G. Double. Tube and sepals crimson; corolla violet with crimson at base. Foliage of medium size but young leaves are tinted gold. Growth vigorous and self-branching. Catalogued by Fuchsialand Nurseries of Birmingham who could not locate the name of the cultivar and rather than discard it named it Gay G. at the nurseries around 1974 or 1975. This cultivar is very similar to Dollar Princess. Raiser unknown – Date unknown.

Gay Garland. Double. Mimosa-yellow tube, sepals neyron-rose inside, white flushed neyron-rose on reverse, long, standing straight out on opening, turning upwards at maturity. Corolla rich ruby-red, with tinges of purple and shaded pale rose to white at base. Large blooms, very free, with occasional petaloids, flowers are single at beginning and end of season. Growth semi-trailer. Monstera × Moon Mist. Reid – Australian – 1975 – A.F.S. No. 1305.

Gay Melanie. Single. Short tube carmine-rose, sepals carmine-rose, held horizontally. Corolla rose-pink edged with carmine-rose. Medium sized flowers, flared and veined carmine-rose with pointed petals. Light green foliage, ovate leaves and serrated. Growth medium upright and bushy, good for bush, and standard, best colour in shade. Tested for 4 years in the vicinity of Maidstone, Kent before release. Sport of Constance. Russell, R. and Saunders, E. – British – 1982 – A.F.S. No. 1673.

Gay Nessier. Semi-double. Tube and sepals red; corolla violet-blue, edged lilac. Medium sized flowers and free. Growth upright. Nessier – American – Date unknown..

Gay Parasol. Double. Short, thick ivory-green tube; ivory sepals with faint magenta streaks down edges, fading to all ivory overlaid magenta. Sepals do not recurve but lift above corolla like a parasol. Dark red-purple corolla fades to bright burgundy-red. Medium sized blooms, fairly short, when in bud and flower the contrast is very sharp, as the bud suggests pastel bloom but the open bloom is dark. Growth semi-upright tested for 4 years in vicinity of Fort Bragg, California, trademarked in California. Introduced into England in 1979. Stubbs – American – 1979 – A.F.S. No. 1501.

Gay Paree. Double. White tube, broad, upturned sepals white, tipped green, flushed pale carmine on outside, soft carmine-pink inside. Corolla with centre petals purplish and some variegation, outside petals phlox-pink with purplish splashes. Largish flowers, early and free, continuous bloomer. Growth lax bush or trailer. Tiret – American – 1954 – A.F.S. No. 206.

Gay Senorita. Single. Short tube and sepals, rosy-red; corolla dark lilac-rose. Bell shaped flowers, very early and free. Growth upright bush. Heron × Pride of Exeter. Schmidt – American – 1939.

Gay Spinner. Semi-double. Tube and sepals pink, very large sepals. Corolla pink at top changing to Imperial purple. Medium sized flowers nicely formed but have few sized petaloids making it a semi-double. Growth tall upright, very suitable as a standard, best as H2. Raised by John Lockyer and introduced by his father C.V. Lockyer in 1978. Lockyer – British – 1978.

Gay Time. Double. Tube and sepals, fuchsia-pink; corolla deep blue, splashed and edged rose. Medium sized flowers and free, growth tall vigorous bush. Niederholzer-Waltz – American – 1949.

Gay Ways. Single. White tube, sepals, rosy-pink; corolla pale blue. Medium sized flowers and free. Growth trailer. Waltz – American – 1952.

Gazebo. Semi-double. Tube and sepals, neyron-rose; corolla salmon-red. Large flowers fairly free, growth trailer. A.F.S. Cert. of Merit, 1972. Tiret – American – 1969 – A.F.S. No. 830.

Gazette. Double. Long tube and sepals, China-rose; corolla methyl-violet with rose petaloids. Flowers large and free, growth lax bush. Baker – British – 1970.

Geboyer. Lemoine – French – 1843.

gehrigeri. Dull red tube, sepals red; corolla dark red. Very few flowers, borne in terminal clusters. Irregular habit of growth, reaching several feet. Munz – 1943 – Venezuela.

Geisha. Single. Tube and sepals, dark red; corolla pale purple. Medium size flowers and free. Growth tall upright bush. Niederholzer – American – 1947.

Geisha Girl. Double. Tube and recurving sepals red; corolla red-purple. Medium size blooms exceptionally floriferous, claimed to be the fullest double to date with no less than 22 petals and no petaloids. Growth medium upright bush, easy grower. Pugh – British – 1974 – A.F.S. No. 1160.

Gem. Single. Crimson and pink. Henderson – British – 1842.

Gem. Single. Cerise and white. Turville – British – 1843.

Gemini. Single. Little known of this cultivar introduced by Hilltop Nurseries of Thornton, Leicestershire in 1981 apart from having red flowers with variegated foliage. Raiser and date unknown.

Gem of Ipswich. Double. Red and purple. Stokes – British – Date unknown.

Gem of the West. Single. Red and purple. Lye – British – Date unknown.

General Bernard Montgomery. Double. Tube and sepals carmine; corolla maroon colour with rolled-in petals. Flowers are large and loose, fairly free. Growth tall upright, very vigorous up to 6 to 8 ft in California. Garson – American – 1944.

General Changarnier. Vermilion self. Miellez – French – 1850.

General Chanzy. Lemoine – French – 1874.

General D'Amade. Double. Rosy-pink. Lemoine – French – 1908.

General De Nansouty. Lemoine – French – 1876.

General Dodds. Lemoine – French – 1893.

General Don Jose Cabrillo. Semi-double. Tube and sepals, darkish crimson; corolla rich lavender, flushed rose. Large blooms, fairly free. Growth upright bush. Raiser unknown – American – Date unknown.

General Douglas MacArthur. Double. Tube and sepals carmine; corolla white, streaked with carmine. Large sized blooms and free, growth upright bush to 4 ft. Garson – American – 1944.

General Drude. Lemoine – French – 1908.

General Felton. Felton – British – 1870.

General Forgemoi. Lemoine – French – 1882.

General Galleni. Double. Red and purple. Lemoine – French – 1899.

General Garfield. Single. Crimson and blue. Williams – British – 1881.

General Grant. Lemoine – French – 1869.

General Ike. Double. Long thin tube and pagoda type sepals crimson; corolla deep aster-violet, splashed white and crimson at base. Flowers are large with plumb-bob buds. Growth lax bush. Walker-Jones – American – 1950.

General Lapasset. Double. Coral and violet. Lemoine – French – 1883.

General Lewal. Double. Red and purple. Lemoine – French – 1885.

General Logerot. Lemoine – French – 1882.

General Lyautey. Lemoine – French – 1908.

General MacArthur. Double. Tube and sepals red, corolla dark blue to purple. Medium sized blooms fully double. Growth upright and bushy up to 3 ft in California. According to reliable American information this cultivar is different to General Douglas MacArthur by the same raiser, Garson, in the same year, 1944. Garson – American – 1944.

General Monk. Double. Tube and sepals, cerise-rose; corolla blue ageing to mauvish-blue. Medium sized blooms, very free and open. Old cultivar, good and still grown. Raiser unknown – French – Date unknown.

General Negrier. Semi-double. Rose and scarlet. Meillez – French – 1848.

General Sassier. Double. Red and purple. Lemoine – French – 1882.

General Tom Thumb. Single. Tube and sepals, white with rose-pink edge; corolla mauve-violet. Smallish flowers but very free, growth upright bush and hardy. Confused with Query and Chillerton Beauty, probably on account of it being sent by Queen Victoria to Osborne House, Isle of Wight, after being used extensively as a bedder in Hyde Park at the time of the Great Exhibition. Bass – British – 1848.

General Voyron. Single. Tube and sepals cerise; corolla violet-magenta. Medium sized flowers, very free and early bloomer. Growth upright and bushy, excels as a bedder, hardy in southern districts, an old cultivar which presents no difficulties. Lemoine – French – 1901.

General Voyron – Empress of Prussia. These two cultivars are almost identical except that G.V. is a little lighter in colour in the corolla and the foliage is definitely a much lighter shade of green, but the chief distinguishing feature is the very long pistil of G.V. Although not recognized as a hardy cultivar G.V. has proved to be hardy in the South Midlands making a huge shrub with long and free flowering laterals.

General Wavell. Double. Tube and sepals, pale cerise; corolla salmon-magenta. Medium sized blooms and free, growth upright and bushy, will produce good half or full standard. Bland's New Striped × Beauty of Exeter. Whiteman – British – 1942.

Genevieve. Double. Tube and wide sepals, deep pink outside, bright pink inside; corolla pale blue and light lavender. Large blooms, fairly free, elegant pastel coloured flowers. Growth cascade trailer. Martin – American – 1957 – A.F.S. No. 321.

Genevieve Gibson. Double. Tube off white, with pink veins, sepals rhodamine-pink curl towards tube. Corolla amethyst-violet, flushed rhodamine-pink. Flowers medium sized, semi-flared, no petaloids, very heavy bloomer. Growth upright bush. Foster – American – 1974 – A.F.S. No. 1171.

Genii. Single. Tube and sepals cerise; corolla rich violet, ageing to dark rose. Small flowers, very free, small foliage light yellowish-green with red stems. Growth upright and bushy, grows better outside, under glass difficult to control and unless conditions are correct, drops both buds and flowers. When first introduced was known as Jeane. Accepted by the B.F.S. as showbench hardy. Reiter – American – 1951.

*Genii-Jeane. Considerable confusion exists between these two cultivars. British authors usually quote Genii as being raised by Reiter in 1951. Reliable American sources quote Reiter as refuting any claim to Genii. As descriptions of both Genii and Jeane (Reiter 1951) are identical in every respect, it is more than possible Jeane is the original and true name, very similar to Golden Gate by Neiderholzer.

Genni. Single. Long tube and sepals red; corolla white. Large flowers and free. Growth lax bush or trailer. Fuchsia-La – American – 1968 – A.F.S. No. 801.

Georgana. Double. Tube and sepals pink; corolla soft pastel shades of pale blue and orchid. Huge blooms, free and continuous. Large bright green foliage, growth upright and bushy, would make fine espalier. Best grown as H1. Tiret – American – 1955 – A.F.S. No. 237.

George Barr. Single. Tube and sepals white; corolla violet-blue. Flowers small, fairly free. Growth upright and bushy, can be most disappointing, but for its white anthers could be an enlarged Venus Victrix. Hazard and Hazard – American – 1930.

George Felton. Double. Red and purple. Felton – British – 1870.

George Humphrey. Single. Thin greenish-white tube with darker veining and slight pinking; long thin sepals white and overlaid with carmine-rose (R.H.S. 52D) on upperside, crepey carmine (R.H.S. 52B) on underneath. Corolla roseine-purple (R.H.S. 68B) overlaid and edged rose-Bengal (R.H.S. 57B). Semi-bell shaped medium sized flowers with white at the base of each petal, pink anthers just clear of the corolla and long pistil with cream stigma. Small to medium midgreen foliage with paler immature

leaves. Lanceolate and heavily serrated leaves. Growth self-branching medium upright, bushy, makes excellent bush or standard, takes full sun. Tested for 4 years in vicinity of Edenbridge, Kent, before release. Holmes, R. – British – 1982 – A.F.S. No. 1670.

George Johnson. Single. Tube rose-pink, slightly recurving sepals rose-pink. Corolla rose-vermilion. Medium-sized flowers have tubular formation in keeping with a well balanced classic flower, red stamens and long pink pistil, flowers measure about ⅝in from ovary to end of stigma. Corolla retains tubular formation and relaxes slightly prior to blossom drop. Growth tall upright and bushy, will make good bush, shrub or standard. Tested for 2 years in Cleveland, England before release. Doyles – British – 1977 – A.F.S. No. 1429.

George Roe. Double. Thin crimson tube, sepals claret-rose, thick and waxy, held well out. Corolla white, extra large and solid. Blooms are exceptionally free for large double, but growth is strong enough to take the extra weight. Growth strong upright bush, fine cultivar which presents no difficulties. Gadsby – Britain – 1972 – A.F.S. No. 1065.

Georges Feydeau. Lemoine – French – 1894.

Georges Lyon. Lemoine – French – 1907.

George Travis. Double. Tube and sepals ivory, edged cerise; corolla silvery-blue. Flowers are largish, full and free bloomer. Growth upright bush. Travis, J. – British – 1956.

Georgia Peach. Semi-double. White tube, sepals pure white, curl back. Corolla very bright peach-pink with white marbling. Flowers seem to glow with fluorescence, petals slightly ruffled, on maturity open three quarters, with four main petals showing white at base, new break-through in colour for a double. Growth lax bush or trailer makes most attractive basket. Castro – American – 1973 – A.F.S. No. 1104.

Gerald. Bland – British – 1882.

Geranium Pink. Single. Tube and sepals rose-pink; corolla deep pink. Largish flowers almost identical to Display but much larger same saucer shape. Growth upright and bushy. Introduced by R. & J. Pacey. Raiser unknown – British – ca 1960.

Gerbe De Corail. F.venusta × Myrtifolia. Lemoine – French – 1896.

Germania. Weinrich – German – 1868.

Gertrude. Double. Tube and sepals, rosy-red; corolla rich blue, with marbled petaloids mauvish-pink. Large flowers and free, growth upright and bushy. Warren – American – 1952.

Gertrude Hannah. Single. No further details other than the cultivar is just another red and purple and very similar to Achievement. McParlin – British – 1976.

Gertrude Pearson. Single. Tube crimson, sepals reddish crimson corolla very deep purple. Medium sized flowers and very free. Growth upright and bushy. One source of information quotes as identical with Pink Pearl which cannot be correct on account of colouring. Dobbie – British – Prior to 1930.

Gesauseperle. This cultivar raised by Karl Nutzinger (Austrian) 1946 according to the Dutch Fuchsia Technical Commission is synonymous with Amelie Aubin (Eggbrecht 1884).

Giant Cascade. Single. Rich carmine self. Large flowers and very free, as the name implies growth is vigorous and cascading. Suitable as greenhouse climber. Nelson – American – 1940.

Giantess. Single. White and rose. Turville – British – 1846.

Giant Falls. Double. Tube and broad upcurved sepals pink, tipped green; corolla creamy-white, slight pink veining at base of petals. Large globular flowers, very profuse bloomer and continuous, very fine cultivar. Deep green foliage, growth trailer, with willowy growth will produce fine espalier. Erickson – American – 1957 – A.F.S. No. 323.

Giant Pink Enchanted. Double. Tube and sepals rose; corolla white, suffused pink. Very large blooms but not very free, good substance. Growth lax bush or trailer, needs support as bush. Raiser unknown – American – Date unknown (about 1965).

Gibraltar. Rozain-Boucharlat – French – 1927.

Gift Wrap. Double. Tube and sepals, white with green tips; corolla dianthus-purple centre with white petaloids and marbling, petals flaring out and turning bright red with maturity. Growth trailer. Kennett – American – 1969 – A.F.S. No. 865.

Gilda. Double. Short tube and broad sepals coral; corolla overlaid rose, each petal edged bright red. Flowers are large, very free flowering with growth that will support the heavy flowers. Foliage golden-green with maroon colouring, stems and veins darker with age. Growth upright. Handley – British – 1971 – A.F.S. No. 986.

Gilt Edge. Single. Small reddish-orange self with unusual foliage. As the name implies has a gold edged leaf and although all leaves do not possess this gilt edge the overall effect is interesting. Introduced by C.S. Lockyer (Fuchsias) of Bristol in 1979. Endicote – British – 1979.

Gina. Double. Tube and sepals rose-pink; corolla white. Large blooms and free for size. Growth natural trailer not inherited from its parents. Introduced by High Trees Nurseries of Reigate, Surrey, in 1980. (Snowcap × Ting-a-Ling) × Snowcap. Hobson – British – 1974.

⁎ Gina Banyard. Single. Neyron-rose tube ½ in long by ¼ in wide, half up sepals neyron-rose (R.H.S. 58C) on top, rose-red (R.H.S. 58B) underneath with recurved and twisted tips. Corolla opens cyclamen-purple (R.H.S. 74A) maturing to magenta (R.H.S. 66B) ¾ in long by ¾ in wide. Quarter flared tubular flowers with sepals nearly twisting into spirals, rose-red filaments and Indian-lake (R.H.S. 58A) anthers, white style and china-rose (R.H.S. 58D) stigma, buds are straight, tubular with lanceolate tip. Mid-green foliage (R.H.S. 146B) scheeles green (R.H.S. 143C) underneath, leaves 1¾ in long by 1 in wide lanceolate shaped, serrated edged, acute tip and rounded base. Growth self-branching medium upright and bushy, good for bush, decorative or standard, prefers full sun and cold weather hardy to 26°F. in Southern England, better as a second-year old plant. Raised in the vicinity of Worthing, Sussex. Hobbs, L. – British – 1984 – A.F.S. No. 1773.

Ginia. Single. Tube and sepals, bright rose, sepals open horizontally with tips upturned at maturity. Corolla bright violet with bright rose base,

opens tight and at maturity petals form rolled tubes. Flowers are smallish, early and very free, foliage light green and small. Growth upright and bushy. Watchorn-Behrends – American – 1970 – A.F.S. No. 1159.

Gipsy. Single. Rose and purple. Barkway – British – 1847.

Gipsy Princess. Double. Little known scarlet and white double cultivar. Listed and introduced by Abermule Nurseries in 1969. Raiser unknown – British – 1969.

Giralda. Single. Chalice-white. Demay – French – 1869.

Giselle. Semi-double to double. Tube white, sepals white, tipped green, pale pink underneath. Corolla lilac-blue, ageing to pinkish-mauve, veined pink, two tiered. Growth upright, needs lot of pinching. Blackwell – British – 1964.

⁎ Gita Nunes. Double. Red tube, sepals rose-red with recurved tips 2 in long by 1 in wide. Corolla white, variegated rose-red 3 in long × 3½ in wide with wavy petal margins. Large blooms square shaped and fully flared with red stamens and pistil. Foliage deep dark green with ovate leaves, large, 4½ in long × 3 in wide, leaf tip acute. Growth natural trailer, will produce huge basket and heat tolerant if shaded. Raised and tested for 3 years in Bolinas, California, and will be trademarked in California. Sport of Vienna Waltz. Guasco Fuchsia Gardens – American – 1983 – A.F.S. No. 1737.

glaberrima. Tube bright red, sepals scarlet; corolla scarlet. Smallish flowers borne in terminal racemes. Upright shrub. Johnston – 1925 – Ecuador.

Gladiator. Double. Red and white. Lemoine – French – 1889.

Glad Rags. Double. Tube and sepals, pink inside, white outside; corolla pale orchid and pink centre, with pink overlay. Flowers are large, compact and fairly free. Growth natural trailer. Fuchsia Forest, Castro – American – 1962 – A.F.S. No. 514.

Gladys. Single. Tube and sepals rose; corolla campanula-violet. Small flowers, free and early. Growth upright bush to 3 ft. Niederholzer – American – 1946.

Gladys Mary Wright. Double. Violet and white tube, sepals are same colour as tube, arch well back. Corolla white with green tips. Large blooms and fairly free for size of bloom. Medium green foliage. Growth tall, upright and bushy, good for bush or standard, best colour develops in shade. Originates from the vicinity of Warwickshire. Seedling of Masquerade. Wright, J.A. – British – 1980 – A.F.S. No. 1600.

Gladys Miller. Single. Short narrow cream tube, sepals cream, flushed pink, tipped green. Corolla white at base shading to pale amethyst-violet. Flowers are large for single, each of the sepals terminate in wide angled point. Growth upright and bushy. Miller – British – 1970.

Glamour. Semi-double to double. Tube and sepals white; corolla orchid-blue. Flowers large and free, growth vigorous trailer. Nelson – American – 1955.

Glenby. Double. Short tube rose-madder, sepals rose-madder, streaked with pale pink, reflexing to tube, then curling downwards. Corolla amethyst-violet, fading to petunia-purple. Medium sized blooms, very profuse, petaloids same colour as corolla. Growth upright and bushy, self-branching. Brazier – British – 1972 – A.F.S. No. 1266.

Glendale. Single. Coral-pink self. Flowers are small to medium, bell shaped, very free, borne in clusters and early. Growth tall bush and vigorous. *F. lycioides* × Fireflush. Evans and Reeves – American – 1936.

Glenn Mary. Double. Short tube and sepals violet, shading to pink; corolla bright pink. Medium sized blooms, very free and early. Dark green foliage, growth lax bush or trailer. Sutherland – American – 1968 – A.F.S. No. 810.

Glitters. Single. Waxy-white tube, sepals waxy-white, inside lovely salmon colour; corolla glowing orange-red. Medium sized flowers, produced in profusion with spreading corolla. One of the parents of Celia Smedley from which it obtains its very vigorous growth. Growth upright and vigorous, heat resistant. Erickson – American – 1963 – A.F.S. No. 579.

Globosa. Single. Tube and sepals, greenish cream, corolla rich plum purple. Medium size flowers, free, rounded as the name implies. Growth upright and bushy. Accepted by the B.F.S. as showbench hardy. Raiser and date unknown. There are many forms of Globosa – see *magellanica* var. *globosa*.

Gloire de Marche. Double. Tube and sepals carmine; corolla white, faintly veined cerise at base. Largish blooms and free for double, well shaped and early bloomer. Growth medium upright and bushy. Crousse – French – about 1853.

Gloire des Blanes. Double. Red and white. Crousse – French – 1864.

Glorious. Single. White tube, sepals white on top, rose underneath; corolla rose-bengal. Large flowers and free. Growth trailer. Niederholzer – American – 1948.

Glororum. Single. Long thin tube neyron-rose, sepals neyron-rose, narrow and flared with upturned tips. Corolla amethyst-violet, flushed pale pink at base, fading to cyclamen-purple with age. Medium sized flowers, very free flowering, bell shaped with distinct wavy edge to petals. Mid green foliage with smooth reddish stems, growth medium upright, bushy and self-branching. Pink Profusion × Lena Dalton. Ryle – British – 1973 – A.F.S. No. 1244.

Glory. Single. Crimson and purple. Banks – British – 1870.

Glory of Bath. Double. Short tube pink, sepals carmine-pink; corolla rosy-purple, veined carmine, rose at base. Very large blooms with lightish green foliage. Growth lax upright. Colville – British – 1965.

Glory of England. Single. White and violet. Harrison – British – 1853.

Glow. Single. Tube and sepals cerise; corolla wine-purple, suffused scarlet at base of petals. Small flowers and free. Growth low bush, hardy, excellent bedder. Accepted by the B.F.S. as showbench hardy. Seedling × Mrs. Rundle (W.P. Wood letter 1952). Wood – British – 1946.

Glowing Embers. Single. Almost self in colour. Tube and sepals watermelon-pink, thick and crepe. Corolla burnt-orange to red. Large flowers and free, sometimes with five to six petals, colouring very similar to Chang. Growth lax bush or trailer. Kennett and Ross – American – 1957 – A.F.S. No. 285.

Glyn Jones. Semi-double. Tube and sepals neyron-rose underside, outside paler pink heavily tipped with green; corolla violet-purple with neyron-rose petaloids. Medium sized flowers, very prolific blooming, delightful colour contrast. Light green foliage, growth medium upright, bushy and strong. Parentage unknown – a chance seedling. George Roe however has used it quite extensively in hybridising. Dr. Manson, Elizabeth Brown, Paul Roe, Pirbright and Southwell Minster have all been produced with Glyn Jones as a parent. Roe – British – 1976.

Goblin. Double. Tube and sepals pink, sepals of crepe texture; corolla blush. Small flowers, free and long lasting. Lush green foliage, growth semi-trailer. Garson – American – 1962 – A.F.S. No. 509.

Gold Brocade. Single. Tube and sepals red; corolla mauve, fading to pink with maturity. Large flowers and very free. Foliage deep gold-green heavily veined purple, slowly changing to pale green with age. Growth upright, bushy and strong, height 1½ to 2 ft. Hardy in Southern England, raised in the Scilly Isles. Tabraham – British – 1976.

Goldcrest. Single. Tube and sepals, light pink, sepals tipped green and deep pink underneath; corolla lavender, veined pink. Foliage golden, ageing to green, growth lax bush. Thorne – British – 1968.

Gold Crest. Single. Red tube, long red sepals; pale mauve and pink corolla. Small flowers borne in profusion. Golden green foliage, new growth is bright gold. Growth is upright but with spreading habit, height 6 to 9 in, real miniature suitable for window boxes and rockeries and troughs. One of a series of new hardy miniatures raised in the Scilly Isles. Not to be confused with Tom Thorne's cultivar of the same name 1968. Tabraham – British – 1982.

Gold Dust. Single. Tube and sepals red, corolla deep purple. Medium sized flowers with golden foliage. Growth upright and bushy. Appears to be exclusive to the Home Counties of England. Raiser unknown – British – *ca* 1970s.

Golden Anniversary. Double. Short thick tube is greenish-white, white sepals, broad and sharply pointed. Corolla is intense black-purple fading to royal purple with maturity. Medium sized blooms with many flaring petals which fade from dark to pale pink at the base of tube. New foliage is very light almost green-gold fading to light green. Growth natural trailer will make excellent basket without weights, self-branching, growth habit is heavy but soft indicating its laxness. Originates from the Fort Bragg area of California. Stubbs – American – 1980 – A.F.S. No. 1532.

*Golden Arrow. Single. Triphylla type hybrid. Long thin tube finely tapered and orange coloured, each short sepal recurves with maturity, tipped green. Corolla has a hue of tangerine. The long flowers are typical of terminal flowering parentage. Growth is rather lax and spreading and eminently suitable for use in hanging pots. Early stopping produces exhibition quality plants living up to its name. Raised in the vicinity of Ipswich, Suffolk, and introduced by the raiser, Gouldings Fuchsias of Ipswich, in 1985. One of a series of ten new introductions named after famous trains in 1985. Goulding – British – 1985.

Golden Border Queen. Single. Short thin tube, rhodamine-pink sepals tipped green, neyron-rose underneath, which flare out and are upturned. Corolla amethyst-violet, flushed pale pink with dark pink veining. Colour slightly lighter than its sister seedling Eden Lady. Identical to Border Queen except for its brilliant yellow foliage without any variegation. Like some other sports, Border Queen produced identical sports in different places, almost at the same time. Introduced by Penhalls Nurseries of Shaw, near Oldham in 1979 and identical to Barry's Queen found by Barry Sheppard in 1980 and introduced by Baker's of Halstead in 1982. Penhall – British – 1979.

Golden Chains. Synonymous with Golden Treasure.

* Golden Cloverdale Pearl. Single. White tube, sepals rhodamine-pink shading to white and tipped green, curling back towards tube. Corolla white, medium sized flowers, well formed and very free flowering. Identical in every way to Cloverdale Pearl except for the golden variegated foliage. Growth is self branching bush. Needs careful cultivation, does tend to 'damp off' and like all the ornamental and variegated cultivars needs all the light possible and as little watering as possible. Introduced by Fuchsiavale Nurseries of Kidderminster in 1983. Sport of Cloverdale Pearl.

Golden Dawn. Single. Tube and sepals, light salmon; corolla light orange, shaded fuchsia-pink. Medium sized flowers and free. Growth upright, needs early pinching. Haag – American – 1951.

Golden Drame. Single to semi-double, Tube and sepals scarlet, corolla violet-purple. Medium sized blooms with exactly the same characteristics as its parent, except in the golden variegated foliage, hardy. Sport of Drame. Introducer unknown – British – ca 1979.

* Golden Eden Lady. Single. Short thin pale rose tube, sepals amaranth-rose (R.H.S. 65A) deeper underneath, shading to white at tips, upturned from the horizontal. Corolla hyacinth-blue (R.H.S. 91A) with slight rose colouring at the base. Medium sized flowers, very similar to Border Queen except for the slightly darker colour. Foliage bright yellow with green patches similar to the golden privet used for hedging. Growth upright bushy and self-branching. Cultivar destined for the showbench, excellent in every way. Sport from Eden Lady found in the Wrexham area in Wales by C. Cater and introduced by J.V. Porter of Southport in 1983. Cater – British – 1982.

Golden Fleece. Synonymous with Golden Treasure.

Golden Gate. Single. Tube and sepals red; corolla rich purple. Flowers small and fairly free the usual combination for ornamental foliage. Dense bright golden foliage. Growth compact and bushy. Niederholzer – American – 1940.

Golden Gate Park. Semi-double. Magenta self. Medium sized flowers and very free. Growth upright bush. Reiter – American – 1948.

Golden Glory. Double. Almost an orange self and most unusual. Flowers medium sized and fairly free, foliage golden colour with red at base of leaves. Growth lax bush or trailer. Gorman – American – 1970 – A.F.S. No. 930.

Golden Glow. Single. Tube and sepals, pale carmine, flushed salmon; corolla yellowish-orange. Medium sized blooms and very free. Growth trailer. Munkner – American – 1958.

Golden Glow. Single. Almost a golden-orange self. Medium sized flowers and free. Growth lax bush. Mrs. Shutt Jun – American – 1968.

* Golden Jessimae. Single. Short china-rose tube, broad china-rose sepals. Corolla pale mallow-purple, medium sized flowers and free flowering. A sport from Jessimae, flower and habit exactly the same as its parent, growth upright and bushy. Foliage green and gold variegated very similar to Golden Treasure. Raised and tested for 2 years without any reversion in the vicinity of North Yorkshire. Introduced by the raiser, Fountains Nurseries near Ripon, in 1984. Sport of Jessimae. Akers – British – 1984.

* Golden Jewel. Semi-double. Tube and sepals neyron-rose, sepals held well back. Corolla wisteria-blue with rose veining passing to violet-blue. Medium sized blooms, very free, the few extra petaloids turning a single into semi-double. Foliage beautiful golden colours without any variegation. Growth upright and bushy, a robust and most attractive cultivar better grown as a second year plant. Tested for 3 years in the vicinity of Northampton. Sport of Cloverdale Jewel. Sayers, E. – British – 1979.

Golden La Campanella. Semi-double. White tube, sepals white slightly flushed pink, corolla is beautiful shade of imperial-purple fading to lavender-blue on maturity. Extremely floriferous and very early, characteristics inherited from its parent. Variegated foliage and could be identical to another sport, found around the same time, from La Campanella under the name of Princess Pat. Growth lax, self-branching but rather straggly and weak in early stages, very suitable for basketwork. Introduced by Fountains Nurseries of Ripon, North Yorkshire in 1981. Anonymous – British – 1980.

Golden Lena. Semi-double. Tube and sepals pale flesh-pink, sepals are half reflexed and slightly deeper in colour underneath; corolla rosy-magenta, flushed pink, paling at base. Medium sized flowers, very free, blooms in flushes, exactly the same as Lena. Foliage resembles that of Golden Marinka with its varying shades of green and gold. Sport from Lena and proved to be hardy in the Midlands after 6 years. Growth lax bush will trail for basket work, a welcome introduction to the variegated foliage cultivars. Introduced by R. Pacey in 1979. Nottingham, M. – British – 1978.

Golden Mantle. Synonymous with Golden Treasure.

Golden Marinka. Single. Probably the most popular and well known of the variegated foliage cultivars. A sport of Marinka introduced in America by Weber in 1955, although not registered by the A.F.S. until 1959 under No. 401. Well grown, this cultivar can be outstanding and eye catching with its brilliant coloured foliage, a combination of green and yellow variegated leaves, some being practically all yellow, others nearly all green, whilst the majority hardly know how to make up their minds, but the attractiveness is that, coupled with the red veining, every leaf is different, banded and splashed creamy-gold. The flowers are identical to that of Marinka and, although sometimes described as semi-double, are single blooms that have the appearance of being semi-double. Tube and sepals are rich red, whilst the corolla is slightly darker red, almost a self. The blooms are medium sized and although fairly prolific, are not as abundant as in its mother; Golden Marinka is a little later to flower, responds to frequent pinching, but from an early planting in late March or early April, will produce a basket full of bloom by mid or late July. The growth is again identical of Marinka and will produce a fine weeping standard, but best grown as a basket as it is a natural trailer; can be trained to almost any shape except a bush, but does lack the vigour of its parent. Like most variegated foliage cultivars, needs the maximum of light to produce the full effect of the brilliant colouring in the foliage, it does need careful watering and better results obtained if the plant or plants are left until the compost has almost dried out before the next watering. When used for basket work, extra care in watering should be exercised, especially in peat based composts when first planted, as over-watering at this early stage, makes it prone to damping off at the base. The idea place for this cultivar is a sheltered spot in the greenhouse, where it can receive the maximum of available light, dislikes draughts and is best grown as H1. Sport of Marinka. Weber – American – 1955 – A.F.S. No. 401.

Golden Melody. Double. Tube and sepals deep pink; corolla blue fading to lavender, medium-sized blooms, very full double. Foliage deep gold-green, slowly changing to pale green with maturity. Growth upright, bushy and strong, height 1½ to 2 ft. Hardy in Southern England, raised in the Scilly Isles. Tabraham – British – 1976.

* Golden Penny Askew. Single. Scarlet tube, recurved scarlet sepals. Corolla magenta, medium sized flowers exactly the same as Brilliant (Bull 1865) except for golden coloured ovary. Foliage olive-green variegated gold. Growth medium upright, self-branching, good for bush or standard, will take full sun but best colour develops in shade. Originates from the vicinity of Leicestershire. Sport of Brilliant. Askew – British – 1983 – A.F.S. No. 1719.

Golden Queen. Single. Tube and sepals red with red corolla, almost a self. Red variegated foliage. Growth upright and bushy. Introduced by John Smith of Hilltop Nurseries, Leicestershire, in 1980. Raiser and date unknown.

* Golden Runner. Single. Tube pale pink, sepals pale pink much lighter colour at tips. Corolla rose-pink, short and straight. Medium sized flowers, very free. Very attractive green and gold variegated foliage, flowers are identical to its parent. Growth upright, strong and short-jointed unusual for coloured leaf cultivar and more resistant to botrytis. Cultivar attributed to the late Wilf Tolley and introduced by Fuchsiavale Nurseries of Kidderminster in 1984. Sport of Runner which was raised from Barbara. Tolley – British – 1984.

Golden Snowcap. Semi-double. Tube and sepals crimson; corolla white, flushed and veined cerise. Small flowers free, similar to Snowcap. Foliage is golden-green and variegated, very similar to Rosecroft Beauty but considered better and superior although this is nothing exceptional as Rosecraft Beauty is not considered to be more

than a mediocre cultivar. Growth upright and bushy. Sport of Snowcap. Howarth – British – 1976.

Golden Swingtime. Double. Tube and sepals waxy-red, corolla white veined red. Large flowers very free. Needs no introduction, identical to its parent, Swingtime, but with golden foliage. Sport from Swingtime which must have occurred in different places around the same time as it was originally introduced by Hill Trees Nurseries of Reigate followed by F.H. Holmes of Beccles, G. Nice of Stowmarket and Rainbow Nurseries of Sandon, Essex, all in 1981.

* Golden Tolling Bell. Single. Short thick scarlet-red tube and sepals with pure white corolla, veined cerise. Perfect bell shaped largish flowers and very free flowering. Inherits all its parent's characteristics with the exception of the pale green edged yellow foliage. Originally found by R. Pacey of Melton Mowbray, Leicestershire, but introduced by Homestead Nurseries of Middlesex, in 1984. Sport of Tolling Bell. Pacey – British – 1984.

Golden Treasure. Single. Tube and sepals scarlet; corolla purplish-magenta. Small flowers not very attractive, rather late to bloom and sparse. Delightful green and gold variegated foliage, with red veins, has the habit of sporting back to green foliage. Growth small low bush, can be used as edging bedder. Another old cultivar which has stood the test of time R.H.S. H.C. Certificate 1929. Carter – British – 1860.

Golden Violet. Double. Short white tube, white sepals open flat, corolla deep violet. Medium sized blooms with round white buds, fairly free, most unusual colour combination for variegated foliage cultivar. Foliage is very attractive, yellow to pale green, veined red, with red stems. Growth trailer. Prentice – American – 1966 – A.F.S. No. 665.

* Golden Wedding. Single. Tube rhodamine-pink, sepals are long and slender rhodamine-pink which turn slightly upwards. Corolla cyclamen-purple. Medium sized flowers, rather long colouring does not fade with maturity. Foliage is lovely golden colour and a great contrast against the attractive flowers. Growth upright and bushy. Found in the vicinity of Gainsborough, Lincolnshire. To be released by the finder, Kathleen Muncaster Fuchsias, in 1985. Sport of Pirbright. Muncaster – British – 1985.

Golden West. Species type with tube approximately 3½ in long, orange self with dark green foliage. Growth lax bush. Classified as a collector's item. Reputed to be a seedling from Fanfare. Early bloomer with cool, crisp green foliage similar to F. arborescens. Flowers with their long tubes and symmetrical star shaped corollas have the appearance of a triphylla type cultivar. Walker and Jones – American – 1955.

Golders Green. Semi-double. Tube and sepals pinkish-red, purple corolla. Medium sized blooms, yellow foliage ageing to green with maturity. Growth upright and bushy. Little known cultivar appears to be exclusive to the Home Counties of England. Raiser unknown – British – ca 1970.

Gold Finch. Synonymous with Golden Treasure.

Goldilocks. Semi-double. Tube and sepals, bright red; spreading corolla white with rose stripes. Medium sized blooms and fairly free, foliage lovely golden-yellow. Growth medium bush. Haag – American – 1950.

Gold Leaf. Single. China-rose tube, sepals China-rose, tipped green, held well back. Corolla clear creamy-white with no shading of the veins. Medum sized blooms of uniform shape and free. Foliage citron-green on fresh growth in cool conditions, giving a golden effect. Growth lax bush, self-branching, bush or basket. Gadsby – British – 1974 – A.F.S. No. 1222.

Goldsworth Beauty. Single. Tube and sepals pale cerise, corolla reddish-purple. Medium sized blooms and free. Growth upright, bushy and hardy in Southern districts. Submitted by raiser for R.H.S. Wisley Hardy Trials 1975–78 but received no award. Slococks – British – 1952.

Goliath. Single. Tube and sepals light red sepals fold back; corolla dark purple. Synonymous with Achievement (Melville 1886). Trwdy – German – 1866?

Golondrina. Single. Tube and sepals, rose-madder; corolla magenta, streaked light pink, dark edges emphasised by crimson blotches. Large flowers and free. Growth lax bush and spreading habit, hardy in Southern districts. Niederholzer – American – 1941.

Gondolier. Double. Tube and sepals, whitish-pink; corolla deep violet-blue. Flowers are large and fairly free, short outer petals are marbled fuchsia-pink, long white buds. Growth upright. Sport of Fluorescent. Pybon – American – 1959.

Good News. Double. Tube and sepals pink; corolla deep rose-pink. Very large blooms, fairly free, with dark green foliage. Growth lax bush or trailer, heat resistant. Fuchsia-La – American – 1967 – A.F.S. No. 697.

Goody Goody. Single. Tube and sepals white; corolla deep purple fading to orchid. Medium sized flowers and free, very showy. Growth upright. Castro – American – 1969 – A.F.S. No. 838.

Gordon B. Lloyd. Tube and sepals red; corolla pink. Medium sized flowers and free. Growth upright and bushy. Fairclo – American – 1947.

Gordon Potton. Semi-double. Pink and white. Bright – British – 1913.

Gordon's China Rose. Single. Tube and sepals white flushed china-rose, corolla magenta-rose. Medium-sized blooms and free. Growth upright. Introduced at 1954 B.F.S. London Show as a new seedling. Raised in Romford, Essex. Lena is one parent. Gordon – British – 1953.

Gotesborgskan. Semi-double. Light red tube, light red sepals, recurved and round; corolla white with light pink veining. Medium-sized blooms with stamens and style deep pink. Foliage mid-green with rather small leaves. Growth upright, bushy and self-branching. This cultivar is grown and cultivated in the Netherlands. Raiser and date unknown.

Göttingen. Triphylla single. Long tube, pale vermilion self. Tube is cylindrical, petals slightly rolled. Dark green foliage, flushed red. Growth upright, dwarf and slow growing. *F. triphylla* × . Bonstedt – German – 1905.

Gouverneur Backer. Crousse – French – 1866.

Gov. 'Pat' Brown. Double. Light pink tube, sepals light pink, tipped pale green, folding back to a graceful curve, back of sepals and tube

creamy-white. Corolla violet with splashes of pink at base of petals. Pale green foliage. Large flowers, fairly free. Growth trailer. A.F.S. Cert. of Merit 1966. Machado – American – 1962 – A.F.S. No. 497.

Grace. Single. Short crimson tube, sepals crimson, tipped green, long, curving upwards. Corolla cyclamen-purple, veined scarlet, light crimson at base of sepals. Flowers are large for a single, bell-shaped, very profuse. Growth lax bush or trailer. Percy Holmes × Jack Acland. Holmes, R. – British – 1974 – A.F.S. No. 1203.

Grace Darling. Single. Short pale pink tube, sepals pale pink, held well back to tube; corolla white. Medium sized blooms, very free, bell shaped. Growth upright and bushy, short jointed. Rosedale × Sleigh Bells. Gadsby – British – 1972 – A.F.S. No. 1066.

*Grace Durham. Single. Short rhodonite-red tube $\frac{1}{4}$ in long, fully up orient-pink sepals, neyron-rose (R.H.S. 55C) underneath, $1\frac{1}{4}$ in long by $\frac{1}{2}$ in wide with recurved tips. Corolla starts purple (R.H.S. 77B) maturing to cyclamen-purple (R.H.S. 74A) 1 in long by $1\frac{1}{4}$ in wide. Medium sized flowers half flared and wide bell shaped, many flowers in each leaf axil. Dark green foliage (R.H.S. 137A). Slightly paler underneath with ovate leaves $1\frac{1}{2}$ in long by 1 in wide. Growth upright and bushy, self-branching, very suitable for all types of tall training and bush, needs little pinching or shaping. Raised in the vicinity of Ipswich, Suffolk, and introduced by the raiser Gouldings Fuchsias of Ipswich in 1984. Goulding – British – 1984 – A.F.S. No. 1779.

Grace Eybel. Semi-double. Short thin tube, green with shades of pink, sepals white at top and bottom, tipped green, shaded with rose. Corolla light blue, shaded with rose, small petaloids of same colouring. Medium sized flowers, fairly free, keep tight form, very attractive colour combination. Growth lax bush, will trail with weights. Pancharian – American – 1975 – A.F.S. No. 1297.

*Grace Groom. Double. Tube and sepals orange, corolla deep pink and lilac. Medium sized blooms, originally known as seedling No. 407. Raised in the vicinity of Guildford, Surrey. Growth upright and bushy. Weeks – British – 1982.

Gracieux. Single. Red and lavender. Lemoine – French – 1881.

gracilis (Sessé and Mocino 1828). Synonymous with *F. microphylla.*

Gracilis. See *magellanica* var. *gracilis.*

Gracious Lady. Double. Tube and long sepals deep rose; corolla maroon with salmon variegations. Large flowers and free, growth trailer. Pennisi – American – 1970 – A.F.S. No. 887.

Graf Witte. Single. Tube and sepals carmine; corolla purple shaded rosy-mauve. Very small flowers, but profuse. Yellowish-green foliage with crimson mid-rib and veins. Growth medium bush to 3 ft, ideal as a permanent bedder. Accepted by the B.F.S. as showbench hardy. Submitted by L.R. Russell Ltd for R.H.S. Wisley Hardy Trials 1975–78 and received Award of Merit. Lemoine – French – 1899.

Granada. Double. Tube and sepals, deep carmine; corolla rich purple. Very large blooms and free, flowers have opulence unmatched by any other purple excepting the old cultivar Royal Purple, but twice as large. Dark green leathery foliage. Growth upright bush. Schnabel – American – 1957 – A.F.S. No. 290.

Grand Duchess Marie. Single. White and rose. Williams – British – 1874.

Grand Duke. Double. Red and purple. Smith – British – 1865.

Grand Horizon. Double. Red and purple. Henderson – British – 1867.

Grandidens. Double. Red and purple. Williams – British – 1874.

grandiflora (Ruiz ex Dahlgren 1940). Synonymous with *F. denticulata.*

Grandiflora Maxima. *F.fulgens × F.grandiflora.* May – British – 1841.

*Grandma. Double. Pink tube, sepals are empire-rose and carmine underneath. Corolla vivid bishop's-violet flushed carmine. Medium sized blooms and free flowering for a double, unusual colour combination, very attractive. Growth upright, medium size and bushy. Raised in the vicinity of Plymouth, Devon. Drake 400 × Merry Mary. Hilton – British – 1984.

Grand Prix. Double. White tube, sepals porcelain-white, rose underneath. Corolla delft-rose at base of petals, shading to pansy-violet with tips edged delft-rose. Medium sized blooms, very free, large foliage. Growth upright and strong. Fuchsia-La – American – 1972 – A.F.S. No. 1020.

Grand Slam. Double. White tube, sepals white topside, pale crepe pink underside, curl and fold back. Corolla pale purple-lavender matures to fuchsia-magenta with pink marbling. Very large flowers, fairly free, very long buds. Large dark green foliage. Growth trailer. Kennett-Castro – American – 1973 – A.F.S. No. 1106.

Grange. Double. Short tube cardinal-red, broad sepals cardinal-red (R.H.S. 53C), dull on underside. Corolla blue with splash or red on outer petals near to sepals (R.H.S. 86B). Medium sized blooms of good character with red stamens. Growth upright and bushy, self-branching will make good bush. Tested for 4 years in the vicinity of Preston before release. Dark Eyes self. Thornley – British – 1981 – A.F.S. No. 1637.

Granpa Bleuss. Double. Tube and sepals white; corolla lavender. Large blooms and free. Growth upright bush. Sport of Papa Bleuss. Roe – British – 1970.

Grasmere. Single. Long thin tube *F.triphylla* type, coral-red, sepals coral-red, tipped green; corolla deep coral-pink, almost a self-coloured flower. Flowers in clusters at apices of stems. Foliage deep green with pink base in younger leaves, large and of *F.fulgens* size and colour. Growth is natural trailer, makes self-branching bush, very vigorous. *F.cordifolia × F.lycioides.* S. Travis – British – 1964 – A.F.S. No. 1151.

Gray Dawn. Double. Tube and sepals, reddish-white, corolla blue-grey, fades to grey. Large blooms, fairly free. Bright green foliage with reddish stems. Growth trailer. Soo Yun Field – American – 1965 – A.F.S. No. 645.

Gray Lady. Double. Tube and sepals, rosy-white; corolla pale campanula-violet, fades to delicate lavender-rose. Flowers large and free, greenish-white buds. Growth upright and vigorous. Reiter – American – 1952 – A.F.S. No. 129.

Grayrigg. Single. Short, thin tube white with green flush, blush-pink sepals, tipped green, have deeper pink underside. Corolla soft pink (R.H.S. 69D). Flowers are larger than parents, heat tolerant if shaded, best colour in shade, very free flowering. Small pale green foliage, growth medium upright, self-branching and bushy. Although raised in 1971 not released or introduced until 1978. Tested for 7 years in the vicinity of Preston. Silverdale × Silverdale seedling. Thornley – British – A.F.S. No. 1468.

Graz. Double. Red tube, red sepals with green tips; corolla white, veined red. Small to medium blooms with pink stamens and style. Dark green foliage, growth upright and bushy. Closely resembles Snowcap. Nutzinger – Austrian – 1949.

Grazer Dirndl. Single. Tube and sepals red; corolla blue. Smallish flowers with pink stamens and light pink style, resistant to heat. Mid green foliage with pointed leaves and red midrib. Gesausesperle × *F.magellanica* var. *gracilis.* Nutzinger – Austrian – 1966.

Great Gable. Double. Tube and broad, long sepals, pale shell-pink, almost white, sepals spiral. Corolla white with faint shell-pink at base. Flowers are large and of extra good substance, free for size. Growth upright and vigorous. Raiser has lost this cultivar but it may be in possession of the North Devon Fuchsia Group. Guinevere × Madame Lantelme. Thornley – British – 1963.

Great Scott. Double. Tube and sepals, carmine-rose; corolla jasper-red with salmon-pink petaloids. Huge flowers and free for size of bloom. Growth upright. Tiret – American – 1960 – A.F.S. No. 433.

Greenfinger. Single. Short tube baby-pink, sepals baby-pink with central green stripe, narrow and rolled. Corolla creamy-white. Medium sized flowers, freely produced and slightly bell shaped. Growth medium bush, short jointed, an exhibitors cultivar. Tolley – British – 1974 – A.F.S. No. 1230.

Green 'n' Gold. Single. Delightful coral-pink self, borne in clusters, flowers are profuse, bell shaped. Foliage is small, cream and yellow colouring provided it has full sunlight, if not will produce just another green leaved plant. Has inherited the growth of Glendale, which has blood of *F.lycioides.* Growth is upright and bushy. Sport of Glendale. Rasmussen – American – 1954.

*Greenpeace. Single. Extremely short tube light absinthe-green (R.H.S. 145C) flushed empire-rose blush in full sunlight (R.H.S. 48C). Sepals light absinthe-green (R.H.S. 145D to 145C), tips of sepals are bowed upwards and held at the horizontal. Corolla ivory-white to very soft pink (R.H.S. 158C) without any sign of veining. Medium sized flowers produced all the year if required, very profuse, hang in clusters on very long pedicels. Stamens rosy-white, leaflets instead of anthers (this phenomenon of anthers degenerating to leaflets often occurs in relation to most hybrids of Speciosa when crossed with unusual cultivars of *F. magellanica* descent), pistil rosy-white large, sometimes with deformed stigma. Large medium green foliage, growth upright and bushy, strong and robust but not self-branching, not short-jointed, detests being trained, stems and foliage slightly hairy. Raised in Holland in vicinity of Lisse and introduced by John Ridding of Fuchsiavale Nurseries, Kidderminster, in 1983. Speciosa × Ting-a-Ling. de Graaff – Dutch – 1981.

Greenrigg Bell. Single. Tube short, neyron-rose, sepals upper surface neyron-rose (R.H.S. 55B) with underside deeper rose (R.H.S. 55A). Corolla rosine-purple (R.H.S. 68A) shading to pink (R.H.S. 68B) at base. Medium-sized flowers compact, bell shape, best colour in shade. Un-usual foliage, new leaves citron-green (R.H.S. 151A) fading to lettuce-green (R.H.S. 144A). Plant was submitted in Seedling Class Manchester 1977 but requested submission to ascertain the fixation of the new foliage characteristic. Growth small upright, self-branching and bushy. Tested for 3 years in Northumberland before release. Lena Dalton × Tennessee Waltz seedling × Border Queen. Ryle – British – 1977 – A.F.S. No. 1435.

Greensleeves. Single. Tube and sepals deep orange, sepals tipped green, corolla deep orange. Medium sized flowers almost an orange self. Growth upright and bushy. Little known cultivar appears to be exclusive to the South of England. Raiser unknown – British – ca 1962.

Greet Altena. Single or Semi-double. Red tube, shining red sepals, tipped green; corolla purple-red. Very short flowers with deep pink stamens and style, best in shade. Foliage medium green with small leaves. Growth upright and bushy. Chang × Marinka. Steevens – Dutch – 1968.

Greg Walker. Double. White tube striped carmine-rose ⅝ in long; sepals carmine-rose 1¾ in long by ¾ in wide, flushed white on upperside, carmine-rose underneath, tipped green (H.C.C. 60/2). Sepals held horizontal on first opening fully, reflexing to cover tube on maturity. Corolla bishop's-violet (H.C.C. 34/1) splashed carmine-rose (H.C.C. 62/1) at the base with magenta veining (H.C.C. 27). Medium sized blooms which mature to imperial-purple (H.C.C. 33/1) 1⅛ in long, stamens magenta with long pistil spiraea-red and white stigma. Lettuce-green (H.C.C. 861) foliage, serrated leaves with magenta-rose mid ribs. Growth semi-trailer, lax bush, will make good basket with weights, best colour requires sun but produces deeper colours in shade. Tested for 2 years in the vicinity of Montrose, Victoria, Australia, before release. Sport of Beryl's Choice. Richardson, L.B. and L.M. – Australian – 1982 – A.F.S. No. 1660.

Grenadier. Double. Red and purple. Bull – British – 1872.

Grenadier. Rozain-Boucharlet – French – 1913.

Grenadine. Single. Red self. Flowers long and free, growth lax bush and spreading. Evans and Reeves – American – 1934.

Grey Lady. Double. Tube and sepals red; corolla grey-blue fading to lavender-pink. Medium sized blooms and very free, dark green foliage. Growth upright and bushy, strong stiff habit, height 1½ to 2 ft, hardy in Southern England, raised in the Scilly Isles. Not to be confused with Gray Lady (Reiter). Tabraham – British – 1974.

Griffin. Single. Tube and sepals rose, corolla purple. Medium sized flowers with yellow foliage. Introduced by Penhalls Nurseries of Shaw, Oldham. Raiser unknown – British – ca 1970.

Grinnell Bay. Single. Thin rose tube ½ in long, rose sepals tipped green, recurved tight against tube at maturity. Corolla red-purple, small to medium sized flowers, edge of each petal opens dark purple fading to medium purple then to rose.

Small to medium dark green foliage with serrated margins and cordate leaf shape. Growth natural trailer will make good basket. Originates from the Coos Bay area of Oregon. This cultivar was introduced in 1964 with little details. Adkins – American – 1980 – A.F.S. No. 1553.

Groene Kan's Glorie. Single. Thick tube rose-orange, sepals orange-salmon, fully reflexed to tube. Corolla light orange at base, shading to deep orange on outer petals. Large flowers and free. Growth upright and bushy. Introduced by High Trees Nurseries of Reigate, Surrey, in 1980. Steevens – Dutch – 1978.

Groovy. Single. Tube and sepals coral; corolla fuchsia-pink to magenta. Medium sized blooms, bell shaped and free. Growth lax bush or trailer. Castro – American – 1969 – A.F.S. No. 839.

Grossherzogin Adeheid. Triphylla single. Long tube, coral-orange; short petals orange-red. Dark green foliage, flushed purple underneath. Growth upright. *F. corymbiflora × F. triphylla.* Rehnelt – German – 1903.

Grotesque. Double. Tube and twisted sepals crimson; corolla white with sharp crimson lines. Flowers are large, loose and fluffy, shy bloomer, similar to Torpilleur. Growth upright and bushy. Niederholzer – American – 1940.

Grumpy. Single. Tube and sepals deep pink; corolla navy-blue. Small flowers but borne in profusion. Growth stiff, branching and prostrate; dwarf, only 9 to 15 in high. Hardy in Southern England, raised in the Scilly Isles. Submitted by the raiser for R.H.S. Wisley Hardy Trials 1975–78 but received no award. Tabraham – British – 1974.

Gruss aus dem Bodethal. Single to semi-double. Tube and sepals, rich crimson; corolla very dark purple, when first opened, almost black, most unusual colouring. Flowers medium to smallish, very free, rather late in flowering. Growth upright and bushy under glass, dwarf bush as bedder, will tolerate indoor conditions. Good old cultivar, the name translated is 'Greetings from the Bode Valley'. Identical with Black Prince. (According to Dutch Fuchsia authorities) parentage is Cupido × Creusa. Sattler and Belge – German – 1838.

Guadalupe. Single. Tube and sepals of a darker pink than the pink corolla, almost a self. Small flowers and very free, growth tall, upright and bushy. American introduction exclusive to California. Raiser and date unknown – ca 1960.

Gualala Blue. Double. Tube and sepals rose; corolla blue to orchid with serrated edges, four protruding swirls in centre. Large green foliage. Large flowers and free for size. Growth lax bush or trailer. Soo Yun Field – American – 1966 – A.F.S. No. 681.

Guardsman. Single. Red and purple. Henderson – British – 1872.

Guiding Star. Single. White and rose. Banks – British – 1856.

Guillaume Grandidier. Lemoine – French – 1898.

Guinevere. Single. Tube and long spreading sepals white, corolla blue-violet, ageing to pale purple. Flowers large and free. Growth lax bush, needs early pinching to prevent spreading habit. Dale – American – 1950.

Gulliver. Single. Tube and sepals, waxy-white; corolla dark Tyrian-rose. Large flowers and free, growth low bush. Reiter – American – 1948.

Gus Niederholzer. Double. Tube and sepals carmine; corolla veronica-blue. Very large flowers and fairly free. Growth upright and bushy. Niederholzer-Waltz – American – 1949.

Gustave Doré. Double. Pink and white. Lemoine – French – 1880.

Gustave Flaubert. Double. Red and purple. Lemoine – French – 1891.

Gustave Heitz. Double. Red and purple. Cornelissen – Belgian – 1866.

Gustave Nadaud. Lemoine – French – 1892.

Guy Dauphine. Double. Tube and sepals carmine; corolla plum-purple. Flowers large and free for size, very similar to Heron. Growth upright and bushy. Rozain-Boucharlet – French – 1913.

Gypsy Baron. Double. Tube and sepals, cardinal-red; corolla dusky blue-violet. Medium sized blooms and free. Growth upright and bushy. Munkner – American – 1952.

Gypsy Girl. Double. Short tube cherry-red with sepals of the same colour, sepals held well out which curve over. Corolla pale phlox-purple, petals heavily veined rose-Bengal at base. Medium sized blooms and quite free flowering. Growth compact bush. Introduced by the raiser in 1980. Pacey – British – 1980.

Gypsy Prince. Semi-double. Tube and upturned sepals, bright red; corolla in four sections of deep rose petals. Large flowers and fairly free. Growth sturdy upright bush. Sport of Gypsy Queen. Ervin – American – 1952 – A.F.S. No. 146.

Gypsy Queen. Double. Scarlet and purple. Bull – British – 1865.

Haggerty Ann. No other details available except that this cultivar was entered in the seedling class at London in the 60's and created some considerable interest with its unusual flower and extra petaloid on each stamen. It was shown by S.J. Wilson and could have been raised by him.

Half and Half. Semi-double. Small red tube, sepals rose, backed red; corolla light cream, red veins from base of petals. Medium sized flowers and free, growth upright and bushy. Brown and Soules – American – 1952 – A.F.S. No. 134.

Hallali. Rozain-Boucharlat – French – 1913.

Hall Mark. Single. White and red. Pince – British – 1883.

Hallowe'en. Double. White and purple. Turville – British – 1893.

Halloween. Single. Tube and sepals, cream-pink; corolla darker pink. Flowers large and free. Sister seedling of Cascade and Claret Cup. Growth vigorous cascade. Rolla × Amy Lye. Lagen – American – 1938.

hamellioides (Sessé and Mocino 1832). Synonymous with *F. arborescens*.

Hampden Park. Double. Tube and sepals, palish-cerise; corolla violet-lilac, flushed rose-pink. Medium sized flowers and very free. Growth upright, rather slow. Named after the famous football ground in Glasgow. Thorne – British – 1960.

* **Hampshire Blue.** Single. Tube and sepals cream flushed with pink, sepals recurve touching the tube. Corolla pale powder blue with white at base of petals. Medium sized flowers, beautiful pastel shaded flowers. Growth upright and bushy. Introduced by Oakleigh Nurseries of Alresford, Hampshire, in 1983. Sport of Carmel Blue.

* **Hampshire Prince.** Double. Pink tube, sepals pink deeper pink underneath, tipped green. Corolla lavender fading to deep pink with maturity. Huge blooms very full double, early and free flowering for a double. Growth lax bush. Introduced by Oakleigh Nurseries of Alresford, Hampshire, in 1983. Sport of Prince of Peace.

* **Hampshire Treasure.** Double. Creamy-pink tube, sepals lovely shade of salmon. Corolla cerise and orange, inner petals are cerise whilst the outer petals together with petaloids are orange with cerise markings. Medium sized blooms, very free flowering for a double, very attractive colouring. Dark green foliage, growth upright. Introduced by Oakleigh Nurseries of Alresford, Hampshire, in 1983. Bicentennial × Lord Lonsdale. Raiser unknown – British – 1983.

Hanna. Double. Tube and sepals red; corolla white. Medium-sized flowers resembles Tausend-schön but with whiter corolla, early flowering. Growth upright and bushy, self-branching. Elsner – German – Date unknown.

Hanora. Single. Long tube, ivory flushed carmine, long sepals, open and horizontal, carmine, warm pink underneath. Corolla claret, rather square in form. Large flowers and very free, very little difference between this and Hanora's Sister. Growth sturdy, upright bush. Travis, J. – British – 1957.

Hanora's Sister. Single. Long tube, ivory flushed rose, long thin sepals, ivory flushed rose, underside glowing pink. Corolla vivid pink, square in form. Deep green foliage, ovate; medium sized flowers and very free, colour may be described as 'Shocking Pink'. Growth upright and vigorous. Mrs. Rundle × Evening Light. Travis, J. – British – 1959.

Hans Neilsen. Single. Turkey-red self, similar to Rufus. Growth upright. Banheur – Continental – 1873.

Hap Hazard. Double. Tube and sepals scarlet; corolla violet-purple, edged white. Largish flowers and free. Growth upright and bushy. Hazard and Hazard – American – 1930.

* **Happiness.** Double. Rose-Bengal tube, sepals rose-Bengal tipped green which curve upwards. Corolla cyclamen-purple shading to rose-Bengal at base of petals. Largish and fully double blooms. Growth upright and bushy. Raised in the vicinity of Bardney, Lincolnshire, and introduced by Pacey's Nurseries of Melton Mowbray, Leicestershire, in 1984. Bellamy – British – 1984.

Happy. Single. Tube and sepals red; corolla blue. Small flowers, star-shaped and erect, very free. Pale green foliage, growth upright and bushy, self-branching habit, dwarf, only 9 to 15 in high. Hardy in Southern England, raised in the Scilly Isles. Submitted by the raiser for R.H.S. Wisley Hardy Trials 1975–78 but received no award. Tabraham – British – 1974.

Happy Birthday. Single. Short rose-pink tube, long thin sepals rose-pink with green tips. Corolla blue changing to rose at base. Very long medium sized flowers and heat tolerant if shaded. Small thin foliage dark green with heavy serrated leaves. Growth medium upright, will make good bush or standard. Originates from Fort Bragg area of California. Introduced by Barbara L. Schneider in 1980 but raiser wishes to be anonymous. The plant was a gift for her birthday, hence the name. Unknown raiser – American – 1980 – A.F.S. No. 1588.

Happy Day. Double. Short, spinel-red tube, crimson sepals, 1 in long × ⅜ in wide, curve up. Corolla white with neyron-rose stripe in middle, marbled at the base 1 in long × ⅜ in wide. Medium-sized blooms with crimson stamens and pistil with brown tips. Scalloped edged foliage. Growth natural trailer without weights, bushy, best colour in shade. Tested for 5 years in vicinity of Sebastopol, California. Soo Yun Field – American – 1978 – A.F.S. No. 1450.

Happy Ending. Single. Tube and sepals white; corolla lilac-pink. Small flowers, very rich colouring and very free. Growth upright bush with open growth. van Wieringen – Dutch – 1970.

Happy Fellow. Single. Tube and sepals, light orange and pale salmon, tipped green, sepals up-turned; corolla orange and smoky-rose. Flowers medium sized, extremely free, especially outside in the border and continuous, corolla has four pleated petals. Light green foliage, rather small. Growth upright and bushy, hardy over a period of four years in the Midlands. Waltz – American – 1966 – A.F.S. No. 655.

Happy Talk. Double. Tube and sepals, white with touches of pink; corolla fluorescent magenta, flares into star shape. Large flowers, growth trailer. Fuchsia Forest – American – 1964 – A.F.S. No. 606.

Hapsburgh. Single. Tube and sepals white, flushed pink; corolla pale parma-violet. Medium sized flowers, very free, growth upright and bushy. Confused with Elsa, Eva Boerg, Lena and Madame Eva Boye. Rozain-Boucharlat – French – 1911.

Harbour Bridge. Double. Short tube and reflexed sepals, pale rose, tipped green. Corolla lavender-blue with phlox-pink blotches on petal base. Growth strong tall upright. Named after the famous one span Sydney bridge. Lockerbie – Australian – 1971 – A.F.S. No. 1001.

Hardy Fred. Single. Short thin bright red tube, long pointed sepals bright red on both upper and under surfaces. Corolla deep magenta fading to cerise with maturity. Medium sized flowers with bright red stamens, red pistil and distinct triangular shaped stigma. Dark green serrated foliage with purple splashes. Growth medium upright and bushy, will make good bush or standard. Tested for 3 years and found to be completely hardy in the vicinity of Cardiff, South Wales. Woolley – British – 1980 – A.F.S. No. 1567.

* Harebell. Semi-double. Tube orange-white (R.H.S. 159D), sepals red-purple (R.H.S. 68D), corolla purple (R.H.S. 77B/78B). New Dutch cultivar raised by Westeinde-Felix in 1983. Nancy Lou × Joy Patmore.

Harlequin. Single. Tube and sepals claret-rose (H.C.C. 021), sepals held very back; corolla white veined claret-rose. Medium sized flowers, very free. Growth strong vigorous bush. Not to be confused with Harlequin by Hazard and Hazard (American). Introduced by V.T. Nuttall of Doncaster in 1979. Joy Patmore × Ice Cap. Roe – British – 1979.

Harlequin. Single. Tube and sepals, dark red; corolla dusky-purple. Long flowers, fairly free. Growth upright bush. Hazard and Hazard – American – Date unknown.

Harmoine. Double. White and mauve. Lemoine – French – 1884.

Harmony. Single. Tube and sepals, light geranium-lake; corolla rose. Medium sized flowers and free. Growth trailer. Niederholzer – American – 1946.

Harmony. Single. Tube and sepals pale pink; corolla deep purple. Medium-sized flowers and free. Growth upright and bushy. Hardy in Southern England raised in the Scilly Isles. Tabraham – British – 1978.

Harriet Lye. Single to semi-double. Tube and sepals, waxy-white; corolla mauve-pink, edged with carmine. Medium sized blooms, very early and very free. Growth upright bush. Lye – British – 1887.

Harriett. Double. White tube, sepals white with light pink on undersides, sepals stand straight up when in full bloom. Corolla blue with centre swirls. Large flowers, fairly free. Growth trailer. Soo Yun – American – 1971 – A.F.S. No. 947.

Harrogate. Single. Tube and sepals red; corolla deep blue. Medium sized flowers, very free, growth upright and bushy, hardy in most districts of Britain. Raiser unknown – Date unknown (about 1950).

* Harrow Pride. Double. White tube, broad and upturned sepals are white with pink flush inside and outside. Corolla dark blue with some fading with maturity to pink sepals and rosy-violet corolla. Medium sized blooms and quite free flowering for a double. Chosen and named after the Harrow Fuchsia Society. Raised in the vicinity of Middlesex and introduced by Woodbridge Nurseries of Hounslow, Middlesex, in 1984. Dyos – British – 1984.

Harry Alis. Lemoine – French – 1894.

Harry Dunnett. Triphylla type single. Long tube, spinel-red, banana shaped; petals neyron-rose, spinel-red at base. Corolla shrimp – red, very small. Foliage medium green with velvet sheen and amber veining. Growth upright of the *F. cordiflora* type. Baker – Dunnett – British – 1974 – A.F.S. No. 1198.

Harry Gray. Double. Rose-pink streaked tube fairly short, slightly recurved sepals white, shading to rose-pink at the base, tipped green. Corolla white, shading to rose-pink (R.H.S. 36B) at base changing to very pale pink with maturity. Small to medium sized blooms very full but compact like a small powder puff, very prolific for a double, could be described as a 'white Marinka', outstanding cultivar with a great future, pink stamens and long white pistil. Dark green foliage small and short-jointed, ovate with red stems. Growth self-branching trailer or lax upright, makes a wonderful dense basket, best colour in filtered shade. Tested for 3 years in the vicinity of Woodbridge, Suffolk before being introduced by Burgh Nurseries of Woodbridge in 1980. La Campanella ×

Powder Puff. Dunnett – British – 1981 – A.F.S. No. 1607.

Harry Hotspur. Single. Pink tube, short and thick, sepals white, flushed pink; corolla violet. Medium sized flowers, free, overlapping petals at outside where the four sepals join at the junction with tube, four small spur-like projections form. Mid green foliage with red stalks, growth medium upright bush. Lena Dalton × Tennessee Waltz seedling × Earl of Beaconsfield seedling × Strawberry Delight. Ryle – British – 1975 – A.F.S. No. 1245.

Harry Williams. Double. Red and purple. Bland – British – 1871.

hartwegii. Red tube, orange-red sepals; red corolla. Small flowers, very free, borne in terminal clusters. Upright shrub. Bentham – 1845 – Columbia.

* Harvest Glow. Single. Orient-pink tube $\frac{1}{4}$ in long by $\frac{1}{2}$ in wide, horizontally held sepals orient-pink on top, French-rose (R.H.S. 49D) underneath $1\frac{1}{4}$ in long by $\frac{1}{2}$ in wide with tips recurved. Corolla orient-pink (R.H.S. 36D) $\frac{3}{4}$ in long by $\frac{3}{4}$ in wide. Medium sized flowers half flared and short bell shaped, neyron-rose (R.H.S. 55A) filaments and anthers with white style and stigma. Foliage yellowish-green (R.H.S. 144C) with burnished tips, leaves $2\frac{1}{4}$ in long by 1 in wide are elliptic, entire edged, acute tips and rounded bases, foliage is especially attractive in early growth. Growth self-branching lax upright on stiff trailer, spreading, will make good basket with weights and suitable for hanging pots, best protected from full effect of wind and sun, best in filtered light. Raised and tested for 2 years in vicinity of Ipswich, Suffolk, and introduced by the raiser, Gouldings Fuchsias of Ipswich, in 1984. Goulding – British – 1984 – A.F.S. No. 1780.

Harvest Home. Double. Red and purple. Henderson – British – 1890.

Harvest Moon. Single. Tube and long, broad, upturned sepals rose-red; corolla white, heavily veined rose-pink near petal base. Medium sized blooms, very free and flat, flaring, raiser claims this is the first hanging fuchsia with a flat white corolla, described as a hanging Citation. Growth trailer. Hodges – American – 1958 – A.F.S. No. 338.

Harvin. Double. Red and purple. Lemoine – French – 1868.

Hathersage. Double. Long pale pink tube, wide sepals neyron-rose, carried well out from corolla; corolla roseine-purple with red veins, shading to amaranth-rose. Medium sized blooms, solid and well formed, fairly free for double. Growth upright and bushy, suitable for most types of training. Joan Pacey × Prosperity. Gadsby – British – 1975 – A.F.S. No. 1282.

Haute Monde. ('Haut' would be correct French.) Single. Tube and sepals, creamy-white, washed with Tyrian-rose; corolla Tyrian-rose. Medium sized flowers and free. Growth upright. Hazard and Hazard – American – 1930?

Haverthwaite. Double. Tube eau-de-nil, sepals shell-pink, flushed rose underside, curving into pin wheel effect. Corolla deep lavender-pink, rose at base of petals. Very small blooms and free, kaleidoscope of colour, unwise to name one colour from time buds open to fall of blooms. Growth medium upright bush. King's Ransom × Hawks-head. Thornley – British – 1966 – A.F.S. No. 1061.

Hawaiian Night. Double. Tube and sepals, waxy-white with light pink undersides. Corolla orchid-mauve. Large flowers, fairly free. Growth trailer. Fuchsia-La – American – 1968 – A.F.S. No. 805.

Hawkshead. Single. Short tube white, suffused green, sepals white, flushed green, broad and very pointed. Corolla white, barrel shaped. Flowers of the *F.molinae* var. *molinae* type but larger and whiter. Small foliage, dark green, compact with serrated leaves. Growth upright and bushy, very hardy, up to 4 ft in height on current year's growth. The first white cultivar raised by a British hybridist. Sister seedling to Silverdale. *F.magellanica* var. *molinae* × Venus Victrix. Travis, J. – British – 1962 – A.F.S. No. 1142.

* Hay Wain. Single to semi-double. Empire-rose (R.H.S. 50C) tube, horizontally held sepals 1 in long by $\frac{1}{4}$ in wide pink (R.H.S. 62C) with a hint of blue on top, rhodamine-pink (R.H.S. 62A) underneath, recurved tips. Corolla opens bishop's-violet (R.H.S. 81A) maturing to cyclamen-purple (R.H.S. 74B) $\frac{3}{4}$ in long by $\frac{3}{4}$ in wide. Medium sized flowers half flared with irregularly shaped corolla, neyron-rose filaments and magenta-rose anthers, empire-rose style and white stigma. Matt green (R.H.S. 138A) foliage with ovate leaves 2 in long by $\frac{3}{4}$ in wide, serrated edges, acute tips and rounded bases. Growth self-branching lax upright or stiff trailer, short jointed producing an abundance of short side shoots, needs little pinching or shaping. Raised in the vicinity of Ipswich, Suffolk; tested for 2 years before introduced by the raiser, Gouldings Fuchsias of Ipswich, in 1984. Goulding – British – 1984 – A.F.S. No. 1781.

Hayward. Double. Short tube and broad sepals, deep red; corolla deepest violet-purple. Large blooms, free for size. Growth upright bush. Brand – American – 1951 – A.F.S. No. 90.

Hazel Marsh. Double. Pale rose tube, broad granular, white sepals, well reflexed, displaying the multiple petalled corolla. Corolla palest orchid. Flowers large and free, and non fading. Growth trailer. Sport of His Excellency. Schnabel-Paskesen – American – 1959 – A.F.S. No. 378.

H. Dutterail. Double. Tube and sepals carmine; corolla purple-violet. Large blooms. Raiser and date unknown.

Healdsburg. Double. Tube and sepals, light red on top with darker red on undersides, tipped light green. Corolla light purple. Flowers are large and free. Growth lax bush or trailer. Soo Yun – American – 1969 – A.F.S. No. 849.

Heart Throb. Double. Tube and broad sepals white, pale carmine-blush underside. Corolla medium blue, white at centre and at base of petals. Large wide spreading flowers almost flat, corolla of large and smaller petals curled and folded, as flowers mature blue and rose petals are interspersed. Growth upright and tall. Hodges – American – 1963 – A.F.S. No. 567.

* Heather. Semi-double. Short thin tube white tinged pink $\frac{1}{2}$ in long by $\frac{1}{4}$ in wide, half up $1\frac{1}{2}$ in long by $\frac{1}{2}$ in wide sepals are phlox-pink (R.H.S. 62B) on top, rhodamine-pink (R.H.S. 62A) underneath, twisted green tips are recurving. Corolla opens deep lilac (R.H.S. 76A) maturing to rose-purple (R.H.S. 73A) 1 in long. Medium sized blooms non-flaring with lilac petaloids $\frac{1}{2}$ in long by $\frac{1}{4}$ in wide, very neat compact flowers contrasting with very curly sepals. Rose-pink filaments and anthers with white style and stigma. Mid-green (R.H.S. 138A) foliage with $2\frac{1}{4}$ in long by $1\frac{1}{4}$ in wide lanceolate leaves, serrated edges, acute tips and rounded bases. Growth lax upright or stiff trailer, good for basketwork with weights, standard or decorative, needs careful watering and cold weather hardy to 32°F. in Southern England. Sister seedling to La Bella Valerie. Tested and raised in the vicinity of Worthing, Sussex, for 3 years before release. *F. microphylla* × Preston Guild. Hobbs, L. – British – 1984 – A.F.S. No. 1774.

Heather Bell. Single. White and rose. Henderson – British – 1869.

Heather Hobbs. Single. Short, crimson (R.H.S. 52A) tube, sepals are (R.H.S. 52A) crimson on outside with inside slightly paler, creped tiny yellow tip, sepals are long and thin, unswept and very occasionally reflexing and twisting. Corolla white, veined neyron-rose (R.H.S. 55A) with overall faint pink cast (R.H.S. 55C). Medium-sized flowers are bell-shaped with crimson stamens and very long crimson pistil. Foliage slightly serrated, ovate, small, yellow-green leaves. Growth medium, upright and bushy, vigorous, good bedder, easy growing, good for bush, standard or decorative. Tested for 4 years in vicinity of Kent. Hugh Morgan × . Holmes, R. – British – 1978 – A.F.S. No. 1460.

Heathfield. Double. Little known cultivar with pink tube and sepals and purple corolla. Appears to be exclusive to the Southern and Home Counties of England although originating from Sussex. Listed by St. Agnes Gardens of Bristol who classify it as hardy. Synonymous with Constance; mistaken identity by South of England nurserymen and incorrect re-naming. Raiser unknown – British – *ca* 1970s.

Heavenly Blue. Single. Tube and long narrow rolled-up sepals, pale pink; corolla pale blue. Large blooms and free. Growth upright and bushy. Niederholzer – American – 1945.

Hebe. Single. Long tube, white flushed pink; sepals long and upswept, white tipped green. Corolla rich purple-violet fading to reddish-purple. Medium sized flowers extremely free; outstanding features are the very long tube and very long upswept sepals. Small medium green foliage, growth lax bush; needs early pinching, can be a most disappointing and untidy plant. The name Hebe was very popular with the early hybridisers causing confusion, but the cultivar grown today is Stokes. Stokes – British – 1848. The other Hebes were (Standish) clear carmine and reddish-violet; (Harrison) slender tube, sepals pointed, corolla cerise-violet. (Bell) tube white, shaded rose and dark crimson corolla; (Mayle) white tube, scarlet corolla. In America, Beauty of Swanley is known as Villa Hebe.

Hecate. Single. Tube and long sepals deep red; corolla delicate pink, heavily red veined. Large flowers, pendulous, bell shaped and free. Foliage light to medium green with dark red stems and delicately serrated leaves. Growth trailer. Foster – American – 1972 – A.F.S. No. 1038.

Heide. Double. Tube and sepals red; corolla reddish-orchid. Large blooms and profuse. Dark green foliage, veined with red. Growth trailer. Bernier – American – 1958 – A.F.S. No. 352.

Heidi Ann. Double. Tube and sepals, crimson-cerise; corolla bright lilac, paler at base, veined cerise. Flowers medium sized, very free and of perfect shape, similar to Mauve Beauty. Dark green foliage with crimson midrib. Growth upright and bushy, needs and responds to early pinching, always to be found upon the show-bench, easy to time, presents no difficulties. Tennessee Waltz × General Monk. Smith (Mrs.) – British – 1969 – A.F.S. No. 818.

Heidi Purpurn. Double. Tube and sepals neyron-rose; corolla violet-purple. Medium sized blooms, very compact and prolific. Growth upright and bushy, responds to frequent pinching, very compact growth. The raiser is carrying out extensive crossbreeding with Heidi Ann and further introductions can be expected. Heidi Ann × Dollar Princess. Roe – British – 1976.

Heidi Weiss. Double. Tube and sepals, crimson-cerise; corolla white, veined scarlet. Flowers, growth and habit exactly the same as Heidi Ann which is a profuse 'sporter', sported White Ann in addition to Heidi Weiss. Exceptionally good cultivar, excels as a specimen bush plant. Sport of Heidi Ann. Tacolneston Nurseries – British – 1973 – A.F.S. No. 1111.

Heinrich Henkel. Synonymous with Andenken an Heinrich Henkel.

Heinzelmannchen. Single. Red tube, red sepals hanging over the crown with young flowers. Corolla purple-pink. Medium to smallish flowers which stand out well, stamens and style deep pink, dark green foliage, growth upright. Cupid × James Lye. Bremback – Nationality unknown – 1911.

Heirloom. Double. Tube and sepals pink; corolla lavender-purple with heavy pink and white marbling. Large flowers, fairly free. Growth lax bush or trailer. Kennett – American – 1968 – No. 779.

Helen Clare. Double. Tube yellowish-green, sepals white with very faint pink on underside. Corolla creamy-white and frilly edge. Growth upright and bushy. Best grown as H1. Holmes, E. – British – 1973.

Helen Hummel. Double. Long slender tube and sepals red and of crepe texture. Corolla purple with some red at base. Flowers are large and serrated, fairly free, dark green foliage. Growth trailer. Gagnon – American – 1969 – A.F.S. No. 845.

Helen McGrath. Double. Tube and sepals cerise; corolla medium violet, marbled phlox-pink. Medium sized flowers and free. Growth upright to 4 ft. Brown-Nessier – American – 1952 – A.F.S. No. 118.

Helen Wilson. No other details except that the cultivar could be of Belgian origin and raised by Duyn – Belgian – 1963?

Helicopter. Single. Tube and long recurving sepals, white of crepe texture, flushed with rose-madder, tipped green. Corolla orchid-purple with a tinting of spiraea-red at the base. Medium sized flowers and free. Growth trailer and exceptional, the long branches will trail 6 to 7 ft, suitable for weeping standard or espalier. Olson – American – 1956 – A.F.S. No. 276.

Heligoland. Double. Red and purple. Henderson – British – 1873.

173

Hellen Cella. Double. Short tube and sepals white; corolla purple, variegated white and pink. Large flowers and fairly free. Growth trailer. Pennisi – American – 1968 – A.F.S. No. 750.

Hello Dolly. Single. Tube and sepals pink, deeper pink underneath; corolla white, slightly veined light pink. Flowers are long budded producing pointed effect, large free and early. Growth upright and bushy. Holmes, E. – British – 1969.

Helvellyn. Double. Long tube and broad sepals cerise; corolla lavender-lilac suffused pink. Large flowers and free for size. Growth upright. Thornley – British – 1962.

hemsleyana. Purplish-rose self. Minute flowers borne solitary in the leaf axials. Member of the Breviflorae section (Encliandra). Upright shrub, growing to several feet in natural habitat. Synonymous with *F. pulchella.* Hardy in most districts. Woodson and Siebert – 1937 – Costa Rica and Panama.

Hendrikje Stoffels. Double. Little known Dutch cultivar raised in the vicinity of Doorwerth, Netherlands. Long tube light rose (R.H.S. 54B); sepals rose-red (R.H.S. 54B), corolla Bordeaux red with orange (R.H.S. 63AB). Growth trailer with medium sized flowers. Checkerboard × Papa Bleuss. Brouwer – Dutch – 1983.

Hendrina Bovenschen. Single. Tube and sepals light red, tube is short, sepals are long standing out horizontally, deep pink underside, crepe de chine-like. Corolla pink at the base to purple-pink at the edge, red veined. Large flowers with pointed buds, stamens and style pink. Dark green foliage, growth upright. Steevens – Dutch – 1972.

Henri de Bornier. Lemoine – French – 1877.

Henri de la Pommeraye. Lemoine – French – 1892.

Henri Dunant. Lemoine – French – 1902.

Henri Etienne. Rozain-Boucharlat – French – 1860.

Henrietta Ernst. Single. Tube and sepals pale Cardinal-red (R.H.S. 53C); corolla bishop's-violet (R.H.S. 81A) maturing to fuchsia-purple (R.H.S. 66B). Medium sized flowers, very free and with longitudinal corrugations in the petals giving a distinctive shape. Growth upright and dwarfish, very slow growing. Ernst – Dutch – 1841.

Henriette Mielhac. Lemoine – French – 1898.

Henri Jacotot. Double. Red and purple. Lemoine – French – 1867.

Henri Lecoq. Dominyana × *F. serratifolia.* Lemoine – French – 1878.

Henri Poincaré. Single. Red tube, sepals crimson-scarlet, curled right back; corolla violet-purple, veined red. Flowers largish and free, bell shaped and early. Can be disappointing with wrong cultivation, blooms tend to 'ball up' in moist conditions. Growth lax bush. Lemoine – French – 1905.

Herald. Single. Tube and recurving sepals scarlet; corolla deep purple. Medium sized blooms, free and good in its colour range. Growth upright and bushy, an old cultivar occasionally still seen on the show bench. Accepted by the B.F.S. as showbench hardy. Sankey – British – 1887.

Herald Angels. Single. Long thin tube ⅔in is red; sepals bright red (R.H.S. 50B) 1¾in long × ½in

wide, twist upward with long point. Corolla pale rosy-lilac (R.H.S. 70D) veined red (R.H.S. 50B). Medium sized flowers 1¾in long × ½in wide open square shape, then flaring to form trumpet shape. Yellow-green foliage (R.H.S. 146A) leaves lightly serrated 1⅞in long by ⅝in wide gradually tapering to long pointed tip, leaves curl backwards with prominent mid rib. Growth natural trailer, will make good basket, weeping standard, pillar or pyramid. Tested in Northumberland N.E. England for 5 years before release. Introduced by R. and J. Pacey of Strathern, Melton Mowbray in 1982. Hall – British – 1982 – A.F.S. No. 1665.

Herbé de Jacques. Single. Tube and sepals red, purple corolla. Small flowers are really insignificant as this cultivar is grown more for its variegated foliage, will take full sun but best colour in shade. Foliage is mottled or spotted, sometimes marked like Sunray or Golden Marinka. Red colour predominates in proper light. Growth is natural trailer without weights, should be kept pinched for best foliage coloration, very hardy as is its parent. Tested for 5 years in California. Sport of Corallina. Schneider, Barbara – American – 1978 – A.F.S. No. 1439.

Hercules. Semi-double. Red and purple. Banks – British – 1872.

Her Highness. Double. Tube and sepals, bright red; corolla lilac, fading to light rose with red veins. Large flowers and large foliage. Growth trailer. Soo Yun – American – 1969 – A.F.S. No. 848.

Heritage. Semi-double. Tube and sepals scarlet; corolla rich purple, ageing to reddish-purple. Flowers fairly large and very free, early, sepals turned right back with maturity, blooms in flushes, excellent in every way. Growth upright and bushy, hardy in Southern districts. Lemoine – French – 1902.

Her Ladyship. Double. Tube and broad recurved sepals, pale pink outerside, deep pink underside. Corolla orchid-blue with splashes of pink at base of petals. Large flowers, free for size, very good pastel colour combination. Growth lax bush or trailer, no improvement upon older cultivars. Waltz – American – 1961 – A.F.S. No. 941.

Her Majesty. Single. Chalice-white. Bull – British – 1863.

Hermione. Double. Tube and sepals, shell-pink; corolla white, flushed pink. Medium sized flowers, free, growth upright, tall and bushy. Hazard and Hazard – American – 1950.

Heron. Single. Tube and sepals, deep scarlet; corolla violet-blue, veined and streaked red. Flowers are large and very free. Growth upright

Heron

174

and bushy, ideal as a bedder, hardy in the Midlands. Another very fine old cultivar. Lemoine – French – 1891.

Hero of Wilts. Single. Pink and purple. Wheeler – British – 1858.

Hesitation. Double. Tube and long sepals, light pink; corolla long, white with small outer petals of soft pink. Medium sized flowers and free, growth lax bush or trailer. Brand – American – 1951 – A.F.S. No. 89.

Heston Blue. Semi-double to double. White tube, long outspread sepals white, flushed pink; corolla smoky-blue. Largish blooms, fairly free. Growth upright and bushy. Rawlins – British – 1966.

heterotricha. (Lundell 1940). Synonymous with *F. michoacanensis.*

Heydon. Double. Blush pink tube, wide swept back sepals off white, flushed pink, tipped green. Corolla pale pink at base, purple-blue at edges. Large blooms and very free for double with white anthers. Deep green foliage with red wood on maturity. Growth medium upright, will make good standard or bush. Raised in the vicinity of Norwich, East England and introduced by Woodbridge Nurseries of Hounslow Middlesex 1981. Nancy Lou × The 13th Star. Clitheroe – British – 1981.

H.G. Brown. Single. Tube and sepals, deep scarlet; corolla dark cake. Small to medium flowers and profuse. Foliage dark, glossy green, growth low and bushy, very hardy. Wood – British – 1946.

Hibernia. Single. Tube and sepals rich rose-pink; corolla lavender-purple with deeper purple at base of petals. Large flowers with fluorescent sheen. First introduced by D. Stilwell in 1978 and named after his nurseries in Hounslow, Middlesex. (Royal Velvet × Gay Fandango) × Texas Longhorn. Hobson – British – 1977.

Hidcote Beauty. Single. Tube and sepals waxy-cream, tipped green; corolla pale salmon-pink, shaded light rose. Flowers medium sized and free, of clean bright appearance, light green foliage, growth upright and bushy, versatile in training, makes stately standard and with careful cultivation a good basket. A.F.S. Honorary Cert. of Merit 1962. This cultivar has always been attributed to the raiser Webb, although he was the introducer rather than the raiser. It was found by Mr. A. Webb, a committee member of the British Fuchsia Society in 1948, growing in Major Johnson's garden at Hidcote Manor, Campden, Gloucestershire, hence the name. It was a seedling raised by his gardener but completely overlooked. Permission was sought by Mr. Webb and readily given to bring the cultivar to the notice of fuchsia lovers. Webb – British – 1949.

Highland Beauty. Double. Tube and sepals, white and dawn-pink, overlaid neyron-rose. Corolla amethyst-violet, edged fuchsia purple. Large flowers and very free, growth upright, needs early support. Clark – British – 1960.

* **Highland Pipes.** Single. New Dutch hybrid with flowers very similar to *F. magdalenae* but with aubergine colouring (R.H.S. 71A) and with green foliage (R.H.S. 138B). One of five new introductions by Herman de Graaff in 1983. Raised in the vicinity of Lisse, Netherlands. *F. magdalenae* (syn. *F. lampadaria*) × *F. excorticata.* de Graaff – Dutch – 1983.

Highlight. Single. Long, tube $1\frac{1}{4}$ in is pink and striped darker pink, sepals are narrow and sharply pointed, very pale pink, curl upwards at tip. Corolla deep magenta, blending to orange-salmon at base. Medium sized flowers, early bloomer, very attractive combination of colours. Dark green foliage with pronounced serrated leaves, red stems and veining. Growth semi-trailer will make good basket with weights, standard, decorative, or spreading bush. Tested for 6 years in vicinity of Derby before release. Handley – British – 1976 – A.F.S. No. 1367.

High Noon. Single. Short thin red tube, sepals red with darker red stripes, usually three thin stripes from base to green tip, underside darker red, long and narrow. Corolla white with red veins at base. Medium sized flowers, very free, white fan shape with red centre, usually with two petaloids. Oblong shape foliage with pronounced veins, growth upright bushy and self-branching, trouble free cultivar. Pancharian – American – 1975 – A.F.S. No. 1292.

High Peak. Double. Tube and sepals white, corolla white, almost a pure white self except for that tinge of pink. Medium-sized blooms, free for a double. Growth lax bush or semi-trailer, short jointed. Brough – British – 1977.

Hi Jinks. Double. Tube and sepals, pale pink on underside and white on top. Corolla dianthus-purple with streaks white marbling. Large blooms and free, growth lax bush or trailer. Kennett – American – 1968 – A.F.S. No. 776.

Hilary. Single. White tube, sepals white with pink flush underneath; corolla pale lavender, overlaid with darker tones from base of petals. Medium sized flowers and very free, growth upright and bushy. Miller, V.V. – British – 1970.

Hilda. Double. Red and purple. Bull – British – 1872.

Hilde Nutzinger. Double. Tube and sepals white; corolla amethyst coloured (lilac). Medium-sized blooms. Taxe Gret × Shy Lady. Nutzinger – Austrian – 1966.

* **Hilde Paschek.** Double. Tube and sepals cherry-red; corolla deep blue. Small blooms but very plentiful, early flowerer. El Camino × Bernadette. Nutzinger – Austrian – 1965.

* **Hilli Reschl.** Single. Tube and sepals pink; corolla lilac-blue. Small dainty flowers, early flowering. Growth short upright. Koralle × F. boliviana. Nutzinger – Austrian – 1975.

Hill Top. Double. Light red tube, light red sepals arch back to tube. Corolla very light pink, mottled with red and darker pink veins. Large blooms and quite free flowering, best colour develops in sun. Medium green foliage and vigorous. Growth tall upright and bushy, will make good bush or standard. Originates from the vicinity of Warwickshire. Seedling of Topper. Wright, J.A. – British – 1980 – A.F.S. No. 1601.

Hilltop Pride. Double. Tube and sepals beautiful bright red, corolla white shading to pink, veined red. Medium sized blooms, growth upright. Introduced by Hilltop Nurseries, Leicestershire, in 1979. Uppadine – British – 1978.

Hindu Belle. Single. Long tube waxy-white, long, broad upcurved sepals white, tipped green, flushed pale carmine underside. Corolla rich plum, changing to red as flowers mature. Flowers are large and very long, very free. Growth upright. Munkner – American – 1959.

hirsuta. Tube fiery-red, reddish sepals; no corolla. Long tubed flowers produced at extreme tips of laterals. Very hairy foliage on both surfaces of the leaves. Climbing, epiphytic shrub with tuberous roots. Hemsley – 1876 – Peru and Brazil.

hirtella. Rose-red tube, red sepals; red corolla. Medium sized flowers, borne in terminal, pendant clusters. Small upright shrub. Synonymous with *F. caracanensis* and *F. miniata.* Kris – 1823 – Colombia.

His Excellency. Double. Short tube and long white sepals; corolla violet, changes to orchid-purple with flecks of rosy-white at base of petals. Large flowers and fairly free. Growth upright. Reiter – American – 1952 – A.F.S. No. 128.

His Majesty. Double. Tube and sepals red; corolla orange-red. Medium sized flowers, free and open. Growth lax bush or semi-trailer. Haag and Son – American – 1952.

Hispano. Single to semi-double. Tube and sepals red; corolla white, tinted smoky-lavender, veined. Largish flowers and free. Growth upright. Niederholzer – American – 1948.

H.O. Barnaby. Double. Tube and sepals red; corolla bright purple, turning to wine-red with age. Large and strong bloomer, fairly free. Growth upright. Hubbard – American – 1967 – A.F.S. No. 704.

Hobson. Double. Tube and sepals pink; corolla creamy-white, red veined. Large blooms and profuse bloomer especially for a double. Growth upright and bushy. Curtain Call × Angela Leslie. Hobson – British – 1976.

Hobson's Choice. Double. Tube and sepals pink; corolla lighter shade of pink with delicate tints and shades. Medium-sized blooms produced in abundance. Growth upright and bushy. Hobson – British – 1976.

Hoche. Lemoine – French – 1886.

Hofrat Dr. Riedl. Single. Tube and sepals red-pink, sepals deeper coloured underneath. Corolla white veined pink at the base. Medium-sized flowers with pink stamens and style. Growth upright and bushy. Nutzinger – Austrian – 1971.

Holiday. Semi-double. Pink tube, sepals very long, curl and twist back, topside pink with pale green and pink streaks, underside glowing pink. Corolla deep purple at centre with overlays of pink and white, outer petals and petaloids white. Very large and long flowers, free for size, colour unchanged in sun or shade. Growth natural trailer. Kennett-Castro – American 1973 – A.F.S. No. 1107.

Holloway's Rival. Double. Red and purple. Williams – British – 1870.

Hollydale Sport. Double. Tube and sepals, dark pink; corolla white. Medium sized flowers, very free small shaped blooms as Winston Churchill. Growth upright and bushy. Sport of Hollydale. Fairclo – American – 1949.

Hollywood. Double. Tube and sepals crimson; corolla white, streaked cerise, outer petals flushed rose. Extremely large blooms and fairly free for

size. Dark green foliage, growth tall, upright bush. Passadena × The Chief. Evans and Reeves – American – 1940.

Hollywood Park. Semi-double. Tube and sepals cerise; corolla white with faint pink blendings. Flowers of medium size, very free, growth upright and bushy. Fairclo – American – 1953.

Holstein. Single. Cerise and pink. Schadendorff – Continental – 1912.

Holydale. Double. Tube and sepals, dark pink; corolla deep pink. Medium sized flowers, very free. Small shaped bloom as Winston Churchill. Growth upright and bushy. Sport of Winston Churchill. Fairclo – American – 1946.

Hombre. Double. Tube and sepals, bright pink; corolla lavender with splashes of pink. Very large blooms, fairly free, growth trailer. Fuchsia Forest – American – 1968 – A.F.S. No. 773.

*Honey. Double. White tube is tinted green, white sepals are held half down with reflexed, green tips $1\frac{1}{2}$ in long by $\frac{3}{4}$ in wide. Corolla opens violet splashed darker violet maturing to darker violet $\frac{1}{2}$ in long × 1 in wide. Full flared bell shaped blooms of medium to small size, with reddish-purple filaments and anthers, white style and stigma. Dark green foliage with elliptic leaves $3\frac{1}{2}$ in long by $1\frac{1}{2}$ in wide with serrulate margins, acute tip and obtuse base. Growth small upright and bushy, rust-free and easy to grow. Raised and tested for 2 years in the vicinity of New Plymouth, New Zealand, before release. Black Prince × unknown. Brightwell – New Zealand – 1984 – A.F.S. No. 1750.

Honey Bee. Semi-double. Bright red tube, sepals bright red, tipped green, corolla white with red veins, four large petals at base and small petals protruding at centre. Large blooms, fairly free, growth upright and bushy. Soo Yun – American – 1968 – A.F.S. No. 766.

Honeychile. Single. Short tube rose-pink, sepals long, narrow and reflexed, rose-pink. Corolla violet-blue. Small flowers borne in clusters, very free and early. Growth trailer. Chiles – American – 1953 – A.F.S. No. 162.

Honeymoon. Semi-double. Tube and sepals red; corolla veronica-blue. Flowers wide open and of medium size, free. Growth upright but slow. Niederholzer – American – 1943.

Honour Bright. Double. Tube and sepals carmine; corolla pansy-violet with petaloids variegated carmine-rose. Large blooms and free, growth upright and bushy. Jones, W. – British – 1959.

Horatio. Single. Long slender pink tube, pale pink sepals; corolla deeper pink (orchid pink). Medium-sized flowers, very free, was greatly admired when introduced at the B.F.S. Manchester Show in 1975. Growth natural trailer, good for basket work. Green, H. – British – 1975.

Hortense. Single. Pink and rose. Harrison – British – 1842.

Hot Pants. Double. Red tubes, sepals light red; corolla white with little red veins at base. Flowers are large and ruffled, beautiful form. Growth natural trailer. Jimenez – American – 1974 – A.F.S. No. 1166.

Howlett's Hardy. Single. Tube and sepals scarlet; corolla violet-purple, paler at base, veined scarlet. Flowers are large for a hardy cultivar, fairly free. Growth medium bush up to 2½ ft. Accepted by the B.F.S. as showbench hardy. Howlett – British – 1952.

Hugh Dutterail. Double. Red and purple. Lemoine – French – 1902.

Hugh Evans. Single. Tube and sepals crimson; corolla burgundy-red. Large flowers, fairly free, bronzy foliage. Growth trailer. Evans and Reeves – American – Date unknown.

Hugh Maitland. Double. Red and purple. Dixon – British – 1895.

Hugh Mollen. Double. Pink and purple. Veitch – British – Date unknown.

Hugh Morgan. Semi-double. Short tube crimson, sepals inside crepe neyron-rose, lined crimson, outside carmine flushed, veined crimson, tipped green, long, broad and reflexed. Corolla white, veined neyron-rose, petaloids heavily flushed neyron-rose. Flowers are long, loose and bell shaped, very free. Growth upright and bushy and hardy. Fascination × Pink Flamingo. Holmes, R. – British – 1974 – A.F.S. No. 1204.

Hugh Tennant. Single. Red and strawberry-red. Stride – British – 1907.

Hula Girl. Double. Deep rose-pink tube, sepals deep rose-pink, stand out flat, do not reflex. Corolla white, shaded pink at base. Flowers are large, very full and very heavy bloomer. Foliage medium green with red veining, shaded red underside. Growth natural trailer. Paskesen – American – 1972 – A.F.S. No. 1023.

Humboldt Holiday. Double. Thin tube pinkish-white, sepals pinkish-white with frosty-pink undersides, gradually curl upward with slight twist. Corolla violet splashed pink, fading to white at base of petals, maturing to predominant rich violet-red colour. Large blooms with thin white line around petal edges, outer petals gradually flare while centre petals protrude, pinkish-white pistil extends 1 in below petals. Medium ovate golden-green foliage, veined magenta, changing to light green with maturity. Growth natural trailer, self-branching will make good basket or weeping standard. Originates from the Eureka area of California. Mary Ellen × Cosmopolitan. Hassett – American – 1980 – A.F.S. No. 1533.

Humdinger. Double. Short tube and sepals, bright deep pink, tipped green; corolla mauve, short with carmine-pink. Large blooms, fairly free. Growth lax upright, enormous blooms but coarse, no clear cut colouring. Fuchsia-La – American – 1960.

***Hurrycane.** Dutch introduction for 1983. Raised in the vicinity of Amersfoort, Netherlands. First Kiss × Pink Bon Accorde. Rijff – Dutch – 1983.

H.V. Kaltenborn. Single. Tube and sepals, dark rosy-red; corolla pale red. Largish blooms and free, open and flared. Growth trailer. Garson – American – 1942.

Hylas. Single. Red and cherry-red. Henderson – British – 1847.

hypoleuca. Red tube, scarlet sepals; reddish-scarlet corolla. Little is known of this species. Upright shrub up to 6 ft. Johnston – 1925 – Ecuador.

***Ian Leedham.** Semi-double. Long neyron-rose (R.H.S. 55B) tube ¾ in × ¼ in; sepals crimson (R.H.S. 52A) held horizontally with recurved tips 2⅛ in × ¾ in. Corolla Tyrian-purple maturing to rose-Bengal 1⅞ in × 1½ in quarter flared. Largish blooms with fluted corolla and cardinal-red petaloids, spinel-red stamens and pistil, amber-yellow stigma. Mid-green (R.H.S. 137A) foliage with ovate serrate shaped leaves 2⅝ in × 1⅜ in. Growth natural trailer produces excellent basket or half basket, best grown from autumn struck cuttings. Much larger and better than Marinka with long arching laterals, continuous flowering and very prolific, well in the exhibition category. Tested for 4 years and raised in the vicinity of Hull, Yorkshire, and introduced by Muncaster Fuchsias of Gainsborough, Lincolnshire, in 1985. *F. decussata* × Lady Kathleen Spence. Bielby – British – 1983.

Icarus. Single. Short white tube, sepals white with slight green tips, horizontal with tips curled back. Corolla purple-rose and four petaloids opposite each other between sepals, petals protrude from centre with white petaloids alongside. Large flowers, most unusual and free, green foliage. Growth natural trailer. Kennett-Castro – American – 1973 – A.F.S. No. 1108.

Iceberg. Single. Carmine tube distinctly striped red, reflexed sepals are white, slightly marked red at outside base. White corolla, medium sized flowers, compact with rolled petals which hold their shape, best colour develops in shade as with all 'whites'. Medium to dark green foliage, elliptical leaves with acute leaf tip, ovate leaf base and serrate leaf margins. Growth medium upright, bushy, will make good bush or standard but capable of all types of training. Awarded the B.F.S. Silver Certificate of Merit at the Northern Show Manchester 1980. Originates from the vicinity of Carlisle. Introduced by J.E. Ridding of Fuchsia-vale Nurseries of Kidderminster in 1980. Norman Mitchinson × Baby Pink. Mitchinson – British – 1980 – A.F.S. No. 1538.

Icecap. Single to semi-double. Tube and sepals, cardinal-red; corolla white with slight red veins. Medium sized flowers, bell shaped, even more profuse in blooming than Snowcap and long lasting. Growth upright and bushy, excels as a bush plant, well in the exhibition class, this is not just another red and white but an improvement upon Snowcap, but does throw the odd extra petal. Gadsby – British – 1968 – A.F.S. No. 971.

Ice Cream Soda. Semi-double. Short tube, light green to white when mature, sepals white, sometimes pink, long and arch back. Corolla white to pink, sometimes full pink, petals flare out making it frizzy looking, the four petals have many petaloids around them that flare out. Large blooms and free, dark green foliage with glossy topside. Growth lax bush or trailer. Castro – American – 1972 – A.F.S. No. 1030.

Iced Champagne. Single. Tube and sepals, dawn-pink, when sepals reflex, a lighter shade of pink. Corolla beautiful shade of rhodamine-pink. Flowers are longish, medium sized and extremely free. Growth low bush, the outstanding feature of this cultivar is the short jointed growth, self branching and compact, but the flowers are apt to lay low in the foliage, especially if growth is pinched too much. Winner of the B.F.S. Jones Cup 1968 and B.F.S. Award of Merit, together with White Pixie. Miss California × Jack Acland or Jack Shahan. Jennings, K. – British – 1968.

Ichiban. Double. Short thick tube, white to pink, sepals broad, white to pink. Corolla spinel-pink at base, fading to cyclamen-purple at tips of petals, maturing to China-rose. Flowers are large, with the largish corolla to date and free for size, foliage large dark green. Growth natural trailer, prefers cool conditions. Fuchsia-La – American – 1973 – A.F.S. No. 1074.

Icicle. Double. White short tube, sepals white; corolla white with pink stamens. Flowers are large and free, light green foliage. Growth trailer, needs a shady position. A.F.S. Cert. of Merit 1971. Paskesen – American – 1968 – A.F.S. No. 760.

Ida Dixon. Double. Red and purple. Dixon – British – 1869.

Ida Mae. Double. Long tube, red; red sepals curve down, very full corolla, variegated lavender and blue. Medium sized blooms with red-black stamens and pistil, long lasting blooms best colour in shade. Red veined foliage, growth natural trailer. Hanson – American – 1976 – A.F.S. No. 1324.

Igloo. Double. Tube pale pink, sepals white, tipped green and reflexed; corolla white. Medium sized blooms, early and free, blooms in clusters. Growth upright and vigorous up to 6 ft in California. Paskesen – American – 1965 – A.F.S. No. 633.

Igloo Maid. Double. White tube, sepals white, tipped green; corolla white with slight touch of pink. Medium to large flowers and free, yellowish-green foliage. Growth upright. Holmes, E. – British – 1972.

Ignea. Lemoine – French – 1848.

Illusion. Semi-double. Tube and sepals white; corolla pale lavender to pale blue shades, streaked with white. Medium sized blooms and free. Growth trailer. A.F.S. Cert. of Merit 1969. Kennett – American – 1966 – A.F.S. No. 676.

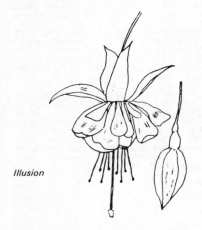

Illusion

Illustration. Lemoine – French – 1875.

Immaculate. Single. Tube and sepals, cherry-red, underlined orange; corolla of slightly darker colour, almost a self. Medium sized blooms and free, dark green, glossy foliage. Growth upright and bushy, hardy. White Queen ×. Wood – British – 1940.

Imperatrice Elisabeth. Cornelissen – Belgian – 1866.

Imperial. Double. Short thick red tube, sepals rosy-red; corolla deep violet-blue with rose streaks at base of petals, fading to Imperial-purple. Large flowers and fairly free. Growth upright. Paskesen – American – 1969 – A.F.S. No. 826.

Imperial Crown. Single. Tube and sepals salmon; corolla rich salmon, almost a self. Medium sized blooms, early and free. Growth trailer and cascade. Haag – American – 1953.

Imperial Fantasy. Double. Greenish-white tube, long curving sepals are broad, white with reddish markings at base. Corolla is imperial-purple. Large blooms flaring with variegated pink, white and coral petaloids. Dark green foliage large leaves 4¼ in long by 2½ in red veined, ovate with lobed base, acute tip and dentate margin. Growth trailer, will make good basket with weights, best colour in filtered sun, needs heat. Tested for 3 years in vicinity of Fort Bragg, Oxnard and Oceanside, California before release where it will be trademarked. Stubbs – American – 1981 – A.F.S. No. 1617.

Imperialis. Semi-double. Red and purple. Salter – British and French – 1845.

Imperial White. Single. White and violet. Carters – British – 1870.

Improved Christine. Single. Light red tube with dark red stripes, rather long; sepals pink, tipped green and rather long. Corolla light purple, pink at base. Medium-sized flowers with lilac-pink stamens and style, very long stamens. Growth upright and bushy. This cultivar grown and cultivated in the Netherlands is of unknown Continental origin.

Improvement. Double. Red and purple. Bland – British – 1877.

Impudence. Single. Tube light red, sepals light red, long and slim; corolla white, veined rose which open perfectly flat. Medium sized flowers, free blooming, corolla is composed of four round petals, much like Citation but flatter and stronger colour. Growth upright, strong and bushy, very aptly named, same raiser as Ting-a-Ling, two remarkable introductions. Schnabel – American – 1957 – A.F.S. No. 291.

Ina. No other details available except the parentage: Bon Accorde × Venus. De Groot – Dutch – 1973.

Ina. Double. Tube and sepals pale cerise, corolla powder blue, streaked pink. Medium sized blooms, prolific flowerer. Growth strong and upright. Raised and introduced by Akers of Fountain Nurseries, Ripon, Yorkshire. Akers – British – 1976.

Ina Buxton. Double. Tube and sepals carmine; corolla petunia-purple. Very large flowers, fairly free, growth trailer. Cultivar appears to be exclusive to California. Raiser and date unknown – *ca* 1960.

Ina Claire. Single. Pink self, flowers very free of medium size. Growth tall upright and vigorous. Hazard and Hazard – American – Date unknown.

Inca Maiden. Single to semi-double. Tube and outside of sepals, shiny rose-pink, inside sepals rose-pink of crepy texture, corolla violet-blue, lighter at base. Flowers free, early and of medium size, growth lax bush or trailer, one of the darkest purple corollas to date. Scarlet Beauty × Patty Evans. Schmidt – American – 1941.

Incomparable. Single. White and purple. Foxton – British – 1845.

Independence. Double. White tube with green streaks, long sepals, white to pink on outside, dawn-pink (R.H.S. 49A) on underside, turn clear back and sometimes twisting. Corolla opens currant-red (R.H.S. 46A) fading to cherry-red (R.H.S. 45C), lighter colour at base. Large blooms, opens into tightly rolled bud which flares slightly but keeps compact form with maturity. Medium foliage with red veins, growth medium upright, will make good bush. Stubbs – American – 1976 – A.F.S. No. 1383.

Indian Maid. Double. Tube and extra long recurved sepals, scarlet-red, corolla rich royal-purple. Large blooms and free, high centred buds open with a blaze of exotic colouring. Dark green foliage. Growth trailer. A.F.S. Cert. of Merit 1965. Waltz – American – 1962 – A.F.S. No. 524.

Indian Prince. Double. Short white tube, sepals white topside, light pink underside; corolla lavender. Medium sized blooms and good bloomer. Slender pointed foliage with serrated edges, growth upright and bushy. Soo Yun – American – 1973 – A.F.S. No. 1094.

Indian Princess. Double. Long tube and long sepals, light red, carmine on underside; corolla ruby-red. Medium sized blooms and free. Growth trailer. Soo Yun – American – 1971 – A.F.S. No. 944.

Indian Summer. Semi-double. Short tube and upright sepals, light magenta, has a tendency to spread into the corolla as it opens. Corolla deep wine-red. Flowers large and free bloomer, dark green foliage. Growth upright and vigorous to 4 ft. Hodges – American – 1957 – A.F.S. No. 303.

Indo-Chine. Semi-double. Red and purple. Lemoine – French – 1885.

* Inferno. Single. Light orange tube $\frac{1}{2}$ in long × 1 in wide, sepals orange held at the horizontal with reflexed tips 1$\frac{3}{8}$ in long × $\frac{3}{8}$ in wide. Corolla reddish-orange shading to orange at base. Medium sized flowers half flared, teardrop shaped buds, stamens and pistil reddish-orange held inside corolla. Medium green foliage, cordate leaves with acute tips 2$\frac{1}{2}$ in long by 1$\frac{3}{8}$ in wide. Growth natural trailer, will produce a fine basket, prefers cool conditions. Raised and tested for 3 years in vicinity of Pacifica, California. Will be trademarked. Storvick – American – 1983 – A.F.S. No. 1741.

Inga. Double. Tube and sepals, rich crimson; corolla white, striped cerise. Flowers largish and fairly free. Growth upright and bushy. Fairclo – American – Date unknown.

Ingegnoli Desiderata. Lemoine – French – 1899.

Ingleside. Double. Short white tube and upturned pink sepals; corolla dark blue, marbled white and pink. Largish blooms and free. Growth trailer. Brown and Soules – American – 1951 – A.F.S. No. 73.

Ingram Maid. Single. White tube, sepals white, flushed neyron-rose (R.H.S. 55A) at base underneath, held horizontally. Corolla creamy-white (R.H.S. 155A), medium-sized flowers, tube-like corolla, very free blooming, best colour in sun, spinel-red (R.H.S. 54A) stamens and pistil both held well clear of corolla. Growth tall upright, bushy, easy to train, tested for 7 years in vicinity of Northumberland before release by J.E. Ridding, Fuchsiavale Nurseries in Kidderminster in 1980. Pink Cloud × Lena Dalton seedling × Sonata. Ryle – British – 1976 – A.F.S. No. 1401.

* Ing. Walter Lukesch. Single. Tube and sepals red; corolla lilac-blue. Medium-sized flowers, free flowering and early bloomer. Growth short, neat upright. Nutzinger – Austrian – 1965.

Inimitable. Single. Scarlet and purple. Carters – British – 1870.

Innocence. Double. Short crimson tube, sepals upturned, palest rose deepening to crimson at base; corolla glistening white, spreading. Largish flowers, fairly free, small leathery foliage. Growth upright, bushy and dense. Reiter – American – 1951 – A.F.S. No. 130.

Insignis. Semi-double. Red and purple. Smith – British – 1841.

insignis (Hemsley 1876). Synonymous with *F. apetala.*

Inspector. Double. Red and purple. Bull – British – 1868.

Inspector. Single. White and pink. Henderson – British – 1874.

Inspiration. Double. Nearly self pink; corolla slightly darker pink. Very profuse bloomer of medium size. Growth lax bush or trailer, very vigorous. Nelson – American – 1952.

Instigator. Single. Red and purple. Bull – British – 1869.

integrifolia (Cambess 1829). Synonymous with *F. regia.*

Intellectual. Double. Small tube, white with green lines, sepals pink, tipped green. Corolla Imperial-purple, lighter in centre of petals. Largish blooms, fairly free, small foliage. Growth trailer. Pennisi – American – 1971 – A.F.S. No. 1016.

Interlude. Double. Slender tube waxy-white, sepals waxy-white with pink flush; corolla violet-purple, outer petals delicate orchid-pink. Medium sized blooms with four basal petals and outer petals, fairly free. Growth trailer and self-branching. Kennett – American – 1960 – A.F.S. No. 429.

Intrepid. Double. Tube and sepals, white with pink edges and green tips. Corolla white, medium sized flowers and free. Medium green foliage with red stems. Growth trailer. Soo Yun – American – 1970 – A.F.S. No. 913.

Invasion. Double. Tube and sepals, light red to rose; corolla purple, fading somewhat to orchid. Very large and very full flowers, fairly free. Growth trailer. Antonelli – American – 1971 – A.F.S. No. 1004.

Iona. Single. Rather long tube creamy wax, sepals pale rosy, underside clear pink, broad. Corolla clear pink at base, suffused lilac-rose, deepening to lilac at edges. Largish flowers of good shape and free, foliage deep green, ovate. Growth upright bush, self-branching good for standard or pyramid. Opalescent × Formosissima. Travis, J. – British – 1958 – A.F.S. No. 1143.

Iphigénie. Lemoine – French – 1854.

Irene. Semi-double. Tube and sepals white, tipped pale green; corolla palest pink, the outer edges of long sepals fold together to form a V. Flowers medium sized and free. Growth lax bush or trailer. Peterson-Fuchsia Farms – American – 1958 – A.F.S. No. 333.

Irene Ryle. Single. Neyron-rose tube, medium sized sepals, neyron-rose with upturned tips; corolla aster-violet with inconspicuous veining at base. Medium sized flowers, free flowering, petals folded in resembling a divided skirt. Lettuce-green foliage, growth tall upright, will produce good bush or standard. Bobby Shaftoe × Goldcrest. Ryle – British – 1975 – A.F.S. No. 1246.

Irene Veach. Double. White tube, sepals white with pale pink tips; corolla beautiful shade of solid pink. Medium-sized blooms, long lasting, heavy bloomer. Self-branching and heat resistant, hardy foliage. Growth upright bush. Gagnon – American – 1971 – A.F.S. No. 1019.

Iris. Single. Pink and purple. Turville – British – 1847.

Iris Amer. Double. Tube and sepals white, flushed pinkish-orange; corolla bright red with shades of carmine, petals splashed with orange markings. Medium sized flowers, very profuse with four or even six from the leaf axils, inherited from its parent Empress of Prussia. Deep green foliage, growth upright and bushy, responds to frequent pinching, feature of the growth is the strong short jointness. This cultivar is similar to Sunkissed but better. Extremely popular for the first few years after introduction, but deserves regaining its popularity. B.F.S. Award of Merit 1966. Empress of Prussia × . Amer – British – 1966.

Irish Rose. Double. Tube and sepals, pale chartreuse; corolla very pale rose. Medium sized flowers and free. Growth upright bush. Reiter – American – 1948.

*Irmgard Morio. Double. White tube, white sepals with pink underneath. Corolla purple-blue. Dark Secret × Bernadette. Nutzinger – Austrian – 1965.

Isabella Cairns. Seedling, no other details available other than the raiser. Clyne – British – 1975.

Isabelle. Double. Red and white. Lemoine – French – 1901.

Isabelle. Rozain-Boucharlat – French – 1913.

Isabel Ryan. Single. Tube and sepals red; corolla white, heavily veined pink. Medium sized flowers borne in great profusion, dark green foliage. Growth upright and bushy, height 2 to 2½ ft, hardy in Southern England, raised in the Scilly Isles. Submitted by raiser for R.H.S. Wisley Hardy Trials 1975–78 and received the Highly Commended Certificate. Tabraham – British – 1974.

Isadora Duncan. Lemoine – French – 1914.

Ishbell. Double. Tube and sepals, napon-rose; corolla napon-rose, overlaid amethyst-violet. Large flowers, very full and free. Growth upright and vigorous. Winner of the B.F.S. Jones Cup 1963 and B.F.S. Award of Merit, can be described as a double Bridesmaid. Clark, D. – British – 1963.

Isidor Raffeiner. Double. Tube and sepals bright red; sepals red, large and star-shaped. Corolla white-pink shaded. Growth upright, strong and vigorous. Koralle × Golden Glow. Nutzinger – Austrian – 1973.

Isis. Single. Crimson self. Lemoine – French – 1880.

Isis. Semi-double. Red and white. Rozain-Boucharlat – French – 1890.

Isis. Single. Tube and sepals red; corolla purple shading to purple-red. Medium to large flowers with red stamens and light red style. Dark green foliage with crimson mid-rib. Growth upright and bushy. This is the third cultivar under the name of Isis, the other two being Lemoine 1880 and Rozain-Boucharlat 1890. De Groot – Dutch – 1973.

Isle of Mull. Single. Tube light magenta with darker veins, sepals baby-pink, veined flesh-pink. Corolla rose-magenta, splashed metallic-pink. Medium-sized flowers, very prolific and the shape of a 'coolie-hat'. Growth upright and bushy, short-jointed and self-branching. Considered to be one of the best introductions by the raiser and one of his last as Tolley died in 1978. Tolley – British – 1978 – A.F.S. No. 1455.

Ismilia. Lemoine – French – 1870.

Italiano. Double. Tube and sepals, salmon to pink; corolla deep purple, fading to burgundy. Medium sized flowers very full and free. Growth trailer. Fuchsia Forest – American – 1966 – A.F.S. No. 668.

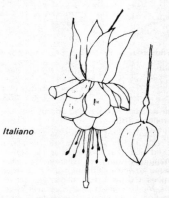

Italiano

Ivan Gadsby. Double. Tube greenish-white, sepals waxy-white; corolla magenta-rose. Very solid flowers, very free flowering for a double. Long, pointed, shiny foliage. Growth upright and bushy. Gadsby – British – 1970 – A.F.S. No. 875.

Ivoire. Double. Crimson and creamy-white. Rozain-Boucharlat – French – 1930.

*Ivy Swales. Semi-double. Short pale pink tube, sepals creamy-white, white underneath held at the horizontal with recurved tips 1¼ in long by ¼ in wide. Corolla pale mauve maturing to rosy-pink 1¼ in long by 1½ in wide. Medium sized flowers half flared with petals wrapped around each other, pale pink petaloids ½ in long by ¼ in wide, white and pink stamens and pistil. Dark green foliage with leaves 2½ in long by 1½ in wide, acute tips and rounded bases. Growth lax upright or stiff trailer, suitable for tall types of training, heat tolerant if shaded. Raised and tested for 4 years in vicinity of Howden, North Humberside. Chance seedling. Swales – British – 1983 – A.F.S. No. 1746.

I.X.L. Semi-double. Tube and upturned sepals, palest rose; corolla white. Flowers free and of medium size, heat tolerant. Growth lax bush or trailer. Walker and Jones – American – 1950.

Jack Acland. Single. Tube and sepals, bright pink; corolla deep rose, ageing to almost same colour as sepals. Large flowers, very free bloomer and fat buds. Growth fairly upright and bushy, with careful training can produce good standard. Although rather stiff will produce magnificent basket 4 to 5 ft across by mid July. Invariably misspelt as Ackland and also confused with Jack Shahan. Although classified by the Americans as a semi-double, flowers in this country are single. Further reference to be found under cultivar Jack Shahan. Haag and Son – American – 1952.

* Jackie Bull. Double. Long shell pink (R.H.S. 36A) tube ¾ in × ¼ in. Rose sepals veined deeper rose (R.H.S. 52C) on top, orange-rose (R.H.S. 50A) underneath held horizontally 2 in long by ⅝ in wide. Corolla is lilac-mauve (R.H.S. 68B). Medium sized blooms but largish and fluffy when matured, requires a little sun to keep the colours. Medium green foliage with ovate shaped leaves 3 in long by 1½ in wide. Growth medium upright and will make good bush, standard or decorative, heat tolerant if shaded, will weep with the weight of blooms. Tested and raised in the vicinity of Chaddesden, Derbyshire, and introduced by Jackson's Nurseries of Tamworth in 1985. Bicentennial × Papa Bluess. Redfern – British – 1985.

Jack King. Tube and sepals crimson, inside of sepals rose-red, nicely creped. Corolla (R.H.S. 76B) lilac, veined rose-red, some petals are overlaid very pale pink at base, fading to (R.H.S. 75B) rose-purple. Blooms are slightly larger than its parent. Growth is more vigorous than General Monk, upright and good for bedding out and pot work. Parentage: Sport from General Monk with all its parent's good characteristics. Holmes, R. – British – A.F.S. No. 1461.

Jack of Hearts. Double. Tube and sepals red; corolla white, with flushes of pink and red to centre, with pink veining. Very large flowers and fairly free for size. Large foliage, growth trailer. Not the best of cultivars, can be disappointing. Fuchsia Forest – American – 1967 – A.F.S. No. 724.

Jackpot. Double. Tube and sepals, light pink; corolla marbled blue, fading to lavender tone. Large blooms, slightly ruffled, fairly free. Growth trailer. A.F.S. Cert. of Merit 1969. Fuchsia Forest – American – 1966 – A.F.S. No. 669.

Jack Shahan. Single. Tube and sepals, pale rose-bengal, corolla rose-bengal. Large flowers and very free, growth inclined to be lax if grown as H1 but under cooler conditions, makes a fine bush plant. With care can be trained as a good weeping standard. Usually listed incorrectly as either Sharon or Sharron and also confused with Jack Acland. Chief differences between the two cultivars are that Acland is more upright and stiffer with bright pink colouring, whereas Shahan is more lax and of a darker pink or rose. Tiret – American – 1948.

Jack Wilson. Single. Tube medium to long, white; sepals white pale pink underneath. Corolla violet-cerise, shading to blue. Mid-green foliage. Medium sized flowers, very floriferous. Growth upright but does tend to become lax. Proved to be hardy in the vicinity of Reading, southern England, since 1967. Introduced by Wills Fuchsias Ltd. of West Wittering in 1980. Wilson, J.W. – British – 1979.

jahnii. Red tube, red sepals; light red corolla. Very small flowers and sparse. Irregular habit of growth, upright shrub. Munz – 1943 – Venezuela.

Jamboree. Double. Tube pinkish-white, sepals salmon-pink, deeper pink underneath. Corolla carmine and salmon-pink. Very large blooms with irregular petals of dazzling colour, free for size of bloom, can be of two different colours under different conditions, becomes deep carmine and orange under cool cultivation. Large, glossy stiff foliage, stems are rather brittle and easily broken. Growth upright and bushy, needs early pinching. Reiter – American – 1955 – A.F.S. No. 231.

James Huntley. Single. White and red. Lye – British – 1885.

James Lye. Double. Tube and sepals cerise; corolla bluish-mauve, flushed pale mauve at base. Medium sized flowers, very free, perfect shaped bloom, similar to Constance but darker. Growth upright and bushy, ideal cultivar for tall training either as standard, conical, pillar or espalier. An old cultivar which should be more popular, very often confused with Constance. Lye – British – 1883.

James Lye – Constance. For information to distinguish between these two similar cultivars see Constance – James Lye.

James Shurvell. Single. Crimson self. Story – British – 1862.

James Travis. Double. Tube and sepals, rich bright-red; corolla rich clear-blue. Largish to medium flowers, early and very free. Growth upright and spreading. Hardy. Susan Travis × Enfante Prodigue. Thorne – British – 1960 – A.F.S. No. 456.

James Travis. Single. Thick glabrous tube, vivid coral, sepals coral, broad, spreading and reflexed. Corolla salmon, fading to dusky-pink 3 to 6 mm long. Tiny flowers, exceedingly free flowering and of Breviflorae type, decorative deep purple berries 4 to 5 mm diameter. Foliage Lincoln green above, paler beneath, glossy. Growth shrublike, will make good bush, excellent as miniature or bonsai. Named by Susan Travis after her famous father. Breviflorae hybrid. S. Travis – British – 1972.

James Welch. Single. Red and purple. Lye – British – 1871.

* Jam Roll. Double. Little known red self cultivar introduced by D.M. Emerson of Cottage Nurseries, Willey, Warwickshire, in 1984. Brough – British – ca 1983.

Jan Bremer. Single. Tube light red, rather long, sepals light red; corolla light red. Medium-sized flowers almost a self, very free flowering. Growth lax bush, very quick grower, branches break very easily. Bremer – Dutch – 1973.

Jandel. Double. White tube, sepals white, reflexed and tipped pink; corolla orchid. Medium sized blooms, fairly free, round and flaring, good colour in both sun and shade. Growth lax bush, makes good basket with weights. Walker-Fuchsia-La – American – 1975 – A.F.S. No. 1264.

Jane Evans. Single. Tube and sepals, coral and salmon; corolla vivid shade of salmon, suffused with orange and cerise. Large flowers, fairly free, light green foliage. Growth upright and bushy. California × Aurora Borealis. Evans and Reeves – American – 1938.

* Jane Humber. Double. Venetian-pink (R.H.S. 49B) tube ½ in by ⅝ in; sepals Venetian-pink (R.H.S. 49B) underneath, fully reflexed with recurved tips 1⅛ in by ½ in. Corolla 1⅛ in by 2⅜ in is rose-purple (R.H.S. 76A) mallow-purple (R.H.S. 73C) at base matures to rose-purple (R.H.S. 75A). Large blooms fully flared, much deeper colour than Blush O' Dawn and free flowering, empire-rose stamens and pistil, amber-yellow stigma extended well below corolla. Mid-green foliage (R.H.S. 137A) with ovate shaped leaves 2¾ in by 1⅝ in. Growth lax upright or stiff trailer, self-branching can make a medium upright, very suitable for basket or tall types of training. Very easy growing cultivar similar to its parent Swingtime making fine pillar or pyramid, more vigorous than Blush O' Dawn and less susceptible to botrytis. Raised in the vicinity of Hull, Yorkshire, and introduced by Muncaster Fuchsias of Gainsborough in 1985. Swingtime × Blush O' Dawn. Bielby – British – 1983.

Jane Lye. Single. Pink and mauve-pink. Lye – British – 1870.

Jane Lye – Lady Kathleen Spence. At a first glance, when flowers of these two cultivars are laid side by side, they appear to be very similar, in fact the colour of both corollas is exactly the same. Closer examination does, however, reveal that L.K.S. is a much smaller flower with a much shorter tube ¼ in as compared with Jane Lye's tube measuring ⅜ in. The pistil of L.K.S. is very long almost 2 in in length whereas J.L.'s is approximately 1¼ in, the stamens in L.K.S. are much shorter and of different lengths, whereas J.L. has much longer stamens of even length. Both cultivars are genuine singles with the same folded petals of the same colour, but J.L. is fuller and larger with a bigger opening for the stamens. The sepals indicate the biggest difference, J.L.'s colour is a much darker pink, although on the pale side, held almost at the horizontal with a slight twist with a much darker colour pink shading, almost to carmine at the tips and darker still underneath the narrower and not so perfect sepals as L.K.S. Apart from the very delicate lavender shade of L.K.S. its main characteristic is the thin, long, sweeping low from the horizontal sepals, standing well out, with nicely curled tips, tipped green. The flowers of L.K.S. do not fade or lose their form, whereas the flowers of J.L do fade and change colour as the flower matures, especially late in the season. The biggest difference between the two cultivars is the habit of growth, Jane Lye can best be described as a lax bush and Lady Kathleen Spence is an upright, self-branching plant which will, however, with careful training make a wonderful specimen basket as was seen at the 1976 B.F.S. Northern Show as a half basket and a full basket at the B.F.S. London/Reading Show 1977.

Janet Corbett. Single. Tube and sepals China-pink, tipped green; corolla lavender-pink.

Large flowers, quite free for size, bell-shaped. Growth upright and bushy. Curtis – British – 1973.

Janet Garson. Double. Tube and reflexed sepals, deep rose; corolla deep garnet with outer petals shaded deep rose half way down. Large flowers, fairly free, growth lax bush, spreading, needs support for upright growth. Garson – American – 1944.

Janet Williams. Double. Tube and sepals red, corolla amethyst blue. Medium-sized blooms, very striking, foliage deep gold-green, slowly changes to pale green with maturity. Growth upright, strong and bushy, height 1½ to 2 ft. Hardy in Southern England, raised in the Scilly Isles. Tabraham – British – 1976.

Janet Wilson. Advance information, new seedling to be introduced in the near future by J.W. Wilson of Reading.

Janie. Double. Tube and sepals white; corolla lavender-blue. Growth trailer. Another unregistered American cultivar with little information. Araujo – American – ca 1970.

Japana. Double. Short thin white (R.H.S. 155A) tube, slightly reflexed sepals, azalea-pink (R.H.S. 38A) tipped green 1¼ in × ⅝ in wide. Corolla azalea-pink (R.H.S. 41C) at base, extends into petal as rose-Bengal (R.H.S. 57B) with beetroot-purple (R.H.S. 72B) edges. Medium sized blooms 1 in × 1¾ in wide ruffled and pleated of thick texture, stamens same colour as corolla, pink pistil with white tip extending ½ in. Medium green (R.H.S. 137A) foliage 2 in × 1⅜ in wide leaves, serrated, centre vein and stems are red. Growth natural trailer, but colour develops in shade. Originates from the Puget Sound area of Washington. Introduced by Linda Tancey of Kent, W.A., U.S.A., in 1980. Eastwood – American – 1980 – A.F.S. No. 1569.

Jason. Single. Deep crimson and black purple. Bland – British – 1878.

Jason. No other details except it is a seedling from Peter Pan. Middlebrook, W.J. – British – 1975.

Jaunty. Double. Carmine tube, short thick and fleshy sepals, carmine. Corolla orchid-pink. Large flowers, square honeycomb effect, blooms in clusters all the way down the stem. Growth upright, strong and sturdy. Weir – British – 1973 – A.F.S. No. 1081.

Jayne Louise Mills. Single. Tube and sepals red; corolla lavender. Medium sized flowers and free. Growth upright bush. Sport of Dutch Mill. Roe – British – 1970.

Jay Pee. Single. Tube and sepals red, corolla violet-purple. medium sized flowers over a long period. Growth upright and bushy. Introduced by the raiser in the vicinity of Southport, England. Porter – British – 1974.

Jean. Single. Tube and sepals white, touched palest pink; corolla deepest Tyrian-rose. Medium sized blooms and free. Growth trailer or espalier. Reiter – American – 1953 – A.F.S. No. 148.

Jean Burton. Single. Tube pale pink, sepals rhodamine-pink held well back. Corolla pure white. Flowers are large, bell shaped and free. Growth strong sturdy bush, prefers shade. Sleigh Bells × Citation. Gadsby – British – 1968.

Jean Campbell. Single. Tube and sepals, rose-pink, suffused pink underneath; corolla rose-red with purple at base. Largish flowers and free, similar to Queen Mary. Growth upright and bushy. Raffill – British – Date unknown.

Jeane Chauvin. Lemoine – French – 1898.

Jeanette Broadhurst. Single. Tube and sepals, rose-madder, sepals short and wide; corolla marbled rose-madder and mauve. Flowers are medium sized and prolific, short rounded petals, stiff and brittle with brilliant hue. Light green foliage. Growth natural trailer, trails well but a little stiffer than Cascade. Sport of Cascade. Broadhurst – British – 1974 – A.F.S. No. 1195.

Jean Ewart. Single. Short china-rose tube, sepals china-rose, short, pointed which curl back to tube. Corolla amaranth-rose (R.H.S. 65A). Medium sized flowers rather small but compact, very free flowering. Medium green foliage, growth upright and bushy, self-branching, good for bush or quarter standard. Named after the current Assistant Secretary of the British Fuchsia Society. Raised in the vicinity of Nottingham and introduced by V.T. Nuttall of Brodsworth Nurseries, Doncaster in 1981. Mipam × Carol Roe. Roe – British – 1981.

* Jeane–Genii. See Genii–Jeane.

Jeanie. Semi-double. Cerise and red. Pince – British – 1871.

Jeanne Benoilon. Lemoine – French – 1886.

Jeanne D'Arc. Double. Red and purple. Cornelissen – Beligan – 1868.

Jeanne D'Arc. Double. White and red. Lemoine – French – 1903.

Jeanne Lisley. Lemoine – French – 1879.

Jeanne Rose. Double. Rose tube, sepals dark rose with creped underside. Corolla mauve with outer petals mixed light rose at base. Medium-sized blooms which stay tight with buds resembling a Turk's turban. Growth natural trailer without weights. Tested for 12 years in vicinity of Coos Bay, Oregon. Registered by Vee Jay Greenhouse in 1978. Prentice – American – 1978 – A.F.S. No. 1486.

Jeanne Samary. Lemoine – French – 1891.

Jean Sisley. Lemoine – French – 1880.

Je Maintiendrai. Single. Tube rose-red; sepals rose-red with green tips. Corolla brown-orange. Medium sized flowers, little other information other than of Dutch origin. Growth upright bush, introduced by Wills Fuchsias Ltd. of West Wittering in 1980. Speciosa x. de Graaff – Dutch – 1979.

Jennie Rachael. Double. Thick, white tube, white, white sepals with tinges of pink, tipped green. Corolla rose-red (R.H.S. 58C) veined rose-Bengal (R.H.S. 57B) with petaloids of the same colouring, often one petal can have white patch. Very large blooms and very full, could be a breakthrough in the large doubles, white stamens and pistil. Dark green foliage with leaves up to 5 in in length. Originally shown as seedling RC2 at Manchester B.F.S. Show 1978, now named after raiser's grand-daughter. Raised in vicinity of Manchester and tested 4 years before release. Cheetham – British – 1979– A.F.S. No. 1526.

Jennifer Hampson. Double. Short, thick, cerise tube, short, fairly thick, cerise sepals; rich purple corolla. Small perfect shaped blooms, free for double, colour develops well both in sun or shade, red stamens and pistil. Small foliage, growth natural trailer. Dollar Princess × . Hilton – British – 1976 – A.F.S. No. 1375.

Jerome. Double. Tube and sepals, light red; corolla lilac-blue. Medium sized flowers, fairly free. Growth low bush or trailer. Raiser unknown – American – Date unknown.

Jerry Copley. Semi-double. Tube and upturned sepals, bright red; corolla white with red veins. Flowers are large and bell shaped, fairly free. Growth trailer. Copley – American – 1966 – A.F.S. No. 694.

Jessie Ryle. Single. Short thick tube, whitish-rose, sepals neyron-rose underneath, whitish rose on top, long and narrow, slightly twisted. Corolla deep mallow-purple, shading to phlox-pink at base, fading to beetroot-purple. Medium sized flowers and free, growth upright and bushy. Complicated parentage involving Howlett's Hardy, Ting-a-Ling, Lena Dalton, Pink Cloud, Golden Dawn and Sonata. Ryle – British – 1975 – A.F.S. No. 1247.

Jessimae. Single. Short china-rose tube, broad china-rose sepals. Corolla pale mallow-purple medium sized flowers and very free flowering. Growth upright and bushy similar to its parent. Raised in the vicinity of Leicester and introduced by R. and J. Pacey of Melton Mowbray in 1981. Seedling from Countess of Aberdeen. White, R.J. – British – 1980.

Jess Walker. Double. Red tube, sepals long and narrow, red, growing straight. Corolla white. Largish blooms, fluffy and flaring, open saucer shape and fairly free. Growth trailer. Copley Gardens – American – 1967 – A.F.S. No. 744.

Jester. Semi-double. Tube and sepals cerise, sepals long, narrow and upturned; corolla rich royal-purple, turning lighter with maturity. Growth upright and bushy, fast grower, hardy. Holmes, E. – British – 1968.

Jester. Single. Tube and sepals pale pink; corolla deep pink. Small flowers, borne in profusion, foliage pale green. Growth upright, bushy and very compact, height 6 to 9 in. Very suitable for rockeries, window boxes and troughs. One of a series of new hardy miniatures. Hardy in Southern England and raised in the Scilly Isles. Not to be confused with a cultivar of the same name raised by Mrs. E. Holmes. Tabraham – British – 1976.

Jet Fire. Double. Tube and sepals, flesh coloured, fading at base and blending into the white tube. Corolla red, petals are surrounded with smaller, shorter petaloids. Flowers are of unusual form, large and free. Growth lax bush or trailer. Reedstrom – American – 1959 – A.F.S. No. 387.

Jewel. Single. Long tube and sepals carmine; corolla darker shade of carmine, almost purple. Flowers are long and borne on long pedicels. Growth low bush, height up to 1½ ft, hardy. Mrs. Rundle × . Wood – British – 1940.

Jewel. Single. Tube and sepals coral-pink; corolla pale mauve. Small flowers, born in profusion, foliage medium green. Growth upright, bushy and very compact, height only 6 to 9 in, very suitable for rockeries, window boxes and troughs. One of a series of new hardy miniature cultivars. Hardy in Southern England, raised in the Scilly Isles. Not to be confused with a cultivar of the same name raised by W. P. Wood. Tabraham – British – 1976.

Jezebel. Semi-double. Short, cherry-red tube, cherry-red sepals, tipped green which cling together while opening showing brilliant corolla like a lantern, opens out on maturity to extra long sweeping arch. Corolla peony-pink, streaked cherry-red. Full, tightly rolled flowers with the extra long sepals make for large blooms. Growth medium upright, raised and tested for 6 years in vicinity of Seal Beach and Huntington Park, California, trademarked in California. Raised by Roy Walker, introduced by Fuchsia-La Nurseries. Walker – American – 1979 – A.F.S. No. 1511.

Jim Dandy. Single. Tube and upper sepal surface, white to flesh colour, lower surface of short broad sepals, flushed brilliant orange. Corolla with four petals of unusual purple-orange colouring. Medium to large blooms, fairly free, growth upright and fast. Kennett – American – 1958 – A.F.S. No. 346.

Jim Fairclo. Single. Tube and sepals, dark crimson; corolla dark burgundy with darker markings at base of petals. Largish flowers and free with large crinkled foliage. Growth upright and vigorous to 4 ft. Hedlund – American – 1951.

Jingle Bells. Single or double. Tube and sepals red, sepals are rather broad and held a little above the horizontal; corolla white with red veining. Smallish to medium-sized flowers with long pistil. Growth lax bush. An American introduction where they seem to have some confusion with another cultivar of the same name, a double having red tube and sepals with violet to purple corolla. Raiser and date unknown – American.

Jinx. Single. Tube and sepals, waxy-white, underside faintly brushed with carmine; corolla deep carmine. Flowers are large for single with broader sepals than normal, free flowering. Dark green leathery foliage, growth lax bush or trailer, heat tolerant. Schnabel-Paskesen – American – 1960 – A.F.S. No. 419.

J.J. Rousseau. Double. Red and purple. Lemoine – French – 1883.

J.N. Twrdy. Double. Red and purple. Lemoine – French – 1868.

Joan Chiswell. Double. Tube rose-pink, sepals deep pink outside, red inside and crepe which reflex with maturity. Corolla nice clear white with red splashes at base. Medium sized blooms of perfect shape with attractive scalloped edged petals. Growth upright and bushy. Introduced by Woodbridge Nurseries of Hounslow in 1980. Swingtime × Joy Patmore. Dyos – British – 1980.

Joan Cooper. Single. Tube and sepals, pale rose-opal, sepals reflex straight back and cover tube, tipped green. Corolla cherry-red, smallish flowers, very free, unusual colouring for hardy. Foliage lightish green, growth upright, bushy and hardy. Accepted by the B.F.S. as showbench hardy. Wood – British – 1954.

Joan Gilbert. Double. Tube neyron-rose, waxy sepals are neyron-rose with distinctive green tips, broad and globe shaped, are uniquely attached to the outer petaloids, extending the very full bloom as they reflex, to reveal fluted and folded inner petals. Multi-coloured corolla, rich violet base

heavily splashed and mottled with salmon and pink right to the tips of both petaloids and inner petals. Growth upright and bushy, self-branching and close jointed, excellent for the training of bush, shrub or standard. Named after the wife of an outstanding Birmingham exhibitor. Introduced jointly by D. Stilwell and J. Ridding in 1978. Gilbert, W. – British – 1977.

Joan Helm. Double. Tube white and pink, curved sepals, white; corolla deep lilac streaked pink. Flowers largish and full, fairly free, growth trailer. Tiret – American – 1972 – A.F.S. No. 1071.

Joan Hurd. Semi-double. Tube white with deep pink flush, sepals white with pink flush and tipped green, deeper pink underneath. Corolla light pink, medium-sized blooms which stand out well, light pink stamens and white style. Dark green foliage, growth upright. This cultivar was named after a past president and founder of the Guildford Fuchsia Group. Originally raised by Bowyers Nurseries and was a seedling of Flirtation Waltz, subsequently grown on at Merrist Wood Agriculture College but eventually disposed of. Was imported into Holland by Dr. Appel around 1974, and has been in cultivation in Holland since that date. Subsequently introduced and listed by High Trees Nurseries of Reigate, Surrey, in the late '70s. Flirtation Waltz ×. Bowyers Nurseries – British – Date unknown.

Joan Leach. Single. Tube and sepals deep pink; corolla light blue, flushed pink. Small flowers, very free, growth upright and bushy, strong branching with spreading habit, dwarfish in height 12 to 15 in. Hardy in Southern England, raised in the Scilly Isles. Tabraham – British – 1975.

Joan Leslie. Double. Tube and broad, upturned sepals deep red; corolla rich royal-purple. Medium sized blooms, free, heat tolerant. Growth upright. Importation from England. Introduced by Victor Reiter – American – 1953.

* Joan Morris. Single to semi-double. Rosy-red tube, sepals rosy-red shading to white, tipped green. Corolla rosy-purple with white or pink streaks on each petal. Medium sized flowers flaring in shape with many petaloids, very eyecatching. Growth medium upright, vigorous and bushy. Good for decorative bush or standard. Raised in the vicinity of Middlesex and introduced by Woodbridge Nurseries of Hounslow, Middlesex in 1984. Named after a very charming and well known fuchsia personality in the Midlands. Dyos – British – 1984.

Joanne. Single. Short, thin tube orient-pink (R.H.S. 36A), sepals red-purple (R.H.S. 61D), tipped green on outside, sepals 1½ in long × ½ in wide Corolla red-purple (R.H.S. 73A) 1 in long × ¾ in wide. Medium-sized flowers with very unusual colouring, growth natural trailer without weights, best colour in shade, will make good basket, bush or small upright. Tested for 2 years in vicinity of Chester. Seedling from Chang. Pugh – British – 1977 – A.F.S. No. 1458.

Joanne Bakker. Single. Pinky-white tube with attractive markings, thick, waxy-pink sepals, shading to white at tips, held horizontally. Corolla white with red veining. Medium-sized flowers very attractive, containing the characteristics of both parents, bell shaped. Growth upright, bushy and self-branching. Originally known as seedling 256A and awarded the B.F.S. Silver Certificate of Merit at B.F.S. Manchester Show 1977. This cultivar was originally named Joanne by the raiser, but it was discovered J.H. Pugh already had a seedling of the same name and this cultivar was consequently changed to Joanne Bakker. First introduced by J. Ridding in 1978. Leonora × Ting-a-Ling. Ryle – British – 1977 – A.F.S. No. 1475.

Joanne Lynn. Semi-double. Short thick tube white with pinkish cast, broad sepals white with pink cast on top, crepey darker pink underneath. Corolla fuchsia-purple (purple with red predominating). Medium sized blooms, medium sized green foliage with serrated margins and ovate in shape. Growth tall upright, originates from the Coos Bay area of Oregan. This cultivar was introduced in 1970 with little detail. Adkins – American – 1980 – A.F.S. No. 1554.

Joan of Arc. Double. Tube and sepals white, tipped green; corolla white with touch of pink, almost a white self. Flowers medium sized and fairly free. Growth lax bush or trailer. Reiter – American – 1947.

Joan Pacey. Single. Long white tube, sepals pink, tipped green. Corolla phlox-pink, veined rose-pink. Flowers are very prolific and of medium size, last well into the autumn, take full sun for best colour. Growth upright and bushy, makes a fine specimen espalier. Has already made a great impression. Gadsby – British – 1972 – A.F.S. No. 1067.

Joan's Delight. Single. Short crimson tube, crimson sepals; corolla rich violet-blue. Small flowers, very freely produced, best colour in shade. Growth is very small dwarf habit, self-branching bush, very attractive in small pots and suitable for 3½ in pot classes. Tested for five years in North Midlands before release. Wee Lass × Cloverdale. Gadsby – British – 1977 – A.F.S. No. 1428.

Joan Smith. Single. Tube and reflexing sepals, flesh-pink; corolla soft pink with a touch of cerise. Medium sized flowers, very early and free but colouring can be very disappointing, very pale. The outstanding feature of this cultivar is the growth, probably the fastest to date, strong upright, vigorous, will reach several feet on current growth, difficult to control. Submited by Vicarage Farm Nurseries in the seedling class at the B.F.S. 1959 London Show and was the first winner of the Jones Cup, also the B.F.S. Award of Merit. Thorne – British – 1958.

Jocelyn. Double. Red and purple. Lemoine – French – 1869.

Jo Chez. Double. Long white tube, very long white sepals with pointed tips. Corolla white, very large. Large blooms with square corolla at bottom and very tight. Petaloids 1 in long ruffled and fluted, edges are rounded looking like extra corolla, long stamens with yellow anthers and long-white stigma. Large medium to dark green foliage, leaves 3 in wide by 5 in long with deep veins. Growth trailer or lax upright, will make good basket and all tall shapes of training, heat tolerant if shaded. Tested for 5 years in vicinity of Washington, N.E. England before release. Cheseldine – British – 1982 – A.F.S. No. 1611.

Joe Kusber. Double. Very full with shortish white tube, faintly striped, the white sepals are large and broad, pointed, held at the horizontal and delicately tipped with pink. Corolla is bluish-purple with very faint pink variegations,

very full and fluffy blooms with many petaloids. The tight blooms open very blue and fade with maturity but held for a long period. The colouring is unusual, a beautiful pastel shade, a real eye catcher which flowers well into the autumn when the flowers are at their best. The foliage is medium green and rather large. Growth is inclined to be lax and would need a little support if grown as a bush, is much better as a second year plant and seen to advantage when displayed on a fairly high pedestal in the greenhouse with blooms at eye level. Would like to see it grown as a weeping standard. Raised in California. This is a cultivar raised by the late Mike Pennisi in 1968 and obviously overlooked by most growers to their disadvantage. Joe Kusber together with White King must be his best two raisings numbering some 55 introductions at nine or more nurseries in Britain. Pennisi – American – 1968 – A.F.S. No. 758.

Joey. Double. Short thick tube light red, veined deeper red; sepals are short and thick, clear red and recurve. Corolla white veined red. Smallish compact blooms with small petals, few small petaloids, red stamens and pistil. Small dark green foliage. Growth self-branching lax upright, suitable for bush or standard, best colour in sun. Tested for 3 years in vicinity of Cardiff, South Wales before release. Adams – British – 1982 – A.F.S. No. 1687.

John. Single. Tube and sepals crimson; corolla reddish-mauve, small flowers and free. Growth dwarf habit and erect, suitable for rockery. Hardy. Wood – British – 1946.

*John Baker. Double. Tube and sepals pink and white, corolla white and pink. Medium sized blooms. Originally known as Seedling No. 408. Raised in the vicinity of Guildford, Surrey. Growth upright and bushy. Weeks – British – 1982.

John Bright. Single. White and mauve. Lye – British – 1886.

John E. Davis. Single. Tube white, sepals geranium-lake; corolla magenta. Medium sized flowers, early and free. Growth lax bush or trailer. Niederholzer – American – 1946.

John F. Kennedy. Double. Tube and sepals, light green; corolla candy-pink. Small flowers and free, growth upright. Pennisi – American – 1968 – A.F.S. No. 751.

John Forbes. Double. Tube and sepals, scarlet-cerise; corolla purple. Largish flowers, fairly free. Growth upright and bush, still grown today. Forbes – British – 1888.

John Fraser. Single. Tube rose-red (R.H.S. 58C) veined (R.H.S. 58B); sepals rose-red at base, paling towards the long green tip, inside sepals are rose-red (R.H.S. 58B), nicely creped with small green tip, semi-reflexed flicking outwards. Corolla Imperial-purple (R.H.S. 78A), rose-red (R.H.S. 58B) at base, veined rose-red, fading to cyclamen purple (R.H.S. 74B). Medium-sized flowers, bell shaped with rose-red stamens and carmine anthers, long pale pink style and yellow stigma. Growth semi-trailer, self-branching and bushy, will trail with weights. Tested for four years in Kent before release, adopted and named by the Guildford Fuchsia Group. Percy Holmes seedling. Holmes, R. – British – 1977 – A.F.S. No. 1419.

John Gibson. Bland – British – 1875.

John Hannon. Semi-double. Tube and sepals burnt orange, corolla orange and pink. Very distinct and attractive cultivar. Growth upright and vigorous. Originated from the area of Stratford upon Avon. Raiser unknown – British – ca 1970s.

John Lindsay. Single. Red and purple. Lemoine – French – 1905.

John Lockyer. Single. Pink tube, upcurled sepals rich pink, tipped green. Corolla pink-purple with red-purple edge and inside. Medium sized blooms, free and early. Growth upright and bushy. Holmes, E. – British – 1969.

John Marsh. Double. Tube and sepals, clear white, tipped green; corolla palest orchid and pink, veined pink. Extra large blooms, tightly packed corolla, exquisite flowers, freely produced. Growth trailer, best grown as H1, difficult. Schnabel – American – 1963 – A.F.S. No. 584.

*John Maynard Scales. Single. Triphylla type hybrid. Very long orange tube, short sepals are also orange. Corolla is brighter shade of orange. Sage green foliage, growth is exceptionally strong and upright. This cultivar is well within the exhibition category. Raised in the vicinity of Ipswich, Suffolk, and introduced by the raiser, Gouldings Fuchsias of Ipswich in 1985. One of a series of ten new introductions named after famous trains in 1985. Goulding – British – 1985.

John McLaren. Semi-double. Red tube sepals very heavy waxy texture, red outside much lighter inside. Corolla light hyssop-violet. Large tight flowers, fairly free. Growth upright and slow. Hazard and Hazard – American – Date unknown.

Johnny. Semi-double. Short red tube, heavy upturned sepals rose; corolla white and pink, blue overcast, heavy red veins from base. Small flowers, very heavy blooming, growth upright and bushy. Brown and Soules – American – 1952 – A.F.S. No. 136.

Johnny Marine. Semi-double. Tube and sepals, bright red; corolla pure white with three large spreading centre petals. Large flowers and free, growth upright, sturdy bush. York – American – 1952 – A.F.S. No. 138.

John Prentice. Double. Tube and sepals, deep rosy-pink crepe; corolla lavender-blue with pink stripe on outer folded petals. Large blooms, fairy free, fade to fuchsia shade with maturity. Growth trailer. Gagnon – American – 1965 – A.F.S. No. 619.

John Sisley. Single. Dominyana × F.serratifolia. Lemoine – French – 1901.

John's Prize. Double. Tube deep rose, sepals of the same colour, very long; corolla deep blue marbled outward. Largish flowers and fairly free foliage small, dark green with red veins. Growth trailer. Prentice – American – 1967 – A.F.S. No. 719.

John Suckley. Semi-double. Tube and sepals, delicate pink; sepals long and pointed. Corolla pale wedgewood-blue. Medium sized blooms very beautiful and free. Growth trailer, makes excellent basket. Suckley – British – 1966.

Joker. Single. Tube and sepals red; corolla violet with reddish shading giving marbled appearance. Medium sized flowers, growth lax and trailing. Introduced by Wills Fuchsia Nurseries in 1979. Lena × . de Graaff – Dutch – 1976.

*Jomam. Single. Rose-pink tube ½ in long by ¼ in wide, half up sepals 1½ in long by ½ in wide, are rose-pink (R.H.S. 52C) with slightly twisted tips and recurving. Corolla opens pale blue-violet (R.H.S. 87C) lightly veined pink, maturing to light violet-pink (R.H.S. 77B), slightly flushed white at base 1 in long by ¾ in wide. Medium sized flowers are quarter flared and slightly bell shaped, symmetrical flowers of clear blue and good colour combination. Rose-pink filaments and carmine (R.H.S. 52B) anthers, rose-pink style and carmine stigma. Dark yellow-green (R.H.S. 146B) foliage with 2¼ in long by 1 in wide elliptic leaves, serrated and with acute tips and bases. Growth small upright and bushy, will make excellent upright bush, very short-jointed, prefers filtered light and cool conditions, Raised in the vicinity of Ponteland, Newcastle-upon-Tyne, and tested for 4 years before release. Blue Elf × Mayfield. Hall – British – 1984 – A.F.S. No. 1767.

Jos'e Joan. Double. Longish white tube, white sepals, tipped green; corolla pale violet. Large blooms, beautiful colour combination and free. Growth lax bush, will make good basket, needs frequent pinching. Bellamy – British – 1978.

Joseph Holmes. Single. Dawn pink tube with darker veins, narrow sepals dawn pink with darker colour edges, tipped green; lower surface creped dawn pink, held out slightly below horizontal recurving slightly at tips. Corolla neyron-rose (R.H.S. 55A), mandarin red (R.H.S. 40B) at base and edges of petals, veined at base dawn pink (R.H.S. 49A). Medium sized flowers slightly flaring bell-shaped with no fading, stamens and yellow stigma are short, just clearing end of corolla. Ovate medium green (R.H.S. 137C) foliage has lighter veins and serrated. Petiole and first quarter of central vein are pink. Growth natural trailer, self-branching, will make good basket, lax bush or weeping standard. Originates from the vicinity of Edenbridge, Kent. Introduced by High Trees Nurseries of Reigate, Surrey, in 1981. Holmes, R. – British – 1980 – A.F.S. No. 1556.

Josephine. Single. White and red. Henderson – British – 1871.

Joseph Sada. Double. Red and purple. Crousse – French – 1867.

Josie. Double. Short tube deep rose, sepals deep rose; corolla rose coloured, variegated pink. Medium-sized blooms, box shaped, will stand and resist heat. Growth lax bush. Pennisi – American – 1970 – A.F.S. No. 892.

*Joy Biolby. Double. Creamy-white tube (R.H.S. 55C) longish, striped with neyron-rose ⅜ in by ³⁄₁₆ in. Sepals are broad, white flushed neyron-rose on top, neyron-rose and tipped green underneath, curling over tube with maturity 1½ in by ¾. Corolla white tipped neyron-rose (R.H.S. 55C). Large blooms flared with skirt with many petaloids, free flowering for large double, almost identical to The Aristocrat not as full but richer in colour, lasts longer and flowers earlier. Neyron-rose filaments, rose-Bengal anthers, neyron-rose pistil and amber-yellow stigma. Mid-green (R.H.S. 137D) foliage with ovate shaped leaves 2⅝ by 1¾ in. Growth lax upright or stiff trailer, self-branching and short-jointed very suitable for basket or tall types of training, very fast grower and elegant! Excellent for cut bloom classes. Raised in the vicinity of Hull, Yorkshire, and introduced by C. and J. Akers of Fountains, Ripon, in 1983.

Swingtime × Blush O' Dawn. Bielby – British – 1982.

Joyce. Semi-double. Tube and long sepals rose-pink; corolla pink. Large flowers and fairly free. Growth trailer. Brand – American – 1949 – A.F.S. No. 48.

Joy Patmore. Single. Short white tube, pure waxy-white sepals, spreading and upturned, reverse side white with a faint pink reflection from the corolla. Corolla, startling shade of rich carmine difficult to describe. Medium sized flowers, very free, when flower is fully open the white centre is most attractive. Growth upright and bushy, easy grower, lovely in every way, the feature of this cultivar is the clear cut colouring, one that will endure for years to come. Turner, E.T. – British – 1961.

Joy Patmore

Joy Patmore – Lye's Excelsior. To distinguish between these two cultivars see Lye's Excelsior – Joy Patmore.

Jubie-Lin. Double. Red tube, long, wide spreading sepals brightest red; corolla deepest purple. Extremely large blooms and fairly free for size. Raiser may exaggerate, but describes the unusual blooms as being the size of tea cups. Bright green foliage. Growth trailer, vigorous and self-branching. Copley Gardens – American – 1964 – A.F.S. No. 616.

Jubilee. Double. Tube and sepals red, corolla rosy-mauve. Growth small upright bush. Sport of Phenomenal and located at the Melbourne Botanic Gardens in Australia in 1888. Still listed and grown in Australia. Introducer unknown – Australian – 1888.

Jubilee. Single. White and red. Lye – British – 1897.

Jubilee. Double. White tube, long spreading white sepals; corolla bright red, petals edged dark Tyrian-rose, fading to lighter shade at base. Large flowers, free for size. Growth strong, upright bush. Reiter – American – 1953 – A.F.S. No. 193.

Jubilee Queen. Single. Tube and sepals creamy-white; corolla reddish-salmon. Medium sized flowers, very free. Growth upright, bushy and vigorous. Raiser unknown – American – Date unknown.

Judith Alison Castle. Single. Creamy-white tube with pink flush; sepals creamy-white, tipped green, reflex to the tube, medium size. Corolla blue (R.H.S. 88B) soft pink at base. Small flowers, very free flowering, petaloids are small and folded on the outside of petals, rounded on the inside, stamens red (R.H.S. 61B) and the style is cream. Medium sized foliage with medium green leaves. Growth medium upright and bushy, makes excellent bush, will take full sun, but best colour develops in shade. Tested for 5 years in vicinity of

Preston, North England before release. Dorothea Flower × Hawkshead. Thornley – British – 1982 – A.F.S. No. 1675.

Judy. Single. Dark pink to rose tube, rose sepals; corolla deep orchid-rose. Medium-sized flowers giving the effect of warm glow. Foliage is variegated with shades of green, white and yellow which is the primary difference of this sport with its original. Growth natural trailer, tested for three years at Huntington Park and Fort Bragg, California before release. Sport from Anapola. Introduced by Fuchsiarama of Fort Bragg. Weaver – American – 1977 – A.F.S. No. 1431.

Jules Daloges. Double. Tube scarlet, sepals scarlet turning right back to reveal corolla; corolla rich bluish-violet. Large blooms, full and free. Growth upright and bushy, an old cultivar and still a favourite with many growers. Lemoine – French – 1907.

Jules Ferry. Single. Red and violet. Lemoine – French – 1881.

Jules Janin. Lemoine – French – 1866.

Jules Noriac. Lemoine – French – 1880.

Julia. Double. Red tube, long and curling sepals, red. Corolla blackish-purple. Very large blooms and free for size, heat resistant. Growth lax bush or trailer. Gorman – American – 1970 – A.F.S. No. 929.

Julia Ditrich. Double. Tube and sepals cream, flushed pink tipped green. Corolla lavender tinged with pink. Introducer describes it as a self. Medium sized blooms. One of the few Australian introductions. Sport of City of Pacifica. Casey – Australian – 1972.

Julie Horton. Semi-double. Pink tube, long pink sepals, tipped green; corolla pink with wide overlapping petals. Largish flowers, free and long lasting. Dark green leathery foliage. Growth trailer. A real beauty. Gagnon – American – 1962 – A.F.S. No. 511.

Julienne de Mahon. Coene – Belgian – 1853.

Juliette Adams. Double. Red and white. Lemoine – French – 1909.

Julius. Single. Tube and sepals scarlet; corolla blue ageing to lavender-blue with maturity. Medium sized flowers, very free and early. Growth medium bush, upright. Spackman – American – 1937.

Jumbo. Double. Thin tube, cardinal-red (R.H.S. 53C), long cardinal-red sepals, finely striped darker red on outside. Long and full corolla, white, flushed crimson at base and veined crimson. Very large blooms, buds 3½ to 4 in long, early, prolific, and fast growing, best grown from cuttings each year, red stamens. Growth natural trailer, self-branching excellent basket cultivar, tested for 6 years in the Derby vicinity before release. Handley – British – 1976 – A.F.S. No. 1368.

Jumbo Blue. Double. Rose-red tube, sepals bright rose-red outside, crepe inside, Corolla lavender-blue, growth upright, stiff and bushy. Unregistered American cultivar with little information. Raiser and date unknown – ca 1960.

June Bagley. Single. Creamy-white tube, sepals light pink topside, pale pink underside, tipped green and held almost horizontal. Corolla rosy-pink, pale pink pistil with creamy-white stigma. Medium-sized flowers, sister seedling of Carol Roe which has almost the same flowers except it has longer and thinner tube with lighter colouring in the flowers. Both show the colouring of both parents. Small light green foliage, growth upright and bushy, very attractive with masses of both flowers and buds. First appeared at the Nottingham and Birmingham Shows of 1976. Eleanor Leytham × Pink Darling. Roe – British – 1976.

June Bride. Single. Tube and sepals pale rose; corolla dark rose. Medium sized flowers and very free. Growth upright bush, vigorous, Raiser unknown – American – Date unknown.

June Carolyn. Single. Tube and sepals, orange-pink, tipped green; corolla coral blended with carmine. Largish flowers, long and free, light green foliage. Growth tall upright and vigorous. Feature of this cultivar is the most unusual colouring inherited from one of its parents. California × Aurora Borealis. Evans and Reeves – American – 1938.

June Elizabeth. Single. Long trumpet shaped red tube, long pointed sepals also red. Corolla purple, flushed pink at base. Medium sized flowers with red petaloids ⅜ in long with rounded edge which do not always grow inwards, stamens red, tipped yellow. Dark green foliage with deep veins, 2 in long heart shaped when young, oval on maturity. Growth trailer of lax upright, will make good basket, bush or standard, heat tolerant is shaded. Tested for 3 years in the vicinity of Washington, N.E. England before release. Cheseldine – British – 1981 – A.F.S. No. 1610.

*June Gardner.** Single. Neyron-rose tube, sepals neyron-rose on upper surface, tipped green (R.H.S. 55A), carmine-rose (R.H.S. 52C) underneath held at the horizontal and recurved tips 1½ in by ⅞ in. Corolla beetroot-purple shading to rose in centre (R.H.S. 71B/61D) with no fading with maturity, ⅞ in by ⅝ in. Medium sized flowers square shaped without flaring, spiraea-red stamens, carmine-rose pistil and amber-yellow stigma well extended below corolla. Scheelesgreen (R.H.S. 144B) foliage with cordate shaped leaves 2½ in by 1¾ in. Growth lax upright or stiff trailer, suitable for basketwork or standards. This golden leaved cultivar needs early pinching for good basketwork, rather late flowering but extremely strong growth and makes very hard wood. Raised in the vicinity of Hull, Yorkshire. Seedling (Empress of Prussia × Autumnale) × Mrs. W. Rundle. Bielby – British – 1982.

June Manley. Single. Tube and sepals, flesh-pink; corolla dark rose-pink, veined dusky pink. Medium sized blooms and very free, dark green glossy foliage. Growth low bush. Fairclo – American – 1944.

June Prentiss. Semi-double. Tube and sepals baby-pink; corolla pink, veined rose. Largish flowers, free flowering. Growth upright and bushy. Rush – British – 1906.

June Revell. Single. Short thin tube pink, sepals deep rose, long and narrow; corolla mauve, pink base, veined crimson with distinctive purple picotee edge. Medium sized flowers with long overlapping petals, very free, take full sun where they develop best colour. Light yellow-green foliage, growth upright and bushy. Handley – British – 1975 – A.F.S. No. 1274.

*June's Joy.** Double. Short thick tube creamy-white, sepals creamy-white; corolla pink. Medium sized blooms, inherits the good characteristics from its parent Seaforth. Found in the vicinity of

Redruth, Cornwall, growth upright and bushy. Sport of Seaforth. Phillips – British – 1983.

Jungle Night. Double. Tube and sepals, waxy-red; corolla dark violet. Flowers are full and free, medium sized, growth low bush. Fuchsia-La – American – 1960.

Junior Miss. Double. Tube and sepals, deep red; corolla blue-mauve, splashed pink. Medium sized flowers, very free and of good shape. Growth upright and bushy. Hodges – American – 1949.

Juno. Double. Tube and sepals red; corolla lavender-purple. Medium sized flowers, free with rolled back corolla. Growth upright. Hazard and Hazard – American – 1930?

Juno. Single. Tube and sepals white, tipped green; corolla dark red, fading to bright red with maturity. Large foliage, light green. Growth trailer. Kennett – American – 1966 – A.F.S. No. 677.

*juntasensis.** Tube rose to flesh coloured, sepals reddish; no corolla. Very few flowers, borne in terminal clusters. Vine-like shrub growing to two or three feet, usually epiphytic. Kuntze – 1898 – Bolivia.

Jupiter. Single. Tube and sepals red; corolla deep rich-purple. Largish flowers and free. Growth upright bush. Greene – American – Date unknown.

Jupiter Seventy. Single. Tube shell-pink, sepals scarlet, tipped green, long, unswept and distinctive. Corolla crimson, mandarin-red at base of petals. Narrow, bell shaped flowers of medium size, profuse bloomer, little or no fading, very heat resistant. Growth very upright and vigorous, self-branching. Excellent cultivar in every way. B.F.S. Award of Merit 1970. Percy Holmes × San Francisco. Holmes, R. – British – 1970 – A.F.S. No. 1209.

Just Fancy. Double. Tube and sepals, claret-rose; corolla dawn-pink, veined crimson. Flowers very free and of medium size, growth upright. Jones, W. – British – 1960.

Justins Pride. Single. Tube and sepals neyron-rose; corolla deep cerise-pink, almost a cerise-pink self. Medium sized flowers and extremely free. Growth upright and bushy and with normal cultivation is self-branching needing no support, strong upright growth as one would expect with a hardy, excellent cultivar in every way. Raised in the Nottingham vicinity and introduced by George Roe of Nottingham. Empress of Prussia ×. Jones, G. – British – 1974.

*Kaboutertje.** Single. Tube and sepals carmine (R.H.S. 52A/B), corolla pink (R.H.S. 61A/B). Very small flowered cultivar characteristic of Minirose; the name in English means 'Gnome'. The plant and flowers are dwarf in every respect. One of five new introductions by Herman de Graaff in 1983. Raised in the vicinity of Lisse, Netherlands. Minirose × Whiteknights Blush. de Graaff – Dutch – 1983.

Kalang Talinga. Semi-double. Long tube neyron-rose (R.H.S. 55B); carmine (R.H.S. 52B) sepals which reflex towards tube, tipped light green. Corolla magenta (R.H.S. 66A) edged on each petal reddish-purple (R.H.S. 67B). Medium sized flowers, slightly bulbous with slight twirl to each petal. Medium green foliage, leaves cordate with very fine serrations. Growth self-branching natural trailer, makes fine basket with weights, best colour develops in either sun or shade. Tested for 3 years in the vicinity of Worthing, South Coast of England before release. Hobbs, L. – British – 1982 – A.F.S. No. 1677.

Kaleidoscope. Double. Tube and sepals red; corolla various shades of purple to pale-lavender, streaked with red and pink. Very large blooms, fairly free for size, blooms change colour and shape during flowering season, hence the name. Growth upright. Martin – American – 1966 – A.F.S. No. 674.

Karen. Single. Tube and sepals, rosy-red; corolla blue-bird blue. Medium sized blooms, very free, held in pairs well out from branches. Growth medium upright bush. Gadsby – British – A.F.S. No. 966.

***Karen Bielby.** Single. Long thin tube Venetian-pink (R.H.S. 49A) $\frac{3}{5}$in by $\frac{3}{5}$in; carmine-rose sepals, tipped green (R.H.S. 52B/C) held slightly below the horizontal with reflexed tips which twist either way $1\frac{3}{5}$in by $\frac{3}{10}$in. Corolla fuchsia-purple (R.H.S. 67A) quarter flared, 1 in by $\frac{4}{5}$ in. Medium sized flowers bell shaped extremely free flowering in flushes with carmine stamens and pistil, amber-yellow stigma. Mid-green (R.H.S. 137A) foliage and ovate serrated leaves 2 in by $1\frac{1}{10}$in. Growth natural trailer only suitable for basketwork, best characteristic is its extremely free flowering habit. Raised and tested for 4 years in vicinity of Hull, Yorkshire, and introduced by Muncaster Fuchsias of Gainsborough, Lincolnshire, in 1985. Arlington Hall × Lustre. Bielby – British – 1983.

Karen Louise. Double. Tube and sepals pink; corolla pink. Very large blooms for a double, lovely self pink. Growth upright, best as H2. Introduced by C.S. Lockyer in 1978. Holmes, E.M. – British – 1978.

Kari Morton. Double. Short, rose-red tube; broad, rose-red sepals curl completely back with the tips curling again. Corolla rose-pink with rose-red veins darkening at tube. Very large blooms, fluffy, open, many petalled corolla has a layer of two short petals then one long petal repeated around base. Medium foliage with sharply pointed leaves. Growth semi-trailer, will make tall upright with support or good basket with frequent pinching. Copley, R. and J. – American – 1976 – A.F.S. No. 1390.

***Karlsruhe.** Double. Tube and sepals white; corolla cardinal-red. Medium sized free flowering blooms. Growth medium trailer. Gesauseperle × Bernadette. Nutzinger – Austrian – 1967.

Kathleen. Single. Tube and sepals cerise, tipped greenish-yellow; corolla rose-pink. Very small flowers but free. Growth dwarf and upright, very hardy. Wood – British – 1940.

Kathleen. Double. Short red tube, flared red sepals; corolla orange-white. Largish blooms with 18 full petals, no petaloids and fairly free. Growth upright and bushy, makes an excellent standard. Pugh – British – 1974 – A.F.S. No. 1163.

Kathleen Colville. Single. Pale pink tube, long sepals pink veined changing to green at tips. Corolla cyclamen-purple, medium sized flowers, beautiful contrasting colour. Growth upright and bushy, best grown as H2. Introduced by C.S. Lockyer of Bristol in 1981. Colville – British – 1981.

***Kathleen Smith.** Double. Venetian-pink tube, sepals white upper surface, tipped green, rhodamine-pink underneath (R.H.S. 62A) fully recurved $1\frac{1}{5}$in by $\frac{3}{5}$in. Violet (R.H.S. 85A) corolla, maturing to bishop's-violet (R.H.S. 81B) fully flared 1 in by $2\frac{2}{5}$in. Largish blooms bell shaped with flared petaloids violet and rhodamine-pink at base, magenta-rose stamens and fuchsia-purple pistil and stigma. Mid-green foliage (R.H.S. 137C) with ovate shaped leaves 2 in × $1\frac{3}{5}$in. Growth lax upright as stiff trailer, very suitable for hanging pot work, more robust than its appearance, similar in growth to Blush O' Dawn but with reflexed sepals and deeper coloured corolla. Raised in the vicinity of Hull, Yorkshire. Swingtime × Blush O' Dawn. Bielby – British – 1983.

Kathryn Maidment. Single. Rose tube, long sepals folding back to cover tube, rose coloured. Corolla violet with deeper violet edges, petals white in centre with red veins then changing to the violet colour. Medium sized flowers which flare out into saucer shape with maturity, beautiful flowers most unusual, very attractive, something between Citation, Swanley Gem and Mission Bells. Growth upright and vigorous. Awarded B.F.S. Bronze Certificate of Merit posthumously at B.F.S. Reading Show 1980. Creer – British – 1982.

Kathy Gorringe. Semi-double. Pink tube, very long pink sepals; corolla grey-blue turning to soft orchid shades. Largish blooms with wide overlapping petals, fairly free and long lasting, colour combination is clear and outstanding. Growth trailer. Gagnon – American – 1962 – A.F.S. No. 510.

Kathy Louise. Double. Raised in Santa Cruz, California, by the Antonelli Bros in 1963, not to be confused with Kay Louise by Gagnon of the same year. Growth is lax and classified as a trailer in the true sense; large double corolla of a very fine shade of soft rose; as the flower matures the corolla becomes fluffy without fading. The slender, upturned sepals are carmine underneath, with a deep carmine on the outside. The large beautiful blooms are nicely displayed on a vigorous trailing habit, with handsome dark green foliage, medium to small and glossy. Maybe the only fault to be found with Kathy is that being so vigorous, care is needed to prevent damage to the stems, which do tend to become brittle. The cultivar is not an early flowerer, but at its peak during August; grown as H1 blooms could be induced earlier. As it does not break very freely, responds to pinching after two pairs of leaves and then for basket work, after every third pair. Will produce a fine fan trained specimen, but is definitely not suitable for bush training. Will produce exceptionally fine baskets with five or six plants in 15 in basket, greatly admired, although a little 'hunting' may be necessary through the catalogues to locate, this cultivar is a 'winner' and an elegant beauty. Antonelli – American – 1963 – A.F.S. No. 558.

***Kathy's Sparkler.** Double. Short flesh streaked green tube $\frac{1}{2}$in by $\frac{1}{4}$in wide, sepals pale to dark pink, coral pink underneath, held horizontally with recurving tips $1\frac{3}{4}$in by $\frac{7}{8}$in wide. Corolla orchid-blue variegated pink maturing to cyclamen-purple (R.H.S. 74B) $1\frac{1}{4}$in long by $1\frac{1}{2}$in wide. Medium sized blooms square shape, fully flared, short and wide spreading with many petaloids variegated orchid and coral-pink of uneven sizes. Lovely pastel shaded cultivar with pink and white stamens and pistil. Dark green foliage (R.H.S 146A) ovate leaves with acute tips $3\frac{3}{4}$ in long by $2\frac{1}{2}$ in wide. Growth lax upright or stiff trailer, will make good basket with weights or standard; received 1st place award in American seedling class Cerritos Show 1982. Raised and tested for 3 years in vicinity of Oceanside, California, and trademarked in California. Hula Girl × Applause. Stubbs – American – 1983 – A.F.S. No. 1734.

Katie. Single. Tube and sepals, creamy-wax flushed rose, corolla lilac-rose. Medium sized flowers, very free. Growth upright. White Spider × Chillerton Beauty. Thornley – British – 1962.

Katrina. Double. Tube and sepals, very pale pink, with same colouring corolla, almost a self. Medium to large blooms, freely produced, rather similar to Queen of Bath, but better grower. Growth upright and bushy. Holmes, E. – British – 1968.

Kay Louise. Double. Tube and sepals, pale pink; corolla snowy-white. Largish flowers open up very lacy, fairly prolific and showy. Small dark green foliage, growth lax bush or trailer. Not to be confused with Kathy Louise. Gagnon – American – 1963 – A.F.S. No. 555.

Keepsake. Double. Pale carmine tube, sepals are short and broad, white above, flushed pink underneath. Corolla dianthus-purple, medium sized blooms with four centre petals perfectly cupped and surrounded by many petals of same colouring as the corolla. Light green foliage, growth upright bush, prone to damping off. Kennett – American – 1961 – A.F.S. No. 477.

Kegworth Beauty. Single. Long white tube, sepals waxy-white, short. Corolla amaranth-rose. Small flowers, free bloomer for long periods. Growth medium upright, bushy and short-jointed. Smith, H.–Pacey – British – 1974 – A.F.S. No. 1226.

Kegworth Carnival. Double. Tube and sepals white and fairly long; shortish corolla Tyrian-purple passing to rose-Bengal. Medium sized blooms, growth lax bush, will trail for basketwork. Almost identical to Duchess of Albany except double flower as opposed to single. K.C. has thicker and shorter tube, sepals wider and longer, recurved below horizontal but colouring identical. D. of A. considered much the superior. Introduced by R. Pacey in 1979. Smith, H. – British – 1978.

Kegworth Delight. Double. Tube and broad short petals are white flushed with carmine and tipped green. Corolla Tyrian-purple, flushed white at base. Medium sized blooms with short petalled corolla, another very interesting cultivar from the Smith 'stable'. Growth vigorous upright bush. Introduced by R. and J. Pacey Nurseries in 1980. Smith, H. – British – 1980.

Kegworth Supreme. Single. Tube and sepals empire-rose, sepals are darker underneath; corolla fuchsia-purple. Very dark foliage, compact upright growth and bushy. Identical to Barbara except for the smaller flowers. Introduced by R. Pacey in 1979. Smith, H. – British – 1978.

*Kelvin Lloyd Hill. Double. Indian red tube, sepals indian red held horizontally with recurving tips 1 in long by $\frac{1}{2}$ in wide. Corolla wine veined cerise with lilac shading, flushed pink at base $1\frac{1}{4}$ in long by $\frac{1}{2}$ in wide. Small to medium sized blooms barrel shaped and almost fully flared, Indian red stamens and pistil. Pale green foliage

leaves are serrulate with acute tips $2\frac{1}{4}$ in long by $1\frac{1}{4}$ in wide. Growth small upright, will produce a good decorative, prefers full sun, blooms best in bright light, self-branching in second year. Raised and tested for 6 years in vicinity of Colchester, Essex. Unnamed seedling × Igloo Maid. Hill – British – 1983 – A.F.S. No. 1738.

Ken Jennings. Single. Short thick rhodamine-pink tube, rhodamine-pink sepals held horizontally. Corolla Tyrian-purple. Medium sized flower of good substance and quite within the range of exhibition purposes. Growth upright, bushy and strong, will make excellent bedder. Named after a well known B.F.S. personality and author. Raised in the vicinity of Nottingham and one of only two cultivars introduced by Jackson's Nurseries of Tamworth in 1982. Bobby Shaftoe × Santa Barbara (synonymous with Lustre). Roe – British – 1982.

Ken Lewis. Single. White tube with pink veins, white sepals, corolla bright rose. Largish flowers bell shaped, fairly free. Growth trailer. Gagnon – American – 1969 – A.F.S. No. 844.

Kenny Holmes. Single. Long tube pale scarlet (R.H.S. 43D) and thin, horizontal held sepals pale scarlet on outer surface and crepey mandarin-red (R.H.S. 40C) on inside, tipped green. Corolla scarlet (R.H.S. 43C), mandarin-red (R.H.S. 40B) at the base with semi-pleated petals. Medium sized flowers with squarish corolla and long pistil. Medium sized foliage with lanceolate leaves, leaf edge is serrated with pale green veins. Growth self-branching medium upright, but will trail, making good basket with weights, bush, standard or decorative. Will take full sun in the vicinity of Edenbridge, Kent where it was raised and tested for 5 years before release. Holmes, R. – British – 1981 – A.F.S. No. 1644.

Kentish Maid. Single. Tube jasper-red (R.H.S. 39B), narrow at waist; sepals carmine-rose (R.H.S. 52D) on outside, rose-Bengal (R.H.S. 61D) inside with distinctive green tip, long and gracefully curve upwards. Corolla beetroot-purple (R.H.S. 71C), edged Indian-lake (R.H.S. 60A) fading to fuchsia-purple (R.H.S. 67B). Medium sized flowers and free, four distinct well-shaped petals form an oval to oblong corolla, very long rose-Bengal stamens with short anthers, blooms held well out from foliage. Growth medium upright, bushy and self-branching, tested for 5 years in vicinity of South East and West of England before release. Percy Holmes × .Holmes, R. – British – 1976 – A.F.S. No. 1339.

Kents Bank. Single. Tube creamy-white of medium length but narrow, sepals creamy-white, flushed pink, narrow. Corolla cyclamen-pink (R.H.S. 74A), short. Medium-sized flowers, very free with soft pink stamens. Growth natural pendulous, will make good basket or weeping standard. Although raised in 1963 not released or introduced until 1978. Hawkshead × Falling Stars. Thornley – British – 1963 – A.F.S. No. 1467.

Kernan Robson. Double. Short pink tube, pale red sepals lie flat against tube, corolla smoky-red. Large blooms. fairly free, change to rosy-red with maturity. Growth upright and bushy. Tiret – American – 1958 – A.F.S. No. 336.

Kerry Anne. Single. Neyron-rose tube, sepals neyron-rose curving upwards. Corolla aster-violet, slightly paler at base of petals. Medium sized flowers very free with red stamens which stand out in contrast. Growth upright, bushy and short-jointed with the same habit as its parent, could prove to be hardy. Raised in the vicinity of Melton Mowbray and introduced by the raisers R. and J. Pacey in 1981. Seedling of Cloverdale Pearl. Pacey – British – 1981.

Keukenhof. Single. Tube light rose; sepals of the same colouring. Corolla cherry-orange. Medium sized flowers of unusual spidery shape. Growth upright bush, introduced by Wills Fuchsias Ltd. of West Wittering in 1980. de Graaff – Dutch – 1979.

Keystone. Single. Pink tube, sepals pale pink, tipped green, deeper pink underneath. Corolla baby pink, almost a pink self. Medium sized blooms, free and longish. Growth medium upright, bushy. Lost some of its popularity. Haag – American – 1945.

Khada. Single. Tube and sepals, rose-red; corolla white, veined rose. Small flowers, but very prolific, held more erect than horizontal, growth upright and bushy, very compact, needs no staking and a mass of bloom, excellent cultivar for 3½ in pot class. Margaret Roe × Snowcap. Roe – British – 1973.

Khedive. Rozain-Boucharlat – French – 1912.

Killiecrankie. Double. Red and purple. Banks – British – 1867.

killipii. Red tube, red sepals; corolla red, tipped yellowish-green. Free flowering of medium size, borne in terminal racemes. Very tall upright shrub up to 12 to 15 ft in natural habitat. Johnston – 1928 – Columbia and Venezuela.

Kim. Semi-double. Short, thin tube, pale green, lined carmine (R.H.S. 52B); sepals carmine-rose (R.H.S. 52B) on inside, outside is pale green over-laid carmine. Corolla rose-Bengal (R.H.S. 57D), sometimes splashed mandarin-red (R.H.S. 41D), veined Indian-lake (R.H.S. 60B), edged rose-Bengal. Medium sized flowers, loosely formed and flared, pistil shows just below corolla and is shorter than stamens. Growth semi-trailer, will trail with weights, self-branching and bushy, good for most types of training, excellent as small standard or wall basket. Percy Holmes ×. Holmes, R. – British – 1976 – A.F.S. No. 1340.

Kimberly. Semi-double. Long tube and very long, broad sepals, white, flushed pink on underside. Corolla deep blue with phlox-pink marbling. Largish blooms, free, with serrated petals, lovely colour contrast. Growth trailer. Munkner – American – 1963 – A.F.S. No. 565.

Kim Hampson. Semi-double. Thick, flesh-pink tube, sepals candy-pink inside, flesh-pink, tipped green on outside, short, fairly broad, upturned and folding back tight to tube on maturity. Corolla violet, candy-pink petaloids are flushed with violet. Medium sized flowers good colour in both sun and shade, pink stamens and pistil. Growth medium upright, bushy and self-branching, short jointed. Parentage: Swingtime × Prelude (A.F.S. No. 348). Hilton – British – 1976 – A.F.S. No. 1376.

Kim Wright. Double. Long, thin pink, tube, long pink sepals; corolla violet with large pink vein. Largish blooms of carnation form, best colour develops in sun. Deep green foliage, growth medium upright, makes good bush, raised in vicinity of Atherstone, Warwickshire. Pink Flamingo × Liebstraume. Wright, J.A. – British – 1976 – A.F.S. No. 1388.

King Alphonso. Bland – British – 1875.

King Charming. Single. Rose and blue. Turville – British – 1858.

Kingfisher. Double. White tube, sepals white, tipped green, neyron-rose inside which fold back tightly to tube. Corolla aster violet, flushed neyron-rose. Very prolific especially for a double, prefers shade for best results. Raised in the vicinity of Plymouth, England. Hilton – British – 1981.

King George V. Single. Tube pink, sepals rose standing out at the horizontal; corolla lightish purple paler at base, veined rose. Large flowers for a single, similar to Queen Mary but of shorter and more compact growth. Foliage light green with crimson mid-rib. Growth upright and bushy. Raised by Charles J. Howlett in 1911, one of two sister seedlings from Mrs. Marshall named after the reigning monarchs of the time. In 1912 Mr. Howlett was commanded by their Majesties to go to Windsor to present a plant of each cultivar. It is said that they flourished 'in the corridor' for many years. Thought to be out of cultivation but recently traced to Moss Lane Nursery of Woolston, near Warrington. Mrs. Marshall seedling. Howlett – British – 1912.

King of Bath. Double. Pale carmine tube, sepals carmine, corolla rich purple, flushed rose. Largish blooms, very full and free, darkish green foliage. Growth lax upright. Colville – British – Date unknown.

King of Fuchsias. Single. Red and purple. Banks – British – 1863.

King of Hearts. Double. Tube and sepals red, corolla pale lavender with splashes of red, pink and white on outer petals. Large flowers, fairly free. Growth trailer, makes lovely basket. Sport of Queen of Hearts. Fuchsia Forest – American – 1965 – A.F.S. No. 627.

King of Siam. Single. Tube and sepals red; corolla fiery purplish-red. Very large blooms and fairly free. Growth lax bush or trailer. Colville – British – 1965 or Fuchsia-La (R. Walker) – American – 1953.

King of the Doubles. Double. Red and purple. Bland – British – 1867.

King of the Stripes. Single. Red and purple. Banks – British – 1868.

Kingpin. Single. Tube and sepals white, flushed pink; corolla magenta-rose, white at base. Medium sized flowers, growth upright and bushy. Jones – British – 1962.

King Size. Double. Reddish tube, upper sepals waxy-white, tipped green, lower surface crepe white, flushed with faint purple. Corolla royal purple centre, outer petals and petaloids white, marbled with various shades of purple. Very large flowers, hence the name, fairly free, good substance and tight. Dark green, glossy foliage. Growth upright. Kennett and Ross – American – 1957 – A.F.S. No. 282.

King's Ransom. Double. White tube; broad recurved granular sepals clear white. Corolla deepest Imperial-purple. Medium sized blooms, very free, globular, strong colour holds up well for a blue. Growth upright bush, vigorous. Schnabel – American – 1954 – A.F.S. No. 195.

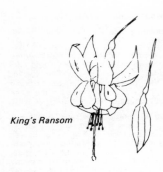

King's Ransom

kirkii (Section IV Skinnera). This is the fifth of the New Zealand species and is less well known than the other four. Prostrate habit of growth and is very similar to *F. procumbens* except the tube is wider, makes good ground cover and in New Zealand used for covering over rocks and scoria walls. Small flowers similar to *F. procumbens* but apart from the tube being wider, the sepals are more oblong and obtuse, style is shorter and the stigma smaller, but has the same growth and habit. Another species very seldom seen in this country not even in Botanical Gardens. Hooker – 1868 – New Zealand.

Kitty O'Day. Double. Tube and sepals, rose-red; corolla white, veined rose red. Very large blooms, fairly free, cupped shape. Growth upright and bushy. Hazard and Hazard – American – Date unknown.

Kiwi. Double. Long white tube, clear white upswept sepals, corolla China-rose with purple. Very large blooms fairly free, growth trailer. Tiret – American – 1966 – A.F.S. No. 687.

Knockout. Double. Long thin tube flesh to white, slightly reflexed, long broad sepals, coral to salmon-pink depending on exposure. Corolla deep magenta-purple with orange markings on outer petals with maturity. Large blooms and free for size, marked colour difference depending on amount of light received, colour more vibrant in sun. Foliage has red veins, leaves 2¾ in long by 2 in ovate shaped with ovate base, obtuse tip and finely serrated margin. Growth trailer will make good basket with weights. Tested for 4 years in vicinity of Fort Bragg, Oxnard and Oceanside, California before release where it will be trademarked. Stubbs – American – 1981 – A.F.S. No. 1622.

*Kocarde. Single. Little known Dutch cultivar raised in the vicinity of Heesde, Netherlands, with the parentage: Kwintet × Cardinal. de Groot – Dutch – 1981.

Kolding Perle. Single. Tube and sepals, waxy-white; corolla pink with cerise and salmon shades. Medium sized flowers, very free, somewhat like Amy Lye. Growth upright bush, vigorous. Originates from Copenhagen. Raiser unknown – Danish – Date unknown.

*Kolding Perle – Lye's Unique. These two waxy-white and salmon-orange cultivars are almost indistinguishable both in colours and habit.

Komeet. Single. Short red tube, red sepals very long; corolla purple changing to red lilac on maturity. Medium-sized flowers with red stamens

and style, medium to dark green foliage, growth upright bush. *F. regia* var. *typica* × Beacon. De Groot – Dutch – 1970.

Komeet Van Halley. Single. White tube rather long and narrow, sepals white with blush pink, long, narrow and curled at tips, tipped green. Corolla deep lilac-pink, lighter at base. Medium-sized flowers with pink stamens and light pink style. Dark green foliage with crimson mid-rib. Growth lax bush or trailer. van Wieringen – Dutch – 1970.

Kon-Tiki. Double. Tube and sepals, pure white; corolla pink-violet. Medium sized blooms and free for size. Growth lax bush, will trail with weights. Tiret – American – 1965 – A.F.S. No. 652.

Koralle. Triphylla single. Long tube, salmon-orange self; short petals. Foliage deep bluish-green, velvety leaves. Growth upright and vigorous, tends to wilt in very strong sun. Received Award of Merit R.H.S. 1929. Also known as Coralle, not very popular in America. *F. triphylla* ×. Bonstedt – German – 1905.

Korean Maid. Double. Red tube, sepals large, bright red, tipped green. Corolla white with red veins and red variegations at base. Large blooms, free for size. Soo Yun – American – 1968 – A.F.S. No. 767.

Kronprinz. Single. Short white tube, white sepals, with blush pink and green tips, deeper pink underneath. Corolla purple, medium-sized flowers with pink stamens and white style. Growth upright and bushy. This cultivar is grown and cultivated in the Netherlands. Raiser and date unknown.

Kuan-Yin. Double. White tube, reflexed sepals, white interlined with pale pink; corolla plum-purple, veined rose, changing to raspberry-rose. Medium sized blooms, fully ruffled, best colour in shade. Light green foliage, growth natural trailer, named for the Chinese Goddess of Mercy. Walker/Fuchsia-La. – American – 1976 – A.F.S. No. 1361.

*Kursal. Double. Tube and sepals white, corolla pale blue. Medium sized blooms, very attractive, very similar to Blush O' Dawn. Growth upright and bushy. Introduced by Rainbow's Fuchsias of Sandon, Essex in 1983. Raiser unknown – ca 1982.

Kwintet. Single. Tube and sepals, rose-pink; corolla rosy-red. Medium sized blooms, very prolific bloomer, rather like Display but with much richer colouring. Growth upright and bushy. van Wieringen – Dutch – 1970.

Kyanos. Single. Red and purple. Rozain-Boucharlat – French – 1911.

*La Belle Valerie. Single. Short tube rose-Bengal ⅓ in long by ¼ in wide, half up 2 in long by ¼ in wide sepals rose-Bengal (R.H.S. 57B) on top, neyron-rose (R.H.S. 58C) underneath, twisted green tips and recurved. Corolla opens lilac-purple (R.H.S. 70A) maturing to imperial-purple (R.H.S. 78A). Largish flowers are quarter flared and bell shaped, very short tube in relation to extremely long sepals, rose-Bengal filaments and anthers, china-rose (R.H.S. 58D) style and stigma. Mid-green (R.H.S. 137C) foliage with 2 in long by 1 in wide lanceolate leaves, serrated edges, acute tips and rounded bases. Growth self-branching lax upright or stiff trailer, will make good decorative or basket with weights, needs careful watering, cold weather hardy to 32°F in Southern England. Raised in the vicinity of Worthing, Sussex. *microphylla* x Preston Guild, sister seedling to Heather. Hobbs, L. – British – 1984 – A.F.S. No. 1775.

La Bergere. Single to semi-double. Tube and sepals white with pink tinge; corolla white with slight pink tinge. Medium sized flowers, growth lax trailer. Submitted in the B.F.S. London Seedling Class 1978, but found little favour with the Floral Committee, too similar to existing cultivars. Introduced by Wills Fuchsia Nurseries in 1979 and 1980. de Graaff – Dutch – 1976.

La Bianca. Single. Tube and sepals white, tipped green, faint green stripe; corolla white, flushed with the faintest pink. Flowers of medium size and fairly free, growth lax upright or semi-trailer. Very popular when first introduced, but with many recent white introductions has lost favour. Tiret – American – 1950 – A.F.S. No. 64.

La Campanella. Semi-double. This delightful cultivar was a chance seedling rather than a deliberate cross, raised and introduced by Blackwells of Swindon in 1968, which they consider to be one of their best of many introductions. Although sometimes classified as a single is definitely a semi-double; the sepals are white, slightly flushed pink, whilst the corolla is a beautiful shade of Imperial-purple and has a delightful colour change to lavender, as the blooms age. This is a very floriferous cultivar, flowers are small, but exceptionally free and profuse. When fully established in a large basket, can lose twenty odd blooms a day and not be noticed, with the quantity still forming and maturing. La Campanella will make an exceptional basket, whether half or full, do not be afraid to use more plants than usual to obtain a show, which cannot help to be admired. The filaments are bright pink and the style pure white; small foliage of medium green colour and does not attract pests. The plant itself is very self-branching and in the early stages

La Campanella

of growth, looks very straggly, weedy and un-fuchsia like; will, however, make a fine plant with little pinching, but responds to heavy pinching, especially for basket work and very suitable for the 3½ in pot classes. Very rapid grower when established and in a normal season, will commence to bloom early July and continue through the summer. The easiest of cultivars to propagate, will make good quarter or half standard and worth considering as an espalier. Blackwell – British – 1968.

Lacédémone. Double. Cerise and white. Lemoine – French – 1911.

Lace Petticoats. Double. Tube and sepals white, topped green; corolla white with the faintest touch of pink at base. Flowers fairly large, very full and free. Darkish green foliage, growth lax upright. Tiret produced many near white cultivars, this one is nearer to white than most, best grown as H1. Tiret – American – 1952 – A.F.S. No. 145.

La Corée. Lemoine – French – 1901.

Laddie. Double. Tube is light carmine, sepals arch back, light carmine with white stripes down middle. Corolla light purple, large blooms and fairly free for size, best colour develops in shade. Large medium green foliage. Growth medium upright and bushy. Originates from the vicinity of Warwickshire. Seedling of Peppermint Stick. Wright, L.A. – British – 1980 – A.F.S. No. 1602.

Ladies Choice. Semi-double. Short white tube, broad, flaring sepals white. Corolla clean orange-rose. Very large foliage, growth upright bush and stiff. Kennett – American – 1959 – A.F.S. No. 399.

Lady. Semi-double. Tube and sepals red; corolla purple with red variegation at base, fading to lighter shade of purple. Medium sized blooms, free, petals protruding at centre. Growth lax bush or trailer. Soo Yun – American – 1968 – A.F.S. No. 764.

Lady Ambersley. Single. Tube and sepals carmine; corolla white. Small flowers, very free. Growth dwarf habit and suitable for rockery, hardy. Introduced by John Smith of Thornton Nurseries 1974. Raiser unknown – British – Date unknown.

Lady Ann. Double. Short tube and broad, spreading sepals white, faintly blushed on underside, tipped green. Corolla purplish-blue marbled phlox-pink. Largish flowers, very free with spreading and curled petals. Growth upright and bushy. Tiret – American – 1953 – A.F.S. No. 155.

Lady Bartle Frere. Semi-double. Cerise and mauve. Williams – British – 1878.

Lady Bath. Double. Tube and sepals flesh-pink, underside cerise; corolla purple, outer petals are splashed cerise. Medium sized blooms, growth lax bush. Longleat Gardens – British – 1966.

Lady Beth. Double. Tube pale rose; sepals palest rose of thick crepe texture; corolla bright violet-blue with phosphorus sheen. Giant blooms, fairly free for size, some of the centre petals roll, giving it the form to resemble an orchid. Growth lax bush or trailer. A.F.S. Cert. of Merit 1961. Martin – American – 1958 – A.F.S. No. 364.

Lady Boothby. Single. Tube and sepals crimson; corolla blackish-purple , veined cerise. Flowers are small but free. Darkish green foliage.

Growth upright and extremely vigorous, suitable for greenhouse climber, hardy in the South and Midlands. The most notable introduction by C.P. Raffill, V.M.H. of Royal Botanic Gardens, Kew. *F. alpestris* × Royal Purple. Submitted by Chingford Nurseries for the R.H.S. Wisley Hardy Trials 1975–78 but received no award. Raffill – British – 1939.

Lady Bower. Double. Tube and sepals, cardinal-red; corolla creamy-white, with outer petaloids heavily flushed crimson. Large blooms and free, growth lax bush or trailer, vigorous. Gadsby – British – 1970 – A.F.S. No. 964.

Lady Claire. Single. Long tube, short sepals and corolla, cerise and orange; flowers short and heavy for type, borne in clusters. Dark, glossy green foliage. Growth upright and vigorous. *F. serratifolia* × . Evans – American – 1934.

Lady C. Sheppard. Single. Pink and purple. Rogers – British – 1845.

*Lady Dorothy. Single. Little known cultivar introduced by Fountains Nurseries near Ripon in 1984. Bright vermilion self and very floriferous. Sport from Beacon with same growth and habit, same coloured foliage but without any serration. Found in 1980 by Don Robinson of Leeds, Yorkshire. Very easy cultivar. Sport of Beacon. Robinson – British – 1980.

Lady Dorothy Neville. Single. Red and purple. Williams – British – 1873.

*Lady Edwards. Double. Tube striped pink and white, sepals pink outside, rose coloured underneath, tipped white. Corolla royal-purple with white shading at base of petals. Good sized blooms of beautiful shape and fairly free flowering for a double. Growth upright and bushy. Raised in the vicinity of Banstead, Surrey, and introduced by Woodbridge Nurseries of Hounslow, Middlesex, in 1984. Hobson – British – 1984.

Lady Franklyn. Single. White and rose. Smith – British – 1859.

Lady Heytesbury. Single. Tube and sepals, waxy-white; corolla deep rose to rose. medium sized flowers and free. Growth upright and bushy. Good old cultivar still in cultivation. Wheeler – British – 1866.

Lady Isobel Barnett. Single. Probably the best introduction raised by the prolific hybridiser Clifford Gadsby of Derby. In the post war years, hybridising was left mainly to the Americans, Cliff Gadsby in recent years is one of the British growers to even out the balance, from his 'stable', has during the early 70s registered no less than 50 cultivars with the American Fuchsia Society. Originally known as Seedling No. 145 was raised in 1968, the same year as his fine cultivar Icecap, but not registered until 1971 under No. 978. This outstanding cultivar was a cross, first between Upward Look and Caroline, which produced Derby Belle and then a cross between Caroline and Derby Belle and is a sister seedling to Margaret Roe. Accepting Cliff is a prolific breeder of cultivars, he describes his introductions as 'special strain bred for freedom and prominence of bloom', this statement is certainly true in Lady Isobel Barnett. A single cultivar, sepals and tube are rosy-red, and the open type corolla where the blood of Caroline is detected, is rose-purple, with edges of flushed Imperial-purple. Blooms are of smallish to medium size, growth of plant is a medium size bush and upright, which carries its flowers semi-erect, with eight or more blooms from the leaf axils, in a similar manner to that fine hardy cultivar, Empress of Prussia. Lady Isobel Barnett is one of the most prolific bloomers to date, will stand moderate sun, best grown as H2, but will produce its best colour with cover or protection of glass, as the delicate pastel shaded flowers are more pronounced in full sunlight or in the open border. In the border the strain of Upward Look can be detected with the blooms carried more erect and with similar colouring. Will make a sizeable plant in its first year, responds to moderate pinching, likes its feed and plenty of it, whilst it will flower to the extent of nearly smothering its foliage, especially if potbound. Excels as a bush plant, magnificent trained as a conical and good specimens can be breathtaking, always to be seen on the showbench, especially in 3½ in pot classes. Caroline × Derby Belle. Gadsby – British – 1968 – A.F.S. No. 978.

Lady Julia. Single. White and crimson. Epps – British – 1846.

Lady Kathleen Spence. Single. Tube whitish pale pink, sepals amaranth-rose underneath, whitish-rose on top, thin, long, sweeping low from the horizontal but standing out well. Corolla delicate lavender shade, fading to light lilac. Medium sized flowers, free, the delicate lavender colour contrasts markedly with the dark anthers, best colour in shade. Growth upright and bushy, originally known as Seedling 244F, B.F.S. Certificate of Preliminary Acceptance, Manchester 1974. The first to receive the B.F.S. Gold Certificate of Merit awarded at the B.F.S. Manchester Show 1976. Bobby Shaftoe × Schneewittchen. Ryle – British – 1974 – A.F.S. No. 1248.

Lady Kathleen Spence–Jane Lye. For further information distinguishing between these two cultivars see Jane Lye–Kathleen Spence.

Lady La Tasha. Double. Short, medium thick crimson tube ½ in long, ¼ in wide; crimson sepals 2¼ in long, ⅜ in wide wide with smooth top and crepe underside, curl up to stem. Corolla violet fading to rose-Bengal, veined crimson and fading to rose-Bengal at base. Largish blooms 1¾ in long, 3 in wide petals, open and flared with many petaloids, streaked crimson, the main four petals scalloped at tips, pistil is red and very long 3 in. Large foliage 2½ in long, 1¾ in wide. Growth lax upright, self-branching will trail with weights. Tested and raised in vicinity of Sebastopol, California, before release. Soo Yun Field – American – 1979 – A.F.S. No. 1492.

Lady Lilian Cash. Double. White tube, sepals long, pinkish-white. Corolla roseine-purple with serrated edges and centres of petals white. Large blooms and free, heat resistant. Growth trailer, produces good basket. Pennisi – American – 1971 – A.F.S. No. 1017.

Lady Magenta. Double. Long tube off-white sepals curl to tube, white on topside with the white underside heavily brushed roseine purple. Corolla magenta brushed with pale roseine purple. Large blooms very full double with skirted effect and serrated petal edges, pale magenta stamens and pistil. Foliage pale lime to lemon as plant matures, serrated leaves and magenta veined. Growth natural trailer, tested for 5 years in Sebastopol, California before release. Soo Yun Field – American – 1977 – A.F.S. No. 1406.

Lady of the Lake. Harrison – British – 1845.

'Lady Patricia Mountbatten. Single. Advance information before release. The raiser, Dave Clark of Merseyside, predicts this cultivar will overtake Border Queen upon release. Considered to be much larger and with a lighter colouring than Lady Kathleen Spence. Requires another year's test on the showbench before releasing to Travis of Preston and Porter of Southport in 1985. Named after the daughter of the late Lord Mountbatten. Eden Lady (sister seedling of Border Queen) × Lady Kathleen Spence. Clark, D. – British – 1985.

'Lady Plymouth. Double. Short empire-rose tube, sepals rhodamine-pink. Corolla phlox-pink. Medium sized blooms and very free flowering for double, beautiful colouring. Growth medium upright, bushy. Raised in the vicinity of Plymouth, Devon. Pink Galore × Drake 400. Hilton – British – 1984.

Lady Ramsay. Single. Short flesh-pink tube, flesh-pink sepals reflex with maturity. Corolla violet and bell shaped. Medium sized flowers very similar to Border Queen but superior and much darker with shorter tube, a real eye catcher and shown with more than considerable interest for first time at B.F.S. London Show 1981. Two or three flowers in each leaf node. Moderate sized foliage with matt surface. Growth self-branching and short jointed medium upright, will make good basket, bush on standard and destined for the showbench. Tested for 2 years in the vicinity of Ipswich, England, before release. Goulding – British – 1981 – A.F.S. No. 1647.

Lady Ransome. Semi-double. Tube and sepals white, corolla white, slightly pink at base. Medium sized blooms and free, growth upright and bushy, heat tolerant. Gorman – American – 1970 – A.F.S. No. 925.

'Lady Rebecca. Double. Very short pink tube, sepals pink broad and creped on underside. Corolla bluish-lilac, heavily veined pink at base of petals. Medium sized blooms, very nice colours combination and free flowering for size of bloom. Mid-green foliage with serrated leaves of medium size. Growth upright, strong and vigorous. H2. Raised and tested in the vicinity of Midford near Bath in Avon and introduced by C.S. Lockyer of Bristol in 1983. Holmes, E. – British – 1983.

Lady Thumb. Semi-double. Tube and sepals, reddish-light carmine, corolla white, slightly veined carmine. Very small flowers, extremely free which tend to drop rather quickly like its parent Tom Thumb. Very small foliage, growth dwarf, upright and hardy. Excellent cultivar for 3½ in pot classes. Accepted by the B.F.S. as showbench hardy. Submitted by Wills Nurseries Ltd and L.R. Russell Ltd for R.H.S. Wisley Hardy Trials 1975–78 and received First Class Certificate. Sport of Tom Thumb. Roe – British – 1966.

Lady Waterloo. Double. Red and purple. Williams – British – 1875.

Lady W. Powlett. Single. Pink and scarlet. Tiley – British – 1847.

La Favourite. Single. Red and purple. Banks – British – 1864.

La Fayette. Lemoine – French – 1896.

La Fiesta. Double. White tube, sepals white, blending into outer petals and petaloids with purple. Corolla light dianthus-purple, flowers fairly large and free, petaloids flare well at flower ma-

turity. Growth trailer and self-branching, very coarse habit and leaves a lot to be desired. Kennett – American – 1962 – A.F.S. No. 535.

La France. Double. Tube and sepals, rich scarlet; corolla rich violet-purple. Very full flowers, large and fairly free. Growth upright and bushy, strong grower. Old cultivar, still grown today for its brilliant colouring. Lemoine – French – 1885.

Laga. Single. Tube and sepals red with white corolla. Small flowers held almost erect very similar in habit to Khada. Growth upright, compact, and vigorous, considered an improvement upon Khada. Introduced by High Trees Nurseries of Reigate. Felix – Dutch – 1978.

La Honda. Semi-double. Tube and sepals, dark pink; corolla rose-purple. Flowers fairly large and free, unusual as it tends to produce six sepals. Growth upright and vigorous up to 8 ft in California. Chiles – American – 1953 – A.F.S. No. 164.

Laing's Hybrid. Single. Red self. From information gathered from *The Garden* Vol IX, page 607, dated 1876 and *The Garden*, Vol XI, page 98, dated 1877, it would appear that Laing's Hybrid and Earl of Beaconsfield are synonymous. The cross being *F. fulgens* and Perfection (Banks). Laing – British – 1873.

La Jungfrau. Lemoine – French – 1875.

Lakeland Princess. Single. Short carmine tube, fully recurving sepals are white, flushed carmine at outside base. Corolla spectrum-violet and white at base of each petal. Medium sized flowers, very free, bright and attractive with bright carmine stamens. Medium sized foliage, leaves ovate with obtuse leaf tips. Growth medium upright, will make good bush. Best colours develops in shade, named for Princess Grace of Monaco on the occasion of her visit to the 1981 Lakeland Show. Tested for 3 years in the vicinity of Carlisle, North West England before release. Introduced by Fuchsiavale Nurseries of Kidderminster in 1981. Eden Lady × Norman Mitchinson. Mitchinson – British – 1981 – A.F.S. No. 1653.

Lakeside. Single. Delightful cultivar raised and introduced by Alf. Thornley of Preston in 1968. The tube and sepals are reddish-pink with green tips, whilst the corolla is bluish-violet, veined bright pink and as the blooms mature, fade to lilac. Filament and style are pink, plant has attractive foliage of medium green with small leaves. Growth although quoted in some catalogues as bushy, is definitely of cascade habit and doubtful whether it could ever make a good bush. Lakeside is extremely vigorous and self-branching and would make a fine quarter or half standard. It is one of the earliest to flower, possible by mid June, remains in bloom until late autumn, one of the few cultivars which will shed both its flowers and seed pods, thereby needing little attention. A cultivar that with good cultivation will show more flowers than foliage, responds with an abundance of flower with frequent stopping, in fact, a pair of shears could be used to either trim or prune and is equally at home, both under glass or out of doors. The raiser has given us many good cultivars. Lakeside is probably his best, although it was almost rejected in its infancy owing to suspected, weak constitution, but now sought after by exhibitors and always found amongst the basket winners and shows. A little beauty! Parentage unknown but raiser considers it could have Lynette blood as it was a chance seedling found

growing at the foot of a Lynette plant, Thornley
– British – 1967 – A.F.S. No. 1062.

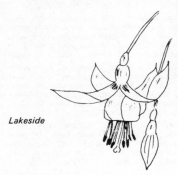

Lakeside

Lakewood. Double. Tube and sepals, turkey-red; corolla violet-blue, variegated lavender and pink. Large blooms and fairly free, growth upright. Fairclo – American – 1954.

Laleham Lass. Single. Tube ivory, sepals ivory flushed pink, underside deeper pink, tipped green. Corolla is a beautiful shade of orange and pink. Foliage dark green, growth lax bush, short jointed and hardy. The first of two cultivars raised by a very successful exhibitor during the 1970's and introduced by D. Stilwell in 1978. Jack Acland × Liebreiz. Dyos – British – 1978.

Lamarck. Lemoine – French – 1880.

Lamartine. Lemoine – French – 1858.

Lameunais. Double. Carmine and white. Lemoine – French – 1883.

L'Amoureuse. Double. Cerise and white. Lemoine – French – 1913.

lampadaria. A new species of fuchsia from Northern Colombia found by John Wright of Reading University. Among fuchsia seed received from South America was a collection by an entomologist, Mike Adams, in Santa Marta, Northern Colombia. One packet contained seeds which grew into a species unlike any previously described, although it showed affinities with some others in Section Fuchsia (Eufuchsia Munz) such as *F. magdalenae* Munz.

Its habit of growth suggests that in the wild it scrambles through other shrubs and it is difficult to train it into a tidy pot plant.

The flowers are long (tube up to 2 in wide at the mouth) and very firm textured. They are bright flame colour (R.H.S. 43A) with a purple shading at the base of the tube. This suggested the specific name *lampadarius*, Latin for torch-bearer, since, held erect, they resemble Olympic torches. The leaves are usually three to a node and large and glossy (up to 2⅝ in × ½ in) with purple petioles (leaf stalk) and veins. The pedicels (flower stalks) and young branches are also purple. A scientific description has appeared in *J. Linnaean Soc., London*, 1978.

La Nation. Double. Red and purple. Lemoine – French – 1877.

*****Lancelot.** Single. Short red tube, sepals red, reflexed with recurving tips. Corolla white with limited red veining. Largish flowers flaring and cup-shaped bell, very free and very similar to Citation

but considered better, destined for the show-bench. First shown at B.F.S. London Show 1982 with great success, one of ten seedlings introduced in 1983 by Goulding. Foliage mid-green of average size. Growth tall upright, self-branching with numerous side shoots, can be trained to most tall types of training. Raised and tested for 2 years in the vicinity of Ipswich, East of England, and introduced by B. and H.M. Baker of Halstead, Essex, in 1983. Goulding – British – 1983 – A.F.S. No. 1728.

Landauer Schonheit. Double. Tube and sepals cherry-red; corolla purple-blue. Medium-sized blooms with extremely rich colouring, growth upright and bushy, excellent as pot plant. El Camino × Winston Churchill. Nutzinger – Austrian – 1968.

La Neige. Double. Red and white. Lemoine – French – 1873.

La Neige. Double. Tube and sepals white, tipped green, with faint touch of pink underneath. Corolla white. Medium sized blooms and free, growth lax bush or trailer. Tiret – American – 1965 – A.F.S. No. 650.

Langley Ford. No other details available other than the parentage: Coxeen × Mrs. Lawrence Lyon. Ryle – British – 1975.

Lansdowne. Single. Red and purple. Lemoine – French – 1895.

La Paloma. Single. Tube and sepals pink; corolla white, faintly veined pink. Medium sized flowers and free, growth vigorous upright. Niederholzer – American – 1940.

La Petite. Semi-double. Short tube pink, fades into pale pink sepals, tipped green. Corolla phlox-pink. Medium sized blooms and free, very showy. Growth trailer. Paskesen – American – A.F.S. No. 662.

La Pompadour. Single to semi-double. Red and purple. Lemoine – French – 1894.

La Porte. Double. Tube and sepals smoky burgundy. Corolla of the same colour. Growth upright and strong grower. Introduced by C.S. Lockyer (Fuchsias), of Bristol, 1979. Holmes, Mrs. E. – British – 1979.

La Quinta. Double. Tube and sepals white; corolla deep purple. Large flowers, fairly free. Growth trailer. Tiret – American – 1970 – A.F.S. No. 899.

La Quintinye. Lemoine – French – 1889.

L'Arlésienne. Semi-double. Tube and long recurving sepals pale pink, tipped green; corolla white, veined pink ageing to palest pink. Long flowers, beautifully shaped, very free, lightish green foliage. Growth upright and bushy, an aristocratic young lady, best grown as H1. Colville – British – 1968.

La Rosita. Double. Tube and recurved sepals, rose-pink; corolla orchid-pink. Medium sized blooms, free, colouring depends upon the extent of light or shade. Growth medium upright. Erickson-Lewis – American – 1959 – A.F.S. No. 406.

Lassie. Double. Short tube, bright crimson, very wide sepals bright crimson, full of substance, glossy above, crepe below, held in about horizontal position. Corolla snowy-white, flowers rather large, very full and compact, all petals about the same length and free. Dark green, glossy foliage, slightly cupped. Considered to be an improvement upon Swingtime, growth natural trailer or lax bush, ideal for both basketwork and standard, best grown as H1. Swingtime×. Travis, S. – British – 1959 – A.F.S. No. 1152.

Late Perfection. Synonymous with Gartenmeister Bonstedt.

La Traviata. Single. Red and purple. Banks – British – 1865.

La Traviata. Double. Tube and sepals, pillar box-red; corolla pale strawberry-pink, veined and marked rose. Medium sized flowers and free. Growth upright and bushy. Blackwell – British – 1967.

Laura. Single. Pink and pale purple. Youell – British – 1846.

Laura. Single. White tube, neyron-rose sepals; corolla fuchsia pink. Long flowers and fairly free, growth upright. Niederholzer – American – 1946.

Laura. Double. Tube and sepals red; corolla sky-blue fading to lavender. Large flowers fairly free, growth lax bush or trailer. A.F.S. Cert. of Merit 1971. Martin – American – 1968 – A.F.S. No. 774.

Laura Sutter. Single. Tube and upturned sepals, pale rose; corolla clear pale silver-blue. Medium sized flowers, bell shaped and free, heat tolerant. Growth lax bush or trailer. Nessier – American – 1950 – A.F.S. No. 122.

Laurent Palmaert. Double. Red and white. Cornelissen – Belgian – 1864.

Laurie. Double. Tube and long, slender sepals, pale pink, tipped green; corolla soft rose and rhodamine-pink. Large blooms, fairly free, heavily petaled at the base with four large petals protruding from centre. Lush dark green foliage, growth trailer, strong and vigorous. A.F.S. Cert. of Merit 1967. Antonelli – American – 1963 – A.F.S. No. 557.

Lavender and Old Lace. Single. Tube and sepals pink; corolla light lavender. Medium sized flowers and free, growth upright and bushy. Hazard and Hazard – American – Date unknown.

Lavender Basket. Double. Tube and sepals red; corolla rosy-mauve. Medium sized blooms and free, growth trailer. Hazard and Hazard – American – Date unknown.

Lavender Beauty. Semi-double. Tube and sepals scarlet; corolla beautiful shade of clear lavender. Largish blooms and very free. Growth medium upright bush. Raiser unknown – American – Date unknown.

Lavender Blue. Single. Tube and sepals pale pink; corolla blue, fading to lavender. Medium sized flowers and very free. Pale green foliage, most attractive, growth upright and bushy, strong, but dainty branching habit, height 1½ to 2 ft. Hardy in Southern England, raised in the Scilly Isles. Tabraham – British – 1974.

Lavender Girl. Double. Tube and sepals pale rose-pink, corolla lavender-orchid. Medium sized blooms. Little known cultivar exclusive to the North of England. Listed and introduced by Penhall's Fuchsia Deeside Gardens of Shaw. Oldham in the 1970s. Raiser unknown – British – ca 1970s.

Lavender Kate. Double. Tube and sepals pink; corolla lavender-blue. Largish flowers and fairly free upright and bushy. Holmes, E. – British – 1970.

Lavender Lace. Single. Short white tube, pink sepals turn flat between petals. Corolla light lavender turns darker with maturity. Miniature flowers of unusual colouring, notched petals, white pistil. Foliage small with serrated leaves. Growth natural trailer, self-branching, will make good basket, tested for 2 years at Fort Bragg, California before release. Francesca – American – 1977 – A.F.S. No. 1421.

Lavender Lady. Double. Tube and sepals pale pink; corolla pale pink and lavender. Medium sized blooms, very free for double, very lovely colouring. Growth upright and bushy, introduced by R. Winkley of Birmingham, not to be confused with Pugh's cultivar dated 1974. Senior – British – 1972.

Lavender Lady. Single. Short red tube, sepals shaded red on top, bottom frosted red, recurving on to tube. Corolla purple-violet with rays of red-purple. Flowers medium sized, free, with long pistil, best colour in shade. Growth medium upright to lax bush. Pugh – British – 1974 – A.F.S. No. 1164.

Laylee. Double. Tube and sepals, light pink, sepals frosted underneath; corolla white. Large flowers, fairly free and long, growth trailer. Wilson – American – 1959 – A.F.S. No. 414.

Lazy Lady. Semi-double. Tube light red, sepals extra long and curly, light red. Corolla medium blue, shading to light blue near sepals. Medium sized blooms, free and continue to flower in a lazy lady fashion, growth trailer. Martin – American – 1960 – A.F.S. No. 444.

Leading Lady. Double. Tube and sepals, flesh-pink; corolla violet-purple. Flowers are large and free, growth upright and sturdy. Jones, W. – British – 1960.

Leah. Single. White and purple. Bull – British – 1871.

Le Berger. Single. White tube, sepals white with faint trace of pink tracing. Corolla white, medium sized flowers and very floriferous. Growth trailer, very suitable for basket work. Introduced by Wills Fuchsia Nurseries of Sussex in 1979. La Campanella×.de Graaff – Dutch – 1976.

Le Chinois. Salter – British and French – 1841.

Le Chinois. Single. White and violet. Rendatler – Continental – 1870.

*Lechlade Apache. Single. Long thin tube, red 1⅛ in long (R.H.S. 52A). Fully recurved sepals red (R.H.S. 52A) ½ in by ⅛ in. Red corolla (R.H.S. 52A) with pink filaments, cream anther, red pistil and white stigma, ½ in by ¼ in. Small flowers in florescence terminal. Foliage medium green (R.H.S. 137B) with acuminate and obtuse leaves 5 in by 2½ in and maroon petiole and stems. Growth is medium upright, good for bush or standard, heat tolerant prefers overhead filtered light. New interspecific cross with terminal raceme flowers similar to both parents, but not so rampant as F. boliviana or climbing like F. simplicicaulis. Tested for 3 years under glass in the vicinity of Reading, hardy to 40°F. F. simplicicaulis × F. boliviana. Wright, J.O. – British – 1984 – A.F.S. No. 1788.

*Lechlade Chinaman. Single. A most unusual species hybrid with small amber flowers and trailing habit suitable for basketwork. Raised in the vicinity of Reading, Berkshire, and introduced by Lechlade Fuchsia Nursery in 1984. F. splendens × F. procumbens. Wright, J.O. – British – ca 1983.

***Lechlade Debutante.** Single. Long cylindrical tube clear pink (R.H.S. 55D) greenish-brown at base (R.H.S. 146C) $1\frac{1}{5}$in by $\frac{1}{5}$in. Sepals held at horizontal with reflexed tips, pale pink (R.H.S. 55D) tipped green $\frac{2}{5}$in by $\frac{1}{5}$in. Corolla clear pink (R.H.S. 55B) flowers held horizontally and axillary $\frac{2}{5}$in by $\frac{2}{5}$in. Filaments pale pink, cream anthers, pink pistil and pink stigma. Green (R.H.S. 143B) foliage paler green underneath (R.H.S. 138B) ovate leaves with little serration $3\frac{1}{2}$in by $1\frac{2}{5}$in. Growth tall upright over 6 ft, good for pyramid and most types of tall training, prefers overhead filtered light. Tested for 3 years under glass in vicinity of Reading. A new interspecific cross with flowers of a clear pink, very floriferous and comparable to birthday cake candles. *F. paniculata* × *F. lampadaria.* Wright, J.O. – British – 1984 – A.F.S. No. 1789.

***Lechlade Fire-Eater.** Triphylla single. Long crimson like (R.H.S. 50A) tube $1\frac{1}{2}$in by $\frac{1}{10}$ to $\frac{3}{10}$in. Sepals held below horizontal with recurved tips, crimson like (R.H.S. 50A) tipped green on upper surface, salmon (R.H.S. 38A) underneath $\frac{1}{2}$in by $\frac{1}{4}$in. Corolla brilliant orange (R.H.S. 32A) $\frac{1}{4}$in by $\frac{1}{4}$in with red filaments, cream anthers, red pistil and pink stigma. Dark olive green (R.H.S. 137A) foliage, reddish-purple underside obovate leaves 4 in by $1\frac{3}{4}$in with velvety look of triphylla hybrid. Growth lax upright, heat tolerant prefers overhead filtered light. Tested for 3 years under glass in vicinity of Reading. The second true triphylla to be bred in Britain. A new interspecific cross with the dark *F. triphylla* foliage and contrasting crimson and orange colouring of *F. denticulata. F. triphylla* × *F. denticulata.* Wright, J.O. – British – 1984 – A.F.S. No. 1790.

***Lechlade Gordon.** Single. Very recent species hybrid with an unusual crossing of *F. arborescens* × *F. paniculata*. Introduced by Muncaster Fuchsias of Gainsborough, Lincolnshire, in 1985. Wright, J.O. – British – 1985.

***Lechlade Potentate.** Single. Long tube $1\frac{1}{5}$in by $\frac{1}{4}$in upper part red (R.H.S. 44A) lower part brown (R.H.S. 187A). Sepals held below horizontal with reflexed tips red 44A uppermost, salmon (R.H.S. 40E) underneath $\frac{7}{10}$in by $\frac{1}{4}$in. Corolla salmon (R.H.S. 40C) petals $\frac{3}{10}$in by $\frac{4}{10}$in, flowers axillary. Pink filaments, palest pink pistil and cream stigma. Foliage green (R.H.S. 143A) paler underneath (R.H.S. 138B), ovate leaves $\frac{1}{2}$in bt $2\frac{2}{5}$in. Growth tall upright over 6 ft, good for pyramid, trellis or tall training, prefers overhead filtered light. A new interspecific hybrid with a striking new colour combination. Tested for 3 years under glass in the vicinity of Reading. *F. splendens* × *F. lampadaria.* Wright, J.O. – British – 1984 – A.F.S. No. 1791.

***Lechlade Rajah.** Single. One of a series of unusual species hybrid raised in the vicinity of Reading, Berkshire. Long purple flowers and introduced by Lechlade Fuchsia Nursery of Lechlade in 1984. *F. boliviana* × *F. excorticata.* Wright, J.O. – British – *ca* 1983.

***Lechlade Rocket.** Single. Long, thick cylindrical tube pale orange-red (R.H.S. 32E) brownish at base $2\frac{3}{4}$in by $\frac{1}{2}$in. Fully reflexed sepals held well below horizontal, orange-red (R.H.S. 32C) on upper half, green (R.H.S. 144B) on other half, $\frac{3}{4}$in by $\frac{2}{5}$in. Corolla orange-red (R.H.S 32A) flowers held horizontally axillary, $\frac{3}{5}$in by $\frac{2}{5}$in. Filaments pale pink, cream anthers, pale pink pistil and four lobed stigma palest pink. Dark sage green (R.H.S. 138A) foliage much paler underneath (R.H.S. 138C) with pale red veining, obvate leaves $5\frac{1}{2}$in by $2\frac{3}{4}$in. Growth lax upright, prefers overhead filtered light; heat tolerant. Tested for 3 years under glass in vicinity of Reading. A new interspecific hybrid with flowers of the brilliant orange of *F. lampadaria* but larger and heavier. Habit of plant is lax and not a climber. *F. lampadaria* × *F. fulgens.* Wright, J.O. – British – 1984 – A.F.S. No. 1792.

***Lechlade Tinkerbell.** Single. Encliandra type of introduction with tiny pink flowers which could attain treelike proportions. Introduced by Lechlade Fuchsia Nursery of Lechlade in 1984. *F. arborescens* × *F. thymifolia* ssp. *thymifolia.* Wright, J.O. – British – 1983.

***Lechlade Violet.** Single. Long, thin cylindrical pale purple (R.H.S. 80C) tube, olive-green at base (R.H.S. 73A) $\frac{1}{2}$in by $\frac{1}{10}$in. Sepals held well above horizontal with recurved tips, pale violet (R.H.S. 80B) tipped green on upper side, violet (R.H.S. 77A) deepening to red-purple at base underneath (R.H.S. 72C) $\frac{1}{4}$in by $\frac{1}{5}$in. Corolla almost fully flared blackish-purple (R.H.S. 79A) flowers in small terminal on lateral inflorescences, held erect or horizontal, $\frac{1}{4}$in by $\frac{1}{5}$in. Filaments purple, cream anthers, purple pistil, green stigma. Pale green (R.H.S. 144A) foliage, darker with age (R.H.S. 147A) lighter green underneath (R.H.S. 138B) ovate leaves 2 in by $1\frac{1}{5}$in. Growth tall upright over 6 ft, self branching, good for upright bush, standard or pyramid, heat tolerant, prefers overhead filtered light. Tested for 3 years under glass in vicinity of Reading. A new interspecific hybrid, the first fuchsia with violet tube and sepals. Although not spectacular, its unique colouring gives a great novelty value. *F. paniculata* × *F. colensoi.* Wright, J.O. – British – 1984 – A.F.S. No. 1793.

Leeanna Bell. Single. Tube and sepals pink; corolla violet, edged red. Flowers free of medium size, growth lax bush or trailer. Hazard and Hazard – American – Date unknown.

Leenado. Single. Tube and sepals pink, corolla purple. Little known American cultivar by a prolific raiser. Tiret – American – 1957.

Le Florifère. Lemoine – French – 1862.

Le Gaulois. Lemoine – French – 1874.

Le Globe. Crousse – French – 1866.

lehmannii. Red tube, scarlet sepals; scarlet corolla. Small flowers borne in terminal racemes. Upright shrub 5 to 6 ft high in native Ecuador. Munz – 1943 – Ecuador.

***Lemacto.** Single. Short tube orient-pink $\frac{1}{4}$in long, with darker streaks; fully up $1\frac{1}{4}$in long by $\frac{1}{2}$in wide sepals orient-pink on top, neyron-rose (R.H.S. 55D) underneath with recurved tips. Corolla $\frac{1}{2}$in long by $\frac{1}{2}$in wide is orient-pink. Smallish flowers are quarter flared and short thick bell shaped, neyron-rose filaments and magenta-rose anthers, neyron-rose style and white stigma. Foliage is sap-green (R.H.S. 150A) lighter on lower surface with $2\frac{1}{4}$in long by 1 in wide elliptical shaped leaves, entire edges, acute tips and rounded bases. Growth self-branching medium upright, good for bush, upright or standard, prefers filtered light in cool conditions, uses fertilisers and water more readily than others, considered by the raiser to be different and better than existing lime-green foliage cultivars. Found by the raiser of the original cultivar in the vicinity of Ipswich, Suffolk, and introduced by Gouldings Fuchsias of

Ipswich in 1984. Sport of Camelot. Goulding – British – 1984 – A.F.S. No. 1782.

Lena. Semi-double. Tube and half reflexed sepals, pale flesh-pink, slightly deeper underneath; corolla rosy-magenta, flushed pink, paling at base. Medium sized flowers, very free, blooms in flushes. One of the most versatile of cultivars, can be trained to almost any shape and often confused with Elsa, Eva Boerg, Hapsburgh and Madame Eva Borg. Growth lax bush and hardy. Accepted by the B.F.S. as showbench hardy. In every enthusiast's collection. Bunney – British – 1862.

Lena Dalton. Double. Tube and recurving sepals, pale pink; corolla crispy blue, ageing to rosy-mauve. Medium size flowers, very free, with four cupped centre petals and shorter petals around outside, well in the show class category. Darkish green foliage, rather small. Growth upright and bushy, very popular cultivar and deservedly. Reimers – American – 1953 – A.F.S. No. 169.

Lena-Elsa. To distinguish between these two cultivars see Elsa–Lena.

L'Enfant Prodigue. Synonymous with Enfant Prodigue.

Le Notre. Lemoine – French – 1867.

Leo. Double. Very long tube, deep pink; sepals recurved, scarlet. Corolla white, veined rose and carmine. Very large flowers, fairly free for size, borne in clusters. Dark green foliage, growth upright bush, heavy blooms need support. Santa Monica × Graphic. Evans and Reeves – American – 1939.

Leo Delibes. Single. Red and purple. Lemoine – French – 1898.

Leonard de Vinci. Double. Red and purple. Lemoine – French – 1859.

Leonard de Vinci. Double. Red and purple. Rozain-Boucharlat – French – 1914.

Leon Carvalho. Lemoine – French – 1898.

Leonora. Single. Very soft pink self, flowers of medium size, extremely floriferous, bell shaped. probably the best self pink to date. Growth upright, vigorous and bushy. One of the best singles from America, excellent in every way. A.F.S. Cert. of Merit 1964. Tiret – American – 1960 – A.F.S. No. 434.

Leonora Rose. Single. Tube and sepals pale pink, tipped green; corolla blush-pink, flushed with white. Medium sized flowers and extremely free, growth upright and bushy. Sport from Leonora. Stilwell – British – 1974.

Le Pascal. Double. Red and purple. Rozain-Boucharlat – French – 1909.

Le Phare. Lemoine – French – 1874.

Le Prophète. Banks – British – 1860.

leptopoda. Tube dark red, rich red sepals; glowing red corolla. Long flowers produced solitary in upper leaf axils. Light green foliage, strong upright shrub. Synonymous with *F. siphonantha*. Krause – 1905 – Peru.

Le Robuste. Double. Red and violet-blue. Lemoine – French – 1904.

Les Hobbs. Single. Tube is glossy crimson, crimson sepals glossy on upper surface and arch down one and half times the length of the corolla.

Corolla claret-rose (R.H.S. 50A). Medium and compact flowers with very long pistil, distinctly hairy on top two-thirds, free flowering. Medium sized foliage darkish green (R.H.S. 147B), leaves roundish with serrated edges and red mid ribs. Growth tall upright, will make excellent bush, ends of branches arch under the weight of terminal bloom custers. Will take full sun at Worthing, South Coast England, where it was tested for 2 years before release. Hobbs, L. – British – 1981 – A.F.S. No. 1645.

Le Siamois. Lemoine – French – 1862.

Letty Lye. Single. Tube and sepals, flesh-pink; corolla carmine-crimson. medium sized flowers, very free. Growth upright, vigorous and bushy, like most of Lye's introductions, good for standard. Arabella Improved × James Lye. Lye – British – 1877.

Letty Palmer. Double. White and carmine. Palmer – British – 1891.

Leucantha. Single. White and red. Wright – British – 1846.

Leverhulme. Synonymous with Leverkusen.

Leverkusen. Triphylla type single. Longish tube, rosy-cerise self. Short drooping sepals, flowers shorter than the usual *F. triphylla* hybrid, very free, but react quickly to any change of atmosphere by losing its buds or flowers. Normal foliage, growth upright. F2 hybrid with F. triphylla and Andenken an Heinrich Henkel parentage. Rehnelt – German – 1928.

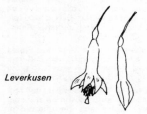

Leverkusen

Lewald. Bull – British – 1872.

Liberty Bell. Single. Light red tube, recurved sepals light red; corolla white, lightly veined pink. Flowers large for single, free and perfect bell shape, continuous bloomer. Growth upright and bushy. Hodges – American – 1954 – A.F.S. No. 197.

Libra. Semi-double to double. Pink tube, white sepals pink underside with white on top. Corolla pale blue to lavender, with splashes of pink. Large flowers, fairly free, growth trailer. Castro – American – 1971 – A.F.S. No. 952.

Libuse. Single. Cerise and scarlet. Lemoine – French – 1879.

Lido Isle. Double. Tube and sepals, rhodamine-pink; corolla rich blue. Medium sized blooms, fairly free, growth lax bush or trailer. Lee – American – 1950 – A.F.S. No. 57.

Liebesfreud. Single. Tube and sepals, rosy-pink; corolla deep crimson. Medium sized blooms and free. Growth upright and bushy. Also known as Love's Joy in California. Niederholzer – American – 1945.

Liebesleid. Single to semi-double. White tube, sepals pale ivory, faint pink inside. Corolla pale Imperial-purple, largish flowers and free. Growth climbing habit. Niederholzer – American – 1945.

Liebestraume. In addition to the cultivar by Blackwell (1966) it is possible that another cultivar of the same name was raised by Niederholzer in America in the 1930s. Tube and sepals white; corolla mauve, growth upright bush. It is possible that the correct spelling of both cultivars is Liebstraume.

Liebestraume. Double. Tube and sepals white, with pink flush, tipped green. Corolla pale lavender, white at base, with deeper marking and splashed palest pink. Largish flowers and free; foliage darkish green. Growth upright. Blackwell – British – 1966.

Liebriez. Semi-double. Tube and sepals, pale cerise; corolla pinkish-white, veined pink. Small flowers but very profuse, blooms continuously. Growth upright and bushy, very hardy, found favour with exhibitors in recent years as a specimen bush plant. Accepted by the B.F.S. as show-bench hardy. Kohene – German – 1874.

Liebstraume. See Liebestraume.

*Liemers Lantaern. Double. Little known Dutch sport from Dusky Rose found in the vicinity of N.W. Wehl, Netherlands. Giesen – Dutch – 1983.

Light Heart. Single. Red and purple. Bull – British – 1865.

Lightning. Double. Long tube ivory, sepals long, ivory, tipped green. Corolla orange-red; flowers very long, large and free. Dark green, foliage, growth lax bush or trailer. Gorman – American – 1970 – A.F.S. No. 934.

Lilac. Single. Tube and sepals, light pink, tipped green; corolla pure lilac. Largish flowers and free. Growth low spreading bush, only wants to grow horizontally. Haag and Son – American – 1952.

Lilac Dainty. Double. Tube and sepals dull red, corolla lilac with small red patch on petal. Small blooms but very double and free flowering. Growth upright medium size, will make good standard. Hardy in Southern Counties of England. Raised in the vicinity of Banstead, Surrey and introduced by Woodbridge Nurseries of Hounslow, Middlesex, 1982. Hobson – British – 1982.

Lilac Gem. Single. Short thick tube creamy-pink; sepals deep rose, long, thin and twisting. Corolla pink-lilac, flushed pink at base with red veining. Medium sized flowers with loosely held petals, occasional petaloids, red stamens and pink pistil. Mid green foliage with rounded serrated leaves. Growth medium upright and bushy, makes excellent bush plant, best colour in sun. Tested for 3 years in the vicinity of Cardiff, South Wales, before release. Adams – British – 1982 – A.F.S. No. 1688.

Lilac Lustre. Double. Short tube and broad, up-turned sepals, rose-red. Corolla powder-blue or lustrous-lilac. Medium to large blooms which appear in profusion, broad pleated petals. Rich green foliage, growth medium, upright bush. Beautiful pastel shaded cultivar. Munkner – American – 1961 – A.F.S. No. 480.

Lilac 'n' Rose. Double. Tube and long, pointed sepals, white, flushed pink; corolla lilac changing to beautiful shade of bright clear rosy-pink. Large blooms, free blooming with folded petals. Growth natural trailer. Waltz – American – 1958 – A.F.S. No. 353.

Lilac Pearl. Single. This cultivar grown and cultivated in the Netherlands is identical to Fiona.

Lilac Princess. Single. Short, thick, greenish-white tube; sepals greenish-white outside, flushed pale pink inside, held well out. Corolla deep lilac (R.H.S. 79B) shading to pink (R.H.S. 55C) at base of petals, short overlapping petals. Medium sized flowers with stamens and pistil pink tipped deep rose (R.H.S. 55A). Dark green foliage. Growth upright, small short stemmed flowers held at right angles, short jointed with vigorous growth. Early flowering, with blooms in fours at each pair of leaf axils. Raised and tested for 8 years before release in vicinity of Derby. Introduced by Jackson's Nurseries, Tamworth, in 1979. Handley – British – 1979 – A.F.S. No. 1502.

Lilac Queen. Double. Tube and sepals, bright crimson; corolla white flushed and veined lilac. Large blooms and free, growth upright and bushy very suitable for standard. Raiser unknown – European – Date unknown.

Lilac Sceptre. Double. Tube and sepals deep pink; corolla lilac. Medium-sized blooms, free for double, very full corolla. Growth upright and bushy. Hardy in Southern England and raised in the Scilly Isles. Tabraham – British – 1978.

Lilac Time. Double. Short tube white, sepals white with green tips; corolla pale lilac. Very large blooms, fairly free; growth trailer. Pennisi – American – 1967 – A.F.S. No. 714.

Lila Horizontalis. Single. White tube with green shine, sepals white, tipped green; corolla lilac-purple, white at base. Smallish flowers with light pink stamens and white style. Foliage is matt green softly haired. Growth lax bush. Marin Glow × Venus. De Groot – Dutch – ca 1970.

Lilani. Double. Tube and sepals, dark crimson; corolla rhodamine-purple. Largish flowers and free with scalloped petals. Growth upright, tall and vigorous. Niederholzer – American – 1947.

Lilian Alderson. Single. Spinel-red tube, long slender sepals, neyron-rose tipped green, recurve abruptly as flower matures. Corolla ruby-red with neyron-rose at base of petals. Medium sized flowers, free, corolla is short relative to sepals, start compact, flaring with maturity. Very large foliage measuring 5 in and over, deeply serrated, growth tall upright and bushy, good for all types of training. Travis, J. – British – 1975 – A.F.S. No. 1319.

Lilian Lampard. Synonymous with Trewince Twilight.

Lillah. Double. Red and purple. Bull – British – 1872.

Lilla Wright. Double. Pink tube, bright pink sepals, tipped green, broad and upturned almost hiding tube. Corolla blush lilac with touch of bright and pale pink. Medium frilly blooms with many petaloids, pink stamens and pistil. Growth upright, vigorous and self-branching. Named after a founder member of Dorking Fuchsia Society the first local society to be formed in England in 1964. Raised in the vicinity of Surrey. Hobson – British – 1977.

Lil Lee. Double. White tube, long white sepals, pink at base, tipped green; corolla pure white, pink at base. Large, heavy blooms, fairly free, ruffled, spooned petals. Growth trailer. Gagnon – American – 1968 – A.F.S. No. 782.

Lillian Grace Paca. Single. Pale pink-orange tube, delicate salmon-pink sepals, tipped pea green; corolla pale pink-orange. Medium sized flowers, very delicate, flaring with serrated petals, long stamens and pistil. Dark green foliage with serrated leaves. Growth tall upright, self-branching, good for bush or standard. Hodges – American – 1976 – A.F.S. No. 1358.

Lillibet. Double. Long tube white, recurved and spiraling white sepals, flushed pale carmine. Corolla soft rose, flushed geranium-lake. Long pointed green tipped buds; flowers very large, fairly free for size, prominent central petals and shorter outside petals. Growth strong pendant, best as trailer. A.F.S. Cert. of Merit. Hodges – American – 1954 – A.F.S. No. 199.

*Lilo Vogt. Single. Tube and sepals pink, sepals tipped green. Corolla pink. Small triphylla type flowers very free flowering and a sister seedling to Erika Köth. Growth trailer, basket type. Koralle × F. boliviana. Nutzinger – Austrian – 1976.

Lily Boulanger. Lemoine – French – 1914.

Lima. Double. Red and purple. Rozain-Boucharlat – French – 1871.

Lime Sherbert. Double. Tube and sepals white, tipped green; corolla white. Medium sized blooms, free and long lasting. Growth dwarf upright. Gagnon – American – 1966 – A.F.S. No. 660.

Linda Copley. Double. Clear pink self. Largish flowers, free and continuous. Growth lax bush or trailer. Copley – American – 1966 – A.F.S. No. 691.

Linda Goulding. Single. Short waxy-white tube, pink sepals reflex to cover tube and ovary. Corolla white with pale pink veining. Medium sized flowers, tight bell shaped, very attractive, stamens and pistil ruby red, two flowers in most leaf nodes. Medium sized foliage is plain green with no trace of redness. Growth self-branching medium upright, will make good bush, standard or pillar. Tested for 2 years in vicinity of Ipswich, East England before release. Goulding – British – 1981 – A.F.S. No. 1648.

Lindhope Sprite. Single. Long thin tube, rose-bengal, sepals phlox-pink, hang downwards with slight curve at angle of about 45°. Corolla rich violet-purple, medium sized flowers in continuous succession. Medium green foliage with coarsely, serrated leaves and light red stems. Growth trailer, produces excellent basket without weights. Coxeen × Mrs. Lawrence. Ryle – British – 1975 – A.F.S. No. 1249.

Lindisfarne. Semi-double. The short, thick tube is the palest of pinks, sepals held horizontally are also pale pink, flushed darker pink at the edges and tip. Corolla is a rich, dark violet (R.H.S. 87A) deeper at the edges, flushed palish pink at the base. Stamens rather short in contrast to the long pistil. Flowers are rather small but prolific and a blue which seems to hold its colour without fading, something previously lacking in the blues. Can best be described as an upright La Campanella (Blackwell 1968) but a decided improvement. Very short jointed, another desirable characteristic, and a strong grower with self-branching habit. The raiser has quoted that under different composts and feed, the normal green foliage can take on a really heavy, flushed reddish cast. Raised by Dr. M. Ryle of Morpeth, Northumberland, in 1974, he introduced only two that particular vintage year: Border Queen and Pink Lady. Although described by the raiser as a semi-double, can produce single flowers and needs that careful consideration if entering for exhibition purposes in single classes. Unfortunately the parentage is unknown and could be a chance seedling, was tested for 2 years at 945 ft above sea level in the vicinity of Consett, before release. Ryle-Atkinson – British – 1974 – A.F.S. No. 1168.

Lindisima. Double. Tube and sepals, deep rose; corolla blending of rose and mauve. Very large flowers, fairly free; growth trailer makes heavy wood in second year. Niederholzer – American – 1941.

Lindsey Victoria. Single. Short creamy-white tube. Sepals creamy-white flushed evenly pink, lower surface matt finish of crepe texture, inclined to turn back to tube. Corolla deep pink to fuchsia-purple (R.H.S. 67A). Foliage has leaves with distinct veins and serrated edges. Growth self-branching medium upright, will make good bush, best colour develops in shade. Tested for 4 years in vicinity of Preston, North England, before release. White Queen self. Thornley – British – 1981 – A.F.S. No. 1638.

Lindy. Double. Tube and sepals, flesh-pink flushed carmine; corolla turkey-red, flushed dianthus-purple. Medium sized flowers, very free, growth upright. Thorne – British – 1964.

Lindy. Double. Tube and sepals, very palest of pink; corolla white mottled and veined with pale pink. Large flowers and very full, fairly free; growth trailer. Antonelli – American – 1965 – A.F.S. No. 634.

*Linet. Single. Tube and sepals chrome-yellow and neyron-rose. Corolla imperial purple changing to magenta as flowers mature. Medium sized flowers, very floriferous especially near the branch ends. Scheele's green foliage. Growth upright, stiff and arching, benefits from above average nitrogenous feeds. Named with a Round Table theme. Raised in the vicinity of Ipswich and introduced by Gouldings Fuchsias of Ipswich in 1984. Goulding – British – 1984.

*L'Ingenue. Single. Tube and sepals carmine (R.H.S. 52B), corolla pink (R.H.S 61B). Flowers and habit of growth have the same characteristics of its parent Locky, makes excellent show plant. One of five new introductions by Herman de Graaff in 1983. Raised in the vicinity of Lisse, Netherlands. Locky × Mazda. de Graaff – Dutch – 1983.

Lisa. Double. Tube and sepals, bright rose; corolla rich lavender, fading to orchid. Huge blooms, fairly free for size. Growth trailer. Antonelli – American – 1965 – A.F.S. No. 637.

*Liselotte Buchenauer. Triphylla type single. Red and orange triphylla type cultivar very similar but lighter colouring than Schönbrunner Schuljubiliäum, both are sister seedlings. Koralle × F. fulgens var. rubra grandiflora. Nutzinger – Austrian – 1976.

Little Alice. Double. Red and white. Bland – British – 1870.

Little Beauty. Single. Tube and sepals flesh-pink; corolla lavender blue. Smallish flower, very free and very early, best colour in shade. Growth upright, very compact and bushy. Could be an American introduction. Raiser and date unknown.

Little Bit. Double. Short thin tube crimson, sepals light crimson with some white showing on topside, tipped green, crimson on underside, sepals curve back to tube. Corolla royal-blue fading to light purple. Medium sized blooms, free, petals have light grey edge with crimson variegation at base, with crimson veins in the lower half only, one petaloid. Largish foliage with red stems and branches, growth lax bush, will trail with weights. Soo Yun – American – 1975 – A.F.S. No. 1267.

Little Bobby. Double. Red and purple. Bland – British – 1874.

Little Bo Peep. Single. Red and purple. Rogers – British – 1862.

Little Catbells. Single. Short white tube, very small rose sepals are reflexed. Very small white corolla changing to rose. Very small flowers typical of the Encliandra cross measure only $\frac{1}{4}$ in, berries are jet black, heat tolerant if shaded. Medium to light green foliage with ovate leaves. Growth medium upright, will make a bush. Originates from the vicinity of Preston, Lancashire. Encliandra cross. Travis, J. – British – 1980 – A.F.S. No. 1582.

Little Cutie. Single. Long tube 1 in long, light pink with darker pink veins; pink sepals, white on top with light green tip. Corolla purple with light reddish-purple at base. Smallish flowers $\frac{7}{8}$ in long, tight, compact with the occasional petaloid, brown anthers with long pistil. Light green foliage with red stems and branches, growth natural trailer. Registered by Soo Yun Fuchsia Garden. Palko – American – 1976 – A.F.S. No. 1349.

Little Fellow. Single. Red tube $\frac{1}{2}$ in long, sepals red, slender and curve outward; corolla red, small and compact. Small flowers, very free, colour and leaves unusual for so small a fuchsia. Dark green foliage, serrated edges. Growth lax bush or semi-trailer. Soo Yun – American – 1973 – A.F.S. No. 1095.

Little Frosty. Double. White tube $\frac{1}{4}$ in × $\frac{1}{2}$ in long, green tipped sepals white on top and light pink underneath, $\frac{1}{2}$ in wide × $2\frac{7}{8}$ in long. Corolla bright rose-pink changing to pale orchid with white spots at base. Long blooms with four petaloids a quarter the size of petals are pale orchid also with white spots, stamens deep pink, white pistil and yellow stigma $1\frac{1}{2}$ in long. Light green foliage with light green stems, leaves $1\frac{1}{8}$ in × $2\frac{1}{4}$ in long. Growth lax bush, will make basket with weights or lax bush, prefers a warm situation best as H1. Originates from the Sebastopol area of California. Soo Yun Field – American – 1980 – A.F.S. No. 1562.

Little Gem. Single. White and blue. Henderson – British – 1872.

Little Gene. Single. Short tube and sepals, carmine; corolla deep campanula-violet. Medium sized flowers, flared and free. Growth upright and bushy. Baker – British – 1970.

Little Giant. Single. Tube and sepals red; corolla purple. Small flowers and small foliage, just another red and purple which appears to be exclusive to California, could be an old established cultivar with another name. Raiser and date unknown.

Little Hardy. Bland – British – 1870.

Little Jewel. Tube shiny, dark carmine, sepals shiny, dark carmine on top, dark flat carmine underneath, star shaped, standing well out. Corolla light purple with carmine variegation at base. Medium sized flowers, very free, bright red pistil with white stigma divided into four dots. Large foliage, growth upright, bushy and vigorous, very strong grower. Soo Yun – American – 1975 – A.F.S. No. 1268.

Little Langdale. Single. White tube and sepals; corolla pastel pink. Flowers small, very free. Growth upright, vigorous and hardy. Sister seedling to Silverdale and Hawkeshead. *F.magellanica* var.*alba* ×. Travis, J. – British – 1967.

Little Leo. Double. Tube and sepals light pink; corolla magenta, marbled pink. Attractive small flowers with trailing habit, suitable for basketwork. Imported by Fuchsialand Nurseries of Birmingham. Gallegos – American – 1975.

***Little Miss Muffet.** Single. Short rose-pink tube $\frac{1}{8}$ in long, sepals rose-red, spear shaped, recurved $\frac{3}{4}$ in by $\frac{1}{4}$ in wide. Corolla dark lilac $\frac{1}{2}$ in long by $\frac{1}{4}$ in wide. Very small flowers with rose-pink stamens 1 in long. Dark green foliage with serrated leaves $1\frac{1}{2}$ in × $\frac{3}{4}$ in wide. Growth small upright, very suitable for miniature standard, small bush or even bonsai training, will take full sun in Cheshire. Raised and tested for 3 years in vicinity of Timperley, Cheshire. Lilac Lustre ×. Howarth – British – 1983 – A.F.S. No. 1715.

Little Pewee. Double. Tube and sepals, rose, tipped green; corolla deep purple with variegations of rose. Miniature double, very free, box type blooms. Very small foliage, heat resistant. Growth trailer. Pennisi – American – 1970 – A.F.S. No. 894.

Little Pinkey. Single. Thick, pink tube $\frac{5}{8}$ in long, $\frac{5}{16}$ in wide; sepals are smooth, light pink, tipped green on top, darker pink underneath, calyx horizontal with tips curling up, sepals $1\frac{1}{8}$ in long, $\frac{5}{16}$ in wide. Corolla lilac-purple fading to deep pink red veined $\frac{3}{4}$ in wide, $\frac{5}{8}$ in long. Smallish flowers, open and bell-shaped, red stamens and pink pistil with white stigma. Light green foliage with serrated leaves 2 in long, 1 in wide. Growth small upright, self-branching makes good bush or standard and will trail with weights. Raised and tested for 5 years before release in vicinity of Sebastopol, California. Soo Yun Field – American – 1979 – A.F.S. No. 1493.

Little Rascal. Single. Small, short tube bright red, sepals red; corolla purple, red at base, no petaloids. Small blooms and free; foliage dappled light green and dark green, young leaves light red, stems and branches red. Growth trailer, heat tolerant. Soo Yun – American – 1974 – A.F.S. No. 1182.

Little Ronnie. Semi-double. Short tube light rose, short broad and upturned sepals, rosy-crimson; corolla dark blue ageing to mauvish-blue. Smallish flowers, very profuse, remains full like small rosette, identical to Lorna Doone except for colouring. Small bright green foliage, growth medium upright, bushy and stiff, requires the minimum of pinching for shaping. Sport of Lorna Doone. De Cola – American – 1975 – A.F.S. No. 1310.

Little Sister. Single. Waxy tube and upturned sepals, light phlox-pink, tipped green. Corolla palest orchid-pink, deepening to rose-lilac at petals edges. Growth upright and bushy. Pybon – American – 1959.

Littré. Single. Rose-pink and purple. Lemoine – French – 1879.

Liver Bird. Single. Tube flesh-pink (R.H.S. 39B), sepals flesh-pink (R.H.S. 39B); corolla claret-rose (R.H.S. 50A). Small flowers the same colouring as Chang but smaller, remaining upright. Chang seedling. Although raised in 1966 this cultivar was not released or introduced until 1978. Thornley – British – 1966 – A.F.S. No. 1469.

Liz. Double. White tube, sepals palest pink, deeper unerneath, tipped green; corolla palest pink, veined and splashed deep pink. Largish flowers very long stamens and free; growth upright bushy and vigorous, hardy in Kent. This cultivar was originally named Yvonne. Holmes, R. – British – 1970 – A.F.S. No. 1379.

Lizzie Hexham. Single. Red and blackish-purple. Banks – British – 1866.

llewelynii. Red tube, sepals pinkish-red; corolla violet. Medium sized flowers, but very sparse. Medium sized upright shrub. MacBride – 1941 - Peru.

Loch Catrine. Single. Red tube, sepals with bright coral-red on crimson-scarlet, broad and recurved. Corolla very deep violet, almost black, cup-shaped, very beautiful cultivar. Raiser unknown – British – Date prior to 1858.

*Lochinver.** Semi-double to double. Pale pink tube ½ in by ¼ in wide, sepals pale pink, rhodamine-pink underneath, held horizontally with reflexed tips 1½ in long by ¾ in wide. Corolla imperial purple shading to pale pink at base with darker purple edges 1 in long by 1 in wide. Medium sized blooms rather loose and open but lovely colour combination, quarter flared and very free, pink filaments, pale pink style with creamy-white stigma. Dark green foliage, ovate leaves with serrated edges, acute tips 2 in long by 1 in wide. Growth medium upright, self-branching, will produce excellent standard or upright bush, prefers cool conditions but heat tolerant if shaded; very short jointed, holds its flowers well on top of plant. Raised and tested for 4 years in vicinity of Carlisle, Cumbria, and introduced by Fuchsiavale Nurseries of Kidderminster in 1983. Seedling × Valerie. Mitchinson – British – 1983 – A.F.S. No. 1745.

Loeky. Single. Short thick tube rosy-red, broad upturned sepals rosy-red hiding tube. Corolla lavender ageing to rose-pink on maturity. Medium sized flowers almost identical in shape to Impudence with the flat open saucer shape petals and long evenly spaced red stamens. Lightish green foliage, growth upright and very bushy. Probably de Graaff's best introduction from Holland. Joy Patmore seedling. Introduced and well recommended by High Trees Nurseries of Reigate, Surrey in 1981. Joy Patmore × Impudence. de Graaff – Dutch – 1981.

Lohengrin. Double. Red and white. Twrdy – German – 1873.

Loie Fuller. Lemoine – French – 1909.

Lolita. Double. Tube and sepals white, tinted rose and tipped green; corolla porcelain-blue,

ageing to lilac with maturity. Growth trailer. A.F.S. Cert. of Merit 1967. Tiret – American – 1963 – A.F.S. No. 574.

Lollypop. Single. Tube pink, upcurling, velvet sepals, spinel-pink. Corolla brilliant plum to deep peony-purple. Long flowers, free and large petals, heat tolerant. growth trailer. Walker-Jones – American – 1950.

Lonely Ballerina. Double. Tube and sepals, dark carmine; corolla white, veined and splashed carmine. Medium sized blooms and free, red and white trailers are conspicuous with their absence, this cultivar is excellent. Blackwell – British – 1962.

Lonesome George. Double. Tube pale pink, sepals pale pink inside, white outside with green tips. Corolla medium maroon, variegated in light salmon. Large blooms, fairly free, growth trailer. Pennisi – American – 1970 – A.F.S. No. 886.

Long Beach. Double. Tube and broad, upturned sepals, rich carmine; corolla white, veined and shaded carmine at base. Large blooms with the red shading extending downward along the petal edges, fairly free for size. Growth vigorous upright, self-supporting. Walker and Jones – American – 1956.

Longfellow. Single. Light rose self. Very long flowers, free with sepals pinwheel shaped. Growth upright. Haag – American – 1946.

longiflora (Bentham 1845). Synonymous with *F. macrostigma.*

Longiflora. See *magellanica* var. *globosa.*

Longipedunculata. See *magellanica* var. *longipedunculata.*

Loraine. Double. Tube and sepals, deep red; corolla pink with rose veining. Medium sized flowers and free. Growth strong, upright bush. Munkner – American – 1952.

Loralei. Double. Deep rosy-red tube, very wide rosy-red sepals; corolla opens pale lavender-blue, with rose-pink at base of petals. medium to large flowers, free; growth lax bush or trailer. Martin – American – 1957 – A.F.S. No. 316.

Lord Byron. Single. Short tube and recurved sepals, deep cerise; corolla very dark purple. Medium sized blooms, free, very expanded somewhat similar to buttercup shape. Growth upright and bushy, this cultivar can throw semi-double flowers. Lemoine – French – 1880?.

Lord Clarendon. Single. Cerise and violet. Epps – British – 1847.

Lord Derby. Single. Red and purple. Banks – British – 1868.

Lord Elcho. Single. Red and purple. Banks – British – 1862.

Lord Falmouth. Single. Red and purple. Banks – British – 1866.

Lord Hill. Single. Dark red self. Gaines – British – 1845.

Lord Lonsdale. Single. Tube and sepals, light apricot colour; corolla orange-peach, slightly lighter than Aurora Superba but petals are larger. Beautiful flowers of medium size, length from seed pod to end of stigma approximately 6 in, one inch longer than Aurora Superba and more profuse. Foliage is lighter green than Aurora Superba and less crinkled, but still suffers from leaf curl but more robust. Flowers are more of a tangerine colouring and on this account sometimes confused with the cultivar Tangerine. Lord Lonsdale is frequently confused with Aurora Superba and has the same habit and growth, sometimes described as a tangerine self, one colour difference being that Lord Lonsdale flowers are less green at the sepal tips. Growth lax but bushy, rather difficult to grow to perfection, best grown as H1. Raiser unknown – British – Date unknown.

Lord Lyons. Lemoine – French – 1888.

Lord Nelson. Smith – British – 1849.

Lord of the Islet. Wheeler – British – 1858.

Lord of the Manor. Fry – British – 1864.

Lord Roberts. Single. Short tube and horizontal sepals, scarlet; corolla rich purplish-violet. Flowers largish, early and free. Growth upright and bushy, good for pyramid training, one of Lemoine's best red and purples. See Royal Purple for further information. Lemoine – French – 1909.

Lorna Doone. Semi-double to double. Tube and short, broad upturned sepals, rich crimson. Corolla rosy-mauve. Medium sized blooms, very profuse. Growth upright and bushy, seldom makes a big plant. Sport of General Monk. Erickson – American – 1954 – A.F.S. No. 410.

Lorraine. Rozain-Boucharlat – French – 1913.

Los Angeles. Single. Tube and sepals, waxy coral-apricot; corolla deep orange, suffused with vermillion. Large flowers, free and long, borne in clusters. Lush green foliage. Growth upright and vigorous. California × Aurora Borealis. Evans and Reeves – American – 1938.

Lothario. Semi-double. Tube pink, very long sepals pink; corolla fuchsia-purple. Large flowers and free; growth trailer. Kennett – American – 1971 – A.F.S. No. 954.

*Lottie. Semi-double. White bulbous tube 1 in long, white sepals held horizontally 1 in by $\frac{1}{4}$ in wide. Corolla lavender-pink non-fading. Medium sized blooms, delightful colour combination especially with the non-fading characteristic, white stamens and pistil 2 in long. Mid-green foliage with leathery broad shades leaves of medium size. Growth small compact upright, short jointed has all the characteristics of a well balanced and delightful cultivar with good parents. Raised and tested for 4 years in the vicinity of Timperley, Cheshire. White Spider × Lena Dalton. Howarth – British – 1983 – A.F.S. No. 1716.

Lottie Hobby. Single. Tube dull scarlet, sepals same colour, tipped with rose; corolla scarlet. Very small flowers, very free, small glossy foliage. Growth upright and dwarfish. Very often taken to be a species, but is a Breviflorae hybrid from the "Enclindra" section. Hardy in most districts. Edwards – British – 1839.

Lottie Routledge. Semi-double. Almost a pink self. Stride – British – 1873.

Louisa Balfour. Single. Light coloured cultivar, used extensively by Lye as a seed parent. Lye – British – Date unknown.

Louis Blanc. Lemoine – French – 1883.

Louise Emershaw. Double. Thin white tube, long white sepals; corolla jasper-red. medium sized flowers, very full and free, dark green foliage, heat tolerant if shaded. Growth natural trailer. Tiret – American – 1972 – A.F.S. No. 1072.

Louis Faucon. Double. Red and purple. Rozain-Boucharlat – French – 1889.

Lovable. Double. Short tube and broad sepals, deep red; corolla orchid-pink, veined deeper pink. Large blooms, fairly free and heavy; small foliage for size of plant and blooms. Growth lax bush or trailer, needs support as bush plant. Erickson – American – 1963 – A.F.S. No. 580.

Love in Bloom. Double. Flesh-coloured tube, long sepals, white to pale flesh pink are broad and tapering, turn up and reflex slightly at maturity. Corolla magenta to brilliant coral. Largish blooms opens very full with many petals some serrated, flaring into huge well formed blooms. Dark green foliage, new growth red stems. Growth natural trailer, tested for 3 years at Fort Bragg, California before release. Stubbs – American – 1977 – A.F.S. No. 1412.

Love It. Double. Tube and sepals pink; corolla orchid and pink. Medium sized blooms, growth upright. An unregistered American cultivar which has been overlooked. Gorman – American – 1964.

Love Knot. Double. Medium rose-madder tube, stiff, wide, upturned sepals, rose-madder, edges brushed with amethyst-violet. Largish blooms ruffled and curled with outside petals adhered to arched sepals, results in full open square-shaped blooms. Foliage is bright lime-green, matures to spinach-green. Growth medium upright makes good bush or basket with weights. Raised and tested for 6 years before release in vicinity of Seal Beach and North Long Beach, California, where it is trademarked. Raised by Roy Walker and introduced by Fuchsia-La Nurseries. Walker – American – 1979 – A.F.S. No. 1512.

Loveliness. Single. White waxy tube and recurving sepals; corolla rosy-cerise. Medium sized flowers, extremely floriferous and early. Growth upright and bushy, will produce excellent stiff standard. Lye – British – 1869.

Lovely. Single. Tube and sepals, creamy-white; corolla carmine, flushed magenta. Medium sized blooms and free; growth upright and bushy. Lye – British – 1887.

Lovely Blue. Double. Tube off-white, slightly veined light roseine-purple, white sepals brushed pale roseine-purple at base. Corolla roseine-purple at base, darkening to violet-purple at tips. Large and very full blooms with roseine-purple stamens and pistil, best colours in shade. Foliage slight serrated with fairly wide leaves red-veined. Growth semi-trailer, bushy will make basket with weights, tested for 5 years at Sebastopol, California before release. Soo Yun Field – American – 1977 – A.F.S. No. 1407.

Lovely Lady. Double. Tube pale pink, sepals white, tinged with pink; corolla carmine-rose with outer petals splashed pale pink. Large flowers, fairly free and full. Growth upright, vigorous, up to 6 ft in California, Paskesen – American – 1967 – A.F.S. No. 700.

loxensis. Longish tube, deep red, scarlet sepals; corolla dull red. Large foliage, flowers not very attractive, seem insignificant to the foliage produced. Strong upright shrub. Synonymous with *F. apiculata* and *F. umbrosa*. Kris – 1823 – Peru.

Lucerowe. Double. Tube and sepals cerise, corolla lilac. Medium sized blooms and a new introduction to the range of hardies. Introduced by

J.A. Wright of Hilltop Nurseries of Atherstone. Wright, J.A. – British – 1979.

Lucien Daniel. Double. Red and purple. Lemoine – French – 1904.

Lucienne Breval. Double. Cerise and white. Lemoine – French – 1912.

Lucille. Double. Long, thick pink tube, very long, curved, pink sepals; corolla is all white. Medium-sized blooms, beautiful and very showy with pink stamens and pistil. Small dark green foliage. Growth natural trailer. Hanson – American – 1976 – A.F.S. No. 1325.

Lucille Lemoine. Single. Pink and rose. Lemoine – French – 1908.

Lucinda. Semi-double. Whitish-pink tube, recurving sepals white tipped pink on outside, pale pink inside. Corolla pinkish-lilac. Large blooms and prolific flowerer. Medium sized foliage, ovate leaves with obtuse leaf tip and serrated margins. Growth lax bush, will excel as half basket, best colour develops in shade. Tested for 3 years in the vicinity of Carlisle, North West England, before released. Introduced by Fuchsiavale Nurseries of Kidderminster in 1981. Baby Pink × Norman Mitchinson. Mitchinson – British – 1981 – A.F.S. No. 1654.

Lucky Finnis. Double. Tube and sepals, rich cerise; corolla pure white. Large blooms, fairly free with incurving petals. Growth upright and bushy. Greene – American – 1939.

Lucky Strike. Semi-double. Tube and sepals, light ivory-pink, sepals darker on inside; corolla inside petals, solid bluish-purple, outer petals pink with purple markings. Large flowers and free; growth upright bush, fast grower. Niederholzer – American – 1943.

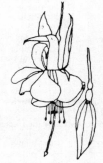

Lucky Strike

Lucky '13'. Single. Tube carmine, sepals brilliant carmine; corolla campanula-violet with red veining on a lighter base. Medium sized flowers with trailing growth suitable for basketwork. An unregistered American cultivar. Fuchsia-La (Roy Walker) – American – 1951.

Lucy Dyos. Single. White tube, long, narrow sepals slightly reflexed are white, veined pink outside, pale pink inside. Corolla delicate shade of lilac, maturing to rose-pink. Small to medium sized flowers good quality and long lasting. Growth upright and arching. Introduced by Woodbridge Nurseries of Hounslow in 1980. Joy Patmore × Madame Cornelissen. Dyos – British – 1980.

Lucy Mills. Single. White and pink. Banks – British – 1865.

Luella. Semi-double. Pink tube, sepals pink and white with deeper pink at base, very pointed. Corolla white, turns lacy as it matures. Largish blooms and free, corolla is formed with four slim petals and four scalloped petals at base and two white spooned petals under each scalloped petal, unusual bloom resembling snowflakes. Growth lax bush or trailer. Gagnon – American – 1969 – A.F.S. No. 842.

Lula Bell. Semi-double. Tube and sepals red; corolla white. Small flowers, very free, growth upright and bushy. Haag and Son – American – 1953.

Lullaby. Double. White tube, sepals near white, crisp and recurved; corolla warm rose, heat tolerant. Flowers medium sized and free, growth trailer. Reiter – American – 1953 – A.F.S. No. 191.

Lunado. Double. Tube and sepals, rose-pink; corolla petunia-purple, fades to spiraea-red with maturity. Very large blooms, fairly free, early flowerer, with numerous extra petals of rose pink. Growth lax bush or trailer. Tiret – American – 1957 – A.F.S. No.294.

Lunar Light. Double. Tube and sepals, light salmon; corolla light orange-red. Large, globular blooms, fairly free. Growth lax bush or trailer. Antonelli – American – 1971 – A.F.S. No. 1005.

Luscious. Double. Tube and sepals, dark red, sepals very wide; corolla dark wine and red marbled with orange. Very large blooms, fairly free for size, but long lasting and rather fluffy. Dark green foliage with red veins. Growth lax bush or trailer, does not live up to its name. Martin – American – 1960 – A.F.S. No. 445.

Luscombe's Choice. Double. Tube and sepals pink, tipped green; corolla pink. Large, loose flowers, with long over-lapping petals, heavy but long lasting, long pink buds. Growth trailer. Prentice – American – 1968 – A.F.S. No. 791.

Lustre. Single. Tube and sepals, creamy-white; corolla salmon-pink, slightly tinted orange. Flowers rather small but exceptionally free and somewhat erect. Growth upright and bushy, outstanding cultivar, should be seen more often, especially on the showbench, easy grower. Bull – British – 1868.

Lustre Improved. Single. Tube and sepals, creamy-white, lightly suffused pink; corolla bright scarlet with shade of salmon. Flowers are larger than Lustre, but not so free. No improvement upon Lustre either in colour or habit or growth. Growth upright and bushy. Carter Page – British – 1870.

*Lustre–Santa Barbara. Confusion exists between the cultivars Lustre (Bull 1868) and Santa Barbara (unknown American ca 1930). Both cultivars grown side by side possess the unusual characteristics of the 'nodding tube' and the holding of pistil on one side of the stamens, in addition to exact colouring, shape and size. This could be another instance of a new introduction from California of an old English established cultivar. Lustre has been used extensively by George Roe to produce Amanda Jones, Ken Jennings, Micky Goult, Pirbright with Ron Ewart as the pollen bearer, male parent. Roe although using the name

Santa Barbara in his records recognises the fact that it is Lustre.

Luther King. Double. Extra long red tube, sepals box type are red with tips turning inward. Corolla deep purple; growth trailer. Pennisi – American – 1970 – A.F.S. No. 893.

Luv. Single. Pink tube, very long sepals, pink. Corolla blue, fading to lavender. medium sized flowers, bell shaped and free. Growth trailer. Kennett – American – 1969 – A.F.S. No. 866.

Luzelle. Single. Short, tube white in bud, turning to scarlet before bud opens, recurled scarlet sepals; pale violet corolla. Tiny flowers, short and compact, tiny skirted corolla, short scarlet stamens, long scarlet pistil. Small to medium-foliage, growth small upright, suitable for good bush or bonsai, needs heavy pinching to keep compact, tiny but not miniature flowers. Smith, N.F. – American – 1976 – A.F.S. No. 1360.

lycioides. Red tube, red sepals; purplish corolla. Smallish flowers, not very free, produced solitary in the leaf axils. Stout branches with short, knobby laterals, leaves are lance-ovate to ovate. Upright shrub attaining a height of 9 to 10 ft in native Chile. Hardy in this country. Synonymous with *F. rosea, F. rosea spinosa* and *F. spinosa.* Andrews – 1807 – Chile.

Lydia Götz. Single cultivar with red tube and sepals; lilac corolla. Growth upright and bushy very suitable as bedder. According to reliable German sources, this cultivar is of German origin and not Austrian. Götz – German – 1958.

Lye's Elegance. Single. Waxy-white tube with faint touch of yellow, sepals waxy-cream. Corolla rich cerise; flowers medium sized, very free and early. Growth upright bush, not one of the well known of Lye's introductions but good. Lye – British – 1884.

Lye's Excelsior. Single. Tube and sepals waxy-white, sepals slightly tinted pink. Corolla rich scarlet-cerise; flowers very free and of medium size. Growth upright and bushy but not as tall as most of Lye's cultivars. Lye – British – 1887.

Lye's Excelsior – Joy Patmore. These two cultivars are very similar and may be confused with each other, especially when the late Tom Thorne quoted that Joy Patmore (Turner 1961) is identical with Lye's Excelsior (Lye 1887). There are however several differences which should help to identify both cultivars. The feature of Joy Patmore is the very clear cut colouring with its slightly deeper cerise-pink corolla, darker at the edge with slightly white at base, the petals are larger which do not fold into each other and are a little more open than Excelsior. Joy Patmore's tube is very short and pure white, whilst L.E.'s is a thick tube, slightly tinged pink and tapers a little at the ovary and is a typical Lye's tube. Excelsior has a very long pedicel whereas J.P.'s is exceptionally short. The sepals of both cultivars are almost identical although Patmore's are longer, both are recurved, tipped green and curl slightly at the horizontal. The larger anthers of Joy Patmore and a larger stigma both help to identify it more clearly. The petals of Lye's Excelsior are slightly fluted and fold into each other whilst the colouring is a little paler cerise-pink, is not so dark at the edge and very slightly white at the base. Joy Patmore is much more floriferous but not so early, the habit of growth is much the same in both cultivars, although as one might expect Lye's Excelsior is very upright and vigorous.

Lye's Favourite. Single. Tube and sepals, flesh-pink, corolla orange-cerise. Flowers very free and of medium size; growth upright and bushy. May have been Lye's favourite but not amongst the fuchsia growers. Arabella Improved × James Lye. Lye – British – 1886.

Lye's Own. Single. Tube and sepals, waxy-white, corolla pinkish-lilac. Medium sized flowers, very free, long and early. Growth upright, strong bush, very suitable for a standard. Submitted by Chingford Nurseries for the R.H.S. Wisley Trials 1975–78 but received no award. Lye – British – 1871.

Lye's Perfection. Single. Tube and sepals waxy-white, corolla bright carmine. Flowers very free and of medium size, growth upright and bushy. Lye – British – 1884.

Lye's Rival. Single. Tube and sepals red, corolla parma-violet, ageing to purple. Medium sized blooms and very free, pale green foliage. Growth upright and bushy. Lye – British – 1891.

Lye's Unique. Single. Tube and sepals, waxy-white, corolla delightful shade of salmon-orange. Medium sized blooms, very free, growth upright bush, very strong. One of Lye's best. Lye – British – 1886.

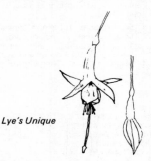

Lye's Unique

*Lye's Unique–Kolding Perle. See Kolding Perle–Lye's Unique.

Lynda. Double. Pale pink tube, sepals extra long, pale pink; corolla marbled violet. Flowers large, fairly free and flaring. Growth trailer. Tiret – American – 1970 – A.F.S. No. 900.

Lynette. Double. White tube, sepals long and twisted pin-wheel fashion, white flushed pink. Corolla white, flowers very full, large and free, could be described as a double White Spider. Growth lax bush or trailer. Guinevere × White Spider. Thornley – British – 1961.

Lynette. Double. Tube and sepals rich red, corolla white, blotched red. Medium sized blooms freely produced and profuse for a double. Growth upright best as H2. Another addition to the congested red and white range. This cultivar should not be confused with Thornley's 1961 introduction of the same name. Introduced by C.S. Lockyer of Bristol in 1981. Holmes, E. – British – 1981.

Lynn Ellen. Double. Tube and broad upturned sepals, deepest rose-pink; corolla rose-purple, changing to glowing rose as the flower opens. Large spreading blooms, free and continuously in bloom, heat resistant. Growth upright. Erickson – American – 1962 – A.F.S. No. 541.

Lynne Marshall. Single. Tube and sepals pale pink; corolla lavender-blue. Medium sized flowers, continuous flowering, pale green foliage. Growth upright and bushy, strong, height 2 to $2\frac{1}{2}$ ft. Hardy in Southern England raised in the Scilly Isles. Submitted by raiser for R.H.S. Wisley Hardy Trials 1975–78 but received no award. Tabraham – British – 1974.

Lyric. Double. White tube, sepals white with touches of pink; corolla orchid-rose, fades into various shades. Large blooms with long thin corolla with unusual petaloids, sometimes looks like notes on a scale. Growth trailer. Kennett – American – 1964 – A.F.S. No. 612.

Mabel Greaves. Semi-double. White and green stripped tube, white sepals which fly back to cover tube, tipped green. Corolla white and veined pink, medium sized blooms producing three blooms in each leaf axil. Growth very strong upright, with pale green foliage. Very suitable for training as standard. Named after a founder member of the Merseyside Fuchsia Society; raised and tested for 4 years in the Merseyside vicinity before release. Seedling from String of Pearls ×. Clark, D. – British – 1982.

Mabelle Edwards. Single. White tube, sepals frosty-white, curl inward; corolla pale pink. Medium sized blooms, bell shaped and free, four overlapping petals with a few folded petals inside. Outer petals are scalloped with flare slightly as flower matures, buds are long white and pointed, borne in clusters. Growth medium upright. Waltz – American – 1957 – A.F.S. No. 311.

Ma Cat. Double. Thick, medium long tube, white with pink stripe, sepals phlox-pink on backside and phlox-pink to orchid-pink on inside, $1\frac{1}{2}$ in long × $\frac{5}{8}$ in wide, long, recurved and cup shaded. Corolla cyclamen-purple fading to mallow purple at the sepals. Medium-sized blooms 1 in long × $\frac{3}{4}$ in wide, tight corolla with rhodamine-pink stamens and pistil with brown tips, heavy bloomer best colour in shade. Growth natural trailer without weights. Tested for 3 years in vicinity of Richmond, California. Registered by Soo Yun Field in 1978. Palko – American – 1978 – A.F.S. No. 1445.

Machell. Double. Short, thin tube rose-Bengal (H.C.C. 25), $\frac{5}{8}$ in × $\frac{1}{4}$ in, sepals rose-Bengal (H.C.C. 25), 1 in long × $\frac{3}{8}$ in wide. Corolla spectrum-violet (H.C.C. 735/2) with magenta base. Smallish blooms $\frac{5}{8}$ in × $\frac{5}{8}$ in with spectrum-violet petaloids. Light green foliage with scalloped leaves $1\frac{3}{4}$ in long and $\frac{3}{4}$ in wide. Growth lax upright, will trail with weights, tested and raised for 4 years before release in vicinity of Richmond, California. Raised by Stephen Palko and introduced by Soo Yun Fuchsia Gardens. Palko – American – 1979 – A.F.S. No. 1497.

Machu Picchu. Single. Orange self-coloured flowers, need a lot of stopping and will flower even in the autumn and winter. Will stand full sun. Growth lax trailer, awarded best basket at Dutch Fuchsia Show, 1978. Entered in the B.F.S. London Seedling Class, 1978, but Floral Committee considered it to be too similar to Coachman and Tangerine. Introduced by Wills Fuchsia Nurseries in 1978. de Graaff – Dutch – 1977.

MacMahon. Double. red and purple. Lemoine – French – 1871.

Macombre. Single. Tube and sepals bright red; corolla violet with lighter colour at base. Growth trailer. Cultivar which appears to be exclusive to California. Raiser and date unknown.

macrantha. Rosy-red to coral or scarlet tube, sepals of the same colouring with yellowish-green tips; no corolla. Very beautiful flowers, often 5 or 6 in long produced in short branchlets. Trailing or epiphytic shrub. Hooker – 1845 – Peru.

macropetala (Presl 1835). Synonymous with *F. corymbiflora.*

macrophylla. Tube scarlet, sepals red with green tips; corolla bright red, small flowers. Upright shrub up to 12 ft in height in native Peru. Johnston – 1925 – Peru.

Macrostema. See *magellanica* var. *macrostema.*

macrostigma. Tube reddish purple, sepals purplish red, spreading; corolla long, cerise to crimson. Smallish flowers produced singly in upper leaf axils. Upright shrub reaching 4 to 5 ft in natural habitat. Synonymous with *F. longiflora* and *F. spectabilis.* Bentham – 1844 – Ecuador.

Madame Aubin. Single. Pink and orange. Cornelissen – Belbian – 1866.

Madame Boucharlat. Double. Red and dark purple. Lemoine – French – 1863.

Madame Butterfly. Double. Tube and sepals red; corolla, white. Medium sized blooms, similar form corolla to Pink Quartet only larger, fairly free. Growth lax bush. Red Jacket ×. Colville – British – 1964.

Madame Carnot. Double, Red and purple. Lemoine – French – 1895.

Madame Chang. Single. Tube and sepals, orange-red, tipped green, corolla pink. Exactly the same as Chang except for corolla. Hazard and Hazard – American – Date unknown.

Madame Cornelissen. Semi-double. Tube and sepals, rich scarlet; corolla white, veined cerise. Smallish flowers but extremely free, dark green foliage. Growth, strong, upright and bushy, hardy and suitable for hedges, height 3 ft. Cornelissen specialised in red and white cultivars, this is probably his best and the most well known. Accepted by the B.F.S. as showbench hardy. Received R.H.S. Award of Merit at Wisley Hardy Trials 1963–65; re-submitted by L.R. Russell Ltd and Sunningdale Nurseries for 1975–78 Trials and received First Class Certificate. Cornelissen – Belgian – 1860.

Madame Danjoux. Short tube and broad, long sepals carmine-red; corolla pinkish-white splashed with carmine. Largish flowers and free, growth upright and bushy, good for standard. Observe the date of introduction and still being grown today, still holding its own. Can throw semi-double flowers. Salter – British – and French – 1843.

Madame Eva Boye. Single. Tube and sepals, flesh-pink, touched cerise, corolla deep wine-purple, streaked purple. Flowers are large and very free, growth upright and bushy, often misquoted as Madame Eva Borg and confused with Elsa, Eva

Boerg, Lena and Hapsburgh. Lemoine – French – 1908.

Madame Garronne. Double. Tube and sepals bright red; corolla rich purple with rose streaks at base. Growth upright and bushy, another cultivar which appears only in California, and could be an old cultivar misnamed. Raiser and date unknown.

Madame Jacques Feuillet. Single. Cerise and white. Lemoine – french – 1913.

Madame Jules Chretien. Double. Red and white. Bonnet – Continental – 1888?.

Madame Lanteime. Double. Crimson and white. Lemoine – French – 1912.

Madame Lemoine. Double, Carmine and white. Twrdy – German – 1872.

Madame Moire. Double. Crimson and blue. Lemoine – French – 1894.

Madame Queen. Double. Tube and recurved sepals, light red; corolla deep purple. Largish flowers of unusual form with extra long stamens and pistil, borne in clusters and free. Growth upright. Hodges – American – 1958 – A.F.S. No. 344.

Madame van der Strasse. Single. Tube and sepals, light reddish-cerise; corolla white, veined and flushed cerise. Medium sized blooms, free, growth upright bush, good bedder. Hazard and Hazard – American – – 1930?.

Mademoiselle. Single. Pale pink self, similar to Countess of Aberdeen. Small flowers, very free and continuous. Growth upright bush, vigorous. *F.lycioides* × Mrs. Rundle. Reiter – American – 1941.

magdalenae. Red tube, purplish at base, red sepals; corolla scarlet. Strong upright shrub. Munz – 1943 – Columbia.

magellanica. Red tube, deep red sepals, purple corolla, small flowers, very free. The hardiest of all fuchsias and has played an important role in the evolution of the present fuchsia, extensively used by the early hybridists. There are numerous forms and natural variants which are themselves amongst the hardiest of fuchsias. *F. magellanica* was found on the mountains of Magellan, the Southernmost part of South America where the climate is often very much worse than our own. Lamark – 1768 – Chile and Argentina. (Those marked with an asterisk below are accepted by the B.F.S. as showbench hardies.)

var. *alba*.* Synonymous with *F. m.* var. *molinae.*

var. *americana elegans*.* With smaller flowers, scarlet and purple. This variant was submitted by Mr. G.S. Thomas for the R.H.S. Wisley Hardy Trials 1975–78 and although awarded a Highly Commended Certificate in the 1929 Trials did not receive any further award.

var. *aurea.* Single. Tube and sepals red, corolla purple. Identical with *F. m.* var. *gracilis* but with small golden-yellow foliage. Needs a sunny location for best results.

var. *conica.* With more rounded and fatter buds, light green foliage.

var. *discolor*.* Of dwarf habit with red and mauve flowers, very hardy. Raised from seed from a plant found at Port Famine in the Straits of Magellan.

var. *globosa*.* Small rounded and fatter buds as *F. m.* var. *conica* with scarlet and purple flowers. Much stouter form of habit and growth. Has been stated to have been raised from the seeds of *F. m.* var. *conica.*

var. *alba.* With white flowers turning to pale mauve.

var. *atkinsoniana* (Lowe 1862). Scarlet and purple flowers with long stamens and stigma. Form of *F. m. globosa* var. *elegans.*

var. *chandlerii.* This is the old French *F. globifera* and is identical to *F. g. magnifica.*

var. *coccinea.*

var. *dealbata.*

var. *Dunrobin Bedder** (Melville 1890). Bright scarlet and dark purple, small flowers of dwarf habit. Similar to *F. m. globosa* var. *perfecta.*

var. *Dunrobin Castle.* Similar to *F. m. globosa* var. *variegata* but with bright coral-red foliage.

var. *elegans.*

var. *longiflora.*

var. *magna.*

var. *magnifica.* Synonymous with *F. m. globosa* var. *chanderii.*

var. *pallida.*

var. *perfecta.* With flowers identical to *F. m. globosa* var. *Dunrobin Bedder.*

var. *ranunculiflorae plena.* With small double red and purple flowers.

var. *rosea.* With rose-coloured corolla.

var. *smithii.* With mauvish-red tube, red sepals and very dark red corolla.

var. *variegata.* With red and purple flowers and variegated foliage.

var. *gracilis*.* Flowers are slightly longer with deep purple corolla, habit of more slender growth but rampant and arching. This variant also known as Senorita in the West Coast State of Washington, U.S.A. Received the R.H.S. Highly Commended Certificate at the Wisley Hardy Trials of 1929, was re-submitted by Mr. G.S. Thomas for the 1975–78 Trials but received no further award.

F. magellanica
var. *gradiis*

alba. With white tube and sepals, corolla flushed pink.

multiflora.

tenella. Deep red tube and sepals, short blue corolla. Slender and wiry growth.

variegata*. Identical to *F. m.* var. *gracilis* but with silvery variegated foliage. Received the

R.H.S. Highly Commended Certificate at the 1960–62 Wisley Hardy Trials was re-submitted by L.R. Russell Ltd. for the 1975–78 Trials but received no further award.

var. **longipedunculata***. Very long flowers with lilac-mauve corolla.

var. **macrostema.** Much larger both in habit and flowers.

var. **molinae.** Probably the best known and widely grown as *F. m.* var. *alba*. Small flowers with white tube and very pale lilac sepals and corolla. Very hardy. This variant is also known as Maiden's Blush in the West Coast State of Washington, U.S.A.' in addition to being synonymous with *F. m.* var. *alba*.

F. magellanica
var. *molinae*

var. **multiflora.**

var. **myrtifolia.** Scarlet and purple flowers, extremely small.

var. **prostrata***.

var. **pumila***. Very small flowers, scarlet and mauve, tiny plant.

var. **riccartonii***. Probably the best known of hardy fuchsias, the name may sound of Spanish origin but originated from the garden at Riccarton, the seat of Sir William Gibson Bart. near Edinburgh; it has no connection with Riccarton near Kilmarnock as once supposed. It was raised by James Young, a well known plantsman between 1830 and 1835 and is said to have been raised from seed of Globosa. The flowers are single, tube and sepals scarlet, with dark purple corolla, very long narrow sepals recurved and held well below the horizontal; prolific with bloom, long for size with bronze to reddish cast on the foliage. This charming and deservedly popular deciduous shrub, the hardiest of all its tribe was often regarded as a hybrid but is now widely accepted as a variant of *F. magellanica* which was introduced from South American by Lamark in 1788. This species grows wild in its natural habitat near the Straits of Magellan and along the west coasts as far as Peru. Though it's hardy enough to grow in any garden in Britain, the fuchsia from Riccarton does best where rainfall, humidity and temperature are similar to those its parent enjoys. So it flourishes particularly in the West Country and in Southern Ireland, where it is pressed into service for thicket hedges up to 8 ft high. These are a sight to behold when in flower in summer and early autumn.

Elsewhere it is liable to be cut back in winter, its shoots die back almost to ground level. Cold drying winds do more damage than merely low temperatures, so this shrub differs most away from the milder moister west coast, particularly in the eastern counties. Yet it seldom expires

F. magellanica
var. *riccartonii*

altogether and in spring, fresh young shoots appear from the base. These grow 4 or 5 ft tall and bear the familiar drooping turkey-red and purple blooms, so aptly named lady's eardrops. In the east they come rather later than in Cornwall or Kerry.

The radically symmetrical hermaphrodite flowers are borne singly in the axils of the lance-shaped leaves, and nod on slender pendulous reddish stalks. They are frequently visited by bees for their nectar. In favourable conditions they may be followed by black berries, which are edible but not remarkable for their flavour. This cultivar received the R.H.S. Award of Merit for hardiness in 1966, was re-submitted again by L.R. Russell Ltd. for the 1975–78 Wisley Trials and received the R.H.S. First Class Certificate. This fuchsia is accepted by the British Fuchsia Society as a showbench hardy. Young – British – 1830.

var. **robertsii.** Similar to *F. m.* var. *riccartonii* but slightly smaller.

var. **thompsonii***. With very bright coloured flowers, tube and sepals scarlet, corolla palish purple. This variant received the Award of Merit at the R.H.S. Hardy Trials of 1963–65. Was re-submitted by Mr. G.S. Thomas for the 1975–78 Wisley Hardy Trials but received no further award.

var. **versicolor**. Submitted by Sunningdale Nurseries for the R.H.S. Wisley Hardy Trials 1975–78 and although it gained the Award of Merit in the 1963–65 trials for flowers and foliage, it received no further award.

var. **virgata.** Flowers borne in sprays.

Magenta. Rozain-Boucharlat – French – 1934.

Magenta Flush. Double. Tube spinel-red, sepals spinel-red, tipped green, held well back. Corolla magenta-rose, flushed rose-red. Large flowers, free for size, dark green foliage with serrated edges. Growth upright. Gadsby – British – 1970 – A.F.S. No. 878.

Magenta Magic. Double. Ivory tube, sepals neyron-rose, with reserve camelia-rose; corolla magenta-rose, flushed and edged camelia-rose. Large star-shaped flowers and free, large long foliage. Growth upright bush. Crockett – British – 1967 – A.F.S. No. 825.

Maggie Little. Single. Short tube crimson, streaked pale pink, sepals crimson on both sides, upper side shiny, tipped white. Corolla Imperial-purple shades rapidly to Tyrian-purple, fading with age to dark mallow-purple. Small but very neat flowers, prolific bloomer, best colour develops in sun. Largish foliage with saw toothed edged leaves, growth tall upright and bushy.

Ruthie × Schneewittchen. Ryle – British – 1975 – A.F.S. No. 1250.

Maggie Makepiece. Double. Tube and sepals turkey-red, corolla violet-purple. Flowers are fairly free and quite large. Growth upright and bushy. Holmden – 1953.

Magic. Double. Tube and sepals white, tipped green; corolla dark magenta, marbled. Large foliage, growth upright bush. Gorman – American – 1970 – A.F.S. No. 923.

Magic Flute. Single. Very thick waxy-white tube, sepals white, tipped chartreuse, narrow, thick and crisp, held at right angles from tube. Corolla clear coral-rose, white near tube. Medium sized flowers, early and very free, funnel shaped with overlapping petals. Bright green foliage, growth natural trailer. Handley – British – 1975 – A.F.S. No. 1275.

Magic Lantern. Single. Long, salmon tube 1¼ in long, sepals salmon outside, orange-salmon inside, thick and held at right angles to tube. Corolla clear orange at the base, blending to flame with a crimson edge. Medium sized flowers, clear brilliant colouring, early bloomer, best colour in sun. Growth upright and bushy, good for summer bedding, tested in the vicinity of Derby for 3 years before release. Handley – British – 1976 – A.F.S. No. 1369.

Magna. See *magellanica* var. *globosa*.

Magnate. Single. Red and purple. Story – British – 1870.

Magnet. Single. Cerise and purple. Smith – British – 1853.

Magnifica. See *magellanica* var. *globosa*.

Magnifica. Single. Carmine and crimson. Smith, G. – British – 1841.

Magnifica. Double. Short tube and heavy sepals, dark red; corolla light pink. Huge blooms living up to its name, fairly free, petals veined bright red from a bright red centre, late bloomer. Growth upright, bushy and tall. Soules – American – 1959 – A.F.S. No. 377.

Magnificent. Single. Rose and purple. Epps – British – 1843.

Maharaja. Double. Pink tube, sepals pink to salmon, tipped green; corolla dark purple with salmon and touches of orange marbling. Large blooms, free for size. Growth upright. Castro – American – 1971 – A.F.S. No. 950.

Maiden's Blush. Double. Tube and sepals, apple blossom-pink; corolla white. Medium sized flowers, very free and early. Growth low bush. Niederholzer – American – 1945.

Maiden's Blush. This is the name under which F. *magellanica* var. *molinae* is known and sold in the west coast State of Washington, U.S.A., creating utter confusion as Niederholzer produced a pink cultivar under the name of Maiden's Blush and F. *magellanica* var. *molinae* is synonymous with F. *magellanica* var. *alba*.

Maid of Kent. Single. Red and white. Banks – British – 1855.

Majestica. Semi-double. Rose and lilac. May – British – 1841.

Major Barbara. Double. Tube and sepals, pale rose. corolla light blue-violet, changing to muted old-rose with maturity. Large blooms and free, the pale rose buds open disclosing multi-petaled corolla. Growth lax bush or trailer. Schnabel-Paskesen – American – 1958 – A.F.S. No. 329.

Major Heaphy. Single. Tube and sepals, brick-red, tipped green, corolla reddish-scarlet. Small flowers but very free delightful cultivar that possesses one bad fault, will drop both buds and flowers in anything like a dry atmosphere. Growth upright and bushy. Raiser unknown – British – Date unknown.

Major Ingold. Double. Carmine and purple. Stride – British – 1911.

Malibu. Single. Tube and sepals, coral-pink, corolla rose-madder. Medium sized flowers, bell shaped, heat tolerant and free, borne in large sprays. Growth upright, vigorous and bushy. Evans – American – 1953 – A.F.S. No. 183.

Mama Bleuss. Double. Tube and sepals pink; corolla pale blue, streaked deep blue. Large flowers and free, a soft blue and pink Enchanted. Growth lax bush or trailer. Tiret – American – 1959 – A.F.S. No. 383.

Mamie. Double. Tube and sepals, coral-pink; corolla lovely cerise shade. Large blooms and free, inner petals extended down in four separate loops, outer petals slightly variegated with soft pink. Growth lax bush or trailer. Herron – American – 1954.

*Mancunian. Double. Tube longer than average starts white turning to red with maturity, long sepals are white recurving with age. Corolla white with pink veining. Medium sized blooms with unusual shape described as 'Parrot Beak' type, continuous flowering and floriferous. Growth is pendant and very suitable for basketwork, multiple side shoots are formed naturally. Raised in the vicinity of Ipswich, Suffolk, and introduced by the raiser, Gouldings Fuchsias of Ipswich, in 1985. One of a series of ten new introductions named after famous trains in 1985. Goulding – British – 1985.

Mandarin. Double. Red and purple. Bull – British – 1872.

Mandarin. Semi-double. Tube and sepals, pale salmon-pink, tipped green. Corolla glowing orange-carmine. Largish blooms and heavy, need support, free. Dark leathery green foliage, heat tolerant. Growth lax bush or trailer. Schnabel – American – 1963 – A.F.S. No. 582.

Mandy. Double. Tube and sepals, rich carmine; corolla pastel blue, ageing to rosy-pink and margined pastel blue with maturity. Large flowers and free growth upright and bushy. Thorne – British – 1964.

Manhattan. Double. Pink tube, heavy, slightly reflexed sepals, inside soft coral-pink, outer ivory with delicate pink veining. Corolla spectrum-violet, with faint pink glow at base of petals. Large blooms, compact and free. Broad foliage, olive green. Growth upright and stiff. Smith-Araujo – American – 1956 – A.F.S. No. 277.

Mantancira. No other details available other than its origin in Rio de Janeiro and could be a species.

Mantilla. Triphylla type single. The 1948 catalogue of La Rochette Nursery of Victor Reiter quotes Mantilla as a sensational new trailer with soft willowy branching growth and beautifully shingled with bronzy foliage, covers itself with long flowers of pure deep carmine, the flowers have the longest tubes, some measuring $3\frac{1}{2}$ in in length. Petals are spreading and the sepals pagoda like. The entire flower, tube, sepals and petals are of one colour, deep carmine, and during the trying American 1947 summer Mantilla alone seemed to revel in the heat. Growth unusual, cascade, will produce excellent basket; best grown as H1. The first fuchsia to be registered under the system introduced by the American Fuchsia Society in 1948. Raised by Victor Reiter Junior. Reiter – American – 1948 – A.F.S. No. 1.

Mantle. Double. Red and purple. Bland – British – 1880.

Maori Chief. Single. Red and purple. Bull – British – 1873.

Maori Maid. Double. Tube and sepals red; corolla purple. Large blooms, free for size. Growth trailer. A.F.S. Cert. of Merit 1969. Tiret – American – 1966 – A.F.S. No. 690.

Marando. Semi-double. Tube and sepals crimson; corolla rosy-purple. Medium sized flowers, fairly free and with loose corolla. Growth trailer. Fairclo – American – Date unknown.

Marcellin Berthelot. Double. Cerise and purple. Lemoine – French – 1905.

Marchioness of Anglesey. Double. Red and white. Bland – British – 1872.

Marchioness of Camden. Single. Pink and crimson. Henderson – British – 1869.

Marchioness of Cornwallis. Single. Scarlet and white. Epps – British – 1849.

*Marco Boy. Semi-double. Little known Dutch cultivar except for parentage. La Campanella seedling. *Ca* 1980.

Mardi. Double. Red and rose-pink. Similar to Fascination (Emile de Wildeman) in colour but corolla is more compact and regular, sepals do not reflex. One of the very few Spanish introductions, imported from Madeira by H.A. Brown of Chingford Nurseries in 1938. Fesco – Spanish – 1938.

Mardi Gras. Double. Tube and sepals red; corolla dark purple, heavily mottled pink. Large blooms of striking colour contrast, fairly free. Growth upright bush, vigorous. Reedstrom – American – 1958 – A.F.S. No. 358.

*Maresi. Single. Tube and sepals whitish-pink; corolla purple. Medium sized flowers, very free flowering. Growth trailer, very suitable for basketwork. Gesäuseperle × *F. magellanica* var. *gracilis.* Nutzinger – Austrian – 1971.

Margaret. Semi-double. Tube and sepals, carmine-scarlet, corolla violet, veined cerise.

Margaret

Medium sized flowers, large for hardy, very free when established. Growth upright, bushy and vigorous, suitable for hedge, height up to four feet, very hardy. One of Margaret's selfed seedlings produced by Mrs. W.P. Wood. Accepted by the B.F.S. as showbench hardy. *F.magellanica* var. *alba* × Heritage. Wood – British – 1937 or 1943.

Margaret B. Herron. Double. Tube and recurved sepals, crimson. Corolla purple. Largish flowers with ragged shaped petals, very free. Growth trailer. Fairclo – American – 1947.

Margaret Brown. Single. Tube and sepals, rose-pink, corolla light rose-bengal. Smallish flowers and very free, lightish green foliage. Growth upright, bushy and vigorous, very hardy, will make a low hedge, height up to 2 to 3 ft, not as vigorous as Margaret. Named after Mrs. Margaret Slater, Past president of the B.F.S. Accepted by the B.F.S. as showbench hardy. Wood – British – 1949.

Margaret Ellen. Single. Short thick tube light rose, medium length sepals are broad held horizontal, light rose, tipped green. Light rose-pink corolla, petals edged deep rose and flushed pink at base with deep rose veining. Medium sized flowers $\frac{3}{4}$ in long almost a self colour, pink stamens, white stigma and light pink style. Midgreen foliage, broad with pointed and heavily serrated edges. Growth medium upright and bushy will take full sun. Tested for 3 years in vicinity of Cardiff, South Wales before release. Adams – British – 1982 – A.F.S. No. 1689.

Margaret Hepburn. Double. Crimson tube, fluffy, reflexed sepals crimson with lower surface crepe textured. Purple corolla with crimson veining and flushed crimson at the base. Medium sized ruffled blooms $1\frac{1}{2}$ in long with long crimson filaments and style. Pale green foliage with denticulated spear shaped leaves. Growth medium upright and bushy, very suitable for bush and standard, best colour in shade. Tested for 2 years in vicinity of Midlothian, Scotland, before release Royal Velvet × Fascination. McGuigan – British – 1982 – A.F.S. No. 1682.

Margaret Hines. Single. Pink and red. Strutt – unknown – 1910.

*Margaret Pilkington. Single. Tube and sepals waxy-white with rose-Bengal veining. Corolla bishop's violet, maturing with age to mallow purple. Very free flowering with great showbench potential. Tested and proved on the Northern showbenches under its original name Euston before release. Named after the wife of the Northern showman Ken Pilkington of Blackpool. Growth upright, bushy and short jointed. Raised in the vicinity of Merseyside and introduced jointly both by J.V. Porter of Southport and P. Chilton of Castledyke Nurseries, Lincolnshire, in 1984. Clark, D. – British – 1984.

Margaret Piper. Double. Red and white. Dixon – British – 1896.

Margaret Roe. Single. Tube and sepals, rosy-red; corolla pale violet-purple. Medium sized blooms, very free, held upright. Growth upright bush, hardy in Midlands, makes excellent bedder. Sister seedling of Lady Isobel Barnett. Caroline × Derby Belle. Gadsby – British – 1968 – A.F.S. No. 975.

Margaret Rose. Single. Short, thick tube, neyron-rose, sepals neyron-rose (R.H.S. 55B) with green tips, broadly open to almost horizontal.

Corolla neyron/rose with spinel-red (R.H.S. 54A) picotee edge. Medium sized flowers, best colour in shade. Growth tall, upright and bushy. Named after Princess Margaret, Countess of Snowdon on the opening of the Manchester Silver Jubilee Show 1975. Hobbs, N. – British – 1976 – A.F.S. No. 1380.

Margaret Susan. Single. Thin tube carmine, sepals outside crimson, inside carmine, tipped green. Corolla fuchsia-purple, carmine-rose at base of petals. Flowers medium sized, very free, well shaped with little fading. Growth upright and self-branching. Hugh Morgan × Melody. Holmes, R. – British – 1973 – A.F.S. 1205.

Margaret Swales. Semi-double. Ivory tube, shading to pink, sepals ivory, tipped green. Corolla carmine-rose, shading to white at base. Medium sized blooms with loose petaloids, striped carmine-rose to white. Dark green foliage, broad with smooth edges. Growth trailer. Sport of La Fiesta. Swales – British – 1974 – A.F.S. No. 1177.

Margaret Thatcher. Single. White tube and sepals, sepals tipped green and curved back; corolla bluebird-blue passing to spectrum-violet. Medium-sized flowers, growth is sturdy, upright and bushy. Named after the famous politician. One of the last introductions to be raised by the hybridist. Christine Clements × Forward Look. Gadsby – British – 1978 – A.F.S. No. 1482.

Margarita. Single. Tube and sepals carmine; corolla short, orchid-purple. Large bell shaped flowers and free for size. Growth upright and bushy. Niederholzer – American – 1940.

*Margarite. Double. Tube very pale pink, striped pale rose, sepals pale rose fading towards tips. Corolla white with pale rose veining at base. Large box shaped blooms and very free for size and for a double. Growth upright and bushy, considered to be a breakthrough in the hardy range. Tested for 7 years and proved to be hardy in the vicinity of Weybourne, Norfolk. Introduced by Kerrielyn Fuchsias of Cambridge in 1984. Dawson, H. – British – 1984.

*Marge Gentry. Single. Longish rose-red tube, half down sepals ⁷⁄₃₂ in long by ₆⁄₁₆ in wide red-rose on top, slightly lighter (R.H.S. 50B) underneath, white tipped are recurved. Corolla opens rose-red (R.H.S. 50A) maturing to red (R.H.S. 45A) ½ in long by ⅜ in wide. Small encliandral shaped flowers, deep colouring, stamens do not extend below corolla, white filaments and anthers, pink style and stigma. Foliage medium green with ovate leaves 1 in long by ½ in wide, serrated and with obtuse tips and bases. Growth natural trailer, will produce good basket, pyramid or decorative. Trademarked in California, U.S.A. Raised in the vicinity of Oxnard, California, U.S.A. Chance Encounter seedling. Schneider – American – 1984 – A.F.S. No. 1754.

Margery Blake. Single. Tube and sepals scarlet; corolla solferino-purple. Flowers small but very profuse continuous bloomer, growth upright, bushy and hardy. Accepted by the B.F.S. as showbench hardy. Wood – British – 1950.

Margharita. Double. Pale pink tube, sepals palest creamy-pink of good firm texture. Corolla white, of immaculate form. Medium to large blooms and free, fully double with centre petals folded in forming tubes, outer petals are pleated.

Growth upright and bushy, strong habit. Miller – British – 1970.

Margie. Double. Tube and sepals, flushed pink; corolla lavender-orchid. Large flowers and free, ruffled petals with serrated edges. Growth upright and willowy. Reimers – American – 1953 – A.F.S. No. 170.

Marginata. Single. Blush-white and pink. Banks – British – 1862.

Marginata. Single. Tube and sepals vermillion; corolla rose-Bengal, dark edge. Large flowers and free. Growth trailer. Niederholzer – American – 1946.

Margo. Double. Tube and sepals red, white corolla. Medium sized flowers but beautifully proportioned and firm. Introduced by John Smith of Hilltop Nurseries Leicestershire 1980. Raiser and date unknown.

Mar-Greta. Double. Long tube bright red, long sepals bright red; corolla white with red markings upside. Large blooms with serrated petals, free and long lasting. Dark green foliage. Growth trailer. Gagnon – American – 1968 – A.F.S. No. 784.

Marguerite. Bull – British – 1865.

Maria Louisa. Single. Pink and crimson. Miller – British – 1846.

Marianne. Semi-double. Tube and sepals deep pink; corolla light violet-blue. Medium sized flowers, very free, growth upright bush. Curtis – British – 1973.

Marianne. No other details except this cultivar grown in the Netherlands was raised by van Wieringen in 1970 and is also known in Holland as Pink Marianne. Not to be confused with the Marianne by Curtis, T.J., 1973.

Maria Papke. Double. Pink tube, sepals pink, curling around tube; corolla blue splashed with salmon-pink. Large blooms resemble an orchid, pleated petals at base. Dark green foliage with red veins. Growth trailer. Prentice – American – 1968 – A.F.S. No. 787.

Marie Cornelissen. Single. Scarlet and purple. Cornelissen – Belgian – 1861.

Marie Juillard. Semi-double. Tube and sepals pink, tipped green; corolla pink with light green markings. Medium sized flowers, not very free which refuse to open under wrong conditions, growth lax bush. Greene – American – 1929.

Marie Louise. Double. Tube and sepals, bright red, wide and thick. Corolla white, veined red. Large blooms with serrated petals, free blooming. Growth lax bush or trailer. Martin – American – 1957 – A.F.S. No. 315.

Marietta. Double. Carmine tube, broad upturned sepals bright carmine; corolla dark magenta-red with splashes of carmine on outer petals. maturing to dark clear red. Large blooms, free for size, growth upright. Uncle Jules × . Waltz – American – 1958 – A.F.S. No. 354.

Marie Weinrich. Single. White and rose. Weinrich – German – 1867.

Marilyn. Double. Tube and broad sepals, pink, quarter way down long tube, each sepal curls partially. Corolla white. flowers very compact with petaloids at each corner of each sepal giving oval shape, fairly free. growth lax bush or trailer. Martin – American – 1961 – A.F.S. No. 463.

Marin Belle. Single. Salmon-pink tube, sepals salmon-pink; turn gracefully back covering tube, ovary and petiole. Corolla pansy-violet, veined pink, medium sized flowers, bell shaped and free. Growth upright and vigorous, makes good standard. Reedstrom – American – 1959 – A.F.S. No. 388.

Marin Glow. Single. Raised and introduced by Phil F. Reedstrom in Novato, California in 1954 is probably one of the best single introductions to be sent over to this country. The tube and sepals are pure waxy-white, whilst the corolla is Imperial rich purple, ageing slowly to magenta and whilst in its prime, seems to be almost phosphorescent. The blooms are of medium size and extremely profuse, of a classic fuchsia shape. Medium green foliage is clean, but does seem to attract the white fly under unsuitable conditions. The growth is strong and upright, develops into a shapely bush without much attention. It is vigorous and self-branching and for normal decorative purposes, two stoppings are sufficient, if required for the showbench, will respond to frequent pinching; a well grown plant will require a lot of beating when used for exhibition purposes. This charming cultivar is easy to propagate, easy to grow and one of the easiest to time for any particular show. Although mainly grown as a bush plant, will produce excellent half or full standard and fine material for a pyramid. Is best grown as H2 with the protection of glass and shade, which brings out the deep purple colouring, not too good as a bedder, where the sun bleaches the corolla to a pale mauve. One slight fault is that Marin Glow does tend to shed its blooms quickly, but with the profusion of flowers, is hardly noticed. Reedstrom after his success with this cultivar, produced Marin Belle in 1959, but nothing to be compared with Marin Glow, he also introduced Marin Monarch in 1955 and Marin Jewel in 1956, but none of these can compare with a cultivar which should be in every fuchsia grower's selection, a cultivar which the beginner can grow with every chance of success. Reedstrom – American – 1954 – A.F.S. No. 204.

Marin Jewel. Double. Flesh-pink tube, up-turned sepals, flesh-pink, slightly darker and iridescent on underside. Corolla mallow-purple, with apricot to pink shadings at base of petals. Flowers are large and free with almost rectangular buds. Light green foliage. Growth upright, bushy and vigorous. Reedstrom – American – 1956 – A.F.S. No. 255.

Marinka. Single. Tube and sepals, rich red; corolla slightly darker red, almost a self. Medium

sized flowers, extremely profuse, has the appearance of a semi-double, beautifully shaped. Growth vigorous cascade, versatile for all types of training except bush, has become the standard upon which all baskets are judged, excellent as a weeping standard or pyramid. Will still be taking red cards for many years to come, probably the raisers best introduction. H.R.S. Award of Merit 1929. Best grown as H1. Rozain-Boucharlat – French – 1902.

Marin Monarch. Double. Red tube and sepals; corolla royal purple, fading quickly to dark red with shades of purple remaining. Large blooms but not very free, odd, but regal fuchsia. Growth upright, vigorous and fast, best grown as H1. Reedstrom – American – 1955 – A.F.S. No. 239.

Marion Clyne. Single. No details available other than it is very similar and no improvement upon Mieke Meursing. Mieke Meursing × Pink Galore. Clyne – British – 1975.

Marionette. Double. Tube and sepals, white changing to pink; corolla white. medium sized flowers and free. Growth upright and bushy. Reiter – American – 1946.

Marion Young. Double. Short red (R.H.S. 16B) tube, broad red (R.H.S. 61B) sepals reflex up to cover tube and ovary. Corolla pink (R.H.S. 74D) shaded lilac (R.H.S. 75A). Medium to large blooms with petaloids same colour as petals, stamens and pistil rose coloured. Medium sized foliage yellow-green (R.H.S. 144A). Growth tall upright, will make good bush or standard. Originates from the vicinity of Kearsley, Bolton. Sport of La France (Lemoine). Young – British – 1980 – – A.F.S. No. 1572.

Mariposa. Single. Tube and sepals satiny-scarlet fusing to geranium-lake at base; corolla dark carmine changing to geranium-lake at sepal joints. medium sized blooms and free. Growth trailer. Mme Aubin × Ballet Girl. Reiter – American – 1942.

Marjon Wit. Single. Tube and sepals red, corolla dark blue. Medium-sized flowers, early and free flowering, growth upright and bushy. Steevens – Dutch – 1972.

Marjorie Hillgers. Double. Tube and sepals, dark rose, flushed pink; corolla shell-pink, veined dark rose. Medium sized flowers and free. Growth trailer. Evans and Reeves – American – 1939.

Marjory. Single. Tube and sepals pink; corolla bluish-purple. Medium sized flowers and free. Growth trailer. Hazard and Hazard – American – Date unknown.

Mark MacDougall. Double. Tube and sepals waxy-red; corolla parma-violet, flushed and veined red. Large blooms, very free and early. Growth upright, bushy and very fast. Thorne – British – 1962.

Marlboro. Semi-double. Tube and wide sepals, deep scarlet; corolla white, veined red. Medium sized flowers and free. Dark green foliage, growth upright and tall. Evans and Reeves – American – 1937.

*Marlies. Double. Little known Dutch cultivar with the parentage of Swingtime × Celebrity. van de Beek – Dutch – 1983.

Marinka

Mars. Semi-double. Short, thick tube rose-pink, sepals are also short and thick, pink (R.H.S. 49A) outside of good substance, rose (R.H.S. 52B) inside. Corolla cardinal-red (R.H.S. 53C) with edges and base a lighter red (R.H.S. 50A). Medium-sized blooms, best colour in shade, early bloomer, growth natural trailer, self branching, will make good basket without weights, tested for eight years in Derbyshire before release. British hybridiser did raise a cultivar named Mars in 1863 but is now considered to be out of cultivation. Handley – British – 1977 – A.F.S. No. 1414.

*Marshside. Semi-double. Thin tube Naples yellow suffused green; sepals are French rose on outside and Venetian pink underneath. Corolla lilac-purple, veined turkey-red; white at base of petals. Medium sized blooms and very free flowering. Growth upright, bushy and strong vigorous habit. Raised in the vicinity of Southport, Lancashire, and introduced by the raiser J.V. Porter of Southport in 1983. Porter – British – 1982.

Martha. Single. Pink and crimson. Barkway – British – 1847.

Martha Auer. No other details known except the parentage: Koralle × Golden Glow. Nutzinger – Austrian – 1972.

Martha Brown. Double. Short glossy red (R.H.S. 53B) tube, reflexed sepals glossy red on outside, dull red (R.H.S. 52A) underneath 1¼ in long by ½ in wide. Corolla greyish-purple veined red (R.H.S. 52A). Medium sized blooms of about 1 in, with distinctly shaped eight petalled corolla surrounded by four petaloids with very short stamens and pistil. Glossy dark green foliage, small leaves but heavily veined. Growth self-branching small upright, will make good bush, standard or decorative. Will take full sun in Ventura, California where it was tested for 2 years before release, will be trademarked in California. Registered by Barbara Schneider of Oxnard. Brown – American – 1981 – A.F.S. No. 1659.

Martha Marie. Single. Tube and sepals, white with bluish tinge; corolla violet-blue. Large flowers and free. Growth trailer. Waltz – American – Date unknown.

Martha Werle. Double. Tube and sepals, bright red; corolla cyclamen-purple. Medium sized flowers and free, early. Growth upright and bushy, small. Werle – American – 1940.

Martha Wolger. Double. Tube and sepals dark pink; corolla pure white. Medium-sized blooms very early with rich colouring. Growth lax bush, suitable both for basket or pot work. F. corymbiflora × Golden Glow. Nutzinger – Austrian – 1973.

Martin. Double. Short tube light pink, sepals white, shaded light pink. Corolla white, variegated light pink. Large flowers, fairly free, petaloids have spots of green. Small, darkish green foliage, growth trailer. Pennisi – American – 1968 – A.F.S. No. 756.

Martina. Single. Short white tube, sepals white, Flushed bluish-pink on inside. Corolla lilac with white at base. Medium sized blooms, very prolific, do not fade with maturity. Growth upright and bushy, good pot plant. Handley – British – 1971 – A.F.S. No. 987.

Martin's Magic. Double. Tube and sepals, reddish-pink to pink; corolla bright magenta-red.

Large flowers, fairly free. Growth lax bush or trailer. Martin – American – 1962 – A.F.S. No. 518.

Martin's Midnight. Double. Tube and sepals, bright red, corolla deep India-blue. Large flowers, full and free, continuous bloomer. Growth upright. Martin – American – 1959 – A.F.S. No. 370.

Marty. Double. Tube and sepals pink, corolla orchid-pink. Large blooms, fairly free. Growth lax bush or trailer. Tiret – American – 1962 – A.F.S. No. 527.

Martyn Smedley. Single. Tube and sepals, waxy neyron-rose; corolla blue-bird inside, wisteria-blue, shaded white outside. Medium sized blooms held horizontal, free, will stand dull sun. Growth upright and bushy. Gadsby – British – 1968 – A.F.S. No. 974.

Marvel. Semi-double. Red and purple. Raiser unknown – Continental – Date unknown.

Marvellous. Double. Red and purple. Banks – British – 1866.

Mary. Triphylla single. Long tube, vivid bright scarlet self. Short petals, very free, flowers up to 3 in long. Sepals are fully reflexed as flower matures and like most triphyllas, loses some lower leaves through yellowing, even before the plant matures. Very dark sage-green foliage, veined magenta and heavily ribbed, purplish underneath. Often confused with Superba. Growth upright. F. triphylla × F. corymbiflora. Bonstedt – German – 1894.

Mary

Mary Ann. Single. White and red. Barkway – British – 1846.

Marybeth. Single. Tube and sepals white, tinted lilac; corolla soft salmon. Medium sized flowers, long and free, light green foliage. Growth lax bush or trailer. Patty × Blue Boy. Evans and Reeves – American – 1939.

Mary Clare. Semi-double. Short tube creamy-white, reflexed sepals creamy-pink; white at base. Corolla shaded pink to rosy-claret, white at base. Medium sized blooms and free, growth upright. Sport of Blue Moon. Schulte – American – 1951 – A.F.S. No. 93.

Mary di Barnardo. Double. Short white tube, sepals white; corolla light pink with variegated edges and blue dot on tips. Large flowers, fairly free, dark green foliage, require shade. Growth upright and bushy. Pennisi – American – 1969 – A.F.S. No. 816.

Mary Ellen. Double. Tube and sepals, light pink; corolla lavender-blue, fading slightly with age. Large blooms, early and very profuse. Growth trailer. Antonelli – American – 1971 – A.F.S. No. 1006.

Mary E. Ware. Double. Self coloured solid pale pink. Largish blooms and free. Growth medium bush. Niederholzer – American – 1945.

Mary Fairclo. Single. Deep pink self. Medium sized blooms and free, real novelty with corolla shaped like a Christmas bell, heat resistant. Growth trailer. Fairclo – American – 1955.

Mary Flanders. Semi-double. Long white tube, sepals white with bright green tips; corolla peachy-pink. Growth natural trailer. Gagnon – American – 1969 – A.F.S. No. 846.

Mary Gates. Single. Pink and blue. Dixon – British – 1904.

Mary Horder. Single. White and rose-pink. Rogers – British – 1896.

Mary Joan. Double. Long rose madder tube ⅝ × ¼ in sepals rose madder ⅞ in × 1¾ in. Corolla light and deep lavender streaked light and dark cerise, fading with maturity. Medium sized blooms approximately 1¾ in long formed of a minimum of twelve petals with four longer ones in centre giving two stage effect, four petaloids same colour as corolla but more streaked with cerise. Medium sized foliage with lanceolate leaves with serrated edges and red mid-ribs and stems. Growth self-branching tall upright, will make good bush or standard. Will take full sun in Nottinghamshire where tested for 3 years before release. Caunt – British – A.S.F. No. 1632.

Mary Kipling. Single. Short tube white suffused neyron-rose, short sepals are white, heavily suffused neyron-rose on top surface, creped neyron-rose underneath, tipped green. Corolla methyl-violet with prominent rose veins turning to rose with maturity. Bell-shaped medium sized flowers, edges of petals turn in towards stigma, extremely floriferous. Small dark green foliage with red main veins. Growth medium upright, self-branching will make good bush or standard, best colour develops when shaded. Originates from the vicinity of Knitsley in County Durham. Atkinson – British – 1980 – A.F.S. No. 1548.

Mary Lockyer. Double. Red tube, broad sepals red, underside has crepe appearance, tipped green. Corolla pale lilac, marbled red from top downwards. Large blooms, fairly free. Growth strong upright and bushy. Colville – British – 1967.

Mary Lou. Double. White tube, sepals white, washed rose-red of crepe texture; corolla creamy-white. Medium sized blooms, long pointed and free. Growth upright. Hazard and Hazard – American – Date unknown.

*Mary Marie. Double. Short red tube, red sepals (R.H.S. 50A) on top, crepey red (R.H.S. 50B) underneath, held horizontally with recurved tips 1 in long by ½ in wide. Corolla opens creamy-white (R.H.S. 155B) maturing to creamy-white with pink splashes 1 in long by 1 in wide with smooth petal margins. Medium sized blooms full flared with corolla held flat against the sepals, pink filaments and anthers, same colour style and stigma. Pale lime-green foliage (R.H.S. 151A) slightly lighter (R.H.S. 151B) underneath, ovate leaves 2¾ in long by 1½ in wide with entire margins, acute tip and rounded base, veins and branches burgundy colour. Growth lax upright or stiff trailer, makes good basket with weights, standard, pillar or decorative. Trademarked in California, U.S.A., where it received

first award in 1982/83 N.F.S. Show for unintroduced seedling class. Raised in vicinity of Oxnard, California, U.S.A. Unknown seedling. Schneider – American – 1984 – A.F.S. No. 1755.

Mary Miloni. Double. Tube and sepals, pink inside, white with pink stripes outside. Corolla deep purple with pink marbling. Small foliage, heat resistant. Growth upright. Pennisi – American – 1969 – A.F.S. No. 813.

Mary Murray. Single. Short thick light pink (R.H.S. 50C) tube, sepals light pink on upper surface, dark pink (R.H.S. 50B) underneath. Corolla pink (R.H.S. 55A). Small flowers but very free flowering. Dull dark green foliage with small heaert shaped leaves. Growth self-branching small upright, will make good bush or decorative. Tested for 2 years in vicinity of San Diego, California, and 1 year in vicinity of Oxnard, California, before release where it will be trademarked. Anonymous raiser but registered by Barbara Schneider of Oxnard. Raiser unknown – American 1981 – A.F.S. No. 1658.

Mary Pennisi. Double. Short white tube, sepals white, tipped green. Corolla purple with light rose at base. Large flowers, fairly free, heat resistant. Small and thick foliage. Growth trailer. Pennisi – American – 1971 – A.F.S. No. 1014.

Mary Poppins. Single. Tube and sepals pale apricot, tipped pink; corolla orange-vermilion. Medium sized flowers and free, growth bushy. Need – British – 1967.

Mary Reynolds. Double. Tube rhodonite-red (R.H.S. 51A). Medium long, recurving rhodonite-red (R.H.S. 51A) sepals. Violet (R.H.S. 83B) corolla. Medium to large blooms, free flowering, corolla opens out wide when mature, long pistil, best colour in shade. Growth upright and bushy, good for most types of training. Raised in the vicinity of Leyland, Lancashire. Awarded B.F.S. Bronze Certificate of Merit at Manchester 1976. Angel's Flight × Royal Velvet. Reynolds – British – 1976 – A.F.S. No. 1363.

*Mary Rose. Double. Fairly long and thin tube rose-Bengal, sepals rose-Bengal, tipped green. Corolla white flushed and veined purple, medium sized blooms of good shape. Growth very strong upright and bushy, excellent for either bush/shrub or standard. Raised in the vicinity of Melton Mowbray, Leicestershire, and introduced by the raiser, Pacey's Nurseries in 1984. Pacey – British – 1984.

Mary Thorne. Single. Tube and sepals, turkey-red; corolla violet. scarlet at base, ageing to purple. Medium sized flowers, very free, large foliage and darkish green. Growth upright, bushy and hardy in the Midlands. Lovely cultivar, one of Thorne's best, makes delightful bush plant. Thorne – British – 1954.

Mary Wright. Double. Bright pink tube, sepals very bright pink arch back to tube. Corolla bright pink. Medium sized blooms and a self-coloured cultivar. Medium green large foliage. Growth tall, upright and bushy, will make good standard, best colour develops in the sun. Originates from the vicinity of Warwickshire. Seedling of Lace Petticoats. Wright, J.A. – British – 1980 – A.F.S. No. 1603.

Masquerade. Double. Short tube and sepals, flesh colour to pink; corolla medium purple, outer petals pleated, marbled pink. Very large blooms, petals flaring wide with maturity, fairly free.

Growth trailer. A.F.S. Cert. of Merit 1965. Kennett – American – 1963 – A.F.S. No. 590.

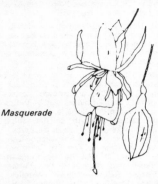

Masquerade

Masterpiece. Single. Red and purple. Henderson – British – 1891.

Master Stroke. Double. White tube, broad horizontal sepals white, corolla white, composed of large pendant centre petals and shorter ones attached to sepals, forming a large bloom as the sepals flare. All petals curl and twist, pink flush on shorter petals and on outside. Flowers are large; fairly free, big, round ornamental white buds. Growth trailer or espalier. Hodges – American – 1957 – A.F.S. No. 297.

Matador. Single. Tube and sepals pink, corolla purple. Medium sized flowers of intense colour, hence the name. Raised and introduced by J.A. Wright of Hilltop Nurseries, Atherstone in 1979. Wright, J.A. – British – 1979.

Matchless. Bland – British – 1882.

mathewsii. This is a species of which little is known except for the fact that it comes from Amazonas, Peru. MacBride – 1940 – Peru.

Maureen Munro. Single. Tube and sepals neyron-rose (H.C.C. 623/1), sepals held horizontally, short tube. Corolla amethyst-violet (H.C.C. 35/2). Small flowers and very free-flowering, growth strong, vigorous and bushy, excels as an outside bedder, growth 12 in to 15 in high. Alison Ewart × Carol Peat. Roe – British – 1980.

Mauve Beauty. Double. Tube and sepals cerise; corolla lilac-mauve. Medium sized flowers, one of the best and most free flowering doubles. Growth upright and bushy. Beautiful cultivar aptly named, easy to grow. R.H.S. Award of Merit 1929. Banks – British – 1869.

Mauve Lace. Double. Tube and sepals red; corolla mauve. Large blooms, continuous flowering, dark green foliage. Growth upright and bushy, height 2 to 2½ ft. Hardy in Southern England, raised in the Scilly Isles. Tabraham – British – 1974.

Mauve Poincaré. Single. Tube and sepals crimson; corolla clear mauve. Largish flowers, early and free, long and bell-shaped. Growth upright and bushy. Sport of Henri Poincare. Rawlins – British – 1951.

Mauve Princess. Semi-double. Tube and sepals, rich red; corolla lilac-mauve. Medium bell shaped flowers, very free. Growth upright bush. Coene – Belgian – 1873.

Mauve Queen. Double. Red and mauve. Banks – British – 1872.

Mauvette. Single. Waxy tube dark pink, sepals dark pink. Corolla mauve-pink, very profuse and long lasting. Long pointed blush-white buds turn gracefully and when fully open seem almost twisted. Small foliage and described as a dainty trailer. Reedstrom – American – 1955 – A.F.S. No. 238.

Mauve Wisp. Double. Tube and sepals deep pink; corolla lavender-blue. Small flowers borne in profusion and continuous. Foliage medium green, growth upright bushy and dainty, height 6 to 9 in. Very suitable for rockeries, window boxes and troughs. One of a new series of hardy miniature cultivars, hardy in Southern England and raised in the Scilly Isles. Tabraham – British – 1976.

Maxine Elizabeth. Single. Thick waxy tube, sepals broad and long, flushed pink outside, salmon-pink inside. Corolla rose-red with orange flushed petal edges. Medium sized flowers, bell shaped, early and free. Growth upright bush. Tiret – American – 1950 – A.F.S. No. 65.

*****Max Jaffa.** Single. New seedling raised by David Burns of Bungay to commemorate the centenary of the Scarborough Horticultural Society. Tube and sepals orient-pink, sepals held slightly below the horizontal. Corolla mandarin-red, medium sized flowers. Produced in great numbers near the perimeter of the plant, early to appear and produced continuously. Foliage attractive dark green. Growth is on the lax side, very suitable for full standards, can also be trained with success in hanging container. Raised in the vicinity of Bungay, Suffolk, and introduced by Sturdley Royal Nurseries of Ripon in 1985. Margaret Roe × Chillerton Beauty seedling × Santa Barbara. Burns – British – 1985.

*****Mayblossom.** Double. Tube and sepals rose-Bengal; corolla white fused rose-Bengal. Small round foliage, small fully double blooms, very free flowering. Growth trailing but short jointed and compact, excellent for basketwork will trail well without weights. Raised in the vicinity of Melton Mowbray, Leicestershire, and introduced by the raiser, Pacey's Nurseries in 1984. Pacey – British – 1984.

May-Dalene. Double. Tube and sepals, heavy crepe bright red; corolla and petals lush pink, veined with bright rose. Large blooms of unusual shade of pink, fairly free. Growth tall, upright bush. Gagnon – American – 1964 – A.F.S. No. 603.

Mayfayre. Double. Short tube and very broad sepals, red. Corolla white, shaded carmine, largish blooms, petals with rolled edges and fairly free. Growth upright. Colville – British – 1967.

May Felton. Double. Red and purple. Felton – British – 1870.

Mayfield. Single. Red (R.H.S. 52A) tube, deep rose-pink (R.H.S. 52B) sepals 1¾ in by ⁵⁄₁₆ wide crepe texture underneath, immature flowers are tipped green. Corolla violet-blue (R.H.S. 91B) edged darker (R.H.S. 91A) fading to purple (R.H.S. 78B) with darker edge. Bell shaped flowers 1¼ in long by 1½ in wide, red vein in centre of each petal and lighter veins at base, long red (R.H.S. 52C) pistil long stamens red (R.H.S. 52B) with red-purple (R.H.S. 71C) anthers. Medium green (R.H.S. 137B) foliage 1½ in long ×

$\frac{7}{16}$ in wide, serrated leaves with light veins. Growth self-branching medium upright, compact and short-jointed, suitable for the showbench with major awards in 1981. Raised and tested for 8 years in vicinity of Newcastle-on-Tyne before being introduced by R. and J. Pacey of Stathern, Melton Mowbray, in 1982. Hall – British – 1982 – A.F.S. No. 1666.

Mayflower. Single. Red and red-white. Smith – British – 1866.

Mayflower. Double. Tube and sepals, deep pink to rose, conspicuously tipped green; corolla light pink. Largish blooms and free, larger and softer pink than Southgate, flaring and spreading. Growth trailer. Hodges – American – 1956 – A.F.S. No. 248.

May Prentice. Double. Tube and sepals, rose-pink; corolla white at base and veined pink. Large blooms, fairly free, non fading, large long buds of rose-pink. Growth upright. Prentice – American – 1966 – A.F.S. No. 667.

May Queen. Single. White and rose. Bull – British – 1869.

May Queen. Double. Tube and sepals, pinkish-white; corolla pale blue centre, pink on outer edge. medium sized blooms, very free, continuous and early. Growth lax bush or trailer. Martin – American – 1962 – A.F.S. No. 519.

Maytime. Double. Tube and sepals, rosy-pink; corolla lilac. Large blooms, fairly free, growth lax bush or trailer. Tiret – American – 1965 – A.F.S. No. 649.

Mazda. Single. Tube and sepals, pale orange with pink; corolla carmine-orange, paler at base. Medium sized blooms, free, darkish green foliage. Growth upright bush, vigorous, needs early pinching. Reiter – American – 1947.

Mazie. Double. White tube, sepals white with pink flushes and bright red tips; corolla orchid with pink at base. Medium sized blooms with rose filaments and bright red anthers. Growth lax can be trained either as trailer or bush. Hanson – American – ca 1970.

Meadowlark. Double. Tube long white, sepals white tipping green, recurved and held at the horizontal and sit on the corolla. Corolla purple to bright rose, streaked white. Large flowers with white stamens and style. Growth trailer. Some confusion exists in the registration with the A.F.S. – described as red and white whereas raiser confirms colouring as above. Kennett – American – 1971 – A.F.S. No. 956.

*Medalist. Double. Short thick tube bright pink striped darker pink $\frac{1}{2}$ in long by $\frac{1}{4}$ in wide. Fully up sepals bright pink on top, slightly deeper pink underneath 2 in long by 1 in wide, with recurving tips. Corolla is white 2 in long by 4 in wide. Corolla white with white streaked pink petaloids $\frac{3}{4}$ in long and from $\frac{1}{2}$ in to 2 in wide, the corolla itself measures 2 in long by 4 in wide. Very large blooms, ruffled and fully flared, pink filaments and dull red anthers, pink style and ivory stigma. Large dark green foliage with elliptic leaves $3\frac{1}{2}$ in long by 2 in wide. Growth lax upright on stiff trailer, prefers cool conditions. Raised in the vicinity of Oceanside, California, U.S.A. This cultivar together with Roxanne Belle were the only two introductions by the hybridiser in 1984. Cyndy Robyn x Trade Winds. Stubbs – American – 1984 – A.F.S. No. 1753.

Medallion. Double. Short tube near white, sepals pale pink; corolla pale pink. Largish blooms and free, needs shade, light green foliage. Growth upright and bushy. Paskesen – American – 1968 – A.F.S. No. 761.

Meditation. Double. Tube and sepals red; corolla creamy-white, veined carmine. Medium sized flowers, very early and free. Growth upright and bushy, hardy in southern districts. Blackwell – British – 1956.

Medora. Banks – British – 1863.

Medusa. Semi-double. Tube and sepals red; corolla white with snake-like petaloids. Large flowers and very free for size, very striking flowers. Prefers cool conditions, growth upright and bushy. Introduced by Wills Fuchsia Nurseries in 1979. Centrepiece x. de Graaff – Dutch – 1976.

Meg. Semi-double. White long tube, sepals white, tipped green, long and narrow. Corolla roseine-purple. Medium sized blooms, growth lax trailer and needs staking for bush training. Raised and tested for three years before release in the vicinity of Melton Mowbray, Leicestershire. Raised and introduced by R. and J. Pacey of Stathern, Melton Mowbray, in 1982. Pacey – British – 1982.

Mei Ling. Semi-double. Tube and sepals pink; corolla very pale purple. medium sized flowers, early and free, blooms in flushes. Growth trailer. Niederholzer – American – 1947.

Mein Lieberling. Semi-double. Tube and sepals, pale cerise; corolla pinkish-white, veined pink. Small flowers but very free. Growth upright dwarf, very compact, hardy. Kohler – German – 1927.

Mel Newfield. Double. Short red tube, long sepals, reflexed turkey-red; corolla amethyst-violet, marbled carmine, matures to deepest cyclamen-purple, largish flowers, fairly free, heat tolerant. Growth upright, very vigorous, up to 5 ft in California. Schnabel – American – 1952 – A.F.S. No. 109.

Melody. Single. Tube and recurved sepals, pale rose-pink; corolla pale cyclamen-purple. Medium sized flowers, very free. Bright green foliage, growth upright and bushy. Easy cultivar, one of the best American introductions but seems to have lost favour. Good for all shapes, especially as a standard. Patty Evans x Mrs. Victor Reiter. Reiter (Sr.) – American – 1942.

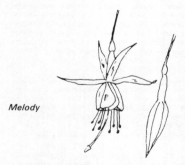

Melody

Melody Ann. Double. Tube and sepals, white with pink at base; corolla light pink. Large blooms, very free and continuous. Growth lax bush or trailer. Gagnon – American – 1966 – A.F.S. No. 657.

Melpomene. No other details except the parentage: *F. regia* var. *typica* × Bon Accorde. De Groot – Dutch – *ca* 1970.

Mel Riha. Semi-double. Thin dark pink tube, sepals pink with dark pink veins on upperside, dark pink on lower side, tipped green, extend outward and downward, twisting in pink wheel fashion with maturity. Corolla blue with pink variegation at base. Medium sized flowers, free, flare out and blue fades to lavender with age, six petaloids. Large foliage with red branches and stems, growth lax bush, will trail with weights. Soo Yun – American – 1975 – A 1269.

membranacea. Tube and sepals greenish to red; no corolla. Glabrous shrub, very little known about this species. Hemsley – 1876 – Ecuador and Venezuela.

Mendocini Mini. Single. Thin white tube, very tiny sepals, white on back, pink on front; corolla light purple, turning to dark pink. Miniature sized flowers approximately ⅝ in and very free. Very small serrated foliage, with thin drooping branches. Growth natural trailer, raiser describes this cultivar as a collector's treasure. Francesca – American – 1975 – A.F.S. No. 1290.

Mendocino Rose. Double. Thin, pale pink tube, long, broad sepals carmine-rose (R.H.S. 52D), somewhat lighter on outside. Corolla carmine-rose to salmon, variegated with reddish-purple (Indian-lake/R.H.S. 58A). Very large blooms, heavy, flare out when mature. Large foliage, makes a big plant quickly but needs support. Growth tall, upright and bushy. Stubbs – American – 1976 – A.F.S. No. 1384.

***Meols Cop.** Single. Tube and sepals blood red; corolla white with very slight veining. Smallish flowers but borne in great profusion. Growth upright and bushy. Raised in the vicinity of Southport. Introduced by J.V. Porter of Southport in 1983. Porter – British – 1980.

Mephisto. Single. Tube and sepals scarlet; corolla deep crimson, almost a crimson self. Smallish flowers but extremely floriferous, borne in clusters, early. Growth is terrific, vigorous and rampant, no use under glass except as climber, makes a good bedder and hardy in the Midlands. *F.lycioides* × Mrs. W. Rundle. Reiter – American – 1941.

Mercurius. Single. Short, red tube, red sepals, rather long and wide; corolla purple changing to deeper shade with maturity. Medium-sized flowers with red stamens and style. Medium green foliage with red mid-rib and metallic shine, hence the name. Growth upright and bushy with horizontally growing branches. *F. regia* var. *typica* × Beacon. De Groot – Dutch – 1971.

Merle Hodges. Double. Red tube, sepals rosy-red, broad and upturned; corolla soft powdery-blue. Largish flowers, free, large and fluffy, lightly veined and flushed pink, rather heavy, needs support. Growth lax bush or trailer. Hodges – American – 1950 – A.F.S. No. 70.

Merlin. Single. Short thin tube bright red, short sepals recurve at tips, bright red tipped green. Corolla deep purple flushed pink with pink veining. Small flowers with pink stamens and pistil. Dark green foliage with small narrow serrated leaves. Growth self-branching tall upright and

bushy, suitable for bush or standard, has survived 4 winters in vicinity of Cardiff and tested for 5 years before release. Adams – British – 1982 – A.F.S. No. 1690.

Merry England. Double. Rose-red tube, sepals waxy-white on top, pink on undersides. Corolla dark violet-blue, fading to Bishops-violet, flushed pink on outer petals. Large blooms and free, a true red, white and blue flower. Growth upright and bushy. Gadsby – British – 1968 – A.F.S. No. 980.

Merry-Go-Round. Double. Tube and upturned, long sepals bright red; corolla deep petunia-purple, overlaid and splashed light salmon on outer petals. Largish flowers and free. Growth lax bush or trailer. Munkner – American – 1952.

Merry Maid. Single. White and rose-red. Banks – British – 1854.

Merry Mary. Double. Pink tube, sepals pink, near white at tip, deeper pink underneath. Corolla white, veined and splashed pink, flowers large and fairly free for size, very showy. Growth lax bush or trailer. Fuchsia Forest – American – 1965 – A.F.S. No. 624.

Merry Widow. Double. Tube and sepals, bright-red; corolla pink and white with rose veining. Medium sized blooms, free, growth trailer. Munkner – American – 1952.

Merseyside. Semi-double. Long tube and long sepals, tangerine; corolla tangerine, variegated in rose. Growth trailer, named after the Merseyside Fuchsia Society. Pennisi – American – 1970 – A.F.S. No. 906.

Meteor. Double. Tube and sepals carmine; corolla red, almost a red self and insignificant. Flowers medium sized and not free. Foliage rich golden-yellow, variegated with crimson and bronze. Growth lax bush or trailer. Carter and Co. – British – 1862.

Me-Tu. Single. Tube and sepals carmine; corolla pale blue with purple. Medium sized flowers and very profuse. Growth lax bush or trailer. Machado – American – 1958 – A.F.S. No. 403.

Mevr. Goyaerts. Semi double or double. Tube white, sepals are long, white with red blush, green tips. Corolla centre petals deep purple, outer petals are shorter, orange with light blotches of orange. Medium-sized blooms with pink stamens and soft pink style. Medium green foliage with large leaves. Growth lax bush or trailer. Goyaerts – Dutch – *ca* 1970.

mexiae. Tube and sepals reddish; white corolla. Tiny flowers and a member of the Breviflorae section (Encliandra). Very little known of this species. Munz – 1943 – Mexico.

Mexicali Rose. Double. Tube and wide sepals, dark red; corolla deep magenta, marbled with orange-red. Large flowers, free, very showy. Light yellow-green foliage. Growth upright. Confusion with this cultivar when first sent over from America which was in fact Orange Drops. Fuchsia Forest, Castro – American – 1962 – A.F.S. No. 515.

Mia van der Zee. Single. Tube and sepals rose-pink; corolla rich magenta, rose-pink at base. Growth lax trailer. Introduced by Wills Fuchsias Ltd. of West Wittering in 1980. La Campanella ×. de Graaff – Dutch – 1978.

Michelangelo. Double. Tube and sepals crimson; corolla rich purple, veined red. Very large blooms, quite free for size, corolla opens flat.

Growth upright and bushy. Rozain-Boucharlat – French – 1914.

Michelle. Single. Short tube slightly darker pink than sepals which are blush-pink, reflexed to stem. Corolla clear bluish-pink. Largish blooms almost self coloured and free, good substance. Dark green foliage, growth upright and bushy. Handley – British – 1972 – A.F.S. No. 1055.

michoacanensis. Red tube, red sepals; coral corolla. Tiny flowers borne singly in the leaf axils. Another species within the Encliandra (Breviflorae) section. Upright shrub attaining 4 to 9 ft in its natural habitat. Synonymous with *F. biflora, F. chiapensis* and *F. heterotricha.* Sessé and Mocino – 1887 – Costa Rica and Mexico.

Micky Goult. Single. Short white tube, short broad sepals white on top, very pale pink underneath toning down to deeper pink, held at the horizontal and slightly tipped green. Short corolla mallow purple (R.H.S. 73D) with slight veining and lighter colour at edges. Small flowers, true single are held semi-erect $1\frac{1}{4}$ in long by $1\frac{1}{2}$ in wide, do not fade even with maturity. Very early flowering, very free and held in clusters, pale pink style and cream stigma. Buds held totally erect, long pedicel enabling flowers to be held well away from foliage. Beautiful and elegant, could be described as a superior and improved Eleanor Leytham, must be a winner on the showbench and probably George Roe's best introduction after Celia Smedley. Light green foliage with ovate-cordate leaves $2\frac{1}{2}$ in long by $1\frac{1}{2}$ in wide and very distinct serration, held at the horizontal. Growth very upright and bushy, neat and compact if frequently pinched, a definite requirement for showbench purposes, needs shade for best results, short jointed. Whole plant gives a very fresh and pleasing effect. Raised in the vicinity of Nottingham before release to Jackson's Nurseries of Tamworth who introduced in 1981. Bobby Shaftoe × Santa Barbara (Syn. Lustre). Roe – British – 1981.

microphylla. Tube deep red, sepals red; corolla rosy-pink, flowers when grown under glass can come almost white. Tiny flowers, borne singly in the leaf axils and subject to colour variation. Flowers are cylindrical in shape. distinguishing them from *F. thymifolia* which are funnel-shaped. Foliage deep green and paler underneath, fern-like in appearance, leaves usually less than $\frac{1}{2}$ in long. Member of the Encliandra (Breviflorae) section. Hardy in most districts. Upright shrub, varies in height from 1 ft upward. Synonymous with *F. gracilis* and *F. minutiflora* var. *mixta.* Kris – 1823 – Mexico.

Midge. Double. Tube and small, broad recurved sepals, flushed pink on outside, deeper pink underside. Corolla lovely, clear silver-blue. Small flowers, fully double, free. Growth upright and bushy, height only 12 in, a little gem. Farrington-Waltz – American – 1961 – A.F.S. No. 490.

Midnight Cowboy. Single. Short dark red tube, sepals dark red, short and stubby, flares to right angle from corolla. Deep rich purple corolla. Flowers are small, delicate, fairly compact, slight flair as bloom matures and free. Lightish green foliage with red stems. Growth upright and bushy. Foster – American – 1973 – A.F.S. No. 1092.

Midnight Sun. Double. Tube and broad, up-turned sepals, pink outside, bright carmine underside. Corolla very dark burgundy-purple. Large blooms, fairly free, shorter outer petals dark shade of burgundy-red, with splashes of carmine and salmon-pink at base of sepals. Foliage rich shade of green. Growth upright and tall. Waltz – American – 1960 – A.F.S. No. 440.

Mieke Meursing. Single to semi-double. Hundreds of new introductions have been introduced over the past few years, but none have received such a terrific impact. Could be described as both the exhibitor's and nurseyman's "dream", for the exhibitor has everything needed for a specimen plant, especially when grown as a bush, for the nurserymen throws "thousands" of cuttings, roots easily and in great demand. As yet unregistered, was a chance seedling found growing on the staging under a plant of R.A.F. by F.G. Hopwood at Hurstbourne Park, Whitchurch, Hants in 1968. Although a single cultivar when introduced, should now be considered as a semi-double; the sepals are red, whilst the corolla is pale pink with deeper veining and long stamens, extremely free flowering, but colouring can be dull and insipid, its growth is exceptional, extremely vigorous and bushy, with a mass of growth from the base of the plant, will respond to any amount of pinching and capable of making a large plant within 6 months of cutting being rooted. With its short jointedness, needs very little or no staking. Will make a fine standard or conical, foliage is medium green and not attracted to many pests. This cultivar received an Award of Merit by the B.F.S. at the August 1968 London Show; the following week was chosen by the Netherlands Fuchsia Society to be named after their first President Mrs. M. Meursing upon retirement from office in 1969. In 1969 the raiser took first award in a class for plants introduced after 1965 at the B.F.S. London Show, but did not make its real showbench debut until the next year, when top exhibitors seeing its possibilities, successfully exhibited, either at Manchester or London. Ever since that date, the showbenches have been crowded with this cultivar to such an extent, that some enthusiasts advocate its isolation into a class of its own. Always considered as a single until the summer of 1972, when exhibitors found their cards marked 'N.A.S.'. For some unknown reason 'M.M.' was throwing semi-double blooms, presumably throwing back a little of the blood from its parent R.A.F. Although when first introduced as Mrs. Mieke Meursing, the name during its short existence appears to have been shortened, by the exclusion of the 'Mrs'. Makes a very good bedder; prefers its roots in the moist shade and best grown as H2, will be with us for a very long time, a cultivar the beginner can hardly go wrong with. Hopwood – British – 1968.

Mignon. Semi-double. Tube and sepals white; corolla red shading to claret. Largish flowers, free with pink stamens. Very small foliage, loves the shade. Growth trailer. Munkner – American – 1954.

Mikado. Rozain-Boucharlat – French – 1912.

Mikado. Double. Tube and sepals, claret-rose; corolla rose-opal. Medium sized blooms and free. Growth upright and bushy. Jones – British – 1960.

*Mike Oxtoby. Single. True triphylla. Long thin vermilion (R.H.S. 41A) tube $1\frac{5}{8}$ in by $\frac{7}{16}$ in, sepals vermilion (R.H.S. 41A), recurved below the horizontal $\frac{3}{4}$ in by $\frac{7}{16}$. Corolla mandarin-red (R.H.S. 40B) $\frac{5}{8}$ in by $\frac{7}{16}$ in. Typical triphylla type flowers with definite bulge and more robust than *F. triphylla*. Dark green (R.H.S. 139A) foliage or upper surface dark green flushed crimson (R.H.S. 139B) underneath with lanceolate shaped leaves $3\frac{3}{4}$ in by $1\frac{1}{2}$ in with puberulent surface. Growth lax upright on stiff trailer will make good basket or upright bush, will take full sun, needs heat and frost shy needs minimum temperature of 40°F. This cultivar has all the beauty of *F. triphylla* but is much stronger and thrives outdoors; like all triphyllas best wintered at 50°F in leaf, with its rather lax growth is unusual as looks best in basket. Raised in the vicinity of Hull, Yorkshire, *F. triphylla* × Fanfare. Bielby – British – 1984.

Mildred. Double. Red and purple. Bull – British – 1864.

Miles. No details available for this cultivar other than its parentage: Citation × Checkerboard. Powell – British – 1975.

Milford Queen. No details available for this cultivar other than its parentage: Pink Cloud seedling × Lena Dalton × Goldcrest. Ryle – British – 1975.

***Milkmaid.** Semi-double. Little known Dutch cultivar except for parentage. La Campanella seedling. *ca* 1980.

Milky Way. Double. White tube, sepals palest pink which fade into corolla; white corolla. Large blooms, free for size, the more shade provided the whiter the blooms. Growth trailer. Paskesen – American – 1967 – A.F.S. No. 702.

***Millie's Tie Dye.** Single. Cardinal red tube $\frac{3}{8}$in long by $\frac{1}{8}$in plus wide, sepals cardinal red (R.H.S. 53B) slightly lighter colours (R.H.S. 53C) underneath $\frac{3}{4}$ in long by $\frac{1}{4}$ in wide. Corolla violet (R.H.S. 83B) cardinal red at base, maturing to cyclamen-purple (R.H.S. 74A) veined red. Small flowers, each petal has slight indentation near base which billows out and curls under. Corolla is small $\frac{3}{4}$ in long by $\frac{5}{8}$ in wide and quarter flared with cardinal red stamens and style. Medium green foliage (R.H.S. 137B) with ovate leaves $1\frac{1}{2}$ in long by $\frac{3}{4}$ in wide, serrated edges and acute tips. Growth self-branching lax upright as stiff trailer, will be suitable for miniature training or bonsai, heat tolerant if shaded; chance seedling. Raised and tested for 5 years in the vicinity of Palos Verdes Peninsula, California. Drapkin – American – 1983 – A.F.S. No. 1739.

Millionaire. Double. Short tube and broad sepals, rose-red. Corolla deepest violet-purple. Very large blooms and fairly free, raise claims it to be the richest colouring of any double to date. Growth trailer. Tiret – American – 1955 – A.F.S. No. 235.

Mima Garson. Double. Tube and reflexed sepals, coral-red; corolla deep garnet. Very large blooms, fairly free, petals are toothed and serrated. Growth lax bush or trailer. Garson – American – 1942.

***Mimi Kubischta.** Double. Tube and sepals cherry-red; corolla white. Medium sized blooms, early flowering. Growth medium upright, very compact. Koralle × *F. boliviana* × *F. splendens*. Nutzinger – Austrian – 1976.

Mindrum Gold. Double. Tube rose-bengal, sepals rose-red on upperside, neyron-rose underneath, curve slightly upwards. Corolla violet, fading to violet-purple. Smallish to medium sized blooms, very free, light coloured foliage, young growth is absinthe-yellow. Growth dwarf, compact, bush. Pink Cloud × Lena Dalton seedling × Sonata seedling × Goldcrest. Ryle – British – 1975 – A.F.S. No. 1251.

Minerva. Single. Red and purple. Bland – British – 1878.

Ming. Single. Tube and sepals, orange-red flushed cerise; corolla cherry-red, paling at base. Flowers rather small, but very free, have exactly the same characteristics as its parent Chang. Lightish green foliage. Growth upright and bushy, delightful cultivar but can be disappointing under wrong conditions, very susceptible to botrytis, excellent outside as a bedder. Chang ×. Jennings, K. – British – 1968.

Mini. Single. Tube and sepals, white with flushes of pink, tipped green. Corolla pinkish-lavender to magenta-rose. Flowers small and free, growth upright and bushy, small cultivar as the name aptly implies. Castro – American – 1969 – A.F.S. No. 840.

miniata (Planch and Linden 1852). Synonymous with *F. hirtella*.

Miniature. Single. Cerise and purple. Hardy cultivar. Myrtifolia ×. Lemoine – French – 1894.

Miniature Jewels. Single. White or whitish-pink tube, whitish-pink sepals turn darker pink with maturity, very small, pointed, fit between petals when first open, then fold back over tube. Corolla whitish-pink turns dark pink or red. Very small flowers as name implies, white stamens and pistil, four in tube and four above the petals, very profuse blooming, unique in that blooms are in alternating sets of white and pink. Small foliage with serrated leaves. Growth natural trailer, self-branching, good for most types of training. Francesca – American – 1976 – A.F.S. No. 1386.

minimiflora. Tube whitish to reddish, sepals red with white edges; corolla white to red. One of the tiniest of flowers, borne solitary in the leaf axials. Classified with the Breviflorae section (Encliandra). Upright shrub attaining 10 to 12 ft in natural habitat. Hemsley – 1880 – Mexico and Honduras.

Minirok. Single. Tube and long sepals red; corolla purple. Small flowers and very free darkish green foliage with small leaves. Growth lax bush or trailer, horizontal grower. Minirok translated into English is 'mini skirt'. Steevens – Dutch – 1970.

***Minirose.** Single. Long fluted tube very pale rose colours, sepals pointed and held well down, opening enough to see corolla, very pale rose on top, slightly darker underneath, each sepal tipped with distinct dark rose. Corolla dark rose slightly veined lighter rose, very small flower $1\frac{5}{8}$ in long by 1 in wide. Very profuse and long lasting, off standing with rose stamens, cream anthers, pale rose style and cream stigma. Light green foliage with ovate leaves and acuminate tip $2\frac{1}{8}$ in long by $1\frac{1}{8}$ in wide. Real novelty, delightful and very petite, very similar to Twinkling Stars but much smaller. Growth upright, bushy and short jointed, excellent as a bush or miniature standard, dwarf. Raised in the vicinity of Lisse in the Netherlands and introduced by John Ridding of Fuchsiavale Nurseries, Kidderminster in 1983. Rose of Castile ×. de Graaff – Dutch – 1983.

Mini Skirt. Double. Short thin greenish-white tube, slightly curved broad pointed sepals are white with green tips. Corolla smokey mauve-grey rose (R.H.S. 185B). Medium sized blooms with very short open corolla, stamens and pistil are long for length of bloom. Dark green foliage with ovate leaves and obtuse tip, slightly serrated margin. Growth small upright, will make good bush, best colour develops in filtered sun. Tested for 4 years in vicinity of Fort Bragg, Oxnard and Oceanside, California before release, where it will be trademarked. Stubbs – American – 1981 – A.F.S. No. 1618.

Minister Bouchier. Double. Red and purple. Lemoine – French – 1898.

Minnesota. Semi-double. Tube and sepals ivory, flushed rose; corolla deep purple, shaded carmine. Medium sized blooms and free, very similar to Rose of Castile. Growth upright. Garson – American – 1938.

Minnie. Single. White and rose. Bull – British – 1862.

Minos. Semi-double. Red and magenta. Lemoine – French – 1896.

Minos. Double. Scarlet and purple Rozain-Boucharlat – French – 1902.

Minstrel. Double. Carmine and white. Lemoine – French – 1889.

Minuet. Single. Tube and sepals red; corolla brilliant purple. Large flowers, fairly free, wide and open, very early. Growth upright. Niederholzer – American – 1943.

minutiflora. Red tube, cerise petals; white corolla, flushed cerise. Tiny flowers approximately $\frac{1}{4}$ in long are borne solitary in the leaf axils. Another species of the Encliandra (Breviflorae) section. Fern-like foliage with thin wiry fronds. Small shrub. Hardy in most districts. Hemsley – 1878 – Mexico.

var. *hidalgensis.* White tube and sepals.

var. *typica.* Shiny flowers.

Mipan. Single. Tube pale carmine, sepals carmine-pink and reflexing; corolla magenta-pink flushed carmine-pink at base. Medium-sized flower, very floriferous, distinctive serrated foliage. Growth upright and bushy, considered to be a good show bench cultivar. Gubler – British – 1976.

Mirabilis. Semi-double. Crimson and violet. Turner – British – 1848.

Miracle. Single. Tube and long sepals, almost white; corolla striped pink and white, deeply serrated. Flowers medium sized and free, growth trailer. Niederholzer – American – 1945.

Miracle. The red and white double cultivar with sepals which 'sit down' on the corolla; grown in Rhodesia under the name Miracle, could be the British cultivar Lassie.

Mirage. Double. Tube and sepals white; corolla medium blue fading to pale orchid. Large blooms, very free with light green foliage. Growth trailer. Martin – American – 1966 – A.F.S. No. 675.

Miramar. Single. Ivory tube, sepals neyron-rose; corolla solferino-purple. Medium sized flowers, free with wide open corolla. Growth upright. Niederholzer – American – 1946.

Miranda. Single. Almost pink self. Knight – British – 1847.

Mirandy. Semi-double. Tube and long, recurving sepals dark pink; corolla water melon-pink.

Medium sized flowers, free, very large foliage. Growth trailer. Fairclo – American – 1947.

Miss America. Double. Tube and sepals red; corolla white with no veining. Large blooms, fairly free, wide open corolla. Growth upright and bushy. Haag – American – Date unknown.

Miss B. Hesse. Double. Deep scarlet and white. Crousse – French – 1853?.

Miss California. Semi-double. Short tube and long pointed sepals, medium pink, shaded deeper pink. Corolla white with faintest pink glow inside and light pink veining near base. Flowers are long, medium in size and very free, growth lax bush, lovely cultivar in every way, much better as a second year plant. Hodges – American – 1950 – A.F.S. No. 71.

Miss California

Miss C.E. Newman. Double. Tube and sepals bright rosy-crimson, corolla pure white. Medium sized but very full blooms. Growth upright, probably one of the first Australian introductions raised and introduced by C.F. Newman & Sons of Houghton, South Australia. Was listed up to World War I and then vanished. Newman – Australian – ca 1894.

Miss Frills. Double. Tube and upturned sepals rose-pink; corolla soft orchid-lilac under cool conditions, otherwise more blue. Largish blooms with spreading and scalloped petals, fairly free. Deep green foliage, growth upright. Tiret – American – 1954 – A.F.S. No. 207.

Miss Great Britain. Single. Tube dark pink to rose-red, sepals creamy-white, tipped green, each having distinct twist. Corolla wisteria-blue, fading to Imperial-purple. Largish flowers very free flowering but late. Growth upright and bushy, another of the raisers red, white and blue cultivars. Gadsby – British – 1968 – A.F.S. No. 981.

Miss Harney County. Double. Tube and sepals red; corolla dark blue. Large flowers, very free. Growth trailer. Gagnon – American – 1967 – A.F.S. No. 706.

Mission Bells. Single. Tube and sepals scarlet; corolla rich purple, splashed cerise near base. Flowers medium to large, bell-shaped and very free. Flowers can come semi-double especially with overfeeding. Growth upright and bushy, hardy in the Midlands. One of the most delightful cultivars sent over from America, excellent in every way and should be seen more on the show-benches. Walker and Jones – American – 1948.

Miss Jacqueline. Single. Tube and sepals, dark red; corolla dark violet with glossy sheen. Largish bell-shaped flowers with flaring petals, very free. Dark green foliage, growth upright and bushy. Evans and Reeves – American – 1933.

Miss Janice Tennant. Double. Red and purple. Stride – British – 1908.

Miss Leucadia. Double. Pink tube sepals pink, tipped green; corolla soft pink. Large blooms with flaring and picotéed edged petals, fairly free for size. Growth trailer. Stubbs – American – 1971 – A.F.S. No. 999.

Miss Louise. Double. Tube and sepals pink; corolla clear pink, almost a self. Flowers are very large and fairly free. Growth trailer. Tiret – American – 1964 – A.F.S. No. 594.

Miss Lye. Single. Tube and sepals, ivory-white; corolla magenta-rose. Medium sized blooms, free and early. Growth upright and bushy. One of Lye's little known cultivars. Lye – British – 1870.

Miss New York. Double. Tube and sepals, bright red; corolla pink. Very large blooms and very free, likes cool conditions. Growth upright. Sport of Swingtime. Sweet – American – 1961 – A.F.S. No. 457.

Miss Norway. Double. Pink tube, sepals coral-pink, long and curled. Corolla dark bluish fading to dark rose. Large blooms, fairly free, growth upright and bushy. Gorman – American – 1970 – A.F.S. No. 922.

Miss Oklahoma. Double. Long, pure white tube, long, pure white sepals; corolla deep rose-pink. Medium sized blooms, very full, white stamens and pistil. Large dark green foliage, growth medium upright, bushy. Hanson – American – 1976 – A.F.S. No. 1326.

Miss Prettyman. Semi-double. White and red. Miller – British – 1844.

Miss Prim. Semi-double. Tube and sepals carmine, pagoda pattern; corolla Imperial-purple, solferino at base. Large flowers for semi-double, very free and early. Growth medium upright and bushy. Reiter – American – 1947.

Miss Rue. Semi-double. Tube creamy-white, sepals pink-carmine, tipped green, sweeping broadly back. Corolla coral with crimson and flame markings, petaloids overlaid with orange. Large blooms and fairly free, growth upright, strong, vigorous and bushy. Woakes – British – 1977.

Miss San Bruno. Double. Tube and sepals red; corolla ivory-white. Flowers largish and free, base of corolla lies flat with pleated petals in variegated red and white, a new form in red and white cultivars. Growth trailer. Bernier – American – 1961 – A.F.S. No. 468.

***Miss Suza.** Single. Red tube with thin white stripes $\frac{1}{2}$ in long by $\frac{1}{4}$ in wide, horizontally held sepals are madder-red on top, vivid red underneath with recurving tips $1\frac{1}{4}$ in long by $\frac{1}{2}$ in wide. Corolla white with red veins and wavy petal margins $\frac{1}{2}$ in long by $\frac{5}{8}$ in wide. The smallish flowers are quarter flared with red filaments and geranium-red anthers, pink style and stigma. Dark green foliage, bracken green underneath with ovate shaped leaves 2 to 3 in long by $1\frac{1}{2}$ in to 2 in wide, serrated with acute tips and rounded bases. Growth lax upright or stiff upright, will make good basket with weights, upright or standard,

cold weather hardy to 25°F. in California, U.S.A. Tested for 10 years and raised in the vicinity of Crescent City, California, U.S.A. before registration and release to the trade in 1976. Unknown parentage could be associated with Swingtime. Anderson – American – 1984 – A.F.S. No. 1797.

Miss Universe. Double. Pink tube, long pink sepals which curve gracefully back against stem. Corolla brightest pink. Largish flowers and free, growth lax bush or trailer. Reedstrom – American – 1958 – A.F.S. No. 359.

Miss Vallejo. Double. Tube and sepals, light pink, tipped green; corolla deep pink suffused with wide streaks of rose-pink. Large blooms, free, of globular shape. Growth lax bush, makes good bush plant but blooms need support. Exquisite cultivar, best grown as H1. Tiret – American – 1958 – A.F.S. No. 334.

***Miss Verity Edwards.** Triphylla type single. Tube and sepals ruby-red; corolla turkey-red, foliage almost identical in colour and shape as Thalia. Tested for $8\frac{1}{2}$ years in the vicinity of Woodbridge, Suffolk, and proved to be hardy. This cultivar is a breakthrough in the hardy triphylla range. Will be released and introduced by Burgh Nurseries of Woodbridge, Suffolk, in 1985. Dunnett – British – 1985.

Miss Wales. Single. Short thin tube very pale pink, long slender sepals light pink, flushed deeper pink on upper surface, same deeper pink underneath, sepals recurved to tube. Corolla light plum, flushed pale pink at base, turning to deep rose with maturity. Small to medium sized flowers with rounded petals flaring out to horizontal and tips turning up with maturity, pink stamens and style. Small light green foliage with very narrow pointed serrated leaves. Growth small upright and bushy, will produce excellent standard. Raised and tested for 3 years in vicinity of Cardiff, South Wales before release. Adams – British – 1982 – A.F.S. No. 1691.

Miss Washington. Double. Tube and sepals light red; corolla white, lightly veined red, slight shading at base of orchid at base of petals. Large blooms and free. Growth trailer. Sport of Fort Bragg. Mouncer – American – 1961 – A.F.S. No. 458.

Missy Myrt. Double. Crimson tube, long sepals crepe crimson; corolla deep orchid and blue. Largish blooms with loose long petals, fairly free. Growth trailer. Gagnon – American – 1966 – A.F.S. No. 661.

Missy Wiltshire. Double. Short tube and sepals, dark pink; corolla lilac. Large blooms, free for size. Growth trailer. Pennisi – American – 1971 – No. 1011.

Mistoque. Single. Long fluted tube very white, long sepals white edged rose, held at the horizontal and then slightly upturned. Long pleated corolla lilac-blue tinged light pink at the base. Long white pistil with rose stamens. Very similar to Carmel Blue and Bonnie Lass. Introduced by S. Orton of Derby in 1980. Raiser unknown – British – *ca* 1978.

Misty Blue. Double. Tube pale pink, sepals pink at base changing to white with green tips. Corolla misty lilac-blue. Medium sized blooms very full, containing up to fifteen petals and free flowering. Growth upright and bushy. Raised in the vicinity of Middlesex and introduced by Woodbridge Nurseries of Hounslow, Middlesex, 1982. Dyos – British – 1982.

*Misty Haze. Double. Very long white tube, pure white sepals which curve upwards, tipped green. Corolla mineral-violet slightly flushed amethyst-violet. Large blooms and free for size, very striking and attractive colour combination. Growth trailer, makes beautiful basket and weeping standard. Raised in the vicinity of Bardney, Lincolnshire, and introduced by R. and J. Pacey of Melton Mowbray, Leicestershire, in 1983. Bellamy – British – 1983.

*Misty Pink. Double. White tube streaked green $\frac{3}{4}$ in by $\frac{1}{4}$ in, sepals white on top, white with greentips underneath, pinkish toward base, $1\frac{3}{4}$ in long by $\frac{3}{4}$ in wide. Corolla pale pink to almost white maturing to pale pink (R.H.S. 56C) $1\frac{1}{4}$ in long by $1\frac{1}{4}$ in wide. Medium sized blooms three quartered flared with wavy petals and many petaloids pale pink, red filaments white anthers and pale pink pistil. Should be outstanding with such lovely parents. Foliage dark green with ovate leaves and acute tips $2\frac{1}{4}$ in long by $1\frac{1}{4}$ in wide. Growth natural trailer, tested and raised in Oceanside, California, trademarked in California. Bicentennial × Capri × Blush o' Dawn. Stubbs – American – 1983 – A.F.S. No. 1735.

Mitford Queen. Double. White tube, downswept sepals white upperside with faint pink tinge and green tips on underside. Corolla creamy-white (R.H.S. 155A) with very little veining at base of petals. Medium-sized blooms, best colour in shade. Growth upright, tall, self-branching, tested for 3 years in Northumberland before release. Awarded the B.F.S. Bronze Certificate of Merit at B.F.S. Manchester Show 1976. Pink Cloud × Lena Dalton seedling × Sonata × Nancy Luo. Ryle – British – 1976 – A.F.S. No. 1436.

mixta (Hemsley 1878). Synonymous with *F. microphylla.*

Mme. Carolyn. Double. Tube and sepals red; corolla mauve. Largish blooms and free. Growth upright vigorous bush. Sport of Purple Phenomenel. Pidwell – American – 1938.

Mme. Chang. Synonymous with Madame Chang.

Model. Single. Blush-white and orange-scarlet. Meillez – French – 1847.

Model. Single. Red and purple. Banks – British – 1868.

Modern Times. Double. Tube and sepals, rose-madder; corolla mauve. Largish blooms and free with marginated petals. growth upright and bushy. Jones – British – 1960.

Molesworth. Double. Tube and sepals, bright cerise; corolla creamy-white, veined cerise. Medium sized blooms, very free and early, very

Molesworth

full corolla. Growth lax bush, needs support as bush training, somewhat straggly, but excellent cultivar suitable for all types of training, especially as pyramid or standard. Lemoine – French – 1903.

Molinae. See *magellanica* var. *molinae.*

Mona Lisa. Single. Tube and sepals, very pale pink; corolla pure white. Small flowers, very free. Growth upright, short and bushy. Neiderholzer – American – 1947.

Money Spinner. Single. Neyron-rose tube, sepals neyron-rose with underside slightly deeper colour, long and curling. Corolla Imperial-purple. Large flowers, free and of very rich colouring, early flowering. Growth trailer, suitable for basket work or standard. J. Lockyer – British – 1974.

Monsieur Alphard. Double. Cerise and violet. Lemoine – French – 1892.

Monsieur Bouchier. Double. Cerise and mauve. Lemoine – French – 1899.

Monsieur Fillon. Double. Crimson and purple. Crousse – French – 1868.

Monsieur Gladstone. Double. Cerise and blue. Lemoine – French – 1895.

Monsieur Hermite. Double. Red and white. Lemoine – French – 1893.

Monsieur Joule. Single. Tube and sepals curled right back to tube, crimson. Corolla violet-blue. Smallish flowers, very free, petals smaller than sepals, very dainty and similar to Abbé Farges. Growth upright and bushy, good old cultivar, still seen today. Synonymous with Duchess of Fife (Clarke 1948). Lemoine – French – 1890.

Monsieur Molier. Double. Red and purple. Lemoine – French – 1897.

Monsieur Thibaut. Single. Tube and long, recurved sepals cerise-red; corolla magenta, paler at base, veined cerise. Largish flowers and free, can throw semi-double blooms. Growth upright, vigorous and bushy, massive habit, produces a large bush very quickly, good for standard, still holds its own with the modern cultivars. Lemoine – French – 1898.

Monsieur Thibaut–Empress of Prussia. To distinguish between these two cultivars see Empress of Prussia–Monsieur Thibaut.

Monsoon. Double. Tube and sepals, palest pink, tipped green; corolla sky-blue. Largish blooms, fairly free and flaring, under cool conditions corolla has short twisted appearance. Growth upright. Lockerbie – Australian – 1971 – A.F.S. No. 1002.

Monster. Bland – British – 1867.

Monstera. Semi-double. Tube and sepals, deep crimson; corolla magenta, mottled and slightly paler at base. Growth trailer. Reedstrom – American – 1956 – A.F.S. No. 256.

Montana. Semi-double. Scarlet and white. Stokes – British – 1847.

Montara. Double. Tube and sepals, bright cerise; corolla creamy-white, veined cerise. Flowers smallish, very similar to Molesworth, very free. Small foliage, growth upright and bushy. Niederholzer – American – 1947.

Monterey. Single. Tube and sepals, white flushed pink; corolla bright vermillion, shaded orange. Medium sized blooms and free, growth upright. Greene – American – Date unknown.

Monte Rosa. Double. Pink tube, sepals pink, tipped green, curling upwards; corolla white with pink veining. Very large blooms and fairly free, lightish green foliage. Growth upright and sturdy. Colville – British – 1966.

Montezuma. Double. Tube and sepals, carmine-rose, tipped green, corolla Tyrian-rose, edged with smoky hue and base of petals carmine-rose. Large blooms, free for size. Growth trailer. A.F.S. Cert. of Merit 1970. Fuchsia-La – American – 1967 – A.F.S. No. 698.

Montmartre. Single. Long tube and sepals, light red to light bengal-rose; corolla dark red to bengal-rose. Medium size blooms, very free. Growth natural trailer. Evans and Reeves – American – 1954 – A.F.S. No. 220.

Montrose. Bland – British – 1869.

Monument. Double. Carmine and purple. Story – British – 1865.

Moody Blues. Double. Tube and sepals scarlet; corolla bluish-purple, ageing to reddish-purple, veined scarlet. Largish flowers and free. Growth upright bush. Homan – British – 1967.

Moonbeam. Double. Short yellow-green (R.H.S. 144A) tube shaded pink. Long sepals 2 in long by $\frac{5}{8}$ in wide pale pink (R.H.S. 55D) on upper surface, crepe textured and deeper pink underneath, the vertical sepals are tipped yellow-green (R.H.S. 144A). Corolla white with pale pink splashes and veining at base. Large blooms 3 in wide by 1¾ in long and frilly with petaloids same colour as corolla 1 in long and almost horizontal, bright pink stamens and long pistil. Dark green (R.H.S. 137B) foliage with large 2½ in long by 1½ in wide leaves, lightly serrated with strong veins. Growth medium upright making good bush or standard. Raised and tested for 10 years in vicinity of Newcastle-upon-Tyne before release. Hall – British – 1982 – A.F.S. No. 1667.

Moonlight. Semi-double. Short tube and long frosted sepals, greenish-white, tipped green. Corolla palest flesh-pink, overlapping petals, veined pale rose. Medium sized blooms and free. Growth lax bush or trailer, self-branching. Waltz – American – 1963 – A.F.S. No. 167.

Moonlight Sonata. Single. Tube and sepals, bright pink, recurling; corolla light-purple, flushed and veined pink at base. Medium sized flowers and very free. Growth lax bush, best grown as basket but will make good weeping standard. Blackwell – British – 1963.

Moonraker. Double. Long tube off-white, sepals held high outside off-white, flushed rose-pink and tipped green, inside white to rose at base. Corolla pale blue (R.H.S. 97B fades to 91C with maturity) pale blue petaloids attached to sepals and flare as sepals lift. Petals and petaloids have unusual 'ragged' edge giving pleasing look to rather long flowers which need space to hang, free-flowering. Foliage medium green with ovate leaves. Growth strong, upright and bushy with red wood. Introduced by D. Stilwell in 1979. Northumbrian Belle × Blush O' Dawn. Clitheroe – British – 1979.

*Moonshot. Semi-double. Tube and sepals roseine-purple, sepals are fairly long and broad, deeper colours on the underside, tipped green. Corolla bishop's-violet flecked roseine-purple at base of petals, very attractive colour combination, medium sized blooms, free flowering. Growth

upright, strong and bushy excellent for bush or standard. Raised in the vicinity of Melton Mowbray, Leicestershire, and introduced by the raiser, Pacey's Nurseries in 1984. Pacey – British – 1984.

Moorland Beauty. Semi-double. Red tube, sepals neyron-rose topside, frosted neyron-rose underneath, tipped white and recurving. Corolla violet, shading to red-purple. Medium sized flowers, fairly free, best colour in shade. Growth upright, bushy and self-branching, enchanting plant when in full bloom. Pugh – British – 1975 – A.F.S. No. 1237.

*Mordred. Single. Long narrow flesh coloured tube, pink sepals long, thin and recurving with age. Corolla dull red with faint hint of blue. Largish flowers, long, thin and bell-shaped, very free flowering, not very impressed with the colour combination. Foliage quite large with lanceolate leaves. Growth self-branching lax upright with long internodes, which could shorten by growing as second or third year plant, possible to train as basket, best colour in sun, will stand both heat and wind. This plant is a large Curly Q with the same quaint reflexing sepals formed almost in circles. Raised and tested in the vicinity of Ipswich, Suffolk, and introduced by B. and H.M. Baker of Halstead, Essex in 1983. Goulding – British – 1983 – A.F.S. No. 1729.

More Beauty. Double. White tube, sepals white, pale pink at base; corolla pale lavender with rose veining. Large blooms, fairly free, growth lax bush or trailer. Gorman – American – 1970 – A.F.S. No. 940.

Morning Glory. Single. Creamy-white tube, sepals upturned pale pink to creamy-white. Corolla clear orchid-pink. Medium sized blooms and free, cup shaped. Growth upright bush and vigorous. Niederholzer-Waltz – American – 1951 – A.F.S. No. 92.

Morning Glow. Semi-double. Tube neyron-rose, sepals neyron-rose, held well back to tube; corolla pale wisteria-blue, shading to gentian-blue. Medium sized flowers, prolific over a long period, light green foliage. Growth upright and bushy, easy to grow and shape. Rosendale × Albion. Gadsby – British – 1975 – A.F.S. No. 1302.

Morning Light. Double. Tube and base of petals coral-pink, sepals white, tipped green, broad upturned, pink at base and edged palest pink underneath. Corolla lavender, splashed pale pink and deep pink. Flowers are large, fully double and exquisite, similar to Sierra Blue, but loses colour very quickly, fairly free. Additional feature of this cultivar is the lettuce-green foliage, growth lax bush, best grown as H1. Waltz – American – 1960 – A.F.S. No. 441.

Morning Mist. Single. Long tube and sepals, orange-pink; corolla orange-red, suffused purple. Largish flowers, very free and long. Growth lax bush or trailer. Berkeley Hort. Nurseries – American – 1937 or 1951.

Morrells. Double. Tube crimson (R.H.S. 52A). Sepals rose-red (R.H.S. 58B), neyron-rose inside, boat-shaped, held horizontally. Corolla lavender-violet (R.H.S. 80D), light veined neyron-rose. Medium-sized blooms of squarish shape, tending to flare open when mature. Foliage darkish green (R.H.S. 137A) with mid rib cardinal-red (R.H.S. 53A). Growth upright and vigorous but not self branching, will make neat bush with pinching, good as standard. Hobbs, L. – British – 1977 – A.F.S. No. 1463.

Mosedale Hall. Single. Short tube cream, flushed green in shade, sepals same colour, flush of pink underneath. Corolla violet. Smallish flowers, very free, compact and barrel shaped. Dark green, ovate foliage. Growth upright and bushy. Silverdale × Silverdale. (Silverdale is *F.magellanica* var. *molinae* × Venus Victrix). Thornley – British – 1974 – A.F.S. No. 1216.

Moth Blue. Double. Short red tube, long red sepals; corolla deep lilac-blue. Largish flowers very free. Foliage dark green with coppery hue. Growth lax bush or trailer. Tiret – American – 1949.

Moulin Rouge. Double. Tube and sepals pink; corolla pale blue and pink. Large blooms, fairly free. Growth lax bush or trailer. Tiret – American – 1960 – A.F.S. No. 435.

Mountain Haze. Double. Tube and short, narrow sepals pale pink; corolla smoky-blue. Flowers largish and free, dark green, glossy foliage. Growth upright and bushy. Haag – American – 1950.

Mountain Mist. Double. White tube, sepals white. flushed rose at tips; corolla pale silver grey-mauve, pink at base. Large flowers and very free, unusual pastel colouring. growth upright. Crockett – British – 1971 – A.F.S. No. 960.

Mount Edgcumbe. Single. White tube, sepals white outside, pink inside, deeper pink-white at base, tipped green. Corolla spiraea-red orange with pencil edge, waxy. Medium-sized flowers and prolific. Growth upright and bushy. Hilton – British – 1978.

Mount Hood. Synonymous with Catalina and White Wonder. Sport of Gypsy Queen. Raiser unknown – American – Date unknown.

Moz. Double. Scarlet tube, scarlet sepals which arch right back to tube. Corolla bishop's blue and bright red. Large blooms and free for size of bloom. Medium green large foliage. Growth tall, upright and bushy, good for either bush or standard. Originates from the vicinity of Warwickshire. Seedling of Swingtime. Wright, J.A. – British – 1980 – A.F.S. No. 1604.

Mozart. Semi-double or double. Red tube, sepals red, wide with green tips. Corolla soft purple, darker at the edges. Medium-sized blooms, very free, both the stamens and style are light red. Raiser unknown – German or Austrian – 1970.

Mr. A. Huggett. Single. Short tube is scarlet-cerise, sepals of the same colour are recurved and stand out horizontally whilst the nicely formed corolla is of mauvish pink with petals edged purple and pink at the base. Both the stamens and the style are pale pink whilst the small foliage is in keeping with the strong, upright and bushy growth. The flowers are single and never troubled with the odd petal to make it semi-double, smallish and extremely floriferous, in fact, when well grown will cover itself with bloom, an early flowerer and continues to flower throughout the whole summer and one of the last to rest in the autumn. Growth upright and bushy. This lovely, smallish cultivar is at home both under glass and outside as a bedder, requires little stopping and may well prove to be hardy in most districts. There are a few outstanding cultivars which have been grown for many years yet we know neither the date of introduction or the raiser. Mr. A. Huggett falls into this catagory, others which spring to mind are General Monk, Aurora Superba, Lord Lonsdale, Major Heaphy and Muriel. We do know that Mr. A. Huggett was a British introduction and the only reference one can find is its listing in an old catalogue of H.A. Brown of Chingford in 1930. Mr. Huggett was 'discovered' by the southern exhibitors in the '70s particularly by Don Stilwell and Allan Dyos who produced magnificent specimen plants grown on the biennial method, needing little or no staking and is now being used by many exhibitors as a 'banker'. This British cultivar has recently been rediscovered by exhibitors and is now frequently seen on show-benches on account of its extreme floriferousness and compact growth. It will still be grown for many years to come. Raiser unknown – British – Date unknown.

Mr. Big. Double. Tube and box type sepals, magenta inside, pink outside; corolla purple. Very large blooms, fairly free; lower skirt of corolla variegated magenta which drops inch below rest of bloom. Growth trailer. Pennisi – American – 1970 – A.F.S. No. 888.

Mr. F. Glass. Single to semi-double. Red and purple. Lye – British – 1870.

Mr. J. Huntly. Single. Red and purple. Lye – British – 1874.

Mr. J. Lye. Single. White and scarlet. Lye – British – 1873.

Mr. J. Stoddart. Single. Rose and lilac. Harrison – British – 1848.

Mrs. Anthony Lipp. Double. Tube and sepals, neyron-rose, sepals are broad and crepy. Corolla alternating petals of violet and smoky-blue. Large flowers, free, large globular buds. Growth upright. Chiles – American – 1953 – A.F.S. No. 161.

Mrs. Ballantine. Double. Red and purple. Bland – British – 1871.

Mrs. B. Hesse. Synonymous with Miss B. Hesse.

Mrs. C.B. Hallmark. Double. Tube and sepals white, flushed coral-pink, sepals very pointed, recurved and tipped green; corolla creamy-white, oval shaped flowers, free and of medium size. Growth lax bush or trailer. Gagnon – American – 1963 – A.F.S. No. 553.

Mrs. Chas. Soules. Double. Short, stiff white tube, light pink sepals. Corolla blue, marbled pink and white with short narrow outer petals. Largish flowers, fairly free, growth trailer. Brown and Soules – American – 1951 – A.F.S. No. 74.

Mrs. Churchill. Single. Tube and sepals, cherry-red; corolla pinkish-white; blotched deep pink and veined cerise. Largish blooms, fairly free and can come semi-double. Growth upright and bushy. Garson – American – 1942.

Mrs. Desmond. Double. Tube and sepals red; corolla purple, veined rose. Largish flowers and free. Growth upright bush. Hazard and Hazard – American – Date unknown.

Mrs. E. Bennett. Single. Scarlet and white. Bland – British – 1872.

Mrs. E.G. Hill. Double. Scarlet and white. Lemoine – French – 1887.

Mrs. Ellen OBrien. Single. Tube and sepals, light red; corolla magenta. Large flowers, fairly free, bell shaped. Growth trailer. Niederholzer – American – 1948.

Mrs. F. Glass. Single. White and pink. Lye – British – Date unknown.

Mrs. Florence Adams. Single. Short tube creamy-pink, narrow sepals creamy-pink on underneath, slightly upturned with green tips. Corolla lilac-pink, flushed at base. Small but compact flowers, very free showering, filaments deep pink, plum anthers, pale pink style and cream stigma. Pale green foliage, medium sized with serrated leaves turning up at sides to tilt over the tip. Growth medium upright and bushy, takes full sun in the vicinity of Cardiff, South Wales where it was raised and tested for 3 years before release. Adams – British – 1982 – A.F.S. No. 1692.

Mrs. Florence Turner. Single. Tube and sepals. China-rose; corolla magnolia-purple. Flowers early and free, medium sized. growth upright and bushy. Turner, E.T. – British – 1954.

Mrs. Frederick Millbank. Single. White and purple. Jackson – British – 1846.

Mrs. Gascoigne. Double. Tube and sepals white, flushed pink; corolla clear violet. Largish blooms, fairly free. Growth upright. Raffill – British – 1939.

Mrs. George Martin. Single. Tube and sepals, pale pink; corolla orange-pink. medium sized flowers and free. Variegated foliage with light yellow band around leaves. Flowers similar to Prince of Orange but larger. Growth lax bush or trailer. Sport of Prince of Orange. Garson – American – 1944.

Mrs. G.G. Henry. Single. Tube and sepals white, flushed pink; corolla pinkish-white. Medium sized flowers, free, bell shaped. growth upright. Niederholzer – American – 1946.

Mrs. Gideon Brown. Double. Tube and sepals scarlet, corolla purple. Fairly large blooms and quite free. Growth upright and bushy. Raiser unknown. Prior to 1930.

Mrs. Gladstone. Double. Red and white. Bland – British – 1867.

Mrs. Hellier. Double. Tube and sepals red; corolla purple. Large blooms, fairly free. Growth upright. Gorman – American – 1970 – A.F.S. No. 933.

Mrs. Hilton. Semi-double. Thick, white tube; broad, upturned sepals are white outside and flushed pink inside. Corolla lilac with lilac marbled flesh petaloids. Medium sized flowers, open saucer shape, red stamens and white pistil, as flowers mature fold into the shape and colour of a rhododendron and inside of sepals turn rose-pink. Growth medium to tall upright bush, self-branching. Prelude (A.F.S. 348) × Swingtime. Hilton – British – 1976 – A.F.S. No. 1377.

Mrs. Huntley. Single. White and carmine. Lye – British – 1882.

Mrs. Ida Noach. Single. Red and magenta. Leomine – French – 1911.

Mrs. Jago. Single. Tube and sepals cerise; corolla delicate shade of blue, beautiful shaped flowers. Growth upright bush. Wright, J.A. – British – 1970's.

Mrs. J. Bright. Single. White and orange. Lye – British – 1882.

Mrs. J.D. Scannavino. Single. Tube and sepals, pale white; corolla of the same colour, almost white-orchid. Medium sized flowers and free. Growth upright. Niederholzer – American – 1945.

Mrs. J.F. Larsen. Double. Tube and sepals, light orangey-red; corolla bright orange and red. Largish blooms, very free, dark green foliage. Growth lax bush or trailer. Gagnon – American – 1968 – A.F.S. No. 780.

Mrs. J. Lye. Single. White and scarlet-pink. Lye – British – 1880.

Mrs. John D. Fredericks. Single. Tube and sepals, salmon-pink; corolla darker pink. Flowers medium sized, very profuse, borne in great clusters. Light green foliage, growth upright and extremely vigorous. *F.lycioides* × Firebush. Evans and Reeves – American – 1936.

Mrs. K. Harling. Semi-double. Pink and salmon-pink. Dixon – British – 1910.

Mrs. Lawrence Lyon. Semi-double. Tube and sepals, ivory-pink; corolla pale fuchsia-purple. Medium sized blooms remarkable for their profusion. Growth upright and bushy which is contrary to raisers description. Excellent cultivar makes fine specimen bush or shrub. Sport of Nonpareil. Named after a great fuchsia grower, Mrs. Lawrence Lyon of Pacific Grove, California; in 1951 her collection of fuchsias totalled no less than 927 different kinds; she took 34 years to get the collection together with the object of preserving old cultivars for future reference. Reiter – American – 1952 – A.F.S. No. 132.

Mrs. Lovell Swisher. Single. Long tube flesh-pink, sepals pinkish-white, tipped green, deeper pink underneath. Corolla deep old rose, small flowers very profuse, similar to Checkerboard but smaller, very early bloomer. Growth upright very vigorous, good for pyramid, conical or standard. Cultivar for the beginner, too easy. Evans and Reeves – American – 1942.

Mrs. Mabel Gorman. Double. Tube light bright-red, sepals of the same colour, creped on underside. Corolla deep violet with blue centre and four pink and white petaloids of various shapes. Large blooms, fairly free, growth upright. Gorman – American – 1970 – A.F.S. No. 920.

Mrs. Marshall. Single. Tube and sepals, waxy creamy-white; corolla rosy-cerise. Medium sized flowers, very free, fairly early. Growth upright and bushy, very versatile for all shapes, especially as pyramid or standard. Been with us since early part of this century and still a great favourite. Very similar to the old cultivar Arabella. In early days of introduction was sent out as Grand Duchesse Marie. R.H.S. Award of Merit 1929. Jones – British – 1862?

Mrs. Marshall – Beauty of Trowbridge. To distinguish between these two cultivars see Beauty of Trowbridge – Mrs. Marshall.

Mrs. Minnie Pugh. Semi-double. Short tube salmon (R.H.S. 27B); sepals frosted crimson (R.H.S. 52A) on inside, outer surface carmine-rose (R.H.S. 52C). Corolla shading outwards from crimson (R.H.S. 52A) to ruby-red (R.H.S. 61A). Smallish flowers, very free, produced on a very compact plant. Growth medium upright, bushy and self-branching. Introduced by Lockyer of Bristol in 1969 but not registered until 1976.

Seedling from Abbé Farges. Pugh – British – 1969 – A.F.S. No. 1331.

Mrs. Palmer. Semi-double. Rich red sepals with magenta corolla, listed and classified as a hardy by High Tree Nurseries of Reigate, Surrey, and considered to be synonymous with Royal Purple. Raiser and origin unknown – *ca* 1890.

Mrs. Phyllis Reid. Double. Short carmine (R.H.S. 52B) tube, red-rose sepals (R.H.S. 58B) rather shortish, broad and reflexing to tube, sepals smooth on upperside with crepe on reverse. Corolla delicate neyron-rose (R.H.S. 56D) blotched rose-red (R.H.S. 58B) and magenta (R.H.S. 66B) at base, with pronounced magenta veining extending to tips of petals. Extremely large blooms, fully double and globular, two tier blooms with outer petals billowing well out. Dark green foliage. Growth upright and bushy has proved to be hardy in Australia, tested for 3 years in vicinity of Sydney before release. Reid – Australian – 1977 – A.F.S. No. 1438.

Mrs. Popple. Single. Tube and sepals scarlet; corolla purple-violet, cerise at centre, veined cerise. Medium sized flowers, free, large for hardy cultivar. Growth upright, bushy and vigorous, very hardy, makes a good hedge up to 3 ft. Very similar to the old cultivar Duke of York (Miller 1845), the corolla of which tends to saucer shape and is of a lighter blue. Received the R.H.S. First-class Certificate at the Wisley Hardy Trials 1963–65; re-submitted for some unknown reason by Sunningdale Nurseries, Jackman's Nurseries and L.R. Russell Ltd. and could not receive any higher award. Accepted by the B.F.S. as show-bench hardy. Elliott – British – 1899.

Mrs. Roberts. Synonymous with The Doctor.

Mrs. Routledge. Double. Cerise and white. Strutt – British – 1907.

Mrs. Story. Semi-double. Reddish-pink and white. One of the first cultivars with a white corolla. Story – British – 1855.

Mrs. Susan Pugh. Single. Medium tube is striped orient-pink (R.H.S. 36C) and azalea pink (R.H.S. 38A) sepals pink (R.H.S. 38A) tipped green, matt surface underneath, shining on top, curving outward the entire length. Corolla red-purple (R.H.S. 58B) with very faint veining 1 in long × 1 in wide. Medium-sized flowers, brighter in colour than Chang, red stamens and long pistil. Growth tall, upright and bushy, exceptionally vigorous could be easily trained as espalier, self-branching. Tested for 2 years in vicinity of Chester. Chang × . Pugh – British – 1977 – A.F.S. No. 1459.

Mr. Storey. Single. Cerise and pink. Story – British – 1858.

Mrs. Vera Letts. Single. Tube and sepals cerise; corolla bluish-violet. Medium-sized flowers, very free. Growth upright and bushy. Identical with Three Counties. Spackman – British – 1934.

Mrs. Victor Reiter. Single. Tube and sepals, creamy-white; corolla pure crimson. Largish flowers, free and longish with Mrs. Rundle form. Foliage light green and brittle. Growth lax bush, slow growing, rather weak. Amy Lye × Mrs. Rundle. Reiter – American – 1940.

Mrs. W.H. Ware. Single. Tube and long sepals. white flushed pink; corolla blue-violet, pink at base. Medium sized flowers, very free. Growth tall

upright and bushy. Hazard and Hazard – American – Date unknown.

Mrs. W.P. Wood. Single. Tube and sepals pale pink; corolla pure white. Flowers very small but very profuse, small lightish green foliage. Growth upright and bushy, hardy. Selfed seedling from Margaret, and a hybrid from *F.magellanica* var. *alba*. Much too vigorous for cultivation under glass. Wood – British – 1949.

Mrs. W. Rundle. Single. Very long tube and reflexed sepals, flesh-pink; corolla rich orange-vermillion. Flowers largish and long, very free, features as the very long tube and equally long pistil, referred to as "the epitome of grace and beauty". Foliage lightish green. Growth lax bush, produces a magnificent weeping standard, or even a hanging basket. The best of the only three cultivars by the raiser Alfred Rundle. Introduced by H. Cannell, Earl of Beaconsfield × Lady Heytesbury. Rundle – British – 1883.

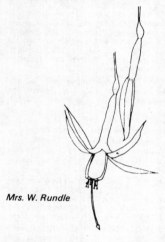

Mrs. W. Rundle

Mr. West. Single. Flowers red and purple, best described as a variegated Corallina. Variegated foliage particularly new growth, leaves mottled in various shades of green and cream, new leaves flushed red and pink. Low bushy plant. One Californian nursery had plants prior to 1939 but did not sell until 1941. Mr. West was listed as 1941 introduction in William Schmidt's catalogue of Palo Alto Nursery in California. It was thought that Mr. West and Tom West were identical and synonymous but reliable American information now seems to prove that they are different cultivars. Tom West could be a sport from *F. magellanica* var. *riccartonii* and Mr. West a sport from Corallina. West – American – 1941.

Mr. W. Rundle. Single. Tube and sepals, pale rose, tipped green; corolla orange and vermilion. Medium sized blooms, very early and very free, longish, colouring somewhat similar to Mrs. W. Rundle, but tube is nowhere near the same length and sepals are not reflexed. Growth upright bush and sturdy. Reputed to be seedling from Earl of Beaconsfield. Rundle – British – 1896.

Mr. W. Rundle – Mrs. W. Rundle. Two very lovely cultivars easily identified side by side, but difficult to distinguish separately. Both are single flowers and reputed to be seedlings from the East of Beaconsfield. Mrs. Rundle has longer tube 1½ in and thinner ¼ in, whereas Mr. Rundle is thicker ⅜ in darker in colour with more pronounced fluting ¾ in long. Mrs. Rundle has very long pistil, slightly lighter in colour and the overall length of bloom 4 in against 2½ in. Another marked difference in the sepals is that Mr. Rundle has recurved sepals almost at the horizontal whereas Mrs. Rundle sepals are much longer, thinner and sweep upwards, both are tipped green but Mr. Rundle more pronounced. Colouring almost identical, Mr. Rundle is slightly darker vermilion corolla and larger ⅜ in wide, Mrs. Rundle measures ⅝ in wide, stamens and anthers almost identical. Both have very long pedicals, Mr. Rundle is only half the size as Mrs. Rundle ⅝ in against ⅛ in. Both have lax habit of growth needing support if trained as a bush, very suitable for half or full basket work. Mrs. Rundle is elegant, feminine and beautiful whilst Mr. Rundle is not so graceful, more masculine and slightly stiff.

Mu Lan. Single. Rose tube, sepals light rose-red inside, waxy dark rose outside. Corolla creamy-white, veined light rose-red. Largish to medium sized flowers, very free, early, petals picotéed. Growth tall, upright bush. Hazard and Hazard – American – Date unknown.

Multa. Single. Tube and sepals red; corolla purple. Small flowers but very free. Growth lax bush, very easy grower. van Suchtelen – Dutch – 1968.

Multiflora. May – British – 1841.

Multiflora. See *magellanica* var. *multiflora*.

Multiplex. Double. Crimson and purple. This cultivar and Duplex are considered to be the first double flowered hybrids and mutations. Story – British – 1850.

Mumtaz. Double. Tube and sepals carmine; corolla creamy-white. Long pointed flowers, fairly free, feature is the foliage, yellowish-green, touched pink in early growth. Growth upright. Hazard and Hazard – American – Date unknown.

munzii. Red tube, sepals reddish-cerise; corolla purplish-red. Very few flowers in irregular and loosely terminal racemes. Very little information available on this species. Upright shrub. MacBride – 1941 – Peru and Chile.

Muriel. Semi-double. Long tube and sepals scarlet; corolla light purple, veined cerise. Largish flowers, very free, not the brightest of colouring. Growth lax and cascade, extremely vigorous and very fast, suitable for greenhouse climber, weeping standard or pyramid. Exhibited at Chelsea Shows for many years by Russells as magnificent arches. Raiser unknown – British – Date unknown.

Muriel Evans. Single. Rich scarlet self. Medium sized flowers, early and free. Light green foliage. Growth upright, bushy and vigorous. Evans and Reeves – American – 1934.

My Baby. Semi-double. Long tube, rhodamine-pink; pale rhodamine-pink sepals curve upward, tipped light green, ⅞ in long and ½ in wide. Corolla magenta-rose fading to spiraea-red at the sepals. Medium sized blooms and rather loose, phlox-pink stamens and pistil with beige tips. Light green foliage with scalloped edges 2 in wide by ¾ in long. Growth lax bush, will make good basket, prefers warm conditions. Tested in vicinity of

Richmond, California, for 3 years before release. Registered in 1978 by Soo Yun Field. Palko – American – 1978 – A.F.S. No. – 1446.

My Beauty. Double. Short, thin, pink tube ⅜ in long, sepals light pink on top with darker pink underneath 1½ in long × ¾ in wide, folding back with ends dropping over, umbrella shaped corolla. Corolla campanula-violet fading to light purple. Medium sized blooms with two to five small petaloids on edge of corolla, very heavy flowerer. Dark green foliage with lighter green on underside, red stems and branches. Growth semi-trailer, needs weights for basket work. Soo Yun – American – 1976 – A.F.S. No. 1354.

My Bette. Double. Bright pink self. Medium sized flowers held in semi-erect position, very free and continuous. Growth upright and bushy. Wilson – American – 1959 – A.F.S. No. 415.

My Cherie. Double. Pale pink tube, broad recurved sepals white, tipped green on top surface, coral-pink underneath. Corolla white shaded slightly pink at base. Largish Blooms with three cupped petals in centre and surrounded by many ruffled petals. Dense dark green foliage. Growth tall upright, will make good bush, best colour develops in shade. Tested for 4 years in vicinity of Colchester, Essex before release. Hill – British – 1981 – A.F.S. No. 1627.

My Darling. Double. Red tube, broad sepals light red; corolla red and white, variegated at base with centre petals reddish-white with red veins. Large blooms, fairly free. Growth trailer. Soo Yun – American – 1970 – A.F.S. No. 910.

My Dear. Double. Short white tube, sepals recurved, flushed white. Corolla clear lavender, fades to pinkish-lavender with an iridescent undertone. Small dark green foliage. Growth upright. Waltz – American – 1959 – A.F.S. No. 392.

My Delight. Single. Short red (R.H.S. 50B) tube, long deep rose-red sepals taper to long point 1⁷⁄₁₀ in long by ⁷⁄₁₀ in wide, curling down then levelling upward with base of tube. Corolla pale-lilac (R.H.S. 70D) very lightly veined deep pink. Medium sized flowers 1½ in long with cylindrical shape, both stamens and pistil extend ¾ in below corolla. Foliage yellow-green (R.H.S. 146A) with lanceolate leaves, lightly veined 2 in long by 1 in wide with long point. Growth lax upright, will trail with weights, best colour in sun. Raised and tested in the vicinity of Newcastle-upon-Tyne for 5 years. Hall – British – 1982 – A.F.S. No. 1680.

My Dream. Double. Crimson tube, crimson sepals 1½ in long, curling upward to tube; corolla orchid pink, blending to light pink. Large blooms very full, flared and ruffled effect, 1½ in long, stamens and pistil crimson, very heavy bloomer. Growth semi-trailer and tested for 5 years at Sebastopol, California, before release. Soo Yun Field – American – 1977 – A.F.S. No. 1408.

My Fair Lady. Double. Tube and sepals, strawberry-red; corolla lavender ageing to rosy purple, pink at base. Largish blooms and free. Growth upright bush. Colville – British – 1966.

My Honey. Single. Thin, triphylla type tube, white; long sepals are pink on underside and light pink to white on top with light green tips. Corolla light cyclamen-purple with carmine variegated base. Smallish flowers, tight, anthers dark brown, white stigma. Dark green foliage, green stems turn red. Growth natural trailer without weights, very heavy bloomer makes beautiful basket. Registered by Soo Yun's Fuchsia Garden. Palko – American – 1976 – A.F.S. No. 1351.

My Keepsake. Double. Tube and sepals, frosty-pink; corolla clear pink. Flowers very large, free for size, petals are pleated, ruffled and picotée-edged, same colouring as Pink Galore. Growth trailer. Fuchsia-La – American – 1961.

My Love. Double. Tube and sepals, deep rose; corolla light orchid. Small flowers, very free. Growth lax bush or trailer. Soo Yun Field – American – 1966 – A.F.S. No. 683.

Myrtifolia. See *magellanica* var. *myrtifolia.*

My Sport. Single. Tube and sepals red; corolla purple. Small flowers, very free. Small dark green foliage with red veins, curled. Growth trailer. Gorman – American – 1970 – A.F.S. No. 924.

My Valentine. Double. Tube and sepals, dark pink; corolla light pink. Medium sized blooms, very full and free. Dark green foliage, growth lax bush or trailer. Martin – American – 1964 – A.F.S. No. 608.

Nananice. Single. Tube and sepals are pure white but splashed with carmine. Corolla rose-pink. Largish flowers and free for size. The outstanding characteristic is the very lush golden-green foliage which is maintained throughout although a red veining does appear with maturity. Considered to be a sport of China Lantern, found in the vicinity of Stowmarket, Suffolk. Introduced by G. Nice of Stowmarket in 1983. Nice – British – 1983.

Nancy. Lemoine – French – 1887.

Nancy. Single. Carmine tube, sepals strongly reflexed, carmine; corolla phlox-pink and flaring. Medium sized flowers and free, early. Growth upright and sturdy. Niederholzer – American – 1948.

Nancy Lee. Single. Tube and sepals pink; corolla blue. Small flowers, free and early. Growth upright and bushy. Hazard and Hazard – American – Date unknown.

Nancy Lou. Double. Pale pink tube, sepals deep clear pink, turned right back. Corolla brilliant white. Large blooms of perfect shape, free for size. Growth upright. Stubbs – American – 1971 – A.F.S. No. 998.

Napoléon. Single. White and crimson. Meillez – French – 1846.

Narcissus. Single. Tube and sepals, ivory-white; corolla orchid-purple. Medium sized flowers and free. Growth upright. Niederholzer – American – 1946.

*Nathalie Louise. Double. Short thin tube white with green stripes, fully up sepals white on top, pink blush underneath with recurved tips 1½ long by ½ in wide. Corolla opens rose-red (R.H.S. 51A) maturing to pale rose (R.H.S. 51C) 1 in long by 1 in wide with smooth petal margins. Half flared medium sized blooms both heat tolerant and pest resistant. Green (R.H.S. 138A) foliage with ovate leaves 2 in long by 1 in wide, serrated margins, acute tip and rounded base. Growth lax upright or stiff trailer. Raised anonymously in the vicinity of Oxnard and Downey, California, U.S.A. and registered by Betty Cole of Downey. Parentage unknown. Raiser unknown – American – 1984 – A.F.S. No. 1759.

Native Dancer. Double. Tube and sepals, bright red; corolla deep purple. Large blooms, free for size. Growth lax bush or trailer. Tiret – American – 1965 – A.F.S. No. 648.

Nautilus. Double. Tube cerise, sepals cerise, curving right back to hide tube; corolla white, veined carmine. Large blooms and free, extremely disappointing unless conditions are perfect, white becomes a 'dirty white'. Growth upright and bushy. Lemoine – French – 1901.

Navajo. Double. Thick, short tube, light rose-opal, wide, crisp sepals of the same colour. Corolla smoky-rose, maturing to vivid rose-opal. Very large blooms, fairly free and of good substance, long lasting. Rich dark green foliage, growth upright and bushy. Blooms are extensively used in America for corsage work, Nelson – American – 1956 – A.F.S. No. 261.

Navy Blue. Single. Tube and sepals deep pink; corolla navy-blue. Medium sized flowers in profusion, pale green foliage. Growth upright and bushy, branching habit, height 1½ to 2 ft. Hardy in Southern England, raised in the Scilly Isles. Submitted by raiser for R.H.S. Wisley Hardy Trials 1975–78 but received no award. Tabraham – British – 1974.

Neapolitan. Semi-double. Tube and sepals, rosy-red; corolla creamy-white. Medium sized blooms and free. Growth upright and bushy. Jones – British – 1961.

Neil Clyne. Single. Short thick tube, neyron-rose; sepals neyron-rose, reflexing with crepe reverse; corolla violet, fading to cyclamen. Medium sized flowers, short and compact, profuse and continuous flowering, best colour in shade. Narrow foliage, spinach-green, growth upright, bushy and self-branching, short jointed habit. B.F.S. Certificate of Preliminary Acceptance, London 1973. La Campanella × Winston Churchill. Clyne – British – 1973 – A.F.S. No. 1285.

Nell Gwyn. Single. Thick, orange-salmon tube, thick, waxy orange-salmon sepals; bright orange corolla edged vermilion. Medium sized flowers, early, with overlapping petals. Bright green, heart shaped foliage. Growth upright and bushy, tested for 6 years in vicinity of Derby before release. Handley – British – 1976 – A.F.S. No. 1370.

Nellie Eastwood. Double. Short light pink (R.H.S. 56C) tube, sepals rhodamine-pink (R.H.S. 62A) with lighter pink tips and light pink (R.H.S. 56C) at base, slightly curling, narrow 1½ in long. Corolla cyclamen-purple (R.H.S. 74B) with light pink to white markings on outer petals, 1 in long × 1¼ in wide. Medium sized blooms are slightly ruffled and remain compact, hold their colour well, cyclamen-purple and white stamens, pistil is 1 in longer than corolla. Medium green (R.H.S. 137A) foliage, red veins and stems, leaves 1½ in long × ⅞ in wide. Growth natural trailer, self-branching. Originates from the Puget Sound area of Washington. Introduced by Linda Tancey of Kent, Washington, in 1980. Eastwood – American – 1980 – A.F.S. No. 1570.

Nellie Nuttall. Single. Very small brilliant red tube, deep crimson small sepals, pointed and held slightly below the horizontal. White corolla with red veining. Smallish flowers of the Upward Look type, very erect and early flowering. Very prolific bloomer always in flower and self cleaning, pink filaments, bright red pistil, stigma and anthers. Small lightish green foliage with ovate leaves and acute tip, little serration 1¼in long by ⅞in wide. Growth upright and bushy, very short jointed makes neat, compact plant, responds to frequent pinching. The introducer's description of being outstanding and to outgrow Snowcap and Mieke Meursing has been fully justified. One of the most exciting cultivars of the 70s and always to be found amongst the red awards in the showbench. Dainty, floriferous, clean and outstanding cultivars. Raised in the vicinity of Nottingham before release to Markham Grange Nurseries of Doncaster who introduced it in 1977. Khada × Icecap. Roe – British – 1977.

Nellie's Lantern. Double. Pale cerise tube with white veining, sepals flesh-pink, suffused darker, descend on corolla. Corolla different shades of geranium-pink. Largish blooms, very full and tight, free but heavy, needs support. Growth upright and willowy. Tolley – British – 1973 – A.F.S. No. 1157.

*Nellie Wallace. Single. Tube white and green (R.H.S. 145D), sepals flushed pink (R.H.S. 155C), corolla creamy-white veined light rose (R.H.S. 158D). Medium sized flowers having the same characteristics, apart from colour, of its parent Fiona; flowers profusely. Growth trailer, received a diploma in the Dutch Fuchsia Society at Aalsmer August 1983. Named specially after the wife of a prominent member of the Enfield Fuchsia Society. One of five new introductions by Herman de Graaf in 1983. Raised in the vicinity of Lisse, Netherlands. Fiona seedling. de Graaff – Dutch – 1983.

Neon. Single. Tube and sepals ivory, flushed rose; corolla rhodamine-purple edged geranium-lake. Small flowers, very free and early. Growth tall upright. Schnabel – American – 1949.

*Neopolitan. Single. Interesting addition to the Encliandra section, very unusual and classified as a novelty, with instability in the chromosomes controlling flower colour. Flowers much larger than the usual Encliandra but still miniature in size; ⁷⁄₁₆in long by ⅛in wide. Unusual colouring with white, pink and red seperate flowers all at the same time. Sepals reflex back to tube, corolla opens flat saucer like. Usual Encliandra fern like foliage. Raised in the vicinity of Merseyside, Lancashire and introduced by J.V. Porter of Southport in 1984. Clark, D. – British – 1984.

Nero. Single. Scarlet and purple. Lemoine – French – 1889.

Nestor. Single. Red and purple. Bland – British – 1878.

Nestor. Single. Red and mauve. Lemoine – French – 1899.

Nettala. Single. Short thick tube, dark red; sepals dark red. Corolla violet-red, petals look like petaloids. Smallish flowers, very free. Growth upright, strong and vigorous. Sport of Chang. Francesca – American – 1973 – A.F.S. No. 1090.

Neue Welt. Single. Tube and sepals, rich red; corolla dark parma-violet. Small flowers, very free. Growth upright and hardy. Mahnke – German – 1912.

Neville Young. Double. Short thin tube shell-pink tinged light green, long apple blossom pink (R.H.S. 65B) sepals cover tube and ovary, tipped white. Corolla shell-pink (R.H.S. 69A), medium

to large blooms but compact, petals have slightly darker veins at base, stamens and pistil pink (R.H.S. 70C). Mid-green (R.H.S. 137C) foliage, medium size with ovate leaves and serrated edges, matt texture. Growth natural trailer. Found in the vicinity of Bolton, Lancashire and tested for 7 years. Sport of His Excellency. Young – British – 1982 – A.F.S. No. 1678.

New Cara Mia. Semi-double. Tube and sepals brilliant white, corolla bright crimson. Medium sized flowers, nothing unusual just another red and white. Lax growth very suitable for basketwork or weeping standard. Raised and introduced by J.A. Wright of Hilltop Nurseries, Atherstone. Wright, J.A. – British – 1976.

New Constellation. Double. Tube and sepals cream, corolla cream, self coloured cultivar. Very large blooms and fairly free for large double, very attractive. Growth upright and vigorous. Raised and introduced by J.A. Wright of Hilltop Nurseries, Atherstone. Wright, J.A. – British – 1976.

New Fascination. Double. Reddish-pink tube, sepals bright red; corolla rose-pink, heavily flushed and veined red. Flowers are large, fairly free, very open and wide, not so compact as Fascination. Growth upright and bushy, needs early pinching. Fascination × Pink Balloon. Niederholzer – American – 1940.

Newhope. Double. Tube and sepals white; corolla rich white, almost a self white but for the slight touch of pink, especially the stamens. Large full blooms, free for size. Growth trailer. Davis – American – 1970 – A.F.S. No. 903.

New Horizon. Double. Tube and sepals, palest rose; corolla lobelia-blue. Largish blooms and free. Growth upright. Reiter (Jr.) – American – 1950 – A.F.S. No. 59.

Newton. Lemoine – French – 1880.

Niagara. Double. Tube and broad, thick granular sepals. white with very pale pink edges. Corolla rose veined on clear white base. Huge flaring near-white blooms, fairly free. Growth trailer. Schnabel-Paskesen – American – 1961 – A.F.S. No. 459.

Nicholas Hughes. Single. Pink tube, pink sepals, underside has scarlet line running down centre giving the appearance of a scarlet cross, tipped green. Corolla cream colour with scarlet anthers. Medium sized flowers of perfect shape from opening to maturity and almost a classic single. Dark green foliage with heavily serrated leaves. Growth upright and self branching with semi-erect flowers produced in two's in each leaf axil. Named after a person lost in the Tenerife Air Disaster of 1980. Raised and tested for 4 years before release in the vicinity of Merseyside. Seedling of Lady Isobel Barnett ×. Clark, D. (Merseyside) – British – 1982.

Nicholsii. Single. Red and purple. Nichols – British – 1846.

Nicola. Single. Tube cerise, sepals cerise, fully reflexed and hiding tube; corolla violet-purple, paler at base, veined cerise. Medium sized blooms and very free, larger edition of Swanley Gem with same flat petals. Growth upright and bushy. Swanley Gem × Citation. Dalgliesh – British – 1964.

Nicolaas Aalhuizen. Single. Tube and sepals red; corolla purple. Small flowers, very free, both stamens and style red. Small medium green foliage. Growth upright, bushy and self branching. Peter Pan×. Steevens – Dutch – 1973.

Nicola Jane. Double. Cerise tube, sepals cerise-pink and upturned; corolla blush-pink, flushed and veined cerise. Medium size blooms and free for hardy. Growth upright and bushy, well in the showbench class, excellent for bush training. Accepted by the B.F.S. as showbench hardy. Dawson – British – 1959.

Nicolette. Single. Thick tube pale pink, outside sepals pale pink, inside deeper pink, changing to white half-way down, tipped green, thick and crisp. Corolla pink at base, blending to broad margin of fuchsia-purple. Medium sized blooms, very prolific, produces six or more blooms at leaf axils. Bright green foliage, heart-shaped. Growth upright and vigorous. Handley – British – 1973 – A.F.S. No. 1135.

Nicolina. Single. Rosy-red tube, sepals rose-bengal, rosy-red underneath, curved back to tube. Corolla white with picotée edge of cyclamen-purple. Medium sized blooms, very free, open bell-shaped. Rich dark green foliage, growth upright and wiry. Bishop's Bells × White Bride. Gadsby – British – 1973 – A.F.S. No. 1123.

Niel. Single. Tube and sepals cream, flushed jasper on outside, pale delf-rose inside. Corolla delf-rose, flowers smallish but very free. Growth upright and bushy. Watson – British – 1967.

Night and Day. Double. Long waxy-white tube and sepals; corolla dark heliotrope. Smallish blooms and free, lovely contrast of colour. Growth trailer. Reedstrom – American – 1959 – A.F.S. No. 389.

Nightcap. Single. Tube and upturned sepals cerise; corolla rich creamy-white, slightly veined pink. Medium sized flowers, very free and shaped like a nightcap. Growth upright and compact. Plummer – American – 1961.

Nightingale. Double. Short tube and sepals white, flushed pink; corolla deep purple centre. Large frilly blooms, free for size and of heavy texture, long lasting. The first of raisers tri-coloured cultivars, deep purple, as the flower matures, centre turns bright magenta with outer petals of pink, white and coral tones. Dark green foliage, growth natural trailer. Waltz – American – 1960 – A.F.S. No. 442.

Night Light. Single. Long creamy-pink tube, sepals creamy-pink upturned at green tips. Corolla deep red, small flowers ¾ in long and compact with red stamens, pale pink style and white stigma. Foliage dark green, long leaves, narrow, slightly serrated with red veining. Growth tall upright and bushy, good for standard. Raised and tested for 3 years in the vicinity of Cardiff, South Wales. Adams – British – 1982 – A.F.S. No. 1693.

nigricans (Linden 1849). Synonymous with *F. sylvatica*.

Nikki. Single. Tube and sepals pale flesh pink. Corolla deeper shade of salmon-rose. Medium sized flowers, free-flowering, very easy cultivar. Growth upright and bushy. Raised and introduced by High Trees Nurseries of Reigate, Surrey, in 1979. Sport from Elizabeth (Whiteman). Head – British – 1979.

Nildesperandum. Single. Red and purple. Youell – British – 1858.

*Nimue. Single. Short flesh to pink tube, sepals pale flesh to cream on top, pink underneath, fully recurved, narrow, held well away from tube and ovary. Corolla pink to mauve with pronounced darker blue edge in each petal. Very small flowers on opening, maturing to larger flowers 1½ in long by 1¼ in wide with pink filaments and pistil, cream stigma, tightly rolled at early stage with a deep contrast of colour. Flowers held horizontally until maturity, very free flowering, graceful and beautiful. Light to mid-green foliage with matt surface, ovate leaves with dentate serration, 1¾ in long by 1⅛ in wide. Growth upright and bushy, self-branching, short-jointed, making a good symmetrical bush with little training. Raised in the vicinity of Ipswich, Suffolk and tested for 2 years before release to B. and H.M. Baker of Halstead, Essex who introduced it in 1983. Parentage unknown. Goulding – British – 1983 – A.F.S. No. 1730.

Nina. Double. Pink tube, broad, upturned sepals, soft pink; corolla picotéed and flaring, white. Largish flowers, quite free, very open. Growth trailer. York – American – 1953 – A.F.S. No. 189.

Nina Wills. Single. Short, thin tube, soft, baby-pink, sepals very pale flesh-pink, upturned. Corolla soft baby-pink, medium sized flowers, very free and of neat form. Growth small upright bush. Sport of Forget-Me-Not. Wills-Atkinson – British – 1961 – A.F.S. No. 1129.

Nino. Double. Long white tube, sepals white and long; corolla ruby-red. Medium sized flowers and free, small foliage. Growth trailer. Pennisi – American – 1971 – A.F.S. No. 1018.

Niobe. Semi-double. Tube and sepals, pale rose,flushed pale pink, sepals upturned and twisting. Corolla Tyrian-rose, medium sized blooms, very free, similar both in colour and shape as Cascade. Growth natural trailer. Reiter (Jr.) – American – 1950 – A.F.S. No. 61.

Nobby Adams. Single. Short thick creamy tube, sepals creamy-pink, very short, deeper pink underneath. Corolla pinky-orange with deeper colour at edge of petals. Small flowers with pink stamens and white pistil. Medium sized foliage, mid-green leaves, rounded and slightly serrated. Growth medium upright and bushy. Raised and tested for three years in vicinity of Cardiff, South Wales. Adams – British – 1982 – A.F.S. No. 1694.

Nobility. Double. Tube and sepals, dark red; corolla very light blue or orchid-pink. Large blooms, fairly free and of good substance. Growth lax bush or trailer. Martin – American – 1961 – A.F.S. No. 464.

Noel. Double. Tube and sepals white, corolla purple. Little known cultivar exclusive to California. Growth trailer suitable for basket. Araujo – American – *ca* 1970.

Nola. Single. Short tube and sepals, pink to white; corolla pink, shaded lavender. Medium sized blooms and free, growth tall, upright bush. Hazard and Hazard – American – Date unknown.

No Name. Double. Tube and sepals, white outside, pink inside; corolla deep violet, fading with maturity. Largish flowers and free. Growth upright and bushy. This cultivar was sold by raiser, prior to 1970 as a seedling with no name, hence the name. Bakers – British – 1967.

Nonpariel. Synonymous with Gypsy Queen.

Nora. Double. Red and purple. Bull – British – 1871.

*Norah Henderson. Single. Long thin pale pink tube ½ in long by ⅛ in wide, horizontally held sepals pale pink (R.H.S. 55D) on top, crepey pink underneath, pale green tips which recurve and slightly twist 1⅜ in long by ½ in wide. Corolla opens white slightly veined pink with wavy petal margins 1 in long by ⁷⁄₁₀ in wide. Quarter flared medium sized flowers, bell shaped, very symmetrical and delicately coloured flowers, rose-pink filaments and light pink anthers, light pink style with primrose stigma, long narrow pointed buds. Dark yellow-green (R.H.S. 146B) foliage with elliptic leaves 3 in long by 1½ in wide, serrated, with acute tips and obtuse bases. Growth is natural trailer, will make good basket or weeping standard, prefers filtered light and cool conditions, needs frequent pinching to produce strong stems. Raised in the vicinity of Ponteland, Newcastle-upon-Tyne. Blue Elf × Mayfield. Hall – British – 1984 – A.F.S. No. 1768.

Norfolk Giant. Synonymous with Norfolk Hero.

Norfolk Hero. Double. Red and purple. Henderson – British – 1867.

Norma. Double. Red and rich lavender. Hardy cultivar. Lemoine – French – 1896.

Norma. Double. Tube and sepals red; corolla deep lavender. Similar in every way to Lemoine's Norma. Hazard and Hazard – American – Date unknown.

Normandy Bell. Single. Tube and sepals, pinkish-white; corolla light orchid-blue. Large perfect bell-shaped blooms, very free, fades to orchid-blue. Light green foliage, growth lax bush or trailer. excellent cultivar, habit and blooms of Citation. Martin – American , 1961 – A.F.S. No. 465.

Norman Mitchinson. Single. Tube pinkish-white, waxy-white sepals tipped green, slightly pink at base; corolla rich purple, very occasionally splashed and flecked pink and white. Variegated foliage, originally known as 5UKB seedling and as such was awarded B.F.S. Silver Certificate of Merit at the B.F.S. Manchester Show in 1976. Introduced by J. Ridding of Kidderminster in 1978. Parentage unknown. Ryle – British – 1976 – A.F.S. No. 1477.

Norrie Roth. Semi-double. Tube and sepals white, tipped green; corolla parma-violet with white centre. Largish flowers, free, form of rosette. Growth trailer. Roth – American – 1956.

Northern Light. Single. Scarlet and purple. Banks – British – 1864.

Northern Light. Double. Tube and sepals, pure white; corolla dark purple. Large flowers, fairly free, very light green foliage. Growth lax bush or trailer. Gorman – American – 1970 – A.F.S. No. 931.

Northern Pride. Double. Pink tube, sepals rhodamine-pink (R.H.S. 62A) inside and phlox-pink (R.H.S. 62B) outside. Corolla fuchsia purple (R.H.S. 67B) with smaller outer petals beetroot-purple (R.H.S. 71A). Medium sized blooms with long, white style and chrysanthemum-pink (R.H.S. 185A) anthers. Growth upright and strong, self-branching. Selected by the raiser to commemorate the 21st anniversary of the B.F.S. Northern Show at Manchester, 1978. Introduced by J. Ridding in 1979 and tested for 3 years in

Northumberland before release. Ryle – British – 1979 – A.F.S. No. 1528.

Northern Queen. Double. Rhodonite red tube ⅝ in long × ¼ in wide, sepals also rhodonite red (H.C.C. 00/22) 2 in long × ⅝ in wide. Corolla spectrum-violet (H.C.C. 735/2) with scarlet (H.C.C. 19/1) base. Large blooms with six petaloids same length and colour as the petals, 2¾ in wide × 1½ in long corolla, pink filaments and brown anthers, pistil is 3 in long with brown stigma. Light green foliage with 2 in and 1¼ in wide leaves. Growth upright, will make good bush, heat tolerant if shaded where best colour develops. Originates from the Sebastopol area of California. Introduced by Soo Yun Fuchsia Gardens in 1980. De Francisco – American – 1980 – A.F.S. No. 1558.

Northumbrian Belle. Single. Short, thick tube, neyron-rose, sepals bright neyron-rose, fairly long and narrow. Corolla aster-blue, fading to petunia-purple. Medium sized blooms, free flowering, growth medium upright and self-branching. Lena Dalton × Citation. Ryle-Atkinson – British – 1973 – A.F.S. No. 1115.

*Northumbrian Pipes. Single. Tube and sepals burning rose; corolla same colour making the flower a rose self. Flowers are very similar to F. magdalenae (synonymous with F. lampadaria) but smaller. One of five new introductions by Herman de Graaff in 1983. Raised in the vicinity of Lisse, Netherlands. F. arborescens × F. magdalenae (syn. F. lampadaria). de Graaff – Dutch – 1983.

Northway. Single. Short, thick tube light pink, short reflexed sepals, light pink. Corolla cherry red, nice break from the red and purple. Small flowers similar in shape to Lustre, very profuse, pink pistil with white stigma, small light green foliage. Growth rather lax but will produce bush or shrub without the need of supports. La Campanella × Howlett's. Hardy. Golics – British – 1976.

Norvell Gillespie. Double. White tube, long sepals, white on top, light pink on bottom. Corolla dark orchid, large sized blooms and free growth trailer. Pennisi – American – 1969 – A.F.S. No. 832.

Not So Big. Double. White tube, sepals pale pink, corolla blue. Largish blooms, quite free. Growth upright. Machado – American – 1962 – A.F.S. No. 500.

Nouveau Mastodonte. Double. Red and purple. Lemoine – French – 1880.

Novar. Semi-double. Tube and sepals white, flushed rose-pink, tipped green, sepals are upturned. Corolla mauve-pink ageing to deep pink and marbled with maturity. Medium sized blooms extra long and free flowering. One of the few Australian introduction. Sport of Flirtation which itself is a sport of Lucky Strike. Smith – Australian introductions – 1970.

Novato. Single. Long, thin tube, white faintly tinged green, sepals white with light green tips, underside white, faintly tinged pink. Corolla pale scarlet, shading to salmon. Foliage very light green. Medium sized blooms and free, growth lax bush or semi-trailer. Similar to the cultivars of the Lye family with the same colour as Rundle's Duchess of Albany. Novato tube differs in being the same width at the top and bottom. Soo Yun – American – 1972 – A.F.S. No. 1042.

Novella. Double. Tube and sepals, rosy-pink; corolla salmon-orange. Large blooms, fairly free. Growth trailer. A.F.S. Cert. of Merit 1971. Tiret – American – 1968 – A.F.S. No. 796.

Novelty. Single. White and purple. Nichols – British – 1846.

Novelty. Epps – British – 1853.

Novelty. Wyness – German – 1865.

Novelty. Single. Red and purple. Clark – British – 1950.

Noyo Star. Double. Short, thin tube, carmine; sepals pink on top side with carmine streaking, tipped green, lighter pink inside shading to green, star shaped, narrow and very long, at full maturity twists around the tube. White corolla with pink streaks the full length. Medium sized blooms, exceptionally long buds, tight when first opens, then slightly flared, pink stamens and .pistils. Ovate foliage with acuminate tip and rounded base, upper surface dark dull green under surface medium green, red stems and green veins. Growth natural trailer, self-branching, will make good basket. Registered by C. Ebeling and B. Barnes. Walker – American – 1976 – A.F.S. No. 1364.

Nutshell. Single. Tube and sepals reddish-orange, sepals spread wide; corolla reddish-orange almost a self. Medium sized flowers very profuse, will stand heat but does not tolerate full sun. Growth lax trailer, needs frequent stopping. Introduced by Wills Fuchsia Nurseries in 1979. La Campanella × . de Graaff – Dutch – 1976.

Nymph. Single. Cerise and whitish-pink. Epps – British – 1845.

Oakland. Double. Crimson tube, short upright sepals crimson; corolla rosy-white, heavily veined crimson. Very large blooms, fairly free for size, very similar to Phyrne. Growth upright, compact and strong. Suzanne Pasquier × Mrs. Victor Reiter. Reiter – American – 1942.

Obergartner Koch. Triphylla single. Long tube, vermilion, small petals, orange-red. Foliage pale yellowish-green. Growth upright. Emile de Wildeman × Gartendirektor Hample. Sauer – German – 1912.

Oberon. Single. Red and violet. Banks – British – 1864.

Oberon. Single. Long waxy tube, mauve-pink, sepals mauve-pink, small, pointed and reflexed. Corolla mauve-pink in shade, coral in sun, pointed petals. Flowers are tiny and free, colour and shape of *F.parviflora*. Very small foliage, Breviflorae type, similar to *F.minutiflora*. Growth upright but frond-like, good for usual types of training including bonsai. Breviflorae type with the smallest flowers amongst the hybrids. Travis, J. – British – 1958.

Ocean. Rozain-Boucharlat – French – 1931.

Ocean Beach. Single. Light salmon tube, sepals light salmon upperside, salmon underneath, stiff and flat, tipped green; corolla salmon-orange, mottled with salmon-rose. Small flowers, very free, anthers often twist out, dark green foliage with dark red tint at growing tip. Growth upright, bushy and small, compact with short joints. Krogh – American – 1975 – A.F.S. No. 1298.

Ocean Mist. Single. Thin, long white tube, white sepals; white corolla. Tiny miniature flow-ers, stamens white at base of petals and in tube, pistil flares open. Foliage fern-like dark green. Growth natural trailer, tested for 2 years at Fort Bragg, California before release. Francesca – American – 1977 – A.F.S. No. 1422.

Odd Ball. Double. Very long tube, pale pink; sepals pale pink opening flat. creating square frame. Corolla pale blue. Largish flowers, free and of irregular, crumpled shape, fading to light orchid. Small foliage, growth lax bush or trailer. Prentice – American – 1966 – A.F.S. No. 666.

Odd Beauty. Double. Short, thick tube, light red, sepals light red, tipped green, broad opening out with slight curve upwards. Corolla blue, variegated with pink. Large blooms, fairly free, variegation is mostly at base of petals, pink streaks at times to tip of petals. Large, serrated foliage, growth lax bush or trailer. Soo Yun – American – 1973 – A.F.S. No. 1096.

Oddfellow. Double. Tube and sepals delicate shade of pale pink with green tips throughout. Corolla pure white, medium size blooms, fully double and very free, good form and substance. Growth upright, short-jointed and vigorous, versatile can be trained into practically all types of growth. In its initial year outside has survived its first year in Middlesex. Selected by the Independent Order of Oddfellows to bear their name. Introduced by Woodbridge Nurseries of Hounslow, Middlesex 1982. Dyos – British – 1982.

Oetnang. Double. Tube and sepals pink; corolla maroon, growth upright bush. The first recorded Austrian cultivar. Listed by High Trees Nursery, Reigate, Surrey, classed as hardy. Raiser unknown – Austrian – Date unknown.

Oh Boy. Double. Tube and sepals, bright red; corolla white with red veining. Huge flowers, fairly free for size with loose corolla. Growth upright. Hazard and Hazard – American – Date unknown.

Old Del Monte. Single. Tube and sepals carmine; corolla red to purple. Medium sized blooms and free. Growth trailer. Hazard and Hazard – American – Date unknown.

Old Fashioned. Semi-double. Tube and long, twisted, upturned sepals, cerise-rose; corolla of the same colouring, almost a self. Largish blooms and free, spreading corolla, diluted to white at base of petals. Dark green foliage, growth trailer. Hodges – American – 1958 – A.F.S. No. 342.

Old Lace. Single. Tube and sepals, rosy-pink; corolla dark blue blending to orchid at petal base. Largish flowers, fairly free, with scalloped petals and long corolla. Growth upright. Brown and Soules – American – 1953.

Old Rose. Double. Tube carmine-rose, sepals neyron-rose (R.H.S. 55B); corolla neyron-rose. Medium sized blooms with twenty large petals and seven small petals, neyron-rose stamens. name suggests both colour and form, best colour in shade. Growth tall upright, bushy, good for bush or standard. Pugh – British – 1976 – A.F.S. No. 1332.

Old Smoky. Double. Tube and outspread sepals. flesh-pink, pink on underside; corolla old rose with smoky cast. Largish flowers and free, growth lax bush or trailer. Schmidt – American – 1952 – A.F.S. No. 112.

*Old Somerset. Single. Variegated foliage cultivar. This cultivar was listed exclusively in 1982 by Clapton Court Gardens of Crewkerne in Somerset. Very little known and could be an old cultivar under a localised name. It is described as a red self with small flowers and beautiful pink variegated foliage. It could be a sport from Corallina and is very similar to the modern Herbé de Jacques.

Olive Jackson. Semi-double. Short, thick tube, deep rose, sepals deep rose and reflexed. Corolla hyacinth-blue, centre of petals white, matures to lilac. Small to medium sized flowers, prolific and early. Bright green foliage. Growth upright and bushy, compact. Handley – British – 1974 – A.F.S. No. 1193.

Olive Smith. Single. Tube and sepals carmine, sepals curve upwards. Corolla rich crimson, small flowers, very colourful and free, holding its flowers for a long time. Similar in shape to Chang, almost a self, flowers hang in clusters. Growth medium upright, short-jointed, will make good bush and one destined for the showbench. Raised in the vicinity of Kegworth, Derby and introduced by R. and J. Pacey of Melton Mowbray in 1981. Lye's Unique cross. Smith, H. – British – 1981.

Olympia. Single. Rose-pink and carmine. Rozain-Boucharlat – French – 1913.

Olympiad. Double. Red tube, sepals red, long slender and curling; corolla white, veined red, flared tips of petals slightly serrated. Large flowers and free, lightish green foliage with dark red stems, delicately serrated. Growth trailer. Foster – American – 1973 – A.F.S. No. 1087.

Olympic Lass. Double. Long slender white tube, sepals white, completely recurving, developing rose edge stripe and tip. Corolla pinkish-purple with pencilled purple picotée edge. Large blooms, free for size, long white buds, corolla two inches, long pear shaped, most unusual bloom. Medium saw-toothed and lacy foliage. Thunderbird ×. Sutherland – American – 1967 – A.F.S. No. 745.

Omar Pasha. Single. Crimson and violet. Smith – British – 1855.

Omeomy. Double. Tube and long sepals pale pink; corolla dianthus-purple, overlaid with coral-pink marbling. Large tight flowers, fairly free. Growth robust trailer. Kennett – American – 1963 – A.F.S. No. 591.

One in the Ring. Single. White and vermilion. Turville – British – 1847.

*OOS. Single. Tube and sepals red, corolla red. Very small flowers of the Breviflorae type. Foliage medium green very small and serrated. Growth bush. *F. parviflora × F. microphylla.* Van der Grijp – Dutch – 1973.

*Oosje. Single. Tube and sepals red ageing to dark red. Corolla whitish-red ageing to dark red. Very small flowers of Breviflorae type. Foliage small and serrated, medium green. Growth upright and bushy. Introduced by W.A. Thipp of Homestead nurseries, Uxbridge, in 1983. *F. parviflora × F. microphylla.* Van der Grijp – Dutch – 1973.

Opalescent. Double. Tube and sepals. China-rose; corolla pale violet blended with opal and rose. Largish blooms and free, need support. Growth upright and willowy. Fuchsia-La – American – 1951.

Oracle. Double. Red and purple. Bull – British – 1871.

Orange Cocktail. Single. Tube pale salmon and waxy, sepals pale salmon with long, narrow pale yellow-green tips. Corolla centre and base, clear orange, blending to outer margins cardinal-red, long over-lapping petals. Large multi-coloured blooms, very floriferous and early. Growth lax bush or trailer. Handley – British – 1972 – A.F.S. No. 1056.

Orange Crush. Single. Tube waxy orange-salmon, sepals orange-salmon, thick and spiky. Corolla bright orange, paler at base with overlapping petals. Medium sized blooms very free, four blooms at each pair of leaf axils. Growth upright, bushy and short-jointed. Handley – British – 1972 – A.F.S. No. 1057.

Orange Crystal. Single. Orange (R.H.S. 33C) tube, sepals orange tipped green held at right angles to tube, 1 in long × ⅜ in wide. Corolla orange (R.H.S. 33A) with overlapped petals, length of corolla 1 in. Medium sized flowers, very free and exceptionally clear colouring, very similar to Lord Lonsdale, stamens and pistil orange (R.H.S. 40D). Mid-green foliage with small serrated leaves 1½ in long × 1 in wide. The raiser has been trying for years to produce a really good orange and now looks as if succeeded, tested for 10 years before release. Growth upright and bushy, self-branching, short pointed and compact, requires usual protection but will take full sun. Introduced by Jackson's Nurseries of Tamworth in 1980. Handley – British – 1980 – A.F.S. No. 1541.

Orange Drops. Single. Good orange cultivars are rather conspicuous by their absence, but this cultivar is probably the deepest orange yet introduced. Raised by Martin in California, introduced in 1963 and registered by the American Fuchsia Society under No. 572. The single flowers of medium size have light orange sepals, held out almost horizontally, whilst the nicely formed corolla is a darker rich orange; the blooms tend to hang in clusters and when in full bloom appear to be fluorescent. Best described as a semi-trailer, although most catalogues describe it as a bush; does incline to grow outwards and does not produce a good bush plant. Foliage is medium green and with over-feeding does produce large leaves; needs pinching back quite regularly in the initial stages of growth. It is tolerant to heat, best grown under glass as H2, when grown outside; the sun bleaches the colouring and needs a shady corner of the garden. Responds to that little extra cultivation as it is prone to botrytis in late spring and

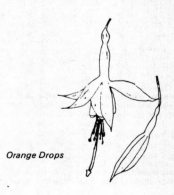

Orange Drops

234

early summer; however, a cultivar once grown, will always be in your collection. Confusion did arise when first introduced from America into this country, coming in as Mexicali Rose. Hybridists of recent years have been concentrating upon this colour range, particularly Mrs. Enid Handley of Derby who in recent years has introduced Orange Cocktail, Orange Crush and Orange Flare; other orange cultivars which did appear, but failed to stay the course were: Orange Glow by Munkner 1957, Orange Queen by Waltz 1949 and Orangy by Reedstrom 1962 and did not last in popularity. Will produce a good, fairly stiff basket and has possibilities of making a good weeping standard. A.F.S. Cert. of Merit 1967. Martin – American 1963 – A.F.S. No. 572.

Orange Flare. Single. Short, thick tube, orange-salmon, sepals orange-salmon short and thick. Corolla light orange at base, shading to deep orange at outer margins of petals, flared. Medium sized flowers, early and free flowering, heat resistant if shaded, best colour in sun. Growth upright, bushy and self-branching. Handley – British – 1972 – A.F.S. No. 1058.

Orange Glory. This cultivar is listed in American catalogues and grown in California with the same description as Mrs. W. Rundle with no hybridiser or date and is confirmed as being synonymous.

Orange Glow. Single. Tube and outside of sepals reddish, inside of the upturned sepals deep orange. Corolla brilliant deep orange, flowers medium sized and very free with flaring corolla. Growth upright and bushy. Munkner – American – 1957.

Orange King. Semi-double. White tube, sepals pale pink arching back, underside rich frosty-pink; corolla opens orange, maturing to rich smoky-pink with rich orange mottling at base. Large flowers, fairly free, carnation type, very bright and eye catching. Heavily serrated foliage, growth lax bush. Wright, L.A. – British – 1975 – A.F.S. No. 1306.

Orange Mirage. Single. Tube and sepals salmon; corolla smoky-orange with touches of salmon. Light green foliage. Growth trailer. Tiret – American – 1970 – A.F.S. No. 896.

Orange Pip. Single. Short thin tube orangey-pink, horizontal short thin sepals cream, flushed orange on lower surface, tipped green. Corolla light orange, small flowers with orangey-pink stamens and style, white stigma. Light green foliage, small with rounded slightly serrated leaves. Growth lax upright, will make basket with weights and bush with certain amount of support. Raised and tested in vicinity of Cardiff, South Wales for 3 years. Adams – British – 1982 – A.F.S. No. 1695.

Orange Queen. Single. Tube and sepals, creamy-white, corolla bright orange-red. Smallish flowers very free, small dark green foliage, growth lax bush or trailer. Waltz – American – 1949.

Orange Queen. Single. Long tube and sepals, porcelain-rose; corolla bright orange. Flowers of medium size and free, similar to Orange Glow. growth upright and bushy. Jones, W. – British – 1960.

Orang-U-Tan. Single. Short thin cream tube, slightly recurving small thin sepals, cream flushed light orange on upper surface, deeper orange underneath, tipped green. Corolla lovely shade of orange, very small flowers but very free flowering, pinky-orange stamens and style, large stigma and anthers, both white. Light green foliage with slightly serrated rounded leaves. Growth tall upright and bushy. Takes full sun in vicinity of Cardiff, South Wales where raised and tested for 3 years before introduction. Adams – British – 1982 – A.F.S. No. 1696.

Orangy. Single. Tube and sepals, pinkish-orange; corolla pale orange. Medium sized blooms and free, foliage attractive with yellow cast. Growth natural trailer and vigorous. Reedstrom – American – 1962 – A.F.S. No. 547.

*Oranje Boven. Single. Tube and sepals rich orange-red, sepals are tipped green. Corolla pure orange, long and slender medium sized flowers and one of the best oranges to date very free flowering, will take full sun. Dark green foliage. Growth upright, one of the few cultivars able to be trained as a climber, not an easy cultivar to grow. Raised in the Netherlands in the vicinity of Lisse. Speciosa × Machu Picchu seedling. de Graaff – Dutch – 1980.

Oranje van Os. Single. Tube and sepals white with deep pink-orange blush, both the tube and sepals are rather long, sepals tipped green. Corolla orange, rather large flowers and very free flowering. This cultivar grown and cultivated in the Netherlands was discovered by J. van Os in the Experimental Garden at Venlo and probably originates from Germany. Raiser and date unknown.

Oregon. Single. Long thin tube and sepals, flesh-pink with white stripes; corolla crimson. Flowers are the same as America but with sepals having white stripes. Growth trailer. Sport of America. Bacher – American – 1947.

Oregon Trail. Single. Tube and sepals crimson; corolla light amparo-purple. Largish flowers, early and free, hoop-skirt corolla opens flat saucer shape. Growth medium bush, spreading. Hodges – American – 1949.

Organza. Double. Tube and sepals rose-pink; corolla heliotrope-blue. Largish flowers and free, growth upright. Nessier – American , 1953.

Oriental Lace. Single. Short tube, soft light red, sepals soft light red, tipped chartreuse-green; corolla deep purple. Very small flowers, very free and blooms continually, gives fine-lace appearance. Small, slender dark green foliage, growth upright and bushy, will produce most types of training. Francesca – American – 1975 – A.F.S. No. 1291.

Oriental Lantern. Double. White tube, sepals white with tinge of pink on undersides. Corolla cerise with buds opening in lantern shape. Medium sized blooms and free. Growth trailer. Soo Yun – American – 1970 – A.F.S. No. 912.

Oriental Princess. Semi-double. Tube and sepals, pale pink, opening to pagoda shape with upcurve. Corolla white, medium sized blooms, very free, bell shaped. Small pale green foliage. Growth trailer. Macado – American – 1963 – A.F.S. No. 560.

Oriental Sunrise. Single. Short thin tube, light orange, sepals light orange, tipped green, dark orange underneath, protruding straight out; corolla dark orange. Medium sized flowers, free, flare out where petals just separate, star shaped. Medium sized foliage with red stems, growth semi-trailer. Soo Yun – American – 1975 – A.F.S. No. 1270.

*Orient Express. Single. Triphylla type hybrid. Long tube with a mixture of pink and white, sepals of similar colour but tipped red. Corolla rose-pink, the long flowers are typical of terminal flowering parentage. Growth is upright and stiff, early stopping will promote branching, although the flowers are of a novelty type they are almost bi-coloured, will make good show plant. Raised in the vicinity of Ipswich, Suffolk, and introduced by the raiser, Gouldings Fuchsias of Ipswich, in 1985. One of a series of ten new introductions named after famous trains in 1985. Goulding – British – 1985.

Oriole. This cultivar is listed in American catalogues and grown in California with the same description as Golden Treasure with no hybridiser or date and is confirmed as being synonymous.

Orion. Single. Dark crimson and purple. Smith – British – 1864.

*Ornamental Pearl. Single. White tube, sepals rhodamine-pink shading to white, tipped green, curving back towards tube. Corolla white of medium size and well formed, extremely floriferous. Has all the characteristics of its parent except for the foliage, which is a most attractive grey-green, edged with cream with a red hue over the young growth and is not the same as Golden Cloverdale Pearl. Growth upright, self-branching bush. Raised in the vicinity of Aldershot and introduced by Oldbury Nurseries of Ashford, Kent in 1984. Sport of Cloverdale Pearl. Gubler – British – 1984.

Ortenburger Festival. Single. Short thick red tube, broad outspread sepals are showy deep red. Corolla blue-violet turning reddish with maturity. Medium-sized flowers, very early and very free. Dark green foliage. Growth upright and bushy. Introduced to the trade in Germany in November 1973. Introduced by Fuchsiama in America, tested for 5 years in Germany and 3 years at Long Beach and Fort Bragg, California before release. Topperwein – German – 1973 – A.F.S. No. 1432.

osgoodii. Dark red tube, red sepals; red corolla. Smallish flowers borne in terminal racemes. Tall upright shrub with height of up to 12 ft in native Peru. MacBride – 1941 – Peru.

O Sole Mio. Single. Tube and sepals, deep red; corolla dark purple, marbled reddish-pink. Medium sized blooms, very free, growth upright. Blackwell – British – 1960.

Othello. Semi-double. Cerise and purple. Lemoine – French – 1869.

Other Fellow. Single. Tube and sepals, waxy-white, tipped green; corolla coral-pink, white at base. Small flowers with profusion of bloom, very dainty. Growth upright and bushy. Exceptionally good cultivar. Hazard and Hazard – American – 1946.

Otto. Single. Tube and sepals deep crimson; corolla blue-purple. Growth upright and bushy. Listed and grown in California and could prove to be a very old English cultivar from the 1800s.

Otto Furst. Triphylla single. Long tube, pink, small petals, pale pink. Foliage bluish-green, growth upright, best grown as H1. *F. triphylla* ×. Bonstedt – German – 1904.

Otto Krunze. Triphylla single. Long tube, orange shaded green, petals orange and vermilion. Long flowers, very free, reddish-green foliage.

Growth upright. *F. triphylla* ×. Rottengen – German – Date unknown.

Otto Nordenskjold. Triphylla single. Long tube, coral-red, short petals cinnabar-red. Very thin tube, free flowering, foliage dark green, flushed purple underneath. Growth upright. *F. tri̱phylla* ×. Rehnelt – German – 1903.

*Our Darling. Single. Deep rose tube ⅔in long by ¼in wide, fully up sepals deep rose on top, crepey, dark rose underneath with recurved tips, 1¾in long by ⅜in wide. Corolla opens deep violet-blue (R.H.S. 87A) veined rose-pink (R.H.S. 52C) maturing to heliotrope (R.H.S. 80A), base flushed rose-pink (R.H.S. 52D) 1 in long by 1¼in wide. Half flaring, bell shaped, medium sized flowers with pronounced basal flush colour and red veining. Olive-green foliage (R.H.S. 146A) with elliptic leaves 3 in long by 1½in wide, serrated edges and acute tips with rounded bases, veins pale green. Growth medium upright, bushy and vigorous, short-jointed with blooms clear of foliage, will make any tall shaped plant. Raised in the vicinity of Ponteland, Newcastle-upon-Tyne. Mayfield × Silver King. Hall – British – 1984 – A.F.S. No. 1769.

*Our Secret. Semi-double. Tube and sepals waxy-white with rose-madder veining. Corolla deep intense purple. Medium sized blooms and very free, growth lax suitable for basketwork with weights. Raised in the vicinity of Rugby in Warwickshire and introduced by F. Sheffield in 1983. Sheffield – British – 1983.

ovalis. Scarlet tube, scarlet sepals; purplish corolla. Smallish flowers, borne in racemes from the upper leaf axials. Foliage dark green. Upright shrub of approximately 3 or 4 ft. Synonymous with *F. polyanthella.* Ruiz and Pavón – 1802 – Chile and Peru.

ovata (Sessé and Mocino 1828). Synonymous with *F. thymifolia.*

Ovation. Double. Thin long ivory tube, long broad sepals ivory to pink. Corolla deep red with some orangey-pink colour in outer petals. Short medium sized blooms and free for double. Rather large foliage 3½in long by 1¾in elliptic shaped leaves and ovate base, obtuse tip and dentate margin. Growth trailer, will make good basket with weights, best under cool conditions, best colour in filtered sun. Tested for 4 years in vicinity of Fort Bragg, Oxnard and Oceanside, California, where it will be trademarked. Stubbs – American – 1981 – A.F.S. No. 1614.

Oxenholme. Single. White tube, narrow white sepals, flushed pink on upper surface, deeper pink underneath, sepals inclined to fold back and twist slightly. Corolla violet (R.H.S. 86). Medium sized flowers of good form and substance, stamens indian lake (reddish) (R.H.S. 59B). Growth medium upright, will make good bush, standard and any tall type of training. Will take full sun in vicinity of Preston where it was tested for 10 full years before release. Named after beauty spot in Cumbria, Lake District, North West England. Sister seedling to Dorothea Flower (1969). Hawkshead × Venus Victrix. Thornley – British – 1981 – A.F.S. No. 1639.

Pacifica. Semi-double. Tube and slightly twisted sepals, crimson; corolla orchid-purple, lighter at base, darker on edges with fine crimson lines. Medium sized flowers and free, growth large, spreading bush, brittle branches. (1915 × Rolla) × Rolla. Niederholzer – American – 1941.

Pacific Grove. Single. Coral and purple-mauve. Synonymous with Evelyn Steele Little. Greene – American – 1930.

Pacific Grove. Double. Tube and sepals, dark crimson; corolla Bishop's-violet with smaller petals outside, crimson. Fairly large blooms, quite free, growth tall, upright and vigorous, up to 8 ft in California. Niederholzer – American – 1947.

Pacific Queen. Double. Tube and wide sepals, phlox-pink tipped white; corolla warm shade of old rose, fading to brighter shade. Large blooms, fairly free, growth upright. Waltz – American – 1963 – A.F.S. No. 587.

Pacquesa. Single. Short deep red tube, reflexing sepals, deep red with crepe reverse; corolla pure white with faint trace of deep red veining. Largish flowers and extremely free, petals are of classic shape, very similar in shape to Ballet Girl. Foliage parsley-green with almond shaped leaves, growth upright and bushy, self-branching, strong short-jointed habit. This is not just another red and white cultivar, but an improvement and a welcome addition to the existing colour range; created great attention when shown at B.F.S. London Show 1974. Pacific Queen × Sheryl Ann. Clyne – British – 1974 – A.F.S. No. 1286.

Pageant. Double. Short tube and broad sepals, white to pale carmine; corolla violet-purple with deep coral marbling extending to petal margins in outer petals. Large blooms and free, flaring with maturity. Growth lax bush or trailer. Kennett – American – 1960 – A.F.S. No. 430.

Pagoda. Single. Tube and sepals bright red; corolla blue changing to dark purple. Flowers nearly 4 in long and well reflexed. Growth upright and bushy. Batten – British – ca 1850.

Pagoda. Single. Tube and sepals bright red; corolla dark red, flowers are pagoda shaped. Growth upright and bushy. An unregistered American cultivar. Fuchsia-La (Roy Walker) – American – 1954.

Painted Desert. Double. Tube and sepals deep red; corolla smoky-blue overlapped with rose to red. Growth upright, this is an unregistered American cultivar and should not be confused with Painted Desert by Paskesen – (A.F.S. 664). Fuchsia-La (Roy Walker) – American – 1954.

Painted Desert. Double. White tube, sepals white, tipped green; corolla blue-purple splashed with pink and white, fading into clear iridescent carmine. Largish blooms and free, growth trailer. Paskesen – America – 1966 – A.F.S. No. 664.

Painted Lady. Single. Tube and sepals, pink to white; corolla pink shaded purple. Medium sized blooms, free and flaring, growth upright. Hazard and Hazard – American – Date unknown.

Pale Beauty. Double. Short tube and sepals, fully reflexed, pale pink; corolla almost white, with faint blush-pink in sun. Very large blooms, free for size, very full, early and of good substance. Growth lax bush, raiser claims this to be his best cultivar to date. Lockerbie – Australian – 1971 – A.F.S. No. 1000.

Pale Face. Double. Almost a pure white self with touch of pink. Large blooms and free, similar in shape and size to Swingtime. Growth lax bush or trailer. Haag – American – 1956.

Pale Flame. Double. Short, medium thick pale carmine tube, pale carmine-rose sepals are very long, twisting into curls or eccentric shapes. Corolla opens claret-rose to carmine-rose at base, fading to delft-rose to azalea-pink. Largish blooms flare slightly at maturity, a novelty with its pale flame colours and the effect of sepals is flame-like. Foliage is dark green with red veins, new growth has red stems. Growth semi-trailer will trail with weights, best colour in shade. Tested for 3 years in vicinity of Fort Bragg, California. Stubbs – American – 1978 – A.F.S. No. 1441.

Pallas. No other details except the parentage: *F. regia* var. *typica* × Bon Accorde. De Groot – Dutch – 1970.

Pallas Athene. Single. Short thick tube and sepals same colouring as corolla which is eau-de-nil (light green) when first opens, changing to red (R.H.S. 55A). Small reflexed flowers $\frac{1}{2}$ in to $\frac{3}{4}$ in in length and typical of its crossing. Light green foliage is ovate. Growth medium upright and self-branching, will make good bush, pyramid or decorative. Heat tolerant if shaded where it develops best colour. Originates from the vicinity of Preston, Lancashire. Encliandra cross. Travis, J. – British – 1980 – A.F.S. No. 1583.

pallescens. Tube pale carmine, white sepals; corolla purplish. Smallish flowers, not very free. Upright shrub of medium size. Diels – 1938 – Ecuador.

Pallida. See *magellanica* var. *globosa*.

Palomar. Double. Tube and curled, twisted sepals, waxy flesh-pink; corolla palest lilac, washed with pink. Largish blooms, very free and flaring, growth upright, bushy and compact. Evans and Reeves – American – 1953 – A.F.S. No. 184.

Pamela. Single. Tube and sepal white, tipped green, tinted lilac on underside; corolla rose-lilac, edged scarlet. Medium sized flowers, early and free. Growth upright and vigorous. Patty × Blue Boy. Evans and Reeves – American , 1939.

Pamela Hutchinson. Single. Pale pink tube sepals are cyclamen-rose with green tip. Corolla light hyacinth-blue. Medium-sized flowers, early flowerer from early July onwards. Large dark green foliage. Growth medium upright, strong, bushy and close-jointed, needs regular stopping for best results, will make good bush or decorative. Tested for 4 years in the vicinity of Derby. This cultivar was the very last to be introduced by the raiser before his death in 1978. Gadsby – British – 1978 – A.F.S. No. 1483.

Pamela Knights. Double. Short cream to flesh with pink tube, sepals pink reflexed with recurved tips. Corolla lavender-blue with lovely pastel shaded colouring. Medium sized blooms and extremely floriferous for a double, bloom in every leaf axil, frilly with irregular petals. Medium green foliage with medium sized leaves. Growth medium upright, self-branching, can be trained to almost all types of training, will even make good basket with weights. Raised and tested for 2 years in the vicinity of Ipswich, East of England and introduced by B. and H.M. Baker of Halstead, Essex, in 1983. Goulding – British – 1983 – A.F.S. No. 1731.

Panama. Rozain-Boucharlat – French – 1927.

Pan America. Double. Tube and sepals red; corolla pale pink. Very large blooms, fairly free, growth of scandent habit. Reiter – American – 1942.

paniculata –arborescens. To distinguish between these similar species *paniculata* has loose panicles of purplish flowers much darker than the tighter, brighter pink flowers of *F. arborescens*, but identical except for colour and being larger. Leaves of *F. paniculata* are slightly toothed along the margins; *F. arborescens* does not possess the tooth-like edges. Separate male and female plants; *F. arborescens* has hermaphrodite flowers. Few berries formed as opposed to abundant berries. *F. paniculata* is found in South Mexico to Panama, *F. arborescens* is found only in Central Mexico. Both plants are easily confused with one another when not seen together.

Pantaloons. Semi-double. Pink tube, light red sepals; corolla plum-burgundy with many petaloids. Medium sized blooms, free, sepals do not reflex. Growth trailer. Fuchsia Forest – American – 1966 – A.F.S. No. 670.

Papa Bleuss. Double. Tube and recurved sepals, pale rose and ivory on outside, carmine-rose inside; corolla deep Bishop's violet, slightly marbled at base delicate crimson. Huge blooms but not very plentiful, excellent for cut bloom classes. Growth lax bush or trailer, best grown as H1. Tiret – American – 1956 – A.F.S. No. 253.

Paper Dolls. Double. White self, with slightest touch of pink, according to the amount of shade afforded. Largish blooms, very free, heat tolerant, similar but larger and whiter than Flying Cloud, same raiser, but has lost all favour. Growth upright and bushy. Reiter – American – 1956 – A.F.S. No. 273.

Papoose. Semi-double. Tube and sepals, bright red; corolla, very dark purple. Small flowers, prolific, more flowers than foliage. Growth low bush, versatile for any type of training, delightful as half standard, will even produce a wonderful basket, hardy. Accepted by the B.F.S. as showbench hardy. A.F.S. Cert. of Merit 1963. Reedstrom – American – 1960 – A.F.S. No. 423.

Parachute. Single. Scarlet and violet. Lemoine – French – 1882.

Parasol. Single. Tube china-rose, broad sepals china-rose held well back from corolla. Corolla imperial-purple, paler at base. Medium sized flowers, very free flowering, four petalled corolla of the coolie hat type. Growth upright, bushy and vigorous, short jointed will make excellent bush or standard. Raised in the vicinity of Bardney, Lincolnshire and introduced by R. and J. Pacey of Melton Mowbray 1981. Bellamy – British – 1981.

Parisienne. Double. Tube and sepals, deep pink; corolla blue-violet rosette with outer petals ruffled with various shades of pink overlay. Medium sized blooms, extremely free, growth lax bush or trailer. Seedlings from Lady Beth (Martin 1958). Fuchsia Forest-Castro – American , 1953 – A.F.S. No. 568.

Parkside. Single. Tube and sepals, palest carmine; corolla doge-purple. Flowers are bell shaped, large and fairly free. Growth trailer. Schnabel – American – 1949.

Partner. Single. Thick white tube ⅞in long and ½in wide; pale pink sepals, tipped green, 1¾in long and ⅝in wide. Corolla bishop's violet (H.C.C. 34) fading to fuchsia-purple (H.C.C. 28). Medium sized flowers with pink stamens and white pistil, petals ⅞in long and ⅝in wide, petaloids attached to sepals. Light green foliage with large leaves 3 in long and 2½in wide, red stemmed. Growth trailer, self-branching. Raised and tested in vicinity of Richmond, California, and introduced by Soo Yun Fuchsia Gardens in 1979. Palko – American – 1979 – A.F.S. No. 1498.

Party Frock. Single to semi-double. Tube and long, upturned sepals, rosy-pink, tipped green. Corolla pastel blue, splashed pink, with outer petals soft pink. Flowers are large, free for size. Growth upright and bushy, needs early pinching delightful cultivar of true pastel shades. Walker and Jones – American – 1953.

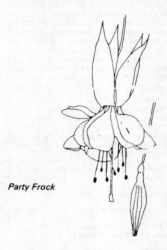

Party Frock

Party Gown. Double. Tube and long, recurved, curling sepals, pink; corolla pale blue. Medium sized blooms, very long and free. Growth trailer. Reimers – American – 1953 – A.F.S. No. 171.

parviflora (Lindley 1827). Synonymous with *F. thymifolia*.

parviflora (Hemsley 1880). Synonymous with *F. encliandra*.

Pasadena. Double. Tube and sepals, deep rose; corolla snowy-white, lightly veined with pink. Large, flaring blooms, free, light green foliage. Growth upright and vigorous, up to eight feet in California. Rolla ×. Evans and Reeves – American – 1938.

Pascal. Lemoine – French – 1881.

Passing Cloud. Single. Tube and sepals, rose-madder; corolla amethyst-violet, marbled white. Largish flowers and free, growth upright and bushy. Jones, W. – British – 1959.

Pastel. Single. Tube and sepals, pale neyron-rose; corolla pale lavender. Medium sized flowers, very free. Growth upright and bushy, disappointing cultivar, belies its name. *F.lycioides* × Brentwood. Reiter – American , 1941.

*Pastell. Double. Neyron-rose tube, sepals neyron-rose which curl up tightly to tube. Corolla fuchsia-purple, heavily flushed azalea-pink. Growth medium upright, raised in the vicinity of Plymouth, Devon. Drake 400 × Devonshire Dumpling. Hilton – British – 1984.

Pasteur. Double. Red and white. Lemoine – French – 1893.

Pat. Double. Tube and sepals rose; corolla light purple. Small blooms, very free, growth trailer. Soo Yun Field – American – 1966 – A.F.S. No. 684.

Pathetique. Double. Tube and sepals, dark red; corolla white, veined carmine. Large blooms, fairly free, similar to Swingtime. Growth lax bush. Blackwell – British – 1952.

Pathfinder. Semi-double. Tube and sepals rosy-red. Corolla fluorescent pink, flushed rose. Medium sized blooms and quite prolific. Growth medium upright self-branching, will make excellent bush or standard. Raised in the vicinity of Banstead, Surrey, and introduced by Hill Trees Nurseries of Reigate, Surrey, 1981. Hobson – British – 1981.

Pat Meara. Single. Tube and sepals, pale rosepink; corolla veronica-blue with white band down centre. Medium to large flowers which can come semi-double, very free, same open saucer shaped as Citation. Growth upright and bushy, resents overwintering and overpotting, has lost favour over recent years and has not lived up to its early expectations. Winner of the B.F.S. Jones Cup 1962 and B.F.S.Award of Merit. Citation × Uncle Charlie. Miller, V.V. – British – 1962.

Patricia. Single. Tube and sepals. waxy pale-salmon; corolla rosy-cerise. Smallish flowers and free, growth upright and bushy, hardy in Southern districts. Wood – British – 1940.

Patricia. Sinngle. Tube and sepals, geranium-lake; corolla magenta. Large flowers and free, growth very strong, upright bush. Niederholzer – American – 1946.

Patricia Ann. Double. Long tube striped neyron-rose and rose-pink, long sepals white striped faint pink on top, pale pink underneath. Corolla neyron-rose shading to rose-pink at base of petals, veined dark pink. Large and very full blooms with long large pinkish-white buds, both stamens and pistil are neyron-rose. Medium to large foliage, medium green with ovate shaped leaves with obtuse tip, ovate base and serrated edges. Growth natural trailer, very suitable for basketwork, vigorous, heat tolerant if shaded. Raised in the vicinity of Coseley, West Midlands and tested for 8 years before being introduced by Fuchsiavale Nurseries of Kidderminster in 1982. Clements – British – 1982 – A.F.S. No. 1702.

*Patricia Bardgett. Single. Short dark rose tube (R.H.S. 54A), sepals the same dark rose colour, slightly reflexed, pointed. Corolla violet-purple (R.H.S. 82A) shading to light pink (R.H.S. 62C) at base of petals. Medium sized flowers and floriferous. Foliage forest green (R.H.S. 137B) with medium sized leaves slightly veined red. Growth lax upright or stiff trailer, self-branching will produce good basket but may need weights. Raised and tested for 4 years in the vicinity of Carlisle, Cumbria and introduced by Markham Nurseries of Doncaster in 1982. Mitchinson – British – 1983 – A.F.S. No. 1721.

Patricia Ewart. Single. Tube and sepals crimson (H.C.C. 22), sepals curl right back to tube. Corolla rhodamine-pink (H.C.C. 025) veined crimson. Medium sized, long, slender flowers. Growth strong, vigorous and bushy, excellent cultivar for the outside border and created very favourable acceptance from fuchsia experts on its pre-release, height 12 in to 18 in. Mieke Meursing × Mipan. Roe – British – 1980.

Patricia Harvey. Single. pink and blue. Dixon – British – 1897.

Patrician. Double. Short white tube and white crepe sepals; corolla red. Largish blooms and free, many short petals with white opposite sepals, joined half the length of sepals. Holly-like foliage, growth upright bush. Kennett – American – 1958 – A.F.S. No. 347.

Patricia Stanmaur. Single to semi-double. Short tube spinel-pink with slight touch of rose-Bengal at base. Slightly reflexed sepals phlox-pink marbled sightly Tyrian-rose at tops and edge. Corolla phlox-pink with slight veining. Medium sized flowers with square shaped corolla, stamens and pistil Tyrian-rose. Small foliage with ovate leaves acuminate tips and red main veins 1¼ in long by ½ in wide. Growth self-branching natural trailer, will make basket without weights. Tested for 2½ years in vicinity of Ramsgate, South East England Coast, before release. Symphony × Alwin. Standen – British – 1981 – A.F.S. No. 1640.

Patriot. Bland – British – 1874.

Patriot. Lemoine – French – 1874.

Pattie Anderson. Single. Tube and long upturned sepals, red; corolla royal purple. Large flowers, fairly free, the four petals curl out at edges. Growth upright stiff and strong. Hubbard – American – 1967 – A.F.S. No. 705.

Patty Evans. Semi-double. Tube and waxy sepals white; lightly tinted pink; deeper pink on underside; corolla white, flushed pink. Large blooms, free and of excellent shape, light green foliage. Growth tall, upright and vigorous. One of the best of early American introductions and still a beauty. Rolla ×. Evans and Reeves – American – 1938.

Patty Monk. Single. Pink and blue. Rogers – British – 1896.

Paula Grogger. Double. Tube and sepals pink; corolla light blue. Medium-sized blooms very early and very free. Bernadette × *F. fulgens* var. *rubra grandiflora*. Nutzinger – Austrian – 1968.

Paula Jane. Semi-double. Short tube, venetian-pink, sepals carmine-rose, arching upwards over corolla hiding the tube. Corolla beetroot-purple, changing to ruby-red with maturity, pale pink flush near sepals. Medium sized flowers, very free, small and compact at first, flaring outwards like a skirt as flower develops. Growth upright and bushy. Tite – British – 1975 – A.F.S. No. 1263.

Paul Baylis. Single. Tube and sepals red; corolla lavender-pink. Medium sized flowers, continuous flowering, dark green foliage. Growth tall, upright and bushy, branching habit, height 2 to 2½ ft. Hardy in Southern England, raised in the Scilly Isles. Submitted by raiser for R.H.S. Wisley Hardy

Trials 1975–78 but received no award. Tabraham – British – 1974.

Paul Cambon. Double. Blooms are as perfect as can be produced with a perfect rosette corolla very free for size, 'a real beauty' would sum up the description admirably. The shortish tube is scarlet, broad, reflexed sepals are also scarlet and sit right down in the corolla in an unusual manner. Short petals, very full. The corolla is of an intense, rich parma-violet, the scarlet stamens are of average length, but the scarlet style is short and the same length as the stamens. Foliage is medium green with crimson mid-rib and heavily serrated. Whilst the growth is upright and sturdy, defies that needed shape, needing only moderate stopping with cool shady conditions, requires H1 conditions and in spite of all attention is one of the slowest of growers. One of Lemoine's best introductions, an excellent bloom for the six cut bloom classes, if you can only produce the elusive plant for the show bench, would create havoc and a sensation. Should you require stock, both Baker's at Halstead and Chingford Nurseries list this very desirable cultivar. If ever a cultivar offered a challenge to the grower to produce a well-shaped plant it is Paul Cambon. In this respect it is similar to Gruss aus dem Bodethal, exciting perfect flowers but defies the best of growers to produce a specimen bush or shrub plant. Lemoine – French – 1909.

Pauline Rawlins. Double. Tube and sepals, pale flesh-pink, tipped green; corolla rich pink, deeper at base. Medium sized blooms, very free, similar to Seventeen, dark green foliage. Growth upright and bushy. Bridger – British – 1959.

*Paul Roe. Double. Short crimson (R.H.S. 52A) tube, sepals narrow slightly upturned crimson. Violet corolla (R.H.S. 83B) veined crimson. Medium sized blooms, free flowering nice distinct colouring. Light green foliage, growth upright and bushy quite vigorous. No breakthrough in colour just another red and purple, but a very clean and attractive plant. Raised in the vicinity of Nottingham and introduced by Jackson's Nurseries of Tamworth in 1981. Glyn Jones × Brutus. Roe – British – 1981.

Pavola. Single. Tube and sepals, deep rose-pink, washed with rose-red; corolla light rose-pink veined rose-red. Large flowers, very free and flaring. Growth upright. Hazard and Hazard – American – Date unknown.

Peace. Double. Tube and sepals white, tipped green; corolla white with very pale pink line on each main petaloid. Flowers of medium size, very free. Growth upright, but like all near whites needs careful cultivation, real beauty. The Bride × Brentwood. Thorne – British – 1968.

Peachy Keen. Double. Tube and sepals rose; corolla salmon-orange. Largish blooms, fairly free. Growth trailer. Tiret – American – 1967 – A.F.S. No. 734.

Peacock. Double. Tube and sepals scarlet, sepals very broad, corolla rich violet-blue. Medium sized blooms freely produced, lovely vivid contrast between sepals and corolla, hence the name. Dark green shiny foliage, growth upright and bushy, best grown as H2. Introduced by C.S. Lockyer of Bristol in 1981. Colville – British – 1981.

*Pearl Drops. Single. Long thin white tube, white sepals, fairly long held well away from tube, tipped green. Corolla white, heavily veined pale violet-purple at base of petals. Medium sized flowers, very free flowering with red stamens contrasting well with rest of flower. Growth trailer, short-jointed, makes very attractive basket without weights. Raised and introduced by R. and J. Pacey of Melton Mowbray, Leicestershire, in 1983. Pacey – British – 1983.

Pearl Farmer. Single. Carmine tube, sepals carmine tipped green. Corolla amethyst-violet, veined carmine at base of petals. Fairly large flowers, a true single, opening out saucer shaped and very free flowering. Growth upright and bushy, raised in the vicinity of Melton Mowbray for 3 years before release. Raised and introduced by R. and J. Pacey of Stathern, Melton Mowbray, in 1982. Pacey – British – 1982.

Pearl Lustre. Double. White tube, broad granular pink sepals, corolla pearl-white, veined pink. Extra large blooms, free, spreading and flaring, similar to Patty Evans only double, heat resistant. Growth trailer. Schnabel-Paskesen – American – 1958 – A.F.S. No. 327.

Pearly Queen. Semi-double. Red tube, sepals red outside, tipped green, pink inside and held horizontally. Corolla, each petal has a pearly sheen which spreads from base, hence the name, changing to light blue halfway. Smallish flowers very delicate, held up and out at right angles, very free-flowering. Growth upright and bushy, introduced by Woodbridge Nurseries of Hounslow in 1980. Tristesse × Snowcap. Dyos – British – 1980.

Pebble Beach. Single. White tube, sepals pale rose; corolla dark solferino-purple. Medium sized flowers and free. Growth trailer. Niederholzer – American – 1947.

Peculiarity. Double. Rose and purple. Story – British – 1862.

Pee Wee Rose. Single to semi-double. Tube and sepals, rosy-red; corolla very pale rose, almost a self. Small flowers but profuse, very small foliage. Growth lax bush, willowy, extremely vigorous under glass, good for espalier training. Submitted by Chingford Nurseries for the R.H.S. Wisley Hardy Trials 1975–78 and received the Award of Merit. *F.magellanica* var.*molinae* × . Niederholzer – American – 1939.

Peggy Ann. Double. Tube light red with darker red veined sepals light red, fold back to tube. Corolla lilac-purple, fading to magenta, no petaloids. Large blooms, fairly free, young foliage light green tinged with red. Growth trailer. Soo Yun – American , 1974 – A.F.S. No. 1183.

Peggy King. Single. Tube and sepals, rosy-red; corolla peony-purple. Small flowers but very free, growth upright, bushy and hardy, suitable for low hedge up to 3 ft. Accepted by the B.F.S. as showbench hardy. Wood – British – 1954.

Pelléas et Mélisande. Single to semi-double. Tube and sepals deep pink; corolla pale pink. Medium sized flowers, very free, growth upright. Blackwell – British – 1968.

Peloria. Double. Tube and sepals, dark red; corolla purple in centre, red petals on outer side. Large blooms, free, star shaped. growth upright and bushy. Martin – American – 1961 – A.F.S. No. 466.

pendula (Salisbury 1796). Synonymous with *F. coccinea.*

Pendula. May – British – 1841.

Pendula Terminali. Single. Red and purple. Mayne – British – 1839.

Penelope. Single. White and pink-purple. Lemoine – French – 1857.

Penelope. Single. Coxeen × Beauty of Swanley. Whiteman – British – 1941.

Penelope. Single to semi-double. Tube and sepals, deep pink tipped green; corolla rosy-pink. Medium sized flowers, very free, similar to Enchanted, wide open and flaring. Small serrated foliage, growth upright, considered to be an advance in pink fuchsias when first introduced. Tiret – American – 1958 – A.F.S. No. 335.

Pennine. Single. Tube carmine striped red, white sepals red at base, inside of sepals shaded pink. Corolla dark violet-blue, paler at base. Medium sized flowers and very free. Growth upright and bushy. Received the B.F.S. Bronze Certificate of Merit at the B.F.S. Northern Show at Manchester, 1979. Introduced by Fuchsiavale Nurseries of Kidderminster in 1981. Norman Mitchinson × Eden Lady. Mitchinson – British – 1979 – A.F.S. No. 1655.

Penrith Beacon. Single. Thin white tube, very narrow near ovary, broadens half way down. Sepals white, tipped green, underside flushed pink, narrow. Corolla beetroot-purple, fading to spiraea-red, short. Smallish flowers, free, growth medium upright and bushy. Chang × . Thornley – British – 1974 – A.F.S. No. 1217.

Peper Harow. Single. Tube neyron-rose, sepals neyron-rose, tipped green, gracefully unswept, sometimes form circle. Corolla mallow-purple, rose-bengal base, veined rosy-red. Medium sized flowers, very free, the four neatly shaped petals form perfect bell. Growth upright. Percy Holmes × Lakeside, R. – British – 1974 – A.F.S. No. 1206.

Pepi. Double. Tube and sepals, rosy-red; corolla orange-red. Large blooms, fairly free. Growth upright. Tiret – American – 1963 – A.F.S. No. 578.

Pepita. Single. Tube and sepals, rose pink; corolla deep blue. Small flowers, very free. Growth upright and vigorous. F.magellanica var. molinae × . Niederholzer – American – 1939.

Peppermint Stick. Double. Tube and upturned sepals. carmine with distinct white stripe running down the middle. Corolla centre petals rich royal-purple, outer petals light carmine-rose with purple edges. Medium sized blooms, free and very solid, very aptly named. Growth upright and bushy, excellent cultivar of showclass quality. Walker and Jones – American – 1950.

perbrevis (Johnston 1925). Synonymous with F. verrucosa.

Percy Holmes. Single. Thin tube azalea-pink, sepals azalea-pink outside, scarlet inside, tipped green, short and at right angle to tube. Corolla rhodonite-red, nasturtium-red at base. Medium sized flowers, very free, four slightly ruffled petals form almost square shaped bloom. Large lush foliage, growth upright and bushy, better as second year plant for bush work. Coachman × Sunset. Holmes, R. – British – 1960 – A.F.S. No. 1207.

*Pèredrup. Semi-double. Little known Dutch cultivar with lax habit and medium sized blooms, raised in the vicinity of Doorworth, Netherlands.

Tube light rose (R.H.S. 58C), sepals light rose (R.H.S. 58B) corolla deeper rose (R.H.S. 63AB). Orange Mirage × Orange Mirage. Brouwer – Dutch – 1983.

Perfecta. See magellanica var. globosa.

Perfection. Single. Red and purple. Banks – British – 1848.

Perfection. Semi-double. Red and mauve. Meillez – French – 1849.

Periwinkle. Single. Tube and long, recurved sepals pink; corolla medium lavender-blue. medium sized flowers, free and long, growth upright and willowy. Hodges – American – 1951 – A.F.S. No. 86.

Perky. Single. Tube white, sepals waxy-white with sharp pointed, deep pink tips. Corolla pink, flowers small and free, small foliage. Growth upright. Hazard and Hazard – American – 1930.

Perky Pink. Double. Tube and short, broad sepals pink, pale green tips; corolla white with palest pink flush and pink veining. Medium sized blooms, very free, heat tolerant. Growth upright, well in the show class category. Erickson-Lewis – American – 1959 – A.F.S. No. 407.

Perky Pink

Perle Mauve. Semi-double. Pink and mauve. Rozain-Boucharlat – French – 1913.

Perle Von Oesterreich. Double. Tube and sepals deep red; corolla pure white. Medium-sized blooms very early and very free. Growth lax bush, suitable for pot work or basket. El Camino × Gesauseperle. Nutzinger – Austrian – 1967.

Perry Park. Single. Short, thick pale pink tube, thick sepals reflexed to stem, pale pink outside with deeper pink (R.H.S. 48C) inside. Corolla bright rose (R.H.S. 52A) shaded (R.H.S. 53D) and paler at base. Medium-sized flowers with overlapping petals, very early and prolific with up to six flowers at each pair of leaf axials, rose-pink stamens and pistil. Growth upright, bushy and short jointed, good for outdoor bedding, tested for 8 years in Derbyshire before release. Handley – British – 1977 – A.F.S. No. 1415.

perscandens (Section IV Skinnera). Red tube with greenish to reddish sepals, purple corolla. Flowers very similar to F. colensoi except that the petals are larger and narrower; produces large dark purple berries on maturity. The tube has the same restriction as the other New Zealand species. Leaves ovate and acute, normal green upperside and whitish underneath. Climbing shrub, vigorous but with slender growth. Not widely distributed and very rarely seen in this country. Cockayne and Allen – 1927 – North Island, New Zealand.

Persia. Double. Tube and sepals white, flushed pale purple; corolla strong violet, outer petals marbled and washed pale purple. Large blooms, fairly free but very late, loose buds are waxy-white. Growth upright bush. Evans – American – 1955.

Persian Queen. Double. Tube and sepals creamy-chartreuse; corolla orchid colour. Growth lax upright, will trail with weights. Unregistered American cultivar grown in California. Raiser unknown – American – ca 1960.

Personality. Double. Short, thick tube and long sepals, bright rose-red; corolla magnolia-purple, changing to spiraea-red. Large blooms and free. Growth upright. Fuchsia-La – American – 1967 – A.F.S. No. 699.

Petaluma. Double. Short tube white, sepals white with pink on underside; corolla white, large blooms and free for size. Growth trailer. Pennisi – American – 1967 – A.F.S. No. 716.

*Peter Crooks. Single. Triphylla type hybrid. Long red tube, short red sepals. Corolla is intense orange-red. The long flowers are typical of terminal flowering parentage, the raiser claims the plant to be the first true terminal flowering basket type introduction. Green foliage is darkly stained red. Growth lax and ideal for hanging pots on baskets, side shoots are freely produced. Raised in the vicinity of Ipswich, Suffolk, and introduced by the raiser, Gouldings Fuchsias of Ipswich, in 1985. One of a series of ten new introductions named after famous trains in 1985. Goulding – British – 1985.

Peter Pan. Single. Tube and upturned sepals pink; corolla orchid and lilac.Largish flowers, prolific bloomer and continuous, heat tolerant. Growth trailer, very much like Pixie. Erickson – America – 1960 – A.F.S. No. 450.

petiolaris. Red tube, red sepals; deep red corolla. Long flowers, not very free, produced in the upper leaf axials. Tall upright shrub. Synonymous with *F. curviflora* and *F. quinquensis.* Kris – 1823 – Columbia and Venezuela.

Petite. Double. Tube and upturned sepals, pale rose; corolla lilac-blue and pale bengal-rose, fading to lavender-blue. Small blooms, very free and early, well named. Growth upright, bushy and very compact. Waltz – American – 1953 – A.F.S. No. 168.

Petit Point. Single. Tube and sepals carmine-red; corolla mauve. Medium sized flowers, very free-flowering. Growth upright, considered good for training as half standard. Introduced by Wills Fuchsia Nurseries in 1979. Alice Hoffman × . de Graaff – Dutch – 1976.

Petra. Single. Tube red, sepals red, tipped green; corolla purple. Smallish flowers and free, stamens and style red. Dark green foliage, growth upright and bushy. De Groot – Dutch – 1972.

Pharaoh. Single. Tube and edge of sepals, rose-Bengal, sepals white, tipped green. Corolla plum-purple, fading to ruby-red. Medium sized flowers and free, growth upright. Need – British – 1965.

Phenomenal. Double. Scarlet tube, very broad sepals scarlet; corolla rich indigo-blue, paler at base, slightly veined carmine. Large blooms, fairly free, very heavy, needs support and inclined to drop. Growth upright and bushy, one of the most vigorous. Although still grown has lost much of its popularity, excellent for cut bloom classes. Lemoine – French – 1869.

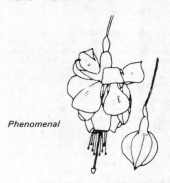

Phenomenal

Phoebe Travis. Double. Tube and sepals, rose-pink; corolla, parma-violet and rose. Large blooms and free, of rosette shape. Growth upright. Travis, J. – British – 1956.

Phoenix. Semid-double. Carmine and purple. Harrison – British – 1842.

Phoenix. Double. Carmine and purple-cerise. Hardy cultivar. Lemoine – French – 1913.

Phyllis. Semi-double. Tube and sepals, waxy-rose flushed cerise, corolla rosy-cerise. Produces sepals other than the normal four and under certain conditions can produce three, five, six or even seven. Smallish flowers, very free and early. Growth upright bush, extremely vigorous, no use for greenhouse, but ideal for large standards or pyramids, very stiff growth, hardy, suitable for hedges up to 3 to 4 ft. A seedling of Continental origin obtained by H.A. Brown from one of his customers in Edinburgh in 1938 and named after one of his sisters. W.P. Wood named Margaret Brown after the other sister (Mrs. Slater). Phyllis is synonymous with the wrongly named Deep Pink Lady in the South of England. Accepted by the B.F.S. as showbench hardy. Brown – British – 1938.

Phyrne. Double. Tube and sepals, rich cerise; corolla white, heavily veined cerise, outer petals also veined. Large blooms, very free, full and of classic shape. Growth upright, bushy and sturdy. Its fault is the spreading habit and needs early and constant pinching. Lemoine – French – 1905.

Pick of the Pops. Double. Tube and sepals, neyron-rose, tipped green; corolla rose-pink. Large blooms and free, growth upright and bushy. Jones, W. – British – 1960.

Picotee. Semi-double. Tube and sepals, phlox-pink; corolla Bishop's-violet, pink at base. Largish flowers, free, petals deeply serrated. Growth upright and very vigorous. Schnabel – American – 1951 – A.F.S. No. 78.

Piedmont. Single to semi-double. Tube and sepals rose; corolla dark Tyrian-rose. Largish flowers and very free with very long corolla. Growth lax upright, will trail with weights. Unregistered American cultivar grown in California. Raiser unknown – American – *ca* 1950.

Pierre Joigneaux. Double. Rose and purple. Lemoine – French – 1879.

pilosa. Scarlet coloured self. Smallish flowers borne in terminal racemes. Low shrub with hairy foliage. Fielding and Gardner – 1844 – Peru and Brazil.

Pinafore. Double. Tube and sepals white; corolla raspberry-pink, lightly marbled. Large blooms, fairly free, very full. Growth lax bush or trailer. Kennett – American – 1966 – A.F.S. No. 678.

***Pinata.** Double. Pink (R.H.S. 50C) tube, fully up pink (R.H.S. 50B) sepals with recurved tips $\frac{3}{4}$in long by $\frac{3}{8}$in wide. Corolla light lavender (R.H.S. 75A) variegated red (R.H.S. 50B) with deeper lavender (R.H.S. 76A) margins maturing to light lavender. Very small blooms, non flaring with multiple colouring, prefers cool conditions and filtered light, dark pink filaments reddish-purple anthers, light pink style and white stigma. Dark green (R.H.S. 139A) foliage with ovate leaves $1\frac{3}{4}$in long by $\frac{1}{2}$in wide, serrated margins, acute tip and obtuse base, veins and branches are green with red stems. Growth small upright, will produce good upright, standard, decorative or bonsai. Trademarked in California, U.S.A. Raised in the vicinity of Oxnard, California, U.S.A. Unnamed seedling cross. Schneider – American – 1984 – A.F.S. No. 1756.

Pinch Me. Double. Tube and sepals, frosty-white; corolla Bishop's-purple. Large blooms, fairly free. Growth trailer. Tiret – American – 1969 – A.F.S. No. 831.

Pinch Me Not. Little information known of this American sport except it was found in California *ca* 1980 and is a sport from Pinch Me.

Pink Antonelli. Double. Tube and sepals dark pink; corolla orchid-pink and streaked. Growth trailer very suitable for basketwork. Unregistered American cultivar grown in California. Raiser unknown – American – *ca* 1950.

Pink Aurora. Single. Tube and sepals, light pink; corolla is a pink form of Aurora Superba with unique orange edging to the petals, forming an orange edge to the corolla. Medium sized flowers and free, growth upright. Endicott – British – 1968.

Pink Ballet. Single to semi-double. Tube short and thin, very light green; sepals white, blushed-pink on top, tipped green, darkens to light pink underside, fold back over tube. Corolla very pale pink, with dark pink variegations, medium pink veins, pale green at base. Medium sized flowers, very free, four petals flare out wide, exposing opening of tube, eight to ten petaloids form a skirt around the corolla. Growth lax bush or trailer. Soo Yun – American – 1972 – A.F.S. No. 1043.

Pink Ballet Girl. Double. Tube and sepals, scarlet-red; corolla pink, flushed light blue. Large blooms, free and very full, large red buds. Possible sport of Ballet Girl. Tom Thorne states that it is identical to Gypsy Queen which was always sporting and responsible for Cataline and White Wonder. Raiser unknown – Date unknown.

Pink Balloon. Single. Tube and sepals, dark red; corolla white, veined pink. Very large flowers, fairly free, loosely shaped. Growth upright and vigorous, up to 6ft in California. Niederholzer – American – 1940.

Pink Beauty. Double. Tube and sepals pink; corolla pink. Blooms are large and square, self colour. Growth trailer, very suitable for basketwork. Unregistered American cultivar. Fuchsia-La (Roy Walker) – American – 1959.

Pink Bon Accorde. Single. Tube pale pink, sepals pale pink, deeper pink underneath, tipped green. Corolla deep pink with touch of rose, paler at base. Small flowers and free, growth upright and bushy. Not of the same habit as Bon Accorde, flowers do not stand out erect and not the profuse bloomer. Always accepted to be a sport of Bon Accorde, but research may prove to find it a Bon Accorde seedling. Thorne – British – 1959.

Pink Bow. Double. Tube and sepals, deep rose; corolla soft pink, flowers medium sized and free, short corolla, inside petals are twisted and curled to form bow shape effect. Growth medium, upright bush. Haag – American – 1948.

Pink Champagne. Double. Tube and sepals white blushed pink, tipped green; corolla white blushed pink. Medium sized blooms, self coloured. Growth trailer, unregistered American cultivar grown in California. Raiser unknown – American – *ca* 1950.

Pink Chiffon. Double. Tube and sepals white, flushed palest pink, tipped green. Corolla soft pink with deeper pinkish tones at base of sepals. Large blooms, free, globular shaped with folded scalloped petals and long lasting. Growth natural trailer, best as H1. Waltz – American – 1966 – A.F.S. No. 656.

***Pink Claws.** Single. Tube and sepals bright red, corolla pale blue fading to pink with early maturity. Large flowers $2\frac{1}{2}$in long, long pendulous claw shaped buds. Very dark green foliage, growth upright, vigorous, strong and arching. Ultimate height 2 to $2\frac{1}{2}$ft. Hardy in Southern England, raised and introduced in the Isles of Scilly by Tabraham's Nurseries. Tabraham – British – 1984.

Pink Cloud. Single. Short white tube, long wide upturned sepals, pale pink, tipped green, deeper pink underneath, curl slightly at tips. Corolla clear pink, veined deep pink, flaring at maturity. Very large flowers and free, corolla has four overlapping petals, at the time of introduction was the largest single pink. Growth upright and bushy, good for standard, pillar or espalier. A.F.S. Cert. of Merit. Waltz – American – 1956 – A.F.S. No. 269.

Pink Cornet. Single. Long pink tube $1\frac{3}{4}$in by $\frac{1}{4}$in wide at mouth enlarging gradually from the ovary spreding to reflexed sepals white and lanceolate $\frac{5}{8}$in × $\frac{1}{5}$in . Corolla bright red $\frac{1}{2}$in × $\frac{1}{5}$in. Miniature flowers with ovate petals falling very early. Large foliage green and no red veining seem to be out of 'proportion to the flower, $5\frac{1}{8}$in × $2\frac{1}{2}$. Growth medium upright, will make good bush, prefers warm climate for best results. *F. boliviana alba* × *F. boliviana* forma *puberulenta.* Round fruit is green flecked with red. Tested for 3 years in the vicinity of Reading, England under glass before release. Wright, J.O. – British – 1981 – A.F.S. No. 1650.

Pink Darling. Single. Tube dark pink, sepals pale pink, deeper underneath; corolla soft lilac pink. Small flowers in great profusion, held semi-erect. Growth upright and bushy will respond to the needed frequent pinching. Excellent cultivar in every way, showclass category. Machado – American – 1961.

Pink Delight. Double. Small tube rosy-red, sepals red; corolla soft pink, faint red veins. Medium sized blooms and free. Growth lax bush or trailer. Brown and Soules – American – 1951 – A.F.S. No. 76.

Pink Delight. Single. Tube and long frosty sepals gracefully curved, sepals white, flushed palest pink. Corolla clear pink with lavender undertones, fading to deeper shade with maturity. Largish blooms, very free, with overlapping petals. Growth natural trailer, best grown as H1. Sport of Guinevere. Waltz – American – 1961 – A.F.S. No. 492.

Pink Dessert. Single. Tube and long sepals white, flushed pink, edged pink, tipped green. Corolla pale pink, almost a self. Flowers are very free and large, heat tolerant, bright green foliage. Growth upright. Kuechler – American – 1963 – A.F.S. No. 551.

Pink Doll. Double. Tube and sepals, pink inside, light pink outside, corolla deep pink. Flowers medium sized and free, box type, heat tolerant. Growth medium bush. A.F.S. Cert. of Merit 1973. Pennisi – American – 1970 – A.F.S. No. 890.

Pink Domino. Double. Tube and sepals red; corolla bright pink. Medium-sized blooms, free for double, very full corolla. Growth pendulous, unusual for a hardy cultivar. Hardy in Southern England, raised in the Scilly Isles. Tabraham – British – 1978.

Pink Easton. Semi-double. Pink and white. Rush – British – 1902.

Pink Elegance. Single. Tube and sepals, light pink; corolla bright phlox-pink. Large flowers and free, long with pleated and rolled petals. Light green foliage, growth trailer. Niederholzer-Waltz – American – 1950 – A.F.S. No. 54.

Pink Fairy. Double. Creamy-white tube, broad recurving sepals, palest rose, tipped white. Corolla clear pink, deeper at base. Large blooms, fairly free, when fully matured open wide with star-like effect, dark green foliage, blooms need support for bush work. Growth upright and bushy. Waltz – American – 1954 – A.F.S. No. 202.

Pink Fandango. Semi-double. Tube and sepals rosy-carmine, sepals are broad and long. Corolla starts rosy-carmine shading to magenta with carmine edges. Medium sized blooms and very free. Growth upright makes excellent standard. Raised by the introducer's son, introduced by C.S. Lockyer (Fuchsias) of Bristol in 1979. Lockyer – British – 1979.

Pink Favourite. Double. Tube and sepals, clear pink; corolla slightly darker, almost a self. Large blooms and free, growth upright. No improvement upon Angela Leslie or Miss Vallejo. A.F.S. Cert. of Merit 1963. Tiret – American – 1960 – A.F.S. No. 436.

Pink Flamingo. Semi-double. Tube pink, sepals dark pink, tipped green; corolla pale pink, veined dark pink from base. Flowers are very long and free, feature is the curling of the sepals into various shapes, giving the effect of flamingoes. Darkish green foliage with bronze flush on new growth. Growth lax bush or trailer, very suitable for half basket but long-jointed. A.F.S. Cert. of

Merit 1964. Fuchsia Forest-Castro – American – 1961 – A.F.S. No. 470.

Pink Foremost. Double. Self fuchine-pink. Very large blooms, fairly free, claimed to be an improvement upon Pink Galore, but never gained any popularity. Growth trailer. Fuchsia-La – American – 1962.

Pink Frosting. Single. Tube and sepals shades of pink; corolla orchid to pink at base. Growth upright, unregistered American cultivar grown in California. Raiser unknown – American – *ca* 1950.

Pink Galore. Double. Cultivar most aptly named, introduced in America by Fuchsia-La Nurseries of Long Beach, California in 1958, registered three years later and received the A.F.S. Cert. of Merit in the same year. Hybridisers have concentrated upon true pinks for many years to the extent that no less than 59 different cultivars have the prefix pink, but Pink Galore perhaps outshines the whole batch. The long tube and upturned sepals are slightly deeper pink than the corolla; the corolla itself is long of a beautiful soft rose or candy-pink, double, of long lasting qualities. This cultivar is a typical American trailer, a type of growth they seem to favour more than any other type and ideal for the planting of baskets; it produces long flowering trails, so ideal for this type of training. It does not, however, provide a large plant and if used for basketwork, the planting of one or two extra plants than normal will produce a breathtaking effect. Foliage is excellent and unusual, dark glossy leaves; the young laterals are easily distinguished, having reddish stems. Although not vigorous in the true sense, it does make a nice weeping standard, looks charming and delicate as a table or quarter standard. Can be used as outside bedder, but excessive sun will play havoc with the pastel pink colours, needing all shade possible. Better grown as H1 for perfect results. delightful, elegant beauty and probably the best of the pinks. Fuchsia-La – American – 1958 – A.F.S. No. 469.

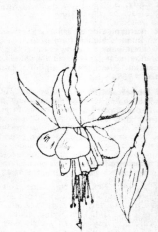

Pink Galore

Pink Globe. Single. Pink and rose-pink. Girling – British – 1847.

Pink Goon. Double. Red tube, broad red sepals, corolla apple-blossom pink, delicately veined deeper pink. Large blooms with flecked rose-pink petaloids which flare back. Growth upright, vigorous and hardy, a real beauty for the garden and a welcome addition to the hardy range. Raised in the vicinity of Banstead, Surrey and introduced by Woodbridge Nurseries of Hounslow, Middlesex 1982. Hobson – British – 1982.

*Pink Haze. Double. Tube and sepals beautiful shade of pink; corolla pink heavily splashed blue. Largish fully double blooms, flowers profusely for a double. Growth upright, vigorous, strong and compact. Ultimate height 2 to 2½ ft. Hardy in Southern England, raised and introduced in the Isles of Scilly by Tabraham's Nurseries. Tabraham – British – 1984.

Pinkie. Double tube and wide, crisp sepals, dark shell-pink; corolla shell-pink. Largish blooms, free and heat tolerant. Growth upright bush. Nelson – American – 1953 – A.F.S. No. 181.

Pink Jade. Single. Tube and upturned sepals pink, tipped green; corolla medium orchid-pink with distinct deeper glowing rose border. Medium sized flowers, free, picotée-edged and saucer shaped similar to Display. Growth lax bush, very low grower, can be disappointing. Pybon – American – 1958.

Pink Lace. Double. Tube and sepals red; corolla pink. Large blooms, very free flowering for double. Growth upright and bushy, strong and branching habit, height 2 to 2½ ft. Hardy in South England, raised in the Scilly Isles. Submitted by raiser to R.H.S. Wisley Hardy Trials 1975–78 but received no award. Tabraham – British – 1974.

Pink Lady. Single. Tube and sepals, dark rose-pink, corolla pink. Flowers are small, very free, borne in clusters. Growth upright and bushy. Raiser unknown – American – Date unknown.

Pink Lady. Single. Tube bright deep crimson, sepals cream, heavily suffused deep pink and red, tipped yellowish-green. Corolla clear pink, dark veins, maturing to darker distinct rhodamine pinkish-purple. Flowers are round, very free, heavy and waxy. growth upright and bushy. B.F.S. Certificate of Preliminary Acceptance. Manchester 1974. Lena × Citation. Ryle-Atkinson – British – 1974 – A.F.S. No. 1169.

Pink Lemonade. Single. Carmine tube, sepals crimson to carmine, tipped greenish-white. Corolla white with carmine veins, medium sized flowers, free, fairly compact. Foliage lemon-yellow with magenta-rose veins. Growth upright and bushy. Foster – American – 1974 – A.F.S. No. 1172.

Pink Marshmallow. Double. Tube and sepals, pale pink, tipped green, blush-pink underneath. Corolla white, blushed and veined pink, almost a self. Large blooms, free for size, sepals turn back and centre of corolla elongates to create double skirted effect, beautiful pastel shaded. Largish, light green foliage. Growth trailer produces huge basket, whether half or full. Stubbs – American – 1971 – A.F.S. No. 996.

Pink Parfait. Double. Strawberry-pink self. Large blooms and very free, somewhat larger and a shade lighter than Dorothy Louise, sepals longer, more wing-like, spreading corolla extends

its petalage between sepals. Growth lax bush or trailer. Dorothy Louise ×. Schnabel – American – 1955 – A.F.S. No. 223.

Pink Pearl. Semi-double. Tube and incurved sepals, pale pink; corolla deeper shade of pink slightly flushed rose. Medium sized flowers, free, can come fully double. Growth upright and bushy. Raised by one of the old great exponents of growing pillars and pyramids, son-in-law of the great James Lye, very easy to grow and specially suitable for the training of standards and any tall type of training. Bright – British – 1919.

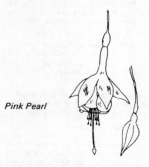

Pink Pearl

Pink Pearl (No. 2). Double. Tube and sepals dark red, corolla pale pink splashed with red. Large full double blooms unusual for reputed hardy cultivar. Growth upright, strong and spreading habit, height 2 to 2½ ft. Hardy in Southern England and raised in the Scilly Isles. Not to be confused with the old established Pink Pearl by Bright (1919). Tabraham – British – 1982.

Pink Perfection. Single. Tube and sepals waxy, creamy-white; corolla mauvish-pink. Medium sized flowers, early and very free. Growth upright and bushy, suitable for standard. Lye – British – 1879.

Pink Perfection. Double. Tube and sepals pink; corolla pale pink. Medium sized blooms and free. Growth medium upright bush. Niederholzer – American – 1947.

Pink Phoenix. Double. Tube and sepals pink; sepals are long and pale pink. Corolla lilac colour. The whole flower is the same shape of its parent, primary difference is the pale pink sepals. Introduced in Rhodesia in 1975. Sport of The Phoenix. Tomlinson – Rhodesian – 1979 – A.F.S. No. 1509.

Pink Poodle. Double. Tube and sepals, pale pink, tipped white; corolla full pale pink. Medium sized blooms and free, growth lax bush or trailer. In spite of name, good cultivar. Kennett – American – 1964 – A.F.S. No. 613.

Pink Popcorn. Double. Long waxy tube and broad sepals, light pink; green tipped; corolla white and phlox-pink. Large blooms, free, with four, white serrated and pink veined central petals, numerous pleated, smaller outer petals of phlox-pink, sepals flare out horizontally as sepals turn up. Growth trailer. Hodges – American – 1955 – A.F.S. No. 243.

Pink Profusion. Single. Tube and sepals, carmine-rose, tipped green; corolla phlox-pink, produces the odd petaloid. Medium sized flowers, very free, sepals are upturned almost hiding tube, with flared corolla. Baker – British – 1970.

Pink Quartet. Semi-double. Tube and upturned sepals, deep pink; corolla very pale pink. Largish blooms and free, aptly named with its four distinct rolls of petals. Growth upright and bushy, makes a fine stiff standard. This cultivar has the classic flower and excels in cut bloom clases, one of the best from America. Walker and Jones – American – 1949.

Pink Roze-II. Semi-double. Tube and sepals white; corolla lacy-white, pink at base and veined pink. Medium sized blooms and free; petals attached to sepals causing bloom to open up flat. Growth trailer. Prentice – American – 1970 – A.F.S. No. 884.

Pink Ruffles. Double. Tube and sepals, cream with pale green tips; corolla pink with light lavender cast. Large blooms, free for size, growth lax bush or trailer. Gorman – American – 1970 – A.F.S. No. 927.

Pink Shower. Semid-double. Tube and sepals, rose-pink; corolla palest rose. Small flowers, very free, growth trailer. Reiter – American – 1948.

Pink Slippers. Single. White tube with very faint pink tinge, sepals pale pinkish-white, tipped green, stand out horizontally with slight curve. Corolla pink with slight veining at base. Medium sized flowers, free, well proportioned and graceful, stay compact. Growth natural trailer, self-branching. Complicated parentage including Earl of Beaconsfield, Lena Dalton and Lye's Unique. Rye – British – 1975 – A.F.S. No. 1252.

***Pink Spangles.** Semi-double. Very little known of this doubtful cultivar. Although listed by several British nurserymen, the origin is difficult to trace, it could be and is very similar to Mieke Meursing. Described as having pale pink tube and sepals and red corolla.

Pink Sport of Bonanza. This sport was found in Los Angeles, California in 1969 and sold under that name. Cultivar was not registered but later introduced in 1977 under the name of Suzy. A.F.S. No. 1430.

Pink Tausendschon. Double. Tube and sepals light red, sepals are bulbous and erect. Corolla white with blush pink and red veins. Medium-sized blooms with deep pink stamens and style. Medium green, small foliage, growth upright and bushy, self-branching. Cultivar grown and cultivated in the Netherlands. Raiser and date unknown.

Pink Temptation. Single. Tjube and sepals, creamy-white with slight touch of pink, tipped green; corolla Tyrian-rose with pale pink centre. Largish flowers for a single, free, sepals almost horizontal. Growth lax upright, good for standard. Sport of Temptation. Wills – British – 1966.

Pink Trumpet. Single. Long pink tube enlarges from the ovary, diameter at the mouth 2 in × ¼ in. Spreading to reflexed white sepals are lanceolate, ¾ in × ¼ in. Bright red corolla has ovate petals ⅝ in × ¼ in petals fall very early. Massively large foliage, green with no red veining or red branches, leaves softly hairy 7⅞ in × 4 in. Growth tall upright, will make good bush or standard, prefers warm climate for best results. Ovoid fruit is green flecked with red. Tested for 2 years in the vicinity of Reading, England under glass before release F. *boliviana* × F. *boliviana* var. *luxurians*. Wright, J.O. – British – 1981 – A.F.S. No. 1630.

Pink Vine. Double. Tube and sepals pink, corolla pink. Medium sized blooms, hang in long racemes, beautiful pink self. Growth natural trailer, introduced by Ron Winkley of Birmingham about 1972. Senior – British – 1972.

Pinky. Single. Tube and sepals, flesh-pink; corolla rich flesh-pink, almost a self. Flowers medium sized and very free. Growth upright bush. Roth – American – 1956.

Pinocchio. Single. Tube and sepals red; corolla dark purple. Small flowers and very profuse, small cordate foliage. Growth trailer. Unregistered American cultivar sometimes spelled Pinnochio and grown in California. Raiser unknown – American – *ca* 1950.

Pinto. Double. Tube and broad upturned tube and sepals, claret-rose; corolla white, splashed with claret-rose. Huge blooms, free for size, pleated arrangement of the petals very pronounced. Growth natural trailer. Walker and Jones – American – 1956.

Pinup. Semi-double. Tube and sepals, pure white; corolla bright pink. Medium sized blooms, free, growth trailer. Kennett – American – 1968 – A.F.S. No. 775.

Pinwheel. Double. Short tube flushed pink, broad pink sepals, pointed and turn back slightly at tips; corolla violet. Large flat blooms, very free, folded petals opening wide in centre, flowers resembles a pinwheel in form. Upright and self-branching, blooms are used for corsage work in America. Almost identical to Blue Pearl. Waltz – American – 1958 – A.F.S. No. 355.

Pio Pico. Double. Short tube and broad, reflexed sepals, palest pink, deep pink inside; corolla opens violet-purple, fading to wine-purple. Very large blooms, free for size, feature is the long corolla and vivid colouring, smaller outer petals splashed with fuchsia-pink. Growth lax bush or trailer. good for espalier. Tiret – American – 1955 – A.F.S. No. 236.

Piquant. Single. Tube and sepals, rose-madder; corolla pale magenta. Medium sized flowers and free. Growth tall upright. Niederholzer – American – 1947.

Pirbright. Single. Rhodamine-pink tube, sepals rhodamine-pink very long and slender which turn upwards slightly. Corolla cyclamen-purple. Medium sized flowers rather long which do not fade with maturity and in the exhibition class. Growth upright and bushy and in addition to exhibition purposes, will make a good bedder. Named after a village in Surrey near Dorking. One of only two cultivars introduced by Jackson's Nurseries of Tamworth in 1982. Glyn Jones × Santa Barbara. Roe – British – 1982.

Pirouette. Semi-double. White tube, sepals white underneath with neyron-rose towards tips, held horizontally. Corolla white with rhodamine-purple (R.H.S. 68D) veining at base. Medium sized flowers with scalloped edges, red-tipped sepals and frilled petticoat combine to make attractive flower, best colour in shade. Growth medium upright, bushy, good for bush or standard, tested for 9 years in vicinity of Northumberland before release. Ryle – British – 1976 – A.F.S. No. 1402.

Pitto. Single. Pale pink and salmon-pink. Turville – British – 1847.

Pius IX. Single. Flesh-pink and dark rose. Salter – British and French – 1849.

Pixie. Single. Tube and sepals, pale cerise; corolla rosy-mauve, paler at base, veined carmine. Medium sized flowers, very heavy bloomer. Foliage yellowish-green with crimson veins. Growth upright, bushy and hardy, vigorous, almost too vigorous for greenhouse, will produce a low hedge, height up to 3 ft. Accepted by the B.F.S. as showbench hardy. Sport of Graf Witte. Submitted by L.R. Russell Ltd for the R.H.S. Wisley Hardy Trials 1975–78 and received the Highly Commended Certificate. Russell – British – 1960.

Pizzazz. Double. Short thick tube, crimson, broad sepals crimson, tipped green, spinel-red on inner side; corolla violet, marbled purple, veined neyron-rose. Medium sized blooms, free for double, fully double and hold colour. Deep green foliage, growth medium upright, bushy and self-branching. Woakes-Fuchsialand – British – A.F.S. No. 1316.

Plato. Double. Red and rich purple. Bull – British – 1872.

platypetala. Red tube, bulbous at base, crimson sepals; corolla crimson with central white blotch. Not very free flowering, borne in upper leaf axials. Reddish foliage with hairy leaves. Tall upright shrub. Johnston – 1939 – Peru.

Playboy. Double. Tube and sepals, red-cerise, corolla bright rose-pink, veined cerise. Growth upright bushy, might prove to be hardy. Phyllis × Fascination. Homan – British – 1969.

Playford. Single. Short baby pink tube, baby-pink sepals turn up with maturity. Corolla bluish-mauve. Small rounded flowers, very prolific, stamens are red at first opening. Medium sized foliage mid-green with no red veining. Growth medium upright, will make good bush or standard. Heat tolerant if shaded, best colour develops in shade, very similar to Estelle Marie but much more vigorous which makes it extremely vigorous and unusual. Tested for 2 years in the vicinity of Ipswich. South East England before release. Goulding – British – 1981 – A.F.S. No. 1649.

Pleiaden. Single. Tube and sepals white with deep pink blush, sepals are long and tipped green. Corolla very light pink, light purple at the edges. Small erect flowers, very free flowering, pink filaments and white style. Small medium-green foliage, growth upright and bushy. Saturnus × Bon Accorde. De Groot – Dutch – 1973.

Plenty. Single. The thick tube is carmine, sepals are neyron-rose (R.H.S. 55A) paler underneath, slightly reflexed and inclined to curl slightly at the tips. The well-shaped corolla, slightly bell-shaped is violet-purple, pink at base and veined carmine, stamens of different lengths are carmine and the style pink. Small to medium single flowers held slightly above the horizontal are so prolific that the raiser could not have named his cultivar better. Lady Isobel Barnett, one of its parents, has always been considered to be one of the most prolific of flowerers but Plenty is even more prolific. The foliage is a little large and a nice dark green colour which does not seem to attract many pests. Growth is upright and bushy, short jointed and responds well to frequent pinching if necessary, as it is naturally self branching and although excelling as a shrub or bush plant would consider it suitable for other types of training except trail-ing or hanging. Whilst it is exceptional under glass, it does make a good bedder and although hardly old enough to be tested thoroughly as a hardy, has stood the test of 3 years in the Midlands. Had the pleasure of obtaining a plant before release in April 1974 and the comments I recorded were 'grown on into 5 in pot with excellent results, holds flowers over long period, seed pods and stalks fall off automatically and smothered in bloom mid-July'. Most exhibitors, particularly in the North and Midlands, now use Plenty as a 'banker' on the show benches, makes a wonderful 3½ in pot plant. Should anyone ever be forced to start afresh with a new selection of fuchsias then the cultivar Plenty would assuredly be foremost for inclusion. Raised and introduced by prolific hybridizer Cliff Gadsby in 1974; probably the best of his single introductions. Cloverdale × Lady Isobel Barnett. Gadsby – British – 1974 – A.F.S. No. 1223.

Pleromet. Single. Tube and sepals, turkey-red; corolla very dark violet. Large flowers and free, corolla open and expanded. Growth upright extremely vigorous, up to 9 ft in California. Niederholzer – American – 1946.

Plumbago. Rozain-Boucharlat – French – 1913.

Plum Glory. Double. Tube and broad, granular recurved sepals, deep carmine; corolla petunia-purple. Large blooms, very free, most unusual for the globular corolla and colour, plum-like hue, no hint of blue with maturity, fading to muted red. Growth natural trailer. Schnabel – American – 1955 – A.F.S. No. 224.

Plum Pudding. Double. Long tube and recurved sepals, deep turkey-red; corolla plum coloured. Large blooms, extremely free, small foliage. Growth natural trailer. Tiret – American – 1959 – A.F.S. No. 384.

Pluto. Single. Tube and sepals red; corolla white, veined red. Medium sized flowers, very free, dark green foliage. Growth upright and bushy, strong branching habit, height 1½ to 2 ft. Hardy in South England, raised in the Scilly Isles. Tabraham – British – 1974.

Plymouth Hoe. Semi-double. Thin tube pale pink, sepals pale pink outside, claret-rose inside. Corolla rhodamine-pink flushed rose. Medium-sized blooms with purple petaloids and marbled azalea pink. Very free flowering, growth upright and bushy. Hilton – British – 1978.

Plymouth Sound. Single. Tube rosy-red, sepals rosy-red and shiny outside, same colour inside but matt. Corolla magenta, medium-sized flowers and very free flowering. Growth trailer. Hilton – British – 1978.

Pocahontas. Semi-double. Tube and sepals, pale rose; corolla smoky red-orange. Medium sized flowers and free. Growth lax blue or trailer. Hazard and Hazard – American – Date unknown.

Poesie. (Poem). Double. Short tube and dark red sepals; corolla deep violet to magenta, mottled red. Very large blooms, very free, dark green foliage. Growth upright. Munkner – American – 1954.

Polar Sea. Double. Tube and sepals white; corolla dark Imperial-purple, marbled white at base. Large blooms, fairly free, growth upright and vigorous. Reiter – American – 1953 – A.F.S. No. 192.

Pole Star. Single. Tube and sepals red; corolla brilliant white. Large flowers borne in great profusion, dark green foliage. Growth upright and bushy, height 2 to 2½ ft. Hardy in Southern England, raised in the Scilly Isles. Tabraham – British – 1974.

Pollux. Single. Tube and sepals reddish-pink; corolla purple, pink at base, red veined. Smallish flowers, free flowering, stamens and style deep pink. Smallish foliage, growth lax bush or trailer. *F. regia* var. *typica* × Frau Henriette Ernst. De Groot – Dutch – 1970.

polyantha. Purplish-red tube, scarlet sepals; crimson corolla. Flowers fairly free, carried in terminal, pendulous racemes. Small shrub up to 3 ft. Killip – 1935 – Colombia.

polyanthella (Johnston 1925). Synonymous with *F. ovalis.*

Polychinelle. Double. Tube and sepals white with blush pink, tube is rather long, sepals deep pink underneath, short and tipped green. Corolla matt purple, pink at base. medium-sized blooms, free flowering, light red stamens and pink style. Growth upright and bushy, a cultivar which is grown and cultivated in the Netherlands. Raiser and date unknown.

Polynesia. Double. Tube and sepals salmon; corolla salmon-orange. Large blooms, fairly free, growth trailer. Tiret – American – 1966 – A.F.S. No. 686.

Pompadour. Double tube and broad, reflexed sepals, pale pink to white; corolla delicate pink. Large blooms, free for size, small foliage. Growth upright. Schnabel-Paskesen – American – 1959 – A.F.S. No. 379.

***Poppet.** Single. Waxy-carmine tube (R.H.S. 52B) short, thick narrowing at sepals, waxy-carmine sepals (R.H.S. 52B) on top, crimson (R.H.S. 52A) base, creped crimson underneath, tipped green, broad and held just above the horizontal. Corolla roseine-purple (R.H.S. 68A) slightly darker edges, crimson base and heavily veined crimson (R.H.S. 52A). Medium sized flowers and very compact with pink stamens, long blush-white pistil, flowers are held semi-erect which hold their colour. Foliage mid-green of medium sized and serrated leaves. Growth medium upright, self-branching, good for bush, standard, pillar or decorative, will take full sun. Parentage: Beacon seedling. Raised and tested for 3 years in vicinity of Edenbridge, Kent. Holmes, R. – British – 1983 – A.F.S. No. 1722.

***Pop Whitlock.** Single. Tube and sepals pale pink, very short tube, corolla beautiful shade of amethyst-violet. Medium sized flower and very prolific. Another sport from Border Queen but different both from Barry's Queen and Golden Border Queen. This cultivar has variegated foliage as opposed to the ornamental foliage of the others. Light greenish-grey with silvery sheen and creamy-white edge. Growth inclined to be lax with bushy habit and self-branching. Very good cultivar and well within the exhibition category, made its first appearance at B.F.S. London Show 1983. Tested for over 2 years during which time held its new characteristics. Sport from Border Queen found by the introducer in vicinity of Reigate, Surrey, and introduced by High Trees Nurseries of Reigate, Surrey, in 1984. Head – British – 1984.

Port Arthur. Semi-double. Red and purple. Story – British – 1869.

Portola. Semi-double. Tube and sepals, pale carmine; corolla Tyrian-rose. Medium sized flowers and free. Growth tall upright. Schnabel – American – 1947.

Port Said. Lemoine – French – 1870.

Poseidon. Single. Light apricot tube is very slender and proportionately long (3½ in), sepals are small and short, light apricot. Corolla apricot short and small. Light sage-green foliage, obovate leaves have acuminate tips. Growth tall upright, will make good bush or decorative, prefers warm climate for best results, has growth habits of its parents, best colour develops in shade. Originates from the vicinity of Preston, Lancashire. Seedling of *F. fulgens* var. *rubra grandiflora*. Travis, J. – British – 1980 – A.F.S. No. 1584.

Postiljon. Single. Tube white with blush pink,* sepals creamy-white, tipped green. Corolla pink-purple, white at base. Smallish flowers, free, stamens and style white. Growth trailer. La Campanella × . van der Post – Dutch – 1975.

Postman. Double. Short tube dull pink, small sepals dull pink and arch back to tube. Corolla smoky-blue with red splashes. Large blooms similar to its parent, best colour develops in the sun. Medium green large foliage. Growth upright, will make good bush or standard. Originates from the vicinity of Warwickshire. Seedling of Lilac Lustre. Wright, L.A. – British – 1980 – A.F.S. No.1605.

Potentate. Double. Long tube, long recurved sepals, rose-madder; corolla deep rose-madder and crimson. Very large blooms and free. Growth lax upright, suitable as a climber, pillar or standard. A.F.S. Cert. of Merit. Reiter – American – 1954 – A.F.S. No. 214.

Potney's Tricolour. Single. Tube and sepals, pale red; corolla blush-purple. Small flowers, not very free, blooms in flushes. Foliage variegated green, white and cream, all suffused red, must have full sunlight, otherwise green. Growth upright. Potney – British – 1842.

Powder Blue. Semi-double. Tube and sepals, Tyrian-rose; corolla palest blue. Medium sized blooms and free, early. Growth tall, upright vigorous, up to 6ft in California. Niederholzer – American – 1947.

Powder Compact. Double. Short pale pink tube, lined magenta, white sepals with magenta veining and edged on upper surface, magenta at the base shading to white underneath and tipped green. Corolla white, splashed magenta (R.H.S. 66C). Medium sized blooms with petaloids same colour as petals, sepals shaped like an outline of a pagoda. Medium sized foliage mid-green with ovate leaves, serrated edges and red veins. Growth self-branching medium upright, compact, very suitable for bush, best colour develops in sun. Raised in the vicinity of Woodbridge, Suffolk. Royal Wedding × Harry Gray. Dunnett – British – 1982 - A.F.S. No. 1706.

Powder Puff. Double. Tube and heavy recurved sepals, Tyrian-rose, shading to rose-madder. Corolla apple blossom-pink, largish blooms and free. Growth trailer. Hodges – American – 1953 – A.F.S. No. 159.

Powder Puff. Double. Tube and sepals red; corolla white. Small blooms, very full double and free flowering for a double. Foliage is dark green.

Growth upright, bushy and very compact, height 6 to 9 in, very suitable for rockeries, window boxes and troughs. One of a series of new hardy miniature cultivars, hardy in Southern England, raised in the Scilly Isles. Not to be confused with the cultivar of the same name raised by the American, Hodges. Tabraham – British – 1976.

*Präsident Walter Morio. Triphylla type single. Pink and orange triphylla type cultivar sister seedling to Liselotte Buchenauer and Schönbrunner Schuljubiliäum. Like all triphyllas will take full sun. Growth upright. Koralle × *F. fulgens* var. *rubra grandiflora*. Nutzinger – Austrian – 1976.

Preference. Double. Tube and sepals white; corolla plum-purple. Large blooms and free, growth upright. Walker – American – 1970 – A.F.S. No. 881.

Prelude. Single. Tube and sepals red; corolla magenta. Medium sized flowers and free carried in large clusters. Growth upright and hardy in Southern districts. This cultivar is totally different to the "American" Prelude. Blackwell – British – 1957.

Prelude. Double. Reddish tube and tapering white sepals, sometimes flushed purple inside, sepals are fully reflexed and almost hide the tube. Corolla purple, splashed pink, white and purple. Large blooms and free, the four centre petals are royal-purple, surrounded by shorter petals of pure white, when bud opens the flower is white, as it matures centre petals are exposed – the prelude of things to come. Growth trailer, rather difficult to control, but beautiful. Kennett – American – 1958 – A.F.S. No. 348.

Premiere. Double. Tube and short sepals, carmine; corolla violet with red marbling, fading to various shades with maturity. Large blooms, fairly free, flares out when developed. Growth lax bush or trailer. Fuchsia Forest-Castro – American – 1961 – A.F.S. No. 471.

Prentice. Double. Short white tube, sepals white, flushed pink, long pointed, open flat and turn back over tube. Corolla bright rose-pink. medium sized blooms and free, corolla opens to outer petals dusky-rose changing to bright rose. Growth natural trailer. Prentice – American – 1974 – A.F.S. No. 1178.

Prentice Clan. Double. Short tube, sepals rosy-lavender, curling around tube; corolla deep blue, marbled pink at base with blue fading to rosy-lavender. Large blooms and free, continuous, rank green foliage, growth trailer. Prentice – American – 1968 – A.F.S. No. 789.

Prentice Encore. Semi-double. Tube and sepals pink; corolla lavender-blue, overlapping and gradually fading to lavender. Medium sized blooms and free, growth trailer. Prentice – American – 1969 – A.F.S. No. 852.

Prentice Frills. Semi-double. Short rosy-pink tube, sepals rosy-pink turn back over tube; corolla ruffled and frilly variegated shades of pink and blue with green in the centre. Medium-sized blooms and very prolific. Growth natural trailer. Prentice – American – 1969 – A.F.S. No. 853.

Prentice Giant. Double. Tube and very long sepals, orange-red; corolla deep blue, marbled with orange-red, fading to rosy-purple. Huge blooms and fairly free for size, can measure 5 in from tips of sepals. Growth upright. Prentice – American – 1968 – A.F.S. No. 785.

Prentice Orchid. Double. Tube and sepals white; corolla light blue with long petals resembling an orchid, changing to pink-orchid shade. Large blooms and free, growth natural trailer. Prentice – American – 1967 – A.F.S. No. 718.

Prentice Pearl. Double. Short tube and pearly-white sepals; corolla pearly-white, often showing tinge of very pale pink. Large blooms and free for size. Growth trailer. Prentice – American – 1968 – A.F.S. No. 788.

President. Single. Tube and sepals, bright red; corolla rosy-magenta, scarlet at base. Medium sized flowers, very free, dark green foliage with distinct red tint. Growth upright bush, very vigorous and hardy. Received an award in R.H.S. Hardy Trials 1965 under the name of Admiration. Accepted by the B.F.S. as showbench hardy. One of the earliest of cultivars and still holds its own with modern cultivars. Formosa Elegans × *F. corymbiflora*. Standish – British – 1841.

President – Admiration. To distinguish between these two cultivars see Admiration – President.

President B.W. Rawlins. Single. Tube and sepals white, underside of petals flushed pink; corolla purple blended with rose. Medium sized flowers, very free, growth cascade. Named after a past President of the B.F.S. during his period of office. Thorne – British – 1966.

President Carnot. Lemoine – French – 1888.

President Charles Unwin. Double. Tube and sepals white, flushed and tipped eau-de-nil; corolla baby pink. Medium sized blooms, very free and of good substance. Growth upright, strong and bushy. Named after a former President of the British Fuchsia Society. Thorne – British – 1963.

President Elliot. Single. Tube and sepals carmine; corolla rich reddish-purple. Medium sized flowers and free, growth upright, bushy and vigorous, hardy in most districts, one of Thorne's lesser known cultivars, also known as Rev. Elliot, named after one of the earlier B.F.S. Presidents. Thorne – British – 1962.

President Felix Faure. Double. Cerise and violet. Leomine – French – 1901.

President Gosselin. Single. Orange-scarlet self. Eggbrecht – German – Date unknown.

President Gunther. Double. Red and white. Rozain-Boucharlat – French – 1902.

President Leo Boullemier. Single. Short fluted tube streaked magenta, white flared sepals which sweep up to angle of 45° and held well away from tube, sepals fairly long and pointed. Bell shaped corolla magenta-blue maturing to blush pink. Medium sized flowers of perfect shape of unusual colouring, flared, well spaced stamens same colour as corolla, white style and stigma. Dark green foliage 3 in × 1¾ in leaves, pointed and with prominent serrated edge. Growth upright and bushy, short-jointed especially when grown cool, well in the exhibition category. Inherits the best features from both parents. Raised in the vicinity of Bungay, Suffolk in 1980 proved to be hardy during 1981–1982 winter. Named after the President of the British Fuchsia Society during his term of office. Introduced and released by High Trees Nurseries of Reigate, Surrey in 1983. Joy Patmore × Cloverdale Pearl. Burns – British – 1983.

President Margaret Slater. Single. Thin white tube, long, narrow and slightly twisted sepals, white, flushed salmon-pink outside, deep salmon-pink underside, tipped green. Corolla mauve-pink, heavily overlaid deep salmon. Medium sized flowers, very free, similar to Cascade. Dark green foliage, red veined with heavily serrated edges. Growth natural trailer, good for standard, fan or espalier. Named after a past President of the B.F.S. during her period of office. Cascade × Taffy. Taylor – British – 1972 – A.F.S. No. 1119.

President Moir. Double. Red tube; coral-red sepals, short and wide, flare approximately 90° from corolla, tips slightly curled. Corolla deep violet flushed coral-red at base. Medium sized blooms, petals large, good shape, fully doubled, fade with age, good exhibition bloom. Growth tall upright, bushy. This cultivar was previously known in New Zealand as The President, raised in 1966, registered by New Zealand Fuchsia Society in 1976. Violet Gem × . Moir – New Zealand – 1963.

President Porcher. Double. Red and blue-violet. Leomine – French – 1862.

President Roosevelt. Double. Tube and reflexed sepals, coral-red; corolla dark violet-blue, occasionally flecked red. Blooms are rather small for a double but very free. Growth shrubbery bush, very good cultivar. Identical in every respect except for smaller blooms to General Monk. Garson – American – 1942.

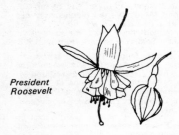

President Roosevelt

President Stanley Wilson. Single. Named after a past president of the B.F.S. during his term of office; was the very last introduction by the late Tom Thorne in 1968 and introduced with another cultivar. A.W. Taylor, in 1969, before he died in December 1969. Tom Thorne, in his later years, used the American cultivar Brentwood (Rolla × Duchess of Albany seedling) extensively for hybridising and President Stanley Wilson is the result of crossing Brentwood with Orange Drops. It is a single, tube colouring is carmine, sepals are carmine turning to pale pink and tipped green, whilst the corolla is rose-carmine. Possesses a most unusual pistil which is deep pink and very pronounced four pointed star shaped. Raiser describes this cultivar as having burgundy and orange colouring, stating it can be either single or semi-double, but throws only single blooms, with the appearance of being semi-double. Extremely free flowering, is one of those desirable cultivars which does not flower in flushes, but has a long continuous production of buds, and is always in bloom, even in the late autumn, especially if the regular feeding programme is maintained. Foliage is clean and of medium green colour, fairly pest free. Growth can be described as vigorous and strong with a natural trailing habit, will produce a magnificent basket, but perhaps excels when grown in the half or wall basket. Produces the desirable long trails and with careful and frequent pinching makes a magnificent specimen for exhibition purposes. Will produce a fine espalier in fan form and a good weeping standard, but not suitable for bush training; best grown under H2 conditions. An outstanding cultivar, considered to be the raisers outstanding contribution, unfortunately not listed in many catalogues and may prove to be a little elusive in finding, but well worth the effort. Brentwood × Orange Drops. Thorne – British – 1968.

President Wilf Sharp. Double. Tube and sepals pinkish-red. Corolla white with slight tinge of pink. Medium sized blooms, very free for a double, rather late flowering but hold both shape and colour. Growth lax bush. Named after a well-known personality in the British Fuchsia Society who held office as President 1973/4/5. Introduced by J. Ridding, 1979. Dorothy Woakes × . Ryle – British – 1979.

Preston Guild. Single. Very long tube with fairly broad sepals which curl right over but at the same time do not hide the tube, both pure white; corolla violet-blue changing to white at base; long stamens with very long pistil; exceedingly long pedicel with long narrow seed pod. Small flowers but very free, does not hold its blooms for a long time and apt to finish flowering rather early in the season. Growth upright and bushy, can be used as a bedder but full sun will take away the brilliance of colour and will cause a flush of pink. Nice cultivar. Dorothea Flower × Hawkshead. Thornley – British – 1971 – A.F.S. No. 1010.

Pretty Baby. Single. Short, thin, Tyrian-purple tube, Tyrian-purple sepals ⅞in long × ⅛in wide, curve slightly upward. Corolla spiraea-red ⅜in long × ⁷⁄₁₆in wide. Small flowers, very prolific, Tyrian-purple stamens and pistil all the same length. Light green foliage ⅞in wide × 1½in long. Growth small upright, bushy. Tested for 5 years in Vicinity of Sebastopol, California. Soo Yun Field – American – 1978 – A.F.S. No. 1447.

Pretty Belinda. Double. Tube deep pink, outside sepals deep pink tipped green, pale pink inside and semi-reflexed. Corolla pure white with the normal slight pink veining at base. Medium sized blooms and quite free. Growth upright and bushy. Introduced by Woodbridge Nurseries of Hounslow in 1980. Tristesse × Snowcap. Dyos – British – 1980.

Pretty Grandpa. Semi-double. Tube and long sepals, pink, tipped green; corolla white with pink veins, flaring when matured, Large blooms and free, growth trailer. Castro – American – 1969 – A.F.S. No. 841.

Preview. Double. Tube blushed-pink fading into white sepals; corolla campanula-violet with outer petals splashed white at base, fading to petunia-purple. Large blooms, free for size, growth upright. Paskesen – American – A.F.S. No. 827.

Pride of Bath. Semi-double. Tube and sepals, pale pink; corolla white. Large blooms, very free, oval shaped and long. Growth upright and bushy. Colville – British – 1967.

Pride of Downey. Double. Tube and twisted sepals, crimson; corolla violet, splashed with crimson. Medium sized blooms and free. Growth upright. Walker and Jones – American – 1949.

Pride of Exeter. Synonymous with Beauty of Exeter in California.

Pride of Orion. Double. Tube and sepals, dark crimson, corolla white, veined cerise. Largish bloom, free and of perfect shape. Growth upright and bushy, very old cultivar and worth finding. Veitch – British – Date unknown.

Pride of Peckham. Single. Crimson and white. Ivery – British – 1846.

Pride of Sheffield. Double. Tube and sepals, scarlet-red, sepals unusual, very vertical, measuring nearly three inches. Corolla pure white with no stripes or markings. Large blooms, free for size. Growth upright and vigorous, suitable for greenhouse climber. Haag – American – 1955.

Pride of the West. Single. Long tube and sepals, palish red, sepals atre narrow, unswept and slightly twisted. Corolla plum-red, flowers largish and free, long, colour combination disappointing. Growth extremely vigorous, suitable as greenhouse climber, no use for pot work, almost as fast as Joan Smith, unusual cultivar for James Lye. Lye – British – 1871.

Pride of Woolwich. Single. Red and dark blue. Banks – British – Date unknown.

Prima Donna. Single. Pale crimson and orange-cerise. Harrison – British – 1845.

Prima Donna. Single. White and dark rose. Smith, G. – British – 1859.

Prima Donna. Single. Tube and curled sepals, pale pink; corolla pure white and long. Medium sized flowers and free, early. Growth upright. Niederholzer – American – 1943.

Prince Albert. Single. White and purple. Banks – British – 1855.

Prince Alfred. Single. White and purple. Banks – British – 1853.

Prince Arthur. Double. Scarlet and dark purple. Jennings – British – 1859.

Prince Frederick William of Prussia. Single. Tube bright carmine-red, sepals carmine-red much recurved; corolla is a wide cup shape of blue changing to plum colour. Raiser unknown – British – Date prior to 1858.

Prince Georges. Double. Crimson and purple. Lemoine – French – 1899.

Prince Leopold. Double. Red and purple with variegated foliage. Williams – British – 1872.

Prince of May. Semi-double to double. Tube and sepals scarlet; corolla blue-violet. Large blooms and fairly free, growth upright, bushy and strong. Grown in California. Raiser and date unknown.

Prince of Orange. Single. Tube and sepals, waxy salmon-pink; corolla deep orange-salmon. Largish flowers, early and free. Growth upright and bushy, hardy in Southern districts. Another old cultivar worth locating. Banks – British – 1872.

Prince of Peace. Double. Tube light rose, sepals frosty-rose and flaring; corolla magenta fading to lustrous rose. Large blooms and free,

growth lax bush or trailer. Davis – American – 1970 – A.F.S. No. 904.

Prince of Wales. Single. cerise and violet-blue. Mayle – British – 1852.

Princess. Double. Slender tube, light green, sepals white with blush of pink, tipped green. very broad. Corolla mauve with white variegation on outer petals, fading to light rose. Large blooms, free for size, with one or two petaloids on outside of petals. Growth lax bush or trailer. Soo Yun – American – 1972 – A.F.S. No. 1044.

Princess Alexandra. Single. White and pink. Smith – British – 1863.

Princess Alexandra. Double. Red and white. Henderson – British – 1872.

Princess Alice. Double. Red tube, sepals red, tipped green; corolla violet, marbled purple with pink veining. Large blooms, very full and prolific flowering. Growth upright and bushy, strong and easy grower both in sun and shade. Woakes – British – 1975.

Princess Dollar. Synonymous with Dollar Princess.

Princesse Dollar. Synonymous in France with Princess Dollar.

Princess Grace. Double. Thick, white tube, medium size white sepals, curve downward; corolla grey-blue. Medium sized blooms, long plum shape, white-red stamens and pistil, prefers warmth, best colour in shade. Growth natural trailer, self-branching, very unusual cultivar and colour, heavy bloomer, good for basket. Hansom – American – 1976 – A.F.S. No. 1327.

Princess Helena. Single, Scarlet and white. Smith – British – 1862.

Princessita. Single. Tube and sepals white, gracefully curved; corolla deep rose. Medium sized flowers and free. Growth trailer. Fandango × Mrs. W. Rundle. Niederholzer – American – 1940.

Princess Louise. Bland – British – 1871.

Princess Margaret Rose. Double. White waxen tube, white upturned sepals; corolla mauve-blue. Medium sized blooms and free, growth lax bush or trailer. Cox – New Zealand – 1940.

Princess of Bath. Double. Tube and sepals, very pale pink; corolla pale pink, almost a self. Very large blooms and free for size. Growth upright and vigorous. Queen of Bath ×. Colville – British – 1968.

Princess of Prussia. Synonymous with Flocon de Neige.

Princess of Wales. Double. Red and white. Bland – British – 1871.

Princess Pat. Semi-double. White tube, white sepals slightly flushed pink. Corolla imperial-purple fading to lavender-blue. Small flowers very floriferous and very early. Has the same characteristics except for the foliage as its parent La Campanella. Variegated foliage, green and creamy-yellow. This cultivar could be identical to Golden La Campanella another sport from La Campanella found around the same time. Growth trailer, self-branching, very suitable for basketwork. Introduced by John Smith of Hilltop Nurseries, Leicestershire in 1980. Early reports claim that the golden variegation can quickly revert back to normal green colouring. Anonymous – British – 1980.

Princess Royal. Semi-double. Pale cerise and purple. Stride – British – 1906.

Princess van Orange. Single. Tube and long narrow sepals, light salmon; corolla rich shade or orange. Medium sized flowers, free and very long. Growth upright. Haag – American – 1951.

Princess Victoria. Single. Pink and vermilion. Story – British – 1845.

Prince Syray. Single. Tube dawn pink, sepals azalea pink; corolla vermillion with shading of neyron-rose on edges. Medium sized flowers and free, growth upright and bushy. Bon Accorde × Lord Lonsdale. White, R.J. – British – 1975.

pringlei. Pink tube, sepals mauvish-pink; corolla mauvish-pink. Tiny flowers, even smaller than *F. thymifolia.* Very similar to *F. thymifolia* except the leaves are closer together. Belongs to the Breviflorae section (Encliandra). Upright shrub to height of 3 ft. Robinson and Seaton – 1893 – Mexico.

pringsheimii. Red tube, sepals and corolla; almost a red self but for a slight colouring of green at sepal tips. Upright, medium shrub. Urban – 1898 – San Domingo.

procumbens (Section IV Skinnera). Although it does not appear to have reached the gardens of Europe until about 1874, it was originally discovered by Robert Cunningham, an Englishman, in 1834 when he visited New Zealand for the purpose of supervising the shipment of naval spares for the Government of New South Wales, his brother Alan having spent a number of years plant hunting in Australia before returning to Kew in 1831.

This trailing species first discovered in 1834 in the North Island of New Zealand growing in the sand along the shoreline, likes growing down banks and will cover an area of around 18 to 20 ft in New Zealand, prostrate in growth, the slender, trailing stems often attain several feet in length. Greenish-yellow tube, red at base; sepals green, tipped purple, no corolla but the stamens bear bright blue pollen. The distinguishing characters are the erect flowers only about ½ in high and the stigma which may appear above or below the level of the stamens.

Seed pods which are green turning to plum purple with maturity are quite large and attractive, covered with plum-like bloom and is one of the very few plants where the berries are left on the plant for exhibition and judging purposes. The flowers are very free, very small and point upwards, very unfuchsia like. The foliage also cannot be recognised as fuchsia, very small leaves, heart-shaped and pretty, borne on slender stalks. Growth consists of long, thin trailing stems which root quite freely, woody and creeping. This species is extremely hardy, even in most parts of Britain, can be used to effect on the larger rockeries or even very suitable for furnishing a hanging basket. Can be best described as more curious than beautiful and most unusual in every way; most specialist fuchsia nurserymen include the plant in their lists. Synonymous with *F. prostrata.* Cunningham – 1834 – New Zealand.

Prodigal. Single. Tube and sepals. pale carmine; corolla carmine. Medius sized flowers and free,

small foliage. Growth bushy and shrubby. Pastel × Aurora Superba. Reiter – American – 1942.

Prodigue. See Enfant Prodigue.

Prodigy. Synonymous with Enfante Prodigue.

Prof. Anton Eipeldauer. Double. Tube and sepals light red; corolla pure white. Medium-sized blooms free for double. Growth upright. Bernadette × *F. fulgens* var. *rubra grandiflora.* Nutzinger – Austrian – 1968.

*Prof. Ernst Hagen. Single. Tube and sepals red; corolla violet-blue. Small flowers, growth short upright. Koralle × *F. boliviana.* Nutzinger – Austrian – 1975.

Professor Roentgen. Single. Carmine and purple. Lemoine – French. 1902.

Profusion. Single. Red and violet. Lemoine – French – 1887.

Profusion. Single. Tube and sepals scarlet; corolla violet-purple. Small flowers, very free. Growth upright and bushy, low and hardy. Wood – British – 1938.

Prosperity. Double. Thick tube crimson, sepals crimson, waxy and firm; corolla pale neyron-rose, flushed and veined rose-red. Medium sized blooms, extremely free, fully double of good shape. Dark glossy green foliage, large leaves produced in threes at most joints. Growth upright, bushy and hardy, excels as outside bedder. Created considerable interest and attention when shown at Birmingham 1974 as a fine standard; will prove to be an outstanding cultivar. Bishop's Bells × Strawberry Delight. Gadsby – British – 1970 – A.F.S. No. 1224.

Prostrata. Single. Tube and sepals, dull red; corolla violet; Flowers very small but borne in great profusion. Growth low and spreading, aptly named, ideal for the rockery, hardy. Accepted by the B.F.S. as showbench hardy. For correct name see *magellanica* var. *prostrata.* Scholfield – British – 1841.

prostrata (Baill, 1880). Synonymous with *F. procumbens.*

Psyche. Double. Red and rose-white. Twrdy – German – 1873.

Psychedelic. Single. White tube, pale pink sepals; corolla bright merthiolate-pink with cast of orange in centre, occasional streaks of lighter pink down petals. medium sized flowers and free, petals slightly wavy and flare out, petal edges turn to darker pink with maturity. Large foliage, shiny underside, dull topside. Growth upright and bushy, very unusual colour combination cultivar. Castro – American – 1972 – A.F.S. No. 1031.

pubescens (Cambess., 1829). Synonymous with *F. coccinea.*

Puget Sound. Double. Tube and sepals, rosy-red; corolla milky-white, overlaid pink on top. Large fluffy blooms and free, large centre with smaller spreading petals. Growth lax bush or trailer. Hodges – American – 1949.

Pulchella. Single. Rose and purple. Mayle – British – 1840.

pulchella (Woodson and Seibert about 1937). Synonymous with *F. hemsleyana.*

Pumila. Single. Tube and sepals crimson, corolla mauve-purple. Tiny flowers but very profuse. Growth upright, bushy, dwarf and hardy, ideal for the rockery. Accepted by the B.F.S. as show-bench hardy. It is possible there are two Pumilas, (a) variant from *F.magellanica* or (b) the one generally accredited to: Young – British – 1821.

Pumila. See *magellanica* var. *pumila*.

Puritani. Semi-double. Scarlet and white. Banks – British – 1864.

Purity. Single. White and purple. Mayle – British – 1847.

Purity. Single. Red and pure white. Williams – British – 1872.

Purperprincess. Single. Tube and sepals deep shiny red; corolla purple red at base, red veined with petals that curl outward. Medium-sized flowers, dark red stamens and style. Dark green foliage. Growth upright and bushy. De Groot – Dutch – 1975.

Purple Ann. Double. Tube and sepals red; corolla violet-purple. Medium-sized blooms, very free and tight, similar to its parent, considered to have a great future on the show bench but never found much favour. Growth upright and bushy. One of the raiser's five cultivars for 1977 and introduced by V.T. Nuttall of Doncaster. Heidi Ann seedling. Roe – British – 1977.

Purple Beauty. Double. Short tube and long, wide sepals. bright carmine; corolla purple with splashes of red at base of petals. Large blooms, free for size, beautiful bell shaped. Bright green foliage, growth trailer. Kuechler – American – 1963 – A.F.S. No. 550.

Purple Bowl. Single. Tube and sepals red; corolla luminous purple. Large flowers, bowl shaped and free. Growth medium bush. Jupiter ×. Niederholzer – American – 1940.

Purple Cornelissen. Single. Tube and sepals cerise; corolla dull purple. Mediujm sized flowers and free, early. Growth upright and bushy, hardy, growth is much lower and dense than Madame Cornelissen. Accepted by the B.F.S. as show-bench hardy. Cornelissen – Belgian – 1897.

Purple Emperor. Semi-double. Tube and sepals crimson; corolla violet. Medium sized flowers and very free. Growth upright and bushy. Endicott – British – 1970.

Purple Gem. Double. Tube and sepals crimson; corolla royal-purple, splashed with crimson. Small blooms for a double, very free, growth upright and bushy. Woodley – British – 1910.

Purple Graseing. Semi-double. Long tube red with splashes of purple, sepals are the same colour which arch well back to tube. Corolla light purple with pink splashes. Small blooms characteristic with its parent an old cultivar dating back to 1910, best colour develops in the sun. Dark green foliage is vigorous. Growth upright, will make good bush. Originates from the vicinity of Warwickshire. Seedling of Purple Gem. Wright, J.A. – British – 1980 – A.F.S. No. 1606.

Purple Heart. Double. Tube and pale crimson, sepals long, waxy-crimson; corolla rich violet. Large blooms, fairly free, outer petals of deep rose-red, inner petals rich violet-purple, rather temperamental under wrong conditions. Growth upright and bushy. Beautiful cultivar, best grown as H1. Walker and Jones – American – 1950.

Purple Lace. Double. Tube and sepals red; corolla purple, large blooms, profuse for double, dark green foliage. Growth upright and bushy, strong

branching habit, height 2 to 2½ ft. Hardy in Southern England, raised in the Scilly Isles. Tabraham – British – 1974.

Purple Night. Double. Short white tube, up-turned sepals, frosty-white, flushed pink corolla deep royal-purple centre, outer petals heavily marbled white and phlox-pink. Large blooms and free for size, rich colouring remains during maturity. Growth natural trailer. Waltz – American – 1955 – A.F.S. No. 226.

Purple Parasol. Single. Thin, red tube, long, red sepals turn upward; corolla deep purple with red veining. Medium sized flowers, red stamens and pistil, unusual, looks like a small umbrella, heavy bloomer. Small dark green foliage, growth tall upright, bushy. Hanson – American – 1976 – A.F.S. No. 1328.

Purple Prince. Double. Scarlet and violet. Smith – British – 1854.

Purple Profusion. Single. Tube and sepals scarlet. Corolla violet-purple. Hardy cultivar. Introduced by C. and J.I. Akers of Ripon – *ca* 1970s.

Purple Queen. Double. Carmine and purple. Smith (F. and A.) – British – 1892.

Purple Robe. Double. Rich cerise and purple. Smith – British – 1873.

Purple Saga. Single. Tube and recurved sepals, deep red; corolla deep purple. Mediums sized flowers saucer shaped, opens flat, free. Dark green foliage with purplish branches. Growth lax bush or trailer. Hodges – American , 1951 – A.F.S. No. 87.

Purple Showers. Single. Tube and sepals white, corolla purple. Medium sized flowers, very prolific, nice clean cut colouring. Growth upright and bushy. Raised and introduced by J.A. Wright of Hilltop Nurseries, Atherstone. Wright, J.A. – British – 1979.

Purple Splendour. Double. Tube and sepals crimson; corolla blue-purple, flowers are very similar to Prodigy. Strong, vigorous growth with spreading habit, height 18 in to 24 in, nothing really exceptional about this cultivar apart from the fact it is a hardy double and received an award. Submitted by Sunningdale Nurseries for the R.H.S. Wisley Hardy Trials, 1975–78, and received the Highly Commended Certificate. Sunningdale Nurseries – British – 1975.

Pussy Cat. Single. Long, thick tube orange-pink with slight reddish tinge, fluted. Sepals orange-pink, held at the horizontal, broad and pointed, tipped green. Triphylla type flowers, habit and shape, with very unusual flowers making almost a novelty. Half the stamens are pink to which petaloids are attached at the extremity, the remaining four stamens equally spaced out alternatively are white, very large cream stigma on a very short pink style. Foliage is similar to Countess of Aberdeen but larger, growth upright. Not an impressive cultivar. Introduced from Holland by Wills Fuchsia Nurseries in 1979. Leverkusen × Checkerboard. Felix, C. – Dutch – 1978.

Puts Folly. Single. Thin tube pale pink, non-reflexing sepals, creamy-white, heavily tipped green, flushed pink. Corolla lilac-rose, paler at base, petals are outlined with deep pink. Growth cascade, makes a good half basket. Baker – British – 1971.

*Puts Pride. Single. Tube and sepals coral-pink, corolla paler coral-pink. Medium sized flowers and very free flowering. Growth strong vigorous trailer, very suitable for basketwork. Raised in the vicinity of Rayleigh in Essex and introduced by Rainbow's Fuchsias of Sandon, Essex, in 1983. Putley – British – *ca* 1982.

putumayensis. Tube bright red, sepals bright scarlet; corolla scarlet. Smallish flowers borne in terminal racemes. Not very much information available on this species. Munz – 1943 – Columbia.

Quaser. Double. White tube and sepals, corolla dauphin's-violet with white mixed at base. Large blooms, free flowering, best colour in shade. Growth trailer. Walker – American – 1974 – A.F.S. No. 1180.

Queen. Single. White and vermilion. Pawley – British – 1846.

Queen Barbara. Double. Tube and sepals flushed palest pink; corolla blue, splashed pink near base. Growth lax upright, will trail with weights and trained on trellis in California. Fuchsia-La (Roy Walker) – American – 1957.

Queen Elizabeth. Single. Tube and reflexed sepals, coral-red; corolla rosy-lilac. Large flowers for single, very free, holly-leaved foliage. Growth trailer. Garson – American – 1942.

Queenie. Double. Tube and sepals crimson, sepals twisted, corolla violet splashed with crimson. Medium sized blooms, free, growth medium upright. Hazard and Hazard – American – Date unknown.

Queen Lucie. Double. Tube pale rose, darker at base, sepals white, tipped green. Corolla dark silvery-blue with traces of pink at base, heat resistance. Growth lax bush or trailer. Gorman – American – 1970 – A.F.S. No. 921.

Queen Mabs. Single. Thin tube, crimson (R.H.S. 52A) with creamy striping, narrows down towards sepals, crimson (R.H.S. 52A) sepals, creped inside, tipped pale green, long sepal reflex to form four lovely circles. Corolla cyclamen-purple (R.H.S. 74B) neyron-rose (R.H.S. 55A) at base, veined crimson (R.H.S. 52A), faint edging of neyron-rose. Large flowers, square shaped, with four petals slightly pleated with uneven edge, stamens and long pistil carmine (R.H.S. 52B). Cordate foliage, heavily serrated, growing tips bronze slightly. Growth semi-trailer with arching growth and pinkish stems. Percy Holmes×. Holmes, R. – British – 1976 – A.F.S. No. 1341.

Queen Mary. Single. Pale pink tube, sepals pink, tipped white. Corolla beautiful rose maturing to mauvish-purple. Large flowers for single but not free. Growth upright, bushy and vigorous, can be disappointing as a bedder, makes a good standard. Similar to the cultivar King George V raised by Charles J. Howlett in 1911, one of two sister seedlings from Mrs. Marshall and named after the reigning monarchs of the time. In the following year 1912 Mr. Howlett was commanded by their Majesties to go to Windsor to present a plant of each cultivar. It is said that they

both flourished 'in the corridor' for many years. Mrs. Marshall seedling. Howlett – British – 1911.

Queen of Bath. Double. Tube and sepals are slightly deeper pink than corolla, corolla bright pink, almost a self. Very large blooms, very free for size, at the time of introduction, considered to be the best pink double. Growth upright and bushy. Winner of the B.F.S. Jones Cup 1966 also B.F.S. Award of Merit. Colville – British – 1966.

Queen of Beauties. Single. White and cerise. Epps – British – 1845.

Queen of Derby. Double. Tube and sepals carmine-rose, tipped green; corolla pale violet with pink stripes and pink flushing. Very solid blooms and fairly large, free for size of bloom. Growth upright with spreading habit. Gadsby – British – 1975.

Queen of Gypsies. Double. Red and purple. Bull – British – 1865.

Queen of Hanover. Single. White and rosy-red. Turner – British – 1855.

Queen of Hearts. Double. Short tube and broad, flaring sepals, clear carmine. Corolla of four centre petals violet-purple. surmounted by many petaloids of lighter carmine-pink. Large blooms, fairly free, growth trailer. Kennett – American – 1961 – A.F.S. No. 475.

Queen of Hearts. Single. Tube and sepals red; corolla deep mauve, flushed pink. Medium sized flowers, very free. Growth upright and bushy, height 2 to 2½ft. Hardy in Southern England, raised in the Scilly Isles. Nothing like the cultivar of the same name raised by Kennett A.F.S. No. 475. Tabraham – British – 1974.

Queen of Sheba. Double. Tube and broad, up-turned sepals, palest carmine, deeper near base and tips. Corolla beautiful greyish powder-blue, flesh-pink toward base of petals. Large blooms, fairly free and spreading. Growth upright and bushy. Munkner – American – 1962 – A.F.S. No. 544.

Queen of the Whites. Single. Red and white. Smith – British – 1867.

Queen of Virgins. Semi-double. Cream and purple. Epps – British – 1846.

Queen of Whites. Single. White and rose-pink. Harrison – British – 1848.

Queen's Corsage. Double. Short tube light red, sepals light red with lighter tips. Corolla royal-purple with pink variegations, fading to light purple, very large blooms and fairly free for size, large foliage with red veins and stems. Growth lax bush or trailer. Soo Yun – American – 1971 – A.F.S. No. 943.

Queen's Delight. Semi-double. Tube and sepals, rosy-pink; corolla blue-mauve fading to lilac. Large blooms, free, loose form, growth lax bush or trailer. Martin – American – 1956 – A.F.S. No. 280.

Queen's Park. Double. Tube and sepals, rich waxy-red, corolla parma-violet. Large blooms, very free and of good substance. Growth upright and bushy. Thorne – British – 1959.

Queen Victoria. Double red and white. Story – British – 1855.

Queen Victoria. Double. One occasionally comes across an old cultivar which was thought to be out of cultivation, one such cultivar is that of Queen Victoria by Smith raised as far back as 1843. Smith's 1843 details are tube pale pink, sepals pale pink, tipped green, deeper pink underneath, rather broad and upswept, nearly hiding the tube. The corolla is purple-carmine, pale pink at the base, the blooms are double of perfect shape, very free and with pink stamens which are very short, style is pale pink and rather short. Medium-green foliage, responds to frequent stopping whilst the growth is upright and bushy. This delightful cultivar is well worth growing and is obviously the cultivar being sent out and listed by Baker of Halstead during the 1970s and 1980s although their catalogue description of waxy white and pale lavender is different from the plants received and grown. This cultivar should not be confused with two others of the same name: Queen Victoria (No. 2) raised by Harrison in 1845 which is a single and identical with Princess Victoria, which has pale pink tube and sepals with pinkish-vermilion corolla. Queen Victoria (No. 3) raised by Story in 1855 was a red and white double cultivar. Tube and sepals cerise with a corolla of white, veined and flecked at the edges with cerise. Largish flowers quite free and with vigorous upright growth. This cultivar together with Mrs. Story, are claimed to be the first cultivars introduced with a white corolla. Smith – British – 1843.

Query. Single. Tube and sepals white, edged rose pink, corolla mauvish-violet. Smallish flowers, extremely free and early. Growth upright, bushy and hardy. Considerable doubt about this cultivar, confused and identical to General Tom Thumb and Chillerton Beauty. Bass – British – 1848.

quinquensis (Kris). Synonymous with *F. petiolaris*.

Rachel Catherine. Single. Tube and sepals deep red; corolla rich purple. Medium sized flowers are flared and prolific, held well away from foliage. Growth upright, self-branching bush. Introduced by D.N. Pickard of Huntingdon, 1979. Gadsby – British – 1979.

Racine. Double. Red and purple. Lemoine – French – 1897.

Radcliffe Beauty. Single. Tube and sepals, claret-rose; corolla Bishop's-violet. Medium sized flowers, very free and held out horizontally. Growth small bush, upright and close-jointed, exceptionally good as bedder. Gadsby – British – 1974.

Radcliffe Bedder. Semi-double. Tube and sepals crimson, sepals fold right back. Corolla spectrum-violet. Medium sized blooms, makes perfect bedding plant. Welcome addition to the hardies. Growth upright and vigorous. Introduced by Markham Grange Nurseries of Doncaster 1980. Neil Clyne × Mipam. Roe – British – 1980.

Radiance. Semi-double. Tube and sepals crimson; corolla Tyrian-rose with apricot shadings. Medium sized flowers, very free with irregular petals. Growth upright and bushy. Reiter – American – 1946.

*Radings Inge. Single. Encliandra type of introduction, one of a series of *Fuchsia* × *bacillaris* selections bred by Mev. Reimann of Hollandsche Rading in Holland. A species hybrid with tiny flowers, rosy-red tube, cream sepals and orange corolla. Growth lax bush. To be introduced by Lechlade Fuchsia Nursery of Lechlade. *Fuchsia* × *bacillaris*. Reimann – Dutch – 1980.

*Rading's Karin. Single. Encliandra type of introduction, one of a series of *Fuchsia* × *bacillaris* selections bred by Mev. Reimann of Hollandsche Rading in Holland. A species hybrid with tiny flowers rosy-red tube and sepals and orange-red corolla. Lax bush growth. Being introduced by Lechlade Fuchsia Nursery of Lechlade. *Fuchsia* × *bacillaris*. Reimann – Dutch – *ca* 1983.

*Rading's Marjorie. Single. Encliandra type of introduction, one of a series of *Fuchsia* × *bacillaris* selections bred by Mev. Reimann of Hollandsche Rading in Holland. A species hybrid with tiny flowers with white tube, light red sepals and pink tube corolla. Lax bush type of growth. Being introduced by Lechlade Fuchsia Nursery of Lechlade. *Fuchsia* × *bacillaris*. Reimann – Dutch – *ca* 1983.

*Rading's Michelle. Single. Encliandra type of introduction, one of a series of *Fuchsia* × *bacillaris* selections bred by Mev. Reimann of Hollandsche Rading in Holland. Rose tube, pink sepals and pale rose corolla. Lax bush growth. Introduced by Lechlade Fuchsia Nursery of Lechlade in 1984. *Fuchsia* × *bacillaris*. Reimann – Dutch – *ca* 1983.

Radio. Double. Tube and sepals red; corolla deep purple. Large blooms, free for size, growth lax bush or trailer. Gorman – American – 1970 – A.F.S. No. 937.

R.A.F. (Royal Air Force). Double. Tube and sepals, bright red; corolla rose-pink, splashed and veined cerise. Largish blooms, free, very similar to Fascination but better. Growth lax bush or trailer, needs support and responds to frequent pinching, well in the showbench category but not seen often enough. Very good. Garson – American – 1942.

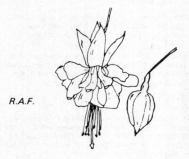

R.A.F.

Raggardy Ann. Double. Tube and sepals, reddish-cerise; corolla bluish-purple inside, changing to magenta, rosy-salmon outside. Largish blooms, fairly free, most untidy bloom with ragged corolla, aptly named. Lightish green foliage, growth lax bush. Brand – American – 1952.

Raggedy Ann. Double. Long rosy-pink tube, sepals white, tipped green with ragged edges. Corolla white, rosy-pink at base, slightly pink at edges. Large blooms, fairly free, growth trailer. Gagnon – American – 1965 – A.F.S. No. 622.

Rahnee. Double. Tube and sepals, deep pink; corolla pink. Medium sized blooms, free for size. Growth upright and bushy. Colville – British – 1966.

Rainbow. Double. Slender tube, carmine; sepals dark pink outside, more vivid underneath. Corolla purple with orange-rose outer petals. Large blooms and free for size, growth lax bush. Nelson – American , 1958.

Rain Drops. Single. Long tube and spreading sepals, white with palest carmine flush. Corolla glowing deep rose-madder. Largish blooms. Composed of four rolled petals, very free. Shiny green foliage, growth upright and bushy. Evans and Reeves – American – 1954 – A.F.S. No. 217.

Raintree Legend. Semi-double. White tube with pale phlox-pink overcast, sepals white, faintly brushed pale phlox-pink at base, absinthe tips, slightly upward curl at tips. Corolla white, medium sized flowers, compact, slightly flared, very profuse and long lasting. Smallish foliage with very finely serrated leaves, growth upright, bushy and self-branching. Foster – American – 1975 – A.F.S. No. 1303.

Rakastava. Single. Tube and sepals, pale pink; corolla white, pink at base. Medium sized flowers very long and free. Growth lax bush. Blackwell – British – 1969.

Ralph Colinson. Single. Rose-pink and purple. Dixon – British – 1886.

Ralph Coutts. Double, Cerise and purple. Strutt – British – 1881.

Rambler. Single. Tube and sepals red; corolla very long, rosy-lilac. Medium sized flowers and very free. Growth upright, suitable only as a greenhouse climber, up to 10 ft in California. Plummer – American – 1953.

Rambling Rose. Double. Soft rose self. Largish blooms, exceptionally free. Lightish green foliage. Growth natural trailer, makes an excellent basket. A.F.S. Cert. of Merit 1962. Tiret – American – 1959 – A.F.S. No. 385.

Ramona. Single. Red tube, long red sepals; corolla magenta. Long flowers, free, very similar to Golondrina. Growth trailer. Niederholzer – American – 1944.

Randy. Single. Tube and sepals pink; corolla amethyst-violet. Small flowers, very free, small foliage. Growth lax bush. Claire Evans × Riccartonii. Evans – American – 1955.

Ranunculiflorae Plena. See *magellanica* var. *globosa*.

Raspberry. Double. Tube and long pointed sepals, pinkish-white; corolla raspberry-rose. Large blooms, fairly free, heat tolerant. Growth upright, needs support as bush. Tiret – American – 1959 – A.F.S. No. 386.

Raspberry Surprise. Double. Tube and sepals are waxy red with pale lilac corolla, veined rose at the base, originally known as seedling No. 2B/69. Growth upright and bushy. Introduced by High Trees Nurseries of Reigate, Surrey, in 1980. (Angela Leslie × Blue Lagoon) × Golden Treasure. Hobson – British – 1978.

Ratae Beauty. Single. Long tube waxy-white, sepals waxy-white; corolla brick-currant-red, gradually fading to lighter colour. Large flowers and very free, growth semi-trailer, vigorous, spreading bush, will make a good half and full standard. Introduced by R. Pacey 1977. Green, H. – British – 1975.

Ravensbarrow. Single. Short thick tube, scarlet; sepals short, scarlet; corolla purple, scarlet at base, short. Small flowers, very free, much smaller but better than its parent. Small foliage, growth upright. Hawkshead × Gruss aus dem Bodethal. Thornley – British – 1972 – A.F.S. No. 1063.

Ray Gagnon. Double. Tube and long pointed sepals, heavily creped bright red; corolla rosy-red. Blooms large and free, swirled bell shaped. Shiny green foliage, growth lax bush. Gagnon , American , 1966 – A.F.S. No. 658.

Ray Weaver. Single. Thick tube reddish-pink, small sepals held horizontal, reddish-pink (R.H.S. 47D) tipped green. Corolla white pink veining at base of petals. Small flowers, very free, resembling Bon Accorde (Esecta Novelty) in shape, stamens and pistil pale pink. Small foliage dark green with pronounced serrated leaves. Growth small upright and bushy, will make good bush or bedder, prefers warmth for best results. Raised in the vicinity of Rancho Palos Verdes, California for 3 years before introduction. Drapkin – American – 1982 – A.F.S. No. 1711.

Razzle Dazzle. Double. Tube and sepals, pale pink; corolla dark purple with darker edge. Large blooms, free for size, sepals curl up very tight, rosette-like petaloids around outer edge. Growth lax bush or trailer. Martin – American – 1965 – A.F.S. No. 630.

Reading Show. Double. Short, red tube ½ in long, thick sepals, red; corolla deep blue, almost purple. Medium sized blooms, fairly floriferous for a hardy double, filaments and style red. Foliage mid-green, tinged red at edges, growth upright, bushy and hardy, tested and proved to be H3 in the vicinity of Reading. Brutus × Swingtime. Wilson, J.W. – British – 1967.

Real Blue. Single. Long ½ in tube white turning to white and lavender stripe. White sepals long and narrow, twist at maturity, 3¼ in long by ½ in wide. Corolla clear blue with white base which ages to lavender-rose. Large sized flowers petals 2 in long by 1½ in wide narrowing to ¼ in at base, buds are long as is the pistil, white 3½ in stamens are pink 2 to 2½ in long. Small to medium foliage 2½ in × 1½ in wide, stems are red when immature. Growth natural trailer, will make good basket without weights but is rather straggly, needs that extra plant to fill. Grown for 10 years in Pacific Grove and Los Altos, California and tested for 2 years in vicinity of Cupertino, California before release. Raiser unknown but registered by Nora Smith of Cupertino. Raiser unknown – American – 1981 – A.F.S. No. 1651.

Rebecca. Single. Short thick tube, eau-de-nil (pale green), sepals white are slightly recurving. Corolla white, large saucer-shaped flower, very similar to its parent. Medium to light green foliage. Growth medium upright, will make good bush and tall shapes of training, as with all near white cultivars, best colour develops in shade. Originates from the vicinity of Lancashire. Seedling of Ting-a-Ling. Singleton – British – 1980 – A.F.S. No. 1580.

*Red Ace. Double. Tube and sepals Post Office red, corolla Indian lake. Medium sized blooms and quite free flowering for a double. Growth upright and bushy, makes a very strong plant. Raised in the vicinity of Nottingham and introduced by Jackson's Nurseries of Tamworth in 1983. Roe – British – 1983.

Redando. Single. Tube and narrow, long sepals red; corolla rose, darker stripe on length of petals. Medium sized flowers and free, growth lax bush or trailer. Haag – American – 1948.

Red Baron. Semi-double to double. Short, thin tube, light green to white when matured. Sepals white, curl back; corolla bright red with marbling of white. Largish blooms and free, petaloids are short, same colour as corolla, petals are loose and tend to follow sepals. Small foliage, growth trailer. Castro – American – 1972 – A.F.S. No. 1032.

Red Buttons. Single, Inflated, shiny tube, red; long pointed outspread sepals, orange-red. Corolla orange-red. Largish flowers, free and heat resistant, growth trailer. Hodges – American – 1961 – A.F.S. No. 481.

Red Cap. Single. Thick tube and sepals, bright red; corolla cerise-rose, flushed orange at the darker petal edges. Large flowers for single, free and flaring. Growth trailer. Hodges – American – 1954 – A.F.S. No. 200.

Red Dangles. Single. Cardinal-red tube, narrow sepals carmen-red; corolla scarlet-red base, red veins with bluish-red blend. Medium sized flowers, free, stiff and hold compact shape. Long oval foliage, dark green top side, lighter underneath, lightly serrated and most attractive. Growth upright, tall and bushy, self-branching. Pancharian – American – 1975 – A.F.S. No. 1293.

Red Devil. Double. Tube and sepals, crimson-red; corolla very dark purple, fading to crimson-red. Very large blooms, free for size, dark green foliage with red stems and veins. Growth lax bush, needs support as bush. Gorman – American – 1970 – A.F.S. No. 938.

*Red Dickenson. Single. Short pink (R.H.S. 55D) tube; pink sepals tipped green (R.H.S. 55D), deep pink (R.H.S. 55A) underneath, sepals are long and spiky, very distinct $1\frac{1}{2}$ in long by $\frac{5}{16}$ in wide. Purple corolla with pink base maturing to purple (R.H.S. 71B) $\frac{3}{4}$ in long by $\frac{5}{8}$ in wide. Medium sized bell shaped flowers with pink stamens and pistil. Foliage mid-green with serrated finely toothed leaves of medium size. Growth medium upright and suitable for bush or decorative, heat tolerant if shaded, very short-jointed with flowers borne in profusion and very distinct spiky sepals. Tested for 3 years and raised in the vicinity of Chaddesden, Derbyshire. Introduced by Jackson's Nurseries of Tamworth in 1985. (Unnamed seedling × Fiona × Sleigh Bells) × Doreen Redfern. Redfern – British – 1985.

Red Flame. Semi-double. Tube and sepals, reddish-white; corolla light lavender, fading to flame-red. Large flowers, very free, heat resistant, dark green foliage. Growth semi-trailer. Soo Yun – American – 1967 –A.F. S. No. 728.

Red Formal. Single. Short tube is Christmas-red, sepals of the same colour narrow, twisting and reflexing tightly against tube. Corolla white, with carmine veins at base. Medium sized flowers, long, tight when first opens, then flares, long style, carmine with white stigma, filaments carmine and burgundy anthers. Dark green foliage,

serrated leaves with red veins and stems. Growth tall upright, raiser describes as a real climber, easy grower and prolific bloomer. Alice Hoffman × Tolling Bell. Registered by B. Barnes and C. Ebeling. Stubbs – American – 1976 – A.F.S. No. 1365.

Redhead. Double. Tube and sepals, deep crimson; corolla cyclamen-purple, matures to fuchsia-purple. Largish blooms and free, wrapped petals have distinct edging when matured. Dark green foliage with serrated edges. Growth upright and bushy, which could prove to be hardy. Nelson – American – 1956 – A.F.S. No. 262.

Red Hot. Double. Tube and sepals, cardinal-red; corolla rich carmine. Medium sized blooms, very free, compact, with sepals standing out gracefully from tube. Lush green foliage, growth upright and vigorous. Reedstrom – American – 1959 – A.F.S. No. 390.

Red Jacket. Double. Tube and long upturned sepals, bright red; corolla pure white. Large fluffy blooms, long buds, very free, extra long pistil and stamens, corolla does not turn brown with age but whiter and larger with maturity. Growth natural trailer. A.F.S. Cert. of Merit 1961. Waltz – American – 1958 – A.F.S. No. 356.

Red Knight. Double. Red self. Large blooms and free. Dark green foliage, growth trailer. Tiret – American – 1967 – A.F.S. No. 735.

Red Monarch. Single. Tube and sepals carmine; corolla red. Medium sized flowers almost a red self. An old unregistered American cultivar, grown exclusively to California. Growth upright, bushy and strong. Raiser and date unknown – American.

Red Petticoat. Single. Long, medium thick rose-Bengal tube curves up, rose-Bengal sepals, tipped light green $\frac{7}{8}$ in long × $\frac{3}{8}$ in wide. Corolla cyclamen-purple (H.C.C.30) $\frac{5}{8}$ in long × $\frac{1}{2}$ in wide, the four petals fade to fuchsia-purple at the sepals. Small flowers with spiraea-red stamens and pistil having plum purple tips. Light green foliage with scalloped edges $1\frac{3}{8}$ in wide × $2\frac{7}{8}$ in long. Growth tall, upright, makes good bush plant. Tested for 5 years in the vicinity of Sebastopol, California. Soo Yun Field – American – 1978 – A.F.S. No. 1451.

Red Princess. Double. Thin white tube, sepals white, very light pink overcast on topside, deeper pink underside. Corolla light lavender to orchid with pink variegations at base of petals. Large blooms, free for size, wrongly named. Growth natural trailer. Soo Yun – American – 1973 – A.F.S. No. 1097.

Red Queen. Semi-double. Dark rose-red self. Dixon – British – 1901.

Red Ribbons. Double. Tube and extremely long sepals, red; corolla stark white. Large blooms and free, sepals are dominate, curling up to form a Christmas bow. Growth lax bush or trailer, little smaller than Texas Longhorn, but better plant. Martin – American – 1959 – A.F.S. No. 371.

Red Riding Hood. Double. Dark red self. Largish blooms, fairly free. Growth upright and sturdy. Hazard and Hazard – American – Date unknown.

Red Rover. Single. Tube and sepals red; corolla purple, flushed red. Medium sized flowers and free. Growth medium upright bush. Hazard and Hazard – American – Date unknown.

Red Rum. Double. Tube and sepals bright red; corolla white. Medium-sized blooms, very floriferous for a double, medium-sized dark green foliage, red veined. Can be described as an improved Snowcap type. Growth upright, bushy and self branching. Named after the famous steeplechaser racehorse of the 1970s. Introduced by D. Stilwell in 1978. Snowcap × (Angela Leslie × Blue Lagoon). Hobson – British – 1977.

Red Sails. Semi-double. Tube and twisting sepals, cardinal red; corolla rose-pink. Medium sized flowers very free. Growth upright, bushy and vigorous. Hodges – American – 1947.

Red Shadows. Double. Tube and upturned sepals, bright crimson; corolla deep burgundy-purple, maturing to ruby-red. Large blooms and very free for size, ruffled, most unusual, seems to change colour three times during maturity. Growth lax bush or trailer. needs support as bush. Very good cultivar, excellent for cut bloom classes. A.F.S. Cert of Merit 1966. Waltz – American – 1962 – A.F.S. No. 525.

Red Spider. Single. Long tube and narrow recurving sepals, deep crimson; corolla deep rose-madder, veined and margined deep crimson. Medium sized flowers, long and extremely prolific, suffers a bad handicap with its name. Growth vigorous trailer, produces enchanting basket. Same raiser introduced Trail Blazer of similar qualities but double. A.F.S. Cert. of Merit 1948. Reiter – American – 1946.

Red Spider

Red Star. Double. Tube cherry-red; sepals cherry on top, claret-rose on reverse side. Corolla Tyrian-purple, veined and flushed claret-rose. medium sized blooms, very free, star shaped. Medium green foliage with red veins. Growth upright and bushy. Crockett – British – 1969 – A.F.S. No. 855.

Red, White and Blue. Single. Red, dark blue and white. Bull – British – 1848.

Red Wing. Single to semi-double. Tube and long sepals red; corolla plum-purple. Large flowers, fairly free, buds reluctant to open under wrong conditions, growth trailer. Tiret – American – 1949.

Redwood Bowl. Double. Short, thick red tube, long sepals, deep red; corolla deep red. Medium sized blooms, all red stamens and pistil. Long narrow foliage. Growth tall, upright. Hanson – American – 1976 – A.F.S. No. 1329.

Reflexa. Single. Tube and sepals red; corolla orange-scarlet. Very small flowers but extremely free. Breviflorae type and not a species but a natural hybrid. Small foliage, growth low bush and dwarf. Raiser and origin unknown – *ca* 1830.

Reflexa plena. Lemoine – French – 1858.

Regal. Single. Rose-madder self. Medium sized flowers and fairly free but very late. Growth extremely vigorous climber, one of the most vigorous cultivars known, will attain a height of several feet in first year. Useless for anything else but a climber. runs up on a single stem with little or no side shoots. Raiser unknown – American – Date unknown.

Regalia. Single. Variegated foliage cultivar with the usual red and purple flowers. Bausie – French – 1869.

Regal Prince. Semi-double. Short thick tube light red, sepals light red, short and broad which recurve over the tube. Corolla dark purple, flushed light red with darker red veining. Medium sized blooms with light red stamens and style, pink stigma. Medium sized foliage, mid-green with slight serratation and deeply veined leaves. Growth medium upright and bushy, best colour in shade. Raised in the vicinity of Cardiff, South Wales. Adams – British – 1982 – A.F.S. No. 1697.

Regal Robe. Double. Tube and upturned sepals, deep bright red; corolla deepest royal violet-purple. Large blooms, prolific bloomer with many scalloped petals, something different. Growth lax upright. Erickson-Lewis – American – 1959 – A.F.S. No. 408.

regia. Tube and sepals red; corolla darker red. Very small flowers, rampant climber attaining a height of 20 ft in its natural habitat, with long and slender branches. Synonymous with *F. integrifolia.* Gardner – 1842 – Brazil.

   var. *affina.*

   var. *alpestris.* Native of Organ Mts, Brazil, at elevation of 5,000 ft, flowers similar in colour and formation to the *magellanica* types usually listed in nurserymen's catalogues as *F. alpestris.*

   var. *radicans.*

Reicharts Sampling. Single. Tube and sepals white; corolla campanulate mauvish-pink. Small flowers, very free, growth upright, compact and dwarfish. Reichart – German – 1866.

Reiters Giant. Double. Short tube and broad sepals, carmine; corolla petunia-purple. Huge blooms, very free for size. Growth upright and vigorous. Grenadier × Jupiter. Reiter – American – 1941.

Rembrandt. Semi-double. Tube and sepals light matt red; corolla light purple. Smallish blooms, quite free, red stamens and style. Small dark green foliage. Growth upright and bushy. Steevens – Dutch – 1974.

*Remus. Double. Tube and sepals rhodamine-purple, sepals deeper colour on underside. Corolla amethyst-violet with little fading. Fairly large blooms and quite free flowering for a double cultivar. Growth upright and bushy, very suitable for bush or standard. Raised in the vicinity of Melton Mowbray, Leicestershire and introduced by the raiser, Pacey's Nurseries, in 1984. Pacey – British – 1984.

Rene. Single. Short crimson tube, sepals crimson on both sides, small, borne horizontally with slight upward curve. Corolla violet with pinkish shading at base with red veins, fading to roseine-purple. Medium sized flowers, very profuse and graceful. Large spear-shaped foliage luttuce green colour, serrated leaves. Growth medium upright bush. Bon Accorde × Strawberry Delight. Ryle – British – 1975 – A.F.S. No. 1253.

Renown. Single. Red and purple. Knight – British – 1869.

Requiem. Single. Longish tube and sepals, red, corolla white; medium sized flowers and free. Growth upright and sturdy. Blackwell – British – 1961.

Resolution. Single. Red and violet. Bull – British – 1867.

Resplendent. Single. Red and blue-violet. Bland – British – 1871.

Rev. Elliott. Synonymous with President Elliott.

Reverend Doctor Brown. Double. Short thick tube, pale pink, sepals pale pink outside, deep pink inside, tipped green, long, folding straight back along stem. Corolla pure white, short pink veins at base of petals. Large blooms and free, wide flaring like a double Citation. Dark green foliage, red veined and glossy. Growth upright and self-branching. Named after one of the three founder members of the British Fuchsia Society 1938. Sophisticated Lady × Citation. Taylor, A. – British – 1973 – A.F.S. No. 118.

Reverie. Double. Pale Tyrian-rose self. Medium sized fluffy blooms and free with recurved sepals, small foliage. Growth upright and bushy. Reiter (Jr) – American – 1951 – A.F.S. No. 84.

Rhapsody. Double. Tube and wide sepals, brilliant red, corolla deep royal-purple with rose marbling on outer side petals. Largish blooms, extremely double and free, growth lax upright. Peterson-Fuchsia Farms – American – 1958 – A.F.S. No. 330.

Rhapsody. Single. Tube and sepals, rhodonite-red, corolla orchid-purple, paling towards base. Medium sized flowers, free, lobed petals. Growth upright and bushy. Jones, W. – British – 1959.

Rhapsody. Double. Tube and sepals, deep blood-red; corolla white. Medium sized blooms and free, growth upright and bushy. Blackwell – British – 1965.

Rhombifolia. Single. Tube and sepals, scarlet-cerise; corolla purple. Small flowers, very free, short corolla, growth upright, bushy and hardy. Accepted by the B.F.S. as showbench hardy. Riccartonii × .Lemoine – French – Date unknown.

Rhythmic. Single. Tube and sepals, dark red, corolla deep maroon. Medium sized flowers and free, growth upright and very vigorous, tall. Plummer – American – 1953.

Riccartonii. See *magellanica* var. *riccartonii*.

Richard Diener. Single. Red tube, extra wide and spreading sepals, red; corolla white, suffused pink, veined red. Huge flowers for a single, fairly free, serrated petals and spreading. Growth strong upright. Niederholzer – America – 1943.

Richard Mumford. Semi-double. Red and pink. Story – British – 1847.

Richard Neville. Semi-double. Rose and blue. Harrison – British – 1877.

Richmond. Double. Tube and sepals, light pink; corolla fuchsia coloured, variegated with salmon and deep rose. Large blooms, fairly free, growth trailer. Pennisi – American – 1968 – A.F.S. No. 752.

Ricky. Double. Tube and sepals, flesh-pink; corolla crisp snowy-white. Largish blooms, very free, heat resistant. Growth upright and bushy, vigorous. Evans and Reeves – American – 1953.

Ric Rac. Single. Tube and sepals, Tyrian-rose; corolla pink, lavender at base of petals. Medium sized flowers, early and free. Growth upright. Tiret – American – 1949.

Ridestar. Double. Tube and sepals, bright red; corolla deep blue, fading to rosy-lavender, pink at base and veined cerise. Largish blooms and free, growth upright, suitable as standard. Blackwell – British – 1965.

Rigoletto. Double. Tube and sepals, deep red; corolla light purple. Largish blooms, fairly free, frilled edges on petals. Growth upright. Blackwell – British – 1967.

Rika. Single. Tube rather long and bulbous, creamy-white, long sepals, creamy-white with blush pink. Corolla orange-red, smallish flowers and very free. Needs early and constant stopping, growth upright and bushy. Mephisto × Water Nymph. van der Post – Dutch – 1968.

*Rikste. Single. Little known Dutch species hybrid introduced by Lechlade Fuchsia Nursery of Lechlade in 1984. *F. lampadaria* × Ting-a-Ling. Raiser unknown – Dutch – *ca* 1980.

Ringwood Market. Semi-double. Tube and sepals neyron-rose; corolla powder blue, fading to lilac, pink at base. Compact habit of growth, easily trained as bush or shrub, floriferous. Named in honour of the 750th year of Ringwood the market town in Hampshire. Introduced by Wills Fuchsia Nurseries in 1977. Tristesse × Susan Ford. Clyne – British – 1976.

rivularis. Tube and sepals, dark, dull red; corolla purple and red. Not very free flowering with flowers produced singly in upper leaf axls. Growth described as spreading shrub. MacBride – 1940 – Peru.

*Robbie. Single. Short pale magenta tube, horizonally held sepals pale magenta on top, fading to white, with green tips and recurving 1¼in long by ⅓in wide. White corolla with little veining ⅞in long by ⅜in wide. Medium sized flowers, half flared and bell shaped, short pedicels give good bloom cover, pale pink filaments and deep pink anthers, pale pink style and pink-magenta stigma. Medium to light green foliage with cordate leaves 1½in long by ⅜in wide. Growth medium upright, bushy, short jointed, needs early and frequent pinching for full bloom coverage. Will make good bush, upright on standard. Raised in the vicinity of Rotherham, Yorkshire, and introduced by Castledyke Fuchsias of Wildmore, New York, Lincolnshire in 1984. Doctor Brenden Freeman × Ting-a-Ling. Lamb – British – 1984 – A.F.S. No. 1771.

Robert Doran. Semi-double to double. Tube and sepals ivory, flushed pink, tipped green and reflexed, underneath tipped green then white, deep rose at base. Corolla white, flushed faint pink. Largish blooms, free and of good size and substance. Growth upright, bushy and erect. Travis – British – 1956.

Robert Hall. Single. Tube and sepals, neyron-rose, held clear from corolla. Corolla magenta-rose, flushed neyron-rose. Medium sized flowers, early and free. Growth strong, upright bush. Gadsby – British – 1970 – A.F.S. No. 871.

Robertsii. See *magellanica* var. *robertsii.*

*Robert Stolz. Semi-double. Tube and sepals red; petals deep blue. Small flowers but very free flowering. Growth neat small upright, bush. This cultivar came to the Netherlands under the name of Rosemarie Isoppe which has now been amended. Koralle × *F. boliviana.* Nutzinger – Austrian – 1971.

Robert Tidmarsh. Semi-double. Pink and violet. Dixon – British – 1900.

Robin. Double. Tube and sepals white; corolla dianthus-purple, fading to bright red. Large blooms, fairly free, growth trailer. Kennett – American – 1967 – A.F.S. No. 741.

Robin Hood. Double. Tube and sepals, bright glowing red; corolla deep crimson, ages to rich self red with maturity. Very large blooms for a hardy, free and carried on exceptionally strong stems. Growth upright, bushy and hardy. Accepted by the B.F.S. as showbench hardy. Colville – British – 1966.

Robin Pacey. Single. Roseine-purple tube, sepals roseine-purple tipped green, Tyrian-purple on underside, long and broad. Corolla campanula violet, shading to white at base of petals and veined rosine-purple. Large flowers of good shape. Growth upright and bushy of good habit and vigorous enough to make the training of a standard. Raised and tested for three years before release in the vicinity of Melton Mowbray, Leicestershire. Raised and introduced by R. and J. Pacey of Stathern, Melton Mowbray in 1982. Pacey – British – 1982.

Rocket. Triphylla type single. Long tube, turkey-red, sepals turkey red; tiny corolla poppy-red. Flowers are similar to Leverkusen, shorter than normal. Foliage reddish-green, deeply veined and suffused red. Growth upright and bushy. F2 hybrid. Gartenmeister Bonstedt × Mrs. Victor Reiter. Reiter – American – 1942.

Roi de Rome. Single. White and rose. Miellez – French – 1856.

Roi des Blanches. Single. White and rose. Harrison – British – 1858.

Roi des Fuchsias. Single. Pink and vermilion. Meillez – French – 1856.

Rolla. Double. Short tube and sepals, pale pink; corolla creamy-white, suffused pink at base. Medium to largish blooms, very free and of good shape. Lightish green foliage. Growth upright and bushy, very suitable for standard, excellent cultivar in every way but lost popularity. This cultivar was exported to America by Rev. H. Brown in 1929 and used extensively in hybridising, many of the modern whites including Flying Cloud can trace their parentage to Rolla. Lemoine – French – 1913.

Romance. Double. Short white tube, sepals white, tipped green, flushed pink underneath. Corolla blue-violet, with pale pink outer petals. Large blooms, very free for size, growth trailer. A.F.S. Cert. of Merit 1970. Paskesen – American – 1967 – A.F.S. No. 701.

Roman City. Double. Long pale pink tube, sepals deeper pink than tube; corolla plum-purple with splashes of deep pink. Extremely large blooms with sufficient substance to feel heavy when held, unusual colour combination, very attractive. Light green foliage, growth arching, best grown as H1 or H2. Endicott – British – 1976.

*Romany Rose. Single. Short thick pink tube, sepals phlox-pink. Corolla neyron-rose, medium sized flowers held semi-erect, very prolific, raiser claims ten to twelve flowers from every leaf axis. Growth medium upright and bushy, proved to be hardy in West of England. Raised in the vicinity of Plymouth, Devon. Mount Edgcumbe × Merry Mary. Hilton – British – 1984.

Romney Girl. Semi-double. Short tube and sepals deep pink. Corolla beautiful shade of rose-pink. Medium sized blooms and very free. Growth upright and bushy. Introduced by Woodbridge Nurseries of Hounslow in 1980. Hobson × Sylvy. Dyos – British – 1980.

Rondo. Single. Short thick tube, pink; long pink sepals, held well back. Corolla cerise, edged red, pink at base. Large flowers, long bell shaped with over-lapping petals, very free. Growth medium upright, bushy. Handley – British – 1973 – A.F.S. No. 1133.

*Ron Ewart. Single. White tube short and thick, white sepals short, broad and recurved. Corolla rose-Bengal (R.H.S. 57C) shaded white at the base. Small compact flowers and very free flowering. Named after the current secretary of the British Fuchsia Society. Small foliage mid-green. Growth upright and bushy, compact and self-branching, well in the exhibition class. Introduced by Markham Nurseries of Doncaster in 1981. Bobby Shaftoe × Santa Barbara (syn. with Lustre). Roe – British – 1981.

Ron Holmes. Single. Medium tube pale pink, medium-sized sepals pale pink outside with carmine-rose (R.H.S. 52C) inside, held at right angles with tips slightly flicking upwards. Corolla mandarin-red (R.H.S. 40B) overlaid with carmine (R.H.S. 25B). Medium-sized round flowers which grow in clusters with long pistil and large pale yellow stigma. Leaves are cordate with heavy serration. Growth medium-upright bush, self-branching makes good bush with early pinching. Tested for 3 years in vicinity of Kent. Percy Holmes × . The hybridiser has named this cultivar after himself. Holmes, R. – British – 1978 – A.F.S. No. 1462.

Ron Honour. Single. Tube and sepals, crimson-red; corolla purple, veined crimson. Medium sized flowers, free, barrel shaped. Growth upright and bushy. Vicarage Farm Nurseries – British – 1969.

Ronsard. Single. Cerise and purple. Hardy cultivar. Lemoine – French – 1897.

Ron's Pet. Single. Long thin tube, shell-pink, sepals shell-pink outside, scarlet inside, tipped green, narrow, follow curve of corolla. Corolla orange with claret-rose base. Small flowers, very free, four petals form square corolla, large compared with tube. Lightish green foliage, young growth yellow-green. Growth lax bush. Percy Holmes × Melody. Holmes, R. – British – 1973 – A.F.S. No. 1208.

Rosabell. Single. Slender white tube, sepals pale neyron-rose, long and held well back. Corolla Imperial-purple, shading to phlox-pink with distinct red stamens. Large flowers and free, growth lax bush or trailer. Gadsby – British – 1968 – A.F.S. No. 970.

Rosa Bonheur. Single. White and rich rose. Todman – British – Date unknown.

Rosalee. Double. Brilliant rosy-red self. Long thick sepals with frilly short side petals, flowers very large and free for size. Growth lax bush or trailer. Martin – American – 1958 – A.F.S. No. 363.

Rosalind. Single. Red tube with red reflexed sepals. Corolla royal purple and pink, Raised and introduced by C. and J.I. Akers Nurseries of Ripon in 1975.

Rosaly Rooney. Single. Long tube and sepals white; corolla orange-red. Medium sized flowers and free, light green foliage. Growth trailer. Niederholzer – American – Date unknown.

Rosamunda. Double. Tube and sepals, dark pink; corolla white with deep pink flushings. Largish blooms and free, growth upright and bushy. Colville – British – 1966.

Rosana. Semi-double. Tube and sepals rose; corolla solferino-purple. Large flowers, free for size. Growth upright and very vigorous, up to 8 ft in California. Neiderholzer – American – 1946.

Rosea. See *magellanica* var. *globosa*.

rosea (Ruiz and Pavón 1802). Synonymous with *F. lycioides*.

Rosea Alba. Single. White and pale rose. Barker – British – 1841.

Rosealba. Single. White and pink. Coene – Belgian – 1853.

rosea spinosa (Reiche 1897). Synonymous with *F. lycioides*.

Rose Aylett. Double. Tube and sepals, pale carmine; corolla bluish-lilac. Large blooms for double, fairly free, growth upright and bushy. Another good old cultivar still in cultivation. Strutt – British – 1897.

Rose Ballet Girl. Synonymous with Fascination.

Rose Bower. Double. Crimson tube, sepals carmine, broad and waxy, tipped green. Corolla lilac-purple, blending to cyclamen-purple, flushed with crimson. Medium size blooms, free bloomer, carries crimson petaloids, attractive colour combination. Growth semi-trailer or medium upright bush. La Fiesta × .Gadsby – British – 1973 – A.F.S. No. 1124.

Rose Bradwardine. Double. Tube and sepals, deep rose-pink; sepals curl up round. Corolla lavender, splashed orchid-pink. Large blooms, free, very full and bell shaped. Growth upright, bushy and very strong. Colville – British – 1958.

Rosebud. Double. Slim white tube, sepals white and flaring. Corolla rosy-orange, white at base of petals. Medium sized blooms, very free and very tight with many petaloids, resembling a rose bud in early stages. Small foliage of light green. Growth lax bush or trailer. Kennett – American – 1958 – A.F.S. No. 349.

Rose Chiffon. Semi-double. Tube and sepals, rose-madder; corolla rose-bengal with apricot overtones. Largish flowers and free, globular, auxiliary petals are apricot tinted giving warm rose-pink cast. Growth trailer. Schnabel – American – 1955 – A.F.S. No. 222.

Rose Churchill. Double. Tube and sepals rose, corolla rose, almost a self. Medium-sized blooms and very prolific. Foliage and growth very similar to Winston Churchill. Introduced into England by John Smith of Thornton, Leicestershire in 1974. According to Dutch information, the cultivar is grown in Holland and could be a sport of Winston Churchill stating the corolla is pink instead of purple-blue. Raiser and date unknown – ca 1970.

Rosecrest. Double. Tube and broad, upturned sepals white, slightly tinged palest pink underside. Corolla deep lilac, turning bright rose with maturity. Medium sized blooms in great profusion, very similar to Silverado. Glossy foliage, growth upright, bushy and compact. Waltz – American – 1957 – A.F.S. No. 312.

Rosecroft. Single. Rosy-red and pink. Robinson – British – Date unknown.

Rosecroft. Double. Tube and sepals, carmine; corolla pink and rose pink. Largish blooms and free, striped and long. Growth upright and bushy. Rosecroft Nurseries – British – 1944.

Rosecroft Beauty. Semi-double. Tube and sepals crimson; corolla white, flushed and veined cerise. Small flowers, free, similar to Snowcap. Foliage pale green, edged golden-yellow with shades of cream and cerise. Growth upright and bushy. Extremely disappointing, both habit and colour have nothing to commend itself, sports back to Snowcap foliage. Sport of Snowcap. Eden – British – 1968.

Rosedale. Single. Short thick tube, carmine, broad sepals carmine, tipped green, underside crimson. Corolla magenta-rose, edged Tyrian-purple. Medium sized flowers, very free, bell shaped, held horizontal from plant revealing parentage. Growth upright and bushy. Upward Look × .Gadsby – British – 1972 – A.F.S. No. 1068.

Rose Dawn. Single. Short tube and sepals rose; corolla solferino-purple. Medium bell shaped flowers, free, growth trailer. Edwards – American – 1948.

Rose de Armour. Single. Pink and purple. Knight – British – 1847.

Rose Harrison. Single. Rose-red and white. Harrison – British – 1861.

Rose Kelly. Double. Tube and sepals scarlet; corolla white, veined red at base. Medium sized blooms, very free, similar to Molesworth. Growth upright and bushy. Nessier – American – 1948.

Rose Lace. Double. Tube and sepals deep pink, corolla rose-pink. Large full double blooms unusual for reputed hardy cultivar. Dark green foliage, growth arching and compact, height 2 to 2½ ft. Hardy in Southern England and raised in the Scilly Isles. Tabraham – British – 1982.

Rose Marie. Double. Tube and sepals pink; corolla lighter shade of pink, almost a self. Very large blooms for a double, beautifully formed corolla with large petaloids. Growth arching and rather lax, best grown as H1 for show purposes. Colville – British – 1976.

*Rosemarie Isopp. Single. Tube and sepals red; corolla blue. Small flowers, very free flowering.

Growth medium upright. Koralle × *F. boliviana*. Nutzinger – Austrian – 1971.

*Rosemary Day. Single. Pale pink tube, sepals pale pink which are both broad and long, much deeper pink underneath. Corolla is the palest of cyclamen-purple. Medium sized flowers, extremely floriferous, inheriting strong characteristics from Melody. Mid-green foliage with well proportioned leaves. Growth upright and bushy will produce good bush or standard. Raised and tested in the vicinity of Bridgwater in Somerset and introduced by C.J. Lockyer of Bristol at Chelsea Show 1983. Day – British – 1983.

Rosemarye. Single. Tube and sepals, pale pink of crepe texture; corolla very pale blue. Medium sized flowers and free, growth upright and bushy. Niederholzer – American – 1941.

Rose Mauve. Double. Tube and sepals, neyron-rose; corolla rose-mauve. Medium sized blooms, free, growth upright and bushy. Schnabel – American – 1951 – A.F.S. No. 80.

Rose of Castile. Single. Tube and sepals, waxy-white, tipped green, bulging tube, sepals very faintly flushed pale pink. Corolla purple, faintly flushed rose, whitish at base. Smallish to medium flowers, free, beautiful colouring. Growth upright and bushy, hardy, produces fine standard. Accepted by the B.F.S. as showbench hardy. H.C. by R.H.S. 1929. Banks – British – 1855.

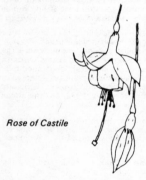

Rose of Castile

Rose of Castile Improved. Single. Tube and sepals, flesh-pink; corolla violet-purple. Medium sized flowers and free, blooms in flushes. Lightish green foliage, growth upright, bushy, hardy and vigorous. Very distinct from Rose of Castile but no improvement, except that flowers are larger and growth more vigorous. Accepted by the B.F.S. as showbench hardy. H.C. by R.H.S. Banks – British – 1869.

Rose of Denmark. Single. Tube and sepals, pale blush-pink; corolla rose-pink edged deep pink. Medium sized flowers, can come semi-double, very free. Growth upright and bushy, better as a second year plant. Banks – British – 1864.

Rose of Encinal. Double. Tube and sepals, rich dark pink; corolla mottled rose, lavender and magenta with outer petals shaded deeper colour at base. Largish blooms and free, growth upright and very stiff. Reimers – American – 1953 – A.F.S. No. 172.

Rose of Monterey. Semi-double. Tube and sepals, rosy-red; corolla rosy-pink. Large flowers, very free, dark green foliage. Growth upright and bushy. Haag – American – 1951.

Rose Petals. Double. Tube and sepals rosy-red; corolla creamy-white and veined red. Medium sized blooms, very little known of this cultivar except that it appears to be exclusive to California. Raiser and date unknown.

Rose Phenomenal. Double. Tube and broad sepals scarlet, corolla rosy mauve-lavender. Large blooms and free, similar in shape and size to Phenomenal. Growth upright. Possibly Banks – British – c. 1850.

Rose Piggot. Single. White and cerise. Letts – British – 1913.

Rose Pillar. Single. Clear neyron-rose self, medium sized flowers, free, similar to Display in shape. Large foliage, growth vigorous climber. Rolla × Aurora Superba. Reiter – American – 1940.

Rose Porter. Single. Rose-pink and violet-blue. Lemoine – French – 1907.

Rose Queen. Single. Tube and sepals scarlet; corolla lavender, flushed rose. Largish flowers and free. Growth natural trailer. Raiser unknown – American – Date unknown.

Rose Red. Single. Deep pink self. Small to medium flowers, free, growth medium upright and bushy. Hazard and Hazard – American – Date unknown.

Rose Red. Single. Deep pink self. Small to medium flowers, free, growth medium upright and bushy. Hazard and Hazard – American – Date unknown.

Rose Reverie. Double. Cream tube, sepals neyron-rose, tipped green; corolla solferine-purple, flushed rose-madder and veined. Large blooms, fairly free; dark green, long pointed foliage. Growth upright. Crockett – British – 1969 – A.F.S. No. 856.

Rosetta. Single. Tube and sepals deep pink corolla rose-pink, heavily veined red. Medium sized flowers and very free flowering. Deep green foliage, growth upright and bushy, strong branching habit, height 1½ to 2 ft. Hardy in Southern England, raised in the Scilly Isles. Tabraham – British – 1974.

Rosette. Double. Tube and sepals, dark rose-madder; corolla dark rhodamine-purple. Medium size blooms, fairly free, rosette shape. Growth upright. Niederholzer – American – 1947.

Rosie O'Grady. Double. Tube and sepals, blushed-white, tipped pale green, pink on underside. Corolla soft rosy-pink, large globular blooms, free and continuous, does not form berries. Growth trailer, much better pink cultivars. Hodges – American – 1960 – A.F.S. No. 453.

*Rosi Oliva. Double. Tube and sepals pinkish-white; corolla purple. Large blooms and free flowering for such large blooms. Growth medium upright. Dark Secret × Bernadette. Nutzinger – Austrian – 1965.

Rosy Frills. Double. Greenish-white tube, sepals are broad and short forming round shiny buds, outside very pale pink, inside pale pink (R.H.S. 49C), tipped pale yellow-green. Corolla rose (R.H.S. 55A and 58C), edged red (R.H.S. 46D), outer petals streaked salmon (R.H.S. 43D). Large blooms, very full yet compact, petals of even length. Dark green foliage with dark red stems. Growth lax, semi-trailer and spreading, early and free-flowering. Raised and tested for 10 years before release in vicinity of Derby. Introduced by Jackson's Nurseries of Tamworth in 1979. Handley – British – 1979 – A.F.S. No. 1503.

Rosy Morn. Double. Tube white, tinged green, pink sepals; corolla smoky-rose. Medium sized blooms, very free, growth strong upright and bushy. Colville – British – 1973.

Rosy O'Grady. Single. Tube and recurved sepals, rose; corolla dark red, changes to old rose. Medium sized flowers, fairly free, very large foliage. Growth upright and very vigorous. Haag and Son – American – 1953.

Rothbury Beauty. Double. Tube and sepals red; corolla pink, heavily flushed rose-pink and cerise. Large blooms, rather similar to R.A.F. and Fascination, did not create much attention when first shown at Manchester in 1976 and 1977. Formerly known as seedling 447A and 47A. Pink Cloud seedling × Lena Dalton × Lady Kathleen Spence. Ryle – British – 1976 – A.F.S. No. 1474.

Rottengen. Synonymous with Andenken an Heinrich Henkel.

Rough Silk. Single. Long tube and large upswept sepals, pale carmine-pink; corolla crimson-red, paling at base. Very large flowers and free, can measure 5 inches across sepals. Lightish green foliage, growth vigorous cascade. This cultivar was originally named Baker's Boy in 1968. Baker – British – 1970.

Roulette. Double. Tube and sepals, pale rose to white; corolla rose-madder, marbled pale rose at base. Medium sized blooms, free, growth lax bush or trailer. Reiter – American – 1950 – A.F.S. No. 60.

Rowena. Single. Tube and sepals, soft pink; corolla soft pink with faint rose edging, almost a self. Flowers extremely small and very free. Growth upright, bushy, compact and hardy. Raiser unknown – American – Date unknown.

*Roxanne Belle. Double. Short thick tube pink (R.H.S. 62A) streaked darker pink ⅜ in long by ½ in wide. Horizontally held sepals pink (R.H.S. 62B to 62C) on top, lighter pink (R.H.S. 62C) underneath with recurved tips 3½ in; long by 1¼ in wide. Corolla pink (R.H.S. 65B) 2¼ in long by 2⅜ in wide. Large blooms almost a pink self, half flared, very large for its colour range. Dark pink filaments, magenta anthers, pale pink style and flesh coloured stigma, buds are long, wide and pointed. Very large foliage dark green (R.H.S. 139A) with elliptic leaves 3½ in long by 2½ in wide, serrated and with acute tips and rounded bases. Growth is natural trailer, will make a good basket or weeping standard, prefers cool conditions. Trademarked in California, U.S.A. Awarded first place in 1983 American N.F.S. show for unintroduced seedling class. Raised in the vicinity of Oceanside, California, U.S.A. Cyndy Robyn × Trade Winds, sister seedling to Medalist, the only two introduced by the hybridist in 1984. Stubbs – American – 1984 – A.F.S. No. 1760.

Roxan Rae. Single. Short medium long red tube, red sepals with darker line down middle, red-purple tipped. Corolla black-purple shows red at base. Small flowers and small foliage with relatively long dark green leaves. Growth trailer

will train without weights. Raised and tested in vicinity of Coos Bay, Oregon, California. Vee Jay Greenhouse – American – 1979 – A.F.S. No. 1489.

Royal Crown. Double. Tube and sepals, heavy waxy-white; corolla deep purple centre with pinkish-white outer petals. Large blooms, fairly free giving the effect of a crown. Large dark green foliage, growth lax bush or trailer. Martin – American – 1960 – A.F.S. No. 446.

Royal Flush. Single. Tube and broad long upturned sepals, deep red; corolla royal-purple, flesh coloured at base. Large flowers, fairly free, open perfectly flat. Growth medium, upright bush. Hodges – American – 1952 – A.F.S. No. 125.

Royal Jester. Double. Short tube red, sepals crimson-red; corolla crimson and ruby-red variegation. Large blooms, fairly free, large foliage. Growth lax bush or trailer. Soo Yun – American – 1969 – A.F.S. No. 847.

Royal Orchid. Single. Tube and extra long, wide spreading sepals white, tinted pale carmine. Corolla blend of orchid and blue shades, fading to deep wine with maturity. Large bell shaped flowers, very free, flaring with age. Growth natural trailer. Hodges – American – 1962 – A.F.S. No. 543.

Royal Pink. Double. Tube light pink with dark veins, sepals light pink topside, dark pink underneath. Corolla amaranth-pink. Large blooms, fairly free, no petaloids. Growth trailer. Soo Yun – American – 1974 – A.F.S. No. 1184.

Royal Purple. Semi-double. Short broad tube and upturned sepals, deep cerise; corolla rich purple, lighter at base, veined red. Flowers are large for semi-double, very free and early. Growth upright and bushy, suitable as bush, standard or pyramid. Lovely cultivar, but correct naming in doubt, confusion with Lord Roberts. Difficulty can be experienced in obtaining the true Royal Purple true to name. Lemoine – French – 1896.

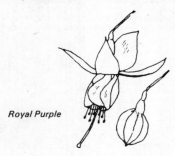

Royal Purple

Royal Robe. Double. Tube and sepals are almost white; corolla dark purple. Largish blooms, growth upright. Appears to be grown almost exclusively in California. Unregistered American cultivar. Fuchsia-La (Roy Walker) – American – 1957.

Royal Ruby. Double. Tube and sepals, claret; sepals held well back; corolla ruby-red. Medium size blooms, free but very late. Growth upright and bushy. Gadsby – British – 1968 – A.F.S. No. 972.

Royal Serenade. Double. Tube and sepals rosy-red with reflexing sepals. Corolla violet-red. Medium to small blooms but very free. Foliage yellowish-green with central veins and stems deep wine red. Growth upright, bushy and short jointed. Introduced by Wills Fuchsia Ltd. of West Wittering in 1980. Clyne – British – 1979.

Royal Sovereign. Semi-double. Tube and sepals crimson, underside spiraea-red; corolla creamy-white. Medium sized flowers and free. Growth upright and bushy. Gadsby – British – 1970 – A.F.S. No. 963.

Royal Standard. Single. Red and purple. Lye – British – Date unknown.

Royal Touch. Double. Tube and sepals rosy-pink; corolla royal-purple. Large blooms, free for size, growth trailer. Needs H1 conditions. Tiret – American – 1964 – A.F.S. No. 597.

Royalty. Single. Tube and sepals red, sepals open flat; corolla royal-blue. Medium sized flowers early and free, opens flat in saucer shape. Growth upright and bushy. Plummer – American – 1951.

Royal Velvet. Double. This cultivar at times becomes confused with Royal Purple; difference is that although the colouring is similar, Royal Velvet is comparatively new and a double of considerable size. Raised in California by Waltz in 1962 is an outstanding cultivar and probably the best double in its colour range. Large double ruffled corolla of luminous deep purple, splashed with crimson, is offset with tube and upturned sepals of crimson-red. As the flower matures, the petals flare open, displaying a contrasting crimson centre and colour changes to rosy-purple. The long crimson pistil adds to the beauty of this fuchsia, whilst the excellent foliage is of medium green. Growth is quite vigorous and upright; although grown mainly as a bush plant, will produce a good stiff standard. Needs regular pinching back; if left to its own devices will search for head room, needing the support of canes, but if kept bushy, is of the self-branching type, that will need little support. For maximum flowering, likes to be slightly pot bound and does better in its

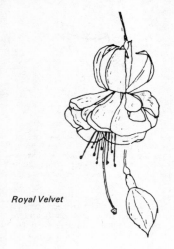

Royal Velvet

second or third year. Excellent cultivar for the showbench and excels with its classic bloom in the cut bloom classes. Best grown as H1 for perfection, but quite happy when grown as H2; performs well outside in the beds, preferring the semi-shade, where the full sun does not extract any of its rich colouring. Elegant beauty! Puts VooDoo in the shade. Waltz – American – 1962 – A.F.S. No. 526.

Royal Wedding. Single. White tube striped pink, sepals white tinged pink (R.H.S. 69B). Corolla ivory-white and as with all near whites best colour in shade. Medium sized flowers with bell shaped corolla and sepals shaped like outline of a pagoda. medium sized foliage, mid-green (R.H.S. 137B) ovate leaves, slightly serrated. Growth medium upright, self-branching and short noded with thick stems. Raised and tested for 3 years in the vicinity of Woodbridge, Suffolk. Introduced by Burgh Nurseries of Woodbridge, Suffolk in 1982. Norman Mitchinson seedling cross. Dunnett – British – 1982 – A.F.S. No. 1707.

Roy Joyce. Single. Tube and sepals, pure white; corolla light blue. Medium sized flowers, early and free. Light green foliage, growth low spreading bush. Haag – American – 1954.

Roy Walker. Double. Small to medium sized with white corolla, round shape and flaring. Sepals are reflexed, white tinged with the palest of pinks, very similar to Harry Gray – a very beautiful cultivar. Pedicel and white tube are short, corolla is fluffy with pink stamens and pistil and like all the 'near whites' the more shade afforded the whiter the flower. Blooms are clean and remain in good condition for a long period. Mid-green cordate foliage with medium sized leaves and very little serration, fairly short jointed with very clean appearance. Needs resting well during the winter, responding to hard pruning. When grown on the biennial method needs more heat than average to prevent leaf drop during the cold months, much better as a second and third year plant. Responds to frequent pinching to make a compact plant which requires 10 to 12 weeks from the last stop to full flower. A heat lover, likes a soil based compost in preference to a soil less one, where the high peat content tends to render the plant susceptible to botrytis, a fault with most 'whites' and pastel shaded cultivars. Growth is upright and bushy, very free flowering and given the correct growing conditions needs no support on staking. Likes warmth, shade and feed. Although raised and introduced in the 1970s was late in finding the exhibition benches but when it did so made a great impact and proved to be well within the exhibition class. Registered and introduced by Fuchsia La Nursery of California. Not difficult to locate being listed by at least twelve specialist fuchsia nurserymen. Walker-Fuchsia La – American – 1975 – A.F.S. No. 1265.

Rozell. Double. Long tube, pale pink, long sepals pink, turn right back. Corolla orchid-pink, streaked with coral. Largish blooms and free, some petals fold back. Growth natural trailer. Prentice – American – 1968 – A.F.S. No. 786.

Rubens. Single. Tube and sepals, scarlet-rose; corolla purple, medium sized flowers, quite free, late in flowering. Foliage description is the same as Autumnale. This cultivar is synonymous with both Burning Bush and Autumnale, the latter was introduced by Berkeley Horticultural Nurseries of America in 1930 and since been given its considered right name of Rubens. Meteor – Date unknown.

Rubeo. Semi-double. Tube and sepals, pale carmine; corolla rose-Bengal, marbled geranium-lake. Large flowers, fairly free, terrible bud and flower "dropper". Wrinkled foliage, growth upright and bushy. A.F.S. Cert. of Merit 1949. Titret – American – 1947.

Rubil. Synonymous with Rubin.

Rubin. Triphylla single. Long tube, cinnabar-red, short petals pale vermilion. Foliage very deep green, growth upright *F. boliviana* × *F. triphylla*. Vieweg – Germany – 1893.

Ruby Glow. Single. Tube and sepals red; corolla deep purple, maturing to rich ruby red with age, almost a self. Medium sized flowers and very free. Dark green foliage, growth is strong and slightly pendulous, height 2 to 2½ft, hardy in southern England, raised in the Scilly Isles. Tabraham – British – 1979.

Ruby Red. Single. Tube and sepals red; corolla dark red. Medium sized flowers almost a red self. Foliage has reddish cast. Growth lax upright can be made to trail. Little known cultivar which appears to be exclusive to California. Raiser and date unknown.

Ruby's Own. Single. Thin tube neyron-rose with slight rose madder stripe, slightly reflexed sepals neyron-rose at base, changing to cream towards the green tips, edges are rose madder. Corolla paper white with very slight neyron-rose veining. Bell shaped flowers, petals ⅞in × ¾in and slightly pleated inward, stamens and pistil spinel-pink. Light green foliage, leaves 2in × 1¼in wide with acuminate tips. Growth trailer, will make good basket with weights and is self-branching, whole plant possesses a very clean appearance. Tested for 2½ years in vicinity of Ramsgate, South East Coast of England, before release. Standen – British – 1981 – A.F.S. No. 1641.

Ruffled Petticoats. Double. Tube and short sepals, claret-rose; corolla white brushed claret-rose. Largish blooms, free, full and flared, giving ruffled appearance, no petaloids. Light green foliage, serrated leaves. Growth upright and bushy. Foster – American – 1974 – A.F.S. No. 1173.

Ruffles. Double. Short waxy tube, broad upturned, sepals deep pink; corolla deep violet, small outer petals, marbled pink. Large blooms, very free, ruffled and spreading with extra long stamens. Growth trailer. Erickson – American – 1960 – A.F.S. No. 451.

Rufus. Single. Bright turkey-red self. Medium sized flowers, extremely free, always in bloom. Growth upright and bushy, strong grower, excellent bedder. Incorrectly referred to as Rufus the Red. Easy cultivar, one for the beginner. Submitted by Chingford Nurseies for the R.H.S. Wisley Hardy Trials 1975–78 and received the Award of Merit. Nelson – American – 1952 – A.F.S. No. 177.

Rufus the Red. Synonymous with Rufus.

Runner. Single. Tube pale pink, sepals are upturned pale pink, lighter at tips. Corolla rose-pink, short and straight, prolific bloomer. Growth medium upright, bushy and short jointed. This cultivar was originally known as The Runner but

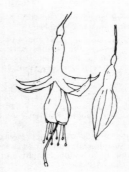

Rufus

the name was not accepted by the A.F.S. when registered. Barbara × seedling. Tolley – British – 1978.

Ruth. Single. Tube and sepals, rosy-red; corolla purplish-red. Medium sized flowers, free, growth upright and bushy, hardy. Accepted by the B.F.S. as showbench hardy. Submitted by the Jackman's Nurseries Ltd for R.H.S. Wisley Hardy Trials 1975–78 and received Award of Merit. Wood – British – 1949.

Ruthie. Double. Tube and short sepals, white, flushed pink on inside; corolla violet-blue, small outside petals fuchsia-pink. Medium sized blooms, very free, growth upright and bushy. Brand – American – 1951 – A.F.S. No. 88.

Ruth King. Double. Tube and sepals pink; corolla lilac and white. Large blooms and free, growth trailer. Tiret – American – 1967 – A.F.S. No. 736.

Rutland Water. Single. Rose-Bengal tube, sepals rose-Bengal tipped green as held horizontal. Corolla amethyst-violet, veined rose-Bengal. Medium sized flowers, very free flowering. Growth medium upright, will make good, compact bush. Named after the huge expanse of man-made water in the Midlands of England. Raised in the vicinity of Melton Mowbray and introduced by the raiser, R. and J. Pacey of Melton Mowbray, 1981. Pacey – British – 1981.

Ruy Blas. Double. Red and violet-blue. Lemoine – French – 1868.

Rydal Water. Single. Long thin tube, pale rose-opal; sepals very long, pale rose-opal above, soft rose underneath, tipped green, pointed and twisted. Corolla lilac-rose, edged deep lavender, silver at base of sepals. Large flowers and free, opens with petals overlapping and twisted to form wide funnel. Growth natural trailer, self-branching. Opalescent × Formosissima. Travis, J. – British – 1960 – A.F.S. No. 1145.

Sabina. Single. Thin tube, pale pink; sepals pale pink, tipped green, prostrate. Corolla pale magenta-pink. Medium sized flowers, free, semi-flared and shortish. Yellow-green foliage, pointed. Growth semi-trailer, better as second year plant. Tolley – British – 1971 – A.F.S. No. 1158.

Sacramento. Single. Self coloured waxy, light carmine; medium sized flowers, free, heat resistant, sepals recurve gracefully. Growth upright and bushy. Reiter – American – 1946.

Sadie Larson. Double. Tube and sepals, coral-rose, tipped white, sepals turn back. Corolla white, looks artificial, like paper. Dark green foliage. Growth trailer. Gagnon – American – 1966 – A.F.S. No. 659.

Sahara. Double. Tube and sepals pink; corolla dianthus-purple centre, with petal overlays of salmon-pink. Medium sized blooms, free and very compact. Growth upright. Kennett – American – 1966 – A.F.S. No. 679.

Saint Lucy. Double. Tube and sepals, bright red; corolla pink, flushed and veined cerise. Darkish green foliage. Growth upright and bushy. Austin – British – 1963.

Saint Teresa. Single. Tube and long sepals, pale pink; corolla pure white. Small flowers, free and graceful. Growth medium upright. Niederholzer – American – 1944.

salicifolia. Tube and sepals yellowish-green; no corolla. Very few flowers which are borne in the leaf axils. Epiphytic shrub. Hemsley – 1876 – Bolivia.

Sally. Double. White tube, sepals white on top, pale pink underneath. Corolla bright pale lavender. Medium sized blooms, free and very full. Growth trailer. Fuchsia Forest – American – 1967 – A.F.S. No. 725.

Sally Ann. Double. White tube, sepals white on top, pink underneath, tipped green, flair straight out. Corolla different shades of rose. Largish blooms and free, growth trailer. Pennisi – American – 1971 – A.F.S. No. 1012.

Sally Brass. The 'famous' yellow fuchsia which was seldom seen and died a very quick death. Double. Tube and sepals cream; corolla primrose. Jones, W. – British – 1963.

Salmon Butterfly. Single. Long tube and long sepals, creamy wax, flushed pink. Long corolla salmon. Medium sized flowers, very free, growth trailer. Raiser unknown – Date unknown.

Salmon Glow. Single. Long, thin pale salmon (R.H.S. 37B) tube, sepals salmon (R.H.S. 41D) tipped green, 1 in long and are held at right angles from tube. Corolla orange-salmon (R.H.S. 40C) shading to (R.H.S. 40D) at base. Medium-sized flowers with short overlapping petals, very clean appearance, a most welcome addition to the orange colour range, does not discolour with age, freely produced, long slender flowers. Light green foliage, growth self-branching lax bush type, will make good basket or bush. Tested for 6 years in vicinity of Derby before being introduced by Jackson's of Tamworth in 1978. Handley – British – 1978 – A.F.S. No. 1454.

Samantha Jane. Single. Pink tube, white sepals, corolla deep lavender. Medium sized flowers and free, growth upright and bushy. Curtis – British – 1974.

Sambo. Double. Tube and sepals red; corolla extremely dark reddish-blue, fading to wine colour with maturity. Largish blooms, early and free, long lasting. Growth lax bush or trailer. Gagnon – American – 1967 – A.F.S. No. 710.

Sampan. Double. Tube and sepals, rose-pink; corolla rosy-red. Largish blooms, fairly free. Growth lax bush or trailer. Tiret – American – 1965 – A.F.S. No. 651.

Sam Parker. Single. Tube and upturned sepals, cherry-red; corolla deep plum-purple with red shading at base of petals. Medium sized flowers, early and free. Growth upright and bushy. Raiser unknown – American – Date unknown.

Sampson's Delight. Semi-double. Tube carmine-pink, sepals carmine-pink on top and coral underneath, medium size which reflex back completely covering the tube. Corolla rose-red streaked with coral. Medium sized blooms slightly flared bell-shaped with deep garnet anthers. Large ovate foliage spinach green with purple madder veins. Growth tall, upright and bushy, will make good bush. Originates from the Seal Beach area of California. Introduced by Fuchsia-La Nursery, California, in 1980. Roy Walker × Orange Glory. Barrett – American – 1980 – A.F.S. No. 1571.

Samson. Double. Extremely long pink tube; wide outer sepals pink, deep rose inside. Corolla dark plum-purple fading to pink at base, pink veined. Large blooms and free, unusual for variegated foliage cultivar. Foliage variegated pale green and pale yellow, heat resistant. Growth cascade and vigorous. Peterson – Fuchsia Farms – American – 1957 – A.F.S. No. 287.

San Carlos. Single. Tube and sepals, rose-bengal; corolla amethyst-violet. Medium sized flowers, very early and very free. Growth upright. Niederholzer – American – 1946.

sanctae-rosae. Red tube, scarlet sepals; orange-scarlet corolla. Flowers are numerous and borne singly in the upper leaf axials. Small compact shrub with plenty of foliage. Synonymous with *F. boliviana* (Britton 1890) and *F. filipes.* Kuntze – 1898 – Bolivia and Peru.

Sandboy. Single. Short thin pink tube, sepals very deep pink, small, narrow, curl well back to tube. Corolla very dark mauve, flushed light mauve at base, fades slightly with age, small bell shaped. Smallish flowers, blooms prolifically. Growth upright and bushy, short-jointed, makes good house plant. Hall-Atkinson – British – 1967 – A.F.S. No. 1117.

San Diego. Double. Tube and sepals, pinkish-white; corolla rosy-red. Large blooms, fairly free for size. Growth trailer. Tiret – American – 1964 – A.F.S. No. 598.

Sandy. Double. White tube with pink veins, sepals light pink top, darker pink underneath, tipped green, very long and wide, curve and twist back to tube. Corolla white, no petaloids. Medium sized blooms free, dark green foliage, growth trailer. Soo Yun – American – 1974 – A.F.S. No. 1185.

San Francisco. Single. Very long tube, carmine-rose, long sepals carmine-rose; corolla geranium-lake. Very long flowers of the Mrs. Rundle type, free and largish. Growth vigorous cascade, very suitable for weeping standard or espalier. Robert Blatry × Mrs. Victor Reiter. Reiter (Sr) – American – 1941.

San Jacinto. Double. Tube and sepals, waxy shell-pink; corolla lilac, fading to lilac-pink. Large blooms, fairly free for size. Growth upright and bushy. Evans and Reeves – American – 1951 – A.F.S. No. 103.

San Jose. Double. Tube and sepals, rose-pink to rosy-red; corolla white. Very large blooms, free for size, colour depends upon exposure. Growth trailer. Sport of San Pablo. Erickson – American – 1955 – A.F.S. No. 409.

San Jose – Williamette. Reliable American sources quote these two cultivars, both sports from San Pablo, as being identical.

San Leandro. Double. Tube and sepals, dark carmine, corolla magenta shading to vermilion. Large blooms and free, very full, beautiful colouring. Growth upright and vigorous, makes a very large specimen plant. Brand – American – 1949.

San Luis Obispo. Double. Tube and wide sepals carmine; corolla light pink, red veined. Largish blooms, sepals open flat, petal edges are notched, free, blooms in flushes. Growth upright and bushy. Nelson – American – 1952 – A.F.S. No. 178.

San Mateo. Double. Tube and sepals, deep pink; corolla very dark violet with pink splashes. Very large blooms, free for size. Growth trailer, makes lovely weeping standard. Niederholzer – American – 1946.

San Pablo. Double. Tube and sepals, deep rose-pink; corolla pink and lilac. Very large blooms, free, long and flaring. Growth trailer. Sport of San Mateo. Crumley – American – 1948.

San Pedrian. Single. Rose coloured self; small flowers very free, borne in clusters. Growth upright and bushy. Fairclo – American – 1947.

San Rafael. Double. Tube and sepals carmine; corolla magenta shading to vermilion. Large blooms, fairly free, growth upright. Niederholzer – American – 1948.

Sanspareil. Single. White and purple. Youell – British – 1846.

Sanspareil. Single. Red and white. Smith – British – 1862.

Santa Barbara. Single. Tube and sepals waxy-white; corolla delicate shade of salmon-orange. Medium flowers, very free, have slight colour resemblance to Lye's Unique. Foliage resembles that of Amy Lye or Billy Green with tinge of purple in the centre of new growth, this cultivar from appearance could easily have been crossed with the Lye's family. Raiser unknown – American – Date unknown. There has been confusion over three other cultivars of the same name.
(a) Single. Tube and sepals pale pink; corolla rose pink. Medium sized flowers and free. Growth strong upright bush. Raiser unknown – American – Date unknown.
(b) Essig quotes a cultivar of a more orange-coloured Speciosa with indefinite local Californian name.
(c) Single, orange self listed in the 1970s by Fuchsialand Nurseries of Birmingham.

Santa Barbara – Lustre. See Lustre.

Santa Clara. Double. Short tube and white sepals, variegated rose; corolla very deep purple, fading to dark rose. Largish blooms, fairly free, box type corolla. Small foliage yellowish-green. Growth trailer. Pennisi – American – 1969 – A.F.S. No. 833.

Santa Claus. Double. Tube and sepals, bright red; corolla white, veined red. Small blooms, very free. Growth upright and bushy. Hazard and Hazard – American – Date unknown.

Santa Cruz. Semi-double to double. Tube and sepals, deep crimson; corolla dark crimson, almost a self. Largish blooms, free, lovely colouring with

little fading. Large foliage with red veining. Growth upright and bushy, good for standard, excellent for cut bloom classes. Submitted by Chingford Nurseries for R.H.S. Wisley Hardy Trials 1975–78 but received no award. Tiret – American – 1947.

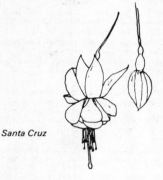

Santa Cruz

Santa Lucia. Double. Tube and broad spreading sepals, deep red; corolla orchid-pink, rose veined, outside petals overlaid salmon-rose. Large blooms, free for size open and round of 'powder puff' appearance. Growth upright. Munkner – American – 1956.

Santa Maria. Double. Tube and wide sepals, red with winged effect; corolla white with red veins, outer petals and petaloids, red. Large blooms and free, heat tolerant, growth upright and bushy. Nelson – American – 1953 – A.F.S. No. 179.

Santa Monica. Double. Tube and sepals, light red; corolla flesh-pink, streaked with cerise. Large blooms, free for size, very late. Dark green foliage, growth tall upright, bushy and vigorous. Rolla × Fascination. Evans and Reeves – American – 1935.

Saphir. Double. Cerise and purple. Rozain-Boucharlat – French – 1930.

Sapphire. Double. Short tube creamy-white, sepals flushed pink outside, clear pink inside. Corolla deep purplish-blue and wide frosty-pink sepals. Medium sized blooms, free, late bloomer, colour matures to rich deep shaded purplish-maroon. Small dark green foliage, growth upright and bushy. Waltz – American – 1954 – A.F.S. No. 203.

Sarah. Single. Tube and sepals flesh-pink; corolla carmine with slight mauvy sheen. Growth trailer. Curtis – British – 1971.

Sarah Bernhardt. Lemoine – French – 1899.

Sarah Churchill. Double. Tube and sepals medium rose; corolla pinkish-white with rose veining. Growth upright, an unregistered American cultivar, grown in California. Hybridiser unknown – American – *ca* 1950.

Sara Helen. Double. Tube and sepals white, turning pink; corolla Tyrian-purple. Large blooms, very full and fairly free, growth upright. Colville – British – 1969.

Sarah Gold. Single. Orange-red and scarlet. Stride – British – 1870.

Sarah Jane. Double. Rosy-pink tube, exceptionally short, sepals rosy-pink; corolla lilac, flushed deeper lilac at base. Small flowers, but extremely floriferous and of a beautiful little rosette shape, superb small double. Growth upright and bushy, good for bush training or pyramid type. Putley – British – 1974.

Sara Jane. Single. Tube and sepals rose-pink; corolla strawberry. Medium sized flowers. Growth trailer. Curtis – British – 1973.

Sarong. Double. Short tube and long twisting white sepals, flushed pink; corolla violet-purple. Large blooms, fairly free, large foliage. Growth lax bush or trailer. Kennett – American – 1963 – A.F.S. No. 593.

Satellite. Single. Tube and sepals white, tipped green; corolla dark red, fading to bright red with streaks of pure white on each petal. Large flowers for single, free, very unusual colouring. Growth upright, tall and vigorous. Kennett – American – 1965 – A.F.S. No. 642.

Satin's Folly. Single. Long tube and extremely long, silky sepals, maroon; corolla reddish-purple. Extra long flowers, free, resemble long red icicles, most unusual and colourful. Growth lax or trailer. Martin – American – 1962 – A.F.S. No. 520.

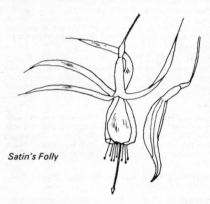

Satin's Folly

Saturnus. Single. Short red tube, red sepals rather long and stand erect as flowers mature. Corolla light purple with red veining, lighter at base changing to lilac on maturity. Smallish flower very free, light-red stamens and style. Growth upright and bushy. *F. regia* var. *typica* × Frau Henriette Ernst. De Groot – Dutch – 1970.

Saxondale. Semi-double. Long tube and short sepals, crimson; corolla amaranth-rose, veined rose-red. Small flowers, free bloomer, heat tolerant. Growth dwarf, upright bush, ideal for the rockery, suitable for miniature or bonsai training. Sister seedling of Sherwood. Trase × Lady Thumb. Gadsby – British – 1973 – A.F.S. No. 1125.

Scabieuse. Double. Red and purple. Rozain-Boucharlat – French – 1928.

scabriuscula. Bright red tube and sepals; corolla red. Flowers approximately an inch long borne solitary in upper leaf axils. Very low spreading shrub. Bentham – 1845 – Ecuador.

scandens (Krause 1905). Synonymous with *F. decussata.*

Scapino. Double. Tube and sepals, pale pink; corolla white. Medium sized blooms and free. Growth upright. Blackwell – British – 1966.

Scarcity. Single. Fairly short but tapering tube deep scarlet cerise, sepals slightly reflexed with a quaint little curl, colour the same as tube. Corolla purple, scarlet at base, fading to rosy purple and rather short. Stamens scarlet and short whereas style is fairly long and again scarlet in colour. Flowers are single and smallish to medium in size and very similar in shape and colouring to Gruss aus dem Bodethal, which in its self should make Scarcity worth growing, but is not such a dark purple in the corolla; very early and very free, can be in flower by the end of June. Excellent in every way; will respond to frequent pinching and presents no problems. The foliage is a nice medium green and slightly large for the size of the flower, the growth is upright, bushy and compact and as with most of Lye's introductions will make an excellent standard, and especially as a half standard. Proved to be hardy and performs well as an outside bedder, accepted by the B.F.S. as a showbench hardy; if you like singles and the best of the red and purples, this is a cultivar you cannot be without. This cultivar is one of Lye's best and now aptly named, seldom grown today, but still listed and obtainable from Bakers of Halstead and Chingford Nurseries. One of the good old cultivars and although red and purple, is a different red and purple. Raised by James Lye way back in 1869; what a pity this grand raiser did not record or hand down the parentage of his wonderful raisings, but would suggest or suspect it may have *F. magellanica* blood in its veins. Lye – British – 1869.

Scarlet Baby. Single. Tube and sepals, brilliant carmine; corolla deep purple-violet, carmine at base. Medium sized flowers, free, growth tall, upright and vigorous. *F.magellanica* var. *molinae* × . Niederholzer – American – 1941.

Scarletina. Single. Scarlet self. Rush – British – 1896.

Scarletina Reflexa. Single. Cerise and purple. Sheriff – British – 1847.

*Scarlet Ribbons. Single. Long thin tube scarlet red, fully reflexed sepals scarlet-red (R.H.S. 46A) with green recurved tips ⅞in long by ⅛in wide. Scarlet-red (R.H.S. 45A) corolla ½in by ¼in wide. Triphylla type flowers quarter flared, red filaments and white anthers, red style and white stigma, extremely floriferous with as many as 50 or more flowers per cluster, a very welcome addition to the triphylla type range. Extremely large foliage, yellowish-green (R.H.S. 145A) with cordate leaves 5½long by 3in wide, new growth is blush red, veins pale pink with green stems. Growth tall upright and will take varying conditions, cool or warm, cold weather, hardy to the mid 20°F in California, U.S.A. Raised in the vicinity of Oxnard, California, U.S.A. *F. boliviana* × Mary. Schneider – American – 1984 – A.F.S. No. 1757.

Schiller. Double. Tube and sepals, pale carmine; corolla bluish-purple. Medium sized blooms and fairly free, growth upright. Reiter – American – Date unknown.

Schiller. Single. Blush-white and purple. Banks – British – Date unknown.

Schnabel. Semi-double. Tube and sepals, salmon-orange; corolla orange. Largish flowers, very free, beautiful colouring. Large foliage, growth vigorous trailer. Antonelli – American – 1971 – A.F.S. No. 1007.

Schneeball. Semi-double. Tube and sepals, bright pink or pale red, according to exposure. Corolla white, veined pink or red. Small flowers, very free, ball shape. Light green foliage. Growth upright and bushy. Twrdy – German – 1874.

Schneekoppen. Semi-double. Tube and sepals, pale red; corolla white, flushed and veined pale red. Small flowers, very free, very similar to Snowcap. Growth upright and bushy. Twrdy – German – 1866.

Schneepyramide. Double. Red and white. Twrdy – German – 1870.

Schneewittchen. Single. Tube and sepals, deep pink; corolla purplish-pink. Small flowers, very free, similar to Brilliant. Growth upright and bushy, hardy in Southern districts. Name means 'Little Snow White'. Klein – German – 1878.

Schneewittcher. Single. Tube and sepals, rich waxy-red; corolla rich violet-blue. Medium sized flowers, very free, open and wide. Growth upright and bushy, hardy in Southern districts. Name not orthodox German and could be a doublet for Schneewittchen. Hoech – German – 1884.

Schönbrunner Schuljubiläum. Triphylla type single. Little known coral red and orange triphylla hybrid listed in German literature with long, largish flowers of a very brilliant red and remarkable substance. Rather a late flowerer and to counteract the stiff and lanky habit needs more pinching than other triphyllas. Raised in Austria and is a sister seedling to Präsident W. Morio. Introduced into Britain in 1984 by B. and H. M. Baker of Halstead, Essex, having been acquired from the President of the Dutch Society N. Aalhuizen in the summer of 1983. Koralle × *F. fulgens* var. *rubra grandiflora*. Nutzinger – Austrian – 1976.

*Schöne Landauerin. Semi-double. Tube and sepals red; corolla violet-blue. Growth is lax bush. Nutzinger – Austrian – 1965.

Schwabenland. Double. Tube and sepals white with red blush, sepals are bulbous, standing well out, deeper red blush underneath with green tips. Corolla blue-violet, colouring to red-purple. Fairly large blooms especially for a double with light pink stamens and style. Growth upright and bushy, this cultivar is grown in the Netherlands. Schmid – Germany – 1959.

Schwan. Single. Red and white. Twrdy – German – 1866.

Schweizer Gruss. No other details available except the parentage. Koralle × Golden Glow. Nutzingen – Austrian – 1973.

Scintillation. Single. Tube and sepals, dark rose; corolla Tyrian-rose with white centre. Largish flowers and free, serrated petals. Growth upright and bushy. Hazard and Hazard – American – Date unknown.

Scotch Heather. Double. Tube white, streaked with pink; sepals top side white, flushed pink underneath, tipped green, short, wide and flaring. Corolla hyacinth-blue to mallow-purple, slightly flared. Medium sized blooms and free, light green foliage. Growth upright and bushy. Foster – American – 1974 – A.F.S. No. 1174.

Scottie. Double. Tube and sepals, deep pink; corolla deep violet blue. Large blooms, fairly free, growth trailer. Brand – America – 1949.

Sea Foam. Semi-double. Tube and sepals white, flushed rose; corolla marbled petunia-purple, tinted rose. Small flowers, very free. Growth small, compact bush. Reiter – American – 1948.

Seaforth. Single. Short thick tube creamy wax; sepals slightly rose flush. Corolla lilac-pink, deepening towards edges. Large flowers, very floriferous. Growth upright and bushy. Need – British – 1964.

Sealand Prince. Single. Tube and long upturned sepals light red, corolla violet-purple fading to reddish-purple. Medium sized flowers, free. Growth upright and bushy, Hardy in the Southern districts. Received R.H.D.S. Award of Merit in 1965 for hardiness; resubmitted by Chingford Nurseries in Wisley Hardy Trials 1975–78 but received no further award. Walker-Bees Nurseries – British – 1967.

Sea Shell. Double. Tube and fully reflexed sepals, whitish-pink; corolla pink, veined deeper pink. Large blooms, very free, dark green foliage. Growth upright and bushy. Evans – American – 1954.

Sea Sprite. Double. Tube and long spreading sepals, white; corolla pale violet-blue. Largish blooms and free, petals mould into globular mass, inner base of blue petals fading to deep rose. Growth upright and strong. Reiter – American – 1955 – A.F.S. No. 229.

Sebastopol. Double. Short tube and long sepals, white and pink; corolla white variegated in pale pink. Largish blooms, free for size. Growth trailer. Pennisi – American – 1968 – A.F.S. No. 755.

Sebastopol Belle. Single. White tube with tinge of green, red veins; sepals long, white, tipped green. Corolla light purple to very light purple at base. Large flowers for single and very free, growth lax bush or trailer. Soo Yun – American – 1967 – A.F.S. No. 732.

seleriana (Loesener 1913). Synonymous with *F. tetradactyla.*

Seneca. Double. Tube and sepals, dark turkey-red; corolla pansy-violet, splashed phlox-pink. Largish blooms, fairly free, growth stiff, upright and very vigorous. Lee – American – 1948.

Senorita. This is the name under which *F. magellanica* var. *gracilis* is known and sold in the west coast State of Washington, U.S.A.

Sensation. Single. Carmine and rose pink. Bull – British – 1882.

Sensation. Single. Tube and long, narrow sepals, shiny pink outside, medium pink underneath, tipped pale green. Corolla deep violet-blue. Huge flowers, fairly free, petals slightly waved, sepals measuring over 5 in across. Growth trailer. Munkner – American – 1962 – A.F.S. No. 545.

Sentinel. Double. Tube and sepals cerise; corolla lavender-blue. Large flowers, fairly free, growth semi-trailer. Lampard – British – 1970.

September Morn. Double. Rose-madder self. Sepals are broad, thick and recurving. Large blooms and free, growth trailer. Hodges – American – 1953 – A.F.S. No. 158.

Sequoia. Double. Tube and sepals red; corolla light lavender with pinkish cast. Large blooms and free. Growth upright and bushy. Sport of Honeymoon. Pape – American – 1948.

Seraphine. Single. Tube and sepals, phlox-pink; corolla cyclamen-purple, flushed white. Large flowers, wide, open and free. Growth upright and bushy. Niederholzer – American – 1941.

Serena. Single. Tube and sepals, cherry-red; corolla lightish purple, streaked with dull orange. Largish flowers and free, growth upright and bushy. Whiteman – British – 1944.

Serenade. Single. Tube and sepals, waxy shell-pink; corolla clear cerise. Flowers large for single, free blooming, heat tolerant and early. Growth upright and vigorous. Evans and Reeves – American – 1951 – A.F.S. No. 101.

Serendipity. Single to semi-double. Pale pink tube, sepals pink both sides, tipped green, fold back. Corolla lavender-pink, merthiolate-pink edge on petals, fading to brighter pink. Large flowers and free, petaloids vary, sometimes inside, other times outside, often form rosette. Coarse foliage with serrated edges, heart shaped. Growth trailer. Sister seedling of Circus. Castro – American – 1973 – A.F.S. No. 1105.

Serervine. Double. Pale cerise and white. Lemoine – French – 1911.

serratifolia (Hook 1845). Synonymous with *F. austromontana.*

serratifolia (Ruiz and Pavón). Synonymous with *F. denticulata.*

sessilifolia. Scarlet tube, sepals greenish-red; corolla scarlet. Flowers produced quite freely are approximately an inch long and borne in clusters at the end of pendant laterals. Upright shrub, making small trees in natural habitat. Bentham – 1845 – Columbia.

Seventeen. Double. Rose-madder to pink self, medium sized blooms and free. Small leathery foliage. Growth upright bush, at the time of introduction considered to be the best pink and still good. Reiter – American – 1947.

Seventh Heaven. Double. Short thick tube greenish-white with green streaks, long broad curving sepals white shading to pink as bloom matures. Corolla orange-red shading to orange and white at base of petals. Large blooms and free for size, best colour develops in filtered sun and warm climate. Medium foliage, leaves with red veins 2¾ in long × 2 in ovate with ovate base, obtuse tip and serrated margin. Growth trailer, will make basket with weights. Tested for 4 years in vicinity of Fort Bragg, Oxnard and Oceanside, California, before release and will be trademarked in California. Stubbs – American – 1981 – A.F.S. No. 1620.

Severn Queen. Single. Thin very pale pink tube, sepals very pale pink of medium size and not upturned. Corolla rose-Bengal (H.C.C. 25/1). Medium-sized flowers are semi-flared and very free flowering. Oval foliage. Scheele's green (H.C.C. 860/2. Growth tall upright and bushy, very short jointed, best in bush form. Tested for 3 years in the Birmingham area before being introduced and registered by Fuchsiavale Nurseries in 1978. Barbara × .Tolley – British – 1978 – A.F.S. No. 1456.

Shades of Space. Double. White tube, tinged with red and red veins, sepals white on top, light pink underneath. Corolla light purple, fading to old rose. Large blooms, free for size, requires shade. Growth lax bush or trailer. Soo Yun – American – 1967 – A.F.S. No. 730.

Shady Blue. Single. Short broad tube and wide sepals, carmine-rose; corolla shades from bluebird blue at edges to spectrum-violet on to carmine. Largish flowers and free, prefers shade, large foliage. Growth upright. Gadsby – British – 1970 – A.F.S. No. 880.

Shady Lady. Double. Tube pink, broad sepals, pink, creped on undersides. Corolla white, very large blooms, fairly free, very full with slightly serrated petals. Growth upright. Stubbs – American – 1970 – A.F.S. No. 901.

Shady Lane. Double. Tube and long, broad, recurved sepals, clear coral-pink, tipped green. Corolla lilac-blue, splashed with coral-pink. Large blooms, flaring with overlapping petals, exceptional lasting qualities in blooms, fade slowly to pleasing shade of lilac-rose. Growing trailer with graceful willowy branches. Waltz – American – 1959 – A.F.S. No. 393.

Shalimar. Double. White tube, sepals white on outside, palest pink blush underneath. Corolla dense pale lavender-blue, marbled with rose. Huge blooms, fairly free, globular shape. Growth lax bush, very heavy blooms need support. Schnabel-Paskesen – American – 1959 – A.F.S. No. 380.

Shangri-La. Double. Tube and sepals, dark pink to red; corolla pale pink to white, heavy pink veining. Very large blooms, free for size, growth lax bush or trailer. Martin – American – 1963 – A.F.S. No. 573.

Shanley. Single. Tube and sepals, bright orange, corolla slightly deeper orange, almost a self. Medium to large flowers, very free, extremely good orange with little fading. Growth upright and bushy. Mrs. Shutt (Jnr) – American – 1968.

Sharon. Semi-double. Tube and sepals, palest scarlet; corolla rose-bengal, splashed geranium-lake. Medium sized flowers and free, growth semi-trailer. Tiret – American – 1948.

*Sharon Allsop. Double. Tube and sepals carmine, corolla white. Medium sized blooms, well shaped and free flowering for a double. Growth upright, bushy very compact and short-jointed, makes an exceptionally good pot plant. Raised and introduced by R. and J. Pacey of Melton Mowbray, Leicestershire, in 1983. Pacey – British – 1983.

Sharpitor. Single. Tube and sepals pale mauve, corolla pale. Very small flowers but extremely free. The outstanding feature of this cultivar is the small variegated foliage and flowers very similar to those of *F. magellanica* var. *molinae* (*alba*) and Mrs. W.P. Wood. The foliage is an attractive cream and pale green which greatly impressed the B.F.S. Sub Committee for Hardy Cultivars; could be a welcome addition to the ornamentals. Submitted to the R.H.S. 1976 Hardy Trials for 3 years by the National Trust establishment at Sharpitor, hence the name. Received Highly Commended Certificate at R.H.S. Wisley Hardy Trials 1975–78. National Trust – British – *ca* 1974.

Shasta. Semi-double to double. Tube and sepals, pale pink to white edges; corolla white with touches of pink on petaloids. Large blooms and free, growth lax bush or trailer. Kennett – American – 1964 – A.F.S. No. 614.

Shawnee. Double. Tube and sepals, rosy-red; corolla rosy-red and white. Large blooms and free, growth trailer. Tiret – American – 1971 – A.F.S. No. 994.

Sheila. Double. Pink tube, sepals deep pink, crepe on underside, topside shiny pink. Corolla lavender, veined pink with pink outer petals. Large blooms, free for size, dark green foliage. Growth upright and bushy. Francesca – American – 1973 – A.F.S. No. 1091.

Sheila Montalbetti. Single. Tube and sepals claret-rose (H.C.C. 021); sepals held horizontally. Corolla Venetian-pink (H.C.C. 420/2) with pink veining. Medium sized flowers and very free. Growth strong, vigorous and bushy, excellent cultivar for the outside border, growth 12 in to 15 in. Snowcap × Ice Cap. Roe – British – 1980.

Sheila Orr. Semi-double. Tube and sepals rhodamine-pink (H.C.C. 025), sepals held horizontally, short tube. Corolla amethyst-violet (H.C.C. 635/3). Medium sized flowers and very free. Growth strong, vigorous and bushy, excels as outside border cultivar, growth 12 in to 15 in height. Susan Ford × Neil Clyne. Roe – British – 1980.

Sheila White. Single. Tube and sepals, pale cerise; corolla purple, streaked and veined cerise. Medium sized flowers and free, growth upright and bushy. Thorne – British – 1959.

Shell Beach. Semi-double. Tube and sepals, clear pink; corolla shell-pink. Smallish flowers very free, dainty and cone-shaped, petals have serrated edges. Growth upright and bushy. Nelson – American – 1956 – A.F.S. No. 263.

Shelley Lyn. Double. Tube and sepals, clear white; corolla clear deep-lilac. Largish blooms and free, growth trailer. Tiret – American – 1968 – A.F.S. No. 795.

Shelley Renee. Double. Short tube pale pink, sepals pale pink; corolla lavender-blue, turning to dark rose-pink. Large blooms with long pink buds, very free. Dark green foliage with serrated edges. Growth lax bush or trailer. Prentice – American – 1971 – A.F.S. No. 990.

Shell Pink. Tube and sepals pink; corolla pale blue quickly changing to shell-pink. Medium sized flowers, very free flowering. Growth upright and bushy, spreading but dainty habit, medium height 1½ to 2 ft. Hardy in Southern England, raised in the Scilly Isles. Tabraham – British – 1975.

Sherwood. Single. Short tube and sepals, carmine; corolla neyron-rose with carmine veins. Small flowers, very free and very early, sister seedling of Saxondale. Small foliage, growth dwarf bush, very suitable for the rockery or training as miniature or bonsai. Trase × Lady Thumb. Gadsby – British – 1973 – A.F.S. No. 1126.

Sheryl Ann. Double. Red tube, very thick bright red sepals; corolla white, centre of each petal flushed red with red veining. Large blooms, very free, full with little fading, very similar to Swingtime, but even larger. Growth upright and vigorous, excellent cultivar – Peterson – American – 1958 – A.F.S. No. 331.

* Shirley. Single. Tube and sepals waxy crimson, corolla cardinal red. Medium sized flowers and very free flowering. Best described as a larger version of Flash. Foliage light green and can be variegated when grown under glass. Tested for 7 years and proved to be hardy in the vicinity of Weybourne, Norfolk. Introduced by Kerrielyn Fuchsias of Cambridge in 1984. Dawson, H. – British – 1984.

Shirley Savage. Single. Thin crimson tube, horizontally held crimson (R.H.S. 52A) sepals are short and wide. Corolla violet (R.H.S. 83B), veined neyron-rose (R.H.S. 55A). Small compact flowers, very free flowering. Small foliage lightish green (R.H.S. 137D). Growth medium upright, will make good bush, standard or decorative, self-branching. Will take full sun in vicinity of Worthing, South Coast of England, where it was tested for 2 years before release. Hobbs, L. – British – 1981 – A.F.S. No. 1646.

Shirley Thompson. Double. Tube and sepals red, corolla white, flushed pink. Large blooms and very free for size of double. Growth upright and bushy, will make good bush. Raised in the vicinity of Banstead, Surrey, before release. Introduced by High Trees Nurseries of Reigate, Surrey, 1981. Hobson – British – 1981.

Shocking Pink. Double. Tube and sepals, pink with darker stripe from base to tip; corolla bright pink, almost a self. Medium sized blooms and very free, growth upright, compact and bushy. Nelson – American – 1958.

Shooting Star. Semi-double. Tube and sepals, salmon-red; corolla purple centre, outer petals purple to salmon-red. Medium sized star-shaped flowers, very free and of striking colour. Growth lax bush or trailer. Martin – American – 1965 – A.F.S. No. 631.

Shooting Star. Double. Cream tube, sepals pale rose; corolla magenta-rose with petaloids of brighter shade. Large blooms and free for size, growth upright and bushy. Baker – British – 1970.

Shot Silk. Double. Tube and sepals red-pink; corolla shot silk. Large flowers and large foliage. Growth upright and bushy. Raiser unknown – Date unknown.

Shot Silk. Double. Short, pink tube, sepals cream, tipped green, pink at base of tube, broad. Corolla is a fusion of pink and blue creating as its name implies, shot silk effect. Although raised in 1964 was not released or introduced until 1978. Pink Galore × Deepdale. Thornley – British – 1964 – A.F.S. No. 1506.

Showboat. Double. Tube and sepals, light rose; corolla blended and marbled with shades of rose and hyacinth-blue. Large blooms, fairly free, compact and full, growth trailer. Walker and Jones – American – 1950.

Showers of Stars. Double. Red and purple. Cannell – British – 1900.

Show Girl. Semi-double to double. Tube and sepals, white with tinges of pink; corolla delicate light pink. Large blooms, free for size, growth trailer. Kennett – American – 1967 – A.F.S. No. 742.

Show Off. Single. Tube and sepals, rose-pink; corolla deeper pink, almost a self. Large flowers for a single, very free, flat and saucer shape, very similar in colour and shape as Display, but almost twice as large. Growth upright and bushy. Hodges – American – 1957 – A.F.S. No. 299.

Shuna. Single. Tube warm pink; sepals broad and short, warm mid-pink. Corolla warm mid-pink, compact, spreading very slightly with age. Smallish flowers, very free. Foliage deep green, dull not glossy. Growth upright and bushy, good for any tall type of training. Sport of Countess of Aberdeen. Travis, J. – British – 1973 – A.F.S. No. 1146.

Shuna Lindsay. Single. Thick red (R.H.S. 52A) tube, narrow sepals red (R.H.S. 51B) at base, green tipped (R.H.S. 138). Corolla orange-red (R.H.S. 32A), slightly recurving. Foliage dark green, growth small upright (2 ft) will make good bush or decorative. Heat tolerant if shaded where best colour develops. Cultivar can best be described as a dwarf *F. denticulata*. Originates from the vicinity of Preston, Lancashire. Travis, J. – British – 1980 – A.F.S. No. 1585.

Shy Lady. Double. Short tube, broad pointed upturned sepals, ivory white. Corolla creamy-ivory, opens into symmetrical formal bloom, as it matures, its numerous petals turn to entirely new delicate shade of pale peach. Medium sized blooms, free, extremely lovely pastel colouring, dainty, yet full and of rose-like shape. Dark green foliage, growth upright and bushy, well in the showclass category, needs little pinching, best colouring under glass as H1. Raiser could not have found a better name. Waltz – American – 1955 – A.F.S. No. 227.

Shy Lady

Shy Look. Single. Short thick tube rose; sepals crimson, almost horizontal. Corolla roseine-purple, paler at base, medium sized flowers, very free, held upright inherited from its parent, open, heat tolerant if shaded. Growth upright and bushy, short jointed. Upward Look × .Gadsby – British – 1972 – A.F.S. No. 1069.

Siboney. Double. Waxy tube and broad recurved sepals, soft pink; corolla blue-violet with centre petals longer, outer petals marbled phlox-pink. Large blooms, free for size, good colour contrast. Growth trailer. Erickson – American – 1963 – A.F.S. No. 581.

Side Show. Double. Tube and broad upturned sepals, deepest red; corolla white with palest pink undertone, veined rosy-pink. Large fluffy blooms, very free and long lasting. Deep green foliage, growth trailer. Erickson – American – 1957 – A.F.S. No. 324.

Sierra Blue. Double. Short tube white, sepals white, flushed inside with palest pink; corolla silvery-blue. Large blooms, gradually fading to soft lilac, free for size. Growth trailer. Waltz – American – 1957 – A.F.S. No. 313.

Signora. Single. Rose-white and violet. Banks – British – 1862.

Silverado. Double. Tube and broad recurved sepals, creamy-white flushed pink; corolla silvery pink with lavender undertone of slightly deeper shade at base of tube. Large blooms, well formed and full to centre, fairly free. Large green foliage, growth lax bush or trailer. This cultivar was formerly Cinderella. Waltz – American – 1956 – A.F.S. No. 270.

Silverbell. Single. Short tube and sepals, bright pink; corolla silvery-orchid. Very small flowers but profuse, very light green foliage. Growth tall, upright and vigorous, up to several feet in California. Evans and Reeves – American – 1942.

Silver Blue. Double. Short waxy tube and broad white sepals, rose-pink at base, tipped green; corolla soft silvery-blue, paler toward centre, near white at very base of petals. Large blooms, fairly free, very full, deep green foliage. Growth upright bush. Hodges – American – 1957 – A.F.S. No. 298.

Silverdale. Single. Short ivory tube, long sepals for small flower, eau-de-nil, flushed very soft pink, tipped green. Corolla pastel lavender. Small flowers, very free, compact barrel shape. Small pale green foliage, growth upright and bushy, hardy, will take sun but best colour in shade. Accepted by the B.F.S. as showbench hardy. Sister seedling of Hawkshead, *F.magellanica* var. *molinae* × Venus Victrix. Travis, J. – British – 1962 – A.F.S. No. 1147.

* Silver Dawn. Double. Long white tube, long white sepals, broad and heavily tipped green. Corolla beautiful shade of aster-violet, shading to rhodanite–red at base of petals with the whole corolla passing to imperial-purple with maturity. Large blooms and quite free for size, very attractive. Growth upright, compact bush. Raised in the vicinity of Bardney, Lincolnshire, and introduced by R. and J. Pacey of Melton Mowbray, Leicestershire, in 1983. Bellamy – British – 1983.

* Silver Dollar. Single. Tube, sepals and corolla are white, as near white as any so called white cultivar. Medium sized flowers with rolled petals which hold their shape, needs shade for the white intenseness. Growth upright, bushy and self-branching. Raised in the vicinity of Carlisle, Cumbria, and the only new introduction in 1985 by Fuchsiavale Nurseries of Kidderminster. Mitchinson – British – 1985.

Silver Jubilee. Double. Short tube, rhodonite-red (R.H.S. 51A), sepals rhodonite-red (R.H.S. 51A), paling to green tips, underside claret-rose (R.H.S. 50C), broad, short, very reflexed. Corolla white, veined in centre, neyron-rose (R.H.S. 55C). Medium to large blooms, very full with almost round short petals, rosette type, petaloids same colour as petals, claret-rose (R.H.S. 50C) stamens. Light green foliage with yellow cast, red stems. Growth medium upright, bushy, named to commemorate the Manchester Silver Jubilee Show 1975. Hobbs, N. – British – 1976 – A.F.S. No. 1381.

Silver King. Single. Long thin red tube (R.H.S. 50B), red sepals (R.H.S. 50B) 1$\frac{7}{10}$ in long by $\frac{1}{2}$ in

272

wide are held horizontal. Corolla white, veined rose-red (R.H.S. 50B). Very large flowers with cylindrical corolla, petals $1\frac{1}{2}$in long by $1\frac{1}{4}$in wide, very long red (R.H.S. 54B) pistil $3\frac{1}{2}$in long, stramens same colour $2\frac{1}{2}$in long. Overall dimensions of flower 4 $\frac{1}{2}$in long by $2\frac{1}{2}$in wide. Dark green foliage (R.H.S. 137C) leaves $2\frac{1}{2}$in long by $1\frac{1}{2}$in deeply veined and serrated except for the first 4 in. Growth lax upright, will make all tall types of training and basket with weights. Raised and tested for 12 years in the vicinity of Newcastle, Northumberland. Hall – British – 1982 – A.F.S. No. 1668.

Silver Pink. Single. Tube and sepals deep pink; corolla silver-pink. Medium-sized flowers and very free. Growth upright and bushy. Hardy in Southern England, raised in the Scilly Isles. Tabraham – British – 1978.

Silver Queen. Semi-double. Tube and sepals, deep rose; corolla silver-blue. Medium sized flowers, early and very free, growth dwarf upright and bushy. Haag and Son – American – 1953.

Silver Slipper. Double. Tube and long, narrow upcurved sepals, soft pink, deeper pink at base of sepals. Corolla white, slightly veined light pink near petal base. Largish blooms, very free, very long buds. Deep green foliage, growth trailer. Hodges – American – 1957 – A.F.S. No. 301.

Silver Wings. Double. Short magenta tube $\frac{1}{4}$in wide × $\frac{3}{8}$in long, sepals magenta (H.C.C. 27) $\frac{3}{4}$in wide × $1\frac{1}{4}$in long. Corolla rose-purple (H.C.C. 533), long blooms with rose-purple petaloids on every petal 1 in long, pink pistil $2\frac{1}{2}$in long. Medium green foliage with red centre veins, leaves $2\frac{1}{4}$in long × $1\frac{3}{8}$in wide. Growth natural trailer without weights. Will make good basket, but colour develops in shade. Originates from the Sebastopol area of California. Soo Yun Field – American – 1980 – A.F.S. No. 1563.

Silvia. Double. Tube and thick sepals, light rose; corolla pure white. Medium sized blooms, free, growth upright and bushy, strong. Schnabel – American – 1951 – A.F.S. No. 79.

Simon Side. Single. Short, red (R.H.S. 63A) tube, short horizontally held sepals are white with greenish tips. Corolla ruby-red (R.H.S. 64A). Compact, tube-like flowers, best colour in shade. Foliage is woodpecker green (R.H.S. 47A). Growth upright, medium bush or shrub, self-branching. Tested in Northumberland for 2 years before release. Pink Lady × Coxeen. Ryle – British – 1977 – A.F.S. No. 1437.

simplicicaulis. Tube purplish-red, sepals red; corolla purplish-red. Flowers are long $2\frac{1}{2}$ to 3 in in length, borne in clusters at the end of dropping shoots. Long, linear lanceolate leaves. Tall upright shrub reaching 12 to 15 ft in native Peru. Ruiz and Pavón – 1802 – Peru.

Sincerely. Double. White tube and sepals; corolla clear white with small, delicate touches of pink on outer petals. Medium sized blooms, free, good substance, growth trailer. Kennett – American – 1961 – A.F.S. No. 476.

Sincerity. Double. Tube and sepals, waxy-white; corolla of the same colour, under some conditions this cultivar may be creamy. Medium sized blooms and very free, hold colour outside. Growth upright and bushy. Holmes, E. – British – 1968.

Siobhan. Semi-double. Rose (R.H.S. 65C) tube, horizontally held sepals, white shaded at base with rose (R.H.S. 65C) and underneath with rose. White corolla has slight tinge of pink at base. Medium sized flowers with neatly curled petals, stamens (R.H.S. 72C) and long pink pistil held well clear, well proportioned white and rose, attractive. Growth medium upright, bushy. Introduced by Jackson's Nurseries of Tamworth in 1979. Joe Kusber × Northumbrian Belle. Rye – British – 1976 – A.F.S. No. 1403.

siphonantha (Krause). Synonymous with *F. leptopoda.*

***Sir Alfred Ramsey.** Single. Empire-rose tube (R.H.S. 50D) $\frac{1}{4}$in long by $\frac{1}{2}$in wide; sepals neyron-rose (R.H.S. 55B) with recurved tips, turning partly up maturity $1\frac{1}{4}$in long by $\frac{1}{2}$in wide. Corolla opens violet-purple (R.H.S. 77A) maturing to Tyrian-red (R.H.S. 61B). Large flowers quarter flared and bell shaped, corolla $\frac{3}{4}$in long by $\frac{3}{4}$in wide, unusual colouring, neyron-rose filaments, magenta-rose anthers, empire-rose style and white stigma, blunt shaped buds. Pale green foliage (R.H.S. 145A) with large ovate leaves $3\frac{1}{4}$in long by $1\frac{1}{2}$in wide. Growth self-branching tall upright, very strong grower needs ample fertiliser, good for all tall types of training, especially standard or pyramid, prefers cool conditions, well in the showbench category. Named after the famous World Cup football personality and President of East Anglian Fuchsia Society. Raised in the vicinity of Ipswich, Suffolk, and introduced by the raiser, Gouldings Fuchsias of Suffolk, in 1984. Goulding – British – 1984 – A.F.S. No. 1784.

Sir Colin Campbell. Double. Crimson and purple. Wheeler – British – 1858.

Siren. Double. Tube and sepals, deep cloud; sepals curl right back; corolla violet with red veins. Large blooms and free, growth upright and bushy. Baker – British – 1970.

Siren. Double. White tube, sepals white, tipped green, curl up. Corolla light lavender-blue with heavy white overlay of petals and petaloids, matures to darker purple-lavender. Large blooms, fairly free for size, open tight and flare with maturity. Glossy green foliage topside, growth trailer. Kennett-Castro – American – 1973 – A.F.S. No. 1109.

Sir Garnet Wolseley. Single. Red and dark purple. Williams – British – 1874.

Sir George McKenzie. Single. Pink and vermilion. Youell – British – 1846.

Sir Robert Peel. Semi-double. Rose and cerise. Bull – British – 1845.

Sissy Sue. Semi-double. Tube and sepals, peachy-pink; corolla pale blue, fades to lavender. Medium sized blooms, fairly free, petaloids peach-pink beautiful colouring. Growth trailer. Fuchsia Forest – American – 1965 – A.F.S. No. 626.

Sister Esther. Double. Tube and sepals, light pink; corolla amethyst-violet, fading to petunia-purple. Large blooms, free for size, unusual foliage with growth which curves to the left, encircling basket or container. Growth trailer. Machado – American – 1960 – A.F.S. No. 449.

Sister Ginny. Semi-double. Tube light pink with dark pink veins; sepals light pink topside, darker pink underneath, light green, curling tips. Corolla campanula-violet to light fuchsia-purple.

Medium sized flowers, free, with no petaloids. Dark green foliage, leaves narrowing to a point. Growth trailer. Soo Yun – American – 1974 – A.F.S. No. 1186.

Skinny. Single. Tube and sepals, rose-red; corolla violet-purple. Small flowers, very free, growth trailer. York – American – 1952 – A.F.S. No. 139.

skutchiana. White tube, sepals pink, white at base; corolla pinkish-white, red in age. Tiny flowers, similar to *F. tacanensis* except for variation in colour and foliage, has more hairy appearance. Minute flowers, member of the Breviflorae (Encliandra) section. Upright shrub to a height of 12 ft. Munz – 1943 – Guatemala.

Skylark. Single. Short white tube, very long tapering sepals, reflexing, white on topside, pink underneath. Corolla violet-blue. Large flowers, free for size, square size when bud opens, retains the form as petals elongate. Dark green serrated foliage, growth trailer. Probably the largest single 'blue' trailer. A.F.S. Cert of Merit. Kennett and Ross – American – 1956 – A.F.S. No. 259.

Skyway. Single. Tube and sepals, rhodamine-pink; corolla hyacinth-blue edged blue-bird blue, inside wisteria-blue. Medium sized flowers, very free, distinct red stamens, prefers shade. Growth upright and bushy. Gadsby – British – 1970 – A.F.S. No. 965.

Sleepy. Single. Tube and sepals pale pink; corolla lavender-blue, fading to pink. Small flowers but continuous, pale green foliage. Growth upright and bushy, dwarf habit only 9 to 15 in high. Hardy in Southern England, raised in the Scilly Isles. Submitted for R.H.S. Wisley Hardy Trials 1975–78 but received no award. Tabraham – British – 1954.

Sleigh Bells. Single. An all white beautiful flower. Long slim white tube, long thin pointed, upturned white sepals, slightly tipped green. White corolla forms itself into a perfect bell. Foliage rather small, long pointed leaves. Growth upright and bushy, ideal for standard, espalier or pyramid. Clem Schnabel of San Francisco, California, the raiser of this outstanding cultivar once

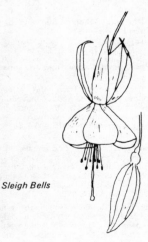

Sleigh Bells

wrote of his introduction 'Mrs. Susie Waltz named Sleigh Bells for me and everybody grows it better than I do. Mark MacDougall grew it through the roof of his lath house, Ted Paskesen gets it up to eight feet tall. Mine is barely two feet high and I have seen it as an espalier and a standard that were breathtaking. Sleigh Bells is a disguised "orange" on which a white corolla has been superimposed and as such is very sensitive to any frost, needs pruning with care or the plant will not come back the following year satisfactorily.' This is a very lovely cultivar and should be grown more, like all whites is rather susceptible to botrytis, needs plenty of ventilation and grown cool, the growth is extremely upright and suitable for training to tall types of cultivation and contrary to the raiser's remarks about hardiness, he did grow this cultivar for many years in the garden border withstanding some winters. One of the first single whites from America, better than La Bianca. A.F.S. Cert. of Merit. Schnabel – American – 1954 – A.F.S. No. 196.

Slender Lady. Single. Tube and long pointed sepals, waxy-white flushed pink. Corolla violet-purple, fading to fuchsia-purple. Large slender flowers, very free, prefers partial shade. Bright green foliage, growth medium upright bush. Gadsby – British – 1970 – A.F.S. No. 879

Smiles. Semi-double. Tube and upturned sepals, brilliant red; corolla light pink, heavily veined carmine. Medium sized flowers, free, unusual arrangement of long and short petals, somewhat resembling an Abutilon flower in form. Dark green foliage. Growth trailer. Hodges – American – 1958 – A.F.S. No. 343.

smithii. Pinkish red tube, to purplish red. Sepals light to deep red; corolla dark red, medium sized flowers. Upright shrub. Munz – 1943 – Columbia and Venezuela.

Smithii. See *magellanica* var. *globosa.*

Snappy. Single. Tube and sepals, turkey-red; corolla heliotrope. Small to medium sized flowers, very free, growth upright and vigorous. Niederholzer – American – 1946.

Sneezy. Single. Tube and sepals red; corolla deep blue-purple. Small flowers and very free, light green foliage. Growth upright and bushy, dainty but branching habit, dwarfish, only 9 to 15 in high. Hardy in Southern England, raised in the Scilly Isles. Tabraham – British – 1974.

Snooks. Semi-double. Tube and sepals, deep pink; corolla white with light pink shadings. Very small flowers, very floriferous and compact. Growth upright, compact and bushy. Whitemost × . Edwards – American – 1957 – A.F.S. No. 402.

Snowball. Double. White tube, long white reflexed sepals, flushed pink at base of sepals and tube; corolla creamy-white. Large blooms, free for size, very large foliage. Growth vigorous upright, needs H1 conditions. Reiter – American – 1952 – A.F.S. No. 127.

Snow Bunny. Double. Waxy-white tube, broad upturned white sepals, rose edging at base of sepals. Corolla creamy-white with faintest pink flush, particularly near base of shorter outer petals. Medium sized blooms, fully globular, very free. Small light green foliage, growth trailer. Hodges – American – 1957 – A.F.S. No. 302.

* Snow Burner. Double. Tube and sepals bright red. Corolla white with red veining. Huge blooms need support. Growth lax bush, will make basket but may need weights. Raised in the vicinity of Merimbula, New South Wales, Australia. Lockerbie – Australian – *ca* 1975.

Snowcap. Semi-double. An easy but lovely cultivar; should form the basis of every beginner's collection. Raised many years ago by Henderson in England, actual date unknown, but considered to be around the 1880 period, is a semi-double and must be considered as a double for show purposes. The tube and sepals are bright red with a pure white corolla, slightly veined cerise and although the flowers are smallish in size, it is a most profuse bloomer and considered one of the most free flowering cultivars in cultivation. Snowcap is a cultivar belonging to the 'old school' and although termed by many as old fashioned, for floriferousness, colour and habit, is yet to be paralleled. Growth is both vigorous and upright and, apart from making an exceptionally good bush specimen, can equally be trained as a standard and is one of the cultivars which will produce an exceptionally good pyramid or pillar. Easy to grow as a cutting and a young plant, will grow into a strong, well branched bush without much effort; but as it makes a vigorous root system, will respond to hard pinching and will make a 'tight head' if necessary, by pinching at every pair of leaves. It is a cultivar which is so prolific in blooming, that when exhibited on the show-bench, the judge will expect a complete mass of bloom before considering an award, so much so that those in some fuchsia quarters, advocate a class to exclude Snowcap. Is very seldom troubled with pests and very rarely bothered with botrytis; can be used with effect as an outside bedder, will stand sunshine, but prefers semi-shade and is more hardy than previously thought, for although considered as H2 is definitely hardy (or H3) in many parts of the British Isles, especially in Southern and Midland districts. Henderson – British – Date unknown.

Snowcap Improved. Synonymous with the cultivar Arlendon.

Snowdrift. Double. Tube and sepals, rosy-red, curved downwards; corolla white. Medium sized blooms, free, very tightly formed, not very deep. Growth upright and bushy. Colville – British – 1966.

Snowdrift. Semi-double. Tube and sepals white; corolla snow-white with tinges of pink. Large flowers, free for size, flare open resembling snow-flakes. Dark glossy green foliage. Growth trailer. Kennett – American – 1966 – A.F.S. No. 680.

Snowdrop. Single. Blush-white and purple. Harrison – British – 1849.

Snowdrop. Single. Red and white. Henderson – British – 1868.

Snowdrop. Single. Red and white. Lye – British – 1897.

Snowfire. Double. Pink tube, sepals white are wide and tapering, approximately same length as corolla, recurve at maturity. Corolla bright pink to coral, variegated white in different patterns. Medium-sized blooms with buds having rose streaks before opening, best colours in shade. Dark green foliage, growth medium upright, bushy, will make good bush or standard. Tested for 4 years in vicinity of Fort Bragg, California. Stubbs – American – 1978 – A.F.S. No. 1442.

Snowflake. Single. White tube, sepals turn straight up, white with pink tinge at base. Corolla white, medium sized flowers, early and free, bell shaped. Growth trailer. Walker and Jones – American – 1951.

Snow Flurry. Semi-double. A near white with rosy flush at base of tube and sepals; corolla white. Medium sized flowers and free, heat tolerant. Light green foliage, growth lax bush or trailer. Schnabel – American – 1952 – A.F.S. No. 115.

Snow Queen. Double. Short thick, white tube, sepals white, short and broad; white corolla, very full. Large blooms for double, free produced, heavily petaled and of good substance, well shaped and ruffled. Mid-green foliage with crinkled leaves, growth upright and bushy, vigorous, but may need support to carry the heavy blooms. Handley – British – 1975 – A.F.S. No. 1276.

Snowstorm. Semi-double. Thin, greenish-white tube, white, tipped lime-green sepals, reflexed to stem. Corolla white with even length petals. Medium sized flowers early and prolific. Growth upright, will produce a good bush or standard. Raised and tested in vicinity of Derby before release. Handley – British – 1976 – A.F.S. No. 1371.

Snowtime. Double. Tube and sepals scarlet; corolla white. Medium sized blooms and free, dark green foliage. Growth upright and bushy, vigorous, needs frequent pinching, raiser claims this cultivar to be very hardy in Central England. Swingtime × Snowcap. Wright, J.A. – British – 1975 – A.F.S. No. 1307.

Snow White. Double. White tube with very faint pink streaks, white sepals held straight back to tube, tipped green. White corolla with petaloids of the same colour. Semi-full blooms with white stamens and pistil, best colour in shade which is needed to produce the 'whiteness' otherwise always the tinge of pink. Mid-green foliage (R.H.S. 138A) with serrated, lanceolate leaves. Growth natural trailer, produces good basket or weeping standard. Raised and tested for 4 years in vicinity of Woodbridge, Suffolk. Introduced by Woodbridge Nurseries of Woodbridge, Suffolk in 1982. Shelley Lynn seedling cross. Dunnett – British – 1982 – A.F.S. No. 1708.

Snowy Summit. Double. White tube, long and broad white sepals; corolla white. Medium sized blooms and free for double, very full, as with all near whites, will develop some pink colouring according to the amount of shade afforded. One of the few near white trailers, growth natural trailer, will produce good basket without weights. Stubbs – American – 1975 – A.F.S. No. 1259.

So Big. Double. Longish tube, rosy-pink, long upturned sepals, pale pink, often measure 5 in from tip to tip. Corolla creamy-white; huge blooms but not many of them, huge long stemmed pointed buds, open slowly into exotic like blooms. Bright green foliage, best grown as H1. Waltz – American – 1955 – A.F.S. No. 228.

Society Belle. Single. Tube coral; sepals turn all the way back against the stem, coral. Corolla is shade between lilac and rose. Largish flowers for a single, free and bell shaped. Growth upright. Peterson – Fuchsia Farms – America – 1959 – A.F.S. No. 374.

So Happy. Double. Tube and sepals, bright red; corolla dark blue. Medium sized blooms and free, bright green foliage with reddish stems. Growth trailer. Soo Yun Field – American – 1965 – A.F.S. No. 647.

Solana Mar. Semi-double. Peachy-pink tube with pink veining, sepals peachy-pink shades, stand straight out from tube; corolla shades from pink to lavender-pink with dark pink veins. Medium sized flowers, free, semi-bell shape, can throw five sepals. Growth upright and bushy; small and compact growth, very lush growth. Hastings – American – 1975 – A.F.S. No. 1309.

Solano. Single. Tube and sepals, white with pale carmine flush, curved pagoda fashion; corolla deep rose with flame undertone. Medium sized flowers, very prolific, heat resistant. Growth upright and bushy. Evans – American – 1954.

Soldier of Fortune. Semi-double. Tube and sepals scarlet with sepals reflexed back to tube. Corolla white with red veining at the base. Medium sized blooms and free-flowering. Growth upright and bushy. Introduced by High Trees Nurseries of Reigate, Surrey, in 1980. (Angela Leslie × Blue Lagoon) × Golden Treasure. Hobson – British – 1978.

Solent Pride. Single. Thin tube white veined slight pink ½in long, sepals white, tipped pale green on top, 'pale pink underneath, flaring back at maturity. Corolla opens red-purple (R.H.S. 63A), fading to R.H.S. 61B. Medium sized flowers, bell-shaped, long stamens are carmen (R.H.S. 63A), pistil pale pink (R.H.S. 63C). Growth lax bush will make good basket, bush or standard. Originates from the vicinity of Southampton. De Bono – British – 1980 – A.F.S. No. 1534.

Solferino. Double. Red and purple. Lemoine – French – 1860.

Solitaire. Double. Pale pink tube, sepals white veined pink outside, pale pink inside, reflexing back to hide tube. Corolla clear white, medium sized blooms of perfect shape and very attractive. Growth upright, bushy and self-branching. Introduced by Woodbridge Nurseries of Hounslow in 1980. Tristesse × Snowcap. Dyos – British – 1980.

Sombrero. Double. Thick flesh coloured tube, sepals light pink on outside, deeper pink underneath, sepals are large, thick, gracefully recurved, resembling Mexican hat, hence the name. Corolla brilliant rose; very large blooms and fairly free. Growth best grown as espalier, but equally as good as trailer. Nelson – American – 1957 – A.F.S. No. 286.

*Soni. Double. Tube and sepals cherry-red; corolla deep blue. Medium sized blooms, early and free flowering. Growth medium upright. El Camino × Bernadette. Nutzinger – Austrian – 1965.

Son of Thumb. Single. Tube and sepals cerise; corolla lilac. Small flowers but very floriferous. Growth and habit is identical to Tom Thumb. Sport of Tom Thumb. Introduced by D. Stilwell in 1978. Gubler – British – 1978.

Sonota. Double. Tube and sepals pink; corolla white. Very large blooms, fairly free, very full and of good substance, very similar to Collingwood but much larger. Growth lax bush or trailer, can be trained for taller types of training, but heavy blooms need support. Excellent blooms for cut bloom classes, but easily bruise, but not as good as Pink Quarter or Southgate. Tiret – American – 1960 – A.F.S. No. 437.

Sophia. Double. Tube and long sepals, waxy-white, flushed palest carmine on inside. Corolla dubonnet-purple; large blooms, free and continuous. Dark green foliage, growth upright. Tiret – American – 1954 – A.F.S. No. 208.

Sophisticated Lady. Double. Pale pink tube, sepals very long, pale pink; corolla white. Large blooms, free, very full, with shorter corolla than Angels Flight, but better habit. Growth lax bush or trailer, heavy blooms need support, best grown as H1. Martin – American – 1964 – A.F.S. No. 609.

Sophisticated Lady

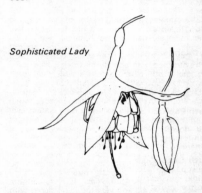

So Pretty. Double. Thin red tube, sepals dark red outside and smooth, slightly lighter red inside and rough. Corolla lavender-blue, blended white at base with red veins. Largish blooms, free for size, ten or more petaloids with red base and red veins, white marbling at base. Oval foliage, dark green outside, lighter green underneath, red stems, most attractive. Growth lax bush, good for bush or basket with weights. Pancharian – American – 1975 – A.F.S. No. 1294.

South Coast. Single. Medium sized tube, ivory (R.H.S. 4D); sepals ivory-white with green tips, deep pink streaks on underside, narrow with pointed tips and turning upward. Corolla open cerise (R.H.S. 64B) fading to deep pink (R.H.S. 63A) with white base and non-flaring. Medium sized flowers with pink stamens and white pistil. Light green foliage (R.H.S. 144A) red vein at base. Growth tall and upright, very strong and vigorous, very suitable as bush. Raised and tested for 3 years in vicinity of Palos Verdes, California. Drapkin – American – 1979 – A.F.S. No. 1507.

South Gate. Double. Tube and upturned sepals, medium pink; corolla very soft powder-pink. Largish blooms, produced in great numbers. Growth vigorous and spreading bush, good for standard or half basket. One of the best American introductions into this country. Best grown as H1. Walker and Jones – American – 1951.

South Lakeland. Single. Tube creamy-white, sepals creamy-white, flushed pink on both sides. Corolla is of similar colouring to Falling Stars (turkey-red) but overlaid with a flush of blue when new. Growth upright and bushy; although this cultivar was raised in 1963 it was not released

South Gate

or introduced until 1978. Hawkshead × Falling Stars. Thornley – British – 1963 – A.F.S. No. 1466.

Southlanders. Single to semi-double. Tube and sepals white; corolla lavender-purple, fading to rose with white marbling. Largish blooms and free, opens and flares almost flat ruffled petals. Growth upright. Castro – American – 1971 – A.F.S. No. 951.

South Pacific. Single. Crimson tube, broad, up-turned crimson sepals; corolla white. Medium sized flowers, free, saucer shaped. Yellowish-green foliage, growth upright and bushy. Hodges – American – 1951 – A.F.S. No. 85.

South Seas. Semi-double to double. Tube and sepals, pale pink to white; corolla beautiful shade of pink, very soft looking. Medium sized blooms, very free, growth lax bush or trailer. Fuchsia Forest – Castro – American – 1963 – A.F.S. No. 569.

Southwell Minster. Single. Tube and sepals rhodanite-red (H.C.C. 0022), sepals held very back from tube. Corolla bishop's violet (H.C.C. 34). Small dainty flowers, extremely free. Growth upright, vigorous and bushy, good for all types of training except baskets. Excellent as outside bedder, growth 12 in to 18 in in height. Named after Southwell Minster in Nottinghamshire. Glyn Jones × Neil Clyne. Roe – British – 1979.

Souvenir de Chiswick. Single. Red and dark violet. Banks – British – 1855.

Souvenir de Henry Henkel. This triphylla is synonymous with Andenken an Heinrich Henkel in California.

Space Shuttle. Single. Tube and sepals red; corolla in addition to the red tone has an exceptional amount of yellow colouring. Medium sized flowers with unusual flowering habit. Flowers the whole year round, summer heat however spoils the yellow colouring, winter and early spring are best periods for this cultivar. Named after the safe landing of Columbia on April 14 1981, the same day the cultivar received the Dutch Award of Merit by the V.K.C. Speciosa × *F. splendens.* de Graaff – Dutch – 1981.

Spangles. Semi-double. Tube and sepals carmine, tipped green; corolla orangy-carmine. Large blooms and free, compact and tight. Growth upright. Fuchsia-La – American – 1959.

Spanish Rhapsody. Double. Tube and sepals red; corolla dark blue with purple shading and satin like sheen. Largish blooms, fairly free and very full. Growth upright and bushy. Winner of

the B.F.S. Jones Cup 1965, also B.F.S. Award of Merit. Colville – British – 1965.

Sparkler. Semi-double. Tube and sepals, palest rose; corolla dark violet. Medium size flowers, very prolific, compact and tight, growth upright. Plummer – American – 1952.

Sparkles. Semi-double. Tube and sepals red; corolla purple. Medium sized blooms, very prolific and heat tolerant. Unregistered American cultivar grown in California. Joyce – American – 1960.

Sparks. Single. Tube flesh to salmon colour, re-curving flesh to salmon sepals. Corolla orangey-carmine ⅜ in to ½ in long. Smallish flowers slightly flaring, good contrast between the sepals and corolla, sepals give thin effect in contrast with corolla, heavy bloomer, entire blooms between 1 in and 1½ in long. Dark green foliage, leaves 1½ in wide × 2 in long. Growth upright but will trail with weights, will make good basket or bush. Originates from the Fort Bragg area of California. Stubbs – American – 1980 – A.F.S. No. 1549.

Special Sampan. Little information known of this American sport except it was found in California *ca* 1980 and is a sport from Sampan.

Speciosa. Probably the name given to a seedling of *F. fulgens* with shorter tubed flowers and more free-flowering. The same beautiful orange-vermilion colouring and very similar to all the other variants and hybrids from *F. fulgens.* Now confirmed to be a hybrid from *F. splendens* × *F. fulgens.*

spectabilis (Hooker 1848). Synonymous with *F. macrostigma.*

Spectacular. Single. Long slender tube, pink turning darker with maturity; corolla white. Largish flowers, free, very unusual with four spooned petals spread evenly at top of sepals which are pink and white. Growth trailer. Gagnon – American – 1969 – A.F.S. No. 843.

Spellbound. Double. Tube and sepals white; corolla purplish-blue. Large blooms, free for size. Growth trailer. Fuchsia-La – American – 1968 – A.F.S. No. 802.

* Spinney. Single. Short tube white tinged green (R.H.S. 157B) ½ in long by ¼ in wide, horizontally held sepals white-magenta (R.H.S. 66C) on top, magenta underneath with recurved tips 1½ in long by ½ in wide. Corolla opens fuchsia-purple (R.H.S. 67A) maturing slightly lighter (R.H.S. 66B) 1½ in long by 1¼ in wide. Largish flowers quarter flared and bell shaped, very similar to Rough Silk but trails better and is more floriferous, magenta filaments and anthers, white tinged purple style and white-cream stigma. Mid to dark green (R.H.S. 147B) foliage with lanceolate leaves 2¼ in long by 1 in wide, serrated edged, acute tips and rounded bases. Growth natural trailer, prefers full sun and is cold hardy to 32°F. in Southern England. Raised in the vicinity of Horsham, Sussex, and registered by Les Hobbs of Worthing. La Tristesse × Mrs. Popple. Dransfield – British – 1984 – A.F.S. No. 1776.

spinosa (Presl., 1835). Synonymous with *F. ly-coides.*

Spion Kop. Double. Short thick tube, rose red; sepals rose-red, reflexed. Corolla white, veined rose red and flared. Medium sized blooms, very free. Growth low bush, very easy, responds to frequent pinching, growth similar to Iced Champagne, but does not hide its blooms, excellent cultivar for 3½ in pot classes. Named after the famous enclosure at Liverpool Football Ground. Jones, G. – British – 1973 – A.F.S. No. 1128.

splendens. Short, vivid scarlet tube, short and almost erect sepals, yellow and green, corolla pale green stamens are exserted. Flowers are borne singly on short crowded branches. Cordate or ovate leaves, rather large, very similar to *F. cordifolia* but are broader, flowers are similar but shorter. Shrub of upright growth, found on Mount Totonoepeque at elevation of 10,000 ft. Flowers very freely when confined to pots. Zuccarini – 1832 – Mexico.

Splendor Falls. Double. Pink tube, extra long sepals, corolla dark lavender-blue, flushed pink at base. Largish blooms, free for size, petals flair outward. Growth trailer. Gagnon – American – 1962 – A.F.S. No. 508.

Sport of Bora Bora. Little information known of this American sport except it was found in California *ca* 1980 and is a sport from Bora Bora.

Spotlight. Single. Tube and sepals pink; corolla white. Large flowers shaped like a Chinese hat. Growth similar to Citation. This cultivar was imported from America by John Smith of Thornton, Leicestershire and received without identification and subsequently named from its appearance in 1974. Raiser unknown – American – 1970s.

Spring Bells. Semi-double. Tube and sepals, bright red; corolla clear white. Medium sized flowers, very free, probably a sport from Snowcap with slightly large flowers and a much longer flowering period. Growth upright and bushy. Kooijman – Dutch – 1972.

Spring Bonnet. Double. White tube, crisp sepals white flushed pink; corolla lavender-blue with extra petaloids. Medium sized blooms, free, heat tolerant. Growth upright and bushy. Brand – American – 1959 – A.F.S. No. 396.

Spring Shower. Semi-double. Short tube and upturned sepals, flesh coloured, underside soft phlox-pink, corolla white and long petaled. Medium sized flowers, very free, growth tall, upright bush. Tiret – American – 1953 – A.F.S. No. 156.

Sputnik. Double. Crimson tube, recurved sepals crimson; corolla violet-blue, spotted with red. Large blooms, profuse and early. Growth lax bush or trailer, heavy blooms need support. Martin – American – 1958 – A.F.S. No. 366.

Square Dance. Double. Pink tube and sepals; corolla light mauve-blue, fading to carmine. Medium sized blooms, free, very full, square shape showing the influence of its parent, late bloomer. Growth upright, bushy and hardy in Southern England. Pink Quartet ×. Smallwood – British – 1973 – A.F.S. No. 1076.

Squarehead. Single. Tube and sepals pink, back of sepals and tube, light red; corolla coral-pink. Smallish flowers, very free, open up square shape. Small dark green foliage, heat resistant. Growth trailer. Machado – American – 1962 – A.F.S. No. 498.

Square Peg. Double. Tube and sepals red; corolla deep violet-blue. Large blooms, fairly free for size and square shaped as name implies. Growth upright and bushy. Clyne – British – 1972.

Stadt Modling. Double. Tube and sepals red; corolla white with pink veins. Smallish blooms with pink stamens and style. Dark green foliage, growth upright and bushy. El Camino × Winston Churchill. Nutzinger – Austrian – 1968.

Stained Glass. Double. Tube is china red to rose-red, short and wide sepals are china rose to rose-red with greenish-white tips and stand at 180° from corolla. Corolla amethyst-violet, streaked rose-red at base. Medium-sized blooms with two tiers of petals with top petals flared, giving a double skirted effect, rose-red stamens and whitish-rose pistil. Growth semi-trailer, will trail with weights, tested for 7 years at Sebastopol and Villa Grande, California before release. Foster – American – 1977 – A.F.S. No. 1417.

Standard. Single to semi-double. Pink and purple. Bull – British – 1862.

Standishii. Single. The only details available are the parentage: *F. fulgens* × *F. magellanica* var. *globosa.* However other useful information is that Standish of Bagshott was one of the earliest of British hybridisers and the cross referred is considered to be the first cross recorded between these two and is the cross that gave rise to all fuchsias except a very few, such as the triphylla hybrids and Fanfare. Pictures of the results of his crosses were appearing in the Botanical Register for 1842 and although not recorded, would presume them to include such cultivars as Aurora, Attraction, Colossus, and the well-known cultivar still in cultivation President. Standish – British – 1840.

Stanford. Single. Tube and sepals, brilliant red; corolla white. Medium sized flowers and free. Dark reddish foliage, growth upright and bushy. Hazard and Hazard – American – Date unknown.

Stanley Cash. Double. Short white tube, short sepals white, tipped green. Corolla deep royal-purple large blooms, free, box shaped. Growth trailer, named after a former editor of the B.F.S. Pennisi – American – 1970 – A.F.S. No. 905.

Star Drops. Double. Tube and sepals red, corolla creamy-white with red veins. Large blooms, free for size, petaloids on stems extend like stamens, opens to star shape. Darkish foliage with red stems. Growth trailer. Soo Yun Field – American – 1965 – A.F.S. No. 646.

Stardust. Single. Thin tube salmon-pink, sepals salmon-pink outside, salmon-orange underneath. Corolla orange at base blending to crimson edges. Small flowers, early and prolific. Foliage mid-green with narrow leaves. Growth upright and bushy. Handley – British – 1973 – A.F.S. No. 1134.

Stargazer. Single. Tube and sepals, pale rose-madder; corolla rose-madder, marbled Imperial-purple. Small flowers, very free and erect, growth upright, compact bush. Reiter – American – 1946.

Starlet. Semi-double. Tube and sepals, pale pink; corolla lavender-pink, maturing to bright rose pink. Large flowers, fairly free and flaring. Growth upright. Kennett – American – 1971 – A.F.S. No. 955.

Starlight. Single. Creamy-white and rose-pink. Bull – British – 1868.

Starlite. Double. Tube and broad, pointed sepals, smoky-rose; corolla deep shade of lilac rose. Large blooms, free for size, most unique opens into square shaped flower with eight pointed star-like centre, extra long pistil. Growth lax bush or trailer. Waltz – American – 1961 – A.F.S. No. 493.

Star of Pink. Double. Short, thin pink tube, sepals light pink topside, dark pink underneath, tipped light green, flare straight with tips curved upwards. Corolla slightly deeper pink flaring out to bell shape with maturity. Medium sized flowers are very free and similar to Display and Beacon, corolla is a little darker than Display but more the shape of Beacon. Feature is the manner in which the blooms are held erect, and improvement upon Display which tends to hide its flowers. Dark green foliage with red stems. Growth upright and bushy, excels in $3\frac{1}{2}$ in pot classes. Raiser describes it as semi-trailer in the U.S.A. First appeared in Britain on B.F.S. Birmingham 1976 showbenches. Soo Yun – American – 1975 – A.F.S. No. 1271.

Star of Wilts. Single. Tube and sepals, waxy-white; corolla violet. Medium sized flowers and free. Growth upright and bushy. Arabella Improved × James Lye. Lye – British – Date unknown.

Starry Trails. Single. Rosy-pink tube, long thin sepals, rosy-pink; corolla has overlapping petals of bright carmine, tipped creamy white at base of tube. Large flowers, prolific, wide spreading sepals give a starry appearance. Dark, glossy foliage. Growth trailer. Waltz – American – 1956 – A.F.S. No. 271.

Static. Double. Tube and thick sepals, rosy-red; corolla dark purple with coral coloured marbling toward base of petals. Large blooms, fairly free, growth trailer. Peterson-Fuchsia Farms – American – 1959 – A.F.S. No. 375.

St. Clare. Semi-double. Carmine and purple. Welham – British – 1842.

Stella Ann. Triphylla type single. Long tube, poppy-red, sepals Chinese-coral, tipped green, rather wide and open. Corolla Indian-orange. Extremely free flowering, olive-green foliage, veining and leaf reverse, strawberry-red. Growth upright and bushy. Baker-Dunnett – British – 1974 – A.F.S. No. 1199.

Stella Engleman. Double. Carmine and pink. Stride – British – 1911.

Stella Marina. Semi-double. Tube and long recurving sepals, crimson; corolla violet-blue, irregularly splashed crimson and white. Large flowers, very free, growth strong, upright bush. A.F.S. Cert. of Merit. Schnabel – American – 1951 – A.F.S. No. 81.

Steve Wright. Double. Pale pink tube, sepals pale pink flushed rose on outer and deeper pink inside, tipped green. Corolla paler pink, veined deeper pink. Medium sized blooms and fairly free flowering. Growth upright. Raised in the vicinity of Banstead, Surrey and introduced by Woodridge Nurseries of Hounslow, Middlesex, 1982. Hobson – British – 1982.

Stop-lite. Semi-double. White tube, short crisp sepals, carmine-rose, lighter at base Corolla lively Tyrian-rose, flecked with geranium-rose, flecked with geranium lake. Medium to large flowers borne in huge clusters. Growth trailer. Schnabel – American – 1956 – A.F.S. No. 266.

storkii. Dark red tube, sepals and corolla. Medium to smallish flowers, borne in irregular terminal clusters. Upright shrub reaching 9 to 10 ft in natural habitat. Munz – 1943 – Brazil and Peru.

Storm. Submitted by the raiser for the R.H.S. Wisley Hardy Trials 1975–78 but received no award. Tabraham – British – 1974. (See also p. 313.)

Storm King. Synonymous with Frau Emma Tauper.

Stormy Sunset. Double. Thin tube, pale pink to white, long, broad sepals phlox-pink on underside, pale pink to white on outside, tipped green. Corolla violet-purple (R.H.S. 80A) and phlox-pink (R.H.S. 62B). Medium sized blooms, very full with serrated edges. Dark green foliage and rather large. Growth trailer. Stubbs – American – 1976 – A.F.S. No. 1385.

Strawberry Delight. Double. Tube and sepals, waxy-crimson; corolla white, heavily flushed petaloids of carmine rose. Medium to large blooms, fairly free. Foliage yellowish-green and bronze, turning green with maturity. Growth upright and bushy, good for outdoor bedding, compact. Gadsby – British – 1969 – A.F.S. No. 873.

Strawberry Festival. Double. Tube and sepals, bright red; corolla pale pink, veined carmine. Large blooms, very free. Growth upright, heavy blooms need support. Haag – American – Date unknown.

Strawberry Fizz. Double. Tube and sepals, clear pink, sepals curl back; corolla deep pink with picotéed edges. Large blooms, fairly free, flaring and frothy looking, hence the name. Dark green foliage, growth trailer. Stubbs – American – 1971 – A.F.S. No. 997.

Strawberry Queen. Single. Tube and sepals red; corolla deep strawberry-red. Small flowers but profuse and early. Growth dwarf, upright and bushy. Haag – American – 1937.

Strawberry Ripple. Double. Long tube, creamy-white with strawberry shading, sepals extra long, wide and stand straight out with downward curvature, creamy-white with strawberry shading. Corolla strawberry and white. Medium sized blooms, very full with very ruffled and serrated edges, strawberry petaloids. Dark green foliage and lush. Growth natural trailer. Hastings – American – 1976 – A.F.S. No. 1333.

*Strawberrys n' Cream. Double. Tube and sepals deep pink, corolla cream and deep pink. Medium sized blooms originally known as seedling No. 379. Growth upright and bushy. Raised in the vicinity of Guildford, Surrey. Weeks – British – 1982.

Strawberry Sundae. Double. Short white tube, white, broad sepals, tipped green, corolla pink with slight touch of lilac. Large blooms, free for size, large foliage. Growth trailer. A.F.S. Cert. of Merit 1962. Kennett – American – 1958 – A.F.S. No. 350.

Strawberry Supreme. Double. Tube and sepals, waxy-crimson; corolla white, flushed carmine-rose well down into outer petaloids. Large blooms, early and free. Growth medium bush, hardy in Southern districts and the Midlands. Gadsby – British – 1970 – A.F.S. No. 874.

Streamliner. Semi-double. Long thin tube and long twisted sepals, crimson, corolla rose-red to crimson. Very long flowers, free, heat tolerant. Growth trailer, especially suitable as weeping standard or espalier. Tiret – American – 1951 – A.F.S. No. 96.

Striata. Single. Red and striped pink and blue. Story – British – 1848.

Striata Incomparabilis. Single. Red and striped purple. Twrdy – German – 1868.

Striata Perfecta. Single. Tube and sepals red; corolla purplish-plum, striped coral-pink. Medium sized flowers and free, bell shaped. Growth upright and bushy, this was considered to be the first fuchsia with striped corolla and sometimes confused with Bland's New Striped. Banks – British – 1868.

Striata Perfecta. Single. White and vermilion, spotted white. Williams – British – 1870.

Striata Splendens. Single. Tube and sepals red; corolla red, spotted red and pinkish-rose. Bland – British – 1872.

Striata Splendida. Single. Tube and sepals red; corolla plum-purple, striped with rose. Raiser and date unknown.

Striata Splendour. Single. Tube and sepals red; corolla plum-purple, evenly striped red. Banks – British – 1872.

Striding Edge. Single. Tube slightly flushed rose, long, narrow strong sepals, ivory, tipped green. Corolla clear pink, long flowers, free, shape very distinct, petals forming claw-like canopy over the corolla. Growth lax bush, vigorous. Don Peralta × Nightingale. Thornley – British – 1965.

Striker. Semi-double. Flesh-pink tube, sepals white with flesh-pink base, slightly upturned, longish, pointed and tipped green. Corolla violet-purple fading to lighter shade. Medium sized flower and very free, pale green foliage. Growth upright with similar habit to its parent. White Spider ×. Tolley – British – 1974 – A.F.S. No. 1231.

String of Pearls. Single to semi-double. Pale rose tube, sepals pale China-rose held well back. Corolla pale rose-purple with lavender veins. Medium sized flowers, uniform-shaped, are carried right down the stem, exceptionally prolific, best colour in shade. Growth strong, upright and bushy, short jointed, most interesting cultivar. Raised and tested in vicinity of Melton Mowbray, Leicestershire for 3 years before release. *F. lycioides* ×. Pacey – British – 1976 – A.F.S. No. 1394.

striolata. Brilliant red self. Tiny flowers not larger than ¼in, borne solitary in leaf axials. Another member of the Breviflorae (Enclaindra) section. Scandent shrub. Lundell – 1940 – Mexico and Guatemala.

Stubby. Single. Short, thick tube, rose to red, sepals of the same colour; corolla purple-violet to magenta. Medium sized flowers, very heavy bloomer, petals slightly convex giving semi-double appearance, the wide, short tube and short flaring corolla combine to make a 'Stubby' bloom. Dark green foliage, growth small upright, bushy, will produce good pyramid. Stubbs – American – 1975 – A.F.S. No. 1260.

Student Prince. Single. White tube, sepals white, tipped green shading to neyron-rose on underside, long and sweeping upwards. Corolla aster-violet, veined roseine-purple and shading to white at base of petals. Fairly large flowers and very free flowering. Growth trailer will make attractive basket without weights. Raised and

tested for 3 years before release in the vicinity of Melton Mowbray, Leicestershire. Raised and introduced by R. and J. Pacey of Stathern, Melton Mowbray, in 1982. Pacey – British – 1982.

Stylish. Semi-double. Short white tube, sepals white on upper surface and veined pink underneath, tipped green, sepals stand well back from corolla. Corolla lavender-blue, marbled pale pink, turns to wistaria-blue with maturity. Short compact blooms, very free flowering. Pale green foliage. Growth medium upright, will make good bush or standard. Will take full sun near Timperley, Cheshire where it was tested for 3 years before release. Howarth, Philip. – British – 1981 – A.F.S. No. 1657.

Subdued. Single. Long tube and sepals, bright salmon; corolla smoky-purple to salmon. Large flowers for a single and free, large foliage. Growth trailer. Fuchsia Forest – American – 1968 – A.F.S. No. 772.

*** Sue Wingrove.** Single. Short pink tube, sepals pink with much deeper shade of pink underneath. Corolla rosy-pink, veined pink at base of petals. Small flowers and very floriferous. Growth upright and bushy with small medium green foliage. Ideal for both small pot work and miniature standard training. Raised and tested for 3 years before release in vicinity of Reading. Introduced by Sinclair Fuchsias of Banbury in 1984. Estelle Marie × Bobby Wingrove. Wingrove – British – 1983.

Suey Ho. Single. Tube and sepals, pale phlox-pink; corolla white with red lines. Medium sized flowers, free and early. Growth upright. Niederholzer – American – 1947.

Sugar Almond. Double. Tube and sepals creamy-white flushed pink, sepals are pink underneath. Corolla pale pink, flushed rose-pink. Medium sized blooms, growth upright and bushy. Introduced by High Trees Nurseries of Reigate, Surrey, in 1980. (Angela Leslie × Blush O' Dawn) × seedling known as No. 77/74. Hobson – British – 1978.

Sugar Blues. Double. White tube, sepals white on topside with touches of pink underneath. Corolla dark blue, fading to violet-blue. Very large blooms, fairly free, extremely long and beautiful with pink blending from the centre into the blue. Growth trailer, best grown as H1. Martin – American – 1964 – A.F.S. No. 610.

Sugar Plum. Single. Short thick tube cherry-red. Sepals bright cherry-red (R.H.S. 50A) crepe textured underneath which stand straight out, curling at the extremities, 1½in long by ⁷⁄₁₀in wide. Corolla pale lavender (R.H.S. 70D) and veined bright pink. Good sized flowers symmetrically bell shaped with petals 1 in long by 1¼in wide, stamens and pistil red (R.H.S. 54B). Yellow-green foliage (R.H.S. 146B) with lightly veined serrated leaves 1⅝in long by ⁷⁄₁₀in wide. Growth lax upright, medium sized, will make basket with weights, bush training may need support. Raised and tested in the vicinity of Newcastle, Northumberland and introduced by R. and J. Pacey of Stathern, Melton Mowbray, in 1982. Hall – British – 1982 – A.F.S. No. 1669.

*** Suikerbossie.** Little known Dutch cultivar other than the parentage: *F. magellanica typica* ×. Brouwer – Dutch – 1982.

Summer Breeze. Double. White tube, sepals pink with green tips; corolla campanula-violet with small groups of petaloids between the petals.

Largish blooms, fairly free, with buds like a round Japanese lantern. Growth trailer. Pennisi – American – 1971 – A.F.S. No. 1015.

Summer Skies. Single. Tube and sepals, pale rose; corolla pale silver-blue. Medium size flowers and free. Growth upright and bushy. Niederholzer-Waltz – American – 1949.

Summer Snow. Semi-double. White tube, recurved sepals, white, tipped green; corolla creamy-white, with a slight suspicion of yellow when bud first opens. Medium sized flowers, free, good substance and long keeping, very similar to Flying Cloud not quite as large but freer. Growth lax bush or trailer, best as H1. Waltz – American – 1956 – A.F.S. No. 272.

Summer Splendour. Double. Tube and sepals, creamy-white turning to red in late season; corolla rose-madder. Medium sized blooms, very free, small dark green foliage, growth trailer. Plummer – American – 1953.

Sunburst. Semi-double. Tube and sepals, pale carmine; corolla crimson. Medium sized flowers, early and free, very short corolla. Growth upright and bushy. Reiter – American – 1946.

Sundance. Single. Light rose tube, sepals light rose, long and held well out. Corolla light burgundy, maturing to cerise. Large flowers, very free, long bell-shaped with overlapping petals. Pale yellow-green foliage. Growth natural trailer. Handley – British – 1974 – A.F.S. No. 1194.

Sunday Best. Semi-double. Tube and sepals white, inner petals flushed pink; corolla bright blue with pink marbling. Large flowers, fairly free, consisting of four large blue semi-spreading petals surrounded by small petals of blue with pink marbling. Very large foliage, growth upright and vigorous, up to 6ft in California. Kenneth and Ross – American – 1956 – A.F.S. No. 258.

Sundown. Double. Tube and sepals red; corolla dark lavender with dark pink streaks out of base and running into petals. Large blooms, fairly free, growth upright and bushy, very heavy blooms need support. Seedling of Lady Beth (Martin 1958). Fuchsia Forest-Castro – American – 1961 – A.F.S. No. 472.

Suneeya. Double. Short tube, sepals white with pink on undersides, tipped green, large. Corolla wisteria-blue, fading to light purple. Large blooms, free for size, growth upright. Soo Yun – American – 1968 – A.F.S. No. 763.

Sun Glory. Single. Tube and sepals, orange-red; corolla glowing vermilion. Medium to large flowers, fere, beautiful shaped with unusual colouring. Rich green holly-like foliage. Growth low spreading bush. Erickson – American – 1954 – A.F.S. No. 411.

Sunkissed. Double. Tube and sepals, azalea-pink, tipped green; corolla jasper-red, spreading to crimson. Medium sized blooms, free and continuous. Growth lax bush or trailer. Tiret – American – 1957 – A.F.S. No. 293.

Sunny. Single. Tube and sepals, pale coral; corolla red with burnt edges. Small flowers but very free, growth lax bush or trailer. Fuchsia Forest – American – 1968 – A.F.S. No. 770.

Sunny Smiles. Single. Long pale pink tube, sepals, carmine-rose, tipped green, underside empire-rose. Corolla crimson, flushed claret-rose. Large flowers for a single, early and very free, will take full sun. Growth lax bush or trailer. Gadsby – British – 1968 – A.F.S. No. 967.

Sunray. Single. This cultivar has been grown for over a hundred years and still seen on the show-benches, which proves its value as an outstanding ornamental. Grown for its attractive foliage rather than the flowers. The leaves are light green, edged creamy-white, suffused cerise, however, if given too much pot-room, will give disappointing results, especially with the bloom, which are rather late and few in number. Like most ornamentals, needs careful watering and plenty of full light to produce the attractive colouring in the foliage which can also contain a silvery cast. The tube and sepals are cerise, darker underneath, corolla rosy-purple and rather smallish in size. Growth is upright and bushy, makes a good bedder and best grown as H2. Has always been attributed to Thomas Milner a nurseryman of Bradford, and thought to be a mutation from Tardif (Lemoine 1856), and sent out as a silver tricolour cultivar in the spring of 1872. Subsequent history, however, reports that this very fine variegated fuchsia previously believed to have originated as a sport was a seedling raised by Mr. G. Rudd of Undercliffe, Bradford. It is also reported to have been obtained from the variegated cultivar Cloth of Gold and fertilised with pollen from a single cultivar with a white tube and sepals with red corolla. Mr. Rudd observing a spot of white on a leaf of one of these seedlings and finding it to be a promise of variegation, cut the plant back in the autumn to that particular leaf and the following spring, broke out in the beautiful variegation form it has never lost. It is now widely grown as one of our best ornamentals, received the R.H.S. Award of Merit in 1929, and is currently listed by most specialist nurserymen.

Sunrise. Single. Tube and sepals white, flushed rose with petals tipped crimson; corolla clear scarlet. Medium sized flowers, early and free. Growth stiff, upright and shrubby. Mme. Aubin × Aurora Superba. Reiter – American – 1942.

Sunset. Single. Tube and sepals, pale pink, tipped green; corolla glowing coral. Medium sized flowers, free, open bell-shaped and early. Light green foliage, growth upright and vigorous. Rolla × Aurora Superba. Niederholzer – American – 1938.

Sunshine. Single. Cardinal-red and violet. Banks – British – 1864.

Sunshine. Single. Tube and sepals, pale rose, tipped green; corolla geranium-lake. Small flowers, very free and early. Growth low bush, compact. Niederholzer – American – 1948.

Sunshine Belle. Single. Tube and sepals flesh-pink; corolla orange, fading to purple. Medium sized flowers, very free and continuous, growth upright and bushy. Thorne – British – 1959.

* Superba. Triphylla single. Triphylla hybrid attributed by reliable German sources as *F. triphylla × F. boliviana*. Veitch & Son – British – 1895.

Super British. Synonymous with White Queen and very similar to Amy Lye. White Queen was sent over from England to America in the early 1930s unlabelled and was renamed in California as Super British. Very vigorous, can reach a height of 6 ft in California under suitable conditions.

Super Colossal. Double. Tube and sepals red; corolla purple. Huge blooms, not very free. Growth upright, vigorous and spreading. Niederholzer – American – 1942.

*Supernova. Single. Very short tube glossy deep pink, sepals glossy deep pink on top, matt mid-pink underneath, opening horizontal. Corolla white veined mid-pink at base, medium sized flowers. Petals flare like a hooped petticoat, very free flowering, stamens and stigma pale pink. The beauty lies in the upward looking flowers with the Swanley Gem type corolla. Growth upright and bushy, short jointed and a strong grower, well in the exhibition category. Raised in the vicinity of Norwich and introduced by Fountains Nursery, near Ripon, in 1984. Cloverdale Pearl × Snowcap seedling × Estelle Marie. Clitheroe – British – 1984.

Super Otto. Single. Tube and sepals red; corolla purple. Large flowers for single, free and long. Growth upright and bushy. Niederholzer – American – 1940.

Surprise. Double. White and purple-crimson. Williams – British – 1875.

Surprise. Single. White and magenta. Lye – British – 1887.

Surprise. Single. Short tube and sepals, bright red; corolla pale hyacinth-blue, carmine at base. Very small flowers, very free and early. Growth tall, upright, vigorous and bushy. *F.magellanica* var. *molinae* × . Niederholzer – American – 1938.

Susan. Double. Tube and sepals, pale rose; corolla light blue, turning to violet with age, upcurving petals. Medium sized blooms, free serrated petals, early. Growth upright, bushy and compact. Niederholzer – American – 1948.

Susan Allen. Single. Short crimson tube, crimson sepals; corolla cyclamen-purple. Medium sized flowers, very free, flowers in pairs. dark green foliage with reddish stems. Growth upright and bushy. Albion × Rosedale. Allen – British – 1974 – A.F.S. No. 1215.

Susan Ford. Double. Short tube neyron-rose, reflexed sepals, neyron-rose, crepe inside. Corolla Imperial-purple, fading to cyclamen-purple. Medium sized blooms, very free, rosette shaped, best colour in shade. Growth upright and bushy. La Campanella × Winston Churchill. Clyne – British – 1972 – A.F.S. No. 1176.

Susan Gilbey. Single. pale pink and purple. Strutt – British – 1901.

Susan Green. Single. Long thin tube white, flushed pale pink, long pale pink and white sepals recurve and twist slightly, held just below the horizontal, tipped green. Corolla rose-pink tapers slightly at bottom, but does not open. Medium sized flowers are long with white pistil and four pointed stigma. Mid green foliage with ovate leaves, edges are serrated, mid-ribs red and stems pale red. Growth medium upright, will make good bush and take full sun in Nottinghamshire where it was tested for 3 years before release. Caunt – British – 1981 – A.F.S. No. 1633.

Susan Olcese. Double. White tube, large, broad white sepals; corolla pale blue. Largish blooms, fairly free, very full and compact. Growth lax bush or trailer. Martin – American – 1960 – A.F.S. No. 447.

Susan Pasquier. Double. Pink and pink-white. Lemoine – French – 1908.

Susan Piper. Double. Pink and violet-purple. Dixon – British – 1899.

Susan Travis. Single. Tube and slightly recurving sepals, deepish pink; corolla rose-pink, paling towards base. Medium sized flowers, prolific, unusual and welcome break in colour for a hardy. growth vigorous, spreading, bush up to 2½ feet, hardy; after a few years horizontal growth as wide as its height. Named after former editor of B.F.S. Accepted by the B.F.S. as showbench hardy. Submitted by Wills Nursery for R.H.S. Wisley Hardy Trials 1975–78 and received Highly Commended Certificate. Travis, J. – British – 1958.

Susan Young. Double. White tube, sepals white, red-purple base to orchid-pink, waxy-white flushed pink, curving back clear of corolla. Purple-lilac corolla, four quarters, four petals in each. Medium sized blooms and free for double growth upright and very bushy. Sport of Blue Pearl. Young – British – 1975 – A.F.S. No. 1261.

Susie Tandy. Double. Dark rose tube, reflexed sepals are waxy-pink, tipped green with darker pink underneath. Corolla cream flushed pale pink. Small compact blooms and very free-flowering, best colour develops in shade. Light to medium green foliage is ovate with obtuse leaf tip and serrate margin. Growth natural trailer, self-branching without weights, strong short jointed carries multiple blooms. Originates from the vicinity of Leicester. Introduced by J.E. Ridding of Fuchsiavale Nurseries of Kidderminster in 1980. Whitehouse – British – 1980 – A.F.S. No. 1537.

Suzanna. Single or semi-double. Tube and sepals pinkish-red, short tube, sepals are a little darker. Corolla blue with small red veins at base. Medium-sized flowers, very free, dark green foliage. Growth strong upright and bushy. Dollarprinzessin × . van der Grijp – Dutch – 1968.

Suzy. Double. Short tube medium pink, deeper than the sepals which are pink, tinged salmon, crepe like and flare upward at maturity. Corolla lilac to pink. Huge blooms with approximately fifteen petals folding into each other, each petal when flat can measure 2 to 2½ in wide, pink stamens and pistil, creamy-anthers. Large, long dark green leaves with red stems. Growth semi-trailer, will trail with weights, tested for 4 years in Pacific Northwest U.S.A. before release. Originally found in Los Angeles in 1969 and sold as a sport of Bonanza but not registered. Introduced by Westover Greenhouse of Seattle. Sport from Bonanza. Carlson – American – 1977 – A.F.S. No. 1430.

Swan Lake. Double. Short tube eau-de-nil; long, broad white sepals with pink flushing at base. Corolla chalk-white with faintest pink tinge. Largish sized blooms, free, globular shape. Growth lax bush. Travis, J. – British – 1957.

Swan Lake. (Blackwell). Synonymous with the above cultivar.

Swanley Beauty. Single. Tube waxy-white, sepals white, faintly tinged pink; corolla soft pink. Medium sized and free, growth upright and bushy. Lye – British – 1875

Swanley Gem. Single. Tube and sepals, rich scarlet; corolla violet; paling at base, veined scarlet. Medium sized flowers, free, the four perfect petals open flat, making a perfect circle. Growth upright and bushy, good cultivar for the showbench, one that will endear for years to come, another old cultivar still holding its own with all newcomers. Cannell – British – 1901.

Swanley Yellow. Single. Long tube and horizontal sepals, orange-pink; corolla rich orange-vermilion. Medium sized flowers, free. Bronze-green foliage. Growth upright and bushy. Name is very misleading, flowers do not contain any yellow colouring whatsoever, often confused with Aurora Superba. Cannell – British – 1900.

Sweepstakes. Double. Tube and sepals red; corolla white, veined red. Large Blooms, very free for size of blooms, heat resistant. Growth trailer, best as H1. Fuchsia-La – American – 1959.

Sweet Dreams. Double. Short thin tube phlox-pink $\frac{3}{8}$in long × $\frac{1}{8}$in wide, sepals phlox-pink (H.C.C. 625/2) 1$\frac{1}{4}$in long × $\frac{3}{8}$in wide. Corolla phlox-pink (H.C.C. 625/2) 1 in long × 2 in wide. Large self-coloured blooms with six petaloids $\frac{1}{2}$in long the same colour, pink pistil 1$\frac{5}{8}$in long with a black stigma. Light green foliage with 2$\frac{1}{4}$in long × 1$\frac{1}{4}$in wide. Growth upright, will make good bush or standard. Originates from the Sebastopol area of California. Soo Yun Field – American – 1980 – A.F.S. No. 1561.

Sweet Elegance. Single to semi-double. Tube and sepals, flesh-pink, tipped green; corolla heliotrope, marbled white. Medium sized flowers, very free, growth upright and bushy. Jones, W. – British – 1959.

Sweetheart. Double. Tube and broad recurved sepals, pink; corolla lavender-blue centre with outer petals, fuchsia-pink. Medium to large blooms, free and of good substance and shape. Growth lax bush or trailer. Walker and Jones – American – 1951.

Sweetheart. Single. Tube white, sepals are pale pink, tipped green. Corolla cherry-pink, white at base. Medium-sized flowers, very free flowering with light red stamens and whitish-pink style. Growth upright, bushy and self-branching. van Wieringen – Dutch – 1970.

Sweet Leilani. Double. Short tube and recurving sepals, pale rose-pink; corolla smoky-blue. Large flowers, free, petals very wide and spreading, heat resistant. Growth lax upright. Tiret – American – 1957 – A.F.S. No. 296.

Sweet Lilac. Single. Long thin tube pale pink, pink sepals are long and thin which recurve over the tube, tipped green. Corolla lilac-blue, flushed pink at base with deep pink veining. Medium sized flowers with red stamens, pink style and white stigma. Medium sized foliage, pale green with rounded serrated leaves. Growth medium upright and bushy. Raised in the vicinity of Cardiff, South Wales, and tested for 3 years. Adams – British – 1982 – A.F.S. No. 1698.

*Sweet Linda. Single. Flesh coloured tube and sepals, pink corolla. Smallish flowers, very free flowering. Growth upright and bushy, self-branching and short-jointed. Shown as a seedling at B.F.S. Midland Show 1983 but not recognised as any breakthrough. Nellie Nuttall × Margaret Roe. Kirby – British – 1983.

Sweet Mystery. Double. Tube and sepals, flesh-pink, tipped green; corolla neyron-rose, fading to rose-madder. Medium sized blooms and free, growth upright and bushy. Jones, W. – British – 1960.

Sweet Mystery. Double. Tube and sepals pink; corolla waxy-white with touch of pink at base. Large blooms, fairly free, good substance. Growth lax bush or trailer. Gorman – American – 1970 – A.F.S. No. 932.

Sweet Red Eyes. Single. Short, crimson tube $\frac{5}{16}$in long and $\frac{6}{16}$in wide; crimson red sepals 1$\frac{3}{8}$in long and $\frac{1}{2}$in wide, curling up and horizontal, sepals smooth top, thick and creped underneath. Corolla white, red veined and red at base. Largish flowers, corolla forms tight bell with the petaloids forming eyes, petals 1$\frac{1}{8}$in long × $\frac{3}{4}$in wide, dark pink stamens and pistil, heavy bloomer at tips of branches, needs frequent stopping. Red veined and red stemmed foliage 1$\frac{3}{8}$in long and $\frac{3}{4}$in wide. Growth small upright but will trail with weights. Raised and tested for 5 years in vicinity of Sebastopol, California. Soo Yun Field – American – 1979 – A.F.S. No. 1494.

Sweet Revenge. Double. Tube neyron-rose, broad sepals, neyron-rose; corolla hyacinth-blue, shading to wisteria-blue. Large blooms, free, good formation with a neyron-rose petaloids, best colour in shade. Growth upright and bushy. Gadsby-Fuchsialand – British – 1975 – A.F.S. No. 1315.

Sweet Serenade. Double. Tube and sepals, neyron-rose; corolla violet; marbled neyron-rose. Medium sized flowers, free, compact and tight. Growth lax bush or trailer. Jones, W. – British – 1960.

Sweet Sixteen. Double. Tube and upturned sepals, neyron-rose; corolla rich pink. Large blooms, fairly free for size. Growth trailer. Walker and Jones – American – 1951.

Sweet Sue. Double. White tube and sepals; corolla light smoky-purple, fading to unusual smoky-orange. Large blooms, free, large foliage. Growth upright. Kennett – American – 1959 – A.F.S. No. 397.

Sweet Violet. Semi-double. Thin, triphylla-type tube, very light pink, over 1 in long, sepals white on top with pink edges and light green tips, pink underneath, curving upward. Corolla violet, turning to light orchid with maturity. Medium sized flowers with three or four petaloids on outer edge of corolla, dark pink stamens, light pink pistil and white anthers and stigma. Dark green foliage, growth semi-trailer, will trail with weights. Soo Yun – American – 1976 – A.F.S. No. 1353.

Swinga-Long. Semi-double. Tube and sepals scarlet; corolla white, veined cerise. Largish flowers, very free, very similar to its parent. Growth upright, bushy and self-branching. Swingtime ×. Austin – British – 1963.

Swingtime. Double. Raised and introduced by Horace Tiret of San Francisco. California in 1950; registered by the American Fuchsia Society under number 66; very quickly received their Certificate of Merit. Horace Tiret has produced scores of excellent cultivars: Angela Leslie, Bridesmaid, Georgana, Lace Petticoats, Miss Vallejo, Sweet Leilani and Voodoo to name only a few, but Swingtime must be considered to be one of the best of his raisings. This delightful cultivar is a full double, the short tube and sepals are a rich, shiny red of crepe texture, the inside of the petals being rosy-red. The very full corolla is milky, but sparkling white, faintly veined pink; the blooms which are very freely produced are largish and perhaps the best in its colour range. Swingtime is a cultivar which produces no difficulties in cultivation, considered to be an extremely fine, show class fuchsia, the growth is upright, vigorous and self-branching, responds well to frequent pinching and can be made to trail if necessary, it will, in fact, make a good basket, an exceptionally fine half basket, although rather on the stiff side. Good red and white cultivars are always eye catchers and until the late 1940s, Ballet Girl by Veitch as far ago as 1894 commanded the scene. Tiret also produced Yuletide in 1948 which although very similar to Swingtime is not considered as good, although a little larger; Red Jacket by Waltz in 1958 created much attention, together with Sheryl Ann by Peterson in the same year and although both these cultivars produced bigger blooms than Swingtime, it still holds its head well above all the other red and whites, not forgetting Lassie by Travis. Swingtime is very suitable as an outside bedder and holds its colour extremely well during all weathers, has proved to be hardy during the late 60s and early 70s in Midlands, but hardly fair to judge owing to the mild winters. Makes a very fine espalier with careful training and produces a stately standard. Foliage is fairly dark of medium size, which does not seem to attract the pests. Swingtime is a cultivar which will 'Swing along' for many a long year and should find a place in every fuchsia collector's selection. Sister seedling of Enchanted Titanic × Yuletide. Tiret – American – 1950 – A.F.S. No. 66.

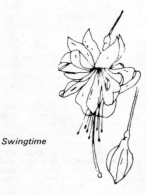

Swingtime

Swiss Miss. Semi-double. Tube and sepals, pink to red; corolla white with pink to red veining. Large flowers, fairly free, flares out to a very skirty effect. Growth trailer and so vigorous that it could be considered as a greenhouse climber, best grown as H1 A.F.S. Certificate of Merit 1965. Fuchsia Forest – Castro – American – 1963 – A.F.S. No. 570.

S'Wonderful. Double. Tube and sepals, pink with splashes of pink at base of bud. Corolla pale lavender inner petals, outer petals of orchid-pink. Medium sized blooms, free, bud carried on extra long stems, open, soft milky-white, whilst sepals flare out and curl up and under. Growth natural trailer. Fuchsia Forest-Castro – American – 1961 – A.F.S. No. 473.

Sydney Mitchell. Double. Tube and sepals red; corolla plum-purple. Large blooms, fairly free. Foliage dark green, veined red. Growth upright

and very slow. Hazard and Hazard – American – 1948.

sylvatica. Tube pink, sepals pink on pale red; corolla crimson to purple-red. Smallish flowers borne in terminal racemes. Low shrub. Synonymous with *F. atroruba* and *F. nigricans.* Bentham – 1845 – Columbia.

Sylvia. Double. Tube and sepals, scarlet-cerise; corolla white, veined cerise. Largish blooms and free, growth upright bush, an old cultivar still grown for its rich colour combination. Veitch – British – 1892.

Sylvia. Double. Tube and sepals rose-red; corolla cream, deep pink at base. Large blooms, dark green foliage with bronze tinted leaves. Growth bush. This cultivar is entirely different to the cultivar of the same name by Veitch. Curtis – British – 1971.

Sylvia Barker. Single. Long, white tube; sepals waxy-white, slightly tipped green, do not recurve. Corolla scarlet with slight smoky cast, petals slightly obtuse. Smallish flowers but very free, reminiscent of Lye's Unique but with deeper shade corolla. Dark small foliage, well serrated with pronounced dark veining. Growth semi-trailer or lax bush. Barker – British – 1973 – A.F.S. No. 1077.

Sylvia Young. Double. Short thick white tube, sepals white (R.H.S. 155A) on top, pale rose underneath, broad and green tipped, maturing to rose colour. Corolla pale mauve (R.H.S. 84A), medium to large blooms with flared corolla, pink stamens and white pistil. Medium green (R.H.S. 137D) foliage, growth medium upright, will make good bush or standard. Originates from the vicinity of Kearsley, Bolton. Susan Young × Arthur Young. Young – British – 1980 – A.F.S. No. 1573.

Sylvy. Single. Tube short barrel shape, bright pink, sepals bright-pink; corolla deep rose. Small flowers borne in profusion. Strong foliage, good in all weather and also for show bench. Growth upright bush, short jointed. The second of two cultivars raised by a very successful exhibitor during the 1970s and introduced by D. Stilwell in 1978. Jack Acland × Liebreiz. Dyos – British – 1978.

Symphony. Single. Tube and sepals, pale phlox-pink; corolla cobalt-violet. Medium sized flowers, free, very gracefully shaped, spreading. Growth tall, upright and bushy. Niederholzer – American – 1944.

syringaeflora (Carr 1873). Synonymous with *F. arborescens.*

Tabu. Double. Pale pink tube, sepals salmon-pink on inside, pale pink outside, stand straight out on early bloom, reflex as bloom matures. Corolla magenta-rose with pale pink marbling at base of outer petals, fading to smoky-rose. Medium sized blooms, very free, heat tolerant if shaded. Growth upright and bushy. Paskesen – American – 1974 – A.F.S. No. 1187.

tacanensis. Tube greenish-white, sepals greenish-white, whte at base; corolla white to pink ageing to red. Tiny flowers borne solitary in the leaf axils. Member of the Breviflorae (Encliandra) section. Upright shrub up to 12 ft in natural habitat. Lundell – 1940 – Mexico and Salvador.

Taddle. Single. Very short tube, deep rose-pink, sepals are fully reflexed completely hiding tube when mature, same colour as tube, rose-pink. Corolla waxy-white with slight pink veining. Medium-sized flowers, extremely free, somewhat similar to Citation but much smaller, stamens and the long pistil are pink. Light green foliage, growth upright and bushy, can produce excellent specimen bush or shrub plant, strong grower. Gubler – British – 1974.

Taffeta. Double. White tube and outer sepals surface pink, blending down into corolla. Corolla violet-purple. Largish blooms, fairly free, the four central petals and reverse pleated. Growth trailer. Kennett – American – 1962 – A.F.S. No. 536.

Taffeta Bow. Double. Short tube carmine-rose; sepals carmine-rose, blends down into base of petals, very broad and long, crepe texture, open straight then curve like a bow. Corolla purple-violet, huge blooms, free, open and compact, gradually flares, some petals serrated, very long pistil. Growth natural trailer and fast. Stubbs – American – 1974 – A.F.S. No. 1196.

Taffy. Single. Pink tube, long pink sepals with stripe down the centre of each sepal, tipped green. Corolla of several shades of pink strip running down the petals. Long flowers, free, with serrated petals. Light green foliage, growth trailer, not worth growing. Martin – American – 1961 – A.F.S. No. 467.

Tahiti. Double. Tube and sweeping sepals, palest pink; corolla vibrant rose-like colourings. Huge blooms, fairly free, growth lax bush. Schnabel – American – 1963 – A.F.S. No. 583.

Tahoe. Semi-double. Tube and sepals, white with touches of pink; corolla light blue to various shades of blue and orchid, with touches of pink. Large flowers for semi-double and free, open out flat, most unusual flowers. Growth upright. Kennett – American – 1964 – A.F.S. No. 615.

Tamalpais. Single. White tube, long white curled sepals, tinged pink; corolla rose. Long flowers and free, growth trailer. Niederholzer – American – 1951 – A.F.S. No. 99.

Tammy. Double. Waxy-white tube, long broad sepals, lovely pink, spreading, twisting and upturned. Corolla mauve-lavender, streaked rose-pink; large spreading blooms, free for size, early and continuous. Growth lax bush or trailer vigorous. Erickson – American – 1962 – A.F.S. No. 542.

*Tam O'Shanter. Double. Tube and sepals flesh pink, corolla dark purple verging on hyacinth-blue, streaked with varying shades of pink. Medium to largish blooms, freely produced. Growth is upright, bushy, strong and short-jointed, will produce excellent bush or standard. Raised in the vicinity of Cumbria in the North of England and introduced by Fuchsiavale Nurseries of Kidderminster in 1984. Mitchinson – British – 1984.

Tamworth. Single. Tube and sepals crisp, pure white, tipped green, sepals curl out to stem: corolla rich purple at outer edge, changing to band of salmon-pink, then to white near tube. Medium sized flowers, early and very prolific, best colour in shade. Light green foliage with no serrations on leaves. Growth upright and bushy, easy to shape. Handley – British – 1976 – A.F.S. No. 1372.

Tangerine. Single. Pink tube, sepals flesh-pink, tipped green, do not reflex; corolla orange, maturing to rose. Medium sized flowers free and longish in shape. Growth upright and bushy. Although this is a lovely cultivar, the name can be very misleading. *F.cordifolia* ×. Tiret – American – 1949.

Tango. Single to semi-double. Clean white tube; long curving sepals, white; corolla rosy-purple. Largish flowers and free, growth upright and bushy. Kennett – American – 1959 – A.F.S. No. 398.

Tanhouse. Single. Light red tube, sepals light red, tipped white, strong of medium size and do not curl. Corolla lilac. Medium sized flowers, very free, blooms for long period, pink stamens and pistil, yellow stigma. Growth very compact upright, vigorous and self-branching. Raised and tested for 2 years in vicinity of Manchester. Royle – British – 1979 – A.F.S. No. 1525.

Tanie Balasam. Double. Short white tube and sepals; corolla pink. Large blooms, free, open up like a camelia, box shaped, very full. Growth trailer. Pennisi – American – 1969 – A.F.S. No. 859.

Tanu Lo Bue. Double. Short red tube, sepals deep red, stand out straight. Corolla pink variegated with white. Large blooms, free for size, very full. Small dark green foliage, growth trailer. Pennisi – American – 1969 – A.F.S. No. 858.

Tanya. Single. Pale pink self, very delicate shade of pink. Medium sized flowers and very free. Growth upright habit and bushy. Holmes, R. – British – 1975.

Tanya Bridger. Double. Tube and sepals white; corolla lavender-blue. Medium sized blooms and profuse. Growth upright and bushy. Bridger – British – 1958.

Tarantella. Single. Tube and sepals red; corolla magenta. Medium sized flowers, free, wide open and recurved. Growth upright. Niederholzer – American – 1946.

Tardif. Single. Reddish-purple self; medium sized flowers, not very free. Growth upright and bushy. This cultivar was used extensively by Lemoine for hybridising, it has also mutated several variegated leaf cultivars, including Sunray. Lemoine – French – 1856.

Tarn Haws. Double. Tube and sepals scarlet-cerise; corolla veronica-blue. Large blooms, free, with pink petaloids. Growth trailer. Travis, J. – British – 1960.

tasconiiflora (Krause 1905). Synonymous with *F. denticulata*.

*Task Force. Single. Long white tube, sepals held well above the horizontal, white on top white flushed pale lilac (R.H.S. 73D) underneath, recurved tips, sepals $1\frac{1}{2}$ in long by $\frac{1}{2}$ in wide. Square shaped corolla $1\frac{1}{4}$ in long by $1\frac{1}{4}$ in wide opens cyclamen-purple (R.H.S. 74B) maturing to magenta (R.H.S. 66A). Large flowers with characteristics inherited from its parent Celia Smedley, long lasting and same type of growth. Magenta stamens with pale lilac anthers, lilac style and stigma. Foliage forest-green (R.H.S. 136A) $4\frac{1}{2}$ in long by $3\frac{1}{2}$ in wide leaves, cordate shaped with serration, the very large foliage is apt to distract from the beauty of the plant. Growth upright, vigorous and bushy, makes a lot of wood quickly, needs frequent pinching for full head on a standard, will produce excellent bush/shrub plant. Raised in the vicinity of Chaddesden, Derbyshire, and introduced by R. and J. Pacey of Melton Mowbray in 1983. Cloverdale Pearl × Celia Smedley. Redfern – British – 1984 – A.F.S. No. 1796.

Tausendschön. Double. Tube and sepals lacquer-red; corolla soft pink. Large blooms and early flowering. Growth upright and bushy, this cultivar is still grown in the Netherlands, Nagel – Probably German – 1919.

Teddy. Semi-double to double. Tube and sepals, ivory-white, flushed pink; corolla violet blue, soft pink at base. Very large blooms, free for size, could be described as a double Rose of Castile Improved. Growth upright and bushy. Travis, J. – British – 1957.

Ted Heath. Double. Tube and sepals cream with suffused tints of delicate pink; corolla soft cream with faint pink shading at base. Large blooms, fully double, very lovely flower. Good foliage, growth upright, bushy and short jointed. Named after the famous politician of the 60s and 70s. First introduced by D. Stilwell in 1978. Clark – British – 1977.

Ted's. Single. Short, thick tube, shell-pink (R.H.S. 37C), veined slightly darker; sepals neyron-rose (R.H.S. 55B), overlaid neyron-rose (R.H.S. 55A), creped inside, tipped green, held out at right angles to tube. Corolla beetroot-purple (R.H.S. 71B) with edges of cyclamen-purple (R.H.S. 74A), base azalea-pink (R.H.S. 38A). Medium sized flowers, bell shaped with 4 medium sized petals, crimson stamens, carmine-rose pistil is tipped yellow, practically no fading. Growth medium upright, self-branching and bushy. Percy Holmes × Hapsburgh. Holmes, R. – British – 1976 – A.F.S. No. 1342.

Ted's Rainbow. Single. Thin, pink tube, short and flared sepals are pink; corolla purple. Short and round medium-sized flowers with pink stamens and white pistil. Variegated foliage lemon-yellow with light to dark green leaves and red veins, the leaves become more yellow in full sun. Growth medium upright bush, self branching. Hardy in California and tested for 5 years at Eureka, California before release. Cultivar is a sport of an unknown cultivar. Zerlang – American – 1977 – A.F.S. No. 1404.

Teepee. Single. Tube dark, dull red; sepals dull red, long narrow and twisted; corolla Indian-red. Medium sized flowers, not very free, but very unusual in shape, sepals lie on top of corolla. Growth upright and bushy. Tolley – British – 1974 – A.F.S. No. 1232.

Telegraph. Double. Red and pure white, Twrdy – German – 1874.

Telegraph. Single. Tube and sepals red; corolla purple. Small flowers and free, growth upright and bushy, very hardy. Riccartonii ×. Lemoine – French – 1886.

Television. Double. White tube, sepals white outside, pale pink underneath; corolla deep orchid, splashed with fuchsia-pink. Medium sized blooms and free, growth semi-trailer. Walker and Jones – American – 1950.

Telstar. Single. Tube flesh pink sepals white, long and thick. Corolla cobalt-violet. Large and long flowers, sepals are overlaid with rose with maturity. Growth upright with arching fronds.

Introduced by R. Pacey and raised by W.J. Jones of Tettenhall, Wolverhampton. Jones, W. – British – ca 1960.

Tempest. Double. Tube and sepals, rosy-pink; corolla jasper-red. Large blooms, fairly free, growth trailer. Tiret – American – 1968 – A.F.S. No. 793.

Temple Bells. Single. Tube and sepals red; corolla mauve, flushed pink. Medium sized flowers, very free. Growth upright and bushy, inclines to be slightly pendulous, strong and branching habit, height 2 to 2½ft. Hardy in Southern England, raised in the Scilly Isles. Tabraham – British – 1974.

Temptation. Single. White tube, long white sepals; corolla white with orange-rose throat. Longish flowers and free, continuous bloomer. Growth upright. Peterson-Fuchsia Farms – American – 1959 – A.F.S. No. 376.

Temptation. Double. Tube and sepals white; corolla purple-blue. Growth trailer, very suitable for basketwork. This cultivar should not be confused with one of the same name by Peterson, A.F.S. No. 376. Fuchsia-La (Roy Walker) – American – 1967.

Tenella. See *magellanica* var. *gracilis*.

Tennessee Waltz. Semi-double to double. This lovely cultivar should be in every collection, primarily because it is considered the yard-stick by which double flowered cultivars are measured. Raised by Roy Walker and Buddy Jones of Long Beach, California in 1951 and surely one of the finest fuchsias to reach this country. Growth is strong and upright with medium green foliage; flowers are double, although can sometimes be semi-double, the reason why some nurserymen catalogue as such. Blooms are of medium size and very free, with upcurved sepals, clean rose-madder colour, the corolla is lilac-lavender, splashed with rose, whilst the squarish flowers have centre points on the petals, the filaments and style are both rose coloured. Very easy cultivar to grow and strongly recommended to the beginner for their attempt in training either a bush or standard; self-branching plant and will make a reasonable bushy plant even after the initial pinching. Will produce a perfect showbench plant with regular pinching, three or four stops being sufficient and can be in full bloom within six months of a rooted cutting. Once in flower, will

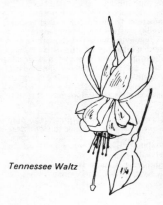

Tennessee Waltz

286

remain in bloom for the duration of the entire season and be one of the last to hold them through into November if required. This cultivar was awarded a Highly Commended Certificate of hardiness by the R.H.S. in September 1965 as the result of their Hardy Trials at Wisley from 1963 to 1965, although for some unknown reason, has yet to be recognised by the B.F.S. as hardy; was resubmitted by Wills Nursery for the 1975–78 Trials but received no further award. Walker and Jones have introduced many fine cultivars, but Tennessee Waltz together with Checkerboard and Pink Quartet must be rated as their finest. Walker and Jones – American – 1951

Tenor. Single. Tube and sepals crimson, corolla reddish-purple. Small flowers, very free, growth upright and bushy. Known as seedling No 97 by Hazard and Hazard – American – Date unknown.

Teresa. Double. Bright pink self; large blooms, free for size. Dark green foliage, growth trailer. Taylor – American – 1969 – A.F.S. No. 811.

Terracotta. Single. Tube and sepals, turkey-red; corolla magenta. Medium sized flowers, early and free. Growth upright and bushy. Niederholzer – American – 1946.

Terry Bayes. Double. Ivory-white tube, broad sepals ivory, tipped green, underneath suffused rose-pink, very reflexed and curving to hide tube. Corolla very rich deep violet-purple. Large and long blooms, fairly free, growth upright and bushy, very erect. Travis, J. – British – 1956.

Terry Mott. Double. Pale orange tube (R.H.S. 38D) streaked red, long 1⅜ in twisted sepals pale orange tipped green with deep pink edge (R.H.S. 38A). Corolla 1 in long pale pink (R.H.S. 73A) marbled deeper pink (R.H.S. 73B) mauve (R.H.S. 73A) and blue (R.H.S. 91B). Large blooms and free flowering with pale pink stamens, red anthers and pink pistil. Foliage is woodpecker-green (R.H.S. 147) with lanceolate leaves 3 in long. Growth natural trailer no weights required, will make good basket or weeping standard. Tested for 4 years in vicinity of Woodbridge Suffolk before release. Dunnett – British – 1981 – A.F.S. No. 1608.

*Terrysue. Single. Long light salmon-pink tube 1 in long by ¼ in wide; horizontally held sepals salmon-pink on top, a little deeper colour underneath with green tips and recurved, 1¼ in long by ½ in wide. Corolla opens deep salmon-pink, deeper at the base, maturing to slightly paler colour. Medium sized flowers are half flared and square shaped, characteristics are the long tube and very square corolla, very free flowering. Deep salmon-pink filaments and anthers, pale salmon-pink style and white stigma, longish buds, very pointed. Mid-green foliage with ovate leaves 2½ in long by 1⅜ in wide, serrated edges, acute tips and rounded bases, veins green, stems pinky-green. Growth lax upright or stiff trailer taking the characteristics from both parents, needs frequent pinching to obtain full plant. Raised in the vicinity of Worksop, Nottinghamshire. Coachman × Lye's Unique. Caunt – British – 1984 – A.F.S. No. 1765.

Tessie. Double. Red and white, veined red. Jardine – British – 1902.

Tessie. Single. Short tube light pink, sepals pink inside, light pink on outside, reflexed. Corolla light rose, shading to deeper rose at petal edge. Medium sized flowers, early, free and continuous,

very long pistil. Dark green foliage, close nodes, growth semi-trailer, excellent as a standard. Keaster – American – 1937 – A.F.S. No. 1078.

Tetrad. Double. Short red tube, short red cupped sepals; corolla dark blue. Largish blooms and free, square shape, growth upright and bushy. Brown and Soules – American – 1951 – A.F.S. No. 77.

tetradactyla. Red tube, red sepals; rose-scarlet or paler corolla. Tiny flowers borne solitary in the leaf axils. Foliage bicoloured, dark green leaves with pale green underneath and slightly hairy. Belongs to the Breviflorae (Encliandra) section. Lowish shrub with a height of 2 ft upwards. Synonymous with *F. seleriana*. Lindley – 1846 – Guatemala.

Tettenhall Supreme. Semi-double. Long tube and sepals, delft-rose; corolla Tyrian-purple, flushed rose. Medium sized flowers, fairly free, growth upright. Jones, W. – British – 1960.

Texas. Single. White tube, long white sepals, pink tips; corolla violet-red. Medium sized flowers, free and open shape. Light green foliage, growth trailer. Hazard and Hazard – American – Date unknown.

Texas Longhorn. Semi-double to double. Tube and sepals, bright red; corolla pure white veined red. Huge blooms but sparse, buds can be produced up to 5 in long, opening up to a 9 in bloom. Growth cascade, with careful cultivation can be trained as a standard. If it must be grown, better as H1; offers nothing but huge vulgar blooms, will never make a good plant. Fuchsia-La – American – 1960.

Thais. Lemoine – French – 1913.

Thais. Single. Tube and sepals crimson; corolla white, veined crimson. Medium sized flowers and free, growth upright. Blackwell – British – 1969.

Thalia. (Attributed to Turner 1855). Triphylla single. Probably the most popular of *F. triphylla* hybrids, this impressive hybrid is always quoted as being introduced by Turner, a Slough nurseryman, in 1855; although keen fuchsia students in history have considerable doubt whether the Thalia grown today is the hybrid attributed to Turner, some believe it could have been introduced much later. Reliable German sources now confirm that the Triphylla Thalia is a German introduction raised by Bonstedt in 1905. In 1855 there was a Thalia attributed to Turner, but this was a white tubed cultivar, considered to be raised from Venus Victrix (Gardener's Chronicle, 1875, Vol. 4, p. 324). However, the hybrid grown over the past years has flowers which are single, very long tube with tiny sepals and small corolla, the colouring is a self, rich orange-scarlet. The long flowers are borne in profusion in terminal racemes, whilst the most attractive foliage is a dark olive-green, the ribs and veins being of a pronounced magenta.

The habit of Thalia is vigorous, usually grown as an upright bush and apart from producing fine specimen plants under glass, is used very extensively for summer bedding. Will bloom continuously, but dislikes draughts and revels in the sun.

Very popular on the Continent, particularly in Germany, Holland and Austria, but cannot stand frost or low temperatures and to overwinter this hybrid must have a winter temperature of at least 40°F. Best grown as H2, needs a warm sheltered position to produce its best, is a hybrid from the species *F. triphylla*. Thalia is often confused with

Gartenmeister Bonstedt, raised by Bonstedt in Germany in 1905, with almost identical colouring both in the flowers and the same foliage and habit, the distinguishing features separating the two are: Thalia has straight sided tube, Bonstedt tube is slightly bulbous at the sepal end, Thalia leaf is darker and more pointed, whereas Bonstedt has a bloom to the leaf. The name Thalia is found in Greek Mythology, one of the nine sister goddesses; the name of the muse of comedy. *F. triphylla* ×. Bonstedt – Germany – 1905.

Thalia

Thames Valley. Semi-double. Tube pale pink, sepals pale pink, deeper pink on reverse; corolla mauve with pink shading. Medium-sized blooms and quite free. Small foliage, growth is of a branching habit. Named by the raiser after the local society to which she belonged. Clyne – British – 1976.

Thanet. Single. Tube and sepals, cardinal-red, sepals rose-opal on reverse side, reflex over tube and broad ovary. Corolla camelia-rose centre to royal-purple, edged royal-purple. Large flowers, free, open flat with wide petals, best colour in semi-shade. Growth upright and bushy, good for all types of training. Bennett-Thanet – British – 1975 – A.F.S. No. 1262.

That's It. Double. Tube and sepals, smoky orange-red; corolla orchid-purple, shading to smoky orange-red. Large blooms, free for size. Growth lax bush or trailer. Fuchsia-La – American – 1968 – A.F.S. No. 809.

That's of You. Double. Long tube light red, sepals light red; corolla reddish-white with red veins. Large blooms, fairly free, heat resistant but requires shade. Growth lax bush or trailer. Soo Yun – American – 1967 – A.F.S. No. 729.

The Aristocrat. Double. Longish tube creamy-white, upturned pagoda sepals, pale rose, tipped white. Corolla creamy-white, veined rose with outer petals of pale rose. Large blooms, free for size, flaring, serrated petals, good substance, very similar to Sonata. Growth upright, vigorous and bushy. Elegant beauty, exceptionally fine blooms very suitable for cut bloom classes. Waltz – American – 1953 – A.F.S. No. 165.

The Aztec. Single. Tube and sepals, cherry-red; corolla dianthus-purple, marbled and margined rose. Largish flowers for a single, long and free. Growth trailer. Jones, W. – British – 1961.

The Blue Boy. See Blue Boy.

The Bride. Semi-double. Tube and sepals, white with touch of pink, corolla pure white. Medium sized flowers, not very free. Growth upright and slow. This cultivar was used extensively by the raisers for hybridising. Hazard and Hazard – American – Date unknown.

The Cape. Semi-double. Tube and sepals pink; corolla carmine-red. Smallish flowers, very free, growth bush. Curtis – British – 1974.

The Chief. Double. Tube and sepals, dark carmine; corolla dark violet, outer petals flushed cerise. Very large blooms, fairly free, growth upright and vigorous to 6 ft in California. Graphic ×. Evans and Reeves – American – 1936.

The Classic. Single. Tube and sepals rose colour, tipped green; corolla mallow purple. Medium-sized flowers with magenta pencil edging. Very free flowering. Growth trailer. Hilton – British – 1978.

The Continental. Double. Tube and sepals, heavy waxy-white; corolla very dark maroon-purple, slightly marbled pink. Large blooms, free, very full. Dark green foliage, growth trailer. Martin – American – 1962 – A.F.S. No. 521.

The Diplomat. Double. Tube and sepals bright waxy-carmine; corolla purple. Large blooms, fairly free, very full and unlike most purples, holds its colour. Bright green foliage, growth lax bush or trailer. Kuecher – American – 1962 – A.F.S. No. 505.

The Doctor. Single. Longish tube and recurved sepals, flesh-pink deeper underneath; corolla rosy-salmon. Medium to large flowers, free, good clean cut colour combination, long pistil. Growth lax, makes fine standard and will even produce a good basket. Excellent cultivar in every way. Synonymous with Mrs. Roberts. Castle Nurseries – British – Date unknown.

The Dowager. Double. Tube and sepals, magenta-red; corolla blue-purple. Huge blooms, but not free. Growth vigorous upright. Reiter – American – 1949.

The Franciscan. Double. Tube and broad sepals pink; corolla bright pink, faintly veined rose. Largish blooms, free, very full, non fading self pink. Growth trailer. Schnabel-Paskesen – American – 1960 – A.F.S. No. 460.

The Indian. Double. White tube, recurved sepals, dark crimson; corolla crimson. Large blooms, free, large white buds, clean cut bicolour flowers. Growth semi-trailer and willowy. Reiter – American – 1954 – A.F.S. No. 213.

The Jester. Double. Pale red tube, white sepals; corolla Dubonnet-red. Large blooms, fairly free. Growth tall upright. Tiret – American – 1972 – A.F.S. No. 1073.

Thelma. Semi-double. Cream tube with faint flush of pink; sepals cream, flushed pink. Corolla ruby-red with splashes of pink near calyx, fading to lavender-blue with maturity. Medium sized flowers and free, best colour in shade. Large foliage with heavily serrated edges. Growth semi-trailer. Sayers – American – 1974 – A.F.S. No. 1161.

The Madame. Double. Tube and sepals, pale red; corolla burgundy-red. Largish blooms, very full and free, growth upright. Tiret – American – 1963 – A.F.S. No. 576.

The Marvel. Single. Tube and sepals white, crepe texture, tipped green; corolla pink with lavender sheen. Large flowers, free, solid and long lasting. Growth upright bush. Vicarage Farm Nurseries – British – 1968.

Themesong. Semi-double. Tube and sepals red; corolla orange-red. Largish flowers and free, large lush green foliage, growth lax bush or trailer. Fuchsia-La – American – 1968 – A.F.S. No. 803.

The Midlander. Single. Tube and sepals, flesh-pink to ivory; corolla orange. Small flowers but very full. Growth trailer. Jones, W. – British – 1958.

The Monster. Double. Light green tube, sepals rose with green line in centre, tipped green. Corolla blue-purple, fading to shades of magenta. Very large blooms, fairly free, growth trailer. Gorman – American – 1970 – A.F.S. No. 939.

The Observer. Double. Tube and sepals white; short corolla bright pink. Medium sized blooms, very free holds colour well, at time of introduction, claimed to be the deepest, coloured white sepaled pink to date. Dark green foliage, short-jointed, growth upright and bushy. Received B.F.S. Award of Merit 1962, flowers very similar to Toby Bridger. Named after the famous London newspaper. Coals – British – 1962.

The Oregonian. Double. Tube and sepals white, tipped pink; corolla white, opens very wide, showing pink stamens. Largish blooms, fairly free and flared. Dark green foliage, growth upright. York – American – 1952 – A.F.S. No. 140.

The Patriot. Double. Tube and sepals, pale pink corolla white. Large free for size, growth trailer. Tiret – American – 1971 – A.F.S. No. 995.

The Phoenix. Double. Tube and long sepals, rosy-jointed; corolla lilac. Large blooms, fairly free, very full. Growth trailer. A.F.S. Cert. of Merit 1970. Tiret – American – 1967 – A.F.S. No. 737.

The President. The cultivar known in New Zealand as The President has been renamed President Moir and any reference for full details should be made under that name.

The Queen. Single. Short white tube, sepals pink, white underneath; corolla light blue with four scalloped petals. Growth upright. Brown and Soules – American – 1953 – A.F.S. No. 173.

The Rival. Double. White tube, sepals white and pink; corolla multi-coloured, pink, rose and red. Growth upright. Medium sized blooms and very free. Walker – American – 1970 – A.F.S. No. 882.

Théroigne de Méricourt. Double. Tube and sepals, scarlet-crimson; corolla creamy-white, veined cerise at base. Very large blooms, free for size, extremely full classic shape, very heavy recurving sepals almost hides the tube. Growth

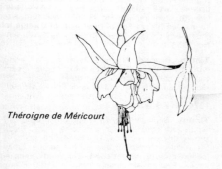

Théroigne de Méricourt

upright and bushy, needs early pinching and support, can be disappointing under wrong conditions, best grown as H1. Well in the showbench class but very rarely seen. Lemoine – French – 1903.

The Shah. Single. Tube and sepals deep cerise; corolla rich pink. Medium-sized flowers and free. Growth natural trailer. One of the very early American introductions. Raiser unknown – American – 1930s.

The Small Woman. Double. Tube and sepals, pale pink; corolla lilac-pink. Medium sized blooms, fairly free, very full, many petaloids. Green foliage splashed with gold, growth trailer. Sport from Lovable. Wagtails – British – 1969.

The Speedbird. Double. Tube and sepals, pure white; corolla deep blue. Largish blooms, very free and full, no red factors so blooms retain blue colouring. Growth upright and bushy. Named after the Speedbird painted on B.O.A.C. Aeroplanes. Dark Secret × Sleigh Bells. Rawlins – British – 1967.

The Spoiler. Double. Tube and sepals, white to pink; corolla blue to plum-purple. Very large blooms, fairly free, growth lax bush or trailer. Fuchsia-La – American – 1968 – A.F.S. No. 806.

The Tarns. Single. Short tube and very long sepals, pale pink with rose reverse. Corolla violet-blue, paling to rose at base. Medium sized flowers, very free, rather long and fairly compact. Dark green foliage, growth upright, bushy and half. Accepted by the B.F.S. as showbench hardy. Venus Victrix ×. Travis, J. – British – 1962 – A.F.S. No. 1148.

Thetis. Double. Tube and sepals red; corolla dark red, almost a self. Medium sized blooms and free, growth upright. Walker and Jones – American – 1949.

The Weaver. Single to semi-double. Red tube, sepals red with slight orange cast; corolla rose-opal with slight purple cast. Medium sized flowers are free, long narrow petals at base bulge out leaving little window-like openings. Growth trailer. Nelson – American – 1954.

The 13th Star. Double. Short, thin tube, neyron-rose, sepals are large 2 in by $\frac{9}{16}$ in. Corolla Imperial-purple on outer edge and lighter purple in centre. Largish blooms, centre petals protrude out from the skirt of the corolla, heavy bloomer. Dark green foliage with green stems and red branches, leaves are large 3 in long. Growth semi-trailer. Soo Yun – American – 1976 – A.F.S. No. 1356.

This England. Double. Longish tube white faintly tinged orchid-pink, broad sepals white, base and tips tinged orchid-pink, recurving up to tube. Corolla white, faintly tinged orchid-pink. (B.C.C. 186) with petaloids present. Large frilly full double blooms with long white pistil. Large foliage golden-green (R.H.S. 145B) maturing to mid-green (R.H.S. 137B). Growth semi-trailer, lax habit enough to make good basket, weeping standard or pyramid. Sport of La France. Located by Miss M. Brackenbury in Essex and registered by Harry Dunnett of Woodbridge, Suffolk. Introduced by Burgh Nurseries of Woodbridge, Suffolk in 1982. Brackenbury – British – 1982 – A.F.S. No. 1709.

Thomas Douglas. Single. White and crimson. Watson – British – 1907.

Thomas Farnes. Double. White and violet. Jardine – British – 1912.

Thomasina. Single. Tube and sepals flesh-pink; corolla terra-cotta and orange. Medium sized flowers and free, dark foliage. Growth upright and bushy. This cultivar is exclusive to California with little information. Raiser and date unknown – ca 1950.

Thomas King. Single. Red and deep purple. Lye – British – 1884.

Thompsoniana. Single. Red and purple. Youell – British – 1841.

Thompsonii. Single. Tube and sepals scarlet; corolla purple. Smallish but long flowers, very free. Growth upright and bushy, with its fine fastigate habit, very suitable for medium hedge, hardy. One of the few of the very early hybrids still in cultivation. R.H.S. Award of Merit 1929. Accepted by the B.F.S. as showbench hardy. F. magellanica ×. Thompson – British – 1840. (See also magellanica var. thompsonii.)

Thornley's Hardy. Single. Tube and sepals waxy-white, corolla red. Small flowers, very free. Growth lax bush or trailer, hardy – unusual for a trailer. This cultivar was another chance seedling taken to the Southport Show 1970 by the raiser for general interest and subsequently taken by W.G. Sharp to Cliff Gadsby with a batch of other cuttings. Unknown to the raiser, Cliff Gadsby named it to distinguish it from others, it was later introduced by George Roe of Nottingham and since proved to be very successful. Submitted by G. Roe for R.H.S. Wisley Hardy Trials 1975–78 but received no award. Thornley – British – 1970.

Thornton Surprise. No details available of this cultivar. Ryle – British – 1975.

Three Cheers. Single. Tube and upswept sepals, bright red; corolla blue with white markings on each petal. Largish sized flowers, free, opening out flat like its parent, firm petals form a perfect circle, very distinct colour break. Growth upright and bushy. Swanley Gem ×. Creer – British – 1968.

Three Counties. Single. Tube and sepals cerise, corolla bluish-violet. Large to medium sized flowers, very free. Growth upright and bushy. Thorne was in error by quoting the raiser as Brown and the date 1947. The British Fuchsia Society Annual of 1938 states the original plant was obtained at the Three Counties Show without a name and being a distinct cultivar from any previously known, the Fuchsia Society called it after the Show at which it came to light. Tom Thorne quoted that the cultivar was identical with Mrs. Vera Letts.

Thumbelina. Single. Short tube, carmine-rose (R.H.S. 52D) lined green, creped sepals, carmine-rose outside and crimson-rose (R.H.S. 52A) inside. Corolla beetroot-purple (R.H.S. 71A), empire-rose (R.H.S. 48C) at base with crimson (R.H.S. 52A) veins. Small flowers, very profuse, consist of four neat petals forming a natural bell, practically no fading. Mid to lightish green foliage, petiole and start of centre of leaves, vein reddish as are the stems. Growth medium upright, good for most types of upright training. Raised and tested in the vicinity of Edenbridge, Kent. Eamer – British – 1976 – A.F.S. No. 1348.

Thunderbird. Double. Tube and extremely long sepals, neyron-rose; corolla vermilion, spreading to China-rose. Large blooms, very early and extremely profuse. Growth trailer. Tiret – American – 1957 – A.F.S. No. 292.

thymifolia. White tube, pinkish-white sepals; pinkish-white corolla, flowers are darker in colour with maturity, tiny, borne solitary in the leaf axils; frequently confused with F. microphylla owing to the variation in the colour of the flowers. Differs from F. microphylla in having somewhat larger foliage and open funnel-shaped flowers. Belongs to the Enclandra (Breviflorae) section. Upright shrub height up to 3 ft, hardy in most districts. Synonymous with F. alternans. F. ovata and F. parviflora (Lindley 1827). Kris – 1823 – Mexico

Tiara. Semi-double. Tube and sepals, pale pink; corolla very light shade of pink-salmon in centre changes to lavender-blue outer petals. Medium sized flowers, free, like Crystal Rose but different colouring. Growth lax bush or trailer. Martin – American – 1965 – A.F.S. No. 632.

Tiburon. Semi-double. Tube and sepals, bright orange; corolla deep orange, almost a self. Medium sized flowers, free and continuous. Growth trailer. Reedstrom – American – 1958 – A.F.S. No. 360.

Tickled Pink. Triphylla type single. Long tube, dark pink, sharp pointed sepals, dark pink, white underneath; corolla bright pink. Normal foliage, growth upright, bushy and compact. Reedstrom – American – 1957 – A.F.S. No. 308.

Tiffany. Double. White tube, upturned sepals, white on upper side, palest pink underneath; corolla pure white. Large blooms, borne in clusters. Dark green foliage producing good background for the white blooms, heat resistant. Growth trailer. A.F.S. Cert. of Merit, 1964. Reedstrom – American – 1960 – A.F.S. No. 424.

Tiffany. Single. Pale pink self. Sport from Leonora. Not to be confused with Reedstrom's cultivar of the same name (1960). Pyemount – British – 1974.

Tiki. Double. Tube and reflexed sepals scarlet; corolla brilliant pink. Large blooms, very free, dark green foliage. Growth upright. Barton – American – 1970 – A.F.S. No. 914

Tillmouth Lass. Single. Thin tube, striped pink, sepals rhodamine-pink underneath, paler colour on topside, twist and curl around the tube from an early stage. Corolla lavender, fading to purple, slight veining at base of petals. Medium sized flowers, well shaped and free in flowering. Growth medium, upright bush. Lena Dalton × Tennessee Waltz × Earl of Beaconsfield seedling × Strawberry Delight. Ryle – British – 1975 – A.F.S. No. 1254.

Timlin Brened. Triphylla type single. Long tube, flamingo, sepals shell-pink, tipped green; corolla coral tint. Deep olive-green foliage with satin sheen, rich red veining, large leaves. Growth upright and bushy. Baker-Dunnett – British – 1974 – A.F.S. No. 1200.

Timmy. Semi-double. Tube and broad upturned sepals red; corolla white with pink veins. Small showy flowers produced in abundance, stamens and pistil extended far beyond the corolla. Small foliage, growth upright and bushy, hardy. Riccartonii ×. Evans – American – 1955.

Timothy Hammett. Single. Longish tube, scarlet; reflexed long sepals scarlet; corolla purple. Medium sized flowers, very free and long lasting, pagoda shaped. Dark green foliage, growth trailer. Tennessee Waltz × Heron. Hammett – British – 1966 – A.F.S. No. 1026.

Tina Head. Double. Tube and sepals rose-pink, corolla white, overlayed with rose-pink petals. Medium sized flowers and free flowering. Very attractive golden foliage. Growth upright, bushy and self branching. Raised in the vicinity of Reigate, Surrey and introduced by the raiser, High tree Nurseries of Reigate, 1981. Head – British – 1981.

Tina Marie. Double. Tube and sepals rich waxy red. Corolla white, veined cerise. Medium sized blooms of perfect shape. Growth lax bush which will trail. Tested for 4 years before release. Raised and introduced by High Trees Nurseries of Reigate, Surrey, in 1980. Dark Eyes seedling. Head – British – 1980.

Tina White. Single. Tube and sepals white, very slightly tinged pink, sepals held semi-erect. Corolla white with the same touch of pink as tube and sepals. Very small flowers, very prolific and perfect shape, stamens very pale pink. Received great attraction when first shown at B.F.S. London Show 1975. Growth upright and bushy, very compact, needs little or no support. Clyne – British – 1975.

tincta. Deep crimson tube, crimson sepals; crimson scarlet corolla. Flowers borne in terminal racemes. Upright shrub reaching 5 ft in natural habitat. Johnston – 1925 – Peru.

Ting-a-Ling. Single. All white self. Largish flowers and free with reflexed sepals and flared petals, best described as a white Display with the same saucer shaped flowers. Like all so called whites, will produce the slightest tinge of pink somewhere and the degree of whiteness will depend upon the amount of shade afforded, very susceptible to botrytis. Growth upright and bushy, one of the best American introductions. A.F.S. Cert. of Merit 1962. Schnabel-Paskesen – American – 1959 – A.F.S. No. 381.

Tinker Bell. Single. Long tube and spreading upturned sepals, white to pink, inside of sepals soft pink, deepening to carmine at tips. Corolla white, veined soft pink; fairly large flowers, long and very free, soft colouring. Growth lax bush or trailer. Hodges – American – 1955 – A.F.S. No. 244.

Tinker Bell. Single. Tube and sepals red; corolla white. Small flowers, bell-shaped, borne in profusion. Foliage dark green, growth dainty and arching, height 6 to 9 in. Very suitable for rockeries, window boxes and troughs, one of a series of new hardy miniatures. Hardy in Southern England and raised in the Scilly Isles. Not to be confused with another cultivar of the same name by Hodges 1955. Tabraham – British – 1976.

Tinker Boy. Semi-double. Short thin tube, pale Tyrian-rose; short sepals, pale Tyrian-rose, white tipped. Corolla lavender-blue to rose with lavender cast as bloom matures. Small flowers, free and delicately flared; light green foliage with red stems. Growth lax bush or trailer. Foster – American – 1973 – A.F.S. No. 1088.

Tintern Abbey. Single. Tube and sepals, light cerise; corolla rosy-lilac. Small flowers, borne in great profusion. Growth upright and bushy, produces good standard or large bush. Gunter – British – 1970.

Tiny Tim. Single. Tube and sepals bright red; corolla violet-purple. Very small miniature blooms as the name suggests, very free. Small foliage light green. Growth trailer, this cultivar should not be confused with Tiny Tim by Gagnon (1967). Walker – American – 1966.

Tiny Tim. Double. Long tube rosy-red, long slender rosy-red sepals; corolla blue, turning to lavender and at maturity to fuchsia colour. Medium size blooms, heavy flowerer all the way up branches, long lasting with long pistil. Growth trailer. Gagnon – American – 1967 – A.F.S. No. 708.

Tiny Tots. Single to semi-double. Short, thin red tube, sepals red on topside, rose colour underneath; corolla blue with pink marbling at base. Smallish flowers but very profuse, sepals are rough spoon shaped, four petals and two petaloids at base of each. Small foliage with oblong shape leaves. Growth upright and bushy, excellent for pot work. Pancharian – American – 1975 – A.F.S. No. 1295.

Tiptop. Single. Short tube and long spreading sepals, dark but bright red; corolla deepest royal violet-purple. Medium crisp flowers, produced in abundance, heat resistant. Growth upright. Hodges – American – 1956 – A.F.S. No. 246.

Titania. Single. Venus Victrix ×. Lowe – British – 1875.

Titania. Single. Tube and corolla, carmine; medium sized flowers and long, very free. Growth upright and bushy. Evans and Reeves – American – 1948.

Titania. Single. Tube and very pointed reflexed sepals, cerise; corolla deep coral, frilled edges, Breviflorae type. Tiny flowers, very free, foliage small but large for Breviflorae, deep green. Growth upright and self-branching, good for all shapes, including miniature or bonsai. Breviflorae hybrid. *F.microphylla* × Golden Dawn. Travis, S. – British – 1966.

Titanic. Double. Tube and sepals carmine; corolla petunia-purple, marbled. Very large blooms, fairly free, growth upright. Reiter – American – 1946.

Titian. Semi-double. Tube and sepals cerise; corolla Bishop's purple. Largish flowers and free, growth upright bush. Crousse – French – Date unknown.

Titus. Semi-double. Rosy-red and purple. Turville – British – 1847.

Toby Bridger. Double. Tube and sepals, bright pink; corolla pink, veined deeper pink. Largish blooms, very free, perfect shaped blooms. Darkish green foliage, growth upright, bushy and compact. Bridger – British – 1958.

*Tolemac. Single. Short $\frac{1}{4}$ in tube, orient-pink with darker streaks; fully reflexed sepals orient-pink on top, neyron-rose (R.H.S. 55D) underneath with recurved tips $1\frac{1}{4}$ in long by $\frac{1}{2}$ in wide. Corolla orient-pink (R.H.S. 36D) $\frac{1}{2}$ in long by $\frac{1}{2}$ in wide. Medium sized flowers quarter flared, short and bell shaped. Scheeles-green (R.H.S. 143C) foliage edged sap-green (R.H.S. 150C) paler on lower surface with elliptic leaves $2\frac{1}{4}$ in long by 1 in wide, entire edges, acute tips and rounded bases, veins, stems and branches are red. Growth self-branching medium upright, prefers filtered light and cool conditions, using more fertiliser and water than most, loses few lower leaves with maturity. Found by the raiser of the original cultivar in the vicinity of Ipswich, Suffolk, and introduced by Gouldings Fuchsias of Ipswich in 1984. Sport of Camelot. Goulding – British – 1984 – A.F.S. No. 1785.

Tolling Bell. Single. Short thick scarlet tube and sepals; corolla pure white, veined cerise. Largish flowers, free, most appropriate name, perfect bell shaped. Growth upright and bushy. Turner, E.T. – British – 1964.

Tom H. Oliver. Double. Short thick tube, rose; sepals claret-rose on top, light rose underneath. Corolla dark ruby-red with base of petals light rose, edges of petals serrated. Largish blooms, free, full box shaped, heat resistant if shaded. Growth trailer. Pennisi – American – 1972 – A.F.S. No. 1046.

Tomico. Single. Tube and sepals, flesh-pink; corolla terra-cotta and orange. Largish flowers and free, dark green foliage. Growth upright and bushy. Hazard and Hazard – American – Date unknown.

Tom Knights. Single. Short white to flesh coloured tube, white sepals shading to flesh on top, flesh-pink underneath 1 in long by $\frac{3}{8}$in wide held at horizontal with recurved tips. Corolla lavender to muted violet with white shading at base of petals. Medium sized flowers $2\frac{1}{2}$ in long by $\frac{3}{4}$ in wide, cup shaped and quite floriferous with more than one flower in each leaf axil, short stamens and long white pistil shading to pink, white stigma. Lightish green foliage with ovate leaves 2 in by $1\frac{1}{2}$ in and obtuse tips, moderate size with no trace of any redness of veins or stems. Growth tall upright, short jointed and vigorous, self-branching, likes plenty of root run, will produce good bush or standard. Rather similar to Melody. Raised and tested for 2 years in vicinity of Ipswich, East of England and introduced by B. and H.M. Baker of Halstead, Essex, in 1983. Goulding – British – 1983 – A.F.S. No. 1732.

Tom Pacey. Double. Pinkish white short tube; sepals white flushed pink, tipped green; corolla very pale pink. Medium sized blooms, free, compact, growth upright and spreading bush. Pacey – British – 1964.

Tom's Chum. Single. Tube and sepals crimson, corolla purple. Small flowers, very free, similar in every way to its parent except the colouring is deeper. Growth upright, bushy and hardy. Tom Thumb × . Catt – 1951.

Tom Thorne. Single to semi-double. Tube and sepals, very pale pink; corolla white. Largish flowers and free, growth upright. Named after a great fuchsia man. Bridger – British – 1959.

Tom Thumb. Single. Tube and sepals carmine; corolla mauve, veined carmine. Very small flowers, very free, blooms are apt to fall rather prematurely, but owing to profusion hardly noticed. Growth upright, bushy and dwarf, ideal for $3\frac{1}{2}$ in pot classes, hardy and suitable for rockeries. Accepted by the B.F.S. as showbench hardy. Received the R.H.S. First Class Certificate at the Wisley Hardy Trials 1960–62, was re-submitted for the 1975–78 Trials but received no further award. The origin of Tom Thumb seems to be obscure being confused with Pumila but generally accredited to Baudinat – French – 1850.

Tom Thumb

Tom West. Single. Tube and sepals red, corolla purple. Small flowers, not very free and late, grown more for its variegated foliage of cream and pale green. Growth lax bush or trailer. Possibly a mutation from Riccartonii. Meillez – French – 1853.

Tom Woods. Single. Short white waxy tube, sepals waxy-white, corolla purple fading to magenta with maturity. Small flowers, very prolific, similar in size to Northway and produced in 'twos' in each leaf axil. Pale green foliage, growth upright and short jointed. Reputed to be a sport from La Campanella but has none of the attributes. Raised in the vicinity of Maghull, Merseyside, Lancashire and introduced by Meadowcroft Nurseries of Huntingdon, 1981. Golics – British – 1980.

Topaz. Double. Tube and sepals, light coral to white; corolla violet-purple and topaz marbling. Medium sized blooms and free, petaloids coral and topaz, marbling with violet. Dark green foliage with roundish leaves. Growth trailer. Kennett – American – 1961 – A.F.S. No. 478.

Topflight. Double. Tube and sepals neyron-rose, tipped green; corolla campanula-violet. Medium sized blooms with ruffled petals, patched with neyron-erose. Growth trailer, very suitable for basketwork. Registered trademark in California, would appear to be exclusive to California. Fuchsia-La (Roy Walker) – American – 1964.

Topper. Semi-double. Tube and sepals red; corolla dark blue with white cloud over centre of each petal. Medium sized flowers and free, slim dark green foliage. Growth tall, upright bush. Brown and Soules – American – 1952.

Top Score. Semi-double. Short cerise tube, sepals brilliant cerise, reflexed to tube, $2\frac{1}{4}$ in long × $\frac{3}{4}$in wide. Corolla rich violet (R.H.S. 80A), cerise at base, $1\frac{7}{8}$ in long. Large blooms with long corolla of good substance and will take full sun, excellent in summer bedding. Dark green foliage with maroon leaf veining and stems, leaves $2\frac{3}{4}$ in long × 2 in wide. Growth upright and bushy, self-branching, this cultivar was tested by the raiser for 12 years before release. Originates from the vicinity of Derby. Introduced by Jackson's Nurseries of Tamworth in 1980. Handley – British – 1980 – A.F.S. No. 1542.

Top Secret. Double. Tube reddish-white, sepals white with red veins; corolla lavender-blue, held closely together by wreath of petaloids of pastel shades. Largish blooms, fairly free. Growth trailer. Prentice – American – 1967 – No. 717.

Topsy. Single. Tube and sepals carmine; corolla deep purple. Small flowers and free, growth upright, bushy, dwarf and hardy. Hazard and Hazard – American – Date unknown.

Torch. Double. Waxy tube, very broad sepals, shiny pink outside, heavily flushed salmon inside. Corolla of two distinct colours, purplish-red in centre with orange-salmon outer petals. Medium sized blooms and fairly free, very showy colouring. Growth tall upright. Munkner – American – 1963 – A.F.S. No. 566.

Torpilleur. Double. Scarlet and white. Lemoine – French – 1909.

Tosca. Double. Tube and sepals, rose-pink; corolla blush-pink with deep pink at base of petaloids. Large fluffy blooms and fairly free, flaring, but fade quickly. Growth trailer. Blackwell – British – 1965.

Tosson Bell. Single. Short tube, rose-red, sepals China-rose on top, lighter colour underneath, carried just below the horizontal. Corolla pinkish plum-purple, shading to lighter colour at base, fading to Imperial-purple. Medium sized flowers, very free, distinct bell shaped, lettuce-green foliage. Growth upright and bushy. Pink Cloud × Lena Dalton seedling × Sonata seedling × Marin Glow. Ryle – British – 1975 – A.F.S. No. 1255.

Touch of Frost. Single. White tube, long sepals white on top, rose pink underneath, tipped green. Corolla old rose with white variegations at base and with a slight frost on outside of petals. Medium sized flowers and free, growth lax bush or trailer. Soo Yun – American – 1969 – A.F.S. No. 851.

Touch of Pink. Semi-double. White tube with pink stripes, ⅝ in long and ⁵⁄₁₆ in wide; sepals faint pink with pink edges and green tips on top flushed pink underneath, sepals are smooth on top, creped underside and twist up when overstretched. Corolla white with pink veining, 1¼ in long and 1½ in wide, flared. Largish flowers with pink stamens and white pistil, very free-flowering. Serrated foliage with beetroot-purple veined leaves 2¼ in long and 1¼ in wide. Growth upright and bushy but will trail with weights. Raised and tested for 5 years in vicinity of Sebastopol, California. Soo Yun Field – American – 1979 – A.F.S. No. 1495.

Tour Eiffel. Single. Tube and sepals orangey-red; corolla of the same colour, almost a self. Medium sized flowers, very profuse bloomer. Small bronzed foliage, growth self-branching trailer. Introduced by Wills Fuchsia Nurseries in 1979. Alice Hoffman ×. de Graaff – Dutch – 1976.

Tourtonne. Single. Almost a red self with slight purple in the corolla. Very long tube and with one of its parents being Leverkusen the flowers are of a triphylla type. Prefers heat, flowers well in the sun but decidedly frost shy. Leverskusen × Waternymph. van Suchtelen – Dutch – 1968.

Tower of London. Double. Cerise and purplish-violet. Bundy – British – 1870.

townsendii. Tube red suffused with green, bulbous at base, sepals red; corolla scarlet. Not very free flowering, produced solitary in leaf axils. Low shrub and spreading. Johnston – 1925 – Ecuador.

Tracid. Semi-double. Short red tube, red sepals broad and upturned. Corolla pale pink veined deeper pink at the base. Medium sized blooms. Growth upright and bushy and proved to be hardy in the West Country of England. The first from the Colville stable for some considerable years. Introduced by C.S. Lockyer at Chelsea Show 1980. El Cid seedling. Colville – British – 1980.

Tracy Wilson. Single. Rose tube, sepals white on outside with pink underside, curl back over tube, tipped green. Corolla deep pink, medium sized flowers and farly free, do not flare, very long pistil. Small dark green foliage, growth trailer. Prentice – American – 1975 – A.F.S. No. 1300.

Trade Winds. Double. Tube white, sepals white and pink; corolla white with pink at base of petals. Small blooms, free, resembling popcorn. Growth lax bush or trailer. Fuchsia-La – American – 1968 – A.F.S. No. 808.

Trafalgar. Semi-double. Red and dark purple. Every – British – 1849.

Trail Blazer. Double. Tube and sepals, pale magenta; corolla dark magenta, almost a self. Largish blooms, very free and long, continuous once in bloom. Growth vigorous cascade, produces a wonderful basket, similar in growth and colour to Red Spider, but double and much larger. Reiter – American – 1951 – A.F.S. No. 83.

Trailing Autumn. Single. Tube and sepals, pale rose; corolla pale magenta with margin of orange-vermillion. Large flowers for a single, very free, growth trailer. Niederholzer-Waltz – American – 1949.

Trailing King. Single. Tube and sepals, rosy-cerise; corolla rosy-magenta. Small flowers but profuse, growth trailer. Brown – American – 1936.

Trailing King. Single. Tube and sepals whitish-pink; corolla orange-red. Small flowers very free, growth is very fast and cascading, similar to the Dutch cultivar Trailing Queen which is synonymous with Balkonkönigin known in England as Balkon. This Dutch cultivar is entirely different to the American cultivar under the same name raised by Brown in 1936.

Trailing Queen. Single. Tube and sepals red; corolla dull red, almost a self. Medium sized flowers, very free. Bronzy-red foliage, growth vigorous cascade, suitable as greenhouse climber or basket. Must have right conditions, can be very disappointing, flowers are dull with premature dropping of both buds and flowers. Kohene – German – 1896.

Trailing Strawberry Festival. Synonymous with Basket Strawberry Festival in California.

Tranquility. Double. White tube, sepals white on top, pink underneath, tipped green and curling back over flower. Corolla purple and pink, changing to ruby-red and pink. Large blooms, fairly free, red stemmed foliage, growth trailer. Soo Yun – American – 1970 – A.F.S. No. 909.

Trase. Semi-double to double. Tube and sepals, carmine-cerise; corolla white veined and flushed carmine-cerise. Medium sized blooms, very free, excellent shape. Growth upright bushy and hardy, height 1½ ft. Accepted by the B.F.S. as show-bench hardy. One of the best hardies and very suitable as specimen bush plant. Submitted by Wills Nursery for the R.H.S. Wisley Hardy Trials 1975–8 and received Award of Merit. Dawson, H. – British – 1959.

Traudchen Bohm. Single. Tube and sepals light red; corolla white with pink veining. Smallish flowers like small trumpets of the *corymbiflora*

type. Very interesting cross. Koralle × *F. corymbiflora*. Nutzinger – Austrian – 1973.

Traudchen Bonstedt. Triphylla single. Long
tube, creamy, pale salmon self. Short petals and
very free. Light green foliage, flushed bronze,
flushed red underneath, slightly hairy leaves.
Growth upright. *F. triphylla* × Bonstedt – German
– 1905.

Traudchen Bonstedt

Travis's Hardy. Double. Tube and sepals pink;
corolla claret-red, flushed pink. Medium sized
blooms and free. Growth upright and bushy and
hardy. Travis, J. – British – 1956.

Treasure. Double. Pale rose tube, sepals
neyron-rose; corolla pale silvery violet-pink. Large
blooms and free, very full. Growth upright and
bushy. A.F.S. Cert. of Merit. 1949. Niederholzer
– American – 1946.

Treasure Island. Single. Tube and sepals, pale
neyron-rose; corolla pale lavender. Medium well
formed flowers, very free, light green foliage.
Growth strong climbing or scandent shrub. *F.ly-
cioides* × Rolla. Reiter – American – 1939.

Tremorfa Pink. Single. Short thick white tube,
broad sepals white, flushed pink on upper surface,
deeper pink underneath. Corolla deep pink
flushed paler pink at the base. Largish flowers
with red stamens, pale pink style and white
stigma. Mid-green foliage, large, broad leaves,
veined red. Growth lax upright. Raised in the vicinity of Cardiff, South Wales. Adams – British –
1982 – A.F.S. No. 1699.

Tresco. Single. Tube and sepals, pale red; corolla purple, pink at base. Small flowers but very
free, large foliage, growth spreading bushy, very
vigorous, hardy, will make low spreading hedge.
Accepted by the B.F.S. as showbench hardy.
Raised and named in the famous Scilly Isles Gardens. Tresco Abbey Gardens – British – Date unknown.

Trewince Twilight. Single. Short tube, sepals
waxy-white, curl back completely with maturity.
Corolla pinkish-mauve, fading to pink. Medium
sized flowers, very free, same shape and form as
its parent. Darkish green foliage, very clean,
growth upright and bushy. Identical with a sport
introduced by Abermule Nurseries. Sport of Marin
Glow. Jackson, R.D. – British – 1972 – A.F.S.
No. 1048.

*Tricia Ann. Double. Tube and sepals
rhodamine-red, sepals are broad and held horizontally. Corolla opens violet-purple, heavily variegated claret-rose and passing through to softer
shades with maturity. Large blooms of almost perfect shape, very attractive. Growth upright and
bushy, very compact. Raised in the vicinity of
Bardney, Lincolnshire, and introduced by R. and
J. Pacey of Melton Mowbray, Leicestershire in
1983. Bellamy – British – 1983.

Tricolorii. Single. Tube and sepals crimson; corolla purple, cerise at base. Small flowers, very
free, variegated foliage of cream and green with pink
flush. Growth upright, bushy and hardy, suitable
as hedge with height up to 3 ft, lower growing
than *F.gracilis variegata* and flowers later.
Accepted by the B.F.S. as showbench hardy. *F.
magellanica* var. *gracilis variegata* ×. Potney –
British – Date unknown.

Tricolour Beauty. Single. Rose and violet.
Henderson – British – Date unknown.

Trimlet. Single. Short spinel-pink tube, slightly
reflexed spinel-pink sepals, tipped green, 1¾in
long. Corolla sea-lavender-pink fades to imperial
purple with mauve centre. Small flowers, very free
flowering with spinel-pink stamens and magnolia
purple anthers, spinel-pink pistil. Small dark green
foliage with blue hue, leaves 1½in long × ⅞in with
red main vein. Growth lax, will trail with weights
and self branching. Will take full sun in Ramsgate,
South East Coast of England, where tested for 2½
years before release. Standen – British – 1981 –
A.F.S. No. 1642.

Trinket. Double. Pale pink tube, sepals rosy-red,
upturned and curved back; corolla dark blue, red
veined. Largish blooms, free, unusual shape with
four wide spreading outer petals and crosswise
centre petals. Growth trailer. Gagnon – American
– 1965 – A.F.S. No. 620.

Trio. Double. Tube and sepals lavender-pink,
corolla rose-pink. Medium sized blooms very prolific especially for a double, beautiful resplendent
flowers. Foliage is pale green and with strong
compact growth very suitable for the showbench.
Growth upright and bushy, best grown as H2.
Introduced by C.S. Lockyer of Bristol in 1981.
Holmes, E. –British – 1981.

triphylla. Triphylla single. Bright red to scarlet
self, long tubed flowers, fairly free. Foliage
coppery-bronze   reddish-purple   underneath.
Growth, erect shrub, lowish and tender, very frost
shy. Always regarded as a difficult plant to cultivate successfully, can be located at Botanical
Gardens such as Kew or Edinburgh. This is the
species on which the genus was founded, originally called *F. triphylla flore coccinea*; the first
fuchsia ever discovered, by Father Plumier, a Je-
suit botanist, in 1703. Plumier – 1703 – San
Domingo.

Triphylla Hybrida. Triphylla single. Very long
tube, reddish-scarlet, short petals, pale vermilion.
Very long flowers, several inches long. Foliage
normal green, flushed red underneath. Growth
upright. *F. triphylla* × *F. boliviana*. Lemoine –
French – 1895.

Trisha. Double. Tube and sepals, near white,
tipped green; corolla burgundy, splashed with
rose and magenta. Large blooms, free for size,
growth upright and strong. Antonelli – American
– 1965 – A.F.S. No. 636.

Tristesse. Double. Tube and sepals, pale rose-
pink; corolla lilac-blue. Medium sized blooms,
free, does not scorch. Growth upright. Lilac
Lustre ×. Blackwell – British – 1965.

Triumph. Semi-double. Pink and red. Miellez –
French – 1849.

Triumphant. Single to semi-double. Tube and
sepals, turkey-red; corolla amethyst-violet. Very
large flowers up to 3 in, not very free, open shape.
Growth upright and extremely vigorous, grows to

several feet high in California. Niederholzer –
American – 1946.

Troika. Double. Tube reddish-pink, much paler
colour with warmth, sepals white. Corolla light
blue to lilac-pink. Medium to large blooms, very
free with the characteristics of its parent, white
style. Growth lax bush or trailer, likes cool conditions. La Campanella×. de Graaff – Dutch –
1976.

Tropicana. Double. Tube and sepals, pale
salmon-pink, tipped green, deep pink underneath.
Corolla orange, large blooms, fairly free and of
unusual colouring. Growth lax bush or trailer.
Tiret – American – 1964 – A.F.S. No. 596.

Tropic Sunset. Double. Tube and sepals carmine; corolla dark purple, splashed pink. Small
blooms and fairly free best, described as a miniature Autumnale. Feature of this cultivar is the variegated small foliage of reddish-bronze leaves
tipped green on strong bold stems. Growth trailer
and self-branching, needs little pinching. Autum-
nale×. Antonelli – American – 1965 – A.F.S. No.
635.

Troubador. Double. Tube and wide sepals, brilliant crimson; corolla dark lilac-purple with
splashes of crimson at base of petals. Large
blooms, free for size with long pointed buds. Dark
green foliage, growth natural trailer. Waltz –
American – 1963 – A.F.S. No. 588.

Troubadour. Double. Cardinal-red and violet.
Bland – British – 1869.

Troutbeck. Single. Short tube salmon, sepals
creamy-white, flushed pink, tipped green. Corolla
aster-violet, short flowers, very free and of good
shape, will take full sun. Growth upright and
bushy. Dorothea Flower×Hawkshead. Thornley
– British – 1967 – A.F.S. No.1064.

Trubell. Single. Tube and sepals rosy-red, corolla Imperial-purple with white flushing veined
scarlet. Very large flowers 4 to 5 in long with extremely long and broad sepals, unswept but held
well away from the tube. Large long petals
cone-shaped corolla. Growth medium upright
bush. Bishop's Belle×. Gadsby – British – 1970
– A.F.S. No. 968.

Trudy. Single. Tube and sepals, rhodamine-
pink, held well back; corolla cyclamen-pink.
Smallish bell shaped flowers, very free, similar,
but an improvement upon Chillerton Beauty.
Growth upright, bushy and hardy in the Midlands
Submitted by Wills Nursery for the R.H.S. Wisley
Hardy Trials 1975–78 and received Highly Com-
mended Certificate. Gadsby – British – 1969 –
A.F.S. No. 969.

True Love. Semi-double. White tube, sepals
white with red veins; corolla blue and variegated pink. Large flowers
and fairly free, corrugated petals with centre protruding from base. Growth trailer. Soo Yun –
American – 1967 – A.F.S. No. 731.

Trumpeter. Single. Crimson and rich purple. Fry
– British – 1882.

Trumpeter. Triphylla type single. Long tube,
pale geranium-lake self. Thick tube, short petals,
colour darkens with age, very free. Rich bluish-
green foliage, growth cascade, makes excellent
basket, best grown as H1. Reiter – American –
1946.

* Tsjiep. Single. Long creamy-white tube, sepals
white on top, slightly flushed pink underneath,
sepals recurved and held well below the horizontal. Corolla orangy-red ¾ in by ½ in wide. Very small
true single flowers 1¼ in long by 1 in wide, sepals
slightly tipped green. Best described as a miniature Amy Lye with pistil held on one side of stamens, short stamens pink with creamy-white anthers. Flowers are very dainty and very free.
Besides having unusual name (pronounced
'chips') has unusual parentage Mephisto×Coun-
tess of Aberdeen. Light green foliage with 1¼ in
long by 1 in wide leaves, ovate with obtuse tip.
Growth upright and bushy, short-jointed, ideal for
miniature standard bush and small pot culture.
Raised in the vicinity of Lisse in the Netherlands
and introduced by John Ridding of Fuchsiavale
Nurseries of Kidderminster in 1983. de Graaff –
Dutch – 1983.

tuberosa. Red tube, green sepals; no corolla.
Flowers borne in the upper axils, with queer-
shaped flattened tube. Epiphytic or terrestrial
roots bearing clusters of roundish tubers. Leaves
may shed at flowering. Shrub attaining 3 ft in
height. Synonymous with *F. chloroloba.* Krause
– 1905 – Peru.

Tulip Time. Double. Tube rose; sepals white on
topside, shell-pink underneath. Corolla lobelia-
blue, fading to cobalt-violet. Large blooms and
profuse. Growth upright and bushy. Kennett and
Ross – American – 1954 – A.F.S. No. 240.

Tumbler. Single. Long flesh-pink tube, sepals
flesh-pink, twisted pinwheel type. Corolla geranium and rose-pink. Barrel shaped flowers, very-
free, best in shade, medium sized. Growth trailer,
long thin arching branches. Tolley – British –
1974 – A.F.S. No. 1233.

Tumbling Waters. Double. Tube and reflexed
sepals, dark crimson outside, light crimson underneath. Corolla cyclamen-purple, medium to large
blooms, fairly free, unusual colour combinations
for trailing cultivar. Growth cascading trailer.
A.F.S. Cert. of Merit. Reiter – American – 1954
– A.F.S. No. 215

tunariensis. Tube red to pinkish, sepals red; no
corolla. Very few flowers borne solitary in the
upper leaf axils. Epiphytic shrub with tuberous
roots. Kuntze – 1898 – Bolivia.

Tuonela. Double. Tube and sepals, bright blue;
corolla powder-blue with touch of pink. Medium
sized blooms and free. Growth lax bush or trailer.
Blackwell – British – 1970.

Turandot. Double. Tube and sepals, white with
shade of purple; corolla violet-purple. Medium
sized blooms, free and flaring. Growth lax bush or
trailer. Blackwell – British – 1970.

Turquoise Lady. Double. Tube and sepals red;
corolla dark blue. Medium sized blooms, free,
fairly early. Growth upright. Plummer – American
– 1952.

Tutone. Double. Tube and sepals pink; corolla
ashen-blue, alternating symmetrically with pink.
Very full blooms, large and free. Dark green, small
foliage, sun resistant. Growth lax bush or trailer,
best as H1. Machado – American – 1963 – A.F.S.
No. 563.

Tutti-Frutti. Double. Tube and reflexed sepals,
pale pink; corolla iridescent magenta-rose. Medium sized blooms, free, the four centre petals well
defined, auxiliary petals are etched and marbled

rose-pink. Growth trailer, too long-jointed will produce 8 to 10 in of stem. Schnabel-Paskesen – American – 1966 – A.F.S. No. 461.

Tutu. Double. Tube and spreading sepals, palest rose inside, greenish white outside. Corolla paler rhodamine-purple, flecked with pale aster-violet. Largish blooms, very flat and free. Growth upright and bushy. Reiter – American – 1952 – A.F.S. No. 131.

*Twiggy. Single. Clear red tube, sepals clear red long and slender, sharp pointed and stand out at 45° angle. Corolla mauve, veined red, small flowers best described as spiderlike, very profuse flowering with grapelike large dark red berries; will produce good fuchsia jam. Medium sized foliage with willowlike twigs, hence the name. Raised in the Netherlands in the vicinity of Lisse. *F. lycioides* × . de Graaff – Dutch – 1980.

Twilight. Double. Tube and upturned sepals, softest pink; corolla deep blue. Medium sized blooms spreading out wide with maturity and fairly free. Dark green foliage, growth lax bush or trailer. Hodges – American – 1958 – A.F.S. No. 339.

Twilight Mist. Double. White tube, sepals white, upturned deep pink; corolla dark violet, marbled fuchsia-pink on outer petals, washed at base with rose-madder. Medium sized blooms, very full and free. Growth lax bush or trailer. Evans and Reeves – American – 1954 – A.F.S. No. 218.

Twinkling Stars. Single. Short, thick tube, blush-pink, narrow sharply pointed sepals, blush-pink outside, pale pink inside. Corolla fuchsia-pink. Small flowers held nearly upright, short even length petals, curved tube gives nodding appearance, early and free flowering. Small foliage, growth upright and bushy, very compact, produces short-jointed pot plant. Raised and tested in vicinity of Derby 6 years before release. Handley – British – 1976 – A.F.S. No. 1373.

Twistie. Single. Tube and sepals rose; corolla pale orchid. Long and twisted flowers, small but free. Growth trailer. Niederholzer – American – 1944.

*Tyfoon. Dutch introduction for 1983. Raised in the vicinity of Amersfoort, Netherlands. First Kiss × Pink Bon Accorde. Rijff – Dutch – 1983.

U.F.O. Single. Short white tube, sepals white, reflexed tight to stem; corolla deep lilac, centre of petals white. Medium sized flowers borne in clusters, very free, open completely flat when matured, saucer shape. Smallish foliage, growth upright and bushy. Handley – British – 1972 – A.F.S. No. 1059.

Ullswater. Double. Long pale pink tube, sepals pale pink, crepe-like and long. Corolla orchid-blue, fading to orchid-purple. Large blooms, very compact and free. Growth upright and bushy. Travis, J. – British – 1958 – A.F.S. No. 1149.

Ultramar. Double. White tube, sepals long, broad and recurving white; corolla delicate pastel grey-blue. Globular blooms, free, creamy-white buds, base of corolla packed with short white-streaked irregular petaloids. Growth upright and vigorous. Reiter – American – 1956 – A.F.S. No. 274.

Ulverston. Double. Tube flesh-pink of medium length and width, sepals are same colour as tube, short, broad, underside stronger shade of pink (R.H.S. 61D) rose-Bengal. Corolla violet-purple (R.H.S. 77A) the edge of each petal showing a gray watermark. Medium-sized blooms and very free for a double. Although this cultivar was raised in 1965 was not released or introduced until 1978. Berkeley × . Thornley – British – 1965 – A.F.S. No. 1470.

umbrosa. (Bentham 1845). Synonymous with *F. loxensis.*

Una. Single. White and rose-pink. Turville – British – 1858.

Una Cochrane. Double. Tube and sepals red; corolla very pale pink, flushed and veined rose. Medium to large blooms, fairly free and open. Growth upright. Spackman – American – 1933.

Uncle Charley. Semi-double. Tube and sepals, rose-red; corolla lilac-lavender, shading to lilac. Largish flowers, free, growth upright and bushy, very good cultivar. Tiret – American – 1949.

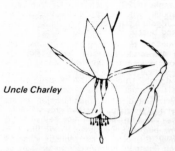

Uncle Charley

Uncle Ike. Double. Tube and sepals, bright crimson; corolla violet. Large blooms, fairly free for size, many petaloids of white and crimson. Growth upright and bushy. Walker and Jones – American – 1950.

Uncle Jeff. Double. Tube and sepals, dark red; corolla purple. Large flowers, not very free but compact. Growth upright and bushy. Tiret – American – 1962 – A.F.S. No. 528.

Uncle Jules. Double. Tube and sepals crimson; corolla campanula blue-violet. Huge blooms, fairly free, good shape. Growth tall, upright with arching branches. Reiter – American – 1947.

Uncle Mike. Double. Tube and sepals white; corolla lipstick-red, maturing to wine-red. Large blooms, fairly free, growth natural trailer. Tiret – American – 1962 – A.F.S. No. 531.

Uncle Nicki. Double. Tube and sepals pale pink to white, corolla purple to red. Medium sized blooms. Little known cultivar exclusive to the North of England. Listed by Penhall's Fuchsia Deeside Gardens of Shaw, Oldham. Raiser unknown – British – *ca* 1970s.

Uncle Steve. Double. Tube and sepals, pale pink; corolla plum-purple. Large blooms, fairly free. Growth trailer. Tiret – American – 1962 – A.F.S. No. 530.

unduavensis. This species is very similar to *F. hirsuta* with the same flowers and climbing epiphytic growth with tuberous roots. The difference is the small, very hairy leaves, which are more developed at flowering time. Munz – 1943 – Bolivia.

Unfinished Symphony. Semi-double. Tube and sepals, bright carmine; corolla blue, veined carmine. Large flowers and free, growth upright and strong. Violet Gem ×. Blackwell – British – 1961.

Unique. Semi-double. Red and very dark purple. Miller – British – 1845.

Unique. Single to semi-double. Tube and very broad sepals, pale rose-madder; corolla rose-madder, marbled Imperial-purple. Medium sized flowers and free. Growth dwarf upright and largish, light green foliage. Hazard and Hazard – American – 1930?

Unique. Single. Tube and sepals, rosy-red; corolla dark red. Medium sized flowers, very free. Growth upright and bushy. Haag and Son – American – 1950.

Universal. Double. Red and purple. Smith – British – 1862.

Unusual. Double. White tube, sepals pure white held at angle of 90° to corolla. Corolla palest pink-lavender with deep pink stripes and blotches. Medium sized blooms and free. Growth upright and bushy, short jointed. Coals – British – 1962.

Upright Anna. Double. Tube and sepals carmine; sepals magenta to light red. Medium sized blooms identical to Anna except for the growth which is upright. Unregistered American cultivar, grown in California. Fuchsia-La (Roy Walker) – American – 1953.

Upward Look. Single. Short carmine tube, short broad sepals, carmine, tipped green. Corolla pale rosine-purple. Short flowers, very full, held erect similar to one of its parents Bon Accorde, but much deeper colouring, prefers shade. Growth upright and bushy. This cultivar was the first real breakthrough of the erect flowers since Bon Accorde. Athela × Bon Accorde. Gadsby – British – 1968 – A.F.S. No. 870.

Urania. Single or semi-double. Light red tube, sepals light red, standing out, tipped green. Corolla purple changing to red-purple with maturity. Smallish flowers, free, with light red stamens and style. Dark green foliage with light hairy leaves, growth upright and bushy. Bon Accorde × Pallas. De Groot – Dutch – 1973.

Ursula Unwin. Semi-double. Creamy-white and rose. Jardine – British – 1902.

Utopia. Single. Tube and sepals, brilliant crimson; corolla dark Tyrian-rose. Exceptionally long and large flowers, free, perfectly shaped early. Growth upright and willowy. Niederholzer – American – 1943.

Uttoxeter Beauty. Single. Creamy-white and pink. Rogers – British – 1847.

Uttoxeter Rival. Single. Creamy-white and red. Rogers – British – 1847.

Vagabond. Double. Short tube and long, broad upturned sepals brilliant carmine; corolla magenta, many outer overlapping petals of magenta splashed with carmine. Largish blooms, buds very large, free. Large foliage. Growth trailer or espa-

lier. Schnabel – American – 1953 – A.F.S. No. 186.

Valencia. Semi-double. Tube and sepals rose; corolla vivid pink. Largish flowers, early and free. Dark green foliage, growth upright. Schnabel-Paskesen – 1962 – A.F.S. No. 533.

Valentina Tjeresjkova. Single. Long light red tube, sepals long and pointed, light red with white running towards tips, tipped green. Corolla deep red-purple. Medium to large flowers with deep pink stamens and style, very long style. Growth upright and bushy. Steevens – Dutch – 1972.

Valentine. Semi-double. Tube and long sepals, white flushed rose; corolla deepest Imperial-purple. Large flowers, free, growth semi-trailer. Reiter – American – 1948.

Vale of Belvoir. Single. Thick tube, neyron-rose, sepals neyron-rose, tipped green, curl back. Corolla spectrum-violet, flushed with rose, fading to pale Imperial-purple. Medium sized flowers, very free, open bell shaped, will take full sun. Growth semi-trailer. Rosendale × Lady Isobel Barnett. Gadsby – British – 1973 – A.F.S. No. 1127.

Valerie. Single. Short tube empire rose (R.H.S. 48B), striped red, fully reflexed sepals white, tipped green. Corolla violet (R.H.S. 83B) flushed pink (R.H.S. 36B) at base of each petal. medium sized flowers, extremely floriferous and will produce large exhibition plant. Medium foliage with ovate leaves and acute tips, Lobed base and serrated margins. Growth medium upright, will make good bush of standard. Named after the introducer's wife, tested in the vicinity of Carlisle, North West England for 3 years before being introduced by John Ridding of Fuchsiavale Nurseries of Kidderminster 1981. Norman Mitchinson × (Simonside × Lindisfarne). Mitchinson – British – 1981 – A.F.S. No. 1656.

Valerie Ann. Double. Tube and sepals, creamy-white, flushed pink; corolla white, flushed pink. Medium sized blooms, free and compact. Growth trailer. Hatt – British – 1963.

Valiant. Single. Cerise and rosy red. Jennings – British – 1850.

Val Secrett. Semi-double. Tube and sepals, rose-madder; corolla rose-bengal. Medium sized flowers and free, dark green foliage. Growth upright. Letts – American – 1936.

Vance Wells. Double. White tube, heavy white sepals; corolla indelible or dark mulberry. Largish blooms, fairly free, ball shaped. Dark green foliage, growth trailer. Gagnon – American – 1967 – A.F.S. No. 707.

Vanessa. Double. Pink tube, long pink sepals curl upwards; corolla pale lavender-blue. Very full blooms, medium sized and free. Lightish green foliage, growth upright and bushy. This cultivar can be difficult and disappointing under wrong conditions, best grown as H1. Colville – British – 1964.

Vanessa Jackson. Single. Tube salmon-red (R.H.S. 43C), long salmon-orange (R.H.S. 41C), sepals held well out, 2 in long × ⅜ in wide. Corolla salmon-orange (R.H.S. 41C) shading to orange-red (R.H.S. 40C) then to cardinal red (R.H.S. 45C) at the edges. Large, long trumpet-shaped flowers with closely overlapping petals, edges flare out sharply resembling a daffodil, very attractive and distinctive shape, prolific flowering, long salmon-red pistil. Lightly serrated mid-green foliage, tinged bronze, leaves are 3 in long × 2 in wide. Growth natural trailer, self-branching does not need weights, will make good basket or weeping standard. Cultivar was tested for 10 years before release. Originates from the vicinity of Derby. Introduced by Jackson's Nurseries of Tamworth in 1980, and named after the introducer's wife. Handley – British – 1980 – A.F.S. No. 1547.

Vanity. Double. Tube and sepals, dark orange, corolla rosy-blue to light orange with deep orange veins. Large blooms, free for size, unusual colour combinations very exciting. Light green foliage, growth trailer should not be confused with Vanity Fair. Martin – American – 1967 – A.F.S. No. 267.

Vanity Fair. Double. Thick tube and upturned sepals, greenish-white, tipped green and flushed with pale pink; corolla pale pink. Very large blooms and free for size, globular and heavily petaled with serrated edges, resembling a carnation. Growth upright and vigorous, produces a fine conical, blooms are excellent for cut bloom classes, best grown as H1. Schnabel-Paskesen – American – 1962 – A.F.S. No. 534.

Variegata. See *magellanica* var. *globosa*.

*Variegated Snowcap. Semi-double. Tube and sepals bright red, pure white corolla with slight cerise veining. Rather small flowers but very profuse and floriferous. Foliage with green and creamy-white variegation nothing like the other sport, Rosecroft Beauty, and far superior. Introduced by Homestead Nurseries of Uxbridge, Middlesex, in 1983. Sport from Snowcap. Locator unknown – British – 1983.

*Variegated Tolling Bell. Single. Short thick scarlet tube, scarlet sepals. Pure white corolla, veined cerise. Largish flowers perfect bell shape, aptly named. Variegated cream, green and red foliage, all other characteristics the same as its parent. Growth upright and bushy. Introduced by Woodbridge Nurseries of Hounslow, Middlesex in 1984. Sport of Tolling Bell. Locator unknown – ca 1983.

*Variegated White Joy. Single. Short tube and broadish sepals held horizontally. White with slight pink flush. White corolla small to medium sized flowers, perfect bell shape, extremely prolific. Foliage is attractive green and gold variegated, the first of many sports from White Joy. Growth upright and bushy, short-jointed and well within the exhibition category. Located in the vicinity of Middlesex and introduced by Woodbridge Nurseries of Hounslow, Middlesex in 1984. Dyos – British – 1984.

Varty's Pride. Double. White tube flushed rose; sepals white, flushed rose, tipped green. Corolla white with slight flush of rose under sepals. Medium sized blooms with red stamens and pink pistil, same size as parent. Foliage is lighter than Swingtime and red veined. Growth trailer, throws two sets of flowers in leaf axil, suitable for training as basket or bush. Tested for 2 years in vicinity of Kendal, Cumbria, before release. Sport of Swingtime. Varty – British – 1979 – A.F.S. No. 1504.

Vee Jay's Orchid. Double. Long tube white shading to pale pink with slight curve, long sepals pale pink on top, darker creped pink underneath, tipped green, curling and twisting towards tube. Corolla rosy-lavender blending rose to pink from edge of petals to base with rose veins. Large curv-

ing blooms with four petaloids originating from each sepal base. Dark green slightly bluish foliage leaves 3 in to 4 in in length. Growth natural trailer, no weights required to make good basket. Tested for 4 years in vicinity of Coos Bay, Oregon before release. Vee Jay Greenhouse – American – 1981 – A.F.S. No. 1625.

Vee Jay's Torment. Single. Short, thin, red tube; red sepals flare in a pin-wheel fashion; corolla violet with red stripes, rose colour at base of petals. Medium sized flowers, but occasionally will produce five or six petals making a semi-double. Foliage yellow-green which turns to normal green in full sun. Growth trailer, tested for 2 years in vicinity of Coos Bay, Oregon, California. Vee Jay Greenhouse – American – 1979 – A.F.S. No. 1490.

Velma. Single. Short off-white tube, sepals off-white maturing to deep pink which turn right back over tube. Corolla deep pink maturing to purple with short and round petals. Medium sized flowers and similar to Fancy Flute. Large light green foliage. Growth upright. Raised in vicinity of Cardiff. Serena Blue × Fancy Flute, although Serena Blue is not known. Adams – British – 1979 – A.F.S. No. 1522.

Veluive Groet. Single. Tube light red, sepals white with red blush and red veined, tipped green. Corolla blue-purple with red veining, paler at base. Medium to large flowers, red stamens and style. Growth upright and bushy. Parentage: Marin Glow × Venus. De Groot – Dutch – 1973.

Ventura. Single. Tube and sepals, coral-pink; corolla rose-madder. Medium sized flowers, very free, bell shaped with terminal cluster habit. Growth upright, sturdy bush. Evans and Reeves – 1951 – A.F.S. No. 100.

Venus. No other details available except the parentage: *F. regia* var. *typica* × Jamboree. De Groot – Dutch – ca. 1970.

Venus. Double. Tube and sepals red; corolla white, veined pink. Medium sized blooms borne in great profusion, light green foliage. Growth upright and bushy yet dainty, branching habit, height 1½ to 2 ft. Hardy in Southern England, raised in the Scilly Isles. Tabraham – British – 1974.

Venus Medici. Single. White and violet-blue. Salter – British and French – 1856.

Venusta. Single. Tangerine and dull red. Not to be confused with the species *F.venusta*. Harrison or Smith – British – 1845.

venusta. Rich red tube, sepals red; corolla carmine. Long flowers borne in a terminal pendant corymbose racemes. One of the most beautiful of the species. Elliptic leaves, acute at base. Growth is upright with slender fronds, Kris – 1823 – Colombia and Venezuela.

Venustrum. Double. Carmine and rose-pink. Harrison – British – 1842.

Venus Victrix. Single. One of the most interesting cultivars, was an unintentional seedling raised by Gulliver of Herstmonceaux in 1840 but was not introduced until 1842 when it was distributed by Cripps of Tunbridge Wells at a price of one guinea. This diminuitive plant has a white tube and sepals, tipped green with a purple-violet corolla, in fact a pure blue when first open. This cultivar was the first white tubed cultivar and on account of its unusual colour combination was extensively used for hybridising and is still being used to try and produce that elusive non-fading blue. It can claim to have its blood, however, diluted, in practically all the white tube cultivars since raised. Venus Victrix is now very difficult to locate and still sought after by most hybridists. Should you be fortunate to obtain it, could be most disappointed with its unattractive habit and growth, tiny flowers which are fairly free and of rather dwarfish growth and straggly. Best grown as H2 but has been known to stand H3 conditions. Venus Victrix is truly one for the genuine collector. *F.magellanica* ×. Gulliver – British – 1840.

Venus Victrix Improved. Single. Somewhat an improvement upon Venus Victrix. Rowson – British – 1887.

Vera. Single. Tube and sepals, rich red; corolla Tyrian-rose. Large flowers and free, growth upright A.F.S. Cert. of Merit 1948. Niederholzer – American – 1946.

Vera Letts. Semi-double. Rich red self. Letts – British – 1882.

Vera Nazeman. Single. Tube and sepals white with red blush, sepals rather long, deep pink underneath, tipped green. Corolla lilac-red, medium to large flowers, very free flowering, pink stamens and white style. Lightish green foliage, growth upright and bushy. Steevens – Dutch – 1973.

Vera Sergine. Semi-double. White and pink. Lemoine – French – 1892.

Verbesserte Henriette Ernst. This cultivar is the same as Frau Henriette Ernst but with improved growth and is self branching. Raiser and date unknown – German.

Verda Evelyn. Double. Short tube and upturned wide sepals, deep pink; corolla pink with petaloids at base, slightly darker. Large full blooms and free, foliage dark green with reddish stems. Growth trailer. Keuchler – American – 1963 – A.F.S. No. 548.

verrucosa. Tube red, green at base, sepals bright red; corolla red. Small flowers, sparse, borne solitary in upper leaf axils. Upright shrub to height of 6 feet in natural habitat. Synonymous with *F. perbrevis.* Hartweg – 1845 – Colombia and Venezuela.

Versicolor. See *magellanica.*

Vesta. Single. Rose-pink and white. Smith – British – 1846.

Vesta. No other details available except the parentage: *F. regia* var. *typica* × Alice Hoffman. De Groot – Dutch – 1970.

Vibrato. Single. Tube and short sepals, salmon-red, flushed orange; corolla rich claret-red. Smallish flowers, very free blooms in terminal clusters. Dark green foliage, young lateral stems are red. Growth natural trailer. Sayers – American – 1974 – A.F.S. No. 1162.

Vicki Putley. Single. Tube and sepals white, flushed carmine; corolla rich crimson-red. Medium sized flowers, very free. Growth lax bush or trailer. Putley – British – 1964.

Victor. Double. Red and violet-blue. Bull – British – 1870.

Victoria. Single. Rose and white. Smith – British – 1855.

Victoria. Double. Red and white. Twrdy – German – 1874.

Victoria. Single. Tube and sepals soft-pink; corolla smoky-orange. medium sized flowers, growth bushy. This cultivar now makes three with same name, the other being raised by Smith and Twrdy. Curtis – British – 1971.

Victorian. Double. Short pink tube; pink sepals; corolla pink. Largish blooms and free, growth upright. Paskesen – American – 1971 – A.F.S. No. 957.

* Victorian Val. Single. Short rose-pink tube, deep rose-pink reflexing sepals. Corolla rose-cerise. Medium sized flowers, very profuse with two or more flowers in each axil. Light green foliage with attractive medium sized leaves. Growth upright and bushy, plant flowers well over a long period. Raised in the vicinity of Banbury and introduced by the raiser, Sinclair Fuchsias of Banbury, in 1984. Elkington – British – 1981.

Victoria Sardou. Double. Scarlet and violet. Lemoine – French – 1861.

Victory. Semi-double. Tube and long recurved sepals, carmine; corolla rose-madder. Long flowers and very free, globular shape. Growth trailer. Suzanne Pasquier × San Francisco. Reiter – American – 1942.

Vie En Rose. Double. Tube and sepals, pale Tyrian-rose; corolla light violet with flecks of white. Medium sized blooms in great profusion, exquisite pastel colouring. Growth upright and bushy. Reiter – American – 1955 – A.F.S. No. 230.

Vielliebchen. Single. Tube and sepals shining red; corolla deep purple changing to red-purple with maturity. Small to medium flowers, very free, pink stamens and pink-red style. Small medium green foliage, growth upright and bushy. Charming × *F.magellanica* var. *gracilis.* Wolf – German – 1911.

Vienna. Double. Tube and recurved sepals, bengal-rose; corolla lilac-blue. Medium sized blooms, long and free, serrated petals. Growth upright. Niederholzer-Waltz – American – 1950 – A.F.S. No. 56.

Vienna Waltz. Double. Tube and sepals, dark pink; corolla rich lavender, splashed red and pink. Large blooms, flaring and fairly free, like filtered shade. Dark green foliage, growth trailer. Sport of Dusky Rose. Nix Nursery – American – 1971 – A.F.S. No. 942.

Vincent d'Indy. Double. Tube and sepals, carmine-cerise; corolla rich violet-purple, suffused carmine. Very large blooms, not free but of beautiful shape and rich colouring. Growth upright and bushy, still has its admirers. Lemoine – French – 1901.

Vindolanda. Single. Short crimson tube, sepals crimson on both sides; corolla violet, fading to cyclamen-purple. Small flowers but very profuse, spear shaped foliage with serrated leaves and pink rib. Growth tall, upright bush, short jointed. Lena Dalton × Tennessee Waltz × Earl of Beaconsfield seedling × Strawberry Delight. Ryle – British – 1975 – A.F.S. No. 1256.

Vinegar Joe. Single. Tube and sepals pink; corolla rosy-purple. Large flowers for single and free, growth trailer. Terrible name for a nice cultivar. Hazard and Hazard – American – Date unknown.

Viola. Single. Tube and pinwheel shaped sepals, pink; corolla blue. Medium sized flowers and free, early. Growth low bush, very hardy. Dale – American – 1950.

Viola. Single. Waxy-white to pale pink tube, sepals waxy-white to pale pink on topside, bright pink fading to soft pink on maturity on underneath, tipped green. Corolla dark bluish-purple with splashes of pink, fading to lavender-pink. Medium sized flowers with four separate incurved petals forming corolla slightly ruffled with some serrated edges, very narrow, twisting bright pink petaloids forming on the inside and outside of corolla, sometimes with white whiskers. Flaring stamens and pistil are very long and pink. Very dark green foliage. Growth trailer, will make good basket with weights. The first real introduction from Robert Castro for 10 years, tested in the vicinity of Oakland, California before release. Castro – American – 1981 – A.F.S. No. 1634.

Violacea. Double. Tube and sepals white; corolla orchid-pink, blooms, fairly free, growth trailer. Fuchsia-La – American – 1968 – A.F.S. No. 804.

Violet. Double. Tube and sepals scarlet; corolla Bishop's violet. Medium sized blooms, fairly free, growth upright and bushy. Niederholzer – American – 1947.

Violet Adams. Single to semi-double. Tube and sepals, soft red; corolla white, veined red. Largish flowers, fairly free, foliage attractive yellow to lettuce-green. Growth upright and bushy. Barton – American – 1970 – A.F.S. No. 917.

Violet Bassett-Burr. Double. Short greenish-white and pink tube, very long upswept sepals completely hiding tube, white, tipped green, pink at base. Corolla pale lilac, paler at base. Very full blooms, free; dark green foliage. Growth upright. Holmes, E. – British – 1972.

Violet Flush. Double. Red tube, broad bright red sepals which do not sweep back. Corolla blue-violet splashed deep pink. Small blooms with pale pink petaloids, red stamens and very long red pistil. Small mid-green wiry foliage is lanceolate (spear-shaped) with serrated leaf margins. Growth lax bush, self-branching, will make good basket or bush, best colour develops in the sun. Originates from the vicinity of Timperley, Cheshire. Masquerade × Pink Ballet Girl. Howarth – British – 1980 – A.F.S. No. 1579.

Violet Gem. Semi-double. Tube and sepals carmine; corolla deep violet. Large spreading flowers and free. Growth upright and bushy. Niederholzer-Waltz – American – 1949.

Violetkoningin. Semi-double or double. Tube and sepals white with red blush, sepals are pink underneath, tipped green. Corolla blue-purple changing to red-purple with maturity, pink-red at base. Medium to large blooms, stamens and style are light pink. Growth upright, bushy and self branching. Cultivar grown and cultivated in the Netherlands. Raiser and date unknown.

Violet Lace. Double. Red tube and sepals, corolla violet splashed with pink. Large full double blooms unusual for reputed hardy cultivar. Dark green foliage, upright and bushy growth, makes compact plant, height 2 to 2½ ft. Hardy in Southern England, raised in the Scilly Isles. Tabraham – British – 1982.

Violet Nymph. Double. Carmen-rose tube, sepals greenish white, pure white on reverse side,

reflexing against stem. Corolla shades of campanula-violet, fading to petunia-rose. Small blooms, very free, good shape; small foliage. Growth medium bush. Crockett – British – 1969 – A.F.S. No. 822.

Violet Quartette. Semi-double. Tube and sepals, geranium-red; corolla rich violet. Medium sized flowers, free, centre of corolla has four tubes formed by the rolling of petals. Growth medium upright and bushy. Machado – American – 1959 – A.F.S. No. 404.

Violet Rosette. Double. Tube and short wide sepals, bright carmine, sepals growing straight back. Corolla deep violet, touch of red at base of petals. Large blooms, free for size very full and of beautiful shape. Bright green foliage, growth upright, makes fine conical, blooms are winners in cut bloom classes. Kuechler – American – 1963 – A.F.S. No. 549.

Violet Roth. Double. Short tube and sepals, greenish-white; corolla almost the same colour with more pronounced green, fading to lighter shade with maturity. Medium sized blooms and fairly free, growth upright. Pennisi – American – 1967 – A.F.S. No. 711.

Violetta. Single. Tube and slim, curved sepals, ivory-white; corolla Bishop's-violet, light blotch at base of each petal. Long bell-shaped flowers, fairly free but continuous. Growth upright and vigorous. Schnabel – American – 1952 – A.F.S. No. 114.

Violette Szabo. Single. Blush-white tube, long slender green tipped sepals reflex up, upper surface blush-white (R.H.S. 62D) with creped rhodamine pink (R.H.S. 62A) underneath. Corolla rose-purple (R.H.S. 75A), rhodamine-purple (R.H.S. 68D) at base with roseine-purple (R.H.S. 68A) edges. Bell-shaped flowers which fade to roseine-purple with maturity, red anthers, blush-white pistil and yellow style. Medium green foliage with paler veins, heavily serrated lanceolate leaves have pink petioles first third of main vein is pink. Growth medium upright, good as either bush or standard, self-branching, most flowers borne in terminal nodes often as many as eight to ten flowers. Tested for 10 years before release. Named specially after the British agent in World War II who was awarded the George Cross and French Croix de Guerre for bravery. Introduced by High Trees Nurseries, Reigate, Surrey. Originates from the vicinity of Edenbridge, Kent. Holmes, R. – British – 1980 – A.F.S. No. 1557.

Virgata. See *magellanica* var. *virgata*.

Virginia Bruce. Double. Tube and sepals, waxy-pink, soft pink on underside; corolla free for size; growth upright and bushy. Evans and Reeves – American – 1942.

Virginia Chiles. Double. Short tube and broad crepy upturned sepals, neyron-rose; corolla hyacinth-blue, splashed with lilac and phlox-pink. Medium sized blooms, heavy bloomer; dark green foliage with red veins. Growth trailer. Chiles – American – 1953 – A.F.S. No. 160.

Virginia Daly. Semi-double. Spiraea-red tube, tri-coloured sepals, base is spiraea-red to white to agathia-green and completely flare to 180°. Corolla white to violet-purple, changes to rose-purple at maturity, very pale rose-purple veins. Medium sized flowers which flare slightly with maturity, spiraea-red stamens, white pistil, best colour in shade. Growth medium upright, bushy. Foster – American – 1976 – A.F.S. No. 1347.

Virginia Lund. Tube and sepals rosy-pink, corolla white with scalloped petals. Large blooms, fairly free. Looks fragile but in fact quite vigorous. Growth natural trailer. Tiret – American – 1966 – A.F.S. No. 689.

Virginia Norris. Single. Tube and sepals, scarlet-cerise; corolla blue, flushed pink at base. Small flowers but very free. Growth upright and bushy. Greene – American – Date unknown.

Vistor. Semi-double. Short, thin tube, spiraea red, sepals spiraea red 1¼ in long × ⅜ in wide, curve upward. Corolla dark aster violet fading to light cyclamen, 1¼ in long × 1¼ in wide. Largish blooms and fairly free, spiraea-red stamens and pistil, tipped brown. Light green foliage, with light red stems, growth semi-trailer, bushy. Tested for 4 years in vicinity of Richmond, California. Registered by Soo Yun Field in 1978. Palko – American – 1978 – A.F.S. No. 1448.

Vivace. Semi-double. Tube and upturned sepals, turkey-red. Medium sized flowers and free; growth upright and vigorous to 8 ft in California. Nessier – American – 1952 – A.F.S. No. 119.

Viva Ireland. Single. Tube and sepals, pale pink; corolla soft lilac-lavender, touched flesh-pink. Medium sized flowers, very free, delightful colour combination. Growth lax bush, needs support as bush plant. Lovely cultivar, produces excellent basket. Ireland – American – 1956.

Vivien Colville. Single. Narrow pink tube, orange sepals, narrow and upturned. Corolla starts with deeper orange than the sepals edged red. Petite flowers freely produced, similar in shape to Checkerboard with the colouring of Falling Stars but not quite as dark. Very long pistil pink shading to orange. Growth upright vigorous and bushy. The first from the Colville stable for some considerable time. Introduced by C.S. Lockyer at Chelsea Show 1980. Colville – British – 1980.

Vivien Harris. Single. Long thick waxy tube of turkey-red, sepals of the same colour. Corolla is a deeper shade of turkey-red. Long flowers of the triphylla type, very free and showing the characteristics of both its parents. Growth upright and bushy, very suitable as a standard. Tested for 3 years in Leicestershire before release, introduced by R. Pacey in 1978. Rufus × Leverhulme. Harris, A. – British – 1977 – A.F.S. No. 1484.

Vivien Lee. Single. Pale pink self; small flowers but very free. Growth upright and bushy. Niederholzer – American – 1947.

Vivienne Thompson. Semi-double. Rhodamine-pink tube, sepals rhodamine-pink (R.H.S. 62A) edged neyron-rose (R.H.S. 55B) with pale green tips 1¼ in long, reflexed with recurved tips. Corolla white with neyron-rose veins at the base. Medium sized blooms, tightly rolled but loosening with maturity, blooming over a long period, pink filaments and red anthers. Mid-green foliage, leaves are small and ovate. Growth medium upright, self-branching will produce good bush, standard, pyramid, pillar cordon or decorative, heat tolerant if shaded. Raised and tested for 4 years in the vicinity of Leyland, Lancashire. Tolling Bell × Border Queen. Reynolds – British – 1983 – A.F.S. No. 1747.

Vobeglo. Single. Tube short and pink, sepals pink; corolla purple-lilac, darker on edges. Foliage mid-green and very small. Small flowers carried erect have the characteristic of its parent. Growth dwarf bush, short joined. Frau Henriëlte Ernst × F. regia var. typica × Bon Accorde. Introduced into England by Wills Fuchsia Nurseries in 1978. De Groot – Dutch – Date unknown.

Vogue. Double. Tube and sepals, ivory-white tipped green; corolla campanula-violet, fading to Bishop's-violet. Largish blooms, not very free, good shape. Growth trailer, best as H1. Fuchsia-La – American – 1959.

Voltaire. Single. Tube and recurved sepals scarlet; corolla magenta, veined scarlet. Medium sized flowers, expanding, early and free. Growth upright and bushy, very easy cultivar and still grown for its rich colouring. Lemoine – French – 1897.

volutina (Johnston 1925). Synonymous with *F. corymbiflora* and *F. cyrtandroides*.

Voodoo. Double. Short tube and long, wide upturned sepals dark red; corolla deep dark purple-violet. Large blooms, free for size, very full and rich colouring. Growth upright and bushy, may need support for the heavy blooms which excel in cut bloom classes. Maxine's Purple × unknown seedling. Tiret – American – 1953 – A.F.S. No. 157.

Vrouwtje. Single. Very small tube red, sepals red; corolla purple changing to purple-red. Small flowers, very free, growth upright. De Groot – Dutch – *ca* 1970.

Vulcan. Semi-double. China-rose tube, sepals neyron rose inside, China-rose outside, tipped pale green. Corolla neyron-rose at base, shading to ruby red at tip. Medium sized flowers, free six petals, lettuce-green foliage, veined red. Growth upright and bushy, exceptionally vigorous, requires tight pinching. Pugh – British – 1975 – No. 1238.

vulcanica (André 1888). Synonymous with *F. canescens*.

Vyvian Miller. Single. Tube and sepals neyron-rose (H.C.C. 623/1), sepals held horizontally. Corolla aster-violet (H.C.C. 38/2). Medium sized flowers, very free, pale green foliage. Growth strong, vigorous and bushy excellent cultivar for show work and the outside border, growth 12 in to 15 in. Introduced by Jackson's Nurseries of Tamworth in 1980. Cloverdale Jewel × Cloverdale Pearl. Roe – British – 1980.

Wailiki. Double. Tube and curving sepals white, flushed pale pink; corolla spiraea-red. Large blooms, free for size, growth natural trailer. Tiret – American – 1958 – A.F.S. No. 333.

Waldfee. Single. Long spreading tube, soft lilac-pink, sepals soft lilac-pink, silky sheen but not glossy, broad for Breviflorae. Corolla soft lilac-pink, reflexed and squarish of the Breviflorae type. Tiny flowers, very free, colour difficult to describe as tube is semi-translucent with stamens and pistil visible through tube. Foliage matt green with silky sheen. Growth upright, self-branching, good for almost any type of training including miniature or bonsai. German name meaning Wood Fairy. Breviflorae hybrid. *F.michoacanensis* × . Travis, J. – British – 1973 – A.F.S. No. 1150.

Walsingham. Semi-double. Off-white tube, sepals off-white outside, inside rose-pink (R.H.S. 62D) and held horizontal. Corolla pale lilac (R.H.S. 84C) tight bell-shape with crimped edge. Foliage is emerald green, leaves are long, pointed and serrated. Growth upright and self-branching. Named after the famous pilgrimage shrine in East Anglia. Introduced by D. Stilwell, 1979. Northumbrian Belle × Blush O' Dawn. Clitheroe – British – 1979.

Waltz Time. Double. Tube and broad upturned sepals, pure white; corolla pink, flushed pale pink on outer edges. Largish blooms with folded petals, fairly free and non fading. Growth natural trailer. Waltz – American – 1959 – A.F.S. No. 394.

* Walz Brandaris. Little known Dutch cultivar other than the parentage: Chang ×. Waldermaier – Dutch – 1982.

* Walz Bruintje. Single. Little known Dutch cultivar raised in the vicinity of Ichayk, Netherlands, with the following colour combination: R.H.S 58BC, R.H.S 62A and R.H.S. 61C. Growth lax trailer. Achievement × Achievement. Waldermaier – Dutch – 1983.

* Walz Gigolo. Little known Dutch cultivar other than the parentage: Swingtime × Achievement. Waldermaier – Dutch – 1982.

War Dance. Semi-double. Tube and sepals white, tipped green; corolla royal-purple with white marbling, fading to smoky orange-red. Medium sized blooms, fairly free, growth lax bush or trailer. Kennett – American – 1968 – A.F.S. No. 777.

War Paint. Double. Short tube and broad flaring sepals, white; corolla dianthus-purple with coral-pink marbling, fading to reddish-purple. Large blooms, quite free, very large foliage. Growth upright and bushy, very heavy in leaf and very well named. Kennett – American – 1960 – A.F.S. No. 431.

Warrior. Single. Red and violet-blue. Smith – British – 1868.

Warrior Queen. Single. Scarlet and rich purple. Carter and Co – British – 1870.

Warton Crag. Single. Short thick tube flesh-pink, sepals creamy-white, tipped green, thick, opening to reveal set of thick crepe sepaloids, creamy-white. Corolla pink of even form. Most unusual flowers free and very attractive, better in shade. Dark green foliage, growth upright and bushy. Jamboree ×. Thornley – British – 1963 – A.F.S. No. 1100.

Washington Don. Semi-double. Scarlet tube, sepals scarlet and broad 1 in long. Corolla purple with slight veining at base of rounded petals. Fluted, medium to large sized blooms 2½ in across with scarlet stamens and pistil. Olive-green foliage, lightly veined, pointed leaves 1½ in long by ¾ in wide and strong stems. Growth upright, bushy and self-branching. Raised in the vicinity of Washington, Tyne and Wear, North East England for 10 years before release. Thorp – British – 1982 – A.F.S. No. 1685.

Water Nymph. Single. White and crimson. Grown and cultivated in the Netherlands under the name of Deutsche Perle. Story – British – 1859.

* Waveney Gem. Single. Tube and sepals white; corolla pink with mauve flush. Medium sized flowers, very free, continuous and early flowering. Foliage mid green, growth lax upright and versatile, suitable for basketwork, bush or small standards. Seen for the first time at B.F.S. London Show August 1984. Raised in the vicinity of Bungay, Suffolk, and introduced by High Tree Nurseries of Reigate, Surrey, in 1985. Mrs. Lawrence Lyons × Santa Barbara (syn. Lustre). Burns – British – 1985.

* Waveney Queen. Single. Short very pale pink tube, pale pink sepals, tipped green and held just above the horizontal. Corolla baby pink with darker pink veining, will produce almost white colouring when shaded. Lightish green foliage very similar to Border Queen. Growth self-branching bush, has the same habit of growth as its parent, Border Queen, excellent cultivar destined for the showbench and very versatile. Raised and tested in the vicinity of Bungay, Suffolk before release; introduced by High Tree Nurseries of Reigate in 1984. Border Queen seedling, pollen parent unknown. Burns – British – 1984.

* Waveney Unique. Single. Pink tube moderately long and comparatively broad, pink sepals open almost to horizontal position on maturity, darker pink underneath. Corolla pink with a tinge of apricot, each petal has a darker margin. Medium sized flowers of exquisite pastel colouring are carried two or more in every leaf axil and prominently displayed. Growth is stiff upright with plain green foliage with leaves having matt surface. Although clearly destined for the showbench, this cultivar is admirably suited for garden border planting. Raised in the vicinity of Bungay, Suffolk, and scheduled for release by Goulding's Fuchsias of Ipswich in 1985. Margaret Roe × Lye's Unique. Burns – British – 1985.

* Waveney Valley. Semi-double or single. Short white tube, white sepals tipped green which reflex to hide both tube and ovary. Corolla lavender-blue on opening, maturing to baby pink. Medium sized flooms with overlapping petals similar to Brutus in outline but larger, light red stamens. Foliage has unusual colouring of lime green with yellower flecking. Self-cleaning cultivar, flowers dropping after maturity. Growth upright and bushy, will produce good bush or standard, well within the showbench category. Raised and tested in the vicinity of Bungay, Suffolk, and released in 1984 by Goulding's Fuchsias of Ipswich. Margaret Roe × Eden Lady. Burns – British – 1984.

* Waveney Waltz. Single. Short baby pink tube, baby pink sepals held almost at the horizontal. Corolla white with very little veining, medium sized flowers, very free flowering, throws the odd extra petal. Light green foliage, growth upright and bushy, similar habit to Flirtation Waltz, makes excellent exhibition cultivar. Raised and tested in the vicinity of Bungay, Suffolk, before release and introduced by High Tree Nurseries of Reigate, Surrey, in 1982. Mrs. Lawrence Lyons × Flirtation Waltz. Burns – British – 1982.

Wave of Life. Single. Tube and sepals scarlet, corolla reddish-purple. Flowers small, fairly free, feature of the cultivar is the variegated foliage of golden-green leaves with pink stems. Growth low bush or trailer, very suitable for baskets. Henderson – British – 1869.

Waverley. Single. Long tube pinkish-white, sepals long, slim, and pointed light pink, tipped green. Corolla orange-magenta. Medium sized flowers, free, very clear appearance. Rich green foliage with red veins and serrated leaves. Growth upright and bushy, good for standard. The first seedling to be introduced from Scotland for many years. Stewart – British – 1968 – A.F.S. No. 961.

Wawona. Single. Tube and sepals crimson; corolla peony-purple with crimson stripe. Wide open medium sized flowers, free, growth upright and very vigorous, up to several feet in California. Niederholzer – American – 1946.

Waxen Beauty. Double. Greenish-white tube, shaded rose; sepals greenish-white, arched and slightly reflexed. Corolla white with the hint of pale pink in centre. Medium sized blooms, fairly free, waxy camellia shaped petals. Spinach-green foliage with almond shaped leaves. Growth tall, upright bush, strong grower, will make large plant in first year. Ting-a-Ling × (La Campanella × Flirtation Waltz). Clyne – British – 1974 – A.F.S. No. 1287.

Wedding Gown. Double. Tube and dainty recurved sepals, palest blush-pink; corolla white with over petals shading to pink at base. Medium sized blooms, free and very full. Very dark green foliage. Growth lax bush or trailer. Reedstrom – American – 1956 – A.F.S. No. 257.

Wedgewood. Double. White tube, sepals long, glistening white; corolla blue-violet. Spreading blooms, very free, delightful and elegant. Growth upright and bushy. Schnabel – American – 1951 – A.F.S. No. 82.

Wee Lass. Single. Short, thick red tube, sepals are short and thick, cardinal-red; tiny corolla, blue-bird blue, passing to spectrum-violet. Very small flowers, very free, corolla measures only $\frac{1}{8}$ in long and $\frac{1}{8}$ in wide. Small foliage on fine, close jointed growth. Growth is described as bushy, this cultivar can be classified as a midget, plants are 10 in high, ideal for pot work or the rockery. Tiny flowers are held erect. Gambit × Upward Look. Gadsby – British – 1975 – A.F.S. No. 1283.

Wee One. Double. Tube and outside of sepals, pale pink, broad sepals turn up pagoda fashion; corolla and inside of sepals, lovely soft pink. Small to medium sized blooms, free and very similar to Seventeen. Growth upright and willowy, one of Tiret's best introductions. Tiret – American – 1951 – A.F.S. No. 209.

Weigalowi Alba. Single. Pinkish-white self. Miellez – French – Date unknown.

Wellesley Wilson. Single. Red tube, thick sepals also red, corolla clean white. Medium sized flowers and very free, red style and pink filaments. Foliage medium green, edgted red, growth upright and bushy. Brutus × Swingtime. Wilson, J.W. – British – 1967.

Wels. Single or semi-double. Tube and sepals cherry-red; corolla ivory-white with red veining. Very early and free flowering. El Camino × F. corymbiflora alba. Nutzinger – Austrian – 1966.

Welsh Dragon. Double. Tube and sepals, rose-opal; corolla magenta-rose, at times practically a self. Large blooms, fairly free, growth upright, bushy and strong. Baker – British – 1970.

Wendy. Synonymous with Snowcap.

Wendy Harris. Double. Short, thick white tube, striped neyron-rose; sepals pale neyron-rose, tipped green. Corolla white, veined neyron-rose. Medium sized blooms with fairly short petals.

Growth compact bush, suitable as a standard. Introduced by R. Pacey in 1979. Harris, A. – British – 1978.

Wendy Leedham. Double. Delft-rose (R.H.S. 36D) tube $\frac{3}{8}$ in by $\frac{7}{16}$ in; sepals delft-rose (R.H.S. 36D) on top, rose-red (R.H.S. 58B) underneath, held at the horizontal with recurved tips 1$\frac{3}{8}$ in by $\frac{3}{8}$ in. Corolla white flushed rose-red. Medium-sized blooms, very full and three quarters flared, rose-red filament, indian-lake anthers, rose-Bengal pistil and amber-yellow stigma. Midgreen (R.H.S. 139B) foliage with ovate shaped leaves 2 in by 1$\frac{3}{8}$ in. Growth medium upright, self-branching, very suitable for either bush or standard, likes cool conditions. Very suitable for bedding in the border similar to Dollar Princess except for the red and white colouring. Tested for 9 years before release and raised in the vicinity of Hull, Yorkshire, and introduced by Muncaster Fuchsias of Gainsborough in 1985. Dollar Princess seedling. Bielby – British – 1984.

Wennington Beck. Double. Short tube reddish-brown, sepals pink, flushed green, underside clear soft pink, reflex back to tube. Corolla soft violet-blue, blush pink at base. Medium sized blooms, very free, rather late. Foliage of even form with serrated edges. Growth lax bush or basket. Dorothea Flower ×. Thornley – British – 1973 – A.F.S. No. 1101.

Westchester. Double. Tube and sepals red; corolla deep blue. Little information apart from the colouring and the cultivar appears to be exclusive to California. Fuchsia-La – American – 1958.

Westergeest. Single. Tube and sepals flesh-pink, sepals hug the corolla. Corolla rose-pink. Medium sized flowers and very free flowering. Another Dutch introduction considered to be worthwhile introducing to England. Introduced by Hill Trees Nurseries of Reigate, Surrey, 1981. de Graaff 1981.

Westlake. Double. Tube and wide sepals, rose-madder; corolla Bishop's violet to fuchsia-purple, marbled soferino-purple. Large blooms, fairly free, growth trailer. Neisser – American – 1952 – A.F.S. No. 120.

Westminster Chimes. Semi-double. Deep rose tube; rose sepals fade to pale pink spreading but not reflexed, tipped green. Corolla violet-blue, ageing to magenta, pink at base of petals. Smallish flowers, very profuse, fluted and spreading with maturity, best colour in moderate sun. Spinach-green foliage with small to medium almond shaped leaves. Growth cascades naturally with lax habit of growth. Raised and tested for 3 years in vicinity of Uxbridge, London, before release, registered by D. Stilwell. La Campanella × Liebriez. Clyne – British – 1976 – A.F.S. No. 1387.

West Wong. Single. Tube neyron-rose, sepals which are held well back also neyron-rose. Corolla cyclamen-purple and paler at base. Medium sized flowers and very free-flowering. Growth compact bush. Introduced by the raiser in 1980. Pacey– British – 1980.

Westwood. Single. Tube and sepals, vivid red; corolla very light pink. Rather small flowers but very free and long, dark green foliage. Growth tall, vigorous climber. Evans and Reeves – American – 1936.

Whirlaway. Semi-double. Short greenish tube and extra long sepals white, tipped green. Corolla white developing a delicate blush-pink tint with maturity. Large flowers, free and exciting, sepals split on opening whilst tips are still joined, giving lantern effect. Growth lax bush or trailer, makes wonderful basket, best grown as H1. A.F.S. Certificate of Merit 1964. Waltz – American – 1961 – A.F.S. No. 494.

Whirligig. Single. Tube and long twisted sepals, rose-opal; corolla violet-purple overlaid plum-purple and veined rose-opal. Medium sized flowers and free, growth upright; bushy and willowy. Crockett – British – 1969 – A.F.S. No. 857.

Whirlybird. Single. White tube, pink sepals, much darker pink inside, tipped green. Corolla white with pink veining from the base. Medium sized flowers very free flowering. Growth upright, raised in the vicinity of Plymouth, England. Hilton – British – 1981.

White Ann. Double. Synonymous with Heidi Weiss. This is a sport from Heidi Ann with a white double corolla as a contrast to the crimson tube and sepals. Wills-Atkinson – British – 1972 – A.F.S. No. 1130.

White Bouquet. Double. Tube and broad up-turned sepals, ivory-white with touch of pink at base of tube; corolla ivory-white. Medium sized blooms, free, folded scalloped petals of heavy texture, rare in a white fuchsia, white buds with pale pink pistil open into perfect flowers. Growth upright, may need support as a bush. Waltz – American – 1959 – A.F.S. No. 395.

White Bride. Double. Tube and sepals white, tipped green, with slight tint of pink; corolla white. Medium sized blooms and free, growth strong, upright bush. Gadsby – British – 1970 – A.F.S. No. 868.

White Caps. Double. Pink tube and broad short sepals white; corolla white. Medium to large blooms, very free flowering, spreading. Growth upright and bushy. Hodges – American – 1958 – A.F.S. No. 340.

White Countess of Aberdeen. Very similar to and could be synonymous with Countess of Aberdeen in California.

* White Ensign. Double. Long, thin white tube, sepals white flushed pink $1\frac{1}{2}$ in long by $\frac{3}{4}$ in wide. Corolla fluffy white $1\frac{1}{4}$ in long by 2 in wide. Largish blooms which hang $3\frac{1}{2}$ in below the branches, stamens and pistil bright pink. Light green foliage with wide serrated leaves $2\frac{1}{2}$ in long by $1\frac{1}{2}$ in wide, main leaf vein is red. Growth medium upright, will make good bush or standard, heat tolerant if shaded. Raised and tested for 4 years in the vicinity of Timperley, Cheshire. Igloo Maid × White Spider. Howarth – British – 1983 – A.F.S. No. 1718.

White Fairy. Double. Snowy-white self. Medium to large blooms of amazing substance, fluffy double corolla, do not wilt. Small light green foliage. Growth bush or semi-trailer. Waltz – American – 1963 – A.F.S. No. 589.

White Falls. Semi-double. Short baby-pink tube, sepals baby-pink, tipped green, broadish and blunt. Corolla creamy-white with pink veins, bunch type. Bright foliage with oval, crimpled leaves. Growth upright but requires early tie as plant starts rather lax. Tolley – British – 1974 – A.F.S. No. 1234

White Galore. Double. Near white self. Large blooms, fairly free, with the slightest touch of pink. Growth trailer. Fuchsia-La – American – 1968 – A.F.S. No. 807.

White Gigantea. Double. Tube and sepals red; corolla white. Large blooms, fairly free, growth upright. Walker and Jones – American – 1952.

White Gold. Single. Tube and sepals white, tipped green, pink at base; corolla white, pale pink at base. Medium sized flowers, fairly free, petals uneven. Foliage variegated golden, white tipped and ageing to green, like all variegated foliage cultivars, needs sunny exposure. Growth lax bush, not an easy cultivar. York – American – 1953 – A.F.S. No. 190.

White House. Double. Tube and sepals, rich red; corolla white, veined red. Medium sized blooms and free, growth upright and bushy. One of the earliest cultivars raised in America. Raiser and date unknown.

White Joy. Single. Short tube and broadish sepals held horizontally are white with slight pink flush. White corolla, medium sized flowers perfectly shaped with bell shaped corolla, very prolific takes good characteristics from both parents. Attractive green foliage, growth upright and bushy with short joined stems. Will make exceptionally good bush or shrub. Awarded to Bronze Certificate of Merit at B.F.S. 1980 London Show. Well in the exhibition category and destined for the showbench. Introduced by Woodbridge Nurseries of Hounslow 1981. Joy Patmore × Eden Lady. Burns – British – 1980.

White King. Double. Tube and sepals, white with pink tips, corolla white. Very large blooms, not very free but of good substance. Growth upright. Pennisi – American – 1968 – A.F.S. No. 753.

Whiteknights Amethyst. Single. Red-purple tube, slightly triangular sepals are $\frac{7}{8}$ in × $\frac{1}{8}$ in and shade from pale red-purple (R.H.S. 64B) at the base through greenish-white to yellow-green at tip. Tubular corolla is violet (R.H.S. 83A) ageing to red-purple (R.H.S. 64A). The somewhat heart-shaped petals are $\frac{3}{8}$ in × $\frac{1}{4}$ in . Style and stamens red-purple with blue pollen. Foliage dark green with small leaves. Growth medium upright, will make good bush, pyramid, pillar and decorative. Has proved to be hardy in southern England. Formerly known as seedling 9C 502 and received the B.F.S. Silver Certificate of Merit at Reading Show, August, 1977. Most unusual cross. Originates from and was raised at Reading University. *F. magellanica* × *F. excorticata*. Wright, J.O. – British – 1980 – A.F.S. No. 1595.

Whiteknights Blush. Single. Pale pink tube, spreading sepals are pale pink with small green tips and lanceolate shaped. Corolla clear pink, the colour of the flowers is similar to *F. magellanica* var. *molinae* but much larger. Small dark green foliage with green veining on both leaves and branches, leaves are $1\frac{1}{2}$ in × $\frac{3}{4}$ in. Growth small upright, self-branching, will make good bush and ground cover, hardy in southern England, will take full sun. Originates from and was raised at Reading University. Wright, J.O. – British – 1980 – A.F.S. No. 1592.

Whiteknights Cascade. Single. Another unusual hybrid and considered to be a breakthrough in both flower and habit, formerly known as seedling 100C99. Awarded the B.F.S. Silver Certificate of Merit at the London/Reading B.F.S. Show 1977. *F. splendens* × *F. boliviana*. Wright, J.O. – British – 1977.

Whiteknights Cheeky. Single. Triphylla-type tube, dark Tyrian purple, small spreading sepals dark Tyrian purple. Very small corolla is dark Tyrian purple. Small flowers borne horizontally clear of foliage in erect terminal racemes. Foliage dark and velvety with red veining. Growth small upright, will make a good bush, grown in greenhouse conditions and will take the usual protection and full sun, best colour requires sun. Originates from and was raised at Reading University. Whiteknights Ruby × *F. procumbens*. Wright, J.O. – British – 1980 – A.F.S. No. 1593.

Whiteknight's Gem. Single. Tube and sepals pink, corolla rosy-red. Smallish flowers, very free. Growth low bush, this cultivar was raised by the same raiser as the famous Pink Pearl. Bright – British – 1910.

Whiteknights Glister. Single. Red (R.H.S. 53C) tube, small $\frac{2}{8}$ in × $\frac{1}{8}$ in spreading sepals shade from red (R.H.S. 52A) at base to near white at the tip. Small tubular corolla is red-purple (R.H.S. 66A) with rounded petals $\frac{5}{8}$ in across. Filaments and style are pink. Foliage strongly variegated green with a cream border. Growth medium upright or will trail with weights, will make good bush or decorative. Rather slow growing and may throw an occasional green shoot. Originates and found at Reading University. Sport of *F. magellanica* var. *molinae* × *F. fulgens*. Wright, J.O. – British – 1980 – A.F.S. No. 1594.

Whiteknights Goblin. See *denticulata*.

Whiteknights Pearl. Single. Thin white tube $\frac{3}{8}$ in × $\frac{1}{8}$ in, spreading sepals are pale pink (R.H.S. 56D) with small green tips and lanceolate shaped $\frac{7}{10}$ in × $\frac{1}{8}$ in. Tubular corolla is clear pink (R.H.S. 56A) with roundish petals $\frac{3}{8}$ in × $\frac{1}{2}$ in. Filaments are white with cream coloured anthers, style is white with cream-coloured stigma. Colour of flowers is similar to *F. magellanica* var. *molinae* but much larger. Small dark green foliage with no red on veins or branches, leaves 2 in × 1 in. Growth medium upright, will make good bush, pyramid, pillar or decorative. Hardy in southern England, will take full sun. Originates and raised at Reading University. *F. magellanica* var. *molinae* × (*F. magellanica* var. *molinae* × *F. fulgens*). Wright, J.O. – British – 1980 – A.F.S. No. 1591.

Whiteknight's Ruby. Triphylla single. Long tube $\frac{5}{8}$ in long, cardinal red at base, grading to Tyrian-purple at mouth; small, spreading $\frac{3}{8}$ in sepals, Tyrian-purple. Corolla is small about $\frac{3}{8}$ in length of sepals, Tyrian-purple. Filament and style are Tyrian-purple, stamens abortive, stigma four cleft. Dark velvety foliage with red veining, red below, leaves elliptic, stems pink to red with some dark flecking, approximately $3\frac{1}{2}$ in × $1\frac{1}{2}$ in. Growth small upright, self-branching and bushy, tested for 2 years in glasshouse in vicinity of Reading. *F. triphylla* × *F. procumbens* B.F.S. Silver Cert. of Merit at London/Reading Show 1977. Registered by University of Reading, England. Wright, J.O. – British – 1976 – A.F.S. No. 1357.

White Lace. Double. Tube and sepals deep red; corolla white, veined red. Large full double blooms, very free for a double and long lasting. Dark green foliage, growth strong, spreading habit, 2 to $2\frac{1}{2}$ ft high. Hardy in Southern England, raised in the Scilly Isles. Tabraham – British – 1976.

White Magic. Double. Tube and sepals deep rose-red; corolla white, veined deep rose. Medium sized blooms, growth trailer, very suitable for basketwork. Registered trademark in California. Walker – American – 1964.

Whitemost. Single. Tube and sepals, very pale pink; corolla pure white. Large flowers, free for size. Growth upright and strong. Niederholzer – American – 1942.

White Pearl. Semi-double. Tube and sepals, very pale pink; corolla pure white. Medium sized flowers, free, very similar to Pink Pearl but with different colouring. Growth medium upright and bushy. Niederholzer – American – 1945.

White Perfection. Single. White and crimson. Henderson – British – 1846.

White Perfection. Single. White and vermillion. Jennings – British – 1848.

White Phenomenal. Double. Scarlet and white. Lemoine – French – 1873.

White Pixie. Single. Tube and sepals, reddish-carmine; corolla white, veined pink. Smallish flowers very free. Foliage yellowish-green with crimson veins. Growth upright, bushy and hardy, suitable as medium hedge up to 3 ft. This sport has occurred in various places at various times; two other examples, apart from Merrist Wood, are Wagtails in 1966 and B.W. Rawlins (Vicarage Farm Nurseries) date unknown; there are others not recorded in Great Britain. Accepted in the B.F.S. as showbench hardy. Received Award of Merit at B.F.S. London Show in 1968 together with Iced Champagne which also won the Jones Cup. This sport introduced also by B. Rawlins was submitted both by Wills Nurseries and L.R. Russell Ltd. for the R.H.S. Wisley Hardy Trials 1975–78 but received no award. Sport of Pixie. Merrist Wood – British – 1968.

White Princess. Single. Short waxy-cream tube, pointed waxy-cream sepals which recurve downwards, waxy-cream on top, pink flushed underneath and very faintly tipped green. Short corolla rosy-cerise shading to orange at base, maturing to orange vermilion. Small flowers abundantly produced, pale pink stamens and pistil, best colour develops in shade. Small bronzy-green foliage with small ovate leaves. Growth medium upright and bushy, suitable for bush and especially as quarter standard. Tested for 8 years in the vicinity of Dover, Kent, before being registered by Frank Saunders of Whitstable in 1982. Certificate of Preliminary Acceptance B.F.S. London 1973. White Queen × . Gray – British – 1973. – A.F.S. No. 1674.

White Queen. Synonymous with Super British, refer to that cultivar for further information. W.Q. (Doyle) is very difficult to distinguish from Amy Lye, almost the same colouring and size with the same thick, creamy tube. W.Q. (Doyle) is however, fluted. Doyle – British – 1899.

White Queen. Double white self. Medium sized blooms, free, small petals tipped green. Growth medium bush. A.F.S. Cert. of Merit 1973. Pennisi – American – 1970 – A.F.S. No. 885.

White Souvenir de Chiswick. Single. White and rose. Lye – British – Date unknown.

White Spider. Single. Tube and long twisted sepals, baby-pink, tipped green; corolla white veined pink. Medium sized flowers, very free and early, although called White Spider it is never white as the pink colouring always prominent. Growth upright and bushy, always seems to want its way to grow horizontally, good for standard. Another fine American introduction. Haag – American – 1951.

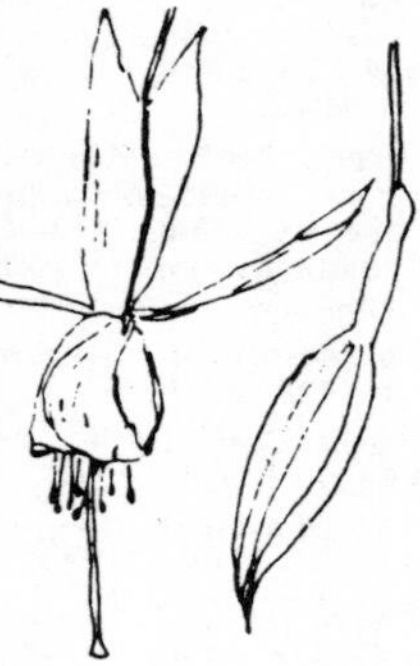

White Spider

White Star. Double. Tube and sepals white, sepals curving to a point; corolla white with deep pink edges. Medium sized blooms and free, resemble a star. Growth upright. Pennisi – American – 1968 – A.F.S. No. 754.

White Swan. Single. Tube and sepals pink; corolla white, slightly veined pink. Medium sized flowers, continuous flowering, pale green foliage. Growth tall upright and bushy, strong, height 2 to $2\frac{1}{2}$ ft. Hardy in Southern England, raised in the Scilly Isles. Tabraham – British – 1974.

White Unique. Double. Red and white. Smith – British – 1874.

White Wonder. Synonymous with Catalina.

Whittier. Semi-double. Tube and sepals, white with faint blush; corolla white variegated at base with delicate shades of orchid-pink. Large loose blooms, fairly free and early. Growth lax bush or trailer. Home Fuchsia Gardens – American – 1955.

Wigwam. Double. Tube and sepals, pale rosy-pink; corolla pale magenta, fading to bengal-rose. Largish blooms, fairly free, dark green leathery foliage. Growth tall upright and vigorous. Paskesen – American – 1966 – A.F.S. No. 663.

Wild and Beautiful. Double. Short, thick white tube, sepals dark neyron-rose inside with light neyron-rose on outside $\frac{3}{4}$ in wide × $1\frac{1}{2}$ in long, sepals turn upward. Corolla dark amethyst-violet fading to china rose at sepals 3 in wide × $1\frac{1}{8}$ in long. Large flowers, aptly named with its very wide blooms, neyron-rose pistil, pale neyron-rose stamens. Light green foliage very large $4\frac{7}{8}$ in long × $2\frac{1}{4}$ in wide. Growth semi-trailer, will make basket or bush. Tested for 5 years in vicinity of Sebastopol, California. Soo Yun Field – American – 1978 – A.F.S. No. 1452.

Wildfire. Semi-double. Short thick tube bright rose, sepals thick, broad and long, bright rose. Corolla salmon-red base, blending to cardinal-red, maturing to intense crimson-scarlet. Prolific, large flowers, with fiery colour combination, will take full sun. Growth lax bush or trailer. Handley – British – 1972 – A.F.S. No. 1060.

Wild 'n' Wonderful. Double. Short red tube, sepals are pink to red with green tips, curl upwards to tube $1\frac{1}{2}$ in long. Corolla white with red stripes. Large blooms, very free for such a large double, corolla is loose with serrated edges and flared, white to pink stamens and pistil. Growth semi-trailer, tested for 5 years at Sebastopol, California before release. Soo Yun Field – American – 1977 – A.F.S. No. 1409.

Wilf Tolley. Semi-double. Short, thick tube, pale pink, sepals China-rose with green tips, waxy, well formed and held well out from corolla. Purple-violet corolla with pale pink base, maturing to cyclamen-purple. Flowers are almost identical to Mrs. Lawrence Lyons when first opened, developing into large blooms of the same colouring. Growth upright and bushy, self-branching. Named after well known British hybridizer. Gadsby – British – 1974 – A.F.S. No. 1225.

William Braas. Double. Tube and upturned sepals, flushed pale pink; corolla rose-madder. Largish blooms, fairly free, growth trailer. Tiret – American – 1951 – A.F.S. No. 97.

***William Caunt.** Single. Creamy-white tube is $\frac{1}{4}$ in long by $\frac{1}{4}$ in wide; horizontally held sepals white on top, flushed pink and slightly paler underneath, tipped green and recurved $\frac{3}{4}$ in long by $\frac{1}{4}$ in wide. Corolla opens rosy to scarlet-cerise flushed white at the base, maturing to slightly paler colour with a pyramidal shape $\frac{3}{4}$ in long by $\frac{3}{4}$ in wide. Medium sized flowers quarter flared, flowers carried in horizontal position, rosy-cerise filaments and white anthers, white style and stigma, oval shaped buds. Dark green foliage with ovate leaves 2 in long by 1 in wide serrated edges, acute tips and rounded bases. Growth self-branching small upright, prefers cool conditions, needs frequent fertilising and very free flowering, easy to shape and grow. Raised in the vicinity of Worksop, Nottinghamshire, and is a chance seedling. Caunt – British – 1984 – A.F.S. No. 1764.

Williamette. Double. Tube and sepals, rose-pink; corolla white with splashes of fuchsia-pink. Largish blooms, quite free for size. Growth trailer. Sport of San Pablo. Pepper – American – 1952 – A.F.S. No. 126.

Williamette-San Jose. Reliable American sources quote these two cultivars, both sports from San Pablo as being identical.

William Silva. Double. Short tube and curved sepals red; corolla red, striped lavender and pink. Small blooms and very free, small foliage. Growth upright, bushy and compact. Weisel – American – 1950 – A.F.S. No. 73A.

William van Orange. Single. Tube and sepals, light apricot; corolla clear shade of orange. Medium sized flowers, free and very distinctive. Growth upright and bushy. Haag – American – 1952.

***Willie Lot.** Single to semi-double. Short thick white tube $\frac{1}{3}$ in long by $\frac{1}{2}$ in wide; horizontally held sepals $1\frac{1}{4}$ in long by $\frac{1}{2}$ in wide are white on top, pale neyron-rose (R.H.S. 56B) underneath with recurved tips. Corolla opens violet (R.H.S. 84A) maturing to violet-purple (R.H.S. 77A). Medium sized flowers barrel shaped with little or no flaring, prefers filtered light and cool conditions, fat buds are pointed. Dark green (R.H.S. 137A) foliage with ovate leaves $2\frac{1}{2}$ in long by $1\frac{1}{4}$ in wide, serrated edges, acute tips and obtuse bases, stems and branches green with some red staining, the spring and early summer foliage has attractive yellow cast. Growth self-branching lax upright as stiff trailer, needs plenty of root space, best as second-year plant, ideal for hanging pots, another cultivar named with the Constable theme. Raised in the vicinity of Ipswich, Suffolk, and introduced by the raiser, Gouldings Fuchsias of Ipswich, in 1984. Goulding – British – 1984 – A.F.S. No. 1786.

Will-O-The-Wisp. Double. Short thick red tube, broad light red sepals recurve back to tube. Corolla very pale lilac flushed red at base. Medium-sized blooms short and compact with red stamens and pistil. Dark green foliage with long narrow serrated leaves and red main veins. Growth small upright no more than 12 in in height, makes bush or bedder. Raised in the vicinity of Cardiff, South Wales. Adams – British – 1982 – A.F.S. No. 1700.

Wilson's Fairfax. Single. Red tube of medium length, red sepals. Corolla violet-blue shading to white at base. Medium sized flowers and free-flowering, very bright appearance. Deep green foliage, growth upright, strong and vigorous. Introduced by Wills Fuchsias Ltd. of West Wittering in 1980. Wilson – British – 1979.

Wilson's Joy. Single. Short tube, white, sepals white tinged pink underneath. Corolla cerise-blue shading to cerise. Medium sized flowers and fairly profuse. Growth upright and bushy. Introduced by Wills Fuchsia Nurseries in 1979. Mrs. Marshall × .Wilson, J.W. – British – 1974.

Wilson's Osborne. Advance information of new seedling to be introduced by J.W. Wilson of Reading.

Wilson's Pearls. Semi-double. Red tube ⅞ in long, sepals same colour as tube, curling back and tending to spiral. Corolla white, veined pink, shading to red at base. Medium-sized blooms with red filaments and creamy-white pistil. Foliage pale green, red centre vein, pointed. Growth lax upright. Introduced by Wills Fuchsia Nursery 1978. Wilson, J.W. – British – 1967.

Wilson's Vera Louise. Advance information of new seedling to be introduced by J.W. Wilson of Reading.

Wilton Gem. Semi-double. Tube and sepals cerise; corolla cerise-pink, veined cerise. Medium-sized blooms, the broad upswept sepals nearly hide the tube, nice frilly flowers and very prolific, cerise filaments with pink style. Light green foliage. Growth upright, very vigorous and bushy. Rapley – British – 1974.

Wilton William. Double. Tube and sepals cerise; corolla bright mauvish-pink, veined cerise. Medium-sized blooms, very prolific, broad sepals sit on top of corolla, very spiky stamens well spaced out with short style of the same length, filaments light cerise, style cerise. Medium green foliage with crimson mid-rib. Growth upright, very vigorous and bushy. Rapley – British – 1974.

Wilton Winkie. Single. Tube and sepals crimson; sepals tipped green, corolla purple, red at base, veined crimson. Medium-sized flowers, the broad reflexed sepals show the whole of thick tube, filaments crimson and carmine style. Very long style, very prolific. Foliage dark green with

crimson mid-rib. Growth upright, vigorous and bushy. Rapley – British – 1974.

Windmill. Single. Short red tube and sepals; corolla deep blue. Small flowers but profuse bloomer, will take full sun. Growth lax upright and self-branching. Paskesen – American – 1967 – A.F.S. No. 727.

Wine and Roses. Double. Short tube rose, sepals broad and turned back, rose coloured. Corolla pleated with rose outer petals, opening to deep wine centre. Large blooms, free for size, flare wide open. Dark green foliage. Growth lax bush or trailer. Walker – American – 1969 – A.F.S. No. 834.

Wingrove's Mammoth. Double. Tube and sepals, turkey-red; corolla white heavily veined and splashed carmine. Huge blooms, exceptionally free for size of bloom, exceeding some of the American giants. Growth upright. Wingrove – British – 1968.

Wings of Song. Double. Tube and fully reflexed sepals bright rose-pink; corolla lavender-pink, veined pink. Largish, solid blooms, very free, foliage medium green with crimson- mid-rib. Growth cascade, vigorous and strong, free branching, excellent cultivar for basket training, a little late in flowering, with extra care and cultivation will make a lax bush but will need support, in the showclass category. Blackwell – British – 1968.

Winifred. Single. Thick tube pale pink, upturned long sepals, deep rose-pink. Corolla cerise-pink, pale pink at base. Medium sized flowers and free, early. Growth upright and bushy, hardy in southern districts. Chatfield – British – 1973.

Winifred Glass. Single. White and carmine. Lye – British – 1887.

Winner's Circle. Double. Short red tube, sepals cranberry-red with smooth top and crepe texture underneath, wide pointed spoon shaped. Corolla cyclamen-purple, blended red at base, changing to vibrant-rose with maturity. Medium sized blooms and free, throw small petaloids of same colouring as corolla. Growth semi-trailer, not an easy cultivar, but good colour and habit. Pancharian – American – 1957 – A.F.S. No. 1296.

Winnie. Single. Tube and sepals pink, corolla blue, fading to light orchid. Medium sized flowers and free, growth upright. Soo Yun Field – American – 1966 – A.F.S. No. 685.

* Win Pettener. Single. Tube and sepals carmine-rose, sepals curve upwards. Corolla amethyst-violet, shading to mallow-purple at base of petals. Medium sized flowers and free, very easy grower. Growth upright, bushy and very short-jointed making the plant ideal for the showbench. Raised and introduced by R. and J. Pacey of Melton Mowbray, Leicestershire, in 1983. Pacey – British – 1983.

Winserii. Single. Rosy-carmine and vermilion. Epps – British – 1843.

Winsome. Single. Tube and sepals white, corolla white to pink. Medium sized flowers and free, growth medium upright and bushy. Hazard and Hazard – American – date unknown.

Winston Churchill. Double. Long tube and broad reflexed sepals pink, tipped green; corolla lavender-blue, maturing to pale purple. Medium size blooms and prolific flowers, tight with many petaloids, well in the showbench class. Growth upright and bushy, very easy cultivar, but may be found difficult to overwinter. Garson – American – 1942

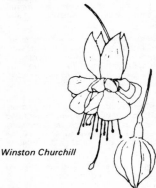

Winston Churchill

Wisteria. Single. Tube and sepals almost white with very pale green tips, tinged phlox-pink inside. Corolla mallow-purple, large irregularly formed flowers, very free. Growth strong willowy climber or trailer. Niederholzer – American – 1941.

Witchingham. Double. Bright candy-pink tube, long twisting sepals bright candy-pink. Corolla white. Medium sized blooms with burgundy anthers. Growth medium upright, rather lax and suitable for all purposes. Raised in the vicinity of Norwich East England and introduced by Woodbridge Nurseries of Hounslow, Middlesex 1981. Nancy Lou × The 13th Star. Clitheroe – British – 1981.

*Woking Fayre. Single. Tube and sepals pink, corolla violet and orange. Medium sized flowers. Originally known as seedling No. 240 and raised in the vicinity of Guildford, Surrey. Growth upright and bushy. Weeks – British – 1982.

Wold. Single. Tube and sepals soft pink; corolla lilac-pink, silky sheen. Growth upright, bushy with self-branching habit. Travis, J. – British – 1973.

Wonder Blue. Double. Tube and sepals, phlox-pink; corolla blue. Large blooms, very full, fairly free, growth upright. Niederholzer – American – 1946.

Wonderful. Double. Scarlet and violet. Epps – British – 1956.

Wonderful World. Semi-double. Tube and sepals, bright scarlet; corolla white, heavily veined red. Growth upright and bushy. Long – British – 1972.

Woodbridge. No details available other than the raiser: Clyne – British – 1974.

*Woodside. Double. Tube and sepals rose-red, slightly lighter shade on underside of sepals. Corolla rich mid-lilac without any fading during maturity. Large blooms and fairly free in flowering, rather a late bloomer in the border. Tested for 7 years and proved to be hardy in the vicinity of Weyborne, Norfolk. Introduced by Kerrielyn

Fuchsias of Cambridge in 1984. Dawson, H. – British – 1984.

Wood Violet. Semi-double. Tube and sepals red; corolla violet-blue. Small flowers, profuse and early, dainty and well formed. Growth upright, bushy and compact, delightful little cultivar. Schmidt – American – 1946.

woytkowskii. Deep vermilion tube, bulbous at base, vermilion spreading sepals; corolla bright red. Long flowers approximately 2 in long, produced singly in the upper leaf axils. Strong upright shrub. MacBride – 1941 – Peru.

W.P. Wood. Single. Tube and sepals scarlet, corolla violet-blue, scarlet at base. Small to medium sized flowers, very free, but late. Darkish green foliage, growth upright and bushy, hardy, height up to two feet, very easy. Accepted by the B.F.S. as showbench hardy. Probably the last cultivar raised by a famous fuchsiaman before his death in 1955. Wood – British – 1954.

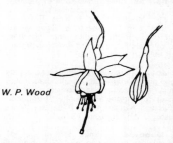

W. P. Wood

W.R. Mould. Single. White and cerise. Lye – British – 1897.

Wurst Park. Triphylla type with Billie Green blood.

W.W. Whiteman. Single. Tube and sepals cerise; corolla pale violet-blue. Medium sized flowers very free, growth upright and bushy. Named after one of the three founder members of the British Fuchsia Society in 1938 Whiteman – British – 1947.

Wyandot. Double. Tube and sepals, rose-madder; corolla doge-purple, outer petals streaked with Tyrian-rose. Large blooms free for size, dark green foliage. Growth upright, bushy and strong. Fuchsia-La – American – 1972 – A.F.S. No. 1022.

Xenia. Single. Tube and sepals, white shaded pink; corolla light violet, edged pink. Medium sized flowers, very free; growth trailer. Hazard and Hazard – American – date unknown.

Xenia Fields. Double. Tube and sepals, pale pink; corolla pink, splashed bright pink. Small blooms, very free; growth upright, bushy compact and dwarfish. Delightful cultivar named after a delightful lady. Although registered with the A.F.S. under No. 455 as Xenia Fields, the correct spelling of the name of the gardening correspondent of the *Daily Mirror* is Xenia Field. Thorne – British – 1960 – A.F.S. No. 455.

Xtra Nice. Double. Rose tube, sepals salmon-rose underside, rose with white on outerside. Corolla lavender with salmon-rose at base. Sepals fold back over the rose tube. Medium-sized blooms, delightful colouring lovely pastel shades, hence the name. Growth natural trailer without weights, will make excellent basket. Tested for 13 years in vicinity of Coos Bay, Oregon. Registered by Vee Jay Greenhouse in 1978. Prentice – American – 1978 – A.F.S. No. 1487.

Yankee Clipper. Double. Short tube and short sepals, carmine; corolla ruby-red and carmine, variegated. Largish blooms, fairly free, large foliage. Growth upright. Soo Yun – American – 1971 – A.F.S. No. 945.

Yankee-Doodle. Single. Short tube and reflexed sepals, deep red; corolla white or white with irregular elongated blotches of blue-purple. Medium sized flowers, very free, open very flat, with seldom the same shape or colour markings. Growth upright and bushy – most unusual cultivar. Hodges – American – 1953 – A.F.S. No. 152.

Ya-Ya. Double. Tube and sepals, bright red; corolla creamy-white, veined red. Medium sized blooms, very floriferous, similar to Snowcap but larger. Growth upright and bushy. Abermale Nurseries – British – 1973.

Yelene Suzanne. Single. Thin tube wine purple, slightly reflexed narrow sepals of the same colour. Longish corolla is lavender to lilac. Long flowers are axillary and bloom in loose terminal spikes, very typical of its parent. Light green foliage with obovate shaped leaves. Growth tall and upright, self-branching, will make good bush or decorative and will take full sun although best colour develops in shade, unusual cross. Originates from the vicinity of Preston, Lancashire. Seedling of *F. arborescens* which was the pollen parent. Travis, J. – British – 1980 – A.F.S. No. 1586.

Yerba Buena. Single. Tube and sepals, pale carmine; corolla Tyrian-rose, shading to rose-madder. Medium sized flowers, free with wavy and serrated petals. (Aurora Superba × Rolla) × Rolla. Reiter – American – 1940.

Yonder Blue. Double. Tube and broad, upturned sepals, rose-red; corolla deep blue. Large blooms, free for size, globular and well shaped. Growth upright and bushy. A.F.S. Cert. of Merit. Tiret – American – 1954 – A.F.S. No. 210.

Yosimet. Double. Tube and sepals white; corolla creamy-pink. Large blooms and free, growth upright. Raiser unknown – American – date unknown.

Youth. Single. Short tube and horizontal sepals, faint pink, flushed green, tipped green; corolla lavender-blue, pink at base. Medium sized flowers, free, petals serrated and edged heliotrope. Growth upright. Travis – British – 1958.

Yuletide. Double. Tube and sepals, rich crimson; corolla creamy-white, veined crimson. Large blooms, free for size. Very similar to Swingtime but even larger. Growth upright and bushy. Uncle Jules × Gypsy Queen (Bull 1865). Tiret – American – 1948.

Yum Yum. Double. Tube and short upturned sepals, light pink, flushed green on outside. Corolla rose-pink with orchid undertone. Medium sized blooms, very floriferous, growth low spreading bush. Erickson – American – 1961 – A.F.S. No. 487.

Yvette. Double. Tube and sepals, bright pink; corolla of the same colour, large blooms, fairly free. Growth trailer. Tiret – American – 1968 – A.F.S. No. 794.

Yvonne. Synonymous with Liz.

Yvonne Holmes. Single. Crimson tube, sepals crimson, tipped green, curved gracefully upward. Corolla cyclamen-purple, carmine at base, veined cherry. Medium sized flowers, perfect bell shape, very free, hold colour. Foliage mid to pale green, veins lighter green, young leaves pale green giving two tone effect. Growth upright, bushy and short jointed. Percy Holmes × Mr. A. Huggett. Holmes, R. – British – 1974 – A.F.S. No. 1210.

Zampa. Lemoine – French – 1882.

* **Zaza.** Single. Tube and sepals light rose; corolla flame-orange. Small flowers but borne in great profusion. Growth upright and bushy. Raised in the vicinity of Southport and introduced by the raiser in 1983. Porter – British – 1981.

Zena. Single. Cerise tube 1 in long, cerise sepals long and thin $2\frac{1}{2}$ in long paling at green tips. Corolla rosy-pink to magenta. Large blooms 5 in across, with 1 in petals veined and edged crimson, but compact. Deep green foliage, leaves 3 in long by $1\frac{1}{2}$ in wide with red mid-ribs and branches. Growth medium upright and somewhat lax as basket can be made with weights. Takes full sun in vicinity of Wallasey, Merseyside where it was tested for 14 years before registration. Grasmere × Hidcote Beauty. Archer – British – 1982 – A.F.S. No. 1704.

Zenobia. Single. Tube and sepals pink; corolla deep pink. Large flowers and free, growth trailer. Hazard and Hazard – American – date unknown.

Zepherine. Single. Tube and sepals, bright cerise; corolla purple. Striped rose-pink. Medium sized flowers and free, growth upright and bushy. Spackman – American – 1922.

Ziegfield Girl. Double. Tube and sepals, darker shade of pink than corolla; corolla beautiful shade of pink. Largish blooms, quite free, shaped like a rosette. Growth trailer, can be disappointing, best grown as H1, A.F.S. certificate of Merit 1969. Fuchsia Forest – American – 1966 – A.F.S. No. 671.

Zody's Dante. Semi-double. Tube and sepals bright cerise; corolla blue, splashed rose. Medium sized flowers, very free. Growth upright, bushy and sturdy. Raiser unknown – American – Date unknown.

'100'. Double. White tube, sepals white, tipped green; corolla lavender-blue turning to bright rose after opening. Medium sized blooms, very heavy blooms, loose and airy. Very dark green foliage with small leaves. Growth trailer. Gagnon – American – 1964 – A.F.S. No. 602.

USEFUL ADDRESSES

AUSTRALIA
Australian Fuchsia Society, Hon. Secretary, Box 97 P.O., Norwood, South Australia

EUROPE
Austrian Fuchsia Society, Mrs Betty Tomsic, Hockegasse 89A, 1180 Vienna, Austria

Mrs Gerda Manthey, Steinberg 21A, 5840, Schwerte-Ergste, West Germany

H.J. de Graaff, Heereweg 315, 2161 BK, Lisse, Netherlands

NEW ZEALAND
E.D. Sweetman, 18 Churton Drive, Churton Park, Wellington, North Island

SOUTH AFRICA
Mrs J. Spurling, Box 193, Hilton 3245

UNITED KINGDOM
British Fuchsia Society, Ron Ewart (Hon. Secretary), 29 Princes Crescent, Dollar, Clack-mannanshire, FK14 7BW

UNITED STATES OF AMERICA
American Fuchsia Society, Hall of Flowers, Garden Centre of San Francisco, 9th Avenue and Lincoln Way, San Francisco, CAL 94122

ADDENDA

p. 95 **Baby Chang**. Only a little larger than a Breviflorae type; colouring identical to Chang but form and shape that of *F. denticulata*.

p. 100 **Bernard Rawlins**. Doubtful if in cultivation as no one ever seems to have seen it.

p. 251 **Princessita**. Now gaining great popularity as an exhibition basket cultivar.

p. 279 **Storm**. Single. Tube and sepals dark red, corolla deep purple flushed rose, medium sized flowers which are continuous. Purple foliage, growth upright and bushy, strong arching habit. Height $1\frac{1}{2}$ to 2 ft. Hardy in Southern England; raised in the Scilly Isles.

p. 296 **Twinkling Stars**. Possesses bad characteristic of producing many flowers with five sepals instead of four.

NOTES